HANDBOOK OF RESEARC

To Joanne
To Denis and Marie
To Diane, Liam, Kate
To Morgan and Spikey

Handbook of Research on Employee Voice

Edited by

Adrian Wilkinson

Professor of Employment Relations, Griffith University, Australia

Jimmy Donaghey

Reader of Industrial Relations and Personnel Management, University of Warwick, UK

Tony Dundon

Professor of HRM and Employment Relations, NUI Galway, Ireland

Richard B. Freeman

Professor of Economics, Harvard University and National Bureau of Economic Research, USA

Edward Elgar
Cheltenham, UK • Northampton, MA, USA

Published by
Edward Elgar Publishing Limited
The Lypiatts
15 Lansdown Road
Cheltenham
Glos GL50 2JA
UK

Edward Elgar Publishing, Inc.
William Pratt House
9 Dewey Court
Northampton
Massachusetts 01060
USA

A catalogue record for this book
is available from the British Library

Library of Congress Control Number: 2013949800

This book is available electronically in the ElgarOnline.com
Business Subject Collection, E-ISBN 978 0 85793 927 2

ISBN 978 0 85793 926 5 (cased)

Typeset by Servis Filmsetting Ltd, Stockport, Cheshire
Printed and bound in Great Britain by T.J. International Ltd, Padstow

Contents

Editors

Adrian Wilkinson

Adrian Wilkinson is Professor and Director of the Centre for Work, Organisation and Wellbeing at Griffith University, Australia. Prior to his 2006 appointment, Adrian worked at Loughborough University in the UK where he was Professor of Human Resource Management from 1998, and he also served as Director of Research for the Business School. Adrian has also worked at the Manchester School of Management at the University of Manchester Institute of Science and Technology. He holds Visiting Professorships at Loughborough University, Sheffield University and the University of Durham, and is an Academic Fellow at the Centre for International Human Resource Management at the Judge Institute, University of Cambridge.

Adrian has written/edited twenty books and over one hundred and forty articles in academic journals. His books include *Managing Quality and Human Resources* (Blackwell, 1997); *Managing with TQM: Theory and Practice* (Macmillan, 1998); *Understanding Work and Employment: Industrial Relations in Transition* (Oxford University Press, 2003); *The Sage Handbook of Human Resource Management* (Sage, 2009); *The Oxford Handbook of Participation in Organizations* (Oxford University Press, 2010); *The Research Handbook on the Future of Work and Employment Relations* (Edwards Elgar, 2011); *New Directions in Employment Relations* (Palgrave, 2011); *The Research Handbook of Comparative Employment Relations* (Edward Elgar, 2011); *The International Handbook of Labour Unions* (Edward Elgar, 2011); *HRM at Work: People Management and Development*, 5th edition (CIPD, 2012) and *Contemporary Human Resource Management* (Pearson, 2013). Adrian is also Editor-in-Chief of the *Human Resource Management Journal* (HRMJ).

Adrian was appointed as a British Academy of Management Fellow in 2010. In 2011 he was elected as an Academician of the Academy of Social Sciences as recognition of his contribution to the field. In 2012 he was shortlisted by HR magazine for the award of HR Most Influential International Thinker (http://www.hrmostinfluential.co.uk/results/hr-most-influential-2012-shortlist-international-thinkers).

Jimmy Donaghey

Jimmy Donaghey is Reader of Industrial Relations and Personnel Management at the University of Warwick. His research interests include social pacts and social partnership, Irish industrial relations, the comparative effects of the Europeanization of industrial relations and the regulation of employee voice in comparative perspective. Recent publications have featured in journals such as the *British Journal of Industrial Relations*, *Economic and Industrial Democracy*, the *International Journal of Human Resource Management* and *Human Relations*.

Tony Dundon

Tony Dundon is Professor of Human Resource Management and Employment Relations and Head of the Management Discipline at the School of Business and Economics, National University of Ireland Galway (NUI Galway). He was previously employed at Manchester School of Management, University of Manchester Institute of Science and Technology (UMIST), where he was also the Programme Director for the Post-Graduate Diploma and MSc in Human Resource Management. Tony has held a number of senior international visiting fellowships at Sydney University; Deakin University, Melbourne; University of Hertfordshire; and Toulouse Business School. He is currently (co)Editor-in-Chief of the *Human Resource Management Journal* (HRMJ), Consulting Editor for the *International Journal of Management Reviews* (IJMR), and a member of the International Advisory Board of *Work, Employment and Society* (WES). Tony's books include *Employment Relations in Non-Union Firms* (Routledge, 2004); *Understanding Employment Relations*, 2nd edition (McGraw Hill, 2011); *Cases in Global Management: Strategy, Innovation and People Management* (Tilde University Press, 2012); and *Global Anti Unionism* (Palgrave, 2013). Tony also serves as the Chief Examiner for the Chartered Institute of Personnel and Development (CIPD) and was awarded the President's Award for Teaching and Learning Excellence in NUI Galway. He has held competitive research grants in excess of €1.8 million from a range of public and private sector bodies, including the IRC, ERSC, HEA, and Enterprise Ireland (among others) and is currently involved in the publication and fieldwork stages with a number of international collaborative research projects.

Richard B. Freeman

Richard B. Freeman is Ascherman Chair in Economics at Harvard University and Faculty co-Director of the Labor and Worklife Program at the Harvard Law School. He directs the Science and Engineering Workforce Project at the National Bureau of Economic Research.

Freeman is a Fellow of the American Academy of Arts and Science and is currently serving as member of two panels of the AAAS, the Initiative for Science and Technology, and the Commission on the Humanities and Social Sciences. He is a member of two panels of the National Academy of Science, the Committee on Assuring a Future US-based Nuclear Chemistry Expertise, and the Committee on National Statistics on Developing Science, Technology and Innovation Indicators for the Future. He is also serving on the Sub-Committee on Biomedical Research Workforce Modeling, an NIH Advisory Committee to the Director.

Freeman received the Mincer Lifetime Achievement Prize from the Society of Labor Economics in 2006, and in 2007 was awarded the IZA Prize in Labor Economics. In 2011 he was appointed Frances Perkins Fellow of the American Academy of Political and Social Science.

His recent publications include: *America Works* (2007), *What Workers Want* (with Joel Rogers, 2007), *What Workers Say: Employee Voice in the Anglo American World* (with Peter Boxall and Peter Haynes, 2007), *International Differences in the Business Practices & Productivity of Firms* (with Kathryn Shaw, 2009), *Science and Engineering*

Careers in the United States (with Daniel Goroff, 2009), *Reforming the Welfare State: Recovery and Beyond in Sweden* (with Birgitta Swedenborg and Robert Topel, 2010), *Shared Capitalism at Work: Employee Ownership, Profit and Gain Sharing, and Broad-based Stock Options* (with Douglas Kruse and Joseph Blasi, 2010), and *The Citizen's Share: Putting Ownership Back into Democracy* (with Joseph Blasi and Douglas Kruse, 2013).

Contributors

Brian Abbott, Senior Lecturer in Management, Kingston Business School, Kingston University

Matthew M.C. Allen, Senior Lecturer in Organisation Studies, University of Manchester

Ariel C. Avgar, Assistant Professor in Labour and Employment Relations, University of Illinois at Urbana-Champaign

Nikola Balnave, Senior Lecturer in the Department of Marketing and Management, Macquarie University; Centre for Workplace Futures, Macquarie University

Alison Barnes, Senior Lecturer in the Department of Marketing and Management, Macquarie University; Centre for Workplace Futures, Macquarie University

Chiara Benassi, PhD Student in Employment Relations and Organisational Behaviour, London School of Economics and Political Science

Jos Benders, Guest Professor, Centre for Sociological Research (CESO), KU Leuven

Chad T. Brinsfield, Assistant Professor of Management, University of St Thomas

Alex Bryson, Visiting Research Fellow with the Centre for Economic Performance, London School of Economics and Political Science and Principal Research Fellow at the National Institute of Economic and Social Research (NIESR)

John W. Budd, Professor of Work and Organizations, University of Minnesota

Shiona Chillas, Lecturer in Management, University of St Andrews

Niall Cullinane, Lecturer, Queen's University Belfast

Tony Dobbins, Senior Lecturer in Human Resource Management, Bangor University

Virginia Doellgast, Associate Professor of Comparative Employment Relations, London School of Economics and Political Science

Jimmy Donaghey, Reader of Industrial Relations and Personnel Management, University of Warwick

Tony Dundon, Professor of Human Resource Management and Employment Relations, School of Business and Economics, National University of Ireland Galway

Janice Foley, Professor of Organizational Behaviour/Industrial Relations, University of Regina

Richard B. Freeman, Ascherman Chair in Economics at Harvard University, Faculty co-Director of the Labor and Worklife Program at the Harvard Law School and Director, Science and Engineering Workforce Project, NBER

Paul J. Gollan, Professor, Macquarie University

Rafael Gomez, Associate Professor at the Centre for Industrial Relations and Human Resources, University of Toronto

Maria González Menéndez, Associate Professor in Sociology, University of Oviedo

Jamie A. Gruman, Associate Professor of Organisational Behaviour, University of Guelph

Bill Harley, Professor of Human Resource Management and Organisation Studies, University of Melbourne

Edmund Heery, Professor of Employment Relations, Cardiff Business School

Peter Holland, Associate Professor in Management, Monash University

Stewart Johnstone, Senior Lecturer in HRM, Newcastle University

Sarah Kaine, Senior Lecturer, University of Technology, Sydney

Bruce E. Kaufman, Professor of Economics, Georgia State University and Adjunct Professor Griffith University and Visiting Professor, University of Hertfordshire

Tobias Kretschmer, Professor of Management, Ludwig-Maximilians-Universität München

David Lewin, Professor of Management, University of California at Los Angeles (UCLA)

Andrew A. Luchak, Associate Professor of Human Resources and Industrial Relations, University of Alberta

Miguel Martínez Lucio, Professor in International Human Resource Management and Comparative Industrial Relations, University of Manchester

Craig MacMillan, Lecturer in the Department of Economics, Macquarie University; Centre for Workplace Futures, Macquarie University

Abigail Marks, Professor of Work and Employment, Heriot-Watt University

Werner Nienhüser, Professor of Human Resource Management, University of Duisburg-Essen

Stacey Owens, PhD Student at the School of Labor and Employment Relations at the University of Illinois at Urbana-Champaign

Mustafa F. Özbilgin, Professor of Human Resource Management and Organisational Behaviour, Brunel University

Glenn Patmore, Senior Lecturer at the Melbourne Law School

Dionne M. Pohler, Assistant Professor in Human Resource Management and Industrial Relations, University of Saskatchewan

Stephen Procter, Alcan Professor of Management, Newcastle University

Amanda Pyman, Associate Professor, Monash University

Alan M. Saks, Professor of Organisational Behaviour and Human Resources Management, University of Toronto

Muhammad Sameer, Lecturer in HRM/OB, University of Bedfordshire Business School, University of Bedfordshire

Jawad Syed, Reader, Kent Business School, University of Kent

Louise Thornthwaite, Senior Lecturer in the Department of Marketing and Management, Macquarie University; Centre for Workplace Futures, Macquarie University

Keith Townsend, Senior Lecturer in Employment Relations and Human Resources, Griffith University

Adrian Wilkinson, Associate Professor, Griffith University

Steve Williams, Reader in Employment Relations, Portsmouth Business School, University of Portsmouth

Paul Willman, Professor, Department of Management, London School of Economics, Senior Research Fellow NIESR and CEP

Ying Xu, Department of Management and Marketing, Macquarie University; Centre for Workplace Futures, Macquarie University

Acknowledgements

Thanks to the ARC LP110200198 and ARC LP 0989151 for their support of research on employee voice and collaborative workplace relations and to the Queensland state government Department of Employment and Industrial Relations for sponsorship of a project on smart workplaces. We also thank the Irish Research Council (IRC) and Economic Social Research Council (ESRC) for a bi-lateral project to examine employee voice which helped to formulate ideas and data contributing to this volume.

PART I

PERSPECTIVES AND THEORIES OF VOICE

1 Employee voice: charting new terrain
Adrian Wilkinson, Tony Dundon, Jimmy Donaghey and Richard B. Freeman

INTRODUCTION

Voice is a term that has been widely used in the practitioner and academic literature on human resource management (HRM) and industrial relations in recent years. Freeman and Medoff (1984) associated voice with union representation and in particular with the role of unions in articulating concerns on behalf of the collective. As union density has fallen in recent years, analysis of voice in workplaces has often focused on how workers communicate with managers and are able to express their concerns about their work situation without a union, and on the ways in which employees have a say over work tasks and organizational decision-making. But researchers from different disciplinary perspectives often use voice in different ways. Some refer to involvement, others to participation, while yet others refer to empowerment or engagement as if they are interchangeable. As Kaufman (Chapter 2) makes clear, few appreciate the historical pedigree of employee voice, for instance, where Karl Marx and Adam Smith expressed interest in the ways and means through which labour expressed its voice. The deeper antecedents to voice have often been forgotten or eclipsed in a rush towards newer managerial fads, such as engagement or other equally abstract notions of labour offering discretionary effort.

This book presents analysis from various academic streams and disciplines that illuminate our understanding of employee voice from these different perspectives. The following chapters show that research on employee voice has gone beyond union voice and non-union voice to build a wider and deeper knowledge base. As the introduction to the book, this chapter provides a guide to the debates about the different dimensions of employee voice and to the research findings in different areas. We review the meanings and purposes surrounding the definitions of voice; consider the role of key actors in the workplace; and evaluate the different forms and processes of voice in different spheres, contexts and organizational settings. We hope that the book will help the reader understand the debates associated with employee voice and appreciate the contribution of the different approaches to our understanding of what goes on in the workplaces that are at the heart of modern economies.

DEFINING AND INTERPRETING EMPLOYEE VOICE

Because research and analysis have grown around the voice concept in a variety of disciplines, 'employee voice' has become an elastic term meaning different things to different policy, academic and practitioner actors (Poole, 1986; Sashkin, 1976; Strauss, 2006; Wilkinson et al., 2010; Budd et al., 2010). In the many disciplines that cover voice, such as human resource management, political science, economics, organizational behaviour (OB), psychology or law, perspectives toward the concept differ. Scholars in one area often know little of the research, connotations or ideological baggage surrounding voice in other areas (Wilkinson and Fay, 2011). For instance, Morrison's (2011: 373) review of voice highlights three common threads running through the voice literature that favour an exclusive OB perspective on the subject:

> One important commonality is the idea of voice being an act of verbal expression, where a message is conveyed from a sender to a recipient. Second, voice is defined as discretionary behavior. Individuals choose whether or not to engage in this behavior at any particular moment in time, a choice that is affected by a variety of factors. A third commonality is the notion of voice being constructive in its intent. The objective is to bring about improvement and positive change, not simply to vent or complain.

These common factors are central to voice considered from a managerial or OB-centric approach which focuses on issues relating to individual verbal communication that is constructive to management. Management introduces voice mechanisms to an organization on management's terms, setting the parameters of what is and is not permissible voice according to employer interests (Donaghey et al., 2011). Morrison explicitly rules out voice as a mechanism 'simply to vent or complain' and, therefore, excludes any conceptualization of employee involvement and participation based on interests other than those of the employer. Thus in excluding complaints, the OB perspective tends to leave out what many other perspectives view as a key component of voice. Yet economic perspectives can also be flawed. Economists often assume voice is about rational actors (employees, employers) making logical decisions in pursuit of a shared performance improvement goal (or economic rent exchange). Neo-classical economists have historically (and mistakenly) treated unions as a constraint disrupting a smooth and natural labour market (Minford, 1985). Of course such a perspective ignores the dynamics of power operating between the buyers and sellers of labour services, not to mention the role that legitimate collective voice structures play in redressing labour market inequalities, particularly trade unions but also including works councils and other institutions (Addison, 2005; Marchington, 2008). Legal scholars, too, often reduce worker voice debates to problems of statutory mandates or infringements on presupposed property rights enshrined in contract law. Importantly, workplace relations tend to dovetail simultaneously into economic, social and psychological paradigms, rendering the notion of a fixed legal contract little more than a figment in the minds of those concerned only with legal juridification (Kahn-Fraund, 1977; Dundon and Gollan, 2007).

In addressing some of these single perspective limitations, the framework in Table 1.1 offers an inclusive structure to capture and assess multiple meanings of employee voice across disciplines. First, voice is an articulation of individual dissatisfaction or concern that aims to address a specific problem or issue with management. Voice may find expression in this way through a grievance procedure or speak-up programme. Second, and often at the same time as individual dissatisfaction, voice takes the form of collective organization, where it provides a countervailing source of power to management. Unionization and collective bargaining are exemplars of pluralist conceptualizations of collective worker voice (Turnbull, 2003). Table 1.1 also recognizes the role of voice as a contribution to management decision-making. Here the purpose is to gain employee input to improve work organization and efficiency more generally, perhaps through quality circles or team work, or by eliciting workforce engagement (Wilkinson et al., 2013). This perspective pervades much of the high performance work system (HPWS) literature, often premised on the view that what is good for the organization is good for the employee (Addison, 2005). In a similar vein, voice can be seen as an instrument for mutual gain, with productive collaboration between capital and labour increasing the long-term viability of an organization and economic well-being of employees (Kochan and Osterman, 1994). Examples of this notion are the US mutual gains idea, European systems of social dialogue and co-determination, and voluntary enterprise-level partnership agreements. A problem facing many organizations is that of reconciling traditional methods of providing a voice for employees, such as collective bargaining and grievance procedures, with more consensual methods such as joint consultation, team working or problem-solving groups. The way employers deal with this issue reflects the purpose it sees in employee voice, which the extant literature has not explored in sufficient depth.

To attach a sufficiently wide but cogent meaning to the employee voice concept which covers the multiple situations in Table 1.1, we define employee voice as the ways and means through which employees attempt to have a say and potentially influence organizational affairs relating to issues that affect their work and the interests of managers and owners. This definition combines a variety of voice mechanisms that analysts often group in separate boxes (for example, involvement or bargaining; union and non-union). It allows for employer implemented non-union employee representative (NER) systems as a collective form of voice, be it chosen to marginalize a union presence or to provide an alternative to union influence (Dundon, 2002; Kaufman and Taras, 2010) as well as union

Table 1.1 Multiple meanings of employee voice

Voice as:	Purpose and articulation of voice	Mechanisms and practices for voice	Range of outcomes
Articulation of individual dissatisfaction	To rectify a problem with management or prevent deterioration in relations	Complaint to line manager Grievance procedure	Exit–loyalty
Expression of collective organization	To provide a countervailing source of power to management	Union recognition Collective bargaining Industrial action	Partnership– Derecognition
Contribution to management decision-making	To seek improvements in work organization, quality and productivity	Upward problem-solving groups Quality circles Suggestion schemes Attitude surveys Self-managed teams	Identity and commitment– Disillusionment and apathy Improved performance
Demonstration of mutuality and cooperative relations	To achieve long-term viability for organization and its employees	Partnership agreements. Joint consultative committees Works councils	Significant influence over management decisions– Marginalization and sweetheart deals

Source: Dundon et al. (2004: 1152).

forms of voice. In economies where trade union membership and bargaining coverage is low and falling, as well as in economies such as that of China where the government established unions as transmission belts for national economic policies, employers generally expect unions to be more in tune with business objectives and use their say to support corporate or national goals. Some independent trade unions engage in dialogue at an enterprise level even in the most management-led interpretations of partnership in the hope that this will benefit their members (Rittau and Dundon, 2010; Johnstone et al., 2010). In general, employee voice is about how employees are able to have a say over work activities and decisions within the organizations in which they work, regardless of the institutional channel through which it operates – whether through speak-up programmes, quality circles, team work, or collective negotiation (Marchington, 2008; Freeman et al., 2007).

Utilizing the above definition helps unpack the meaning of employee voice. Strauss (2006) argues that voice is a weaker concept than other related terms – such as participation – because voice does not denote influence or power-sharing and may thus be no more than 'spitting in the wind'. But Strauss highlights a key element of voice as a defining concept. This is the act of trying to exert influence over management actions, even if desired worker outcomes are not achieved or realized. In a similar vein Harlos (2001) points out that some managements have 'deaf-ear syndrome', where worker exercise of voice becomes a process of little real impact as management pays little attention to resolving issues or changing action.

In recent years, diminishing union density in advanced economies has shifted the form of voice in most organizations and countries from collective and unionized channels of representation to direct and individualized mechanisms, some of which exist alongside unions as a dual method while others are exclusively non-union. The union-only form of voice has all but disappeared in countries where unions once dominated the space of representing worker concerns. In the 2000s, for example, only 5 per cent of British workplaces relied on union-only participation (Willman et al., 2009: 102) Similar trends are evident across much of the rest of Europe, America and Australia (Lewin, 2010; Gomez et al., 2010). In a world in which voice mechanisms go beyond the traditional union mechanism, there is need for more fine-grained and at times more qualitative analysis of how the different mechanisms actually function.

STRUCTURE OF THE BOOK

Theoretical Approaches to Voice

The voice literature finds its roots in several theoretical and methodological paradigms. Part I (Perspectives and Theories of Voice) demonstrates the insight that we gain from complementary and competing approaches towards voice. Importantly, the idea of employees having a say and contributing to work decisions is not in itself new or novel. The recognition that workers tend to know better than managers how best to do a job or how to engage in customer relations existed long before the factory system and the Industrial Revolution. The history and trajectory of worker involvement in industry (voice) is comprehensively examined by Kaufman in Chapter 2, showing that early conceptualizations are central to contemporary developments in the employee voice space.

Allen (Chapter 3) points out that early human resource management (HRM) developments about voice tend to start with the work of Albert O. Hirschman. Hirschman's (1970) classic study of consumers in nationalized African Railways conceptualized 'voice' in the context of the ways in which organizations respond to decline in consumer demand for their products. His definition of voice was 'any attempt at all to change rather than to escape from an objectionable state of affairs' (1970: 30). The point about voice is that its provision may secure general improvements. The absence of good exit options may force the discontented to take action within the organization, hence making voice more powerful (Dundon et al., 2004: Wilkinson et al., 2004). Freeman and Medoff (1984) developed the notion of employee voice in terms of industrial relations and human resource management. They argued that it made good sense for both employer and employee to have a voice mechanism. This had both a consensual and a conflictual potential. On the one hand, participation could lead to a beneficial impact on quality and productivity, whilst on the other it could deflect problems which otherwise might explode (Gollan and Wilkinson, 2007). Freeman and Medoff (1984) saw trade unions as the best agents to provide such voice as they were generally independent of the employer, which adds a degree of voice legitimacy. As Benson (2000: 453) notes, 'for some commentators independent unions are the only source of genuine voice'.

The high performance work system (HPWS) literature has generated different insights into the role of employee voice in human resource management (see Harley, Chapter 6). HPWS theory argues that informing and allowing employees input into work and business decisions can result in better decisions and improve understanding (Boxall and Purcell, 2003). This links to analysis which treats voice as a key ingredient in the creation of organizational commitment (Lewin and Mitchell, 1992; Pfeffer, 1998). It also overlaps with the OB related discussions concerning the idea of employee engagement as something distinct to voice (Emmott, 2005; Welbourne, 2011) and has implications for the management of employee voice in organizations. Among the implications are that hierarchy and compliant rule-following are inappropriate for employees who are expected to expend discretionary effort. As Strauss (2006: 778) observes, giving workers voice 'provides a win-win solution to a central organizational problem – how to satisfy workers' needs while simultaneously achieving organizational objectives'. However, theory and practice can diverge (Harley et al., 2005).

The main aim of the HPWS approach to voice reflects management's desire to increase employee understanding and commitment and raise their contribution to the organization's bottom line. Many such claims are predicated on a positivistic and arguably misplaced method of seeking to validate worker intentions and behaviours through coefficient scores that are detached from context and place. Thus, while some forms of voice in the HRM and HPWS space provide employees with new channels of communication and potential routes to influence issues of concern, facilitating employee voice does not involve any *de jure* sharing of authority or power. Moreover, in the absence of influence and power, any link between voice and the decision-making outcome is always tenuous at best. This is what Kaufman and Taras (2010) nicely suggest is 'voice without muscle'.

The political science literature, which often views voice in terms of rights, links voice to notions of industrial citizenship, legal protection or democratic humanism. The concept of industrial democracy, which draws from notions of industrial citizenship,

sees participation as a fundamental democratic right enabling workers to extend a degree
of control over managerial decision-making in an organization (see Foley, Chapter 5).
Some use the term organizational democracy (Harrison and Freeman, 2004) to describe
a higher form of voice than individualistic channels of communication. This also brings
in notions of free speech and human dignity (Budd, 2004). An important claim is that
workplace democracy allows workers to develop skills and values that then have a role
in broader society (Foley and Polyani, 2006).

The economics approach stemming from the work of Hirschman (1970) and Freeman
and Medoff (1984) finds expression in transaction costs economics (TCE) (see Willman
et al., Chapter 4). Here, voice is premised on an economic exchange that carries with it
certain assumed costs and benefits. TCE assumes workers are like customers in a marketplace. If employees demand a voice and it is not heard, they exit the relationship.
Likewise, managers (employers) may change preferences and opt for one particular
voice arrangement over another, subject to cost implications. For example, managers
may 'make' their own voice system (for example, non-union) rather than 'buying' an
alternative from a contract supplier (for example, recognizing a trade union). In addition, a 'hybrid' dual union and non-union voice can emerge depending on the nature of
the economic transaction, the type of workers, union power, management preference, or
perception of risk. Using TCE to analyse voice trends, Willman et al. (2003) and Gomez
et al. (2010) show that some 30 to 40 per cent of organizations switched their voice
regime between 1980 and 1998, mostly toward non-union and dual hybrid variants over
union-only channels of voice (see Willman et al., Chapter 4).

Labour process theory (LPT – see Marks and Chillas, Chapter 7) offers another
twist on the voice concept. LPT is less forgiving of the neutral nomenclature of the
term 'employee' voice and instead prefers concepts of participation, representation and
countervailing sources of power and collective worker mobilization against the inherent
tensions of a capitalist economic system. Whereas other perspectives noted above have
gravitated to Hirschman (1970) or Freeman and Medoff (1984) as initial anchor points
against which to assess voice, at the heart of LPT is Braverman's (1974) *Labor and
Monopoly Capitalism*. Ramsay's (1977) 'cycles of control' thesis offers insights from this
perspective. It views worker participation as a ruse employed by management threatened
with union power in order to maintain its domination of workplaces – employee voice
as a form of employer control, as it were. But, as Marks and Chillas observe, LPT has a
more complex and nuanced analysis that considers the coexistence of consent and compliance as much as control.

Finally, there are analyses of voice rooted in work psychology and OB perspectives
(see Brinsfield, Chapter 8). Debates in this area connect voice practices with developments and outcomes such as employee engagement (see Gruman and Saks, Chapter
28). Voice as engagement connects with better teamwork, individual job satisfaction or
improved workforce commitment. The creation of semi-autonomous work groups gives
workers a say in task allocation, scheduling, monitoring of attendance, flow and pace
of production and even redesigning work roles and target setting, which ideally pro-
duces better engagement (Wall and Martin, 1987; Morrison, 2011; Welbourne, 2011).
These practices have a long pedigree in seeking to counter the degradation of work and
employee alienation (Proctor and Mueller, 2000), with many schemes formed as part
of a series of work psychology experiments in the 1960s and 1970s (for example, by the

Table 1.2   Employee voice: theory, focus and philosophy

Theoretical strand	Indicative voice schemes	Voice rationale	Form of voice	Philosophy
HRM / HPWS	Focus groups Open door policy	Performance	Individual	Managerial/unitarist: Engender loyalty Enhance performance
Political science	Workers on boards Joint consultation	Citizenship	Representative	Legalistic: Democracy and rights-based
TCE	Dual (union and/or non-union) voice	Cost switching	Representative	Utilitarian: Transaction efficacy
LPT	Collective bargaining Works councils Partnership	Power and control	Collective	Pluralist: Power-sharing Countervailing power
OB	Teamworking Speak-up programmes	Job design	Individuals and groups	Humanist/unitarist: Engagement Commitment

Tavistock Institute and QWL (quality of working life) programmes in the USA and Sweden; see Berggren, 1993).

The above categorization of the diversity of analyses towards employee voice offers potential for greater theoretical specificity within the wide range of perspectives that shape understanding and can help identify conceptual overlap. An alternative way to view the different literatures is to relate them to a series of expected or indicative voice schemes that operate in practice. Table 1.2 presents such an analysis, tying each of the theoretical or disciplinary perspectives to the practices on which they largely focus, the preferred rationale for voice and desired form, all of which may be underpinned by an ideological or philosophical position shared by dominant actors or social groups concerned with employee voice.

There is further scope for refinement and analysis regarding what any specific voice scheme or practice means to the actors involved, and whether various schemes can improve organizational effectiveness and employee well-being or allow workers to have a genuine say in organizational decisions. The way voice initiatives actually work may depend on whether participants perceive them as faddish or as being embedded within the organization (Cox et al., 2006). Clearly, forms of employee voice through participation can differ in regard to the scope of decisions, the amount of influence workers can exercise over management and the organizational level at which the decisions are made. Some forms are purposely designed to give workers a voice but only a modest role in decision-making, while others are intended to give the workforce a more significant say in organizational governance.

Actors in Employee Voice

Studies that examine the importance of voice outcomes and processes from the point of view of different actors include not only workers and employers but line managers, trade unions and other vested interest groups in society. This moves the voice literature from a simple worker–firm or labour–capital approach to incorporate a wider array of agents.

Most studies focus on managers as strategic policy actors operating within a framework of legislation or public policy prescriptions. Management plays a key part in adapting and interpreting legislation, corporate initiatives, consultancy panaceas and benchmark schemes to the workplace. This is important in the context of statutory regulation intent on extending employee voice. In many European countries the state plays a much more active role on top of voluntary collective bargaining. The way actors interpret and affect voice – both as a process of engagement in the workplace and as an outcome of organizational performance – is important in shaping the psychological and economic well-being of employees and indeed the health of families as well as the quality of a country's democratic process (Budd and Zagelmeyer, 2010). Thus the range of actors and their roles in affecting employee voice is of crucial importance, and several key groups can be observed as having a particular vested interest.

First and foremost are employers (and managers) as a distinct group affecting voice processes and outcomes. However, as Kaufman (Chapter 2) points out, management as a distinct function is relatively new in modern business terms, emerging in the late 1800s and developing first in the USA around 1910 and shortly after in Britain, mostly in response to collective organization of labour. Until then management as a distinct discipline was mostly haphazard. Taylor's model of scientific management is even credited as promoting 'equal' voice between worker and manager (Kaufman, Chapter 2); albeit a somewhat twisted understanding of equality given Taylor's core separation between capital/management as those who conceive of the work to be done and labour (employees) as those who carry it out. The idea of voice in terms of the design of jobs or work task involvement was alien to early management theorists.

In addition to the emergence of organized labour pushing management to consider how best to give workers a voice, Holland (Chapter 9) explains a whole set of considerations shaping employer choice around voice. Economic competition and global patterns of restructuring – such as shifts into large-scale bureaucratic organizations at the turn of the twentieth century followed by decline in manufacturing to smaller, more flexible specialization and knowledge and service industries – all affect options for the form of voice that employers may find most appealing. Employers interested in paternalism, social welfare or HRM arrangements would tend to eschew the traditional collectivist adversarial model for direct communications of voice rather than negotiation and bargaining. However, as important as employers are in the voice debate, it is line managers who act as the agents of employers, and as Townsend (Chapter 10) remarks, line managers are the ones who may hear or not hear the employees' voices. Management and employers are far from homogeneous. While a chief executive or human resource function may give strategic direction, line managers form relationships at the workplace level that can frustrate, lubricate or bypass voice opportunities.

Trade unions have probably occupied the lion's share of interest around employee voice in the industrial relations literature. Kaine (Chapter 11) revisits Freeman and Medoff's contention that union voice is most effective given that unionization has all but collapsed in advanced countries (though it is developing from a government-dominated institution in China). Kaine argues that while union voice is often viewed in terms of the diminishing role of collective bargaining, this is only one form of union voice. The point is that unions have adapted and changed considerably. While some criticize Freeman and Medoff's view of collective union power as outdated or a narrow concept of union representation (Turnbull, 2003; Hirsch, 2004), forms of union voice have themselves changed (Heery, 2009), extending beyond the remit of collective bargaining to include articulation of worker concerns at multiple levels: individual, workplace, industry, national, transnational. Moreover, Kaine argues that what matters is what unions or workers qualitatively attain at a particular level and context. Therefore union voice is more nuanced, extends beyond pay and includes grievances, safety, training and workplace learning, among many other matters that have redefined the union voice agenda since Freeman and Medoff's contribution.

The decline of union voice in advanced countries raises a broad intellectual concern about how voice is affected in workplaces that do not have union recognition rights. Pohler and Luchak (Chapter 12) address a range of actor roles (unions, works councils, dispute resolution bodies) that can help fill the gap left by those missing employee voices.

In part because of union decline, and also as a result of employees lacking the opportunity for a formal agent to articulate their concerns, analysts have examined other societal agents who express voice for workers and marginalized groups. Piore and Safford (2006) argued that mission based organizations often substitute for unions in independent advocacy. Similarly, Williams et al. (2011) highlight the growth of social movement forms of employee representation and Heery et al. argue in this volume (Chapter 13) that Civil Society Organizations are based first and foremost on an 'expressive' identity – that is, on celebrating factors such as age or disability, sexual orientation or an ideological stance such as feminism. In contrast, trade unions have tended to portray a more 'instrumental' or 'vested-interest' logic toward benefits for members. However CSOs are also highly diverse which reflects variation towards voice and representation, albeit generally falling into advocacy, identity and issue-based movements in terms of supply of voice. Yet, despite the advocacy provided, these organizations face both representation and legitimacy issues. In representative terms, they often lack democratic foundations. Furthermore, they often seek solutions to issue-based agendas, rather than advocating specific occupational or sector/industry concerns of workers. Finally, there is a possibility of employer capture of initiatives which may compromise the independence of representation.

Forms of Employee Voice

Although in decline in most countries, union bargaining remains an important form of voice for millions of workers and employers around the world. Several chapters of the book re-evaluate unions as institutions of collective voice in a broader, more inclusive way than the labour relations literature has classically viewed them. In addition to collective bargaining (Doellgast and Benassi, Chapter 14) a range of forms includes such institutions as works councils (Nienhüser, Chapter 15) and joint consultative committees (Pyman, Chapter 16). In contrast to collectivist forms there are individualized mechanisms such as individual and grievance voice discussed by Lewin (Chapter 17). Other forms that are not as easily categorized as either collective or individual binaries but tend to dovetail with a more complex web of union and non-union, individual and collective or semi-collective group mechanisms include the likes of task involvement and teamworking (Proctor and Benders, Chapter 18), workplace partnership (Johnstone, Chapter 19), mutual gains voice (Avgar and Owens, Chapter 20) and non-union employee representation (Dobbins and Dundon, Chapter 21).

These contributions analyse the broader changes in voice form from a variety of perspectives. We also see the growth and importance of informal voice, that is, ad hoc or non-programmed interactions between managers and their staff which provide opportunities for information-passing, consultation and the seeking of ideas (Marchington and Suter, 2013). Strauss (1998: 15) specifically defines informal involvement as 'the day-to-day relations between supervisors and subordinates in which the latter are allowed substantial input into decisions . . . a process which allows workers to exert some influence over their work and the conditions under which they work'.

It is important to note that the provision and practice of these different voice forms and mechanisms vary considerably across countries (Lansbury and Wailes, 2008). In European countries government policy and legislation provide for a statutory right to voice in certain areas and in both union and non-union establishments. But this is by no means typical. Other countries, including the USA and Australia, place much less emphasis on statutory provisions for employee voice with more emphasis on the freedom of managers and unions to establish their own preferred arrangements. In many organizations, the result is a mix of direct and indirect voice. It is also worth noting that, depending on the societal regime within which employee voice is situated, the benefits tend to be seen from rather different perspectives. Thus, in liberal market economies, voice is seen in terms of contribution to profit and shareholder value at the organizational level and in customer service, and product quality and staff retention at the workplace level. Issues to do with worker commitment, job satisfaction and alignment with organizational goals are often the proxies used to measure the success of employee voice schemes, but in themselves these may tell us little about the impact of particular schemes on the bottom line or the consolidation of management prerogative. In coordinated market economies, the focus is longer term and more widely defined in terms of a range of stakeholder interests, including that of the government, employers, trade unions and workers. The focus is on peak level institution representation. In these situations the expectation is more likely to be of mutual gains, either at the level of the individual employing organization or more broadly in terms of citizenship and long-term social cohesion (Wilkinson et al., 2010). As Budd and Zagelmeyer (2010) remind us, voice is not necessarily a private affair and it is not simply about improving economic performance.

Evaluating the Future of Employee Voice

Most employees want the opportunity to have a say and to contribute to the work issues that matter to them (Bryson et al., 2006). There are a variety of practices that can be utilized to deal with this desire for voice. Evidence suggests that many of these practices reflect the history of an organization or workplace and consist of ad hoc adjustments to problems rather than a fine-tuned employee voice strategy, which can make employee voice fragile in terms of its structure and efficacy. There is, as Syed (Chapter 26) shows, need for a diversity voice agenda given the many missing and neglected voices from parts of a labour force. There is also (see Balnave et al., Chapter 27) need to supplement traditional voice practices such as face-to-face bargaining, consultation or involvement with social media and modern communication technology. Future generations of workers will almost certainly use new systems of voice and participation, possibly in ways that managers may find alien. As Pyman et al. (2006) have argued, a critical issue will be the configuration of multiple channels of voice and engagement rather than any single method, a configuration that technology will play a role in shaping. They conclude that the interaction and coexistence of multiple channels of voice and plurality of arrangements are most effective and legitimate from an employee's perspective in achieving organizational outcomes. Similarly, Handel and Levine (2004: 14) point out that bundles should be more effective than the simple sum of effects for the individual practices, and hence the existence of voice schemes may tell us little about the quality of the process (Wilkinson and Fay, 2011).

The operation of systems of voice and evaluation inevitably differs according to the power resources held by the respective actors within a firm, the size of the organization, and the constraints of particular legislative frameworks within a country (see Gollan et al., Chapter 22) or across international borders (see González Menéndez and Martínez Lucio, Chapter 23). Small firms where family relations and close personal links exist between management and workers often override employment regulations and policies in determining channels of voice and their success or failure (see Sameer and Özbilgin, Chapter 25).

Many firms have invested in programmes to increase employee involvement or engagement. Practitioner research seems to indicate that employee voice is an important driver of engagement and the former is a necessary prerequisite (process) for the latter (outcome) (Macey and Schneider, 2008). But it has not been without criticism. As Luisa Kroll (2005) notes, when writing for *Forbes* and quoting Randall MacDonald of IBM: 'Soon we'll be talking about marrying all those employees to whom we're engaged.' Welbourne (2011) points out that the beauty of employee engagement is that it can be all things to all people and that most people think employee engagement sounds good. As she argues, employee engagement speaks to something most social scientists, employees and managers truly believe, and that is the fact that when employees go 'above and beyond' and are not robots just doing a simple, repetitive job, then organizations do better (Welbourne, 2011). Likewise, as Gruman and Saks (Chapter 28) point out, many of the best-known organizational disasters – the Columbia space shuttle tragedy or the BP Deepwater drilling rig explosion – were connected to employee disengagement, situations when workers failed to report problems. Some argue that when employees do not speak up and instead remain silent they can be engaging in a type of protest, an active silence. In some contexts remaining silent can carry as much or more of a message than speaking out (see Brinsfield, Chapter 8; Cullinane and Donaghey, Chapter 24). This is the 'thunder in silence' in the Chinese sage Lao-tzu's philosophy about how to voice discontent. But while 'getting-back' or protesting against employer actions by actively not offering ideas may carry the message of discontent, it does not offer the mechanism for finding solutions. Related debates include the idea of employee whistle-blowing as voice, especially given the growth in corporate and government scandals surrounding unethical business conduct – such as the information communicated by Edward Snowden concerning alleged unethical practices at the US National Security Agency (NSA) when he was working there as a contract employee. Therefore how voice is evaluated concerns not just the type of practice, its form and mechanism, or who the particular actors are. More important is the nature of the process, its intended purpose and meaning, and the ethical and moral fibre of those in positions of authority and the degree to which they are interested in power-sharing exercises that can effect change and enable a genuine say. These matters are picked up in the final chapter when Budd (Chapter 29) considers a number of challenges: the conceptualization of voice, and in particular whether voice can have an intrinsic self-determination role or be expressive of aims and interests as outcomes. Future challenges include what happens when there is no voice (or voice is minimal): do employees suffer in silence or exit the relationship? Voice also has to be re-evaluated in relation to time and space so as to capture its relevance and substance in relation to different types of work, occupations and industries. Future issues in this regard include the changing role of government institutions and legislative regimes for voice, corporate governance and business ethics, which affect both individual and collective rights for voice. Above all, the future of employee voice research is vibrant, challenging and intellectually stimulating with implications for policy, practice and theory.

REFERENCES

Addison, J.T. (2005), 'The determinants of firm performance: unions, works councils, and employee involvement/high-performance work practices', *Scottish Journal of Political Economy*, **52** (3), 406–50.
Benson, J. (2000), 'Employee voice in union and non-union Australian workplaces', *British Journal of Industrial Relations*, **38** (3), 453–9.
Berggren, C. (1993), *The Volvo Experience: Alternatives to Lean Production in the Swedish Auto Industry*, Basingstoke: Macmillan.
Boxall, P. and J. Purcell (2003), *Strategy and Human Resource Management*, Basingstoke: Palgrave.
Braverman, H. (1974), *Labor and Monopoly Capital: The Degradation of Work in the Twentieth Century*, New York: Monthly Review Press.
Bryson, A., A. Charlwood and J. Forth (2006), 'Worker voice, managerial response and labour productivity: an empirical investigation', *Industrial Relations Journal*, **37** (5), 438–55.
Budd, J. (2004), *Employment with a Human Face: Balancing Efficiency, Equity and Voice*, Ithaca: ILR Press.
Budd, J. and S. Zagelmeyer (2010), 'Public policy and employee participation', in A. Wilkinson, P. Gollan, M. Marchington and D. Lewin (eds), *The Oxford Handbook of Participation in Organizations*, Oxford: Oxford University Press.
Budd, J., P. Gollan and A. Wilkinson (2010), 'New approaches to employee voice and participation in organizations', *Human Relations*, **63** (3), 1–8.
Cox, A., S. Zagelmeyer and M. Marchington (2006), 'Embedding employee involvement and participation at work', *Human Resource Management Journal*, **16** (3), 250–67.
Donaghey, J., N. Cullinane, T. Dundon and A. Wilkinson (2011), 'Re-conceptualising employee silence: problems and prognosis', *Work, Employment and Society*, **25** (1), 51–67.
Dundon, T. (2002), 'Employer opposition and union avoidance in the UK', *Industrial Relations Journal*, **33** (3), 234–45.
Dundon T. and P. Gollan (2007), 'Re-conceptualising non-union voice', *International Journal of Human Resource Management*, **18** (7), 1182–98.
Dundon, T., A. Wilkinson, M. Marchington and P. Ackers (2004), 'The meanings and purpose of employee voice', *International Journal of Human Resource Management*, **15** (6), 1150–71.
Emmott, M. (2005), 'What is employee relations?', Change Agenda, Chartered Institute of Personnel and Development, London.
Foley, J. and M. Polanyi (2006), 'Workplace democracy: why bother?', *Economic and Industrial Democracy*, **27** (1), 173–91.
Freeman, R.B. and R. Medoff (1984), *What Do Unions Do?* New York: Basic Books.
Freeman, R.B., P. Boxall and P. Haynes (eds) (2007), *What Workers Say: Employee Voice in the Anglo-American World*, Ithaca: Cornell University Press.
Gollan, P. and A. Wilkinson (2007), 'Contemporary developments in information and consultation', *International Journal of Human Resource Management*, **18** (7), 1133–44.

Gomez, R., A. Bryson and P. Willman (2010), 'Voice in the wilderness: the shift from union to non-union voice', in A. Wilkinson, P. Gollan, M. Marchington and D. Lewin (eds), *The Oxford Handbook of Participation in Organizations*, Oxford: Oxford University Press.

Handel, M. and D. Levine (2004), 'The effects of new work practices on workers', *Industrial Relations*, **43** (1), 1–43.

Harley, W.G., J. Hyman and P. Thompson (eds) (2005), *Participation and Democracy at Work: Essays in Honour of Harvie Ramsay*, Basingstoke: Palgrave Macmillan.

Harlos, K. (2001), 'When organizational voice systems fail: more on the deaf-ear syndrome and frustration effects', *Journal of Applied Behavioural Science*, **31** (3), 324–42.

Harrison, J. and E. Freeman (2004), 'Is organizational democracy worth the effort?', *Academy of Management Executive*, **18** (3), 49–53.

Heery, E. (2009), 'The representation gap and the future of worker representation', *Industrial Relations Journal*, **40** (4), 324–36.

Heery, E. and M. Simms (2011), 'Seizing an opportunity? Union organizing campaigns in Britain, 1998–2004', *Labor History*, **52** (1), 23–47.

Hirsch, B. (2004) 'What do unions do for economic performance?', *Journal of Labour Research*, **25** (3), 415–55.

Hirschman, A. (1970), *Exit, Voice and Loyalty: Responses to Decline in Firms, Organizations and States*, Cambridge, MA: Harvard University Press.

Johnstone, S. and A. Wilkinson (2013), 'Employee voice, partnership and performance', in G. Saridakis and C. Cooper (eds), *How Can HR Drive Growth?*, Cheltenham, UK and Northampton, MA, USA: Edward Elgar, pp. 141–69.

Johnstone, S., P. Ackers and A. Wilkinson (2010) 'Better than nothing? Is non-union partnership a contradiction in terms?', *Journal of Industrial Relations*, **52** (2), 151–68.

Kahn-Freund, O. (1977), *Labour and the Law*, London: Stevens.

Kaufman, B. and D. Taras (2010), 'Employee participation through non-union forms of employee representation', in A. Wilkinson, P. Gollan, M. Marchington and D. Lewin (eds), *The Oxford Handbook of Participation in Organizations*, Oxford: Oxford University Press.

Kochan, T.A. and P. Osterman (1994), 'The mutual gains enterprise: forging a winning partnership among labor, management and government', Harvard Business School, Harvard.

Kroll, L. (2005), 'No employee left behind', Forbes.com, New York, 15 September, available at: http://www.forbes.com/home/free_forbes/2005/1003/060.html (accessed 26 November 2013).

Lansbury, R. and N. Wailes (2008), 'Employee involvement and direct participation', in P. Blyton, N. Bacon, J. Fiorito and E. Heery (eds), *The Sage Handbook of Industrial Relations*, London: Sage, pp. 434–46.

Lewin, D. (2010), 'Employee voice and mutual gains', in A. Wilkinson, P.J. Gollan, M. Marchington and D. Lewin (eds), *The Oxford Handbook of Participation in Organizations*, Oxford: Oxford University Press.

Lewin, D. and D. Mitchell (1992), 'Systems of employee voice: theoretical and empirical perspectives', *California Management Review*, **34** (3), 95–111.

Macey, W.H. and B. Schneider (2008), 'The meaning of employee engagement', *Industrial and Organizational Psychology*, **1** (1), 3–30.

Marchington, M. (2008), 'Employee voice systems', in P. Boxall, J. Purcell and P. Wright (eds), *The Oxford Handbook of Human Resource Management*, Oxford: Oxford University Press.

Marchington, M. and J. Suter (2013), 'Where informality really matters: patterns of employee involvement and participation in a non-union firm', *Industrial Relations: A Journal of Economy and Society*, **52** (1), 284–313.

Minford, P. (1985), 'Trade unions destroy a million jobs', in W.E. McCarthy (ed.), *Trade Unions*, Harmondsworth: Penguin, pp. 365–75.

Morrison, E. (2011), 'Employee voice behavior: integration and directions for future research', *Academy of Management Annals*, **5**, 373–412.

Morrison, E.W., S.L. Wheeler-Smith and D. Kamdar (2011), 'Speaking up in groups: a cross-level study of group voice climate and voice', *Journal of Applied Psychology*, **96** (1), 183–91.

Pfeffer, J. (1998), *The Human Equation: Building Profits by Putting People First*, Boston: Harvard Business School Press.

Piore, M.J. and S. Safford (2006), 'Changing regimes of workplace governance, shifting axes of social mobilization, and the challenge to industrial relations theory', *Industrial Relations: A Journal of Economy and Society*, **45** (3), 299–325.

Poole, M. (1986), *Towards a New Industrial Democracy: Workers' Participation in Industry*, London: Routledge and Kegan Paul.

Proctor, S. and F. Mueller (eds) (2000), *Teamworking*, London: Macmillan.

Pyman, A., B. Cooper and J. Teicher (2006), 'A comparison of the effectiveness of employee voice arrangements in Australia', *Industrial Relations Journal*, **37** (5), 543–59.

Ramsay, H. (1977), 'Cycles of control: worker participation in sociological and historical perspective', *Sociology*, **11** (3), 481–506.

Rittau, Y. and T. Dundon (2010), 'The roles and functions of shop stewards in workplace partnership: evidence from the Republic of Ireland', *Employee Relations*, **32** (1) 10–27.

Sashkin, M. (1976), 'Changing toward participative management approaches: a model and methods', *Academy of Management Review*, July, 75–86.

Strauss, G. (1998), 'Participation works – if conditions are appropriate', in F. Heller, E. Pusic, G. Strauss and B. Wilpert (eds), *Organizational Participation: Myth and Reality*, Oxford: Oxford University Press.

Strauss, G. (2006), 'Worker participation – some under-considered issues', *Industrial Relations*, **45** (4), 778–803.

Turnbull, P. (2003), 'What do unions do now?', *Journal of Labor Research*, **24** (3), 491–527.

Turnbull, P. and V. Wass (2000) 'Redundancy and the paradox of job insecurity', in E. Heery and J. Salmon (eds), *The Insecure Workforce*, London: Routledge, pp. 57–77.

Wall, T.D. and R. Martin (1987), 'Job and work design', in C. Cooper and I. Robertson (eds), *International Review of Industrial and Organizational Psychology*, Chichester: Wiley.

Welbourne, T.M. (2011), '50 years of voice in HRM', *Human Resource Management*, **50** (1), 1–2.

Wilkinson, A. and C. Fay (2011), 'New times for employee voice?', *Human Resource Management*, **20** (1), 65–74.

Wilkinson, A., T. Dundon, M. Marchington and P. Ackers (2004), 'Changing patterns of employee voice', *Journal of Industrial Relations*, **46** (3), 298–322.

Wilkinson, A., P. Gollan, M. Marchington and D. Lewin (2010), 'Conceptualising employee participation in organizations', in A. Wilkinson, P.J. Gollan, M. Marchington and D. Lewin (eds), *The Oxford Handbook of Participation in Organizations*, Oxford: Oxford University Press, pp. 1–25.

Wilkinson, A., T. Dundon and M. Marchington (2013), 'Employee involvement and voice', in S. Bach and M. Edwards (eds), *Managing Human Resources*, Oxford: Blackwell.

Williams, S., B. Abbott and E.J. Heery (2011), 'Civil regulation and HRM: the impact of civil society organisations on the policies and practices of employers', *Human Resource Management Journal*, **21** (1), 45–59.

Willman, P., A. Bryson and R. Gomez (2003), 'Why do voice regimes differ?', Centre for Economic Performance, London School of Economics and Political Science.

Willman, P., R. Gomez and A. Bryson (2009), 'Voice at the workplace: where do we find it, why is it there and where is it going?', in W. Brown, A. Bryson, J. Forth and K. Whitfield (eds), *The Evolution of the Modern Workplace*, Cambridge: Cambridge University Press.

2 Employee voice before Hirschman: its early history, conceptualization, and practice
Bruce E. Kaufman

INTRODUCTION

A person reading the scholarly employee voice literature could easily conclude the subject did not exist before Albert Hirschman wrote *Exit, Voice and Loyalty* (1970). His book is repeatedly cited as the root stem of the field (for example, Wall and Wood 2007: 1336; Morrison 2011: 380), with the implication being that no one before him had given articulation to the concept. A Google search on the term 'voice' reveals in a matter of seconds, however, that this is a serious case of historical myopia. Yes, Hirschman deserves credit for being the first to develop a *formal theory* of voice, albeit limited to people in their role as *consumers* in product markets. Accordingly, Freeman and Medoff (1984) also deserve credit because they were the first to take Hirschman's theoretical ideas and apply them to *employees* in labor markets. Unacknowledged and unrecognized, however, is a long train of writing on employee voice that predates Hirschman and Freeman and Medoff by a century and more.

In this chapter I give a brief overview and synthesis of the early writing on employee voice. Part of the mission is to sketch a missing component in the history of thought, a discussion which I believe most readers will find interesting and useful in its own right. This historical analysis also has an instrumental purpose, however, which is to shape, inform, and critique the present-day research program on employee voice. For example, this review reveals that modern-day scholars have substantially re-invented a concept well known and utilized many years ago. More substantively, this early literature not only provides important insights regarding the definition, meaning, and conceptualization of employee voice but also indicates shortcomings in modern work on the subject. Finally, the early literature reveals an empirical pattern of employee voice noteworthy for its diverse organizational forms and breadth and depth of practice.

It is impossible to cover in one short chapter early voice literatures across multiple countries. This review, therefore, is largely limited to American experience and authors, although several writers based in Britain are selectively introduced. An advantage of the American case is a rich documentary record; a drawback is omission of important voice forms and developments in other cultural and political contexts. For Britain, see Fox (1985) and Gospel (1992); for France, see Reynaud (1975) and Despax et al. (2011); for Germany see Spencer (1984) and Milert and Tshirbs (2012); and for Japan see Kinzley (1991) and Totten (1967).

THE IDEA OF EMPLOYEE VOICE

The employment relationship is a team form of production embedded in a capitalist market economy coordinated by a top-down authority structure. It became important in world history with the rise of capitalism and wage labor, the decline of self-employed farmers and artisans, the end of feudalism and slavery, and the development of large-scale factories, mills, and railroads.

Put in this context, it seems strange that the employment relation has existed for hundreds of years and yet the concept and practice of employee voice has only attracted attention in the last thirty years or so (see, for example, Addison 2005; Brinsfield et al. 2009; Holland et al. 2011). Actually, the idea of employee voice goes back more than two centuries to the start of the Industrial Revolution.

Provided below are different perspectives on employee voice drawn from four distinct literature bases, with illustrative quotations. The voice term is italicized in each quotation to give it attention. Since the concept and definition of employee voice in the modern-day literature remains somewhat splintered and contested, I endeavor to inform this discussion and move it forward by supplementing these quotations in places with brief interpretive comments.

Economics

The first writers to use the voice term come from economics. The field was born with the publication of Adam Smith's *Wealth of Nations* (1937 [1776]). In the book Smith specifically discusses the concept of employee voice. He states, 'The laborer['s] . . . *voice* is little heard and less regarded [except] upon some particular occasion, when his clamour is animated' (1937 [1776]: 396–7).

Several noteworthy features deserve highlight. We see, for example, that use of the voice term to connote the employee's act of speaking-up and expressing his or her mind goes back more than two hundred years. Although not explicitly stated by Smith, from the context of surrounding sentences one also sees that he envisions voice as including both individual and group expression. It appears that Smith also defines voice to include more than simple verbal communication, per the idea of 'animated clamour.' Smith further expresses a dichotomy between voice as communication (the message is heard) and influence (the employer takes action). Smith likewise suggests that voice as communication often fails to register with employers and is even less effective as influence. In an earlier chapter of the book, Smith sheds additional light on this matter by noting that the interests of employers and employees 'are by no means the same' and 'masters must generally have the advantage' (1937 [1776]: 66–7). Thus, Smith can be read as suggesting that employers may be 'hard of hearing' either because it serves their interests to ignore employee voice or because they feel little inducement to act on it.

Another economist who uses the voice term is Karl Marx. He writes in Volume 1 of *Capital* (1906 [1867]: 257–9):

> He [the employer], like all other buyers, seeks to get the greatest possible benefit out of the use-value of his commodity. Suddenly the *voice* of the laborer, which has been stifled in the storm and stress of the process of production, rises: The commodity I have sold to you differs . . .

[for it] is the use of my labor-power . . . I will, like a sensible saving owner, husband my labor power [against] an unlimited extension of the working day . . . Hence is it that in the history of capitalist production, the determination of what is a working day, presents itself as the result of a struggle, a struggle between collective capital, i.e., the class of capitalists, and collective labor, i.e., the working class.

Like Smith, Marx indicates that the worker's voice is apt to go unheeded. However, Marx's use of the word 'stifled' suggests that employers actively discourage employee voice, in part because during the 'storm and stress of production' they either have more pressing matters to deal with but also because they regard voice as an unwanted intrusion. Marx also intensifies the divergence of interests between the employer and employee into a 'struggle' and more sharply frames this struggle as diametrically opposed, class-based, and insoluble within the bounds of capitalism. Marx adds the idea that the worker and employer are in a bargaining contest over the terms and conditions of employment and that the worker deliberately holds back effort (labor power) as a bargaining chip and protective response. Finally, Marx emphasizes that workers use voice not only to advance their economic position but also to safeguard their human capital from wear, tear, and exploitation.

Another famous ninetennth-century economist is John Stuart Mill. He states in his autobiography:

> I saw no more reason why women should be held in legal subjection to other people, than why men should be. I was certain that their interests required fully as much protection as those of men and were quite as little to obtain it without an equal *voice* in making the laws by which they are bound. (Mill 1874: 244)

Mill is here calling attention to the fact that the unequal treatment of women originates in part from a tilted regime of law and regulation – including discriminatory laws and regulations affecting women's participation, treatment, and reward in employment. Thus, he suggests that employee voice has to be broadly considered to include giving workers, whether women or other groups, some say and influence on rule-makers at two levels – managers in firms and legislators in national governments.

Trade Unions

A second literature base that used the voice term comes from trade unions and their leaders and supporters. Although trade unions in the USA go back to the start of the nineteenth century and considerably earlier in Britain, it was only in the latter part of the 1800s that unions became permanently established and a national presence.

The voice term quickly became a standard part of the discourse about unions. In late nineteenth-century America, for example, books and pamphlets appeared with titles such as *The Voice of Labor: Some Advice to Workingmen* (Porter 1886) and *The Voice of Labor, Containing Special Contributions by Leading Workingmen Throughout the United States* (Jelley 1888). A number of trade union journals and newspapers also used the voice term in their titles (for example, *The Miner's Voice*; *Wisconsin Voice of Labor*) and in the 1920s the Chicago Federation of Labor started a radio station WCFL called 'Voice of Labor' (Godfried 1997).

Proponents of trade unions used the voice term to explain and justify their mission and activities in economic, political, and human rights terms. They also frequently joined the concept of voice with that of industrial democracy (Derber 1970; Lichtenstein and Harris 1993), as was influentially articulated by Sidney and Beatrice Webb (*Industrial Democracy*, 1897). As trade unionists saw it, the competitive capitalism of that era forced workers to sell their labor as a commodity and, to get and keep jobs in an overstocked market, obliged them to accept poverty wages, twelve hour workdays, and dismissal without cause. Likewise, the common law of the employment relationship, based on the master-servant doctrine and sanctity of private property rights, put the employer in the position of an industrial monarch who had near-unlimited authority to govern, discipline, and terminate employees as he deemed appropriate. Accordingly, when workers are treated as commodities and industrial serfs, it is inevitable that they rebel when basic canons of social justice and human rights are violated. The mission of trade unions, therefore, is to use collective bargaining and political action to restore equality of bargaining power in labor markets, bring industrial democracy to the workplace, and protect and advance workers' human rights in industry.

Henry Demarest Lloyd (1893) in the USA captures these themes when he states, 'it is the share of the majority [the nation's workers] to have *no voice*, to do the hardest work and feed on the crumbs of life . . . In a thousand trades labor is forced by compulsion stronger than that of the British stamp acts to sell labor to a ruler' (1893: 7). He continues 'Democracy must be progressive or die,' 'all must have a *voice*,' and (quoting Abraham Lincoln), 'A house divided against itself cannot stand' (1893: 8).

One of organized labor's most articulate and best-known spokesmen in the late 1800s was John Mitchell, president of the United Mine Workers (USA). He states:

> There is much lip service paid to the ennobling effect of labor . . . but it is the trade union, and the trade union alone, which translates these professions into actual deeds. The same man who . . . discourses eloquently upon the dignity of labor is unwilling that his employees shall have anything to say with regard to the conditions of their work . . . The working man . . . is the ultimate repository of power and the real producer of the wealth of the nation [yet] he is not considered worthy of a *voice* in the disposal of his time. (Mitchell 1903: 158)

Even better known than Mitchell was Samuel Gompers, long-time AFL (American Federation of Labor) president. He wrote:

> The synonyms for 'union' shop and 'non-union' shop respectively are 'democracy' and 'autocracy.' In the union shop the workers are free men . . . Employees in the non-union shop are like cogs in a machine. They have nothing to say as [to] the conditions under which they will work, but must accept any wages, hours and working conditions that may be fixed arbitrarily by the employer. A non-union man who accepts employment in a union shop has the privilege of joining the union which has a *voice* . . . with employers. (Gompers 1920: 2)

Management

Recognition of a distinct functional activity called management did not begin in the USA and Britain until the 1880s and did not blossom into a focused literature until after the turn of the century. A specialized branch of management devoted to personnel/employment took even longer to develop. In America, it first appeared in the early 1910s under the label employment management and then evolved into personnel management and industrial relations in the late 1910s (Kaufman 2008); in Britain it developed more slowly and was more narrowly framed as an industrial welfare function (Gospel 1992; Kaufman 2007). Since in this period personnel management and industrial relations covered overlapping but distinct participants and knowledge/subject domains, I deal with the former here and the latter in the next section.

From the 1880s to the end of the 1910s the United States experienced a growing labor problem. Unions spread and became more militant, many strikes broke out – a number of them quite large and violent, companies experienced very high rates of employee turnover and disaffection, and to many people it appeared that class relations between capital and labor were slowly becoming more polarized. A major impetus behind the development of the modern practice of management, therefore, was to discover ways to reunite employers and employees in order to promote harmony and cooperation, and to raise firm performance.

An employer who devoted considerable attention to improving relations between employers and employees was John D. Rockefeller, Jr. One of his family's businesses, the Colorado Fuel and Iron Company, was rocked in 1914 by a devastating strike – popularly known as the Ludlow Massacre – and this event spurred Rockefeller to investigate new approaches to labor management. Rockefeller's diagnosis of the problem was that labor–management conflict stems primarily from lack of communication, mutual understanding, and proactive resolution of friction; these conditions, in turn, were aggravated by the loss of personal contact between employer and employee as industry evolved from small workshops to huge impersonal factories and mills. He explains:

> Most of the misunderstanding between men is due to a lack of knowledge of each other. When men get together and talk over their differences candidly, much of the ground for dispute vanishes. In the days when industry was on a small scale, the employer came into direct contact with his employees, and the personal sympathy and understanding of each grew out of that contact and made the rough places smooth. (Rockefeller 1916: 13–14)

Rockefeller traveled to Colorado with labor advisor Mackenzie King and spent a number of days talking with managers and workers. He decided to create a representation plan with joint employer–employee committees in order to help rebuild lost communication and personal contact. On this he states:

> The men in each mining camp were invited to choose, by secret ballot, representatives to meet with the executive officers of the company to discuss matters of mutual concern and consider means of more effective co-operation in maintaining fair and friendly relations. That was the beginning, merely the germ, of a plan [of employee representation] which has now been developed into a comprehensive 'Industrial Constitution.'. . . Some have spoken of it as establishing a 'Republic of Labor.' Certain it is that the plan gives every employee opportunity to *voice* his complaints and aspirations, and it neglects no occasion to bring the men and the managers together to talk over their common interests. (Rockefeller 1916: 18–19, 26)

Several points deserve notice. Although trade unionists were the first to frame employee voice as a matter of industrial democracy, by the mid-1910s managers also began to use various governance metaphors. Rockefeller, for example, speaks of 'Republic of Labor' and 'Industrial Constitution' while other management writers (for example, Leitch 1919) called representation schemes 'plans of industrial democracy.' The managerial form of industrial democracy, however, is an employer-created 'inside' form of employee voice rather than an independent 'outside' form as with a trade union. Also noteworthy, Rockefeller illustrates the tendency of management writers to downplay structural sources of conflict, such as divergent interests, unequal bargaining power, and capitalist ownership of industry, and instead to focus attention on strengthening a sense of common interests through improved communication and bilateral resolution of differences. Finally, Rockefeller also emphasizes that the shift from small workshops to large factories and mills requires a parallel shift from personal forms of employer–employee interaction and direct employee voice to organized coordination and indirect forms of voice and involvement.

Other corporate executives of this period also spoke about employee voice in unitarist and mutual gain terms. For example, in an article entitled 'How we brought management and men together,' Chief Operating Officer W.W. Atterbury of the Pennsylvania Railroad says of the company's new representation plan:

> Summarized in one sentence, the gist of the Pennsylvania plan is this: To give employees an opportunity through employee representatives to have a *voice* in the management on all matters affecting our mutual welfare . . . The theory underlying our plan is simply that we are giving our employees a chance to see that only a prosperous company can pay good wages, that the company's success is their success, and its failure is their failure, and that men and management are merely two divisions of the same working forces. (Atterbury 1924: 42)

Although the use of the voice term was frequently associated with the movement to set up works councils and representation plans, it had a more general provenance in the managerial discourse of this period.

Frederick Taylor, for example, claims that his program of scientific management gives 'workers in the end equal *voice* with the employer' (quoted in Hoxie 1916: 836). Taylor, however, conceives of voice not as *ex ante* communication and discussion but as *ex post* influence through 'arbitrament of science and fact' (ibid.). Voice, in his schema, is provided through the medium of neutral, fact-based engineering of workplace practices by scientists and technical experts.

Employers quickly discovered, however, that when they tried to install scientific management their workers strongly resisted the new program and sometimes went out on strike to stop it. One of Taylor's disciples, Robert Valentine, argued that the problem arose from Taylor's too-mechanical and elitist notion of voice. In an influential paper entitled 'The progressive relation between efficiency and consent' (1915), Valentine asserted that scientific management is bound to fail unless it gives workers genuine voice and participation in the process since otherwise they feel the plan is forced on them and will refuse to cooperate.

The marriage of scientific management with a human conception of the worker became the foundation for the new fields of employment management and personnel management in the 1910s in the USA. Employee voice, in turn, was regarded as essential to successful practice of this new approach to people management for reasons Valentine had outlined. Thus, two pioneers in employment management state:

> This attention to the human problems has emphasized the need for the development of a science of employment and personnel management . . . so that some of the waste experienced by both

employers and employees may be eliminated and the personnel function raised to its proper place in industrial management. It is highly important that, as this movement develops, the *voice* of the worker and the *voice* of the social agencies be prominently heard. (Bloomfield and Willets 1916: viii)

By the end of World War I the discussion of personnel management, works councils, and industrial democracy had evolved into the new topic of workers' participation in management (Hotchkiss 1920; Merritt 1920; Kaufman 2001). Here too employee voice was featured. For example, Benge (1920: 237) observes, 'Participation in management has sprung up from many causes . . . Some employers have felt it to be an easy way to combat unionism; others have had sufficient faith . . . to grant a *voice* in the conduct of the business.'

Some management writers also discussed why employee voice, per Adam Smith's observation, is not more actively solicited and acted upon by employers. Lewisohn (1926: 566) observes, for example, that managers find dealing with employee complaints and suggestions 'tinged with an unpleasant emotional state, which makes the whole subject distasteful to them.' Another states that many employers 'never introduce it [representative voice] on the grounds that it infringes on the rights of the foremen, their all-necessary adjunct to the success of the business' (MacNamara 1920: 103). A third observes that many managers are 'unwilling to relinquish the reputation of knowing it all' (Porter 1905: 219).

Industrial Relations

Industrial relations first emerged as a formal academic field of study and business practice area about 1920 in the USA (not until the late 1940s in Britain), although its roots extend to Britain and Germany and writers such as the Webbs and Brentano (Kaufman 2004). Personnel management, or what today is called human resource management, was specifically focused on the management side of the employment relationship, emphasized managerial objectives and practices, and among the more behavioral-oriented in the field drew significant input from psychology. A review of the personnel literature reveals that the closer to the psychology side one goes the less the employee voice concept is encountered.

Industrial relations, by way of contrast, was more broadly focused to cover all sides of the employment relationship, including managerial, labor, and societal interests, and took a more external/macro focus on markets, institutions, laws, and policy. Industrial relations was presented as an integration of employment perspectives and knowledge bases; in practice, although it contained a managerial component, the field's center of gravity was in political economy and law and gave greater weight than personnel management to progressive social reform and helping the worker underdog.

The divergence between personnel and industrial relations, along with attention to the concept of employee voice, is indicated in this passage by American labor economist William Leiserson. He states:

In any plan or policy of labor management for industrial enterprises two sets of labor relations must be clearly distinguished. First, the personal relations which present the personnel management problems; and secondly, the economic collective relations which cover the problems of bargaining and democracy . . . The personal relations in industry cover such questions as hiring, selection, placement, training, . . . These questions . . . are not essentially controversial in nature; they do not involve conflicting interests and they have to be settled by good management and scientific experts . . . The second set of labor relations . . . has to do with the division of the product of industry, with the government or control of industry, with bargaining, wages, hours, unionism, and shop discipline. The return that workers should get for their labor, . . . the *voice* they should have in making disciplinary rules, . . . these are questions that present controversial issues which cannot be settled by technical experts. They are matters which require democratic discussion and about which a wide diversity of opinion will be permitted. (Leiserson 1919: 8–9)

Leiserson goes to say:

Committees of employees may be used by the technical men who handle the personal relations in industry, but they are not the same kinds of organizations of employees that are needed to deal with the economic or governmental relations. The first can be permitted to offer to the management only advice and suggestions. The second must have a veto power on the acts of management and will sooner or later demand an equal *voice* in determining wages and hours and controlling discipline. (Leiserson 1919: 11)

We see here clear recognition that the employment relation contains several dichotomies – integrative vs. distributive, administration vs. bargaining, individual vs. collective, managerial vs. democratic – and therefore requires different expressions and forms of employee voice.

The lead academic figure in American industrial relations was John Commons. He took a group of graduate students on a cross-country tour of thirty companies to study alternative forms of labor management and workforce governance. The case studies were published as a book with the title *Industrial Government* (1921). He summarizes their findings, stating: 'From 10 to 25 per cent of American employers may be said to be so far ahead of the game that trade unions cannot reach them. Conditions are better, wages are better . . . The other 75 per cent to 90 per cent are backward . . . and only the big stick of unionism or legislation can bring them up' (Commons 1921: 263).

As Commons saw it, all employees deserve a baseline of decent wages and hours, job security, opportunity for voice, status, and dignity, and due process protection in dispute resolution. Where management voluntarily provides these, a trade union form of industrial government is not required. For example, he calls the non-union system of labor management at the Ford Motor Company, 'just old-fashioned industrial autocracy tempered by faith in human nature' (Commons 1921: 24). Nonetheless, since Ford's labor practices were in the top 10–25 percent, Commons observes, 'Why should there be any industrial democracy, grievance committee, or labor organizations, when nobody can be fired anyhow . . . and management always has a line on the foremen who have too much trouble?' (1921: 25). He concludes, 'The open shop [non-union workplace] may be either a cloak to hide long hours, competitive wages, and *voiceless* workers, or it may be freedom for the management in furnishing reasonable hours and fair wages for manly workers' (1921: 265). Where the former is the case, Commons argues that labor law and collective bargaining have to provide workers with an outside collective form of voice.

Another industrial relations writer of national prominence was Sumner Slichter. He notes that a transformation took place in labor management philosophy and practice before and after World War I. Before the war, unemployment was extensive and employers could use the threat of discharge to coercively motivate and control workers (called the drive system); after the war, however, threat of discharge lost its power because unemployment was much lower and, hence, employers had to motivate and control workers by building up their morale and commitment through a positive program of good wages, job security, and fair treatment. Thus, one approach to industrial relations gains cooperation through negative coercion while the other gains it through positive inducement. With this in mind, Slichter (1919: 60) states, 'As the importance of labor's cooperation becomes more apparent, the more apparent will become the desirability of making labor an insider in industry with a corresponding *voice* in its direction.'

Slichter thus highlights an external contingency critical to effective employee voice – the level of unemployment – which most management writers neglect. Other industrial relations writers argued that voice is likely to remain under-supplied until labor law and trade unions give workers more power and insider status. For example, Fitch (1920: 2) argues:

> The first noteworthy thing about the worker in his relation to industry is that he has no right to a *voice* concerning it. Often he succeeds in establishing such a right for himself, but he can get and keep such a right only by fighting for it . . . This means that he can have no *voice* in industry without organization, and the whole history of the American trade union movement shows that the right to organize is also a thing for which he must fight.

EARLY FORMS OF EMPLOYEE VOICE

The idea of employee voice, at least in America, was evidently well-known and frequently used a century and more ago. So, what about the practice of voice? Was it also widespread and, if so, how was employee voice organized and provided?

The historical record suggests employee voice options and coverage were quite limited in the USA before World War I. As described below, many employers actively discouraged voice and, thus, a large swath of industry could accurately be described as falling into the 'No Voice' category. Workers who had some kind of formal voice option were typically members of trade unions. Most AFL unions, however, included only workers from skilled trades and crafts and, hence, the mass of unskilled and semi-skilled manual workers were mostly on their own. After World War I, non-union voice options substantially expanded with the birth of the personnel/industrial relations function, the emergence of professional management, the development of the welfare capitalism movement, and the shift from an external to internal labor market strategy by many companies.

As Hirschman posits, an alternative to voice is exit and workers through the war era used the exit option in droves. Turnover rates in American industry in the 1910s – when the first companies started to keep records on the matter – were phenomenally high. Marcus Alexander (1916) did the first quantitative study of turnover and found the number of new hires in twelve plants was roughly *six and one-half times larger* than needed to fill the growth in jobs. A movement quickly developed to stabilize employment; out of this proliferated, in turn, formal internal labor markets and organized voice through employee representation.

Workers also used other tactics besides exit to signal employers about their dissatisfactions, grievances, and unmet demands. Many strikes in that era, for example, were not led by unions but occurred as short and mostly unplanned walk-outs by unorganized workers in a department or plant. Some of these strikes mushroomed into hugely destructive conflicts, such as at Pullman in 1894 with thirty people dead and eighty million dollars of railroad property destroyed. Here are examples of Smith's voice as animated clamour. Other signals included absenteeism (up to 10 percent on Mondays at Ford Motor), deliberately working slowly (Frederick Taylor's much hated 'soldiering'), and a bad and belligerent attitude (called 'kicking').

Presented below is a brief synopsis of alternative voice forms in American industry prior to the New Deal. They are arranged along a spectrum from low to high in terms of extent of organizational breadth/depth, formalization, and influence, starting with 'No Voice' and ending with 'Workers' Control.'

No Voice

Many companies, particularly before World War I, not only did not have a voice option but rejected and perhaps actively discouraged it. The employer adopted the role of army general, absolute monarch, or master of the household – a person with great authority whose orders are to be obeyed without question or talk-back and who uses harsh punishment to maintain compliance and control.

A flavor of the 'No Voice' style of workplace is given in this remembrance by Don Lescohier. He worked in a factory before World War I and recalls:

> Ordinarily a man hired in this process did not know what his pay would be until he got his wages on payday. If you asked the foremen that question when you were hired you would, ordinarily, be shown the gate. Complete submission of unorganized workers to the company was the expectation at the Detroit Stove Works. Like hundreds of other common laborers I had heard the foreman say to me: 'Put on your coat,' which meant that you were fired. You did as he said.' (Lescohier 1960: 32)

Also instructive is this remembrance by Daniel Willard. As a teenager he started out on a railroad track gang and then worked his way up to become president of the Baltimore & Ohio Railroad. He recalls:

> I was young and enthusiastic, and I saw something that seemed to me ought to be done, and it wasn't being done, so I thought the thing to do was to go and tell the officer, the master mechanic or whatever his title was, what I had in mind, and he said, 'Sonny, you had better keep still; when they want your advice they will ask you for it, and I wouldn't volunteer any advice.' And then I learned that there was a definite thought in the minds of the all the men, that if they wanted to get along with management they had better not make suggestions.' (Willard 1927: 263)

Individual Voice

If voice was an option for workers, it first started with informal one-on-one voice in the form of individual discussion, usually on the shop floor with a gang boss or foreman but sometimes higher up such as with the business owner or department head. For example, one writer (Roland 1896: 395) visited six companies and found at most 'an absence of a fixed method and a general policy of individual treatment' with communication and bilateral relations maintained by the 'perpetual and everywhere personal influence' of the owner and lower-level managers (1896: 410).

Other open shop employers gave formal expression to their voice policy. Most often it was called the open door. An open door company was the US Steel Corporation. Its president, Elbert Gary, said:

> Any employee . . . is at liberty at all times to present to the respective foremen and, if desired, the higher appointees and officials, all questions involving the interests and welfare of both employee and employer for discussion and disposition. In this way fair and satisfactory adjustments are made. (Quoted in Levenstein 1962: 61)

Gary opposed collective forms of non-union voice, such as shop committees, because they compromised managerial control and could be 'the beginning of a full and thorough unionization of the industry' (Levenstein 1962: 62).

Henry Ford had an organized grievance resolution committee in the late 1910s but later abandoned it in favor of individual dealing and the open door. On the open door he states:

> Any workman can go to anybody, and so established has become this custom, that a foreman does not get sore if a workman goes over him and directly to the head of the factory. The workman rarely ever does so, because a foreman knows as well as he knows his own name that if he has been unjust it will be very quickly found out, and he shall no longer be a foreman. One of the things we will not tolerate is injustice. (Ford 1924: 92)

In practice, the open door at Ford Motor progressively atrophied over the 1920s, as did all forms of voice (conversing with workmates was forbidden during work hours) as Henry Ford turned toward a lean and mean labor strategy. Other companies, however, actually walked the talk on the open door and direct personal communication between manager and worker.

An example is the Endicott-Johnson Company, the nation's largest shoe manufacturer. Its president, George Johnson, made unity of interest a strategic business objective. To achieve it, Johnson went to great lengths to create a family culture where workers felt materially and emotionally invested in the success of the company. This close connection was fostered by devices such as job security, generous wages, and profit-sharing; also key was giving employees voice through close personal contact and attention to their needs and problems. Thus, Johnson framed successful voice as resting on principles of 'Personal Contact,' 'Putting Yourself in the Other Person's Shoes,' and the 'Square Deal' (Zahavi 1988: 40). Toward this end, Johnson spent hours walking though the company's plants to talk with workers, many of whom he knew by name. His office was also regularly open to employees and a steady stream came in to talk about problems and special needs, many of which Johnson personally took action on. Part of the return on this investment was that the workers remained loyal to the company and did not unionize during the 1930s (ibid.).

Small-Scale Collective Voice

Still within the non-union part of industry but next up the rung of employee voice are employers who formed various kinds of small-scale, decentralized, and informally organized teams and committees. These groups were the beginning of indirect (representative) forms of employee voice.

Here is a brief synopsis of these types of committees and voice forms in the USA as gleaned from periodicals and reports from this era. They reveal a mix of voice and participation functions.

Welfare committees. An industrial welfare movement developed after 1900 in which employers provided new amenities and benefits for workers, such as cafeterias, savings plans, athletic programs, washroom facilities, and recreation halls. In a number of cases they gave groups of employees an opportunity to help create and operate the new programs. A report notes, for example, that some firms 'allow their employees to manage the lunch room . . . The employees quite frequently have a *voice* in the management of the club rooms or houses . . . The administration of the benefit [thrift] associations is in most cases either mutual or in the hands of the employees' (Bureau of Labor Statistics 1919: 121).

Safety committees. A writer states, 'The function of the Workmen's Inspection Committee is to inspect the shop, or one department thereof, for safety, and make recommendations for the removal of hazards . . . The Workmen's Safety Committee is, as far as I know, the first recognition in this country on a large scale of the principle that it is advantageous to give rank and file workmen a *voice* in determining shop conditions' (Williams 1919: 95).

Piece-rate and profit-sharing committees. Employers also created employee voice committees to help administer variable pay compensation programs, such as with piece rates and profit-sharing, in order to promote trust and transparency in the determination of pay-outs and ensure that variable pay is a source of increased mutuality and not conflict. Tead (1917: 253) notes, for example, 'Price committees, perforce, exist already in industries where piece rates have constantly to be set' while Farnham (1917: 765) states, 'an opportunity to share in the profits aroused among the employees such an interest in the company's affairs that they felt they should have a share in the management and determination of the policy.'

Grievance committees. Watkins (1922: 468) describes a four-step process for resolution of grievances, starting with a branch committee composed of equal number of management and employee members. Unresolved grievances move up to committees at the department and firm level and then, if still unresolved, are submitted to an arbitrator.

Expense committee. A temporary committee of four people assigned to review all aspects of operations and policy and make recommendations to senior management. The company president notes that resistance from lower-level managers and supervisors is 'where an economy committee is bound to strike its first snag' (Morgan 1925: 742) since they feel threatened by loss of authority and exposure to criticism.

Special Project Team (see *Iron Age*, 'Improving the Personnel,' 18 May 1916: 1198). The general manager of the Fore River Shipbuilding company relates, 'It was recently determined to see what could be done to improve the quality of the employees and to increase efficiency . . . A committee of employees was carefully selected and sent to inspect fifteen large manufacturing plants, . . . the object of the committee's visits being to obtain as much information as possible relative to both personnel and plant betterment.'

Shop Committees, Works Councils, and Employee Representation Plans

In America the highest level of formal collective voice in non-union establishments before the New Deal was in the form of shop committees, works councils, and employee representation plans (ERPs). These groups provided a permanent basis for voice that included workers across a facility, plant, or company. A few representation plans included employee representatives on the board of directors; some companies used the plans as a substitute for a personnel department.

Employee representation developed into a large and influential industrial relations practice after World War I, encompassing a decade later more than 800 plans and covering roughly 1.5 million workers (Nelson 1982). The American movement was partly an attempt by employers to set up a non-union version of the Whitley Councils introduced in Britain after the war (Gospel 1992). Balderston (1935) assembled case studies of twenty-five of the most advanced employee relations programs in the USA. Twenty companies were non-union and fourteen of these had some form of ERP. Most of the corporate leaders of the welfare capitalism movement, such as DuPont, General Electric, Goodyear, International Harvester, Standard Oil of New Jersey, and Westinghouse, had ERPs (for example, Litchfield 1920).

All ERPs were created and operated by employers; otherwise their specific characteristics and functions varied widely. Some companies set them up as a bilateral communication channel, others billed them as serving an advisory and consultation function, as providing an organized method of employee participation in management, as a form of industrial self-government (industrial democracy), or as a non-union form of collective bargaining. Typically workers voted for representatives in secret ballot elections and the representatives then interfaced with first-level supervisors on an informal day-to-day basis and with upper level management in periodic formal meetings. The advanced ERPs had written constitutions, monthly meetings, discussed all aspects of operational and personnel activities, paid employee representatives for council duties, and created a formal process for dispute resolution. The companies that set up ERPs as an alternative form of collective bargaining frequently entered into written contracts with the employees' organization. By most accounts, on balance, the ERPs had a discernible influence in resolving friction, improving work conditions, promoting mutual understanding, and tempering discipline and discharge (Kaufman 2000); their effects on wages, hours, and other economic matters were less evident but on balance also positive (Fairris 1997; Pencavel 2003).

With the onset of economic depression in late 1929, some ERPs were dropped and others became inactive – either because the plans fell victim to deep cost-cutting or because they no longer seemed needed in an environment of mass layoffs and unemployment. The true believers in representation, however, not only kept the plans going but utilized them to help co-manage layoffs, wage cuts, work-sharing, and relief activities. After coming to office in early 1933, President Roosevelt pushed forward a New Deal economic recovery program which encouraged collective bargaining as a way to raise wages and purchasing power. Several thousand companies responded by quickly setting up ERPs as a non-union form of collective bargaining. Within several years ERP membership mushroomed to 2.5 million (Nelson 1982). This new group of ERPs became quite controversial because they were seen as a crass and mostly illegitimate union avoidance tactic and also a threat to the goals of the president's economic recovery program (Kaufman 2000).

Abetted by widespread public disillusionment with employers and competitive markets, Congress enacted the National Labor Relations Act (NLRA, or Wagner Act) in 1935 which declared all forms of non-union collective dealing with employees over a term or condition of employment – even if only bilateral discussion in a small-scale committee – an illegal unfair labor practice. Hence, many forms of collective worker voice disappeared, in some cases replaced by an independent labor union or a non-union committee focused only on production related matters (Jacoby 2000).

One of the earliest ERPs, established about 1900, was at William Filene and Sons, a Boston retail department store (Kaufman 2010: 58–63). It was called the Filene's Co-operative Association (FCA). The FCA was one component of a pioneering set of advanced human resource practices installed by the company, including an employment management department, profit-sharing plan, and peer review board of arbitration. The author of a case study of the company observes, 'The Filene's Co-operative Association, if not the original plan of employee participation in management, was among the earlier of such plans' (La Dame 1930: 119). La Dame reproduces the written charter of the FCA, which states as the organization's first purpose, 'To give its members a *voice* in their [industrial] government' (1930: 121).

The company selected by Balderston (1935) as having the best employee relations program in the United States was Leeds and Northrup, a manufacturer of scientific instruments and measuring devices. Unusual for a company of that period, it gave all new employees a written employee handbook The table of contents lists twenty-six items, including wages, hours, working conditions, overtime, vacations, lay-off and discharge, lunch room, and attendance bonus. One of the twenty-six is an ERP. The voice plan's relative importance is indicated by the fact that it is listed as the second item in the table of contents, behind only the executive committee. The handbook states that the association's objective is 'to furnish an organization in which the employees may cooperate for their mutual welfare and through which they may work with the management in matters that pertain to their interests' (Balderston 1935: 3). The workers' committee elected a 'board of councilors' which met with the executive committee once a month; most of the association's work, however, was done through twelve sub-committees (including an employees-only grievance appeal board).

Independent Labor Unions

The next gradation in employee voice is the independent labor union. In that period most unions were organized along craft and occupational lines and hence were commonly known as trade unions. The unions portrayed themselves as the organized form of voice for American workers, per Gompers's statement that the labor movement '*voices* the aims and hopes of the toiling masses' (Gompers 1953: 32). Trade union density in the USA started out in the early 1900s at less than 5 percent, rose slightly above 10 percent on the eve of World War I, surged to nearly 20 percent by the end of the 1910s, slowly shrank back to near 10 percent in the early 1930s, and then surged past the 20 percent level during the New Deal period of the 1930s.

Trade unionists were highly critical of ERPs which they contemptuously called company unions. AFL president William Green (1925: 244) attributed the company union to employers' 'desire for autocratic control and managerial domination. They seek to maintain the form of collective bargaining without its substance or its spirit of independence.' Robert Dunn (1926: 15, 33, 38, 51) offered these more pointed critiques of ERPs:

> Many of the plans lie more or less dormant when there are no strikes on the horizon, but in time of industrial disturbance they are revived and dressed up to fool the worker again and keep him away from the real trade union.

> [D]elegates . . . meet to discuss baseball, bowling, picnics and banquets. But never [do] they at any time take up any matter that is of vital interest to the workers, such as wages and hours of labor.

> Any worker who is not close to the company has no chance of getting elected . . . Why don't the workers take up their grievances with their 'ward representative'? . . . The answer is simple: If he did he . . .would be dropped from the payroll the next day.

> When the time came to cut wages, the machinery was at hand with which to do this expeditiously and peacefully.

From the trade union perspective, most of the issues of vital concern to workers, such as wages, hours, and job security, inevitably create a conflict of interest between the employer and employee and thus have a significant element of win–lose. Further, employers are typically in the superior power position since they control who gets the jobs and can thus use the threat of termination to keep workers silent and submissive. In most cases, therefore, workers can only get meaningful voice when they are part of an independent labor union since the workers elect their own representatives, the union's leaders are free to speak up and make demands, and the union has bargaining power through the strike threat and other sanctions to induce the company to make concessions. Union voice is also more effective because it extends common wages across all firms in the market and takes labor cost out of competition; ERPs, on the other hand, have no capacity to create or protect minimum industry labor standards.

When unionism came to the steel industry in the mid-1930s, a magazine article described the transformation in voice terms when it used the title 'A Man Can Talk in Homestead' (Fitch 1936). Similarly, unionism came to the apparel industry in the late 1910s and the industry went from mostly non-union to 90 percent organized. An observer notes:

> The clothing industry, competitive beyond most of the other basic industries, left individual workers at the mercy of the autocratic government of hundreds of employers, themselves driven by the sharpness of the competition of trade . . . Six years ago less than 15 per cent of the garment workers earned as much as $20 a week . . . approximately the lowest sum sufficient . . . for the humble maintenance of a family of five. Last year in New York four-fifths of the workers earned between thirty-five and fifty-five dollars a week . . . [Also], the worker had few rights which the employer had to respect. That too has gone. Every shop where the union is effective has its own leader. In the larger markets judicial and legislative machinery representative both of workers and of employers has been established . . . The clothing makers have citizenship in industry. They have the dignity, the self-assurance, that arises from knowledge of the solid bulwarks of their liberties. (Chenery 1920: 273)

The union just cited, the Amalgamated Clothing Workers of America, was unusual at this time because it entered into an official program of labor–management cooperation with employers in which the union worked with the companies to improve productivity and cost control. Several other American unions also adopted innovative labor–management cooperation programs, the most famous case being on the B&O Railroad with the International Association of Machinists (Lauck 1926; Willard 1927).

The complaint of most employers, however, was that union voice is too focused on conducting a battle to win a larger slice of the economic pie for workers and not interested enough in cooperating with companies to grow the economic pie. As Seager (1920: 334) observed on this matter:

> The introduction of an outside representative means at once emphasis on the conflicting interests of employer and employee. Disagreements are no longer analogous to disputes within the family in which both sides remain conscious of and are restrained by the common family interests. The trade or labor official has little or no concern with the business success of the plant in which the dispute has arisen. His primary concern is for the success of the union which he represents . . . and he is, therefore, anxious to obtain higher wages or more favorable working conditions . . . As found in most industries in the United States, the psychology of collective bargaining through shop committees is predominantly cooperative; that of collective bargaining through trade or labor union officials predominantly contentious.

He suggests that one solution to this problem is to conceive of trade unions and ERPs not as substitutes but as complements (see also Douglas 1921). That is, unions perform the distributive wage-fixing function at the industry level while ERPs perform the integrative cooperation-promoting role at the plant level. This suggestion never gained traction in the USA but was implemented in Germany with a combination of industry collective bargaining and plant level works councils.

Workers' Control

Opposite the no employee voice end of the spectrum is a variant of workers' control (no management voice). It was never more than a fringe movement in the USA (more so in France and some other countries) but deserves mention to round out the story.

The idea of workers' control goes back to the early nineteenth-century anarchist, communitarian, and syndicalist movements associated with people such as Owen, Fourier, and Proudhon. Robert Owen, for example, established a short-lived communitarian experiment at New Harmony, Indiana, with a large measure of worker self-management. Later in the nineteenth century, workers' control became associated with workers' cooperatives as espoused by the Knights of Labor and other reform groups and, also, various versions of state socialism as espoused by Marx, Debs, DeLeon, and other radicals (Derber 1970).

Most of these versions of workers' control faded away by the 1920s. Some exceptions nonetheless remained. For example, workers' cooperatives in the plywood industry were set up in the Pacific Northwest and still operate (Pencavel 2001). Most discussed, however, were companies such as the Duchess Bleacheries and Columbia Conserve Company. Lauck (1926: 286) called the latter, 'the most complete and perfect illustration of direct industrial democracy which exists today.'

The latter company employed about one hundred people. Originally privately owned, the principal stockholder put all the shares into a trust under control of the board of directors and a factory council. The board was composed entirely of employees, including managers, and its members were elected by workers in town hall meetings. The board, acting on behalf of the employees, made all financial, operating, and personnel decisions. Thus, the workers chose the chief executive and top-level managers, approved capital investment expenditures, set hours of operation, and approved all salaries and wages. The company survived until 1953.

CONCLUSION

As this survey indicates, employee voice was a concept frequently discussed and practiced in late nineteenth and early twentieth-century American industry (the historical record in other countries is a topic needing research). Both the conceptualization and implementation were in important respects roughly formed relative to current standards. Nonetheless, attention to this historical experience with voice also yields important ideas and insights that people today can build on for new and improved theory and practice. This survey, for example, highlights the cross-disciplinary nature of the employee voice concept; the different dimensions of voice (for example, communication vs. influence, individual vs. collective, managerial vs. industrial democracy, distributive vs. integrative), and the broad spectrum of voice forms coexistent in the economy. Although research on employee voice has considerably advanced since the pioneering studies of Hirschman (1970) and Freeman and Medoff (1984), this survey also indicates a distressing penchant among modern scholars to ignore the contributions of our forebears, claim credit for rediscovering or dressing-up old ideas and distinctions, take a too narrow and scholastic perspective on a complex and multi-faceted reality, and neglect the rich diversity of voice forms of an earlier era and the lessons they provide for modern practice and policy.

REFERENCES

Addison, John (2005), 'The determinants of firm performance: unions, works councils, and employee involvement/high performance work practices', *Scottish Journal of Political Economy*, **52** (3), 406–50.
Alexander, Marcus (1916), 'Hiring and firing: its economic waste and how to avoid it', *The Annals of the Academy of Political and social Science*, **65** (May), 128–44.
Atterbury, W. (1924), 'How we brought management and worker together', *System*, **45** (January), 42–5.
Balderston, C. Canby (1935), *Executive Guidance of Industrial Relations*, Philadelphia: University of Pennsylvania Press.
Benge, Eugene (1920), *Standard Practice in Personnel Work*, New York: Wilson.
Bloomfield, Meyer, and Joseph Willets (1916), 'Foreword', *Annals of the American Academy of Political and Social Science*, **65** (May), vii–viii.
Brinsfield, Chad, Edwards, Marissa, and Jerald Greenberg (2009), 'Voice and silence in organizations: historical review and current conceptualizations', in J. Greenberg and M. Edwards (eds), *Voice and Silence in Organizations*, Bingley, UK: Emerald, pp. 3–33.
Bureau of Labor Statistics, United States Department of Labor (1919), *Welfare Work for Employees in Industrial Establishments in the United States*, Bulletin 250, Washington, DC: Government Printing Office.
Chenery, William (1920), 'The vanguard of labor', *The Survey* (22 May), 273–5.
Commons, John (1921), *Industrial Government*. New York: Macmillan.

Derber, Milton (1970), *The American Idea of Industrial Democracy*, Urbana: University of Illinois Press.
Despax, Michel, Jacques Rojot, and Jean-Pierre Laborde (2011) *French Labor Law*, Leiden: Wolters Kluwer.
Douglas, Paul (1921), 'Shop committees: substitute for, or supplement to, trade unions?', *Journal of Political Economy*, **29** (2), 88–107.
Dunn, Robert (1926), *American Company Unions*, Washington: Trade Union Educational League.
Fairris, David (1997), *Shopfloor Matters: Labor–Management Relations in Twentieth-Century American Manufacturing*, London: Routledge.
Farnham, Dwight (1917), 'Some experiences with profit sharing', *Industrial Management*, (March), 757–67.
Fitch, John (1920) 'The human factor in industry', address before the Massachusetts Conference of Social Work. John Fitch papers, Box 1, Folder 8, State Historical Society of Wisconsin, Madison.
Fitch, John (1936), 'A man can talk in Homestead', *Survey Graphic* (February), 71–6, 118–19.
Ford, Henry (1924), *My Life and Work*, Garden City, NY: Doubleday.
Fox, Alan (1985), *History and Heritage: The Social Origins of the British Industrial Relations System*, London: Allen & Unwin.
Freeman, Richard B. and James Medoff (1984), *What Do Unions Do?*, New York: Basic Books.
Godfried, Nathan (1997) *WCFL, Chicago's Voice of Labor, 1926–1978*, Urbana: University of Illinois Press.
Gompers, Samuel (1920), *The Union Shop and its Antithesis*, Washington: American Federation of Labor.
Gompers, Samuel (1953), *The American Labor Movement*, Washington: Allied Printing.
Gospel, Howard (1992), *Markets, Firms, and the Management of Labor in Modern Britain*, Cambridge: Cambridge University Press.
Green, William (1925), Address by William Green, *Bulletin of the Taylor Society*, **10** (December), 242–6.
Hirschman, Albert (1970), *Exit, Voice, and Loyalty: Responses to Declines in Firms, Organizations, and Nations*, Cambridge, MA: Harvard University Press.
Holland, Peter, Amanda Pyman, Brian Cooper, and Julian Teicher (2011), 'Employee voice and job satisfaction in Australia: the centrality of direct voice', *Human Resource Management*, **50** (1), 95–111.
Hotchkiss, Willard (1920), 'Participation in management – discussion', *American Economic Review*, **19** (March Supplement), 110–15.
Hoxie, Robert (1916), 'Scientific management and labor welfare', *Journal of Political Economy*, **29** (9), 833–54.
Jacoby, Sanford (2000), 'A road not taken: independent local unions in the United States since 1935', in B. Kaufman and D. Taras (eds), *Nonunion Employee Representation: History, Contemporary Practice, and Policy*, Armonk: M.E. Sharpe, pp. 96–120.
Jelley, S.M. (1888), *The Voice of Labor, Containing Special Contributions by Leading Workingmen Throughout the United States*, Philadelphia: Smith.
Kaufman, Bruce (2000), 'Accomplishments and shortcomings of nonunion employee representation in the pre-Wagner act years: a reassessment', in B. Kaufman and D. Taras (eds), *Nonunion Employee Representation: History, Contemporary Practice, and Policy*, Armonk: M.E. Sharpe, pp. 21–60.
Kaufman, Bruce (2001), 'The theory and practice of strategic HRM and participative management: antecedents in early industrial relations', *Human Resource Management Review*, **11** (4), 505–34.
Kaufman, Bruce (2004), *The Global Evolution of Industrial Relations: Events, Ideas and the IIRA*, Geneva: International Labour Organization.
Kaufman, Bruce (2007), 'The development of HRM in historical and international perspective', in P. Boxall and J. Purcell (eds), *Oxford Handbook of Human Resource Management*, Oxford: Oxford University Press, pp. 19–47.
Kaufman, Bruce (2008), *Managing the Human Factor: The Early Years of Human Resource Management in American Industry*, Ithaca, NY: Cornell University Press.
Kaufman, Bruce (2010), *Hired Hands or Human Resources: Case Studies of HRM Programs and Practices in Early American Industry*, Ithaca, NY: Cornell University Press.
Kinzley, W.D. (1991), *Industrial Harmony in Japan: Invention of a Tradition*, London: Routledge.
La Dame, Mary (1930), *The Filene Store: A Study of Employees' Relations to Management in a Retail Store*, New York: Russell Sage Foundation.
Lauck, W. Jett (1926), *Political and Industrial Democracy, 1776–1926*, New York: Funk & Wagnalls.
Leiserson, William (1919), *Employment Management, Employee Representation, and Industrial Democracy*, Washington, DC: US Department of Labor Working Conditions Series.
Leitch, John (1919), *Man-to-Man: The Story of Industrial Democracy*, New York: Forbes.
Lescohier, Don (1960), *Don Divance Lescohier: My Story for the First Seventy-Five Years*, Madison, WI: Art Brush Creations.
Levenstein, Harvey (1962), 'The Labor Policy of the United States Steel Corporation 1920–1927', MSc, University of Wisconsin, Madison.
Lewisohn, Sam (1926), 'Management: a behavior problem', *Industrial Management*, **56** (September), 565–8.

Lichtenstein, Nelson, and Howell Harris (1993), *Industrial Democracy in American: The Ambiguous Promise*, New York: Cambridge University Press.

Litchfield, Paul (1920), 'The industrial representation plan in the Akron factories of the Goodyear Tire and Rubber Company', *Annals of the American Academy of Political and Social Science*, **90**, 27–31.

Lloyd, Henry (1893), *The Safety of the Future Lies with Organized Labor*, Washington: American Federation of Labor.

MacNamara, M. (1920), 'Shop committee and the foreman', *Industrial Management* (August), 102–3.

Marx, Karl (1906 [1867]), *Capital: A Critique of Political Economy*, Vol. 1, New York: Modern Library.

Merritt, Walter (1920), 'Employee representation as a step toward industrial democracy', *Annals of the American Academy of Political and Social Science*, **90**, 39–44.

Milert, Werner, and Rudolf Tshirbs (2012), *Die andere Demokratie: Betriebliche Interessenvertretung in Deutschland 1848–2008*, Essen: Klartext.

Mill, John Stuart (1874), *Autobiography*, New York: Holt.

Mitchell, John (1903), *Organized Labor, its Problems, Purposes, and Ideals and the Present and Future of American Wage Earners*, Philadelphia, PA: American Book and Bible House.

Morgan, H. (1925), 'Saving $1,000 every business day', *System* (June), 741–6.

Morrison, Elizabeth (2011), 'Employee voice behavior: integration and directions for future research', *Academy of Management Annals*, **4**, 373–412.

Nelson, Daniel (1982), 'The company union movement, 1900–1937', *Business History Review*, **8**, 335–57.

Pencavel, John (2001), *Worker Participation: Lessons from the Worker Co-ops of the Pacific Northwest*, New York: Russell Sage Foundation.

Pencavel, John (2003), 'Company unions, wages, and work hours', in D. Lewin and B. Kaufman (eds), *Advances in Industrial and Labor Relations*, Vol. 12, Greenwich, CT: JAI Press, pp. 7–38.

Porter, H. (1905), 'The suggestion system', *Cassier's Magazine* (July), 218–22.

Porter, Robert (1886), *The Voice of Labor: Some Advice to Workingmen*, New York: Ogilvie.

Reynaud, Jean Daniel (1975), *Les Syndicats en France*, Paris: Editions du Seuil.

Rockefeller, John D., Jr (1916), *The Colorado Industrial Plan*, New York: published by the author.

Roland, Henry (1896), 'Six examples of successful shop management', *Engineering Magazine*, **12** (October), 69–85.

Seager, Henry (1920), 'Needs of industry versus demands of organized labor', *The Survey* (3 January), 333–7.

Slichter, Sumner (1919), 'Industrial morale', *Quarterly Journal of Economics*, **35** (November), 36–60.

Smith, Adam (1937 [1776]), *An Inquiry into the Nature and Causes of the Wealth of Nations*, New York: Modern Library.

Spencer, Elaine (1984), *Management and Labor in Imperial Germany: Ruhr Industrialists as Employers, 1896–1914*, New Brunswick: Rutgers University Press.

Tead, Ordway (1917), 'Employees' organizations and their helpful uses', *Industrial Management* (November), 249–56.

Totten, George (1967), 'Collective bargaining and works councils as innovations in industrial relations in Japan during the 1920s', in Ronald Dore (ed.), *Aspects of Social Change in Modern Japan*, pp. 203–44. Princeton: Princeton University Press, pp. 203–44.

Valentine, Robert (1915), 'The progressive relation between efficiency and consent', *Bulletin of the Taylor Society* (November), 3–7.

Wall, Toby, and Stephen Wood (2007), 'Work enrichment and employee voice in human resource management-performance studies', *International Journal of Human Resource Management*, **18** (July), 1335–72.

Watkins, Gordon (1922), *An Introduction to the Study of Labor Problems*, New York: Thomas Crowell.

Webb, Sidney, and Beatrice Webb (1897), *Industrial Democracy*, London: Longmans, Green.

Willard, Daniel (1927), 'The new executive viewpoint on labor relations', *Industrial Management*, **73** (5), 260–63.

Williams, Sidney (1919), 'Safety', in *Proceedings of the First Annual Convention, National Association of Employment Managers*, pp. 92–7.

Zahavi, Gerald (1988), *Workers, Managers, and Welfare Capitalism: The Shoeworkers and Tanners of Endicott Johnson, 1890–1950*, Urbana: University of Illinois Press.

3 Hirschman and voice
Matthew M.C. Allen

INTRODUCTION

Many recent studies of employment relations have explicitly drawn upon the concept of 'voice' as part of their analytical frameworks (see, for instance, Bryson et al., 2006; Budd et al., 2010; Dundon et al., 2004, 2005; Gollan, 2005; Lavelle et al., 2010; Wilkinson and Fay, 2011; Wood et al., 2009). However, Hirschman (1970), who is credited with introducing the term within scholarly analyses, largely applied the concept to customers within competitive markets and 'customer-members' of organizations such as clubs; he did not draw on it to explain employee behaviour within firms. This is noteworthy, as the relationship between consumers and firms in competitive markets and that between employees and employers are fundamentally different. Most importantly, the issue of power within the latter relationship requires even closer scrutiny than it does within the former. In addition, power and the assumptions that are made about the (in)ability of employers and employees to enter into a non-conflictual relationship and/or into a partnership are of central importance within the broad literature on employment (Ackers, forthcoming; Ackers et al., 2005; Johnstone et al., 2010). By contrast, assumptions that firms, in general, will seek to respond to changed customer preferences is more widely accepted (though compare Crouch, 2011).

This chapter discusses Hirschman's (1970) use of the terms 'voice', 'exit', and 'loyalty'. It will raise and discuss crucial issues for studies that apply these terms within the employment relationship. As firms are, in general, authoritative organizations in which collective rules can be enforced by coercive means, such as disciplinary action (Hamilton and Feenstra, 1997; Whitley, 2003), these discussions emphasize the ways in which power shapes employee behaviour. This, in turn, highlights the need for studies of employee behaviour to include not just voice, exit and loyalty within analyses, but 'neglect', too, as employees with very limited power to voice their views or exit the firm may be neglectful (this constitutes the EVLN model of analysis – exit-voice-loyalty-neglect). Neglect may help to bring working conditions into alignment with employees' preferences. A couple of other corollaries follow from these discussions. Firstly, the strategic objectives of companies should be considered within analyses of voice in the employment context, as the aims of firms will have implications for the power of different employee groups within the company. Secondly, the institutional setting of firms, in terms of employment protection legislation and mandated employee representation, will shape the strategies of firms and the power of employees and employers.

This chapter is structured as follows. It begins by outlining the broad aims that Hirschman set himself in his 1970 book. It then discusses in detail his key terms and crucial issues that emerge from applying them to employees within firms. It subsequently discusses neglect. The discussion then broadens its focus to examine other concerns, such as company competition models and the firm's institutional setting, that are cardinal for analyses of employers and their policies towards workers, but that are not as pertinent for Hirschman's analytical focus. Finally, conclusions are drawn.

HIRSCHMAN'S FRAMEWORK

In a compact, yet wide-ranging publication, Hirschman (1970: 2) sought to understand the means by which firms could learn about a 'repairable lapse' in their performance. This analytical focus, as will be shown, has implications for assumptions that are, in general, made by Hirschman about firms' willingness to improve their offering. In short, it suggests that firms will seek to remedy their shortcomings so that they do not fall behind their competitors. Firms may lose out to competitors if consumers decide 'to exit'; that is, to buy a rival's product. The alternative means by which companies may learn about a rectifiable deterioration in their performance is 'voice'. By communicating their dissatisfaction with a product to the firm, consumers voice their concerns. Both voice and exit will be mediated by consumers' loyalty to any particular company. Key questions for Hirschman (1970: 5) were: 'Under what conditions will the exit option prevail over the voice option and vice versa? . . . In what situations do both options come into play jointly?' These issues are also crucial in the study of employees within companies.

VOICE

The importance of power within the voice construct is evident within Hirschman's (1970) analysis. (See also Butler, 2005; Dundon and Gollan, 2007; Dundon et al., 2004; Poole, 1978; Marchington and Wilkinson, 2000 for other discussions of power in relation to different voice mechanisms.) For instance, Hirschman (1970: 4, 40–1) argued that, in most instances, once consumers or 'customer-members' of an organization had voiced their concerns, decision-makers within the selling organization could be expected to search for the sources of those misgivings and to attempt to remedy the situation. In other words, Hirschman presupposed that consumers had some power and they could expect to 'marshal some influence' (Hirschman, 1970: 41, see also p. 78).

To be sure, Hirschman recognized that there were instances in which consumers were unlikely to wield much power over companies. Importantly, he discussed the effects of voice and exit on monopolies. For monopolies controlled by the state, the loss of customers could be compensated by additional payments from the treasury or from a 'variety of financial resources outside and independent of sales revenue' (Hirschman, 1970: 46). If those who exit are also the most vociferous, the effects of voice will be severely diminished (Hirschman, 1970: 45). For those private sector '"lazy" monopolies' (Hirschman, 1970: 59) that are not significantly affected by the loss of customers who are the most sensitive to quality, exit can enable them to continue in 'comfortable mediocrity' (Hirschman, 1970: 59). This is likely to be especially true if those customers who remain view exit as impractical or too costly (Hirschman, 1970: 60). Under such conditions, voice is likely to be ineffectual. These are important caveats that have implications for the application of the voice concept to the employment relationship. They suggest that companies will react differently to the loss of employees if they can be replaced easily or if those employees who leave are the most sensitive to working conditions and those who remain have few, if any, exit options.

Hirschman's caveats create a nuanced perspective. Notably, they provide important starting points for an analysis of the application of the voice concept to the employment relationship. In that relationship, power plays an even more important role in shaping the voice and exit options open to an individual. For instance, employees may lack the power that consumers have in competitive markets (Hyman, 2005). This may be especially true if the concerns raised by employees are construed either as irrelevant by managers or as a threat to their authority within organizations that can be seen, in fundamental terms, as hierarchies with enforceable collective rules (Hamilton and Feenstra, 1997; Whitley, 2003).

A prominent and early application of Hirschman's (1970) framework to the employment relationship is Freeman and Medoff's (1984) study. They recognized that power had to be taken into consideration within that context. For instance, they noted (1984: 107, emphasis added, see 108, too) that 'one reason for the lower quits under unionism is the *dilution of managerial authority*'. Indeed, one of the reasons why Freeman and Medoff chose to focus on unions (and not, for example, on management-initiated voice mechanisms) as the most effective form of voice was because unions were seen as affording employees a degree of protection from any retaliation that managers may have sought to take against employees who had voiced their concerns. Such retaliation could, for instance, result in the firing of an individual worker who had revealed his or her grievances to the employer (Freeman and Medoff, 1984: 9).

Unfortunately, Freeman and Medoff (1984) and others did not discuss the notion of power explicitly. However, a useful way of framing the discussion is to disaggregate the concept. For instance, it can be broken down into, firstly, the range of issues over which potential voice can be expressed, and, secondly, the extent to which those who make use of potential voice mechanisms are able to exert an influence over those workplace issues. Thus, the power of different voice mechanisms should be conceptualized in terms of both areas covered and the degree of influence (Poole, 1978). The latter aspect may depend on the relative dependence of employers on the resources created or owned by employees.

These two aspects of voice are closely akin to issues raised in the related politics literature. In terms of the issues covered by voice mechanisms, managers may play an important role in determining what can and cannot be addressed by those voice mechanisms. This issue is, perhaps, at its acutest in relation to those mechanisms, such as staff associations and joint consultative committees (JCCs), that have been established by managers and whose remit is often set by managers. Thus, managers may be able to set the agenda – and, hence, what is subject to a decision and what is subject to a 'non-decision' (Bachrach and Baratz, 1963). Employees may be able to shape in a proactive way managers' decisions or they may simply react to proposals put forward by managers or, indeed, they may be excluded from certain decisions (Donaghey et al., 2011).

In terms of the degree of influence of different voice mechanisms, Dahl's (1957: 202) concept of power may be useful. He contended that: 'A has power over B to the extent that he can get B to do something that B would not otherwise do.' The emphasis within this definition on *power over* can, however, be construed to imply a zero-sum game. To be sure, at times this aspect will be present within the employment relationship. For instance, employees may be asked to take on additional time-consuming duties without any commensurate pay increase. Employers may also seek to limit the ability of employees to quit one firm to move to another by means of 'no poaching agreements'. The recent compact between, amongst others, Apple and Google to 'not cold call' one another's employees in certain development areas about jobs is such an example. The agreement may have prevented the affected employees from obtaining higher salaries (Kirchgaessner and Menn, 2010). However, power within the employment relationship does not always have to be expressed in a zero-sum way. For instance, constraints placed on employers that can prevent them from firing employees easily can lead to beneficial outcomes in terms of increased training for employees and higher productivity or other improved company outcomes (Croucher et al., 2012; Harcourt and Wood, 2007; Streeck, 1997).

It can be argued that for a voice mechanism to be defined as such, it must be effective; that is, it must enable employees and/or their representatives who remain in a firm not only to make their views known, but also to influence workplace practices. Determining what is and what is not a voice mechanism is, therefore, an empirical question. To define voice in such a way that excludes a consideration of influence would not enable researchers or practitioners to distinguish between mere talking shops, which enable employees to express their opinions, and those measures that lead to a change in workplace practices. Indeed, it is only by leading to a change in practices that voice is likely to lead to an increase in, for example, workplace trust, which is considered in more detail below under loyalty, and performance outcomes. This does not mean, however, that, to be powerful, voice mechanisms must result in practices that are entirely in accordance with employees' wishes; they must, however, have been altered in a discernible way.

This reference to 'employees' wishes' raises the issue of Lukes's (1974) third face of power; that is, the origins of employee preferences. However, this issue will not be addressed here as it would warrant a fundamentally different chapter. In short, it would require an examination of both employees' and employers' preferences and the ways in which these are formed. This is beyond the scope of this chapter – and of Hirschman (1970). Indeed, most empirical studies and conceptual frameworks that draw on the exit, voice and loyalty typology do not examine the establishment of, and changes to, employers' and employees' preferences. Instead they focus on various voice mechanisms and outcomes.

Although defining voice mechanisms in a way that focuses on changed practices may seem to be applying a strenuous criterion to them, other authors have specified voice in a similar manner. For example, Marchington (2007: 234) has noted that voice gives workers a 'direct say' in how the work they perform is organized. Indeed, Strauss (1998: 779) has written that 'voice is meaningless if the message is ignored'. (See also Kaufman, 2005: 568; Bailey, 2009; Butler, 2005; Hyman, 1997.) Moreover, defining voice in this way has important implications for research, as it places the emphasis on assessing employees' evaluations of their impact on workplace practices. All too often, however, it is managers' assessments of employees' input into the decision-making process that are measured (Marchington, 2007). In addition, it would appear to be appropriate for studies, as is increasingly happening, to approach the effects of various voice mechanisms from the employees' perspective. This is especially true if the aim is to evaluate different forms of employee relations as well as workers' opinion of, and potential subsequent need for, various voice mechanisms (Bryson et al., 2006; Freeman et al., 2007;

Pyman et al., 2006; Ramsay et al., 2000; Timming, 2007). Voice may be needed to share information; it can take different forms.

Information Sharing

Information sharing was a crucial aspect of Hirschman's (1970: 33) voice construct, noting that: 'Voice has the function of alerting a firm or organization to its failings . . .'. Clearly, then, the voice of customers or, *mutatis mutandis*, workers in a company aids the sharing of information between managers and employees; more specifically and mirroring Hirschman's arguments, voice in firms, *sensu stricto*, is concerned with the upward communication of information to managers from employees. This, necessarily, assumes that actors do not have perfect information; that is, employees have information that managers do not. Consequently, voice is seen as a means by which these information asymmetries can be overcome. The amount of information that employees have that may be useful to the organization will depend upon the nature of the work carried out by the organization, its strategic priorities and its institutional location (Brewster et al., 2007; Hotho et al., forthcoming). Similarly, employees' willingness to share that information will depend upon the commitment that employers show to employees and the firms' institutional location (Allen, 2014; Whitley, 1999).

Although Hirschman's (1970: 4) definition of voice could also be construed as covering other means of communication, such as protests, by which a firm is alerted to its failings, these are not defined here as voice, as they can be seen as 'negligent' and adversarial forms of behaviour (see below). It should be noted that such labels do not connote a lack of legitimacy of such forms of behaviour. Protests are, indeed, a possible indication that potential voice mechanisms have failed or are absent (compare Edwards et al., 1995). Voice is usually restricted to employees of the firm. Defining voice and protests in this way enables voice to be bounded: not all forms of communication should be deemed to be voice and the views of protesters who are not employees of the firm should not be taken to be voice.

Furthermore, the definition of voice here is distinct from formulations of voice as 'two-way communication' between employees and managers (see, for instance, Willman et al., 2006). The latter definition may not be precise enough for a number of reasons. Firstly, two-way communication could cover protests as well as suggestion schemes. Secondly, two-way communication assumes that managers enter into a dialogue; however, as shown below, 'managerial response' (Freeman and Medoff, 1984) may depend upon the power of voice mechanisms. Moreover, two-way dialogue may imply that managers respond to employees' concerns by talking about them, rather than by changing workplace practices. Thirdly, two-way communication also presupposes that employees either collectively or individually voice their concerns. As noted above, however, this may not be the case if employees fear being reprimanded by managers (Freeman and Medoff, 1984).

Finally, it stresses neither the most important source and, hence, the direction of information flow nor the degree to which employees' views are taken into consideration. In other words, if managers communicate that they are unwilling to change a company practice, even though employees have expressed their disapproval of it, this should not be deemed to be voice. It can, however, be construed as two-way communication. Similarly, whilst some forums that are seen as 'talking shops' may facilitate two-way communication, they do not provide employees with a voice; that is, with a degree of influence over workplace principles, policies and, most importantly, practices. In other words, defining voice merely as two-way communication overlooks the cardinal importance of power in facilitating or hindering the exchange of information within the context of employment. The varying strengths of voice mechanisms are likely to be related to their form. This was not a primary concern for Hirschman because of his analytical focus.

Forms of Employee Voice

Voice can be expressed by workers directly or by workers' representatives collectively. This issue has been the most contentious, and is, again, underpinned either explicitly or implicitly by the different perspectives on the degree of power that employees need for their opinions not only to be voiced, but also to be acted upon by managers. There are major differences between researchers on the efficacy and value of different forms of voice (Freeman and Medoff, 1984; Hirsch and Addison, 1986; Delaney and Godard, 2001; Wood and Fenton-O'Creevy, 2005). The first of the two main divisions is between indirect and direct voice; the second is, within indirect voice, between independent channels (trade unions or non-union structures, such as works councils) or 'employer-sponsored structures' (Gollan, 2002: 325), such as JCCs. Despite this prevalent dichotomy, different forms of voice are not necessarily mutually exclusive: a combination of different forms of voice could be the most effective for organizations, as one form of voice may be able to complement, or mitigate the deficiencies of, another (Kim et al., 2010; Kochan and Osterman, 1994; Marchington, 2001; Tüselmann et al., 2007).

LOYALTY

Although applying Hirschman's concept of loyalty to the employment relationship might appear to be straightforward, it is not, as the notion of power must, once again, be taken into consideration. If the notion of power is not taken into account, assessments of the influence of voice mechanisms on workplace outcomes may underestimate the role of power within the employment relationship. In Hirschman's model, loyalty was positively related to voice: the more loyal a customer is, the more likely he or she is to voice concerns, and the less likely he or she is to exit (Hirschman, 1970: 77–8). Despite the importance of the concept to his model, Hirschman did not discuss loyalty at length. Hirschman (1970: 77) did, however, note that a customer-member's 'special attachment to an organization [is] known as loyalty' (compare Boroff and Lewin, 1997: 53; Turnley and Feldman, 1999: 899). This definition will be applied here, despite Hirschman's analytical focus being on consumers rather than employees. The advantages of this definition are that it can distinguish between narrow job satisfaction and a broader sense of belonging/commitment to an organization. It suggests a more deep-seated attachment than job satisfaction. It can be interpreted to mean that a person will remain loyal to an organization even if current job satisfaction is low. This may be the case if a person is performing unfulfilling duties in order to benefit from credible promotional opportunities in the future.

Loyalty within the context of employment raises issues that are of less importance to consumers. Although employees who are more loyal might be expected – as more loyal consumers are – to voice their concerns more readily than those who are less loyal, this ignores aspects of power that are inherent in any employment relationship (Edwards et al., 1995; Hamilton and Feenstra, 1997; Whitley, 2003). Organizations are hierarchies in which those higher up can direct those lower down. Therefore, expressions of disapproval as well as suggestions for improving existing practices or products could be seen as attempts to undermine the authority of either individual managers or the organization as a whole. In such a situation, those employees who voice their concerns may be seen as disloyal or as a disruptive influence by managers (Butler, 2005; Upchurch et al., 2006). This is likely to be especially true if concerns are raised in areas that managers view as 'non-decisions'; that is, they affect policies or practices that are deemed to be solely within management's prerogative. Hence, loyal employees may be less – rather than more – willing to express their unease about company practices for fear of appearing to criticize the organization and/or individual managers (Boroff and Lewin, 1997: 57).

However, the relationship between loyalty and exit within the context of employment may be the same as it is within the context of consumption. For instance, Boroff and Lewin (1997) noted that those employees who were more loyal had a lower propensity to leave than those who were less loyal. This latter finding is in line with Hirschman's expectations. It also supports the arguments made above: being more prepared to leave the organization, those employees who are less loyal may be more willing to accept the opprobrium that – from a managerial perspective – may attach to criticisms by employees of their actions. These results, therefore, underline the cardinal role played by power in underpinning voice and loyalty.

There is a further theoretical aspect of loyalty that should be addressed. As Hirschman (1970: 77–8) was well aware, loyalty could be seen as both exogenous and endogenous to voice. In other words, a person's or a group's degree of loyalty could both influence, and be influenced by, voice. If loyalty is to a certain extent exogenous – if different individuals exhibit varying degrees of loyalty in the same situation – and if it influences the willingness of individuals to voice concerns, both researchers and practitioners need to take it into consideration. More broadly, factors outside the workplace, such as employment protection legislation, can also shape employee–employer interdependence and, hence, employee loyalty. An emerging strand of the literature is beginning to analyse these issues (Allen, 2014; Brewster et al., 2007; Croucher et al., 2012).

If loyalty is endogenous, the more effective voice mechanisms are, the higher the level of loyalty employees can be expected to have (Dietz and Fortin, 2007). In addition, firms may be able to influence employees' loyalty by their ability to offer, in a credible way, organizational careers to individuals. In other words, the power that a company may have to offer an employee the prospect of promotion is likely to have an impact on that person's loyalty. In short, employers can 'set the agenda' for a person's career and can take decisions and 'non-decisions' that shape an employee's career prospects. Indeed, employers may be able to persuade an employee that a particular move is in his or her interests, as it may appear to lead to improved career chances, even when it does not. More broadly, employee loyalty will be influenced by the (perceived) availability of alternative jobs both within and outside the firm. Indeed, as (Hirschman, 1970: 82) noted, if internal and external exit opportunities are absent, it would make 'no sense to speak of being loyal to a firm'. Therefore, the availability of attractive careers within and outside the organization needs to be added to those factors that influence loyalty.

EXIT

According to Hirschman (1970: 4, italics removed), if '[s]ome customers stop buying the firm's products or some members leave the organization: this is the exit option.' Again, it may seem a relatively straightforward task to apply this concept to the employment relationship. This is not the case, however. Indeed, even if the concept is applied in a strict way – that is, when employees leave an organization – to the employment relationship, difficulties arise. For instance, changing purchasing habits is easier than changing jobs. Firstly, it may be relatively easy to make assessments of well-known and widely available rival products in non-monopolistic consumer markets. By contrast, information asymmetries about the existence of other jobs (some of which may only be open to candidates from within the employing organization) and the quality of the working environment (including, for example, the work-life balance) make switching employers more onerous.

Secondly, transaction costs are involved in the process of looking for other jobs. Indeed, searching for an alternative job curtails the opportunities available with a current employer, if it becomes known that they are actively seeking a job elsewhere. Thus, employers can use their power to influence the range of options available to employees. Other possible transaction costs include the need to find two appropriate jobs (if the employee comes from a dual-income household) in the same area, which may impose severe constraints upon such moves. Thirdly, it may not be possible to move back to the original employer if the new job does not meet expectations. Obviously, consumers, if they so wish, can easily switch their purchases back to the original supplier if they are disappointed with the alternative provider. Employers can, in short, make the decision to return a 'non-decision'.

An employee's ability to quit a firm might not even be a practical option if opportunities for employment at other organizations do not, for instance, exist as a result of poor labour market conditions. In addition, employer collusion to reduce exit options, by, for instance, using their power to take certain employment options 'off the agenda', can also restrict employees' exit options. Consequently, imbalances in power between employers and employees mean that the 'external exit option' is not as readily available to employees as it is to consumers. Thus, in sharp contrast to Hirschman's (1970: 77) argument that where exit is possible, voice is likely to be determined by 'the extent to which customer-members are willing to trade off the certainty of exit against the uncertainties of an improvement in a deteriorated product', it may, within the context of employment, be the case that the decision to quit will be strongly influenced by the extent to which employees are willing to trade-off the uncertainties and costs of exit against the certainties of staying.

It is important to disaggregate the concept of exit in the employment context further. For instance, if the aim of voice mechanisms is to bring workplace policies and practices into alignment with the views of workers either individually or collectively, then, in much the same way that an individual may seek to improve his or her working conditions by changing employers, some workers may be able to do the same by moving up the hierarchy or by changing jobs within the organization. This can be seen as a form of exit described as 'internal job mobility'. (See Farrell (1983) and Rusbult et al. (1988) for earlier treatments of this aspect of exit.) Whilst Hirschman (1970) did not exclude the possibility that a consumer might respond to a deterioration in a particular product or service from a company by buying a more expensive and higher quality product from the same firm, the way that this process operates for employees within firms is very different to that for consumers.

Once again, power is a significant element. In particular, the asymmetric distribution of power in the employment relationship is likely to influence an employer's ability to offer employees the opportunities to change jobs within the organization. Employees, unlike consumers in their purchasing decisions, cannot 'set the agenda' and cannot, usually, unilaterally determine which post within a firm to have. Additionally, employers may use their power to shape the criteria needed to fulfil the duties associated with a particular post to those they favour.

These insights can help to explain apparent anomalies in empirical studies. For instance, low quit rates may indicate that employees are satisfied with their working conditions. It might, consequently, be assumed that those workplaces with low quit rates will also have reduced rates of absenteeism; however, this is not always the case (March and Simon, 1958; see also Barker, 1993; Godard, 2001). This suggests that disgruntled employees find it difficult to quit the firm that they work for; however, they may be able to vent their dissatisfaction with the company by being absent from work. A further corollary of the difficulty that employees may have in changing employers is that exit should, within the context of employment, be measured not just by quits, but also by the willingness/desire to leave the organization (Naus et al., 2007; Rusbult et al., 1988).

This has important ramifications for researchers and practitioners. Most notably, it means that employees who are not loyal to the firm, unlike disappointed consumers, may have to stay with an employer rather than quit. If employees, either collectively or individually, have a voice that enables them to influence workplace practices, they can contribute towards improving working conditions. In this situation, the lack of an exit option may not pose a problem. If, on the other hand, employees do not have a voice, they may use what power they have to act in a 'neglectful' way; that is, to behave in ways that are at odds with the organization's goals (compare Edwards et al., 1995). This underlines the importance of including the fourth category of the EVLN model in analyses.

NEGLECT

Neglect was not a category that Hirschman or Freeman and Medoff or the majority of later researchers explicitly included in their analyses (compare Donaghey et al., 2011; Farrell, 1983; Mellahi et al., 2010; Rusbult et al., 1988; Si and Li, 2012; Withey and Cooper, 1989). Neglect will be defined here as the wilful failure to perform duties either properly or with a sufficient level of care (see also Turnley and Feldman, 1999; compare Rusbult et al., 1988: 601). This does not have to be covert. Neglectful behaviour may involve an employee showing a lack of interest or not engaging fully in work practices. The definition of neglect here does not have normative connotations. Neglect is different to the withdrawal of goodwill. Employees who are well motivated can be expected to try to exceed the level of performance required of them. Those who withdraw their goodwill may perform their duties adequately. By contrast, neglectful employees wilfully under-perform. Defining neglect in this way means that it can cover not just shirking and protests, but also repeated lateness, medically unjustified absenteeism, silent sabotage, withholding productivity-enhancing suggestions, and the use of the company's time and resources for personal matters (Si and Li, 2012; compare Donaghey et al., 2011). Neglect may enable employees to exert some power over their employers by getting the employer to pay for work that has not actually been done. This is, obviously, not in the employer's interest. It will also be defined to include negative attitudes towards the employing organization.

To be sure, Hirschman did address behaviour that could be seen as neglectful; this behaviour was, however, subsumed under 'voice'. For instance, Hirschman (1970: 16) noted that voice 'can be graduated, all the way from faint grumbling to violent protest'. However, protests would appear to have little to do with voice as their 'properties' are fundamentally different: although both voice and protests communicate employees' attitudes to employers, protests do so in a quintessentially adversarial way. That is not to say, however, that voice cannot be expressed confrontationally at times. It is, however, to suggest that the 'starting points' for voice and protests differ radically (compare Edwards et al., 1995; Hyman, 2005).

Although Freeman and Medoff (1984) do not explicitly discuss neglect, they state that disgruntled employees could either quit or engage in 'quiet sabotage or shirking' (Freeman and Medoff, 1984: 11). Rather than treating sabotage and shirking as relatively unimportant outcomes, such neglectful behaviour should be analysed in more detail, as employees cannot change jobs as readily as consumers can alter their buying habits. Therefore, they may turn to negligent behaviour and express or hold negative attitudes towards their employer if they are dissatisfied and cannot exit.

Previous studies that have examined neglect have focused on behavioural outcomes, such as medically unjustified absenteeism and theft. It is equally possible, however, to see neglect in attitudinal terms. Neglect may, therefore, also be expressed in terms of employees having a negative perception of the organization, a mental predisposition to distrust the actions and statements of managers, or a desire to thwart or hinder the attainment of declared organizational goals (compare Naus et al., 2007). This may result in a discrepancy between the number of those who have thought about sharing information with managers and those who have actually done so.

FIRM STRATEGIES AND COMPETITION MODELS

By focusing primarily, but not exclusively, on consumers in competitive markets, Hirschman (1970) was justifiably able to exclude detailed discussions of the strategies of both consumers and firms from his analysis. It would, for instance, seem reasonable to assume that most consumers would wish to purchase products and services that most closely match their price and quality preferences. If the consumer's usually purchased product suffers a deterioration in, say, quality, he or she can be expected either to buy an alternative product that meets his or her requirements more closely or to raise the problem with the firm's managers. Similarly, firms that operate in non-monopolistic markets can, in general, be expected to react to a fall in revenues, which has been brought about by consumers buying rival products, by trying to remedy the drop in performance. However, within employment studies, companies and their strategies cannot be assumed to be homogeneous (Allen and Aldred, 2013; Whitley, 2010). Importantly, contrasting strategies can be expected to have varying implications for the ways in which employees are treated.

In short, firms can seek to compete along three distinct dimensions: they can focus either on price or quality, they can produce low or high volumes of standardized goods, and they can seek to respond rapidly to changing market and technological conditions. These dimensions can, of course, be combined in company strategies (Whitley, 2010). Firms that compete by pursuing Fordist competition models that focus on reducing costs, providing relatively high volumes of standardized goods, and that do not seek to respond very rapidly to market changes can be expected to provide limited voice opportunities to employees. Employer–employee interdependence is likely to be low. If voice mechanisms are in place in companies pursuing this competition model, they are likely to be employer-dominated and/or focus on channelling the views of individual employees rather than the concerns of workers collectively to managers (Lewin and Sherer, 1993). By contrast, those firms that seek to improve continuously the quality of their products are likely to rely on the skills of their employees to a greater extent. Consequently, they can be expected to grant workers either individually or collectively more voice over workplace issues (Allen and Whitley, 2012; Hall and Soskice, 2001; Harcourt and Wood, 2007; Whitley, 1999).

Along with legislation, managers' attitudes towards voiced concerns and workers' access to information, then, an important source of employees' power is likely to be the degree to which employers are dependent on them and the difficulty that the employer would face in either replacing them or finding other substitutes for them. If the firm's strategy creates a high dependence on employees (either individually or collectively), workers are likely to be powerful. Therefore, workplace practices and policies are likely to adhere more closely to their wishes, as employees may be able to ensure that changes, which the employer may not otherwise make, are implemented.

INSTITUTIONAL SETTING AND DIFFERENT TYPES OF LABOUR MARKETS

Another aspect that was neglected within Hirschman's (1970) framework is institutions. When examining the differences in voice practices across workplaces, it is important to take into consideration the institutional setting of different establishments (Allen, 2014; Allen and Whitley, 2012; Croucher et al., 2012; Harcourt and Wood, 2007; Wilkinson and Wood, 2012). Institutions can shape the power of workers individually and/or collectively. For example, non-union forms of collective voice, such as joint consultative committees and works councils, are often not permitted in the USA, but they exist in Australia and the UK (Freeman et al., 2007). Other countries, such as Germany and the Netherlands, have independent and relatively powerful forms of employee representation. Thus, the power relationship between employers and employees will depend not just on the strategy of the firm, but also on the institutional setting of the establishment.

These institutions can shape the nature of labour markets (Allen, 2014; Whitley, 2007). For instance, employment protection legislation will influence the extent to which firms can rely on numerical flexibility to adjust to product market conditions. If a firm takes advantage of a flexible labour market, a corollary is that some employees are not seen as being of fundamental importance to the firm and the attainment of its strategic objectives. Some activities are likely to be designed so that employees do not need much training or specific skills; employees can, consequently, be replaced easily (Whitley, 2007). By contrast, legislation that hinders firms' ability to use numerical flexibility as an adjustment strategy may lead to a view of employees as a fixed cost and, hence, encourage firms to invest in training to upgrade employee skills (Harcourt and Wood, 2007). Consequently, those lower level employees may become more important to the firm and its ability to achieve its objectives. The voice mechanisms within workplaces in such contrasting institutional settings are likely to reflect the employees' power.

However, it is not merely the presence of particular voice mechanisms that is important, but their influence on a range of employee- and establishment-related outcomes, such as quit rates, levels of absenteeism, innovation, productivity rates and profitability. These have only recently been assessed in detail in comparative studies at the workplace level (Allen and Whitley, 2012; Allen et al., 2011; Brewster et al., 2007, forthcoming; Croucher et al., 2012; Goergen et al., 2012; Harcourt and Wood, 2007). Collectively, these studies demonstrate that voice-related institutions, such as legally supported works councils, do not determine establishment outcomes, but they do exert an influence. In general, establishments in countries with stronger, legally supported voice mechanisms are more likely to be able to share authority and delegate some decision-making discretion to employees than those with weaker institutional forms of voice. This, in turn, can cultivate the provision of firm-specific skills that underpin particular competition models (Allen and Aldred, 2011; Whitley, 2010).

CONCLUSIONS AND IMPLICATIONS

This chapter has sought to illustrate the importance of the notion of power not only to the voice aspect, but also to the exit and loyalty aspects of Hirschman's framework. Moreover, it has shown how that framework should be complemented by a 'neglect' category. This chapter has, in addition, highlighted that there are ways to disaggregate yet further the individual elements of the EVLN framework. For instance, exit may involve leaving the organization or a move to a different job in the same organization. Research has tended to focus on the former (Addison et al., 2001; Allen, 2006; Freeman and Medoff, 1984; Hyman 2005) rather than the latter (March and Simon, 1958). If the internal labour market enables employees to move to more satisfying jobs within the firm, employees may show higher levels of loyalty even if voice mechanisms are absent. However, loyalty tends not to be controlled for in assessments of various voice mechanisms on firm-level outcomes (compare Luchak, 2003).

Moreover, there may be opportunities to assess in even greater detail the extent to which voice mechanisms are associated with different workplace outcomes, such as higher or lower productivity levels. For instance, although Bryson et al. (2006) extended the use of the voice framework to include employees' perceptions of the different voice mechanisms within their empirical analysis, the extent to which those perceptions are shaped by other factors – such as loyalty and internal and external exit – were not included. These omitted variables may bias the results if they are correlated with those factors included in the study. This may be the case if employers are willing to make a trade-off between voice mechanisms that constrain their decision-making abilities and the use of promotional prospects to gain employees' loyalty. In other words, internal exit may be deemed preferable to powerful voice mechanisms by some employers (and employees).

The strategic priorities and institutional context of firms are also important factors that can help to explain levels of voice, exit, loyalty and neglect within the context of employment. Whilst much key work has already been carried out in this area (Allen and Whitley, 2012; Brewster et al., 2007; Croucher et al., 2012; Goergen et al., 2012; Harcourt and Wood, 2007), future research could focus to an even greater extent on analysing the complex relationships between institutional supports for voice and the goals of firms, on the one hand, and outcomes in terms of voice, exit, loyalty and neglect, on the other. Such research could encompass in-depth comparative case studies and cross-national survey data. In short, Hirschman's (1970) voice framework has spawned a great deal of important employment-related research and can continue to do so.

REFERENCES

Ackers, P. (forthcoming), 'Rethinking the employment relationship: a neo-pluralist critique of British industrial relations orthodoxy', *International Journal of Human Resource Management*.

Ackers P., M. Marchington, A. Wilkinson and T. Dundon (2005), 'Partnership and voice, with or without trade unions: Changing UK management approaches to organizational participation', in M. Stuart and M. Martinez Lucio (eds), *Partnership and Modernisation in Employment Relations*, London: Routledge, pp. 20–39.

Addison, J.T., C. Schnabel and J. Wagner (2001) 'Works councils in Germany: their effects on establishment performance', *Oxford Economic Papers*, **53**, 659–94.

Allen, M.M.C. (2006), *The Varieties of Capitalism Paradigm: Explaining Germany's Comparative Advantage?*, London: Palgrave Macmillan.

Allen, M.M.C. (2014), 'Business systems theory and employment relations', in A. Wilkinson, G.T. Wood and R. Deeg (eds), *The Oxford Handbook of Employment Relations: Comparative Employment Systems*, Oxford: Oxford University Press, pp. 86–113.

Allen, M.M.C. and M.L. Aldred (2011), 'Varieties of capitalism, governance, and high-tech export performance: a fuzzy-set analysis of the new EU member states', *Employee Relations*, **33** (4), 334–55.

Allen, M.M.C. and M.L. Aldred (2013), 'Business regulation, inward foreign direct investment, and economic growth in the new European Union member states', *Critical Perspectives on International Business*, **9** (3), pp. 301–21.

Allen, M.M.C. and R. Whitley (2012), 'Internationalization and sectoral diversity: the roles of organizational capabilities and dominant institutions in structuring firms' responses to semiglobalization', in C. Lane and G.T. Wood (eds), *Capitalist Diversity and Diversity within Capitalism*, Abingdon: Routledge, pp. 97–120.

Allen, M.M.C., H.-J. Tüselmann and M.L. Aldred (2011), 'Institutional frameworks and radical innovation: an analysis of high- and medium-high-technology industries in Germany', *International Journal of Public Policy*, **7** (4, 5, 6), 265–81.

Bachrach, P. and M. Baratz (1963), 'Decisions and non-decisions: an analytical framework', *American Political Science Review*, **56**, 632–42.

Bailey, M. (2009), 'Can you hear us? The effectiveness of European works councils as a mechanism of employee voice for Hungarian workers of PrintCo', *Employee Relations*, **31** (2), 197–218.

Barker, J.R. (1993), 'Tightening the iron cage: concertive control in self-managing teams', *Administrative Science Quarterly*, **38** (3), 408–37.

Boroff, K.E. and D. Lewin (1997), 'Loyalty, voice, and intent to exit a union firm: a conceptual and empirical analysis', *Industrial and Labor Relations Review*, **51** (1), 50–63.

Brewster C., G. Wood, R. Croucher and M. Brookes (2007), 'Collective and individual voice: convergence in Europe?', *International Journal of Human Resource Management*, **18** (7), 1246–62.

Brewster, C., M. Brookes, P. Johnson and G. Wood (forthcoming), 'Direct Involvement, Partnership and Setting: a Study in Bounded Diversity', *International Journal of Human Resource Management*.

Bryson, A., A. Charlwood and J. Forth (2006), 'Worker voice, managerial response and labour productivity: an empirical investigation', *Industrial Relations Journal*, **37** (5), 438–55.

Budd, J.W., P.J. Gollan and A. Wilkinson (2010), 'New approaches to employee voice and participation in organizations', *Human Relations*, **63** (3), 303–10.

Butler, P. (2005), 'Non-union employee representation: exploring the efficacy of the voice process', *Employee Relations*, **27** (3), 272–88.

Crouch, C. (2011), *The Strange Non-Death of Neoliberalism*, Cambridge: Polity.

Croucher, R., G. Wood, C. Brewster and M. Brookes (2012), 'Employee turnover, HRM and institutional contexts', *Economic and Industrial Democracy*, **33** (4), 605–20.

Dahl, R.A. (1957), 'The Concept of Power', *Behavioral Science*, **2**, 202–10.

Delaney, J. and J. Godard (2001), 'An industrial relations perspective on the high-performance paradigm', *Human Resource Management Review*, **11**, 395–429.

Dietz, G. and M. Fortin (2007), 'Trust and justice in the formation of joint consultative committees', *International Journal of Human Resource Management*, **18** (7), 1159–81.

Donaghey, J., N. Cullinane, T. Dundon and A. Wilkinson (2011), 'Reconceptualising employee silence: problems and prognosis', *Work, Employment and Society*, **25** (1), 51–67.

Dundon, A. and P.J. Gollan (2007), 'Re-conceptualizing voice in the non-union workplace', *International Journal of Human Resource Management*, **18** (7), 1182–98

Dundon, A., A. Wilkinson, M.P. Marchington and P. Ackers (2004), 'The meanings and purpose of employee voice', *International Journal of Human Resource Management*, **15** (6), 1149–70.

Dundon, A., A. Wilkinson, M.P. Marchington and P. Ackers (2005), 'The management of voice in non-union organisations: managers' perspectives', *Employee Relations*, **27** (3), 307–19.

Edwards, P., D. Collinson and G.D. Rocca (1995), 'Workplace resistance in Western Europe: a preliminary overview and a research agenda', *European Journal of Industrial Relations*, **1** (3), 283–316.

Farrell, D. (1983), 'Exit, voice, loyalty, and neglect as responses to job dissatisfaction: a multidimensional scaling study', *Academy of Management Journal*, **26** (4), 596–607.

Freeman, R.B. and J. Medoff (1984), *What Do Unions Do?*, London: Basic Books.

Freeman, R.B., P. Boxall and P. Haynes (eds) (2007), *What Workers Say: Employee Voice in the Anglo-American Workplace*, Ithaca: Cornell University Press.

Godard, J. (2001), 'High-performance *and* the transformation of work? The implications of alternative work practices for the nature and experience of work', *Industrial and Labor Relations Review*, **54** (4), 776–805.

Goergen, M., C. Brewster, G. Wood, and A. Wilkinson (2012), 'Varieties of capitalism and investments in human capital', *Industrial Relations: A Journal of Economy and Society*, **51** (S1), 521–7.

Gollan, P. (2002), 'So what's the news? Management strategies towards non-union employee representation at News International', *Industrial Relations Journal*, **33** (4), 316–31.

Gollan, P.J. (2005) 'Silent voices: representation at the Eurotunnel call centre', *Personnel Review*, **34** (4), 423–50.

Hall, P.A. and D. Soskice (2001), 'Introduction', in P.A. Hall and D. Soskice (eds), *Varieties of Capitalism: The Institutional Foundations of Comparative Advantage*, Oxford: Oxford University Press, pp. 1–68.

Hamilton, G.G. and R.C. Feenstra (1997), 'Varieties of hierarchies and markets: an introduction', in M. Orru, N.W. Biggart and G.G. Hamilton (eds), *The Economic Organization of East Asian Capitalism*, Thousand Oaks, CA: Sage, pp. 55–96.

Harcourt, M. and G. Wood (2007), 'The importance of employment protection for skill development in coordinated market economies', *European Journal of Industrial Relations*, **13** (2), pp. 141–59.

Hirsch, B. and J. Addison (1986), *The Economic Analysis of Unions: New Approaches and Evidence*, Boston: Allen and Unwin.

Hirschman, A.O. (1970), *Exit, Voice and Loyalty. Responses to Decline in Firms, Organizations, and States*, Cambridge, MA: Harvard University Press.

Hotho, J.J., A. Saka-Helmhout and F. Becker-Ritterspach (forthcoming), 'Bringing context and structure back into situated learning', *Management Learning*.

Hyman, R. (1997), 'The future of employee representation', *British Journal of Industrial Relations*, **35** (3), 309–36.

Hyman, R. (2005), 'Whose (social) partnership?', in M. Stuart and M. Martinez Lucio (eds), *Partnership and Modernisation in Employment Relations*, London: Routledge, pp. 251–65.

Johnstone, S., P. Ackers and A. Wilkinson (2010), 'Better than nothing: is non-union partnership a contradiction in terms?', *Journal of Industrial Relations*, **52** (2), 151–68.

Kaufman, B.E. (2005), 'What do unions do? Evaluation and commentary', *Journal of Labour Research*, **26** (4), 555–95.

Kim, J., J.P. MacDuffie and F.K. Pil (2010), 'Employee voice and organizational performance: team versus representative influence', *Human Relations*, **63** (3), 371–94.

Kirchgaessner, S. and J. Menn (2010), 'Tech firms agree to halt anti-poaching deals', *Financial Times*, September 25, available at: http://www.ft.com/cms/s/2/42294fdc-c82d-11df-ae3a-00144feab49a.html#axzz1sZgIvScr (accessed 27 November 2013).

Kochan, T. and P. Osterman (1994) *The Mutual Gains Enterprise*, Boston: Harvard Business School Press.

Lavelle, J., P. Gunnigle and A. McDonnell (2010), 'Patterning employee voice in multinational companies', *Human Relations*, **63** (3), 395–418.

Lewin, D. and P.D. Sherer (1993), 'Does strategic choice explain senior executives' preferences on employee voice and representation?', in B.E. Kaufman and M.M. Kleiner (eds), *Employee Representation: Alternatives and Future Directions*, Madison, WI: Industrial Relations Research Association, pp. 235–63.

Luchak, A.A. (2003), 'What kind of voice do loyal employees use?', *British Journal of Industrial Relations*, **41** (1), 115–34.

Lukes, S. (1974), *Power: A Radical View*, New York: Macmillan.

March, J.G. and H.A. Simon (1958), *Organizations*, New York: John Wiley.

Marchington, M. (2001), *Management Choice and Employee Voice*, London: CIPD.

Marchington, M. (2007), 'Employee voice systems', in P. Boxall, J. Purcell and P. Wright (eds), *The Oxford Handbook of Human Resource Management*, Oxford: Oxford University Press, pp. 231–50.

Marchington, M. and Wilkinson, A. (2000), 'Direct participation', in S. Bach and K. Sisson (eds), *Personnel Management: a Comprehensive Guide to Theory and Practice*, Oxford: Blackwell, pp. 340–64.

Mellahi, K., P.S. Budhwar and B. Li (2010), 'A study of the relationship between exit, voice, loyalty and neglect and commitment in India', *Human Relations*, **63** (3), 349–69.

Naus, F., A. van Iterson and R. Roe (2007), 'Organizational cynicism: extending the exit, voice, loyalty, and neglect model of employees' responses to adverse conditions in the workplace', *Human Relations*, **60** (5), 683–718.

Poole, M. (1978), *Workers' Participation in Industry*, London: Routledge.

Pyman, A., B. Cooper, J. Teicher and P. Holland (2006), 'A comparison of the effectiveness of employee voice arrangements in Australia', *Industrial Relations Journal*, **37** (5), 543–59.

Ramsay, H., D. Scholarios and B. Harley (2000), 'Employees and high-performance work systems: testing inside the black box', *British Journal of Industrial Relations*, **38** (4), 501–32.

Rusbult, C.E., D. Farrell, G. Rogers and A.G. Mainous III (1988), 'Impact of exchange variables on exit, voice, loyalty, and neglect: an integrative model of responses to declining job satisfaction', *Academy of Management Journal*, **31** (3), 599–627.

Si, S. and Y. Li (2012), 'Human resource management practices on exit, voice, loyalty, and neglect: organizational commitment as a mediator', *International Journal of Human Resource Management*, **23** (8), 1705–16.

Strauss G. (1998), 'Worker participation – some under-considered issues', *Industrial Relations*, **45** (4), 778–803.

Streeck, W. (1997), 'Beneficial constraints: on the economic limits of rational voluntarism', in J.R. Hollingsworth and R. Boyer (eds), *Contemporary Capitalism: The Embeddedness of Institutions*, Cambridge: Cambridge University Press, pp. 197–219.

Timming, A.R. (2007), 'European works councils and the dark side of managing worker voice', *Human Resource Management Journal*, **17** (3), 248–64.

Turnley, W.H. and D.C. Feldman (1999), 'The impact of psychological contract violations on exit, voice, loyalty, and neglect', *Human Relations*, **52** (7), 895–922.

Tüselmann, H.-J., F. McDonald, A. Heise, M.M.C. Allen and S. Voronkova (2007), *Employee Relations in Foreign-Owned Subsidiaries: German Multinational Companies in the UK*, London: Palgrave Macmillan.

Upchurch, M., M. Richardson, S. Tailby, A. Danford and P. Stewart (2006), 'Employee representation and partnership in the non-union sector: a paradox of intention?', *Human Resource Management Journal*, **16** (4), 393–410.

Whitley, R. (1999), *Divergent Capitalisms: The Social Structuring and Change of Business Systems*, Oxford: Oxford University Press.

Whitley, R. (2003), 'From the search for universal correlations to the institutional structuring of economic organization and change: the development and future of organization studies ', *Organization*, **10** (3), 481–501.

Whitley, R. (2007), *Business Systems and Organizational Capabilities: The Institutional Structuring of Competitive Competences*, Oxford: Oxford University Press.

Whitley, R. (2010), 'Changing competition models in market economies: the effects of internationalisation, technological innovations and academic expansion on the conditions supporting dominant economic logics', in G. Morgan, J.L. Campbell, C. Crouch, O.K. Pedersen and R. Whitley (eds), *The Oxford Handbook of Comparative Institutional Analysis*, Oxford: Oxford University Press, pp. 363–97.

Wilkinson, A. and C. Fay (2011), 'New times for employee voice?', *Human Resource Management*, **50** (1), 65–74.

Wilkinson, A. and G. Wood (2012), 'Institutions and employment relations: the state of the art', *Industrial Relations*, **51** (S1), 373–88.

Willman, P., A. Bryson and R. Gomez (2006), 'The sound of silence: which employers choose no employee voice and why?', *Socio-Economic* Review, **4** (2), 283–99.

Withey, M. and W. Cooper (1989), 'Predicting exit, voice, loyalty and neglect', *Administrative Science Quarterly*, **34**, 521–39.

Wood, S. and M.P. Fenton-O'Creevy (2005), 'Direct involvement, representation and employee voice in UK multinationals in Europe', *European Journal of Industrial Relations*, **11** (1), 27–50.

Wood, G., R. Croucher, C. Brewster, D.G. Collings and M. Brookes (2009), 'Varieties of firm: complementarity and bounded diversity', *Journal of Economic Issues*, **43** (1), 241–60.

4 Employee voice and the transaction cost economics project

Paul Willman, Alex Bryson, Rafael Gomez and Tobias Kretschmer

INTRODUCTION

Transaction costs are, in Arrow's memorable term, the costs of running the economic system (1974: 48). To use Williamson's simple analogy, they are analogous to friction in physical systems (1985: 19). In many forms of positive, mathematical economics, they do not exist, just as frictions are assumed away in the abstract modelling of physical systems. Transaction costs are subversive of pure market models because, by definition, they imply something is not working or that there is a cost (over and above that which is determined by supply-demand conditions) involved in making it work.

Voice is at root a transaction cost concept. Markets should work by exit; if consumers or employees are not getting what they want, they should switch supplier or employer. Voice is the obverse of switching. The existence of voice is premised on the empirical observation that people often try to sort out their problems rather than simply finding a better option somewhere else. For Hirschman (1970), there are potentially a large number of such situations in both consumer and labour markets. Moreover, he sees collective voice as more effective than individual voice; but collective voice is difficult to organize, since there are collective action problems. It is not just a matter of what is to be done but a matter of who will do it.

This is quite a disturbing set of observations for some economists because not only do markets sometimes not work, but economic actors are prepared to engage in costly collective action to resolve problems in a wide set of circumstances. The conclusion for an economist (if not for other social scientists) is obvious. If voice is widespread, it must be more efficient for both parties in a wide set of transactions, so one must study the efficiency properties of voice mechanisms.

This is significant for the following reasons. The most widely cited approach to voice used in the employment relations (ER) field is essentially Hirschman's (Morrison 2011), and its import by Freeman and Medoff (1984) into the mainstream of labour relations. More precisely, it is Hirschman's with a few key assumptions added since Freeman and Medoff argued that collective voice is of primary importance and that collective voice is to be equated with trade unions. The first is a stronger version of Hirschman's argument. The second is arbitrary, based probably on overreliance on the American model of legal collective action (the 'Wagner Act' model).

Interestingly, over fifty years prior to Hirschman, William Basset's book *When the Workmen Help You Manage* (1919) included the use of the term voice and did not restrict observations to the union establishment (Kaufman, 2012). What goes missing in the traditional ER conception of voice is central; it is the transaction. Whether it is better to adopt voice or exit depends on the *nature of the transaction* for both parties.

Let us take the employment relation. The strongest voice-sustaining equilibrium is where both parties see voice as preferable to exit. This is likely where both parties have substantial sunk costs. In other circumstances, there is no voice-sustaining equilibrium. Critically, though both sets of authors greatly contributed to the current interest in the voice concept, neither Hirschman nor Freeman and Medoff spend much time examining which transactions sustain voice and which do not.

This chapter will try to do both and to use that approach to explain the emergence of voice and its variance. The next section will look at which types of employment relationship are likely to sustain voice and which not; it develops a model of the employment contract that originates with Oliver Williamson. Based on this, the following section uses a simple cost–benefit model which deals with two related questions. First, where is voice likely to emerge and, second, what type of voice is it likely to be? Next we illustrate how this approach may be developed empirically.

THE EMPLOYMENT RELATIONSHIP

Williamson (1975; see also Willman, 1986: 89–96) identifies three broad types of employment contract: spot contracting, contingent claims contracting and, explicitly borrowed from Simon, an 'authority relationship'. Each are in Williamson's terms, different 'governance mechanisms', and each has different transaction cost properties. He does not deal directly with this, but as we show below, each is likely to lead to demands by one or both contractual parties for voice mechanisms, primarily to control what Williamson terms 'opportunism' ('self interest seeking with guile': Williamson, 1975: 26).

Consider Figure 4.1. In spot contracting, at time t_1 the parties agree a price for the supply of labour services x_1 at the occurrence of the event e_1. They do the same again at t_2 and again at t_3 and so on. This is in effect a description of a casual labour market and its effects have been documented by Willman (1986: 108–44) for two empirically important historical examples, dock (longshore) work and newspaper printing; in many countries, through much of the twentieth century these industries were associated with high levels of collective voice, particularly high union density and high levels of collective conflict. Both were also characterized by high levels of product market volatility which could translate into volatile and uncertain levels of demand for labour. In dock work, ship arrival times were unpredictable, and demand for labour to unload the ship was high, but short lived; particularly if the product was perishable, the employer had incentives for very short spot contracts for large groups of employees. The employer incentive for short-term employment, treating labour as a variable cost, arose since fast unloading meant lower berth costs and better use of capital (the ship and berth). Employees had incentives to extend employment and to control the volatility of earnings. In newspapers, there was similar volatility in demand for labour. This emerges because, although the publication time of the newspaper may not be in question, the content and size of it is; one cannot produce the news element of a paper until as late as possible. The product is highly perishable; no one wants yesterday's paper.

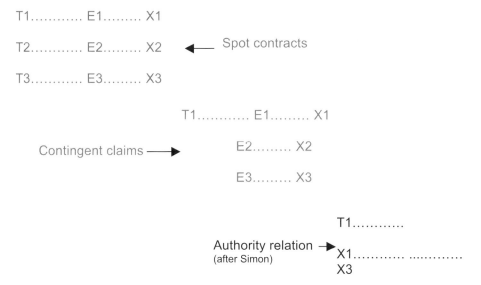

Source: Williamson (1975).

Figure 4.1   Employment contract types

Similar institutional responses emerged in both industries across several countries. The employer wishes to use spot contracts so that all the risk in labour demand volatility is borne by the employee. The employer also has no incentive to build a relationship with any individual employee across a contract sequence. The usual way of implementing this was through the use of casual labour and the 'hiring hall' in which the employer shows up on any event *ej* and picks labour from a pool. The usual response by employees was collective action to implement rules for hiring (work sharing of several forms), setting minimum labour prices and minimum manning levels. Three further points are of interest, both emerging once collective organization is established. First, the union has no incentive to encourage relationships between individual employees and firms (that is, 'decasualization' or long-term employment). Second, collective action needs to cover the whole labour market to be effective, so closed shops are preferred by the union. Third, firms have a strong incentive for collective action in wage bargaining to take labour costs out of competition, so industry bargaining emerges.

So, the contractual pattern, itself a response to product market conditions, encourages strong union voice. However, this is not necessarily an equilibrium. Employers are faced with higher labour costs and have no incentive themselves to invest in voice. Empirically, both cases disappeared when technology was substituted for labour, in circumstances of very high levels of conflict. In general terms, more stable employment contracts emerged.

Let us return again to Figure 4.1 to examine contingent claims contracting. In contingent claims contracting, at time t_1 the parties agree a price for the supply of labour services x_1 to x_3 at the occurrence of the events $e_1 \ldots e_3$. So the underlying assumption is of a longer term employment relationship, but across a specifiable range of events which each lead to demand for a predictable set of labour services ($x_1 \ldots x_3$). Empirical examples of this sort of contract in industries such as shoemaking in a variety of countries go back as far as Commons (1909). In shoemaking they take the form of price lists for particular types or elements of shoe (normally the shoe is priced by the element combination). However, almost all piecework arrangements where prices are attached either to labour inputs or outputs are forms of contingent claims contract. For example, the application of Taylorist production systems would normally be based on a complex contingent claims contract (Braverman, 1974).

This Taylorist example gives a clue to the limitations and also the voice implications of this form of contracting. A key element in Taylorism is the separation of conception from execution; that is, employers decide on, design and specify the tasks and the employee delivers the service. So for this form of contracting to be useful in the employment relationship, the employer must be able, at t_1, to specify both a large set of events $(e_1 \ldots e_j)$ and the specific set of labour services triggered by each event $(x_1 \ldots x_j)$. Where there is product market volatility or technological change, the efficiency of the approach is compromised and it can degenerate into a sequence of spot contracts with similar voice implications to those described above. Williamson uses Simon's term 'bounded rationality' to describe the cognitive limitations of this form of contracting.

However, even in steady state, there are two sets of voice implications. First, what governance mechanism is in place to establish whether a particular e_j generating a requirement for x_j has occurred? Second, what do the parties do in the face of the unexpected (that is, unspecified) event? The first points to some mechanism for consultation and communication backed up by a process such as arbitration to establish what the state of the world is. The second points to a procedural arrangement in which a new event generating a new demand for labour service is identified, classified and priced. These may both be part of a collective agreement between management and union but there is nothing here that excludes the possibility of non-union voice.

However, Williamson still regards contingent claims contracting as either *ex ante* or *ex post* inefficient. By *ex ante* is meant that the parties can spend enormous efforts trying to identify and price contingencies and the complexity of the contract is enormous. By *ex post* is meant that haggling over unforeseen contingencies remains a high probability. Williamson (1975, 1985) regards the 'authority relation' which he also borrows from Simon as more efficient. It is worth quoting his approach.

> The authority relation mode involves capitalist ownership of equipment and inventories coupled with an employment relationship between capitalist and worker. The employment relationship is, by design, an incomplete form of contracting. Flexibility is featured as the employee stands ready to accept authority regarding work assignments provided only that the behaviour called for falls within the 'zone of acceptance' of the contract. (Williamson, 1985: 218–19)

In terms of Figure 4.1, the employee, in return for an employment contract, allows the employer to specify a zone of acceptance, which may be thought of as a range of $(x_1 \ldots x_3)$ services unconnected to specific events. For the transaction cost economist, this reduces costly haggling merely to whether anything falls outside $(x_1 \ldots x_3)$, which is therefore more efficient than the other modes in which haggling is more likely. For other social scientists, it may beg many interesting questions, particularly the general one – why should the authority reside with the employer (capitalist)? And the specific one – what defines $(x_1 \ldots x_3)$? In order to get to the voice-related issues involved in this contractual form, we have to look at two other conceptual building blocks of the transaction cost economics project: first, opportunism and, second, the difference between perfunctory and consummate cooperation. These are both, for Williamson, attributes *only* of employees, but not because they are employees – because they are sellers.

Opportunism, as we noted above, is self-interest seeking with guile. It is a much stronger assumption than simple self-interest. It involves adverse selection *and* moral hazard, and the generation of 'contrived' conditions of information asymmetry. It can destroy the efficiency principles of any contractual form because 'were it not for opportunism, all behaviour could be rule governed' (and we could write the rules). It destroys 'actions of a joint profit maximising kind' (Williamson, 1985: 48). In employment contracts, opportunism is discussed as a property of employees; put colloquially, they get hired by saying they will do the job (adverse selection) and then they do as little as possible (moral hazard) while learning much more about how the job is done than the employer (information asymmetry).

'As little as possible' is perfunctory cooperation. This is performing in a minimally acceptable way; just better than the next available job applicant. The basic idea is that the supplier of labour enjoys discretion within an incomplete contract but chooses the minimum effort. Consummate cooperation is 'an affirmative job attitude whereby gaps are filled, initiative is taken, and judgement is exercised in an instrumental way' (Williamson, 1985: 262–3). Joint benefits and efficiency gains are maximized. In other words, in Fox's (1974) terms, the 'silences' in an authority relationship can be filled by low or high trust, and this is the space for voice. Williamson (1975) opts for Doeringer and Piore's (1971) idea of an internal labour market characterized by, on the one hand, long-term investments and monitoring by the employer and, on the other, promotion and skill acquisition benefits by the employee, as a contractual governance mechanism disposed towards the avoidance of opportunism and the maximization of efficiency gains.

So, in all three forms of employment contracting, there is a clear role for voice as (in Williamson's terms) a 'governance mechanism' to increase efficiency by reducing transaction costs. And the probability of voice increases with the switching costs of both parties; both scarcity of alternative employment opportunities and scarcity of alternative supplies of labour should promote voice.

There have been many criticisms of the Williamson approach. Many concern the assumptions about actors therein; specifically, the assumption about pervasive opportunism (self-interest seeking with guile) embeds a particularly bleak view of human nature (Dietrich, 1994; Donaldson, 1995; Ghoshal and Moran, 1996). It has been seen as ethnocentric, specifically based on Western assumptions (Dore 1983). It ignores power altogether (Francis, 1982), and it is a theoretical construct rather than an empirically grounded set of findings about employment contracts. Most significantly for the present concerns, it sees opportunism in employment contracts as an option only for the employee, when the three mechanisms underpinning it – moral hazard, adverse selection and information asymmetry – are clearly also relevant for the employer (Marglin, 1962, Willman, 1982).

However, for the study of employee voice, it does generate specific predictions.

1. Because voice is a likely outcome of all forms of employment contract, it should be common; specifically, it should be far more common than employment contracting without voice.

2. Because voice can be of benefit to both contracting parties, it may be sponsored and initiated by either employer or employee, or both.
3. Because voice has efficiency properties, the parties should choose the most efficient form of voice, either in terms of the costs of voice provision, or the returns (reduction in transaction costs) to any given form of voice.

In the next section, we develop a model dealing with the costs and benefits of voice.

THE CHOICE OF VOICE REGIME[1]

Transaction cost economics suggests that in exchanges characterized by asset specificity, frequency of interaction and uncertainty, choices about transaction governance structures are required. In particular, the choice whether to make or buy, or, more accurately, own or contract. All else equal, the more idiosyncratic the investments, the greater the frequency of interaction (and duration of exchange), and the greater the uncertainty facing the buyer, the more hierarchy rather than market will be preferred (Williamson, 1975, 1985, 1991).

The choice of governance mechanism is made by parties operating under bounded rationality, faced with the possibility of opportunism, and operating on a risk neutral basis. With single interactions (the temporary employee paid by the piece) and no uncertainty, the employer will not want voice; the classic example above is the longshore hiring hall. However, the employer wanting voice faces a governance choice problem when seeking to 'purchase' a voice-producing workforce. 'Making' involves full provision of those mechanisms which might engender employee voice, including those perceived as legitimate by employees. Specifically, this would involve full provision of non-union voice. 'Buying' would, *in extremis*, involve the subcontracting out to a union of all aspects of voice provision. Hybrid and intermediate forms, which involve a mixture of union and non-union voice, are possible and might be differentiated in terms of variance in the nature of the transaction (asset specificity, frequency and uncertainty) or of the purchasing party (boundedness of rationality, expectation of opportunism and risk preference).

Where voice is not chosen, it may be assumed either that the employer is not concerned by employee exit, or that the costs of voice exceed those of exit. Where voice is chosen, we conceptualize the employer options described above within the transaction cost framework as follows:

(a) Buy (that is, union voice **U**)
   This is closest to the Freeman and Medoff view of voice where the employer subcontracts to one or more unions the responsibility for the generation of voice. This involves, in Williamson's terms, a long-term relational contract in which the employer's direct costs in the production of voice are low but the risks of supplier opportunism are high.
(b) Make (that is, non-union voice **N**)
   This is akin to the 'sophisticated HRM' (human resource management) approach and involves employers choosing directly to provide a set of employee voice mechanisms excluding third-party intervention. Direct costs are correspondingly higher

and, while there is a risk that the approach may not generate the voice required, there are no counterparty risks.

(c)   Hedge (that is, dual channel voice **D**)

Following Williamson (1991) we include a mixed option in which union and non-union voice mechanisms coexist. This may be seen as a form of employer hedging, attempting to control both cost and risk. For simplicity, we treat this as a single option in what follows, acknowledging that a range of hybrids are possible across firms.

Adapting Farber and Western (2002), we consider the choice between the three options above in terms of a cost–benefit framework with three dimensions. Specifically we define the expected value V_i^j to the firm of adopting voice regime j as,

$$V_i^j = \theta_i^j R_i^j - C_i^j, \tag{4.1}$$

where,

θ_i^j = probability that an employee management regime for employer i will meet with success,[2] which inversely proxies the risk associated with regime choice, and where $j = (U, N, D)$ indexes the three voice regimes described above

R_i^j = gross return or benefit from voice regime adoption

C_i^j = the administrative cost of providing or purchasing voice regime j.

A rational employer, i, will adopt voice regime j when its expected value is greater than the next best alternative V_i^*. Thus, 'buying' would occur when:

$$V_i^U > V_i^*. \tag{4.2}$$

When buying or making offer equivalent expected values, the firm may hedge or use other criteria (discussed later) to make its decision. Taking the adoption of union voice as our benchmark example, (4.1) and (4.2) imply that the condition for the firm to undertake a 'buy' decision is given by

$$\theta_i^U > \frac{C_i^U}{R_i^U}. \tag{4.3}$$

The right-hand side of equation (4.3) defines a critical value for the probability of an employer finding union voice adoption successful. The critical value is

$$\theta_i^* = \frac{C_i^U}{R_i^U}, \tag{4.4}$$

and unions will be able to organize employers for which the probability of successfully adopting union voice is greater than the critical value, that is, $\theta_i^U > \theta_i^*$.[3] Assuming R_i^j is similar for all forms of voice – that is, voice is an experience good residing in a competitive 'solution market' that may be secured equally through a variety of institutions[4] – the key variables for the firm become risk θ_i^j and cost C_i^j.

In terms of risk, consider the effect of change in the distribution of θ_i^U without any change to θ_i^*. Suppose for example that there is a negative shock in organizing climate (due to either legal changes or lower employee demand for unionization) which lowers union density at the workplace level. This would reduce the ability of unions to act as voice providers, lowering θ_i^U and reducing the number of firms which would profit from buying voice. The first-order result would be that fewer firms would adopt union voice. However, since the critical value remains unchanged, the success of union-only voice for firms that stick with their buy decision will not alter greatly. That is, pockets of successful union-only voice will persist even as overall union reliability declines. Such an adverse change in the distribution of θ_i^U could account for the sharp decline in union-only voice adoption by British firms that started after 1980 (as shown later in the text) and with the lack of radical changeover for firms started in the earlier period.

Apart from environmental changes, other factors could also affect the risk of voice regime adoption. In terms of non-union voice, the most important risk item for θ_i^N is the probability (running from 0 to 1) that the firm will be able to hire voice-production specialists and generate institutional forms which elicit voice without the existence of a third, independent party. The key risk item influencing θ_i^U (apart from exogenous changes to economic or political climate) is the probability that the firm will find a non-opportunistic or incompetent counterparty. Where both risks are equally high, for example where personnel specialists are rare and unions militant or too weak, the firm may hedge and adopt the hybrid option $V_i^{D}.$[5]

In terms of costs, the key items are as in Figure 4.2, which depicts hypothetical firm A in three possible states. In reverse order, in case 3, the firm experiences C_i^U having entered a long-term relational voice contract with a reliable union $\theta^u=1$. If the union becomes less able to elicit voice and/or more militant, the firm may seek – providing that HRM itself is a reliable alternative $\theta^N=1$ – to move to case 1, with costs C_i^N; this could occur through de-recognition of the union by the employer. Where union and non-union prospects are equally risky, that is, $\theta^u=\theta^N=0.5$, the firm may seek to 'hedge' and adopt a dual channel of union and non-union voice with costs C_i^D, as in case 2.

Figure 4.2 also outlines the variable elements of any C_i^j. They are, for all, market wage and administrative costs α, the former assumed regime-independent (equal for all and thus not included) and the latter regime-dependent. For both C_i^U and C_i^D, there is the possibility of a wage mark-up δ, variations in which might generate regime switching behaviour. Note that the administrative cost of voice is highest in the make case and lowest in the buy case. Hedging, the highest cost option in this illustrative example, is also assumed to be the lowest risk option $\theta^u+\theta^N=1$.

What happens if firms decide to change voice regimes? Two implications regarding the switching behaviour of firms emerge. First, the logic above indicates that switches from wholly union to wholly non-union voice (or the reverse) are less likely than a switch from either to a dual channel. If one form of voice provision is unsatisfactory (perhaps because the union is unreliable) or too costly (perhaps because of the number of personnel specialists required) then hedging to a dual channel is more likely than complete abandonment.

Several factors might induce such a switch. Switching away from union voice is more likely when union voice is fragile (with low union membership), when interruptions to voice supply occur (strikes), where administrative costs – for example those involved in providing union facilities – rise, or where for reasons of competition the firm negatively evaluates the equal supply of union voice to all competitors. Non-union voice is fragile

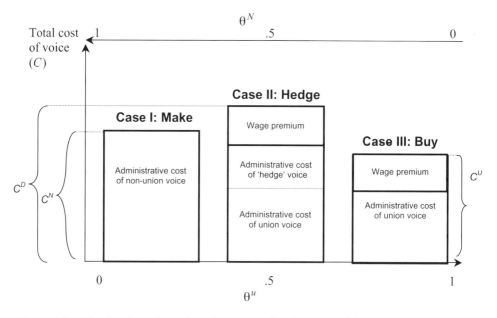

Figure 4.2   The firm's make or buy decision under three possible cases

where there are capability or cost questions, where the union wage premium disappears (thus lowering the relative cost of the buy decision) or where employer-made voice is not viewed as legitimate by employees.

In this regard, an apparent paradox emerges. In Britain and the United States, there is evidence that the union wage premium has fallen. (Blanchflower and Bryson, 2003; Hildreth, 1999). In addition, over the last two decades, the number of strikes has fallen. In other words it would appear that C_i^u and θ_i^u have become more favourable for firms. However, there is no evidence of a switch to union voice – in fact, as shown below, the opposite has occurred. What explains this lack of switching in the face of a seemingly cheaper and more reliable alternative? This question raises the second implication of our modelling above.

We argue for the existence of switching costs S_i^{jk} once a voice regime is adopted, where $j,k=(U,D,N)$ and $j\neq k$ for switching regime j to k. Switching costs encourage inertia; hence movements away from an existing form of voice for an established employer are less likely than the adoption of alternative forms of voice by newly established firms. Switching costs can therefore explain why an employer *remains* non-unionized (unionized) even when a better (non-)union alternative exists. The voice regime choice model (4.1) can therefore be re-written as:

$$V^j = \theta_i^j\, R_i^j - C_i^j + S^{jk}. \tag{4.5}$$

Persistence in regime j in the face of better alternative k occurs as long as S_i^{jk} remains greater than the net-benefit $\Delta V_i^{jk} = V^k - V_i^j$ of changing voice regimes,

$$S_i^{jk} > \Delta V_i^{jk}, \text{ where } \Delta V_i^{jk} > 0. \tag{4.6}$$

Equation (4.6) is one reason why employers often stick with their original voice regime decisions and why switching does not occur simply because expected net benefits of new adoption are positive (as would be the case if equation (4.1) were in effect).

This model adds to the predictions about voice outlined in the previous section.

1.   Although we would expect voice regimes to be stable in the short term, we would expect, long term, that employers would move to the most efficient forms of v oice.
2.   However, we might also expect employers to mix forms of voice to hedge against future changes in the costs of or returns to any particular voice regime.

EMPIRICAL EVIDENCE

The empirical evidence indicating the usefulness of a transaction cost perspective on voice comes from previous studies using the WERS dataset based on a British sample (Bryson et al., 2007, 2012; Gomez et al., 2010; Willman et al., 2006, 2007, 2009). A British dataset on establishments from 1980–2004 has the advantage in a cost–benefit approach that relatively few external influences existed on the choice of voice regime by employers and employees. One can assume with some confidence that efficiency constraints, rather than coercive or normative pressures, had an impact (see Dobbin et al., 1993).

We summarize the key findings as follows.

1.   Willman et al. (2006) found a no voice sector in the UK that was stable both in size and in composition. It had a thinner set overall of employer–employee com-munication channels rather than one different from the voice sector; that is, the no voice sector seemed to do less communicating on every dimension (formal and non-formal). Smaller establishments, lower network externalities and lower asset specificity work against the adoption of a formal voice regime. Overall, this seems to tell a story about the returns to voice (net of costs) being an important determinant of voice adoption. However, this no voice sector was small, below 20 per cent of all establishments throughout the period 1984–88, and falling to under 15 per cent in 2004 (see Gomez et al., 2010: 388). The majority of employment contracts have voice as a governance mechanism.
2.   Figure 4.3 below shows (Gomez et al., 2010: 389) the change in voice regimes across the whole period. It shows clearly that voice mechanisms were sponsored by employers (non-union voice), by employees (union only voice) and by both (dual voice). There was a substantial change in the proportion of each across the period, but the switches appear to be between forms of voice, rather than into and out of the no voice sector.
3.   Bryson et al. (2012), using the same dataset, find that establishments with voice have lower quit rates than those without, confirming the underlying exit-voice proposi-tion. They also find that establishments with non-union voice have lower conflict than those with union voice but better performance in terms of productivity and

(to a limited extent) financial performance. Industrial climate was perceived by managers to be better in establishments with non-union voice than union voice. Overall, they found that non-union voice had a comparative advantage over union voice for many establishments.

4. As one would expect from this finding, the pattern in Figure 4.3 of long-term moves towards the comparatively advantageous non-union voice form is evident, as our transaction cost based model would predict. However, churn is more limited in the shorter term, as our model of switching costs would suggest. Between 1990 and 1998, for example, under 30 per cent of establishments made a switch in voice regime (Willman et al., 2003: 20). There appear to be transaction costs in change.

5. This idea is reinforced by an examination of the switching behaviour itself. For the above period, over 40 per cent of all regime switches were into mixed (dual) forms of voice. This may be seen as a form of hedging, as employers seek to insure against movements in the relative return to different forms of voice.

These findings are presented less as a complete picture of voice patterns in the UK and more as an indication of how five propositions emerging from a transaction cost approach achieve some empirical support from this dataset. It does seem that economic considerations of this sort affect voice choice and switching.

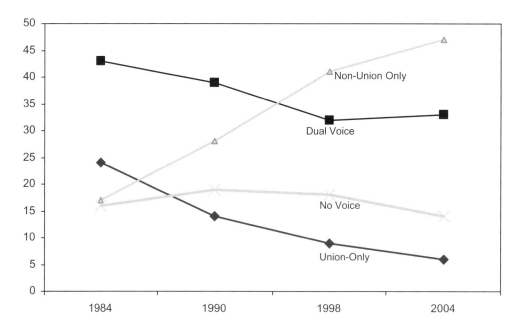

Source: Gomez et al. (2010: 389).

Figure 4.3   Incidence of voice regimes across establishments in UK, 1984–2004

DISCUSSION AND IMPLICATIONS

The exit-voice framework is an attempt to understand the impact of switching costs and the emergence of collective action in markets. The transaction cost economics approach augments this with a primary concern for what goes on in hierarchies, and particularly the governance of intra-firm contracts. The latter contains an analysis of employment contracts that implies the emergence of voice as a governance mechanism. Unlike other approaches within economics which see employment contracts just like any other transaction (Alchian and Demsetz, 1972), Williamson spells out the complexity of employment contracts in ways that predict both the emergence of voice in general and, specifically, what voice regime might be preferred.

The approach rests on fairly rigid, and largely negative, views about human nature in general and employee behaviour in particular; people are prone to opportunism and, because of the nature of employment contracts, employees are particularly prone to it. Efficiency concerns are paramount; power is excluded. So, voice emerges not because of the authority relationship itself, but because it can make the authority relationship work for both parties by improving efficiency.

It is not empirically based, but one can derive predictions from it that are, by and large, supported by data. There seems to be a need for voice by both employers and employees, though perhaps for different reasons. Certain types of voice seem more efficient than others, at least for employers. The decline of union voice may be seen, from this perspective, as the result of competition between voice regimes. Where union membership under collective agreements declines, and where employers are also investing in HRM, which can complement non-union voice, the balance of advantage between the two regimes may shift (Bryson et al., 2012).

Overall, the use of a transaction cost perspective to analyse employee voice empirically will depend on the extent to which economic considerations are paramount. In jurisdictions where voice is either mandated or forbidden, an approach that relies fundamentally on choice will lose explanatory power. It may thus be, for example, that the application of a transaction cost perspective works best where labour markets and the patterns of labour representation are unregulated. Where this is not the case, and voice of a specific form is mandated by statute or external institutions, such choices are constrained and this naturally affects the operation of the model presented here. For example, where statutory union recognition is in place – as was the case in the UK for much of the later twentieth century – the employer may only choose whether to add non-union voice. Similarly, in 2004, the EU Directive on Information and Consultation removed the choice of no voice from the employer's set (EIRO, 2004). What both of these examples illustrate is the old maxim that economic approaches talk about how choices are made and sociological ones spell out what the choices are.

But it is important to recognize this limitation to the transaction cost approach. To return briefly to the spot contracting examples of longshore work and newspapers, we must acknowledge that the voice outcome depends very heavily on the statutory framework. Where the union controls the labour supply through a closed shop, the outcome is union only voice; where this condition is absent, the outcome is no voice.

The logic of the transaction cost approach is that such exogenous legal and institutional frameworks should be designed to allow the contracting parties to make the most efficient voice choices. However, this sits uneasily with the empirical reality that most developed countries have legislation that in some way mandates specific types of voice. The approach outlined here would logically need to accept that there may be efficiency enhancing aspects to this.

This raises some interesting research questions, the most general of which – and central to the future research agenda on voice – concerns the optimal regulation of voice choices. To take a simple example – it may be that mandating some types of voice increases both parties' commitment to the exchange, encouraging skill development by employers and higher commitment to the firm from employees, leading to a positive impact on country competitiveness. The effects may even be exogenous to the firm; there is, for example, emerging evidence that the employee experience of voice may have positive impacts on broader civic commitment and voting frequency. These wider impacts of voice at work require further research both by those interested in the transaction cost approach and those more interested in the development of institutions.

NOTES

1. This section relies on Willman et al. (2007).
2. Where success is measured from the employer's perspective, along a variety of dimensions related to the ability of the voice regime to elicit employee behaviours that are favourable to productivity.
3. The same decision rule could have been applied to the other two voice regime choices.
4. This is an admittedly strong assumption but is relaxed later when we discuss the possibility of inter-firm heterogeneity.
5. In all three cases one can see the experiential characteristics of voice provision (that is, the fact that any form of voice necessitates a trial or sampling period before the payoff can be accurately assessed). This is why voice regimes are experience goods for employers as well as employees (see Gomez and Gunderson, 2002; Bryson and Gomez, 2003).

REFERENCES

Alchian, A. and H. Demsetz (1972), 'Production, information costs, and economic organisation' *American Economic Review*, **62**, 777–95.
Arrow, Kenneth J. (1974), *The Limits of Organization*, New York: Norton.
Bassett, William Rupert ([1919] 2012), *When the Workmen Help you Manage*, Ulan Press (Amazon).
Blanchflower, D. and A. Bryson (2003), 'Changes over time in union relative wage effects in the UK and the US revisited', forthcoming as chapter 7 in *International Handbook of Trade Unions*, John T. Addison and Claus Schnabel (eds), Cheltenham, UK and Northampton, MA, USA: Edward Elgar.
Braverman, H. (1974), *Labor and Monopoly Capital*, New York: Monthly Review Press.
Bryson, A. and G. Gomez (2003), 'Buying into union membership', in H. Gospel and S. Wood (eds), *Representing Workers: Trade Union Recognition and Membership in Britain*, The Future of Trade Unions in Britain, Vol. 1, London: Routledge, pp. 72–91.
Bryson, A., R. Gomez, T. Kretschmer and P. Willman (2007), 'The diffusion of workplace voice and high-commitment human resource management practices in Britain, 1984–1998', *Industrial and Corporate Change*, **16**, 395–426
Bryson, A., P. Willman, R. Gomez, and T. Kretschmer (2013), 'The comparative advantage of non-union voice in Britain, 1980–2004', *Industrial Relations: A Journal of Economy and Society*, **52** (S1), 194–220.
Commons, J.R. (1909), 'American shoemakers, 1648–1895', *Quarterly Journal of Economics*, **24** (4) (November), 39–83.
Dietrich, M. (1994), *Transaction Cost Economics and Beyond*, London: Routledge.
Dobbin, F., J.R. Sutton, J.W. Meyer and W.R. Scott (1993), 'Equal opportunity law and the construction of internal labor markets', *American Journal of Sociology*, **99** (2), 396–427.

Doeringer, P. and M. Piore (1971), *Internal Labour Markets and Manpower Analysis*, Lexington: D.C. Heath.

Donaldson, L. (1995), *American Anti-Management Theories of Organisation: A Critique of Paradigm Proliferation*, Cambridge: Cambridge University Press.

Dore, R. (1983), 'Goodwill and the spirit of market capitalism', *British Journal of Sociology*, **34**, 439–82.

(EIRO) European Industrial Relations Observatory online (2004), 'UK: The impact of the information and consultation directive on industrial relations', available at: http://www.eurofound.europa.eu/eiro/studies/tn0710029s/uk0710029q.htm (accessed 28 November 2013).

Farber, H. and B. Western (2002), 'Ronald Reagan and the politics of declining union organization', *British Journal of Industrial Relations*, **40** (3), 385–401.

Fox, A . (1974), *Beyond Contract: Work, Power and Trust Relations*, London: Faber.

Francis, A. (1982), 'Markets and hierarchies; efficiency or domination?', in A. Francis, P. Turk and J. Willman (eds), *Power, Efficiency and Institutions: A Critical Appraisal of the 'Markets and Hierarchies' Paradigm*, London: Heinemann, pp. 105–17.

Freeman, R.B. and J. Medoff (1984), *What Do Unions Do?*, New York, Basic Books.

Ghoshal, S. and P. Moran (1996), 'Bad for practice; a critique of the transaction cost theory', *Academy of Management Review*, **21** (1), 13–47.

Gomez, R. and M. Gunderson (2002), 'The experience good model of union membership', paper presented at the 28th Middlebury Economics Conference, April.

Gomez, R., A. Bryson and P. Willman (2010), 'Voice transformation: the shift from union to non-union voice in Britain', in Adrian Wilkinson, Paul J. Gollan, Mick Marchington and David Lewin (eds), *Oxford Handbook of Participation in Organizations*, Oxford: Oxford University Press.

Hildreth, A.K.G. (1999, 'What has happened to the union wage differential in Britain in the 1990s?', *Oxford Bulletin of Economics and Statistics*, **61** (1), 5–31.

Hirschman, A. (1970), *Exit, Voice and Loyalty*, Cambridge, MA: Harvard University Press.

Kaufman, B. (2012), 'Strategic human resource management research in the USA: a failing grade after 30 years?', *Academy of Management Perspectives*, **26** (2), 12–36.

Marglin, S. (1962), 'What do bosses do?', *Review of Radical Political Economy*, **6**, 33–60.

Morrison, Elizabeth (2011), 'Employee voice behavior: integration and directions for future research', *Academy of Management Annals*, **4**, 373–412.

Williamson, O.E. (1975), *Markets and Hierarchies*, Glencoe: Free Press.

Williamson, O.E. (1985), *The Economic Institutions of Capitalism; Firms, Markets, Relational Contracting*, New York: Free Press.

Williamson, O.E. (1991),'Comparative economic organization: the analysis of discrete structural alternatives', *Administrative Science Quarterly*, **36** (2), 269–98.

Willman, P. (1982), 'Opportunism and labour contracting: an application of the organisational failures framework', *Journal of Economic Behaviour and* Organisation, **2** (1), 83–98.

Willman, P. (1986), *Technological Change, Collective Bargaining and Industrial Efficiency*, Oxford: Oxford University Press.

Willman, P., A. Bryson and R. Gomez (2003), 'Why do voice regimes differ?', Centre for Economic Performance Discussion Paper 591, London School of Economics.

Willman, P., A. Bryson and R. Gomez (2006), 'The sound of silence: which employers choose no employee voice and why?', *Socio-Economic Review*, **4** (2), 283–99.

Willman, P., A. Bryson and R. Gomez (2007), 'The long goodbye; the rise and fall of union voice in the UK', *International Journal of Human Resource Management*, **18** (7), 1318–34.

Willman, P., A. Bryson and R. Gomez (2009), 'Voice at the workplace 1980–2004', in W. Brown, A. Bryson, J. Forth and K. Whitfield (eds), *The Evolution of the Modern Workplace*, Cambridge: Cambridge University Press, pp. 97–102.

5 Industrial democracy in the twenty-first century
Janice Foley

INTRODUCTION

Voice is said to be the current form of industrial democracy available in the industrialized economies (Marchington, 2007). According to Kulkarni (2010: 443), 'having a voice' means that 'employees are free to achieve what they value'. But the essence of industrial democracy goes beyond voice, because it was workers' search for social justice and the need to reform the inequities of free market capitalism that first gave rise to demands for industrial democracy (Lichtenstein and Harris, 1993). The values being pursued were freedom, self-determination, human dignity and respect in a capitalist environment that was uninterested in workers' needs and desires. It should be recalled that at that time, unions were in their infancy, wages were low, working conditions harsh, and job security at risk for those who dared to challenge their employers. It was not until the onset of World War I that some measure of industrial democracy was introduced into workplaces in an effort to maintain wartime production (Hancock et al., 1991).

Many claims have been made in support of industrial democracy, among them potentially improved decision-making and job satisfaction, more cooperative relationships between workers and management, and increased organizational effectiveness (Huddleston, 1972; Purcell and Georgiadis, 2007). Employees may also be entitled to have a greater say at work because we live in a democratic society, employees are major stakeholders, and the quality of their lives is greatly affected by the decisions made in corporate boardrooms (Deakin and Njoya, 2008; Zammitt, 2001).

Industrial democracy can only be achieved when workers have the recognized right and the real capability to genuinely influence decisions affecting their lives at work and it requires true power-sharing between employees and employers (Foley and Polanyi, 2006). Given this definition, neither opportunities to own company stock and to share in profits through bonus or merit plans, nor short-term voluntary participation schemes that exist at the whim of employers, are considered in this chapter. Worker cooperatives are left out as well because although they are viable mechanisms of industrial democracy, they account for a very small portion of employment worldwide (Dow, 2003).

The structure of this chapter is as follows. First, the various approaches used to advance industrial democracy in the twentieth century in the countries under consideration, which are the UK, Western Europe, The Netherlands, the Scandinavian countries and North America, are examined. For convenience this review is broken into two time periods, before and after World War II. In the next section they are evaluated to see to what degree they advanced industrial democracy as the term is defined above. Then three examples of voluntary initiatives introduced to provide industrial democracy are briefly reviewed. The chapter wraps up with the identification of several preconditions for the success of industrial democracy initiatives and the presentation of some ideas on how to make attempts to democratize workplaces more effective.

EARLY INDUSTRIAL DEMOCRACY INITIATIVES (1900–1945)

German-Style Works Councils

Works councils, the most common and earliest structural innovations introduced to advance industrial democracy outside North America, were introduced by legislation in the Weimar Republic in 1920 (Hall and Marginson, 2005; Helm, 1991). They were to operate at local levels to facilitate labour–management communications and were meant to supplement already existing national or industry-level collective bargaining arrangements. They could be set up at regional and national levels to work with employers' federations to advise on economic matters (Huddleston, 1972).

Works councillors could advise management on a wide range of matters affecting workers, including working conditions, staffing and discipline (Helm, 1991; Horner, 1974). They were entitled to receive information about all matters of interest, and were expected to act in the company's best interests at all times (Helm, 1991). Matters such as wages, which were the subject of collective bargaining, could not be discussed, and strikes could not be authorized. Employers were obliged to attend to workers' concerns, with all disputes to be resolved through an arbitration process or through the labour courts. These works councils were discontinued during the economic collapse and the rise of Fascism that preceded World War II (Horner, 1974).

France and Italy specifically rejected the idea of works councils during this time because they were fighting for worker control, not joint consultation. In Scandinavia, the central labour and employer federations negotiated a social accord in the 1930s that lasted into the 1960s, ushering in a long period of labour peace. It gave workers some representation rights via the establishment of voluntary works councils with some information-sharing and consultation rights (Jain, 1980: Ch. 2).

Collective Bargaining

In North America and in the UK, workers saw collective bargaining and militancy as the best means of improving their lot. Employers in both countries were vehemently opposed to the idea of industrial democracy and to collective bargaining, on the grounds that it interfered with property rights, free markets and management prerogatives (Freeman et al., 2007; Nightingale, 1982). Nevertheless, to ward off the passage of works council-type legislation, some American employers voluntarily introduced more humane work practices and even established company unions during the 1920s and 1930s. The labour relations legislation that was passed in 1935 in the USA and in 1944 in Canada guaranteed workers the right to join unions and to have them negotiate wages and working conditions, which set the stage for the growth of industrial unions in the two countries.

INDUSTRIAL DEMOCRACY INITIATIVES SINCE WORLD WAR II

Workers in the developed countries enjoyed steady improvements in pay and working conditions in the post-war period thanks to buoyant economies and – in most European countries – labour-friendly governments eager to rebuild war-torn economies (Freeman and Medoff, 1984; Horner, 1974). But when the productivity crisis of the 1970s materialized, government priorities changed. Productivity enhancement and cost-cutting became the major concerns and many of the gains workers had made were lost, including unionized jobs and union protection. OECD statistics (2012) indicate that the overall unionization rate, which had been 34 per cent among 20 reporting countries in 1975, with greater than 50 per cent unionization in 11 of those countries, had, by 2008, fallen to 18 per cent in 34 reporting countries. By 2010 only Finland and Sweden had unionization rates above 50 per cent.

Many quasi-industrial democracy initiatives were introduced in this period to address productivity issues through the introduction of quality circles, team production and even high performance workplace systems (Danford, 2005; Heller, 1998), but these initiatives were usually short lived and often ineffective. Interest in works councils, labour directors and collective bargaining continued, and a few other innovations were introduced.

German-Style Works Councils and Labour Directors

Codetermination legislation for the public sector was passed in West Germany in 1951 and 1952 (Addison et al., 1993). The 1951 legislation provided for a two-tier management structure in the iron and steel industry consisting of a management board to run the operation, and a supervisory board to elect the management team and oversee its actions. Equal numbers of labour and shareholder directors were to sit on the supervisory board, and one of the managerial board members was responsible for personnel matters (Helm, 1991), although still constrained to make the company's well-being the top priority.

The 1952 legislation afforded workers outside iron and steel similar rights, including the management director with personnel responsibilities, but with workers entitled to hold only one-third of the seats on supervisory boards and the opportunity to sit on works councils. The works councils were quite similar to those established post-World War I, with somewhat more extensive information, consultation and codetermination rights (Helm, 1991; Garson, 1979). A further legislative change in 1972 allowed trade union officials to sit on works councils, and a 1976 amendment raised labour's share of supervisory board seats to 50 per cent, but permitted the tie-breaking chair to be from management ranks rather than a neutral third party. The codetermination legislation was extended to the private sector at that time (Jain, 1980: Ch. 2).

Works councils based on the German model were introduced in other European and Scandinavian countries following the war (Horner, 1974; Jenkins and Blyton, 2008). In The Netherlands, works councils were set up in 1950, but they settled on a different structure of supervisory board representation, with one-third of the seats reserved for workers, one-third for shareholders and one-third for other interested parties. A voluntary system of works councils in Norway, Sweden and Denmark continued until the 1970s when works council legislation was introduced. Sweden's legislation enabled establishments to introduce labour directors if requested by the trade unions and to negotiate decision-making procedures (Jain, 1980: Ch. 2). Denmark's legislation made provision for one-third worker representation on supervisory boards. France introduced works councils in 1945 but labour did not have any representation on supervisory boards until 1972 when they gained observer status. In 1975 the Sudreau Commission proposed one-third representation but France along with Italy rejected codetermination in 1976 (Garson, 1979).

Worker Investment Funds and Self-Management

Sweden, Denmark and The Netherlands tried unsuccessfully to get employers to create worker investment funds to allow workers to buy into and ultimately gain control over enterprises and industries (Horner, 1974). Yugoslavia from 1949–91 embarked on an experiment in self-management (Dow, 2003), whereby state-owned enterprises were operated and controlled by workers through a system of works councils. The scheme allowed works councillors in each factory to set long-term policy and select a director and a management board to actually run the enterprise (Whitehorn, 1980).

Collective Bargaining

Neither the USA nor the UK embraced works councils or investment funds. In the post-war period, North America continued to pursue collective bargaining as the best route to industrial democracy (Adell, 1986; Yates, 2009) despite a relentless anti-union employer lobby. The legitimacy US unions had gained with the passage of the Wagner Act in 1935 was compromised as concerns grew about union power and their undemocratic and even criminal practices. The 1947 Taft Hartley Act made organizing more difficult (Peirce, 2000). While some joint consultation and joint governance experiments occurred during this period on a voluntary or negotiated basis, few North American employers faced pressures to advance industrial democracy because union density never rose much above 30 per cent in the post-war era (Peirce, 2000: 148).

Multiple Initiatives in the UK

The UK faced significant pressure to consider the German system, particularly as it prepared for entry into the European Economic Community. Joint consultation within nationalized UK industries was evident in the post-war period (Clegg, 1963; Hillard and Coates, 1991; Jones, 1977), intended to give workers more influence. The 1968 Donovan Commission recommended expanding the scope of collective bargaining and letting shop stewards negotiate shop floor working conditions.

The Labour government and some of the trade unions through the late 1960s and the 1970s proposed introducing worker directors onto supervisory boards, despite opposition from other trade unions, the employer lobby and the general public. They were introduced in some of the nationalized industries on a trial basis. A formal structure that would reconcile the disparate views about how supervisory boards and labour directors should operate was sought by the Bullock Commission in 1977 and by the government in 1978, but both attempts failed. Collective bargaining and direct shop floor action remained the major tool of industrial democracy in the UK (Horner, 1974; Jones, 1977).

Much of the interest in industrial democracy faded once the Labour government fell in 1979 and the economy worsened, but experimentation with a variety of methods to increase worker participation in decision-making continued (Heller, 1998). Labour directors and works councils returned to the political agenda in 2002 when the European Union issued a directive urging all member nations to set up information-sharing and consultation arrangements with their employees. While the UK has to date managed to avoid passing works council legislation, employers face ongoing pressure from the European Community to enhance industrial democracy.

THE EFFICACY OF INDUSTRIAL DEMOCRACY INITIATIVES INTRODUCED TO DATE

The foregoing review of formal industrial democracy initiatives has identified the main means employed to date to advance industrial democracy in the UK, the USA, Scandinavia, The Netherlands and Western Europe. The focus now shifts to evaluating their adequacy as mechanisms of industrial democracy using standards developed by institutional economists in the USA in the 1930s (Kaufman, 2000). To meet the requirements, the mechanisms had to provide a method for representation of employee interests with respect to work rules and their administration, to protect employees from arbitrary management treatment, to guarantee due process in the event of disputes and to give workers a reasonable ability to influence outcomes. These standards will now be applied to the current approaches to industrial democracy.

Works Councils

As the German works councils are deemed to have been the most effective (Helm 1991), they will be evaluated here. In theory, the joint consultation arrangements that were institutionalized in the form of works councils met most of the requirements, although generalizations are difficult since they operated differently from country to country (Horner, 1974). The German legislation certainly afforded workers opportunities for representation and, by entitling workers to take disputes to labour courts or to arbitration, forced employers to attend to their concerns. The balance of power may not have been in workers' favour though, impairing their potential for influence for a number of reasons (Garson, 1979; Jenkins and Blyton, 2008).

   A major issue is that the works councils were compelled to act in the best interests of the enterprise, therefore they could not prioritize workers' concerns where a conflict of interest existed. In addition, they could not authorize strikes to achieve what they wanted. While worker representatives could be elected from management ranks, union officials were not allowed to sit on the committees until 1972, which may have restricted the types of concerns raised. Because the elected representatives were not directly accountable to their trade unions and were sworn to secrecy, there was an inconsistent flow of information between the two bodies that may have reduced their effectiveness. Finally, while works councillors may have had some influence, the bulk of employees did not.

   The evidence suggests that works councils did have some positive impacts (Diamant, 1977; Frege, 2002) by providing a measure of representative voice for shop floor workers and allowing favourable agreements to be reached even under unfavourable economic conditions (Helm, 1991). This increased trust and reduced exit, which should have had a positive effect on profits and productivity by improving decision-making, although methodological difficulties make that hard to determine (Frege, 2002; Jenkins and Blyton, 2008). Surveys indicate that works council representatives felt they were valuable even if other workers were relatively unaffected by them (Horner, 1974). They played a role in protecting working conditions and promoting industrial peace (Mohrenweiser et al., 2012).

On the other hand, they might have influenced the process of decision-making more than its substance (Marginson et al., 2004), and their economic effect may have been relatively insignificant (Addison et al., 2004) although the 1998 Codetermination Commission in Germany found that they increased efficiency as well as costs (Deakin and Njoya, 2008). Their effectiveness depended on the make-up of the committees, works councillors' and managements' views of the role of works councillors, how much training the works councillors received, how much access they had to outside expertise, and management attitudes toward sharing information (Garson, 1977: Ch. 7; Hall and Marginson, 2005; Horner, 1974).

Abuses of the system by management in the form of withholding information, bypassing works councils, or limiting their involvement to discussions of how to implement decisions made without their input have been reported (de Jong and van Witteloosttuijn, 2004; Horner, 1974). The IDE International Research Group's study found that 40 years of works councils had had little impact on workers' influence or on decision-making. So they appear to have been ineffective mechanisms of industrial democracy, but they remain an important workplace institution today (Addison et al., 1993; IDE International Research Group, 1993).

Labour Directors

Because the weaker German codetermination legislation was copied in most other countries, it will be the referent point for this discussion. According to the standards set out earlier, labour director appointments to supervisory and management boards potentially allowed workers to influence high-level decision-making. The management board director responsible for personnel matters was usually a union nominee and could only be appointed or dismissed with the majority approval of the worker representatives on the supervisory boards (Diamant, 1977; Helm, 1991). The worker representatives on the supervisory boards were elected. These arrangements protected directors from arbitrary management treatment. However, the constitution of the boards ensured that these directors were at a power disadvantage relative to management, so they did not have an equal ability to influence outcomes (Garson, 1979; Horner, 1974).

In regard to both the supervisory and managerial boards, the biggest issue was that the worker representatives on boards were normally outnumbered, the sole exception being the supervisory boards in Germany's iron and steel industry where parity representation existed. Both boards were required to act in the best interests of the company, which could force them to agree to decisions that did not serve workers well. Furthermore, they were sworn to secrecy, which further constrained their actions. They were not always well trained and since their board duties were part time, they lacked the expertise of the full-time managers on the board regarding the operational and financial matters discussed (Jain, 1980: Ch. 1). They functioned at a level far above the shop floor and their isolation from their unions and from the shop floor predisposed them to prioritize their obligations to management (Davies, 1979; Horner 1974; Strauss, 2001).

According to Hunter (1998), directors on supervisory boards were unable to change the criteria used for decision-making. Jain (1980: Ch. 2) maintained that they did little to address shop floor concerns. In addition, they rarely met, did little advising, received limited information and mostly rubber-stamped decisions made by the managerial board or by subcommittees of the board with little or no labour input. The Norwegian Industrial Democracy Project found that introducing worker directors did not increase productivity or reduce worker alienation (Trist, 1979). The 1970 Beidenkopf report indicated that, even with parity representation, labour directors had little impact on policy (Davies, 1979).

So again, labour directors had limited success at advancing industrial democracy but on a more positive note, Huddleston (1972) concluded that while codetermination did not limit managers' unilateral power in the workplace, it did give workers a better understanding of the industrial challenges their companies were facing and therefore contributed to labour peace.

Collective Bargaining

At first glance, collective bargaining ostensibly meets all four standards. Negotiation is an effective means of representing employee interests because employees elect their trade union representatives and can vote to replace them if necessary. The provisions of the collective agreement protect employees from arbitrary management action and provide grievance and arbitration procedures to deal with disputes. As long as unions are strong enough to act as countervailing forces to management, they can ensure that workers' interests are protected.

Evidence exists that collective agreements do regulate employer behaviour, protecting employees from arbitrary and discriminatory treatment (Freeman and Medoff, 1984; Yates, 2009). They provide protections for employees expressing concerns with management actions, because of job security provisions. They have increased labour's share of company profits and have positively influenced working conditions for their members, as well as for non-unionized workers. But collective bargaining has several limitations as a mechanism of industrial democracy, particularly today.

The basic problem is that the economic, social and political environment affects the balance of power, and since the 1980s, in the UK and elsewhere, employers have increasingly resisted recognizing, consulting with or negotiating with unions (Bacon, 2008). In addition, according to the IDE International Research Group (1993), employers have purposely tried to weaken unions to protect their own interests. This has been accomplished in part by pressuring governments to pass anti-union legislation. Under these conditions trade unions lose their power to protect workers.

Adding to the problem, many sectors of the economy have never been unionized, such as the lower-paid service sectors. Non-unionized workers may be unsupportive of unionized workers due to media messages suggesting that they enjoy an undeserved, privileged position in the labour market (Ross and Savage, 2012). Unions are potentially unattractive to large segments of the work force, such as professionals, who may prefer to rely on professional associations to represent their interests.

Aspects of the labour relations regime can disempower workers and trade unions (Jain, 1980: Chs. 4 and 7). The voluntary nature of collective bargaining in the UK allows employers to refuse to bargain and also allows them to interfere with the certification and decertification processes (Deakin and Njoya, 2008). The legislation seeks to institutionalize conflict (Davies, 1979; Swartz and Warskett, 2012), therefore negotiation of only a limited set of issues is allowed, and work action while the collective agreement is in effect is prohibited. Workers therefore have no avenue to express their dissatisfaction with their employers during the term of the contract except through the grievance procedure. Grievances belong to the union, not to the member, and may not be taken forward. Furthermore, workers are compelled to do the employer's bidding now and express grievances later (Swartz and Warskett, 2012).

While both parties are required to bargain in good faith, management can withhold information that would be pertinent to negotiations and can unilaterally decide any matters where the collective agreement is silent (Jain, 1980: Chs 4 and 6). Trade union leaders are forced to act as agents of the employer, ensuring their members abide by the collective agreement (Camfield, 2011).

Shortcomings of the internal union administration and representation processes can also hamper the efficacy of collective bargaining as a means of advancing industrial democracy (Hemsworth, 1979; Jain, 1980: Ch. 4). Unionized workers are generally fairly apathetic and uninvolved in their unions. Few attend union meetings to make their concerns known. When they do, there is no guarantee that leaders will listen to them, particularly where diverse and conflicting interests exist. Members may have limited ability to influence what issues go to the bargaining table, or to control their elected representatives, as it is difficult to oust incumbent leaders from office when they control the internal political machinery and communications systems. Despite these problems, many believe that strengthening and expansion of collective bargaining is the best path to industrial democracy (Horner 1974; Kaufman, 2000; Yates, 2009).

VOLUNTARY INDUSTRIAL DEMOCRACY APPROACHES

We turn now to a brief review of three voluntary approaches that stand out as apparently sincere efforts to advance industrial democracy that were motivated by religious or philosophical convictions and have been sustained for many decades. They include joint consultation at the John Lewis Partnership in the UK (Flanders et al., 1968), employee ownership and joint control at Scott Bader Commonwealth in the UK (Hadley and Goldsmith, 1995) and joint employee ownership and control at the Dutch Breman Group (de Jong and van Witteloostuijn, 2004). Although not uniformly effective in advancing industrial democracy, they do show that the way in which such ventures are designed affects outcomes for workers. The same standards applied to the previous initiatives will be applied to these examples.

John Lewis Partnership (JLP)

The JLP is a retail department store and supermarket chain founded by John Lewis in the nineteenth century. His son transferred full ownership to a trust on behalf of its employees in 1929 in part because he believed that employees should have an equal share of the profits, knowledge and power in business enterprises. While he also believed that executive control should be retained to ensure businesses remained commercially viable, he felt they should be accountable to employees, and he enshrined that accountability in the JLP's constitution (Flanders et al., 1968).

An elaborate system was set up to provide representation rights, but ultimately it failed to make managers accountable to employees. Managers dominated decision-making and felt entitled to act in ways that privileged their desired outcomes. One example of that was provided by Cathcart (2013: 6), who noted that in 2012 the managers instigated a constitutional change that tripled their salary ceiling, knowing that it would increase their share of profits as profit-sharing was proportionate to salary, and that it would reduce the employees' share. While the decision-making structures ensured that employee representatives would have had to agree to this, according to Cathcart, the rhetoric and the pressure that existed at upper level committee meetings left employees little choice but to do so. Flanders et al. (1968: 28) described JLP's management system as a control system based on coercion, persuasion and manipulation.

Employees did not evince much interest in the democratic structures available, displaying more concern with their supervisors' willingness to consult and share information, because that directly affected their jobs. Pay secrecy was a general concern.

Scott Bader Commonwealth

Scott Bader, a multinational chemical company, was initially established in 1921 in the UK. Thirty years later the company was restructured by the founder to give his employees a 'real' say in its operation. He initially transferred 90 per cent of the family-owned shares in the operating company to a charitable trust, the Scott Bader Commonwealth, to be collectively owned by his current and future employees in perpetuity. The remaining 10 per cent of shares was transferred to employees in 1963 (Hadley and Goldsmith, 1995). Once hired by the operating company all employees could join the Commonwealth. As Commonwealth members they were shareholders of the operating company, able to attend quarterly and annual general meetings, vote on operational matters and elect the governing board.

The company's website states that the governance structure aimed to encourage involvement, commitment, team work and the diffusion of power so that no constitutional body or individual within the operating company had greater influence than another. Nevertheless, as was the case with the JLP, it was pay and benefits rather than democratic structures that appealed to the majority of employees, and only a small minority took advantage of the self-governing and consultation opportunities afforded to them (Hadley and Goldsmith, 1995). Workers explained this aspect of their behaviour in terms of poor understanding of democracy, lack of training to participate on committees effectively, lack of interest in participation, and management actions that had suggested that workers' input was not welcome.

Dutch Breman Group

The Breman Group currently consists of 25 independent firms offering products and services related to construction, utilities and maintenance. It began as a single bicycle shop in The Netherlands in 1925, but in the early 1970s, out of religious conviction and a strong belief that the creativity, commitment and knowledge of their employees should be rewarded, the founding family made employees the collective owner of 50 per cent of the equity in the company. They also set up structures that enabled employees to participate equally with management in the operation and governance of the group, and to share equally with management in profit distributions. An intricate system of checks and balances was created to ensure that the democratic aspects of this governance model were safeguarded. For example, employees were placed in charge of hiring and firing managers and no operating decisions could be made without the approval of both workers and managers. In addition, employees were trained to effectively participate in the democratic structures available.

This example, unlike the others, satisfies the standards for an adequate mechanism of industrial democracy because it did give workers a significant amount of influence, which has worked extremely well for the group and for its employees. It provides evidence that voluntary initiatives that are well designed can effectively promote industrial democracy.

PRECONDITIONS FOR ACHIEVING INDUSTRIAL DEMOCRACY

These three cases and the previous discussion of the more formalized mechanisms used to achieve industrial democracy indicate some preconditions for their success. First, it is clear that a supportive environment is needed, based on positive attitudes on the part of both managers and workers toward industrial democracy. The motivation for introducing industrial democracy initiatives must be a sincere belief in the value of more democratic workplaces whereby managers willingly share power with employees, even though they recognize that employees' and management's priorities may vary. Managers must fully value rather than fear the abilities and potential of their employees and be willing to introduce practices and structures that will unleash them, rather than allow their own priorities to dominate.

Employees, on their part, must genuinely want more say, and be willing and able to expend time and effort to participate in the democratic opportunities extended to them (Rus, 1984). Although paternalistic managers can introduce democratic principles and practices out of a personal sense of what is ethical or desirable, employees may not understand and/or appreciate them, and may fail to do their part to make them successful. A strong social safety net must exist to ensure that employees are able to freely express their preferences, unconstrained by material needs for jobs, housing, food and the like (Clegg, 1963).

Second, the structures must be formalized in some way (IDE International Research Group, 1993) so that the initiative cannot be easily abandoned. A related requirement is that democratic initiatives must be introduced in a holistic rather than a piecemeal fashion, so that together they support the organization's democratic system (Garson,

1977: Ch. 1). Longevity and a holistic approach will create the kind of high-trust organizational culture that supports industrial democracy (Gollan and Markey, 2001).

Within this kind of culture, where democratic beliefs, values and practices permeate all levels of the organization, problems such as information-hoarding or distortion, manipulation of votes, allowing contentious issues to be decided on the basis of recommendations from committees formed without proper worker representation, consultation after decisions have been made, and the other breaches of formal democratic arrangements that research has identified (Jain, 1980: Ch. 7) are less likely to arise. Workers will see that they can improve their working conditions by participating in the democratic processes provided, will be trained and supported to do so effectively, and will feel confident that they can express their true sentiments without fear of reprisal.

This type of culture cannot be legislated and although company founders can attempt to enshrine it in company documents, individuals imbued with the collective beliefs and values of the founders are needed to keep the original culture intact. Ensuring supportive attitudes and beliefs exist is a long-term project requiring education to ensure workers understand the economic and political systems that affect their well-being, as well as their role in protecting democratic ideals. They must also be afforded opportunities to develop the skills of debate, logic, problem-solving, conflict handling and the like that are necessary to the maintenance of a democratic system. Some degree of resocialization may also be required to promote a democratic consciousness (Johnson, 2006). With these preconditions met, a variety of options exist to advance industrial democracy, which will be the next issue considered.

THE PATH TO INDUSTRIAL DEMOCRACY

Before considering options it must be acknowledged that existing political, economic and legal systems as well as unionization rates will have a bearing on what is possible, as well as what is acceptable. The European Community's directives will impact the actions of its member nations. The current fixation in the USA and, to a lesser extent, in Canada on free enterprise and maintaining management prerogatives (Freeman et al., 2007) will limit what is deemed acceptable. Whatever approach is taken, gradual introduction would probably be desirable (Garson, 1977: Ch. 1; Rus, 1984).

Continuation of already-existing arrangements is likely to be preferred, but they must be modified to address current conditions. Collective bargaining is growing more decentralized which, in countries with works councils, is exacerbating tensions between them and trade unions. Keeping consultation arrangements functioning effectively in companies that have operations in more than one country is creating difficulties (Waddington, 2011). Existing codetermination regulations are being flouted in many companies. The reach of this legislation is inadequate as size exemptions mean that only some private and public sector enterprises are covered. Options also exist in terms of what forms of compliance are acceptable, so not all workers have access to the same voice opportunities even where they are legislated. Those whose only forms of voice are employer-determined and wholly voluntary face even more variability in terms of access to and efficacy of voice arrangements.

Strengthen Collective Bargaining

One possibility that exists in all countries is to take legislative steps to facilitate organizing and collective bargaining in order to strengthen trade unions so that they will again have the power to provide effective collective voice to employees. Employment at will legislation would have to be modified and residual rights management clauses replaced with bargaining rights clauses to expand the scope of collective bargaining, so that issues like industrial democracy can get to the negotiating table (Sanderson and LaBerge, 1979). Workers' right to use direct action like sit downs and work stoppages to protest management actions during the term of the contract would have to be established (Camfield, 2011). The requirement to 'bargain in good faith' would have to entitle trade unions to get all pertinent information, including management's future intentions, in a timely manner (Jain, 1980: Ch. 6). Having the help of expert third parties to help lay out the 'facts' could be helpful (Sanderson and LaBerge, 1979).

Unions may have to transform themselves, however, if they wish to attract more members. They need to be less bureaucratic, more democratic and more relevant as part of an international working class movement, better-aligned with community groups and other social movements, and attractive to youth (Camfield, 2011; Freeman et al., 2007; Ross and Savage, 2012). They will have to find a way to organize the burgeoning low-paid service sectors, despite the difficulties posed by small bargaining units, transient workers and language differences. Their uncompromising attitude toward cooperation with management will have to be adjusted (Jain, 1980: Ch. 7), but only where potential exists for mutual benefit, in order to afford protection to workers. To appease the public, they may have to emphasize their voice rather than their monopoly function (Freeman and Medoff, 1984).

Given current levels of trade union density and their past failures, this is unlikely to be an effective option on its own, at least in the short term, and will require state action to implement.

Collective Bargaining and Joint Consultation

One way to supplement collective bargaining as an approach to industrial democracy would be to legislate joint consultation by requiring bodies similar to works councils to be established in all but the smallest of workplaces, with some seats reserved for trade union officials. These bodies would have to be effectively policed to ensure compliance. Provision could also be made for the appointment of worker directors to 50 per cent of board seats at the level where operational decisions are actually made (Jain, 1980: Ch. 7). Limits should be set on their terms and they should have ties to the labour movement, to ward off co-optation. Legislation would have to be changed to allow them greater latitude in advancing workers' interests and the secrecy mandates would have to be relaxed to allow them to provide at least some information to the unions representing the workers. A procedure would have to be set up to regulate how unions deal with any sensitive information brought to the works councils (Gollan and Markey, 2001).

Liaison positions to link national and international works councils would have to be established, with the incumbents of these positions, possibly former trade union officials, held accountable to workers' organizations within their own countries, and having the sole responsibility of representing workers' interests. This combination would support an international workers' movement, give all workers basic voice rights that would be legally enforceable, improve information flows within organizations and could potentially add weight to bargaining priorities, increasing trade union effectiveness.

Trade union leaders would play dual roles in this scenario (Zammitt, 2001), negotiating collective agreements and also ensuring the other participatory arrangements functioned effectively. The scope of the joint consultation or of collective bargaining could be expanded to ensure that all worker concerns could be addressed. A procedure for determining the appropriate venue for any issues raised would have to be established (Jain, 1980: Ch. 7). Strauss (2001) proposes that to avoid jurisdictional disputes, worker directors and works councils could be tasked with looking after longer-term workers' interests and trade unions could negotiate shorter-term interests.

Research has shown that effective works councils in combination with strong legislation protecting workers' rights (Gollan and Markey, 2001) or in combination with collective bargaining (Garson, 1979; IDE International Research Group, 1993) provide effective employee representation and do not undermine unions. Since unions outside the USA normally coexist with works councils, this combination remains a viable option, as long as trade unions can come to accept the existence of multiple forms of voice operating in the workplace and can agree to greater levels of union–management cooperation in areas where priorities overlap.

Legislated Minimum Voice Rights

Another alternative would be to give workers legislative rights to some specified minimum level of voice, giving employees and employers latitude to work out the details themselves. This could potentially consist of a variety of complementary direct and indirect representation options. Employers' compliance could be encouraged through the provision of a tax credit incentive system to set up such procedures (Kochan 2007), or making access to significant government funding contingent on making voice opportunities available to employees (Connaghan, 1979).

This solution could meet the standards set out as long as the specified minimum voice levels were adequate to provide industrial democracy and were enforced. Voice arrangements, however, are deemed to be ineffective in the absence of protections against employer retaliation (Marchington, 2007; Morrison and Rothman, 2009), so unless an effective method of enforcing employers' compliance with the legislation exists, there would still be a need for a strong social safety net coupled with trade union representation or strong workers' rights legislation.

CONCLUSION

This chapter has reviewed and evaluated the main approaches to industrial democracy pursued in the UK, Western Europe, the Scandinavian countries and North America in the twentieth century, and identified several preconditions that must be met before any such initiatives can succeed. It has also offered a few suggestions regarding the path forward. Past experience suggests that any progress along that path will require a long-term, comprehensive strategy, a sustained commitment to and support for democratic goals on the part of governments, trade unions, the public, employers and workers, and a great deal of effort.

REFERENCES

Addison, J. T., K. Kraft and J. Wagner (1993), 'German works councils and firm performance', in Bruce E. Kaufman and Morris M. Kleiner (eds), *Employee Representation: Alternatives and Future Directions*, Madison, WI: Industrial Relations Research Association, pp. 305–38.
Addison, J., C. Schnabel and J. Wagner (2004), 'The course of research into the economic consequences of German works councils', *British Journal of Industrial Relations*, **42** (2), 255–81.
Adell, B. (1986), *Establishing a Collective Voice in the Workplace*, Kingston: Industrial Relations Centre.
Bacon, N. (2008), 'Management strategy and industrial relations', in Paul Blyton, Nicolas Bacon, Jack Fiorito and Edmund Heery (eds), *The Sage Handbook of Industrial Relations*, Thousand Oaks, CA: Sage, pp. 241–57.
Camfield, D. (2011), *Canadian Labour in Crisis. Reinventing the Workers Movement*, Halifax: Fernwood.
Cathcart, A. (2013), 'Paradoxes of participation: non-union workplace partnership in John Lewis Partnership', *International Journal of Human Resource Management*, DOI: 10.1080/09585192.2012.743476.
Clegg, H.A. (1963), *A New Approach to Industrial Democracy*, Oxford: Basil Blackwell.
Connaghan, C. (1979), 'Introduction', in George Sanderson, and Frederick Stapenhurst (eds), *Industrial Democracy Today: A New Role for Labour*, Toronto: McGraw-Hill, pp. 189–97.
Danford, A. (2005), 'New union strategies and forms of work organization in UK manufacturing', in Bill Harley, Jeff Hyman and Paul Thompson (eds), *Participation and Democracy at Work: Essays in Honour of Harvie Ramsay*, Basingstoke and New York: Palgrave Macmillan, pp. 166–85.
Davies, R. (1979), 'Introduction: industrial relations in international perspective', in George Sanderson, and Frederick Stapenhurst (eds), *Industrial Democracy Today: A New Role for Labour*, Toronto: McGraw-Hill, pp. 3–17.
de Jong, G. and A. van Witteloosttuijn (2004), 'Successful corporate democracy: sustainable cooperation of capital and labor in the Dutch Brennan Group', *Academy of Management Executive*, **18** (3), 54–66.
Deakin, S. and W. Njoya (2008), 'The legal framework of employment relations', in Paul Blyton, Nicolas Bacon, Jack Fiorito and Edmund Heery (eds), *The Sage Handbook of Industrial Relations*, Thousand Oaks, CA: Sage, pp. 284–304.
Diamant, A. (1977), 'Democratizing the workplace: the myth and reality of MITBESTIMMUNG in the Federal Republic of Germany', in G. David Garson (ed.), *Worker Self-Management in Industry: The West European Experience*, NY: Praeger, pp. 25–48.
Dow, G. (2003), *Governing the Firm: Workers' Control in Theory and Practice*, New York: Cambridge University Press.
Flanders, A., R. Pomeranz and J. Woodward (1968), *Experimentation in Industrial Democracy: A Study of the John Lewis Partnership*, London: Faber and Faber.
Foley, J. and M. Polanyi (2006), 'Workplace democracy: why bother?', *Economic and Industrial Democracy*, **27** (1), 173–91.
Freeman, R.B. and J. Medoff (1984), *What Do Unions Do?*, New York: Basic Books.
Freeman, R.B., P. Boxall, and P. Haynes (2007), 'Introduction: the Anglo–American economies and employee voice', in Richard B. Freeman, Peter Boxall and Peter Haynes (eds), *What Workers Say: Employee Voice in the Anglo–American Workplace*, Ithaca, NY: ILR Press, pp. 1–24.
Frege, C. (2002), 'A critical assessment of the theoretical and empirical research on German works councils', *British Journal of Industrial Relations*, **40** (2), 221–48.
Garson, G. David (ed.) (1977), *Worker Self-Management in Industry: The West European Experience*, New York: Praeger.
Garson, G.D. (1979), 'The codetermination model of workers' participation. Where is it leading?', in George Sanderson, and Frederick Stapenhurst (eds), *Industrial Democracy Today: A New Role for Labour*, Toronto: McGraw-Hill, pp. 91–100.
Gollan, P. and R. Markey (2001), 'Conclusions: models of diversity and interaction', in Raymond Markey, Paul Gollan, Ann Hodgkinson, Alain Chouraqui and Ulke Veersma (eds), *Models of Employee Participation in a Changing Global Environment: Diversity and Interaction*, Aldershot: Ashgate, pp. 322–43.
Hadley, R. and M. Goldsmith (1995), 'Development or convergence: change and stability in a common ownership firm over three decades: 1960–89', *Economic and Industrial Democracy*, **16**, 167–99.

Hall, M. and P. Marginson (2005), 'Trojan horses or paper tigers: assessing the significance of European works councils', in Bill Harley, Jeff Hyman and Paul Thompson (eds), *Participation and Democracy at Work: Essays in Honour of Harvie Ramsay*, Basingstoke and New York: Palgrave Macmillan, pp. 204–21.

Hancock, M.D., J. Logue and B. Schiller (1991), 'Introduction: the transformation of modern capitalism', in M. Donald Hancock, John Logue and Bernt Schiller (eds), *Managing Modern Capitalism: Industrial Renewal and Workplace Democracy in the United States and Western Europe*, New York, Westport, CN, and London: Greenwood Press, pp. xi–xxi.

Heller, F. (1998), 'Influence at work: a 2-year program of research', *Human Relations*, **51** (12), 1425–56.

Helm, J. (1991), 'Workplace democracy in Germany', in M. Donald Hancock, John Logue and Bernt Schiller (eds), *Managing Modern Capitalism: Industrial Renewal and Workplace Democracy in the United States and Western Europe*, New York , Westport, CN, and London: Greenwood Press, pp. 173–94.

Hemsworth, L. (1979), 'Participation through communication', in George Sanderson and Frederick Stapenhurst (eds), *Industrial Democracy Today: A New Role for Labour*, Toronto: McGraw-Hill, pp. 197–200.

Hillard, J. and D. Coates (1991), 'The challenge of industrial democracy in Britain', in M. Donald Hancock, John Logue and Bernt Schiller (eds), *Managing Modern Capitalism: Industrial Renewal and Workplace Democracy in the United States and Western Europe*, New York, Westport, CN, and London: Greenwood Press, pp. 121–44.

Horner, J. (1974), *Studies in Industrial Democracy*, London: Victor Gollancz.

Huddleston, J. (1972), 'Industrial democracy', *Parliamentary Affairs*, **25** (3), 224–33.

Hunter, L. (1998), 'Can strategic participation be institutionalized? Union representation on American corporate boards', *Industrial and Labor Relations Review*, **51** (4), 557–70.

IDE International Research Group (1993), *Industrial Democracy in Europe Revisited*, Oxford: Oxford University Press.

Jain, H. (1980), *Worker Participation. Success and Problems*, New York: Praeger.

Jenkins, J. and P. Blyton (2008), 'Works councils', in Paul Blyton, Nicolas Bacon, Jack Fiorito and Edmund Heery (eds), *The Sage Handbook of Industrial Relations*, Thousand Oaks, CA: Sage, pp. 346–57.

Johnson, P. (2006), 'Whence democracy? A review and critique of the conceptual dimensions and implications of the business case for organizational democracy', *Organization*, **13** (2), 245–74.

Jones, D. (1977), 'Worker participation in management in Britain: evaluation, current developments, and prospects', in G. David Garson (ed.), *Worker Self-Management in Industry: The West European Experience*, New York: Praeger, pp. 97–151.

Kaufman, B.E. (2000), 'The early institutionalists on industrial democracy and union democracy', *Journal of Labor Research*, **21** (2), 189–209.

Kochan, T.A. (2007), 'What should governments do?', in Richard B. Freeman, Peter Boxall and Peter Haynes (eds), *What Workers Say: Employee Voice in the Anglo–American Workplace*, Ithaca, NY: ILR Press, pp. 198–205.

Kulkarni, S. (2010), 'Sustaining the equality of employee voice: a dynamic capability', *International Journal of Organizational Analysis*, **18** (4), 442–65.

Lichtenstein, N. and H.J. Harris (1993), 'Introduction: a century of industrial democracy in America', in Nelson Lichtenstein and Howell John Harris (eds), *Industrial Democracy in America: The Ambiguous Promise*, Cambridge: Cambridge University Press, pp. 1–19.

Marchington, M. (2007), 'Employee voice systems', in Peter Boxall, John Purcell and Patrick Wright (eds), *Oxford Handbook of Human Resource Management*, New York: Oxford University Press, pp. 231–50.

Marginson, P., M. Hall, A. Hoffman and T. Muller (2004), 'The impact of European works councils on management decision-making in UK and US-based multinationals: a case study comparison', *British Journal of Industrial Relations*, **42** (2), 209–33.

Mohrenweiser, J., P. Marginson and U. Backes–Gellner (2012), 'What triggers the establishment of a works council?', *Economic and Industrial Democracy*, **33** (2), 295–316.

Morrison, E.W and N.B. Rothman (2009), 'Silence and the dynamics of power', in Jerald Greenberg and Marissa S. Edwards (eds), *Voice and Silence in Organizations*, Bingley: Emerald Group, pp. 111–34.

Nightingale, D.V. (1982), *Workplace Democracy: An Enquiry into Employee Participation in Canadian Work Organizations*, Toronto: University of Toronto Press.

OECD (2012), 'OECD StatExtracts', available at http://stats.oecd.org/Index.aspx?DatasetCode=UN_DEN (accessed 27 June 2012).

Peirce, J. (2000), *Canadian Industrial Relations*, Scarborough, ON: Prentice Hall Canada.

Purcell, J. and K. Georgiadis (2007), 'Why should employers bother with worker voice?', in Richard B. Freeman, Peter Boxall and Peter Haynes (eds), *What Workers Say: Employee Voice in the Anglo–American Workplace*, Ithaca, NY: ILR Press, pp. 181–97.

Ross, S. and L. Savage (2012), 'Rethinking the politics of labour in Canada: an introduction', in Stephanie Ross and Larry Savage (eds), *Rethinking the Politics of Labour in Canada*, Halifax: Fernwood, pp. 7–16.

Rus, V. (1984), 'The future of industrial relations', *International Social Sciences Journal*, **36** (UNESCO Special Issue: Industrial Relations), 233–54.

Sanderson, G. and R. LaBerge (1979), 'Introduction', in George Sanderson, and Frederick Stapenhurst (eds), *Industrial Democracy Today: A New Role for Labour*, Toronto: McGraw-Hill, pp. 111–15.

Strauss, G. (2001), 'American experience with union-nominated Boards of Directors', in Raymond Markey, Paul Gollan, Ann Hodgkinson, Alain Chouraqui and Ulke Veersma (eds), *Models of Employee Participation in a Changing Global Environment. Diversity and Interaction*, Aldershot: Ashgate, pp. 97–118.

Swartz, D. and R. Warskett (2012), 'Canadian labour and the crisis of solidarity', in Stephanie Ross and Larry Savage (eds), *Rethinking the Politics of Labour in Canada*, Halifax: Fernwood, pp. 18–32.

Trist, E. (1979), 'Adapting to a changing world', in George Sanderson and Frederick Stapenhurst (eds), *Industrial Democracy Today: A New Role for Labour*, Toronto: McGraw-Hill, pp. 35–43.

Waddington, J. (2011), 'European works councils: the challenge for labour', *Industrial Relations Journal*, **42** (6), 508–29.

Whitehorn, A. (1980), 'Yugoslav worker self-management: some advantages and problems', Case 9 in Hem Jain *Worker Participation: Success and Problems*, New York: Praeger, pp. 310–23.

Yates, Michael D. (2009), *Why Unions Matter*, New York: Monthly Review Press.

Zammitt, E. (2001), 'Efficiency vs democracy in the workplace? A postscript on self-management at Malta Drydocks', in Raymond Markey, Paul Gollan, Ann Hodgkinson, Alain Chouraqui and Ulke Veersma (eds), *Models of Employee Participation in a Changing Global Environment: Diversity and Interaction*, Aldershot: Ashgate, pp. 161–75.

6 High performance work systems and employee voice
Bill Harley

Since the 1990s, 'high performance work systems' (HPWS) theory has risen in prominence in the field of human resource management (HRM) and has become the dominant model of links between HRM and organizational performance. Employee voice has been central to many accounts of HPWS and indeed has been accorded considerable weight in theoretical arguments about how HRM drives organizational performance. This makes a consideration of the role of voice in HPWS essential in understanding the contemporary sphere of HRM.

This chapter considers the theoretical debates and the evidence concerning the role of voice in HPWS. It begins with theoretical concerns and explains how voice has been conceptualized in the HPWS literature as involving both direct and indirect forms of employee input to decisions. The chapter then considers the theoretical debates about direct and indirect forms of voice and highlights the lack of agreement about key issues. Discussion then turns to the research evidence about HPWS and voice. While the research has provided valuable insights, the evidence remains partial, fragmented and ambiguous, restricting the conclusions we can draw about the role of voice in HPWS. Based on recognition of the limits of our current empirical knowledge, the chapter concludes with consideration of possible future trajectories for research.

THEORETICAL DEBATES ABOUT HPWS AND VOICE

This part of the chapter considers how voice is theorized within the HPWS literature. It begins by mapping out the conceptualization of voice which can be found in published work on HPWS, before moving to consider in detail theorizations of the role of direct and indirect or representative forms of voice. This sets the agenda for consideration of the research evidence in the section which follows.

The Concept of Voice in the HPWS Literature

The concept of 'high performance work systems' (HPWS) is now well entrenched in the literature on human resource management (HRM), industrial relations (IR) and management. It came to prominence in the early 1990s in the United States (see Appelbaum and Batt 1994) and since then has received increasing attention in the literature (see Appelbaum et al. 2000; Ramsay et al. 2000). It is arguable that HPWS is now the dominant conceptual model underlying attempts to explain the links between HRM practices on the one hand and organizational performance on the other. Moreover, it is an account that makes employee voice, in at least some of its forms, central to claims about performance gains (Harley 2012).

There is an extensive literature on HPWS and for this reason only a small amount of space will be devoted to explaining what this term means. The debates about how best to specify the components of HPWS are well rehearsed and it is clear that there remains disagreement as to the precise practices which should be included. Nonetheless, there is broad agreement about what constitutes HPWS (Appelbaum 2002; Harley 2005). Most or all accounts of HPWS accept that they comprise 'post-Taylorist' forms of work organization, such as high-scope jobs and autonomous teams, which enhance employee discretion and participation in decisions about production. These forms of work organization are buttressed by provision of skills, chiefly through sophisticated recruitment and selection and the provision of training, which equip workers to utilize their autonomy effectively. In addition, motivation mechanisms, chiefly in the form of performance-based rewards, encourage workers to use their skills and autonomy to enhance production of good and services. Put simply, the argument made for HPWS is that these mutually reinforcing systems of practices deliver performance gains to organizations exceeding those which would result from the sum of the effects of the individual components. Moreover, as will be discussed later in this chapter, this is commonly claimed to go hand in hand with improved quality of working life for employees (see Ramsay et al. 2000).

It has been claimed that employee voice is central to HPWS (Budd et al. 2010: 306). Indeed, it could be argued that a large part of the debate on employee voice and performance in the contemporary HRM literature is framed by the concept of HPWS (Harley 2012). Before considering the debates about voice and HPWS, it is necessary to clarify how the relevant literature defines the former. In his germinal formulation, Hirschman defined voice as:

> any attempt at all to change, rather than to escape from, an objectionable state of affairs, whether through individual or collective petition to the management directly in charge, through appeal to a higher authority with the intention of forcing a change in management, or through various types of actions and protests, including those which are meant to mobilise public opinion. (Hirschman, 1970: 30)

This rather narrow definition, with its emphasis on various forms of expression of dissatisfaction as a means to facilitate change, has been broadened and developed over the past forty years (Budd et al. 2010).

There is a tendency in the literature to use the terms 'voice' and 'participation' interchangeably. Clearly voice and participation are not mutually exclusive terms, but it is important to be precise about what voice means if we are to understand how it relates to HPWS. Based on a review of the relevant literature, Dundon et al. (2004) provide a useful analytical framework to consider the range of meanings of voice in the HRM and industrial relations (IR) literature. They identify four distinct meanings.

First, in line with Hirschman's 1970 definition, voice can refer to the articulation of individual employee grievances with the aim of rectifying a perceived problem, for example by complaining to a line manager. Second, it can refer to mechanisms through which individual employees are able to contribute to management decision-making aimed at improving productivity, for example via organizing work around autonomous or semi-autonomous teams and/or high scope jobs. Third, it can take the form of expressions of collective organization aimed at balancing the power of management, such as collective bargaining. Finally, they suggest, voice can refer to collective practices aimed at demonstrating mutuality of interest and cooperation with management with a view to achieving performance gains and long-term viability, such as partnership agreements or works councils.

This typology suggests two important dimensions on which we can classify different voice mechanisms. The first is the extent to which they can be seen as primarily direct or representative in nature. The second is the extent to which they can be seen as concerned with asserting workers' interests and balancing managerial power (traditional concerns of IR scholars), as opposed to providing mechanisms for improving organizational performances and viability (concerns commonly associated with HRM).

In practice, it makes sense to regard these dimensions as representing tendencies, rather than dichotomous categories. For example, while we might regard partnership arrangements as being primarily focused on organizational performance, this need not exclude the exercise of collective power as a rationale for unions to enter into such arrangements. The HPWS literature tends to focus on those forms of voice, both direct and representative, which have the purpose of enhancing organizational performance.

In most accounts, performance is conceived almost exclusively in terms of *economic* performance. Measures in the extant empirical research cover either or both operational performance (notably productivity, turnover and quality of products or services) and financial performance (commonly based on accounting data or subjective assessments by senior managers) (see Combs et al. 2006; van de Voorde et al. 2012). It is perhaps unsurprising that the focus of theory and empirical research has been so squarely on economic performance, given that demonstrating that HRM drives business success has been something of a 'holy grail' for mainstream HRM scholars ever since the emergence of the field (Legge 2001). Nonetheless, it means that consideration of a broader range of organizational implications has largely been absent from the research and that much of the discussion has been narrowly and uncritically managerialist (Legge 1998). The ethical arguments for the kinds of humanistic and developmental practices associated with HPWS, particularly voice mechanisms, have largely been ignored. To the extent that employees have been considered, this has usually been in the context of their role in delivering performance (van de Voorde et al. 2012), although there has been some research which has considered the implications for employees in their own right (Harley et al. 2007; Harley et al. 2010). In the next section, the debates about the role of individual and collective voice mechanisms and HPWS will be considered.

HPWS and Direct Forms of Voice

Theorizing and empirical research on voice in the context of HPWS has tended to focus more on direct forms of voice than representative ones, reflecting the fact that direct forms of voice are integral to HPWS, while representative forms are not. For this reason, more attention will be devoted to direct than representative forms of voice in the remainder of this chapter. There are three forms of employee voice which consistently appear in accounts of HPWS. The first of these is the presence of high-autonomy jobs. These are jobs which are characterized by relatively high levels of employee discretion concerning production processes. It might be argued that high-autonomy jobs are not, of themselves, an example of voice since they do not involve input to management decisions. This could be countered, however, by the argument that in fact the very nature of high-autonomy jobs is such that they involve a shifting of management decisions (albeit often of a relatively minor kind) to the level of the individual worker. The second is the organization of work into autonomous or semi-autonomous teams, in which employees individually have input to team decisions about production. Again, this can be seen as the shifting of management decisions (albeit, again, often only relatively minor ones) to a team level. These two forms of work organization are at the very heart of HPWS and, as will be discussed below, are conceptualized as the fundamental mechanism through which HPWS contribute to organizational performance gains (Appelbaum 2002; Harley 2012).

Third, some accounts of HPWS also include mechanisms that are more obviously forms of voice (for example, Ramsay et al 2000). These are more 'traditional' forms of communication and participation, such as suggestion schemes, communication programmes and information sharing meetings. While these are commonly discussed in accounts of HPWS, they are not core HPWS practices, but are better conceptualized as practices which might be seen as augmenting them.

As one might expect, the bulk of the literature on HPWS argues that the key effect of direct voice mechanisms is to contribute to organizational performance. Indeed, as implied by its label, the central rationale for HPWS is that voice mechanisms will generate performance gains. The literature suggests that the function of the voice mechanisms associated with HPWS is to enhance employee autonomy and provide employees with the opportunity to influence processes of production (Appelbaum 2002). High-autonomy jobs allow employees to make 'micro' decisions about production, teamwork allows employees to exercise a degree of local level collective influence over production decisions, and communication mechanisms allow employees to provide individual input to more 'macro' decisions about the organization and its activities.

All three of these forms of voice are said to have positive impacts on employees' attitudes to work and through this to performance. According to the HPWS literature, employees who enjoy higher levels of autonomy and influence also enjoy higher levels of organizational commitment, satisfaction and motivation. The result of this is that they are more likely to work effectively and to remain with the organization, thereby increasing productivity and reducing turnover. In the HPWS model, the motivational effects of voice mechanisms are also buttressed by other motivators, such as performance-based pay. As well as positive effects on attitudes, high-autonomy jobs and teamwork have the potential to generate better production decisions. The argument here is that when employees have discretion to influence production, they are able to use their tacit and explicit knowledge of production processes to solve problems and make decisions. Because they are much more familiar with production processes than managers, these decisions are likely to be better than if they were imposed by management. This kind of effect is buttressed by skill provision in the HPWS model, to ensure that employees have the kinds of skills they need to maximize the potential provided by enhanced autonomy.

Historically, a number of rationales have been put forward for enhancing employee voice at work (Lansbury and Prideaux 1980). One has been that voice will contribute to performance and another that there is an ethical rationale for the provision of voice mechanisms. That is, employees ought to have a voice at work because it improves quality of working life (Harley 2012). In the HPWS model, these two rationales are presented as coming together. In meeting the performance needs of organizations, the kinds of voice mechanisms associated with the model are claimed simultaneously and necessarily to improve the quality of working life. The autonomy which results from these voice mechanisms is inherently positive and the positive attitudes to work which result reflect this. Thus, it is the centrality of voice which allows HPWS to address a perennial problem in the management of labour – how to simultaneously improve organisational performance and employees' experience of work.

This overwhelmingly optimistic view of the role of voice in delivering positive outcomes has not been without its critics (Danford et al. 2004, 2008). While there have been some differences among critiques, the fundamental one has been that the kind of 'win-win' scenario put forward by advocates of HPWS overlooks the negative outcomes for employees. The critics generally accept the argument that the voice mechanisms inherent in HPWS contribute to performance gains, but they suggest that this is because the mechanisms shift responsibility for decision-making from managers to employees, thereby increasing pressure on them and intensifying work (Harley et al. 2010).

HPWS and Representative Forms of Voice

While direct forms of voice are characterized for the most part as inherent components of HPWS, the role assigned by the literature to representative forms of voice is different. It is possible to discern two closely related claims in the literature. The first is that unionization facilitates the implementation of HPWS practices. The second is that collaborative labour management relations, exemplified by union–management cooperation, not only facilitate the introduction of HPWS, but also facilitate particular approaches to the implementation and operation of HPWS that deliver mutual gains to management and workers. Each conceptualization will be considered in turn.

Since the literature on HPWS emerged, a number of authors have claimed that such arrangements were more likely to be implemented in unionized workplaces and industries (see Liu et al. 2009). The argument here is that workers have an interest in a better quality of working life, unions recognize this and thus are likely to encourage the implementation of HPWS practices in workplaces where they are active. Further, it may be the case that unions actively pressure management to introduce innovative workplace practices (Verma 2005), because they recognize that productive workplaces are likely to deliver better outcomes for their members in terms of pay and job security. Moreover, there are likely to be gains in terms of legitimacy for unions that promote workplace innovation. From this perspective, collective voice in the form of unions may be a predictor of the presence of direct voice practices of the kind associated with HPWS.

Turning to the second argument that is commonly made in the literature, some authors have gone further and suggested that where there are cooperative relations between unions and management, not only is it more likely that HPWS practices will be introduced, but it is likely that they will be introduced in ways that deliver 'mutual gains' in the form of improved productivity *and* enhanced quality of working life (Edwards et al. 2006; Bélanger and Edwards 2007). This argument recognizes the criticisms of 'win-win' accounts of HPWS highlighted in the previous section and accepts that HPWS can have either positive or negative outcomes for employees, but suggests that in cooperative environments some degree of mutual gain is possible. The argument here is that while labour–management relations necessarily have an element of conflict, there are always potential shared interests, most notably in the continued viability of enterprises. Where there is a cooperative relationship between management and unions, notwithstanding the inevitability of conflict there is a greater likelihood that HPWS will emphasize the kinds of direct voice mechanisms discussed earlier in the chapter, as well as the skill development that is said to be part of HPWS. This is because such mechanisms are recognized by unions as benefiting workers.

The discussion so far has highlighted the fact that there are at least two different categories of employee voice associated with HPWS. Moreover, it has pointed to the fact that there are differing claims in the literature about the role of voice in HPWS. An obvious question is to what extent the evidence allows us to elucidate these claims and resolve differences between different accounts. Discussion will now turn to the evidence.

THE RESEARCH ON VOICE AND HPWS

Before considering the research evidence on voice mechanisms, it is necessary to be clear about the focus of the next part of the discussion. While the term HPWS implies a coherent *system* of practices, the focus in some of the discussion that follows will be on the *voice mechanisms* which are associated with the HPWS model. There are two reasons for this. The first and most obvious one is that the focus of this chapter is on voice, rather than on skill provision or performance management. The second is that there is a good deal of evidence that the use of HPWS as coherent systems is actually relatively rare and that it is more common for organizations to use the practices in relatively fragmented ways (Harley 2002, 2005). There is, moreover, evidence that the different practices associated with the model have quite different outcomes, particularly for employees, which has led some scholars to suggest that they should be studied as individual practices rather than systems (Wall and Wood 2005). Indeed, a number of researchers prefer the term 'HPWS practices' to HPWS (Harley et al. 2010).

Research on Direct Forms of Voice in HPWS

This section can be broken down into three areas of discussion. The first considers the evidence concerning the links between direct voice mechanisms – teamwork, high-autonomy jobs and participation/consultation mechanisms – and organizational performance, while the second examines the evidence on these mechanisms and employee outcomes. The third brings these concerns together by asking what we know about the mechanisms through which performance outcomes appear to emerge. These three themes fit together in a chronological sequence, with the early phase of research focused on performance, a concern with employee outcomes emerging subsequently, and with detailed empirical analyses of causal mechanisms being the most recent phase.

Early empirical work on HPWS and performance focused almost exclusively on the links between HPWS practices and performance, and the 1990s saw the publication of a number of influential studies, emanating chiefly from the USA, which plotted associations between a range of HRM practices on one hand and a range of performance measures on the other (see, for example, Huselid 1995; Delery and Doty 1996; Ichniowski et al. 1997). A stream of research that focused on HRM and performance continued to flow until well into the 2000s, based chiefly on cross-sectional studies of companies, organizations or work units, which tested for associations between practices and performance (Wood and Wall 2007). There have been some studies that have explicitly examined the impact of voice mechanisms on performance, but not within a broader consideration of HPWS (for example, Kim et al. 2010; Levine and Tyson 1990). While the evidence has been mixed, in general the research is consistent with the claim that voice plays a role in delivering performance gains. This is not the same thing, however, as saying that the research conclusively demonstrates that HPWS cause gains in performance. The cross-sectional designs of most studies mean that causal claims are impossible to verify and the small number of longitudinal studies have, if anything, challenged claims of causation (for example, Guest et al. 2003). Further, the ways in which HPWS practices and performance are commonly measured may not provide valid and reliable indicators of the phenomena under consideration (see Wall and Wood 2005 and Guest 2011 for discussion of the limitations of the research). We must, therefore, be sceptical about any claim that we know with certainty that HPWS practices drive performance.

When it comes to studies that focus on voice specifically as part of the HPWS model, difficulties arise in identifying the role of voice. As a means to draw conclusions about the specific impact of voice mechanisms on performance outcomes, the bulk of the published studies have two limitations, highlighted by Wood and Wall's (2007) analysis of refereed, empirical papers on the HRM–performance link published between 1994 and 2005. First, while most studies included measures of consultation mechanisms, relatively few also included items on high-autonomy jobs and teamwork (Wood and Wall 2007: 1357). Second, few tested for the individual effects of practices as opposed to using composite HPWS or system scales for their independent variable (2007: 1360). It is, therefore, difficult to draw particularly confident conclusions about the role of voice in delivering performance gains based on this influential body of empirical work.

This lack of focus on the links between voice and performance in empirical studies of HPWS has been claimed to be of wider significance than just posing a challenge to the conclusions we can draw about findings. According to Wood and Wall (2007) it reflects a shift away from early HPWS models – framed around 'high commitment' and 'high involvement' – which made participation central to performance and explicitly argued that performance gains went hand in hand with enhanced employee experience of work. The focus on voice and on positive employee outcomes as preconditions for performance gains have increasingly been supplanted, according to Wood and Wall, by research underpinned by the resource-based view of the firm and a focus on skills and motivation. This may also reflect a shift within the broader field of HRM, in which theory, practice and research have all become more focused on strategic considerations at the expense of a concern with employee outcomes (Van Buren et al. 2011).

Such claims, at least as they apply to HPWS research, are probably overstated, given the fact that there has been an increase over time in the volume of research that has examined employee outcomes as significant in their own right (Harley et al. 2010). There has also been some growth in work that has included employee responses as potential mediators between HPWS practices and performance (see, for example, Takeuchi et al. 2007; Messersmith et al. 2011; Aryee et al. 2012). The work that has examined the implications of HPWS for employees has, perhaps unsurprisingly, focused a good deal of its attention on direct forms of voice, as practices that could be expected to have a significant impact on employees' experience of work.

It would seem almost axiomatic that direct employee voice would deliver overwhelmingly positive outcomes for employees in terms of both their degree of control over their work and their attitudes to work. As noted above, however, there have been differences of opinion about the ways that HPWS affect employees. Indeed, the research evidence suggests that the links between direct voice mechanisms and employee outcomes may be rather more complex than a simple 'win-win'. It is possible to find studies that show no association, either positive or negative, between voice mechanisms and employee autonomy (for example, Harley 1999, 2001). There are also studies that find evidence of negative outcomes from HPWS (for example, Berg and Frost 2005). Other studies have found positive associations between voice mechanisms and employee outcomes, both in terms of autonomy and attitudes to work (for example, Harley et al. 2007).

The fact that the evidence presents a complex picture of the outcomes of voice mechanisms suggests that the reality is also complex. This has led some commentators to suggest that further debate about whether such practices are 'good' or 'bad' for employees are likely to be fruitless, and that a more sensible focus for future research would be the different contextual factors associated with different outcomes as well as the different causal paths through which outcomes emerge (Harley et al. 2010).

The preceding discussion suggests that the research on the impact of HPWS on employee outcomes does not provide conclusive evidence and that both the outcomes and the causal paths through which they emerge are likely to be complex. When we turn to the evidence on the causal paths from HPWS, via employees, to organizational performance it quickly becomes apparent that it is indeed complex and ambiguous. Scrutiny of some of the few studies that have sought to test apparent causal paths illustrates the lack of unequivocal evidence.

It must be said that it is very difficult to find studies that provide a clear empirical basis for understanding the apparent effects of voice practices, via employees, on performance (see Van de Voorde et al. 2012 for a recent review of relevant work). In the first place, relatively few studies have sought to explore the role of employee responses in mediating between HPWS practices and performance. Further, there are virtually none that have done so and which test for the effects of individual HPWS practices including voice mechanisms. For this reason, when we seek to assess the current state of knowledge of the causal paths from voice mechanisms to performance, we must make inferences based on a handful of studies that have used composite HPWS measures. What this means is that the conclusions that can be drawn must be at best tentative. This can be illustrated with reference to an early study and a more recent one.

Ramsay et al.'s (2000) germinal study sought to test the extent to which employee discretion, satisfaction, commitment and work intensity mediated associations between components of HPWS on the one hand and a series of measures of organizational performance on the other, using data drawn from the 1998 Workplace Employment Relations Survey (WERS). The broad aim of the study was to test competing explanations of the performance effects of HPWS – those of 'labour process' critics and 'mainstream' advocates – by assessing whether performance gains flowed via intensified work effort or via a positive transformation of work. While this study used composite HPWS scales, rather than examining individual practices, one of the three composites comprised a 'subset of practices closest to the HPWS idea of enhancing involvement and development' (Ramsay et al. 2000: 508) which included a number of voice mechanisms.

The results were, at best, ambiguous. While the composite HPWS scale was associated positively with six of the seven measures of organizational performance used in the study, the evidence for a mediating effect of either positive employee experiences or work intensification was weak, leading the authors to conclude that neither mainstream nor labour process models received clear support. Since that time, only a few other studies have been conducted which have sought to test mediation. A notable example is Takeuchi et al.'s (2007) study of Japanese organizations. In this study, the authors also used a composite HPWS scale, but tested quite different mediators from those used by Ramsay et al. (2000). Takeuchi et al. (2007) found that the association between HPWS and performance was mediated by collective human capital and social exchange. These results suggest that as well as individual-level mediating effects, it may well be the case that HPWS practices have an impact via collective social processes within organizations.

A more recent study that sought to test mediation is Ehrnrooth and Björkman (2012). Again, these authors used composite measures, so it is not possible to disentangle the effects of voice practices, but the results highlight the fact that as the research has progressed it has become increasingly clear that simple causal explanations do not grasp the complex paths from HPWS to performance. These authors used employee creativity, core job performance and workload as their performance measures, rather than organizational performance, which must be taken into account in interpreting the results. They then tested for the mediating effect of psychological empowerment. The results of this study indicate that psychological empowerment fully mediates the associations between HPWS practices on one hand and creativity and workload on the other, but that while there was an association between HPWS and core job performance this was not mediated by empowerment. These results are suggestive of the fact that, as argued by Harley et al. (2010), we should not expect the causal paths from HPWS to performance to be via 'good' or 'bad' employee outcomes. Rather, it would appear that the causal paths may be via a combination of both: 'On balance, existing evidence suggests that there may be both positive and negative mediating relationships' (Ehrnrooth and Björkman 2012: 1126).

The preceding discussion suggests that any conclusions we make about causal paths must be tentative at best. The most significant thing they point to is the need for further research to tease out the complex pathways from HPWS voice mechanisms, via employees, to performance. The discussion will now turn to the evidence on representative forms of voice.

Research on Representative Forms of Voice in HPWS

The earlier discussion suggested that there are claims in the literature that representative forms of voice in the form of unions and partnership arrangements facilitate HPWS and that they also tend to lead to outcomes of HPWS which are likely to benefit both management and employees. What is the evidence? If the evidence concerning the role of direct voice in HPWS is limited and fragmentary, that concerning representative forms of voice in HPWS is even more so. As well as the aforementioned fact that direct voice is integral to HPWS, whereas representative voice is not, this may also reflect the fact that a focus on industrial relations and, in particular, institutional industrial relations has been marginalized somewhat by the more micro focus of HRM research in the study of HPWS (see Godard and Delaney 2000).

There has been some research on the extent to which unionization is associated with the adoption of HPWS practices, but the results are mixed and inconclusive. A very useful review of the evidence up until the mid-2000s can be found in Verma (2005). He reviews the research (including that which focuses specifically on voice mechanisms) and, while acknowledging that the evidence is mixed, concludes that the weight of the evidence suggests that unions increase the likelihood of HPWS being implemented at the workplace level (2005: 439). There have been a few papers published on unions and HPWS adoption since Verma's (see for example Liu et al. 2009; Ramirez et al. 2007) but none have conclusively demonstrated either a universal positive or negative impact. It would seem prudent to conclude that in some circumstances collective voice in the form of unions contributes to the adoption of HPWS practices.

There is a similar paucity of research examining the extent to which the presence and involvement of unions in workplaces appears to lead to more 'mutual gains' flowing from the adoption of HPWS. The empirical studies which have been published tend to focus on the extent to which union involvement amplifies productivity gains from HPWS (see for example Cooke 1994). A comprehensive review of research on unions in the USA and works councils in Germany conducted by Addison (2005) provides a useful basis for making empirically-supported inferences about the question of representative voice and the effectiveness of HPWS. Addison's analysis of studies published up to the mid-2000s suggests that interactions between HPWS practices and collective voice contribute to performance gains and on this basis we might cautiously conclude that collective voice can have a role in amplifying the performance gains associated with HPWS. Similarly, Black and Lynch (2001) found that unionized plants which introduced HPWS practices involving enhanced employee input to decisions enjoyed higher productivity than unionized plants which utilized more traditional labour management practices, suggesting that cooperative approaches involving unions and management deliver greater gains.

This brief review of the research evidence points to the fact that, while there has been a good deal of research devoted to HPWS, there are still significant gaps in our knowledge. In the final part of the chapter, emergent and future directions for research will be discussed.

FUTURE RESEARCH AGENDA

HPWS has become increasingly prominent in the debates about HRM and performance, and issues of employee voice have been central to these debates. It is important to recognize that while HPWS might be seen as a new phenomenon, it can also be seen as simply the latest manifestation of a concern with the potential for developmental and humanist approaches to HRM to deliver performance gains while also benefiting employees (Ramsay et al. 2000). To that extent, we can see the debates about HPWS and voice as overlapping with perennial debates about participation and involvement. For this reason, while labels might change it seems highly likely that the issues canvassed in this chapter will remain important for the field of HRM for the foreseeable future.

As the literature on HPWS has evolved, the research agenda has broadened and the approaches to research have become more sophisticated. In the early phase of research, the influential studies were generally cross-sectional firm-level studies of HR practices on the one hand and performance outcomes on the other (for example, Huselid 1995). Subsequently, studies were published which focused on employee outcomes, as a means to bring workers' concerns into the debates (for example, Harley 2002). A handful of studies sought to bring together employee responses and performance outcomes as a means to explore causal paths from HPWS to performance (for example, Ramsay et al. 2000). At the same time, there was a similarly small number of studies that sought empirically to assess the role of collective voice in influencing the adoption and functioning of HPWS (for example, Cooke 1994).

As shown in the discussion of the literature above, while there has been a large and growing body of research either directly concerning, or at least relevant to, debates around HPWS and voice, it must be recognized that the available evidence is fragmentary, partial and inconclusive and much work is still to be done. In the discussion which follows, consideration will be given to two key areas where research has been developing or needs to develop further. The first concerns questions about the processes through which HPWS have their effects on organizations and the second considers the contextual factors, including collective voice, which appear to have an impact on how HPWS operate.

Research on Processes

In spite of the limitations of the extant research on HPWS and performance (see Wall and Wood 2005) the evidence is suggestive of the fact that HPWS practices have a role to play in driving organizational performance gains. While there are limitations in terms of research that focuses specifically on voice mechanisms within HPWS, nonetheless the available evidence suggests that voice may play a part in contributing to performance. What remains much less clear, as shown by the discussion above, is what the causal processes are through which such performance gains emerge.

As noted earlier, the assumption in much of the literature has been that HPWS have their impact via employees, although as we have seen there has been relatively little research that has tested employee outcomes as mediators. There has been to a large extent a polarization of views, with 'mainstream' scholars arguing that voice mechanisms associated with HPWS enhance employee discretion and 'critical' scholars arguing that direct voice simply means shifting responsibility to employees and intensifying work (Harley 2005). The research canvassed above suggests that it is unlikely that performance outcomes emerge universally through either completely positive or completely negative impacts on employees. This has led some scholars to argue that the 'good vs bad' debate has run its course and that we must recognize the diversity of possible causal paths through which HPWS are likely to have an impact on employees and performance (Harley et al. 2010).

This points to the need for research that explores both the ways in which HPWS practices shape employee outcomes and the way that employee outcomes feed into organizational outcomes. Some recent research points to potentially fruitful directions for the future. For example, in terms of the question of how the practices shape employee outcomes, Harley et al. (2010) report that employee perceptions of predictability and order mediate the association between participative forms of work and employee discretion. In a similar vein, Ehrnrooth and Björkman (2012) report that psychological empowerment mediates associations between HPWS practices and employee outcomes. While these two studies cannot be seen as by any means filling the gaps in our knowledge of the way HPWS have an impact on employees, nonetheless they point to potentially fruitful paths for research that seeks to tease out the complex mechanisms by which HPWS shape employee experiences of work.

In terms of the question of how impacts on employees shape impacts on organizational performance, as noted above a growing body of work has sought to test how different employee responses mediate associations between HPWS practices and performance (for example, Takeuchi et al. 2007). This research is beginning to fill in some of the pieces of the puzzle and it points towards two fruitful future directions. The first of these, which underpins the discussion in the remainder of this section, is the use of increasingly complex multi-level statistical modelling to explore the effects of HPWS on employees and organizational outcomes simultaneously (for example, Aryee et al. 2012).

While this kind of complex quantitative research on causal paths is undoubtedly valuable, it can be subjected to a number of criticisms which point to the need to augment it with different approaches (Gahan et al. 2010). First, much of the research is informed by psychological theories and assumes that organizational phenomena can be explained as the aggregation of individual responses and behaviours and fails to grasp causal processes which exist beyond the individual level. In particular, it tends to ignore insights from sociology and political science which suggest that the outcomes of managerial practices reflect in part conflicts inherent in the employment relationship (Harley et al. 2010). Second, reflecting its broadly positivist assumptions, the quantitative research focuses on testing hypotheses and making broad generalizations about causal processes, which tends to downplay the specific contextual factors at work at a local level within organizations.

These criticisms of the extant research point to the potential of more sociologically informed analyses of causal paths, focusing on the way that a range of individual and collective processes work together to produce specific outcomes in specific contexts. Moreover, they point to the need to develop theoretical models which bring together individual and collective attitudes and behaviours to develop holistic understandings of causal processes. It must be said that such research is embryonic at best at present. A promising example of research that has moved in this direction can be found in the work of Gittell et al. (2010). These authors argue for a 'relational model' of HPWS that conceptualizes it as facilitating 'relational coordination', that is, by enabling communication and relationships at work that enhance task integration (2010: 491).

Research on causal paths might also usefully address the question of how particular causal mechanisms explain particular outcomes. It is easily to slip into discussing 'performance' as if it is a single phenomenon, but as previously discussed the empirical research has employed a range of indicators of performance. While this research has pointed to specific associations between HPWS practices and performance outcomes, there remains a need for more detailed research on specific causal mechanisms.

There is also a need to broaden the agenda and to consider a wider range of processes and outcomes. For example, Legge (1998) has suggested that HRM practices which are ethical – underpinned by trust, fairness and justice – are more likely to deliver benefits to both employers and employees than practices that emphasize transactional relations at work. In the increasingly prominent field of corporate social responsibility (CSR), it has been suggested that organizations that implement socially responsible HR practices are likely to perform better than those that do not, in terms of both CSR and environmental sustainability (for example, Pless et al. 2012).

Research on Contextual Factors

The second potentially fruitful area for future research concerns not the internal organizational processes through which voice mechanisms contribute to outcomes, but rather the role of contextual factors in shaping their introduction and outcomes. Given the evidence that HPWS can deliver performance gains and that in the right circumstances this can go hand in hand with gains for employees, there would seem to be a pressing need for research exploring the factors that lead to such positive outcomes (Harley 2012). As already noted above, there is a paucity of research on the role of collective voice, chiefly in the form of unions, in facilitating the introduction of HPWS and their capacity to deliver mutual gains. It seems difficult to feel optimistic about the growth of this kind of research, given the shift in scholarly focus away from institutional industrial relations and towards 'micro' HRM (Godard and Delaney 2000).

In addition to consideration of the role of collective voice in facilitating HPWS, there would appear to be value in considering the role of institutions more broadly defined. The work of Bélanger and Edwards (2007) provides a useful framework for future research on the institutional conditions favouring 'mutual gains' approaches, pointing to the role of technology, product markets and institutional arrangements in fostering effective HPWS. The very small amount of work on the conditions favouring 'mutual gains' approaches to HPWS suggests that the field remains wide open for scholars who wish to pursue research in this area. In particular, there is scope for work that explores the role of governments in driving the adoption of HPWS (see Delaney and Godard 2001). There has been a small amount of work done internationally on the policy settings that appear most likely to facilitate mutual gains (Forsyth et al. 2006). Clearly there is much work to be done on the broad contextual factors and the kinds of policy settings that are likely to foster HPWS and mutual gains.

This brief discussion of potential future directions in research by no means exhausts the possibilities. Nonetheless it points to potentially fruitful avenues. Clearly the augmentation of existing research with work which more fully teases out causal paths and the role of contextual factors will allow us to develop a more complete picture of the workings of HPWS and the roles of direct and representative forms of voice.

REFERENCES

Addison, J. (2005), 'The determinants of firm performance: unions, works councils, and employee involvement/high performance work practices', *Scottish Journal of Political Economy*, **52** (3), 406–50.
Appelbaum, E. (2002), 'The impact of new forms of work organisation on workers', in G. Murray, J. Bélanger, A. Giles and P. Lapointe (eds), *Work and Employment Relations in the High Performance Workplace*, London: Continuum, pp. 120–49.

Appelbaum, E. and R. Batt (1994), *The New American Workplace: Transforming Work Systems in the United States*, Ithaca NY: ILR Press.
Appelbaum, E., T. Bailey, P. Berg and A. Kalleberg (2000), *Manufacturing Advantage: Why High Performance Work Systems Pay Off*, Ithaca NY: ILR Press.
Aryee, S., F. Walumbwa, E. Seidu and L. Otaye (2012), 'Impact of high-performance work systems on individual- and branch-level performance: test of a multilevel model of intermediate linkages', *Journal of Applied Psychology*, **97** (2), 287–300.
Bélanger, J. and P. Edwards (2007), 'The conditions promoting compromise in the workplace', *British Journal of Industrial Relations*, **45** (4), 713–34.
Berg, P. and A. Frost (2005), 'Dignity at work for low wage, low skill service workers', *Relations Industrielles/Industrial Relations*, **60** (4), 657–82.
Black, S. and L. Lynch (2001), 'How to compete: the impact of workplace practices and information technology on productivity', *Review of Economics and Statistics*, **83** (3), 434–45.
Budd, J., P. Gollan and A. Wilkinson (2010), 'New Approaches to Employee Voice and Participation in Organisations', *Human Relations*, **63** (3), 303–10.
Cooke, W. (1994), 'Product quality improvement through employee participation: the effects of unionisation and joint union–management administration', *Industrial and Labor Relations Review*, **46** (1), 119–34.
Combs, J., M. Liu, A. Hall and D. Ketchen (2006), 'How much do high-performance work practices matter? A meta-analysis of their effects on organisational performance', *Personnel Psychology*, **59**, 501–28.
Danford, A., M. Richardson, P. Stewart, S. Tailby and M. Upchurch (2004), 'High performance work systems and partnership: a case study of aerospace workers', *New Technology, Work and Employment*, **19** (1), 14–29.
Danford, A., M. Richardson, P. Stewart, S. Tailby and M. Upchurch (2008), 'Partnership, high performance work systems and quality of working life', *New Technology, Work and Employment*, **23** (3), 51–166.
Delaney, J. and J. Godard (2001), 'An industrial relations perspective on the high-performance paradigm', *Human Resource Management Review*, **11** (Winter), 395–429.
Delery, J. and D. Doty (1996), 'Modes of theorising in strategic human resource management: tests of universalistic, contingency and configurational performance predictions', *Academy of Management Journal*, **39** (4), 802–35.
Dundon, T., A. Wilkinson, M. Marchington and P. Ackers (2004), 'The Meanings and Purpose of Employee Voice', *International Journal of Human Resource Management*, **15** (6), pp. 1149–70.
Edwards, P., J. Bélanger and M. Wright (2006), 'The bases of compromise in the workplace: a theoretical framework', *British Journal of Industrial Relations*, **44** (1), 125–45.
Ehrnrooth, M. and I. Björkman (2012), 'An integrative HRM process theorisation: beyond signalling effects and mutual gains', *Journal of Management Studies*, **49** (6), 1109–35.
Forsyth, A., P Gahan, J. Howe and R. Mitchell (2006), 'Regulating for innovation in workplace production and employment systems: a preliminary discussion of issues and themes', paper presented to the third Australian Labour Law Association annual meeting, Brisbane, 22–23 September.
Gahan, P., B. Harley and G. Sewell (2010), 'How do "high performance work systems" deliver?: Towards an explanatory framework', paper presented to the 2010 Work Employment and Society Conference, Brighton.
Gittell, J., R. Seidner and J. Wimbush (2010), 'A relational model of how high performance work systems work', *Organization Science*, **21** (2), 490–506.
Godard, J. and J. Delaney (2000), 'Reflections on the "high performance" paradigm's implications for industrial relations as a field', *Industrial and Labor Relations Review*, **53** (3), 482–502.
Guest, D. (2011), 'Human resource management and performance: still searching for some answers', *Human Resource Management Journal*, **21** (1), 3–13.
Guest, D., J. Michie, N. Conway and M. Sheehan (2003), 'Human resource management and corporate performance in the UK', *British Journal of Industrial Relations*, **41** (2), 291–314.
Harley, B. (1999), 'The myth of empowerment: work organisation, hierarchy and employee autonomy in contemporary Australian workplaces', *Work, Employment and Society*, **13** (1), 41–66.
Harley, B. (2001), 'Team membership and the experience of work in Britain: an analysis of the WERS98 data', *Work, Employment and Society*, **15** (4), 721–42.
Harley, B. (2002), 'Employee responses to high performance work system practices: an analysis of the AWIRS95 data', *Journal of Industrial Relations*, **44**, 418–34.
Harley, B. (2005), 'Hope or hype? High performance work systems', in B. Harley, J. Hyman and P. Thompson (eds), *Participation and Democracy at Work*, Basingstoke: Palgrave, pp. 38–54.
Harley, B. (2012), 'New work practices, participation and organisational performance: prospects for high performance work systems in Australia', in M. Baird, K. Hancock and J. Isaac (eds), *Work and Employment Relations: An Era of Change*, Sydney: The Federation Press, pp. 93–108.
Harley, B., B. Allen and L. Sargent (2007), 'High performance work systems and employee experience of work in the service sector: the case of aged care', *British Journal of Industrial Relations*, **45** (3), 607–33.

Harley, B., L. Sargent and B. Allen (2010), 'Employee responses to "high performance work systems" practices: an empirical test of the "disciplined worker thesis"', *Work, Employment and Society*, **24** (4), 740–60.

Hirschman, A. (1970), *Exit, Voice and Loyalty: Responses to Decline in Firms, Organisations and States*, Cambridge MA: Harvard University Press.

Huselid, M.A. (1995), 'The impact of human resource management practices on turnover, productivity, and corporate financial performance', *Academy of Management Journal*, **38**, 635–72.

Ichniowski, C., K. Shaw and G. Prennushi (1997), 'The effects of human resource management practices on productivity: a study of steel finishing lines', *American Economic Review*, **87**, 291–313.

Kim, J., J. MacDuffie and F. Pil (2010), 'Employee voice and organisational performance', *Human Relations*, **63** (3), 371–94.

Lansbury, R. and G. Prideaux (1980), 'Democracy in the Work Place: Some Basic Issues', in D. Lansbury (ed.), *Democracy in the Work Place*, Melbourne: Longman Cheshire, pp. 1–13.

Legge, K. (1998), 'The morality of HRM', in C. Mabey, D. Skinner and T. Clark (eds), *Experiencing Human Resource Management*, London: Sage, pp. 14–30.

Legge, K. (2001), 'Silver bullet or spent round? Assessing the meaning of the "high commitment management"/ performance relationship', in J. Storey (ed.), *HRM – a Critical Text*, 2nd edn, London: Thompson Learning, pp. 21–36.

Levine, D. and L. Tyson (1990), 'Participation, productivity and the firm's environment', in A.S. Blinder (ed.), *Paying for Productivity*, Washington: Brookings Institution, pp. 183–244.

Liu, W., J. Guthrie, P. Flood and S. MacCurtain (2009), 'Unions and the adoption of high performance work systems: does employment security play a role?', *Industrial and Labor Relations Review*, **63** (1), 109–27.

Messersmith, J., P. Patel, D. Lepak and J. Gould-Williams (2011), 'Unlocking the black box: exploring the link between high-performance work systems and performance', *Journal of Applied Psychology*, **96** (6), 1105–18.

Pless, N., T. Maak and G. Stahl (2012), 'Promoting corporate social responsibility and sustainable development through management development: what can be learned from international service learning programs?', *Human Resource Management*, **51** (6), 873–903.

Ramirez, M., F. Guy and D. Beale (2007), 'Contested resources; unions, employers, and the adoption of new work practices in US and UK telecommunications', *British Journal of Industrial Relations*, **45** (3), 495–517.

Ramsay, H., D. Scholarios and B. Harley (2000), 'Employees and high performance work systems: testing inside the black box', *British Journal of Industrial Relations*, **38** (4), 501–31.

Takeuchi, R., D. Lepak, H. Wang and K. Takeuchi (2007), 'An empirical examination of the mechanisms mediating between high-performance work systems and the performance of Japanese organisations', *Journal of Applied Psychology*, **92** (4), 1069–83.

Van Buren, H., M. Greenwood and C. Sheehan (2011), 'Strategic human resource management and the decline of employee focus', *Human Resource Management Review*, **21** (3), 209–19.

Van de Voorde, K., J. Paauwe and M. van Veldhoven (2012), 'Employee well-being and the HRM–organisational performance relationship: a review of quantitative studies', *International Journal of Management Reviews*, **14**, 391–407.

Verma, A. (2005), 'What do unions do to the workplace? Union effects on management and HRM policies', *Journal of Labor Research*, **XXVI** (3), 415–49.

Wall T. and S. Wood (2005), 'The romance of human resource management and business performance, and the case for big science', *Human Relations*, **58** (4), 429–62.

Wood, S. and T. Wall (2007), 'Work enrichment and employee voice in human resource management – performance studies', *International Journal of Human Resource Management*, **18** (7), 1335–72.

7 Labour process perspectives on employee voice
Abigail Marks and Shiona Chillas

INTRODUCTION

Employee voice is used as an umbrella term to cover formal and informal avenues through which workers and their representatives are able to contribute to decision-making in organizations. The neutral tone of employee voice masks organizational processes such as participation, engagement, involvement and empowerment, which in some circumstances are used interchangeably and in others are given a specific meaning attached to a particular theoretical perspective on employee relations with associated management practices. Human resource management, for example, casts voice as an involvement mechanism that contributes to worker well-being, whilst simultaneously fulfilling management aspirations for continuous improvement in task-based participation and work organization (Marchington, 2007). Accordingly, perspectives on employee voice can be conceptually arranged along a spectrum ranging from voice as a mechanism for emancipation and engagement, typical of a best practice human resource management view (Gatenby et al., 2011), to voice as a manifestation of exploitation in what Martínez Lucio (2010: 123) characterizes as 'the age of *self-harm* as the socio-economic system turns further inwards onto the body to extract ever more intense levels of worker activity and effort'. The spectrum occurs as a result of the different underlying theoretical perspectives which are subsumed under a neutral term encompassing a range of activities and work organization in contemporary society (Wilkinson and Fay, 2011). Employee voice is a literal term, suggesting channels of communication, yet it is also metaphorical, covering control mechanisms and representing enactments of power relations in organizations.

Dundon et al. (2004) present the concept of voice as having multiple meanings ranging from the articulation of individual concerns to more collective forms of labour action and arrangements of mutuality between management and employees (see Chapter 1 above for details). We are not adhering to this definition of voice precisely; however, we do see voice as both an individual and collective phenomenon. Our purpose in this chapter is to explain employee voice through labour process theory (LPT). Admittedly, LPT adopts a critical perspective on the extent to which employer and employee interests can be in harmony and yet it is precisely this critical standpoint that offers a robust counter to the unquestioned managerialist view of voice that might otherwise prevail. Through the distinctive and critical contribution of analysis based on LPT, it may be possible to advance the ongoing projects of both LPT and employee voice. Indeed, there is clearly common ground in the subject matters of both, including managerial control regimes, work organization, worker responses, and individual and collective representation within contemporary capitalism, which suggests our analysis may be timely.

This chapter will trace the development of LPT and examine its engagement with issues of employee voice. The chapter will commence by examining the relationship between Marx and LPT and early understandings of voice, particularly focusing on the work of Harvie Ramsay. This is followed by an examination of the work of other key labour process theorists of the 1970s and their engagement with issues such as participation and involvement. We then move on to look at how human resource management and Japanization impacted on the relationship between labour process theorizing and employee voice. The chapter ends with an examination of recent trends in LPT, including its engagement with identity and critical realism explaining how these impact on understandings of participation and involvement.

BRAVERMAN AND MARX – LABOUR PROCESS FOUNDATIONS

Regardless of definition or conceptualization, employee voice embodies workplace relations and implicitly or explicitly examines the inherent tensions produced by the indeterminacy of labour, central to labour process debates. As management have increasingly sought to capture the 'hands, hearts and minds' of workers (Warhurst and Thompson, 1998), the articulation and actions of labour have assumed increasing importance both analytically and practically.

At the heart of the labour process debate is Braverman's (1974) critique of American work organization. In *Labor and Monopoly Capital*, Braverman observed occupational shifts in the USA. Broadly speaking, the labour process approach suggests that management is driven to control labour and the indeterminacy of labour is a product of employers purchasing the capacity to work rather than an individual worker, and it is this capacity to work that requires management. Management control and increased technocratization of work leave employees alienated from the products of their labour. Having sold their labour power to the employer, workers lose interest in the labour process and control becomes central to management systems.

Labor and Monopoly Capital, which developed Marx's work (particularly the influence of Capital Volume 1), had a clear focus on structural patterns of conflict in the workplace. However, as Thompson (1990) stresses, core LPT is not a Marxist theory, because it isolates the process of production from broader issues of social transformation, hence separating out workplace conflict from societal conflict (Jaros, 2010). Failing to make the link between the workplace and broader issues of the political economy is one of the key critiques of core LPT. As Rowlinson and Hassard (1994: 70) note, 'the connection with Marxian political economy is largely severed, and it becomes difficult to distinguish labour process theory from radical organisation theory'. Even on a rather superficial level it is clear that the two *must* be related. If we look at debates about the knowledge economy and the change in work, then the movement of more and more people to white collar jobs in Western economies (whether this involves 'better' work or not) leads to a change in the structure of the workplace and in turn leads to further changes in broader society – for example in perceptions of social class and composition of social strata (see Marks and Baldry, 2009).

Another example of potential faux separation between the politics of production and the broader society is persuasively articulated by Jaros (2010). He states that Thompson (1990) describes gender theory as a separate 'sphere of analysis'. Yet, as Jaros notes, patriarchal structures and associated discourses are often reproduced in terms of gender relationships within the workplace. Thompson's argument for the separation of core LPT from the broader political economy is that theories are developed to address particular phenomena and it is not appropriate to use a conceptual tool dedicated to the examination of capital–labour relations to look at other issues. If workplaces are part of broader social forces then they cannot be examined in isolation from them.

Indeed, LPT has now explicitly moved on from the articulated silo based approach of separating issues concerned with the workplace and the broader political economy. Thompson and Smith are keen to delineate the boundaries within which LPT operates and state that 'LPT is neither paradigmatic nor a complete sociology of work in terms of concepts and coverage' (Thompson and Smith, 2010a: 13). Thompson and Vincent (2010) move towards the articulation of LPT as an approach rather than a theory, which makes it less bounded by a specific focus on the micro politics of production. We will return to Thompson and Vincent's work later on in this chapter. Some could argue, however, that LPT never really isolated itself from broader social structures. Burawoy (1983) pointed out that workplace systems are fundamentally embedded within national contexts and that different countries adopt varying perspectives on the regulation of the labour process. Even Thompson (2003) argues that workplace regimes should be situated in corporate strategies and the economy as a whole.

When it comes to an understanding of employee voice, then, labour process influenced work has actually dealt with the wider economy and with broader social structures. The key example of this is the labour process community's recognition of and reverence toward Ramsay's (1977) 'cycles of control' theory of participation.

Early labour process writers were pretty cynical and dismissive of any notion of industrial democracy and industrial participation (Braverman, 1974). The perception being that engagement with participation by management is likely solely to pay lip service to the concept with the ultimate outcome being the extraction of even more surplus value from labour and an increase in managerial control. Indeed, Ramsay notes (1985: 54–5):

> The 'labour process' view of participation, or of any management policies which purport to improve or ameliorate the condition of the worker, derives from this conception of control. Thus these devices are deception, seeking to lure the worker further into collaborating in his/her exploitation ... [giving the worker] the illusion of making decisions by choosing among fixed and limited alternatives designed by a management which deliberately leaves insignificant matters open to choice.

Ramsay's (1985) criticism of core labour process theory is twofold. Firstly, as previously discussed, he argues there is an omission of engagement with the state. Secondly, he argues that if management control is so singular in its intent, then why over time has the process of work organization been adapted to account for participation?

'FIRST WAVE' LABOUR PROCESS THEORY – CYCLES OF CONTROL

Harvie Ramsay's work spanned almost a quarter of a century and its influence continues over a decade after his untimely death. Indeed, an edited collection in honour of Ramsay was published in 2005 with the vast majority of contributors and contributions coming from a labour process tradition (despite the focus of Ramsay's work extending beyond the experience of work at the point of production) (Harley et al., 1995). Ramsay published 'Cycles of control: worker participation in sociology and historical perspective' in 1977. His 'cycles' thesis held the central Marxist position that the relationship between workers and management is fundamentally antagonistic. He suggested that it was important to take a historical view of worker participation and that management's interest in participation initiatives in the UK had been cyclical from the start of the nineteenth century. Ramsay argued that each occurrence of managerial interest in participation was a response to the perception of challenge to managerial authority (as a result of conflict, labour mobilization, low levels of unemployment) and that when labour power declined (or it was necessary to cut costs) then the participation initiatives declined accordingly. In the struggle between capital and labour employers make conscious decisions to cede some control to workers as a response to circumstances where labour seeks to challenge managerial authority. Giving away some control stops the pursuit of full control but results in no real change in the extent to which employees exert real influence. Participation becomes a defensive mechanism on the part of management, introduced to dilute worker power in an instrumental way, rather than a genuine attempt to involve employees in decision-making. Whilst Ramsay (1977) did not suggest that the project of liberation through participation was futile, he was clear that as a response to the inherent conflict between capital and labour, which is a key feature of capitalism, true participation and industrial democracy would only occur – in a true Marxist sense – with the complete transformation of society, economy and the means of production.

One of the motives for Ramsay's initial work on participation was as a response to the somewhat naive optimism about new workplace participation initiatives in the 1970s. He viewed such optimism as reflecting a lack of understanding of the historical and cyclical nature of participation. As Harley et al. (2005: 3–4) note, it is important to understand that the context in which Ramsay's thesis developed was similar to those of the previous cycles that he had discussed and that the development of interest in participation occurred in a period of economic prosperity and full employment. There were also high levels of union membership and strong organized labour so managers were under pressure to seek cooperation and conciliation.

Though Ramsay's cycles predicted the declining interest in participation in the late 1970s and early 1980s – the result of a rise in unemployment, slower economic growth and a decline in union density – his 1977 variant of the cycles thesis did not predict the increase in management-led initiatives on involvement later on in the 1980s.[1] Indeed, the Thatcher government in the UK encouraged organization-led arrangements (frequently ignoring or marginalizing trade unions). These arrangements were a response to concepts such as human resource management and working practices associated with Japanese inward investors, including quality circles and teamworking (Martínez Lucio, 2010; Harley et al., 2005). There was also a substantial influence emanating from the new wave of professional managers influenced by the burgeoning fads of management gurus such as Peters and Waterman. These latter influences on all forms of employee involvement initiatives will be addressed in the next section of this chapter.

As indicated by Ramsay's cycles thesis (and indeed a wealth of earlier and subsequent research too vast to mention) the trade union movement is key to workers' ability to be heard. Yet Marx himself was ambivalent as to the value of trade unions. (Marx believed that the trade union movement legitimizes the power differences between capital and labour.) Indeed, some of Marx's followers were concerned that the trade union movement further assimilated the working class into the socio-economic system (Marcuse, 1964). Collective bargaining and forms of worker participation were seen as vehicles for shaping working-class demands and depoliticizing labour (Martínez Lucio, 2010).

Nonetheless, the broader labour process tradition has operated in parallel and sometimes in collaboration with industrial relations research for a number of years. Issues of central concern to labour process researchers, such as the changing politics of production, are clearly affected by or impact on the trade union movement. As Thompson and Vincent (2010) note, however, there are particular analytical challenges to making links between union behaviour and labour process theory. Thompson and Vincent (2010: 61–2) remind us that whilst the International Labour Process Conference embraces and accommodates papers on trade union organizing, there are limited attempts to 'integrate those studies with traditional concerns about labour agency'. These disconnects are described in terms of the practical separation between individual agency and union organization and also the analytical disconnects which existing theoretical resources can barely accommodate.

'SECOND WAVE' LABOUR PROCESS THEORY – CONTROL, COMPLIANCE, CONSENT

Whether or not practical and analytical linkages between labour process theory and industrial relations can be developed, what is apparent is that even early labour process work addressed the issue of voice and participation. The body of work referred to as 'second wave' analysis (Thompson and Newsome, 2004) is dominated by a triumvirate of writers – Michael Burawoy, Richard Edwards and Andy Friedman. Friedman's (1977) work centred on the fact that employees were not always subject to a process of direct control as typified by Taylorist forms of management. He believed that some workers were allowed a degree of 'responsible autonomy', which 'attempts to harness the adaptability of labour power by giving workers leeway and encouraging them to adapt to changing situations in a manner beneficial to the firm' (Friedman, 1977: 78). Bluntly, employees were given scope to have a voice but only under conditions that were appropriate for management and perhaps only a perception of having a voice rather than really being heard. Moreover, 'responsible autonomy' was often the privilege of skilled workers who were less easily replaced and whose commitment could be bought by offering them preferential terms and conditions and a perception of discretion. Friedman (1977) argues that these two forms of control have a substantial impact on labour power and that they segment and stratify the working class by creating a more privileged group of workers. Whilst there is a substantial variation in the discussion of forms of control Edwards (1979) continued with the theme of control strategies segmenting and subsequently dividing workforces. He argued that the establishment of bureaucratic control, typical of many large-scale organizations, effectively subdivided workforces. Workplaces reinforced these divisions with specialized training, an increase in supervisory jobs, multiple pay grades and diverse work locations. This not only gave those people further up the hierarchy a perception of greater voice, it also facilitated the destruction of mass unionism, as workers within single industrial sectors no longer shared similar goals.

The final member of the triumvirate – Michael Burawoy – argued that the basis of labour process theory, which was founded on conflict between capital and labour, was unable to explain why for the majority of the time there was consent between management and employees. Burawoy, in his book *Manufacturing Consent* (1979), suggested that the interaction between adaptive strategies of workers on the shop floor and the political systems of management generates 'games' that help to make work bearable at the same time as engendering consent to exploitation. Employees believe they have choices but as Burawoy (1979: 27) states, 'it is participation in choosing that generates consent'.

We have only touched upon three key players in 'second wave' research so our discussion is incomplete but from this short review it can be understood that this work had a distinctive focus in terms of the consideration of control, conflict and consent within the workplace. One of the critiques of this period of theorizing is the focus on conflict as a response to managerial control and the perception that resistance can only occur at a collective level (Thompson and Newsome, 2004). Thompson and Newsome (2004) cite Ackroyd and Thompson (1999: 50):

> The differences between events such as absences and strikes is cast in terms of the degree of formal organisation that is needed to develop them and make them effective instruments of class action. Informal practices such as fiddling or sabotage, lacking any formal organisation, are taken to be ineffective surrogates for striking and other acts which have formal organisation as their basis.

This quote suggests that individual acts of resistance or 'voice' can also have power in terms of creating imbalance at the point of production and we will return to this point later in the chapter.

Another criticism of the 'second wave' research is that the context for analysis was often assumed to be the USA (Thompson and Newsome, 2004). This was addressed by 'third wave' research. Whilst much of the work in this next wave originated from Europe, particularly the UK, there was a 'forced engagement' with international forms of work organization with the much talked about (although not as widely implemented as academics and management gurus would have us believe) impact of Japanese work practices in Western economies (Oliver and Wilkinson, 1989).

'THIRD WAVE' LABOUR PROCESS THEORY – HUMAN RESOURCE MANAGEMENT, LEAN PRODUCTION AND PARTNERSHIP

As a result of the crisis with the domestic currency and a prevailing anxiety about European countries using protectionist policies towards Japanese business, there was a blast of Japanese businesses investing in Europe from the middle to the end of the 1980s (Elger and Smith, 1994). The majority of these Japanese transplants came from the motor industry (although there was a later surge in investment from the electronics industry) and in the UK firms were attracted by the Conservative government's low-wage policy.

Similar politically driven incentives were seen in other parts of Europe. With these Japanese organizations came new forms of organizing production and labour.

Whilst Friedman (1977) argued that organizations have always involved a degree of participation for the purpose of legitimation of management strategy, Japanization took this process to a whole new level. Japanese management practices were typified by lifetime employment (securing commitment to the company), job rotation, promotion-based seniority and, at least superficially, practices that promoted participation, involvement and voice – group consensus, just in time, quality circles, teamworking and *kaizen*. Labour process theorists took centre stage in the critique of these practices. As Pulignano (2001: 2) notes, 'Labour process theorists have been in the forefront of analysing the rapid changes in technology, management strategies, and production techniques that have occurred under the term "Japanisation" or lean production.'

As we have indicated, whilst Japanese working practices in their complete package were limited to the Japanese transplants and a few 'forward thinking' domestic companies, elements of lean production percolated into many organizations, particularly in terms of teamworking and a redefinition of industrial relations in terms of partnership and mutual gains. Teamwork was seen as the perfect vehicle for providing employees with the opportunity to have a voice (see Proctor and Benders, Chapter 18 below).

Labour process and associated writers have focused on the outcomes of teamwork for employees and are broadly sceptical of the extent to which the introduction of teamworking has really altered the employment experience for most workers (and indeed provided them with the opportunity for true participation). This has been described as 'the *dark side* of new production systems' (Thompson and Smith, 1998: 210; emphasis added). Although the fundamental premise of teamwork is the reintegration of managerial responsibilities (including enhanced participation and involvement for employees) to the broader workforce, much writing from the labour process perspective perceives teamwork as an alternative management strategy to undermine and broaden control over employees' effort and output. Teamwork can disempower employees by enhancing managerial control and intensifying work activity (for example, Parker and Slaughter, 1988; Garrahan and Stewart, 1992). Critical analysis of teamwork during this period also articulates fears regarding the coercive nature of teams and how these new forms of control assist management in extracting labour from employees using work intensification (Barley and Kunda, 1992). Writers from a labour process perspective have relied heavily on evidence from lean production settings, arguing that the use of off-line quality circles, multi-skilling and JIT production techniques involve little redistribution of responsibility to employees. They claim that as well as intensifying work, lean production settings are also an attempt to mine employees' tacit knowledge for the purpose of continuous improvement (Doellgast and Batt, 2005). Indeed, Adler's (1995) study and Parker and Slaughter's (1988) examination of the NUMMI plant depict teamwork as a form of 'democratic Taylorism' and 'super-Taylorism', respectively. Building upon this, Sewell (1998) suggested that he had identified a new model of labour process control that moves beyond the superficial veneer of teamwork as a form of empowerment to teamwork as 'chimerical control'. In effect, Sewell develops Edward's discussion of technical control to the workplace, and particularly teamwork, leading to the 'constant and supportive interaction of electronic surveillance and the peer group scrutiny of teams' (Sewell, 1998: 422).

This form of control, presenting a gloss of participation, goes beyond teamwork and Japanization to the introduction of human resource management (HRM). Hasegawa (2001: 160) argues that:

> Japanization was in fact an additional and effective route for the diffusion of HRM in Britain, while, at the same time, Japanization owed its success to the timely spread of HRM in Britain. This implies that Japanese management involved elements necessary for the practice of HRM. These can be classified as the employment system (life-time, seniority promotion), techniques/ methods for production management and industrial relations. If the ultimate goal of HRM is the organic integration of employees into corporate objectives, then that of the Japanese management system was similar in principle, and it was the consequence of managerial efforts and strategies taken in the high growth period.

One of the main thrusts of human resource management has been the individualization of the employment relationship both for manual and managerial employees, through, for example, individual contracts, performance related pay and individual and small group bonus payments.

Whilst it is not the purpose of this chapter to review human resource management practices,[2] it is important to summarize the relationship of HRM to voice in order to establish the parameters for critique. If we take the Harvard Business School model of HRM which was developed in the early 1980s (Beer et al., 1984), voice was central to the espoused strategic aims, with the inclusion of voluntary delegation of responsibility, authority and power to both workers and their representative bodies. In Guest's (1987) model of HRM, voice and participation practices via communication and grievance systems were argued to be central to success. Similarly, from the popular management literature Peters and Waterman (1982) identify two of their eight characteristics of excellent organizations as being concerned with employee involvement – 'autonomy and entrepreneurship' and 'productivity through people'. As Wood and Wall (2007: 339) (based on points made by Guest, 1987) correctly note, however, to 'many proponents of HRM, especially those in the USA, "the unions are seen as unnecessary and irrelevant"'. Nonetheless, Guest leaves open the possibility that such high commitment approaches to HRM should still work in settings such as the UK where trade unions are more strongly institutionalized, providing there is mutual adjustment between employers and unions.'

In the context of declining trade union membership and the consolidation of HRM practices, worker representation and, by implication, voice have become central components of assessing employment relationships (Marchington, 2007). The move from indirect to direct voice mechanisms associated with HRM is – from a labour process perspective – a manifestation of individualizing the employment relationship, driven by attempts to marginalize the influence of trade unions, or to replace union representation with 'committee-type structures in which communication and exchange of thoughts is fostered' (Kaufman and Taras, 2010: 259). As the rhetoric of HRM moves employee relations from joint decision-making through negotiation between unions and management to individualized information-sharing, the real influence that employees have beyond the confines of their own tasks becomes further constrained (Blyton and Turnbull, 2004) and control remains in the hands of management.

Yet, HRM and practices such as direct voice mechanisms do present a challenge to trade unionism, ideologically and practically. If unions are marginalized or excluded and can no longer fulfil their role of representing workers' interests in an oppositional manner, then they are forced to adapt or die. Partnership agreements between unions and management have been presented as a 'third way' to operate the employment relationship, but one where the role of unions fundamentally shifts from adversarial to cooperative. Partnership invites unions to actively participate in firms' productivity, quality and flexibility initiatives within a rhetoric of mutual benefits (Guest and Peccei, 2001). Management can continue to assert prerogative and achieve control by consent, while for unions partnership is an opportunity for renewal, whether this is by attracting new types of members in different sectors of industry or by provision of wider services (Blyton and Turnbull, 2004). Partnership, however, assumes a managerially-led system and not a redistribution of power based on divergent interests. While it may give opportunities for union renewal, unions are given a facilitating role, which raises the question of whose interests are best served by these arrangements. It is management who are likely to draw up the terms of the partnership agreement, and with no legal protection for agreements management is just as likely to default when it suits. The emphasis on participating *with* management instead of *against* it creates an ideological debate and dilemma within trade unions. Having a seat at the table is better than none because without that seat employers are left unchallenged, yet the penalties are that unions lose credibility in the eyes of those that they represent and fail to deliver improved working conditions (Gall, 2010). Nevertheless, workplaces where trade unions are present in whatever capacity are consistently found to have better wage rates, better health and safety records and more opportunities for training. Ackers and Payne (1998: 530) suggest that 'partnership combines seductive rhetoric with ambiguous and shifting meaning' and cast doubt on the extent to which partnership is a long-term model for the employment relationship that is grounded in antagonism between employers and employees. Danford et al. (2009: 344) looked at voice in three knowledge-intensive sites and found a 'clear gap between what direct influence workers in the three case workplaces desired and what they actually experienced'. Despite intentions to offer voice to employees, from Danford et al.'s work it was evident that the reality was of low-trust relations, diminished consultation, and disillusionment with unions who were perceived to be excessively collaborative with management rather than representative of worker interests.

Of course, union management interactions are not always predicated on adversarial relations and similar goals. Thompson and Newsome (2004) confidently assert that LPT should not have any problem with the idea of mutual gains in particular circumstances and they also note that the extent of shared interests is shaped by a variety of endogenous and exogenous conditions. Work reform, including opportunities for voice, may simultaneously increase employee discretion and increase stress by shifting responsibility to employees. It may also involve raising targets, leading to work intensification (Thompson and Harley, 2007).

An interrelated by-product of academic analysis of human resource management, high performance work systems and partnership agreements was the rising influence of postmodernism on the labour process debate. Key writers (for example, Knights and Willmott, 1989) focused on the cultural redefinition of work, and the focus on high commitment workplaces developed more mainstream arguments to suggest that employees '"buy in" to the system . . . in processes of seduction (by corporate values, surveillance and self-discipline' (Thompson and Newsome, 2004: 145). This argument is detailed elsewhere (for example, Marks and Thompson, 2010), however, for the purpose of this chapter, one of the key effects of the 'cultural turn' is that an alarming number of writers have taken on board this position and as a result, control is replace by surveillance and the central concept of (colonized) identities means that resistance to managerially imposed cultures has been marginalized (Thompson and Newsome, 2004).

This postmodern position emerges from the belief that consideration of worker subjectivity is missing in Braverman's (1974) analysis (now replaced almost entirely by a belief in the omission of identity). Tinker (2002) argues that this is an ahistorical reading of Braverman and that worker subjectivity is deliberately 'de-emphasized' because the focus on de-skilling and the characteristics of production were essential to counteract the dominant belief that work was being enriched and up-skilled. However, this belief in the corporatization of self, hand in hand with the weakening of trade unions, has, as we stated above, led many writers to argue the death of resistance (Knights and Wilmott, 1989). Ironically, post-structuralist analysis is based on the perspective that power gives rise to resistance, yet worker resistance (and any possibility of voice) has been marginalized in post-structuralist writing despite it being one of the central problems identified by writers such as Knights and Wilmott in their early critique of Braverman (Thompson and Ackroyd, 1995). In this respect, we concur with van den Broek and Dundon (2012: 99) who argue that '[u]ltimately, employee responses outlined in this [post-structuralist] research (largely based around employee cynicism) were analyzed within a structural and regulatory vacuum'.

FINDING THE MISSING SUBJECT: NEW WAVES IN LABOUR PROCESS RESEARCH, IDENTITY, RESISTANCE AND VOICE

The role of identity and particularly the role of identity within labour process analysis is key to any future work on employee voice, and represents conceptual and methodological struggles and new directions within labour process analysis. In part these new directions emerge from an acknowledgement that during the 1990s, too much attention was given to 'a variant of paradigm wars' in the labour process debate (Thompson and Smith, 2010b: 3). Yet a key strength of LPT lies in its ability to develop by recognizing new contexts and conditions in the sociology of work. In particular, the decline of union density has stimulated interest in new forms of collectivism and expressions of resistance, paralleled by a focus on alternative sources of collectivity and voice in the non-union workplace (Dundon and Gollan, 2007).

As we have already discussed, the main critiques of labour process analysis centre on the limited engagement with the political economy and weak conceptualization of the subject. It is crucial for the understanding of employee voice (as detailed earlier in the discussion of Harvie Ramsay's work) to engage with the broader political economy. Whilst there were limitations to Ramsay's cycles thesis, it clearly depicted the relationship between broader structural changes and employees' ability to participate in workplace decision-making. Dundon and Gollan (2007) note that macro environmental factors, such as product and labour markets, and the regulatory framework impact on micro organizational dimensions such as occupational identity as a source of group solidarity, strategies towards trade unions, and trust between management and workers in non-union workplaces. For example, where employers dominate in product markets,

Fitting LPT and CR together

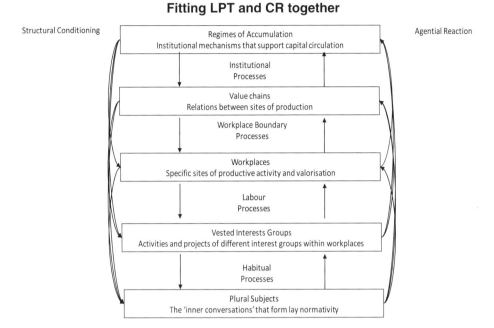

Source: Thompson and Vincent (2010: 63).

Figure 7.1 Fitting LPT and CR together

direct forms of voice may be encouraged to maintain product quality, however voice will be constrained in competitive and unstable markets for goods (Marchington, 2007).

Thompson and Vincent's (2010) work on the interrelationship between critical realism and labour process theory demonstrates the importance of locating labour process analysis within a holistic picture (see Figure 7.1). As they state, this has 'the goal of beginning to articulate a more systematic conception of the multiple embeddedness of labour process analysis' and 'theoretically locate the various strata of phenomena that significantly affect labour process' (Thompson and Vincent, 2010: 63).

This approach both (re)situates labour process analysis within the broader political economy and acknowledges the relationship between labour process theory and identity. Traditionally, positions such as Thompson and Smith's (1998: 562) view that the 'indeterminacy of labour had been replaced by indeterminacy of identity' have tended to sideline labour process interest in identity. Fortunately, that has now changed and there are signs of the development of perspectives on identity which can bring something different to the debate and which are compatible with traditions of labour process analysis (Marks and Thompson, 2010). Similarly, occupational identity is highlighted as 'a potentially potent force in the interplay of factors shaping the pattern and character of non-union forms of employee voice' (Dundon and Gollan, 2007: 1187). A body of work that Jaros (2010) labels 'contextualist' has combined insights from labour process analysis and social identity theory to produce accounts of the varied outcomes of identity construction amongst technical and knowledge workers (Marks and Scholarios, 2007; Marks et al., 2007). As Thompson and Vincent (2010) show, via the labour process, there is a clear interrelationship with employee identity. The reality is that the relationship between identity and collectivism is an issue that is close to the heart of both Marx and core labour process theorists, it just articulated in a different manner. The classic sociological studies of work and workers, such as Nichols and Beynon (1977), were written without explicit reference to identity. What was then referred to as (class) consciousness is now often replaced by identity. One reason that class is a notoriously difficult concept is that it can, and has, been used as a fundamental concept for analysing social structure but is also recognized as an important part of that bundle of loyalties, shared experiences and common values which comprises an individual's social identity (Marks and Thompson, 2010).

As Marks and Baldry (2009) argue, people rarely judge themselves relative to other groups in society by their economic relationships alone; often more explicit and more immediate are all those fine gradations offered by comparisons of occupation, income, consumption and lifestyle and other dimensions of perceived status. Class identity can consist of a complex bundle of symbolic and material resources reflecting personal histories, shared experiences and perceived social status. Such meanings are sometimes revealed when there are tensions between the two. For example, a study of IT employees (Marks and Baldry, 2009) found that whilst many recognized their 'middle-class' occupational position, they 'felt working class'. In choosing a form of identification such employees were, in effect, making a statement about their own personal valuation and sense of esteem as associated with particular political and cultural positions and a collective articulation of their values. From a labour process perspective, McBride and Martínez Lucio (2011: 794–5) present a similar argument that 'collectivism is a flexible and rich concept, which continues to be valid for the study of work and workers in a context of change regardless of the extensive literature on the decline of collectivism'. Work on the sociology of professions and occupations mirrors the theorizing of class identity, with a focus on both the material and symbolic underpinnings of collective identities. With falling trade union density, the professional unit or body becomes an ever more central forum for collective action, employee voice and representation (Baldry et al., 2007). In this manner, the occupational group is seen to be a medium for symbolic power and citizenship, as well as more formal interest based activities (Derkzen and Bock, 2007). As with class, contemporary research illustrates the balancing act between identity and interests. In comparing two groups of software workers, Marks and Scholarios (2007) noted that employees who were more qualified and undertaking complex work 'invested' in a strong professional identity and saw little value in organizational identity. In contrast, the less qualified, lower skilled group had fewer external opportunities and developed a stronger identification with the organization.

Professional/occupational esteem does not in itself require identity work, as membership of some groups, for example, the legal profession, automatically confers it. However, if an individual does not hold the values of the profession or fails to make an investment in their professional identity they are likely to be gaining self-esteem from other identities. This is more likely for employees who do not belong to a high status occupational group. Ashforth and Kreiner (1999) examined a group of 'dirty workers', including sewage workers and cleaners. For them, the availability of externally-derived occupational prestige (Treiman, 1977) – status, power, quality of work, education and income – is a limited resource. Yet, they invest in a different kind of identity work that challenges the stigma of their employment and develops pride in their activities, supported by a strong occupational culture.

Similarly, Fleming (2005), in an examination of an Australian call centre, found that an oppositional identity developed within an all pervasive organizational culture which allowed employees to make fun of the organization. Fleming argues that such cynicism is an effective form of resistance. From more traditional labour process research within a call centre, Taylor and Bain (1998) found collective resistance evocative of responses to traditional industrialized work. This leads to the reasonable conclusion that collective identity exists and that collective identity is a necessary precursor for employee voice and increases the likelihood of being heard. As Krefting and Powers (1998: 271) note, any decrease in collectivism 'gives individuals maximum inducement to avoid blame of any sort since it diminishes the odds of both professional and personal survival'. From labour process work there are a number of more subtle expressions of employee voice, particularly from work on organizational misbehaviour. These expressions of voice are likely to provide more positive value and present a decreased risk to employees (Jermier, 1998) but could not be present without some form of collective identity.

Within a traditional labour process framework of structured antagonism between capital and labour, control is viewed as the dominant aspiration for management but it can never be complete, leaving capacity for expressions of resistance and misbehaviour. The most often cited example of work within this tradition in terms of misbehaviour is Donald Roy's (1959) 'Banana Time'. While Collinson and Ackroyd (2005: 320) observe that 'the field of employee resistance remains far from coherent' and that it encompasses different views on the motives and actual behaviours associated with opposition in the workplace, including collective and individual expressions of discontent, Ackroyd and Thompson (1999) define misbehaviour as anything you do at work that you are not supposed to do. This broad definition was conceived in part to challenge post-structuralist assumptions that workers are 'blank slates' on which management writes its own messages, which are in turn passively received and therefore remove worker agency from the employment relationship (Ackroyd and Thompson, 1999). The critique is developed by identifying the terrains of time, effort, product and identity as sources of resistance and misbehaviour, which draws attention to the persistence of worker resistance, albeit in altered forms outside the traditional formal expression of resistance through trade union action. The key point from this work is that the absence of organized strike action does not equate to industrial harmony and compliance with managerial regimes, nor has the introduction of new surveillance technology and new working practices completely removed the space for worker resistance and misbehaviour (Callaghan and Thompson, 2002).

Van den Broek and Dundon (2012) demonstrate that far from passive acceptance of managerial prerogative, workers find new and innovative ways to express resistance to managerial de-collectivizing strategies. They found that illicit union involvement can itself be a form of resistance in the face of active anti-unionism across different workplace contexts; that call-centre workers made collective representations to register opposition to new work regimes; and that drivers in a water company turned up late for work when management withdrew the use of company vehicles outside working hours. Individual expressions of resistance were also apparent in that skilled technicians reported circumventing company procedures (2012: 108–11) and car mechanics lied about the availability of spare parts. Such empirical work shows that resistance is apparent in different contexts, shaped within the labour process that operates 'within the wider political economy of western de-industrialisation and de-collectivisation' (van den Broek and Dundon, 2012: 114).

Thus expressions of what labour process theorists would term resistance and misbehaviour, via both formal and informal channels, are reflected in literatures on voice, particularly in terms of direct voice. So-called 'silent' forms of voice such as sabotage, absence from work, or shirking (Marchington, 2007) are indeed the same (mis)behaviours associated with labour process analyses of resistance and misbehaviour. In a recent extension to the literature on voice, Donaghey et al. (2011) review the literature on employee silence, recognizing that it lacks depth, is largely unitarist and focuses on individualized choice around expressing or withholding voice. They call for 'an appreciation of how institutions might serve to inhibit voice and enforce silence' (Donaghey et al., 2011: 57), suggesting a framework for studying silence as a relational dynamic resting on the frontier of control which is contingent on variable managerial intent as well as worker resistance and consent (see Chapter 1 by Wilkinson et al. above). In recognizing the frontier of control as a contested terrain, they observe that silence can be a form of resistance to managerially imposed regimes which reduce voice to 'non-threatening issues or issues enhancing productivity or performance' (Donaghey et al., 2011: 61). In these circumstances, management structure the scope and depth of voice with the result that employees may choose to withhold information or actively disengage as a form of resistance. Work on identity and resistance highlights the 'continuum of possible, situationally driven, and overlapping worker responses to relations of ownership and control in the workplace' (Thompson and Harley, 2007: 150).

CONCLUSIONS

This chapter has revealed that manifestations of employee voice in its various guises have been a key element of labour process analysis, which emphasizes actors, interests and contexts at macro and micro levels of analysis. At the macro level labour process analyses operate in drawing political and institutional boundaries between capital and labour and at a micro level in fine-grained accounts of work and workplaces. LPT recognizes that within the constraints of capitalist production, there is room for struggle and negotiation over the organization of work and its outcomes (Thompson and Harley, 2007: 157). Indeed, throughout its development, labour process analysis has sought to challenge a naive optimism which expects new forms of work always or mainly to have positive outcomes, thereby offering a critical view of those who present different forms of voice in terms of a win-win scenario. We would suggest that for effective engagement with employee voice from a labour process perspective, there needs to be a clearer conceptualization of the motivations for, and outcomes of, various voice initiatives and how these fit into the critical framework that labour process analysis provides.

Attention to the broader issues surrounding employee voice has varied throughout different stages of maturity of labour process research, starting with a belief that within a capitalist society there can be no true form of participation and voice, through critique of HRM and the individualization of the employment relationship effectively reducing traditional collective forms of employee representation via trade unions. However, recent work within the labour process tradition offers conceptual and methodological contributions to research on voice. Work on identity, resistance and new forms of collectivism accepts the nuances of different workplaces and the interrelationship between the roles of individual actors and broader structures in the articulation of employees' workplace struggles; critical realism offers a way in which such interrelationships can be understood.

NOTES

1. Ackers at al. (1992) provided a critique of Ramsay's cycles and the initial presentation of an alternative 'waves' thesis. Whilst potentially a useful contribution to debate on voice initiatives, the two perspectives are very different: 'cycles' provides a macro-orientated explanation of participation and 'waves' is concerned with micro-level arrangements at workplace level. We engage with levels of analysis within LPT elsewhere in this chapter.
2. For a thorough labour process critique of HRM, see Thompson and Harley (2007) and Thompson (2011).

REFERENCES

Ackers, P. and J. Payne (1998), 'British trade unions and social partnership: rhetoric, reality and strategy', *International Journal of Human Resource Management*, **9** (3), 529–50.

Ackers, P., M. Marchington, A. Wilkinson and J. Goodman (1992), 'The use of cycles? Explaining employee involvement in the 1990s', *Industrial Relations Journal*, **23** (4), 268–83.

Ackroyd, S. and P. Thompson (1999), *Organizational Misbehaviour*, London: Sage.

Adler, P. (1995), 'Democratic Taylorism: the Toyota production system at NUMMI', in S. Babson (ed.), *Lean Work: Empowerment and Exploitation in the Global Auto Industry*, Detroit: Wayne State University Press, pp. 207–19.

Ashforth, B. and G. Kreiner (1999), 'How can you do it? Dirty work and the challenge of constructing a positive identity', *Academy of Management Review*, **24** (3), 413–34.

Baldry, C., P. Bain, P. Taylor, J. Human, D. Scholarios, A. Marks, A. Watson, K. Gilbert, G. Gall and D. Bunzel (2007), *The Meaning of Work in the New Economy*, Basingstoke: Palgrave, pp. 163–83.

Barley, S. and G. Kunda (1992), 'Design and devotion: surges of rational and normative ideologies of control in managerial discourse', *Administrative Science Quarterly*, **37**, 363–99.

Beer, M., B. Spector, P. Lawrence, D. Quinn Mills and R. Walton (1984), *Managing Human Assets*, New York: Free Press.

Blyton, P. and P. Turnbull (2004), *The Dynamics of Employee Relations*, 3rd edn, Basingstoke: Palgrave.

Braverman, H. (1974), *Labor and Monopoly Capital: The Degradation of Work in the Twentieth Century'*, New York: Monthly Review Press.

Burawoy, M. (1979), *Manufacturing Consent: Changes in the Labor Process Under Monopoly Capitalism*, Chicago: University of Chicago Press.

Burawoy, M. (1983), *The Politics of Production*, London: Verso.

Callaghan, G. and P. Thompson (2002), 'We recruit attitude: the selection and shaping of call centre labour', *Journal of Management Studies*, **39** (2), 233–54.

Collinson, D. and S. Ackroyd (2005), 'Resistance, misbehaviour, dissent', in S. Ackroyd, S. Batt, R. Thompson and P. Tolbert (eds) A *Handbook of Work and Organization*, Oxford: Oxford University Press, pp. 305–26.

Danford, A., S. Durbin, M. Richardson, S. Tailby and P. Stewart (2009), '"Everybody's talking at me": the dynamics of information disclosure and consultation in high-skill workplaces in the UK', *Human Resource Management Journal*, **19** (4), 337–54.

Derkzen, P. and B. Bock (2007), 'The construction of professional identity: symbolic power in rural partnerships in The Netherlands', *Sociolgia Ruralis*, **47** (3), 189–204.

Doellgast, V. and R. Batt (2005), 'Groups, teams and the division of labour: interdisciplinary perspectives on the organization of work', in S. Ackroyd, R. Batt, P. Thompson and P. Tolbert (eds), *Oxford Handbook of Work and Organization*, Oxford: Oxford University Press, pp. 138–56.

Donaghey, J., N. Cullinane, T. Dundon and A. Wilkinson (2011), 'Reconceptualising employee silence: problems and prognosis', *Work, Employment and Society*, **25** (1), 51–67.

Dundon, T. and P.J. Gollan (2007), 'Re-conceptualizing voice in the non-union workplace', *International Journal of Human Resource Management*, **18** (7), 1182–98.

Dundon, T., A. Wilkinson, M. Marchington and P. Ackers (2004), 'The meanings and purpose of employee voice', *International Journal of Human Resource Management*, **15** (6), 1149–70.

Edwards, R. (1979), *Contested Terrain: The Transformation of the Workplace in the Twentieth Century*, London: Heinemann.

Elger, T. and C. Smith (eds) (1994), *Global Japanization? The Transnational Transformation of the Labour Process*, London: Routledge.

Fleming, P. (2005), 'Workers' playtime: boundaries and cynicism in a "culture of fun" program', *Journal of Applied Behavioral Science*, **41** (3), 285–303.

Friedman, A. (1977), *Industry and Labour: Class Struggle at Work and Monopoly Capitalism*, London: Macmillan.

Gall, G. (2010), 'Labour union responses to participation in employing organizations', in A. Wilkinson, P. Gollan, M. Marchington and D. Lewin (eds), *The Oxford Handbook of Participation in Organizations*, Oxford: Oxford University Press, pp. 361–82.

Garrahan, P. and P. Stewart (1992), *The Nissan Enigma: Flexibility at Work in a Local Economy*, London: Mansett.

Gatenby, M., C. Rees, E. Soane and C. Truss (2011), *Employee Engagement in Context*, Interim Report to the CIPD, London: CIPD.

Guest, D. (1987), 'Human resource management and industrial relations', *Journal of Management Studies*, **24** (5), 503–21.

Guest, D. and R. Peccei (2001), 'Partnership at work: mutuality and the balance of advantage', *British Journal of Industrial Relations*, **42** (2), 349–78.

Harley, B., J. Hyman and P. Thompson (2005), 'The paradoxes of participation', in B. Harley, J. Hyman and P. Thompson (eds), *Participation and Democracy at Work: Essays in Honour of Harvie Ramsay*, Basingstoke: Palgrave, pp. 1–19.

Hasegawa, H. (2001), 'Globalization and Japanization: implications for human resource management in Britain', *Japan Forum*, **13**(2), 159–75.

Jaros, S. (2006), 'Skill dynamics, global capitalism, and labour process theories of work', *Tamara*, **5** (1), 5–16.

Jaros, S. (2010), 'The core theory: critiques, defences and advances', in P. Thompson and C. Smith (eds), *Working Life*, Basingstoke: Palgrave, pp. 70–88.

Jermier, J. (1998), 'Critical perspectives on organizational control', *Administrative Science Quarterly*, **43** (2), 235–56.

Kaufman, B. and D. Taras (2010), 'Employee participation through non-union forms of employee representation', in A. Wilkinson, P. Gollan, M. Marchington and D. Lewin (eds), *The Oxford Handbook of Participation in Organizations*, Oxford: Oxford University Press, pp. 258–85.

Knights, D. and H. Willmott (1989), 'Power and subjectivity at work: from degradation to subjugation in social relations', *Sociology*, **23** (4), 535–58.

Krefting, L. and K. Powers (1998), 'Exercised voice as management failure: implications of willing compliance theories of management and individualism for *de facto* employee voice', *Employee Responsibilities and Rights Journal*, **11** (4), 263–77.

Marchington, M. (2007), 'Employee voice systems', in P. Boxall, J. Purcell and P. Wright (eds), *The Oxford Handbook of Human Resource Management*, Oxford: Oxford University Press, pp. 231–50.

Marcuse, H. (1964), 'One dimensional man: studies in the ideology of advanced industrial society', *Boston*, **19**, 48–55.

Marks, A. and C. Baldry (2009), 'Stuck in the middle with who? The class identity of knowledge workers', *Work, Employment and Society*, **23** (1), 49–65.

Marks, A. and D. Scholarios (2007), 'Revisiting technical workers: professional and organizational identities in software industry', *New Technology, Work and Employment*, **22** (2), 98–117.

Marks, A. and P. Thompson (2010), 'Beyond the blank slate: identities and interests at work', in P. Thompson and C. Smith (eds), *Working Life*, Basingstoke: Palgrave, pp. 316–38.

Marks, A., D. Scholarios, C. Baldry and J. Hyman (2007), 'The identity construction of knowledge workers: a study of the call centre and software industries', Paper presented at WES conference, Aberdeen, 11–13 September.

Martínez Lucio, M. (2010), 'Labour process and Marxist perspectives on employee participation', in

A. Wilkinson, P. Gollan, M. Marchington and D. Lewin (eds), *The Oxford Handbook of Participation in Organizations*, Oxford: Oxford University Press, pp. 105–30.

Nichols, T. and H. Beynon (1977), *Living with Capitalism*, London: Routledge.

Oliver, N. and B. Wilkinson (1989), 'Japanese manufacturing techniques and personnel and industrial relations practice in Britain', *British Journal of Industrial Relations*, **27** (1), 73–91.

Parker, M. and J. Slaughter (1988), *Choosing Sides: Unions and the Team Concept*, Labor Notes, Boston: South End Press.

Peters, T. and R. Waterman (1982), *In Search of Excellence: Lessons from America's Best Run Companies*, New York: Harper and Row.

Pulignano, V. (2001), 'Understanding British trends in the sociolo.gy of work: some reflections from an Italian Perspective', paper prepared for the International Workshop, Between Sociology of Work and Organisation Studies: The State of the Debate in Italy and in the United Kingdom (Bologna).

Ramsay, H. (1977), 'Cycles of control: worker participation in sociological and historical perspective', *Sociology*, **11** (3), 481–506.

Ramsay, H. (1985), 'What is participation for? A critical evaluation of "labour process" analysis of job reform', in D. Knights, H. Willmott and D. Collinson (eds), *Job Redesign: Critical Perspectives on the Labour Process*, Aldershot: Gower, pp. 107–41.

Rowlinson, M. and J. Hassard (1994), 'Economics, politics, and labour process theory', *Capital & Class*, **18** (2), 65–97.

Roy, D. (1959), '"Banana Time": job satisfaction and informal interaction', *Human Organization*, **18** (4), 158–68.

Sewell, G. (1998), 'The discipline of teams: the control of team-based industrial work through electronic and peer surveillance', *Administrative Science Quarterly*, **43**, 406–69.

Taylor, P. and P. Bain (1998), 'An assembly line in the head: the call centre labour process', *Industrial Relations Journal*, **30** (2), 101–17.

Thompson, P. (1990), 'Crawling from the wreckage: the labour process and the politics of production', in D. Knights and H. Willmott (eds), *Labour Process Theory*, London: Macmillan, pp. 95–124.

Thompson, P. (2003), 'Disconnected capitalism: or why employers can't keep their side of the bargain', *Work, Employment and Society*, **17** (2), 359–78.

Thompson, P. (2011), 'The Trouble with HRM', *Human Resource Management Journal*, **21** (4), 355–67.

Thompson, P. and S. Ackroyd (1995), 'All quiet on the workplace front: a critique of recent trends in British industrial sociology', *Sociology*, **29** (4), 615–33.

Thompson, P. and B. Harley (2007), 'HRM and the worker: labor process perspectives', in P. Boxall, J. Purcell and P. Wright (eds), *The Oxford Handbook of Human Resource Management*, Oxford: Oxford University Press, pp. 147–65.

Thompson, P. and K. Newsome (2004), 'Labour process theory, work and the employment relationship', in B. Kaufman (ed.), *Theoretical Perspectives on Work and the Employment Relationship*, Champaign, IL: Industrial Relations Research Association, pp. 133–62.

Thompson, P. and C. Smith (1998), 'Beyond the capitalist labour process: workplace change, the state and globalization', *Critical Sociology*, **24** (3), 193–215.

Thompson, P. and C. Smith (2009), 'Waving, not drowning: explaining and exploring the resilience of labour process theory', *Employee Responsibilities and Rights Journal*, **21** (3), 253–62.

Thompson, P. and C.. Smith (2010a), 'Debating labour process theory and the sociology of work', in P. Thompson and C. Smith (eds), *Working Life*, Basingstoke: Palgrave Macmillan, pp. 11–28.

Thompson, P. and C. Smith (2010b), 'Introduction: labour process theory in retrospect and prospect', in P. Thompson and C. Smith (eds), *Working Life*, Basingstoke: Palgrave Macmillan, pp. 1–8.

Thompson, P. and S. Vincent (2010), 'Labour process theory and critical realism', in P. Thompson and C. Smith (eds), *Working Life*, Basingstoke: Palgrave, pp. 47–69.

Tinker, T. (2002), 'Spectres of Marx and Braverman in the twilight of postmodernist labour process research', *Work, Employment and Society*, **16** (2), 251–81.

Treiman, D. (1977), *Occupational Prestige in Comparative Perspective*, New York: Academic Press.

Van den Broek, D. and T. Dundon (2012), '(Still) Up to no good: Reconfiguring worker resistance and misbehaviour in an increasingly non-union world', *Industrial Relations Quarterly Review*, **67** (1), 97–121.

Warhurst, C. and P. Thompson (1998), 'Hands, hearts and minds: changing work and workers at the end of the century', in P. Thompson and C. Warhurst (eds), *Workplaces of the Future*, Basingstoke: Palgrave pp. 1–24.

Wood, S. and T. Wall (2007), 'Work enrichment and employee voice in human resource management-performance studies', *International Journal of Human Resource Management*, **18** (7), 1335–72.

Wilkinson, A. and C. Fay (2011), 'New times for employee voice?', *Human Resource Management*, January–February, 65–74.

8   Employee voice and silence in organizational behavior
Chad T. Brinsfield

INTRODUCTION

Envision yourself in a department meeting planning the launch of a vital corporate initiative. You have serious reservations about a proposed plan, but you hold back and do not express these concerns to your coworkers. Think about what it must have been like to be a young soldier in Iraq stationed at the Abu Ghraib prison in 2004. You have witnessed egregious human rights violations by some of your fellow soldiers toward Iraqi prisoners. Do you speak up, or do you remain silent? Or, imagine you are a line manager for a large manufacturer which is experiencing tenuous employee relations. You recognize the need for employees to be able to express their concerns. However, you are uncertain how, or to what extent, to grant voice to your employees. All of these examples represent situations where voice may be used as an expressive or participative medium in the workplace. Moreover, these scenarios also suggest that the efficacy of voice is not always clear cut, and that sometimes silence is a compelling alternative. In this chapter I explore the study of employee voice and silence within the field of organizational behavior (OB) and propose avenues through which our understanding of situations like these can be further enhanced.

HISTORY OF VOICE AND SILENCE IN ORGANIZATIONAL BEHAVIOR

To explore the study of employee voice and silence in OB we should first examine what these terms mean. This is not an easy task, as these terms have been used in different ways and encompass a broad conceptual space in the OB literature. In addition, there is a rich history of the use of the term voice in the literatures of industrial labor relations (ILR) and human resource management (HRM). Scholars in these areas have used the term voice to describe the formal mechanisms for individual and collective employee input and influence (for example, union participation, ombudsman services, suggestion systems; see Morrison, 2011). While there are notable intersections between voice in these literatures and employee voice and silence in OB, an in-depth review of voice in the ILR and HRM literatures is beyond the scope of this chapter.

OB scholars have used the terms voice and silence in a variety of ways over the years and have developed a considerable number of different constructs to describe phenomena which conceptually overlap with voice and silence. An in-depth review of all the different uses of the terms voice and silence and overlapping constructs would easily take an entire volume. However, an overview of the field indicates that some of these concepts are mainly concerned with describing and explaining different forms of communicative *expression or participation* (see Table 8.1). In contrast, other concepts are more oriented toward explicating different forms of communicative *suppression* (see Table 8.2). Although the distinction in focus between voice or silence is not unequivocal in all cases, it does help illuminate an important difference in perspective regarding employees' communicative behaviors. Voice and silence may indeed be two sides of the same coin, but in order to fully understand the nature of the coin it is necessary to examine both sides. This idea has also generated notable research interest in recent years (for example, Greenberg and Edwards, 2009; Morrison and Milliken, 2000; Pinder and Harlos, 2001), the implications of which I expound upon in a later section.

As is evident from the array of terms and constructs presented in Tables 8.1 and 8.2 (which is not exhaustive), this area of inquiry has an extensive history. In fact, ideas related to voice and silence were significant in the writings of some of the most influential authors in the organizational sciences. For instance, Elton Mayo, in discussions of the famous Hawthorne experiments (see Roethlisberger, 1941), recognized that employees are often reluctant to express themselves across hierarchical levels. Concepts related to voice and silence also emerged early on in other disciplines and have impacted research on voice and silence (for example, pluralistic ignorance, diffusion of responsibility; Allport, 1924; Latané and Darley, 1968). In the next two sections I briefly review the concepts presented in Tables 8.1 and 8.2, and discuss how these areas of research have evolved.

Voice Focused Concepts (Table 8.1)

Research which was influential in popularizing the term *voice* in the management vernacular was the seminal work of Albert Hirschman in *Exit, Voice, and Loyalty* (1970). Hirschman conceptualized voice as an attempt to change rather than to escape from an objectionable state of affairs. This could be through verbal appeal to a higher authority, or through various other types of actions and protests (for example, mobilization of public opinion). Although Hirschman's initial work was grounded in economics and focused primarily on clients of an organization using exit, voice, or loyalty, these concepts steadily gained attention in the OB literature and were adapted to organizational members (Farrell, 1983). Around the time of Hirschman's work, other scholars were also displaying an interest in different facets of voice and silence in the workplace. Other works on the voice side of the ledger include research focused on *upward communication* by Roberts and O'Reilly (1974). They examined the importance of trust, the influence of superiors, and mobility aspirations as important facilitators of open information exchange from lower to higher members in the hierarchy. Another related construct developed around this time was Thibaut and Walker's (1978) concept of *process control*. Although originally examined in the context of legal dispute resolution, this has become very influential in the field of organizational justice. The concept is based on the idea that a disputant's perception of fairness is positively related to the degree to which they can control the development, selection, and presentation of evidence used to resolve the dispute. An important aspect of control in this context is the opportunity to voice one's opinion and position (Blader and Tyler, 2005; Greenberg and Folger, 1983).

In the early 1980s, the term "organizational citizenship behavior" (OCB) was applied

Table 8.1   Voice focused concepts

Terminology/ construct	Description/definition
Voice (Hirschman, 1970)	In response to dissatisfaction, customers and organizational members can exercise three options: exit, voice, or loyalty.
	'Any attempt at all to change rather than escape from an objectionable state of affairs, whether through individual or collective petition to the management directly in charge, through appeal to a higher authority with the intention of forcing a change in management, or through various types of actions and protests, including those that are meant to mobilize public opinions' (p. 30).
Upward communication (Roberts and O'Reilly, 1974)	The transference of information from lower to higher members in an organizational hierarchy and the meaning inferred from that information.
Process control (that is, voice; Thibaut and Walker, 1975)	Originally termed 'process control' by Thibaut and Walker, is now commonly referred to as 'voice' in the procedural justice literature (see Blader and Tyler, 2005).
	The opportunity to express one's opinion or present evidence supporting one's own case with respect to allocation decisions.
Whistle-blowing (Near and Miceli, 1985)	Disclosure by organizational members of perceived organizational wrongdoing to authorities who can take action (p. 2).
Principled organizational dissent (Graham, 1986b)	'Effort by individuals in the workplace to protest and/or to change the organizational status quo because of their conscientious objection to current policy or practice' (p. 2).
Civic virtue (Graham, 1986a)	Suggesting modifications in policies and speaking up about issues for the benefit of the organization.
Employee voice mechanisms (Spencer, 1986)	'Grievance procedures, suggestion systems, employee management meetings, counseling services, ombudsman services, non-management task forces, question and answer programs, and survey feedback' (p. 491).
Excuses, justifications, apologies, disclaimers (Arkin and Shepperd, 1989)	Self-protective tactics where different forms of voice are used in response to feeling threatened.
	Self-promotion tactics where different forms of voice are used to enhance one's image and esteem.
Issue selling (Dutton and Ashford, 1993)	'Behaviors that are directed toward affecting others' attention to and understanding of issues' (p. 398).
Advocacy participation (Van Dyne et al., 1994)	Constructive and proactive behaviors such as expressing high standards, challenging others, and making suggestions for change.
Complaining (Kowalski, 1996)	'Expressions of dissatisfaction, whether subjectively experienced or not, for the purpose of venting emotions or achieving intrapsychic goals, or both' (p. 179).
Voice (Van Dyne and LePine, 1998)	'Promotive behavior that emphasizes expression of constructive challenge intended to improve rather than merely criticize' (p. 109).
Psychological safety (Edmondson, 1999)	'A shared belief that the team is safe for interpersonal risk taking' (p. 354).
Employee voice (Van Dyne et al., 2003)	Intentionally expressing work-related ideas, information, and opinions based on three distinct underlying motives: (a) acquiescence, (b) defensive, and (c) prosocial.
Group voice climate (Morrison et al., 2011)	'Shared beliefs about speaking up on voice behavior within work groups' (p. 184).

Table 8.2   Silence focused concepts

Terminology/ construct	Description/definition
Pluralistic ignorance (Allport, 1924; Katz et al., 1931)	Conditions in which nearly all members of a group privately reject group norms yet erroneously believe that most of the other group members accept them. Therefore they remain silent regarding their true feelings of disagreement.
Diffusion of responsibility (Latané and Darley, 1968)	The mere perception that other people are also witnessing an event will markedly increase the likelihood that an individual will not intervene or speak up about an issue or situation.
Loyalty (Hirschman, 1970)	In response to dissatisfaction, customers and organizational members can exercise three options: exit, voice, or loyalty. Loyal employees may stay and suffer in silence; confident that things will get better.
The 'MUM' effect (Rosen and Tesser, 1970)	Individuals' general reluctance to convey negative information because of the discomfort associated with delivering bad news.
Groupthink (Janis, 1972)	A form of thought exhibited by group members who try to minimize conflict and reach consensus without critically analyzing, evaluating, and testing ideas. Group members remain silent about concerns and doubts they may have.
The spirals of silence (Noelle-Neumann, 1974)	Provides insight into how silence may manifest and perpetuate in the conformance to public opinion, often due to fear of isolation or self-doubt.
Abilene paradox (Harvey, 1974)	Situation where people communicate agreement because they want to conform to the perceived wishes or desires of the group. Group members keep silent with regard to their true feelings and beliefs.
Neglect (Farrell, 1983)	Building on the work of Hirschman, Farrell identified 'neglect' as a fourth response to job dissatisfaction characterized by apathy, passive disengagement, and silence.
Sportsmanship (Organ, 1988, 1990)	Type of citizenship behavior which includes withholding work-related ideas, information, or opinions with the goal of benefiting other people or the organization.
Deaf ear syndrome (Peirce et al., 1998)	Functions as an organizational norm that discourages employees' open and direct expression of their dissatisfaction.
Organizational silence (Morrison and Milliken, 2000)	A collective-level phenomenon of employees withholding information, opinions, or concerns regarding work-related problems or issues.
Climate of silence (Morrison and Milliken, 2000)	'Widely shared perceptions among employees that speaking up about problems or issues is futile and/or dangerous' (p. 708).
Employee silence (Pinder and Harlos, 2001; Van Dyne et al., 2003)	'The withholding of any form of genuine expression about the individual's behavioral, cognitive and/or affective evaluations of his or her organizational circumstance to persons who are perceived to be capable of effecting change or redress' (Pinder and Harlos, 2001: 334). Based on acquiescent and quiescent motives. Intentionally withholding work-related ideas, information, and opinions based on three distinct underlying motives: (a) acquiescence, (b) defensive, and (c) prosocial (Van Dyne, et al., 2003).
Implicit voice theories (Detert and Edmondson, 2011)	'Taken-for-granted beliefs about when and why speaking up at work is risky or inappropriate' (p. 461).

to Katz's (1964) category of extra-role behavior (for example, Bateman and Organ, 1983) and became a basis for much of the subsequent research on voice in OB. OCB entails prosocial behavior that is outside the scope of one's formal job responsibilities, but that is nevertheless important for organizational performance (see Van Dyne et al., 1994). In a related line of research, but focused on contexts of organizational wrongdoing, Near and Miceli (1985) were instrumental in bringing the investigation of *whistle-blowing* to the organizational sciences. According to Near and Miceli, whistle-blowing typically involves communication outside the normal chain of command (that is, to outside authorities), and often represents a challenge to the organization's authority structure. Although there is debate on whether or not whistle-blowing should be considered a form of OCB (see Van Dyne et al., 1995), prior to the work of Near and Miceli, whistle-blowing had primarily been viewed from legal and policy perspectives. Also in a related line of research, Graham (1986b) developed the idea of *principled organizational dissent*. According to Graham, the term *principled* applies to the type of issue at stake (for example, one that violates a standard of justice, honesty, or economy). Building on the work of Hirschman, she proposed a variety of forms that principled organizational dissent can take (for example, constructive criticism, protest expressed within the organization, reports to audiences outside the organization). Also around this time, and building on earlier work on citizenship behavior, Graham (1986a; Organ, 1988) conceptualized *civic virtue* as a type of OCB that included encouraging others to speak up at meetings, sharing informed opinions, and challenging the majority. However, these voice related behaviors are only one facet of a broader civic virtue construct which also includes constructive involvement in the political process of the organization and keeping abreast of larger issues involving the organization.

During this period a number of other voice related concepts were also being investigated. Spencer (1986) looked at *employee voice mechanisms* and their effect on employee retention and problem resolution. In Spencer's research, voice mechanisms consisted of formal 'grievance procedures, suggestion systems, employee management meetings, counseling services, ombudsman services, non-management task forces, question and answer programs, and survey feedback' (p. 491). Not surprisingly, he found a negative correlation between the existence of voice mechanisms and employee turnover. He also found a positive correlation between voice mechanisms and employee expectations for problem resolution and the perceived effectiveness of an organization's procedures for resolving problems. Although research on voice mechanisms has important implications for OB, most of the subsequent research has been in the ILR and HRM literatures. In the late 1980s a different perspective on voice was being investigated by Arkin and Shepperd (1989) based on self-presentation theory (Goffman, 1959) and impression management theory (Tedeschi et al., 1971). Arkin and Shepperd's research looked at how people use different forms of voice behavior (for example, excuses, justifications) as self-protection and self-promotion tactics. However, these forms of voice have by and large been examined in their own distinct lines of inquiry and have not generally been integrated into the domain of voice and silence research. Although, as will be discussed in a later section, self-protection is a commonly cited reason for employee silence.

Throughout the 1990s additional voice related constructs continued to emerge and stimulate related lines of research. Dutton and Ashford (1993) introduced the concept of *issue selling*, which focuses on how middle managers influence where top managers allocate their limited time and attention among potential strategic issues. Although many of the activities they considered to be forms of issue selling (for example, providing important information about issues, framing the issues in particular ways, mobilizing resources and routines that direct top managers' attention to some issues and not others) may involve voice, Dutton and Ashford recognized that issue selling may also involve the concealment of important information. Other voice related constructs derived from research on OCB also emerged during this period. Van Dyne et al. (1994) identified a form of citizenship behavior which they labeled *advocacy participation*. According to Van Dyne et al., advocacy participation involves a range of behaviors aimed at effecting positive change in an organization (for example, challenging others, making suggestions for change). They also recognized that in certain situations (for example, when the "common good" is an issue), advocacy participation may be quite similar to Graham's (1986b) principled organizational dissent.

During this time other researchers were also busy examining different voice related phenomena. Kowalski (1996) looked at *complaining*, which had previously been examined mainly in the context of consumer dissatisfaction. Although her research was initially published in the psychological literature, her work was important in raising awareness of these types of behaviors within organizations. There is little doubt that complaining is an inescapable phenomenon in organizations and can serve multiple functions (for example, catharsis, self-presentational motivations, social comparison processes, a communicative tool to call others to account for their behavior). Whether or not complaining is positive or negative for the complainer, or the organization, certainly depends on the nature of the complaint and the situation. Moreover, for certain functions (for example, calling others to account for ethical shortcomings) complaining appears to share similarities with principled organizational dissent.

Research which has been seminal in the demarcation of the *voice* construct was published by Van Dyne and LePine (1998; see also LePine and Van Dyne, 1998) and was a refinement of earlier work on advocacy participation. They conceptualized helping behaviors and voice as two distinct types of OCB. Helping behaviors were considered cooperative and noncontroversial, aimed at preserving relationships and building harmony. In contrast, they considered voice to involve constructive challenge and improvement of the status quo (for example, making innovative suggestions for change, recommending modifications to standard procedures even when others disagree; Van Dyne and LePine, 1998: 109). And although employee voice has subsequently been defined with subtle distinctions by other scholars (see Morrison, 2011: 367), it is the underlying intent for constructive challenge and improvement that is the primary factor in differentiating "voice" from other forms of verbal expression in the workplace. This general conceptualization has served as a guiding framework in many subsequent studies on employee voice (for example, Morrison et al., 2011; Tangirala and Ramanujam, 2008b; Whiting et al., 2008).

The next concept indicated in Table 8.1 is *psychological safety*, which Edmondson (1999) defined as 'a shared belief that the team is safe for interpersonal risk taking' (p. 354). This construct has also been successfully adapted to measure individual-level perception of psychological safety with the organization as the focus (for example, Baer and Frese, 2003). Psychological safety has had a significant impact on the study of voice as many studies either implicitly or explicitly place it as a mediator between antecedent variables and voice behaviors (for example, Ashford et al., 1998; Detert and Burris, 2007; Miceli and Near, 1992). Moreover, employees' willingness to speak up has been included in some measures of psychological safety (see Edmondson, 2004).

In response to increasing scholarly interest in voice and silence, in 2003 a special issue of the *Journal of Management Studies* was published on the dynamics of voice and silence in organizations from which several important contributions emerged. One particularly noteworthy contribution was Van Dyne et al.'s (2003) conceptualization of voice and silence as multidimensional constructs. They proposed three distinct types of *employee voice* based on different underlying motives (acquiescent, defensive, and prosocial). (They also proposed three parallel forms of employee silence which are discussed in the next section.) This research raised awareness about the role of different motives when considering the nature of voice and silence. As is evident from the different motives they proposed, voice can serve purposes in addition to the challenging and promotive function expressed by Van Dyne and LePine (1998). However, there has not been any subsequent empirical research that has specifically examined the nature and implications of different motives for voice.

The last construct indicated in Table 8.1 is *group voice climate* (Morrison et al., 2011). This research builds upon Morrison and Milliken's (2000) idea of a 'climate of silence' and extends Van Dyne and LePine's (1998) conceptualization of employee voice to the group level of analysis. Prior to this work there had been little empirical examination of the effects of group-level cognitions on voice behavior within work groups. Moreover, most prior research on employee voice has examined voice directed 'up the hierarchy,' which cannot necessarily be generalized to voice directed at other targets (see Kish-Gephart et al., 2009). Kish-Gephart et al. examined voice directed at fellow work-group members and found that group voice climate explained variance in voice behavior beyond the effects of individual-level identification and satisfaction, and procedural justice climate.

The concepts described up to this point broadly focus on different forms of communicative *expression or participation*. As previously mentioned, this perspective represents only one side of the voice–silence coin. To better understand the nature of employees' communicative experiences, some scholars have proposed that silence should not simply be equated to an absence of voice, but rather is often meaningful in and of itself (for example, Morrison and Milliken, 2000; Pinder and Harlos, 2001). Based on this line of reasoning, the focus of this overview now shifts to concepts which are generally more oriented toward communicative *suppression*.

Silence Focused Concepts (Table 8.2)

While some research was examining the voice focused concepts discussed above, concepts more oriented toward communicative suppression were also receiving attention (see Table 8.2). One of the earliest of these was *pluralistic ignorance* which Floyd Allport (1924; Katz et al., 1931) described as a condition in which nearly all members of a group privately reject group norms yet believe that most of the other group members accept them. When pluralistic ignorance occurs people may remain silent regarding their true thoughts and feelings, and/or express agreement when they really do not agree. The idea of pluralistic ignorance subsequently has been integral in the development of notable silence and voice related constructs such as the spiral of silence (see Noelle-Neumann, 1993) and acquiescent voice (Van Dyne et al., 2003).

The next construct indicated in Table 8.2, which is conceptually related to the idea of pluralistic ignorance, is *diffusion of responsibility*. Latané and Darley (1968), in an investigation of bystander intervention in emergency situations, demonstrated that this may be a primary reason for remaining silent. According to Latané and Darley, if a person is alone when he notices an emergency, he is solely accountable for coping with it. If he believes others are also present, he may feel that his own responsibility for taking action is reduced, making him less likely to help. An infamous example of this is the case of the Kitty Genovese murder in New York City in 1964 when 38 people witnessed her killing from their individual apartments, but did not take action. Presumably, because each individual could also see other people witnessing the crime, they all felt that someone else would act, the result being that no one helped her. Although diffusion of responsibility has not received much attention in the recent employee silence literature, it has been acknowledged as a potential reason for failures to express voice (for example, Henriksen and Dayton, 2006; LePine and Van Dyne, 1998) and represents a fertile area for further investigation with respect to employee voice and silence.

In conjunction with his conceptualization of voice, Hirschman (1970) described an aspect of *loyalty* as a conscious and passive state where one stays and suffers in silence hopeful that the situation will improve. This idea has found mixed support in research on organizational loyalty and voice. Some studies have found that loyal employees are more strongly invested in improving their workplaces, making them inclined to speak up about their work-related concerns (for example, Barry, 1974; Olson-Buchanan and Boswell, 2002; Spencer, 1986). However, other studies have found that loyal employees may 'suffer in silence' because they are apprehensive about the potential disruption caused by voicing their concerns (for example, Boroff and Lewin, 1997; Rusbult et al., 1988). To help explain the different effects of loyalty on voice, Tangirala and Ramanujam (2009) proposed that in work contexts unfavorable for speaking up (for example, where there is fear of reprisal for speaking up or perceived low utility in engaging in voice), loyal employees are likely to substitute voice with alternative behaviors aimed at resolving work problems. Around the same time as Hirschman's work on loyalty, Rosen and Tesser (1970) examined employees' reluctance to convey unfavorable information due to the general discomfort associated with doing so. They termed this the 'MUM' effect, which stood for keeping '*M*um [that is, silent] about *U*ndesirable *M*essages' (Rosen and Tesser, 1970: 254). The MUM effect has since been recognized as a possible explanation for why employees remain silent about problems in the workplace (Milliken et al., 2003).

A seminal concept, which has been studied in a wide range of disciplines and is related to employee voice and silence, is *groupthink* (Janis, 1972). Groupthink represents a tendency of cohesive groups working under directive leadership to reach premature consensus and not challenge prevailing views. These groups exhibit a strong confirmation bias in that they tend to focus on information that confirms their initial opinions and disregard information that opposes dominant beliefs. An important characteristic of groupthink involves rebuking anyone who speaks up with a different point of view. Research on groupthink may also help explain why loyal employees sometimes engage in self-censorship and refrain from expressing their concerns (Janis, 1972; Turner and Pratkanis, 1998). Many subsequent studies on employee voice and silence have built on factors that contribute to groupthink (for example, potential risks to one's image or credibility from speaking up about certain issues; Milliken et al., 2003; Piderit and Ashford, 2003).

Not long after Irving Janis first published his work on groupthink, Noelle-Neumann (1974) introduced the concept of a *spiral of silence*. In the context of public opinion, the belief that voicing a disfavored opinion may result in one being isolated or ostracized perpetuates a spiral of silence regarding the unpopular opinion. This process is self-reinforcing and further extends the belief that the unspoken opinion is less favored than it actually may be. This line of reasoning has subsequently been adapted to explain different forms of communicative suppression in organizations (for example, negative effects of diversity on voice; Bowen and Blackmon, 2003). Around this same time, the idea of the *Abilene paradox* was introduced by Harvey (1974), building upon the idea of pluralistic ignorance. In the classic Abilene paradox example, none of a group of four family members really wants to drive 53 miles to Abilene, TX (in the summertime, in a car without air conditioning to eat greasy food in a bad cafeteria), but no one speaks up and admits that they do not want to go. After returning from this unpleasant experience, each hot and frustrated person tries to blame others for the trip. Since no one really wanted to go, no single individual was responsible and no one person could be blamed. Instead, each person's failure to communicate accurately caused the group to do something that no one wanted to do. The Abilene paradox also shares similarities with groupthink and the spiral of silence in that the desire for conformity leads to the suppression of open and honest communication. This concept has also been influential in more recent conceptual research on acquiescent silence (Pinder and Harlos, 2001; Van Dyne et al., 2003).

Building on Hirschman's framework of exit, voice, and loyalty, Farrell (1983) identified *neglect* as a fourth response to job dissatisfaction. In formulating these ideas, Farrell also drew on earlier studies which had extended Hirschman's framework to silence (Kolarska and Aldrich, 1980) and to neglect in the context of romantic involvements (Rusbult et al., 1982). According to Farrell, neglect is exemplified by apathy, passive disengagement, and silence. Moreover, the type of silence that is symptomatic of neglect is distinct from the type of silence that Hirschman considered an aspect of loyalty and further illustrates the need to distinguish between different forms of silence.

The next concept illustrated in Table 8.2 is *sportsmanship* (Organ, 1988, 1990). Sportsmanship is a type of OCB which Organ (1990: 96) defined as 'a willingness to tolerate the inevitable inconveniences and impositions of work without complaining.' Sportsmanship has generally received less attention in the literature than other types of OCB (Podsakoff et al., 2000). And although an aspect of sportsmanship entails self-censorship of certain types of communicative expression (that is, complaining), it has not been notably integrated into research on employee voice or silence. One exception is the idea of prosocial silence (Van Dyne et al., 2003) which involves withholding information or opinions with the goal of benefiting other people or organizations. Beyond this conceptual work of Van Dyne et al. there has been no research which has expressly examined the effects of sportsmanship on employee voice or silence.

The next notable silence related concept to emerge in the OB literature was the *deaf ear syndrome* (Peirce et al., 1998). According to Pierce et al., this phenomenon results when people capable of effecting change in an organization fail to respond to complaints. It was originally developed in the context of sexual harassment cases, but was used subsequently to explain silence in other work-related contexts (Harlos, 2001). Pierce et al. described three themes associated with deaf ear syndrome: (1) inadequate organizational policies and procedures, (2) managerial rationalizations, and (3) inertial tendencies. The deaf ear syndrome later provided conceptual underpinnings in the development of quiescent and acquiescent silence (see Pinder and Harlos, 2001), but otherwise there has been surprisingly little integration with more recent research on employee voice and silence.

Probably one of the most influential articles on intentional silence in organizations was published by Morrison and Milliken (2000) wherein they introduced the term *organizational silence*. Perhaps more than any other single piece of research, this article has been responsible for stimulating research interest in silence in organizations. Although they were not the first to acknowledge that silence may be meaningful in its own right, their article has served as a catalyst for much subsequent research that has viewed silence as a distinct construct and not simply as equivalent to an absence of voice. Morrison and Milliken conceptualized organizational silence as a collective-level phenomenon wherein employees withhold their opinions and concerns about organizational problems (Morrison and Milliken, 2000: 707). It is driven by what they referred to as a *climate of silence* which is characterized by 'widely shared perceptions among employees that speaking up about problems or issues is futile and/or dangerous' (p. 708).

Building partly on the work of Morrison and Milliken, Pinder and Harlos (2001) introduced the construct of *employee silence*. They defined employee silence as 'the withholding of any form of genuine expression about the individual's behavioral, cognitive and/or affective evaluations of his or her organizational circumstance to persons who are perceived to be capable of effecting change or redress' (Pinder and Harlos, 2001: 334). Pinder and Harlos's conceptualization of employee silence differs from Morrison and Milliken's organizational silence in that employee silence is an individual-level phenomenon, whereas organizational silence is conceptualized at a collective level. Moreover, Pinder and Harlos limit their discussion to employee silence as a response to injustice, whereas organizational silence is broader in respect of the types of situations, issues, or concerns to which employees may choose to respond with silence. Perhaps one of the most important developments resulting from the work of Pinder and Harlos was their recognition that silence may represent decidedly distinct phenomenological experiences, depending on voluntariness, consciousness, acceptance, stress level, awareness of alternatives, propensity to voice, propensity to exit, and dominant emotions (Pinder and Harlos, 2001: 348). Based on these factors they proposed two different forms of silence: quiescence and acquiescence. According to Pinder and Harlos, quiescent silence represents a state of disagreement with one's circumstances, awareness of existing alternatives, yet being unwilling to speak up about the situation based on fear. In contrast, acquiescent silence implies a deeply-felt acceptance of organizational circumstances, a taking-for-granted of the situation and limited awareness that alternatives exist (p. 349).

Shortly after Pinder and Harlos proposed quiescent and acquiescent silence, Van Dyne et al. (2003) extended this line of reasoning and proposed three different forms of employee silence (acquiescent, defensive, and prosocial) based on distinct underlying motives. According to Van Dyne et al., acquiescent silence is based on feelings of resignation and being unable to make a difference. Defensive silence is based on fear of consequences associated with speaking up. Prosocial silence is based on feelings of cooperation or altruism, and includes withholding confidential information and protecting proprietary knowledge to benefit the organization. Although influential in advancing our understanding of silence, both the work of Pinder and Harlos and Van Dyne et al. were conceptual in nature, and there has subsequently been little empirical research to substantiate the existence, pervasiveness, or implications of these different forms of employee silence.

The last construct indicated in Table 8.2 is *implicit voice theories* (Detert and Edmondson, 2011). Although this construct contains the term 'voice' in its name, it is included here with silence focused concepts because its emphasis is primarily on why employees are unwilling to speak up about important matters in the workplace. The authors conceptualize implicit voice theories as taken-for-granted beliefs about when and why speaking up at work is risky or inappropriate (Detert and Edmondson, 2011: 461). In an extensive, mixed-methods investigation, they identified five such implicit theories employees may have: (a) a belief in managers' identification with the status quo, which leads to the assumption that managers will hear suggestions as personal criticism; (b) the need to have solid data, polished ideas, or complete solutions before it is safe to speak; (c) the belief that speaking up in ways that challenge the boss in front of his/her superiors will be seen as disloyal and unacceptable; (d) the belief that bosses dislike hearing bad news, or being challenged in front of others without advance, private notice; and (e) that challenging the status quo may lead to managerial retaliation. This research is notable in probing deeper into the reasons employees believe it is risky or inappropriate to speak up, but employees may remain silent for many other types of reasons (for example, out of feelings of futility or to protect a relationship; see Milliken et al., 2003; Morrison et al., 2011; Van Dyne et al., 2003).

Summary of Voice and Silence Focused Concepts

As is evident from the preceding overview, there have been many different voice and silence related concepts examined over the years which have impacted the field of OB. The term employee voice has become widely understood as verbal communication aimed up the organizational hierarchy with the intention of improving a situation (for example, Hirschman, 1970; Van Dyne and LePine, 1998). Although there have been notable differences in the way the term voice has been conceptualized and used (for example, different targets of voice or different kinds of information conveyed in response to different types of situations; see Morrison, 2011), most uses do entail the communication of relevant work-related information with the intent to constructively challenge or improve a situation. In addition, many of the other concepts reviewed overlap considerably with this conceptualization of voice. For instance, whistle-blowing is typically concerned with challenging or improving a situation, albeit the situation is typically of an ethical nature. Principled organizational dissent is intended to protest or change an objectionable situation, with the implicit intent of challenge and improvement. Civic virtue involves suggesting modifications and speaking up about policies for the benefit of the organization. Similarly, advocacy participation includes elements of constructive verbal expression, such as making suggestions for constructive change.

Other concepts in this overview, however, are more distinct from voice as it is widely referred to in the OB literature (for example, Van Dyne and LePine, 1998). Voice in the procedural justice literature is a conceptually different phenomenon, although voice opportunities in the service of fairness perceptions are often improvement oriented. Employee voice mechanisms are also distinct from voice itself, although they are generally viewed as means to facilitate the types of challenging or improvement oriented expression proposed by Van Dyne and LePine. Excuses, justifications, apologies, and disclaimers are based on self-promotion or self-protection motives, rather than on an intention to challenge or improve a situation, and therefore are not forms of voice. Issue selling is related to voice, but is different in the sense that it is focused on directing upper management's attention, rather than on the conveyance of challenging or improvement oriented information. Complaining is also conceptually distinct from voice. Although both represent forms of verbal expression, the intention of complaining is often cathartic and based more on one's own intrapsychic goals.

As we have seen, there are also numerous terms focused more on the explication of communicative suppression. Some of these describe psychological states which may lead to the unwillingness to convey information (for example, pluralistic ignorance). Others are conceptually broad group-based phenomena, which may predispose members of groups toward remaining silent (for example, diffusion of responsibility, groupthink). Other concepts have been specifically developed to focus directly on the phenomenon of silence in organizations (for example, spirals of silence, organizational silence, employee silence). Although this vast body of research on voice and silence related concepts has produced numerous important insights, many scholars contend that there is still much we do not know about situations wherein employees have something meaningful to say, but at the same time feel compelled to remain silent (Edwards and Greenberg, 2009; Morrison, 2011).

UNRESOLVED ISSUES AND DIRECTION FOR FUTURE RESEARCH

What is the employee voice and silence literature all about? What are the central questions guiding research in this area? Not surprisingly, there are no clear and consistent answers to these questions; researchers in this field continue to move in many different directions. Moreover, considering the history and scope of the research reviewed in the previous sections it may seem counterintuitive to say the field is still in an adolescent phase, but in some important ways it is. Just as an adolescent confronts the existential question, 'Who am I?' so too is the field of employee voice and silence in a time of self-discovery. This is evident in OB textbooks from the fragmented way this information is presented, and the relatively little space allocated to such an important workplace phenomenon, if it is discussed at all. From a research perspective, construct ambiguity, construct proliferation and redundancy, conceptual myopia, and methodological issues have all contributed to gaps in our knowledge and notable issues remain unresolved. Unfortunately a detailed discussion of all of these different issues is beyond the scope of this chapter (for more in-depth discussions see select chapters in this volume; Greenberg and Edwards, 2009; Morrison, 2011). Therefore, in the remainder of this chapter I focus on two of the more important (and related) unresolved issues in the field: (1) more fully explicating and leveraging the distinctions between employee voice and employee silence, and (2) the need for an integrative framework for making sense of this diverse body of literature.

As discussed in the preceding overviews, the field now seems in general agreement on what constitutes employee voice (that is, the communication of work or organizationally relevant information with the intent to constructively challenge or improve a situation). There is somewhat less agreement on what constitutes employee silence, but most conceptualizations characterize it as the intentional withholding of seemingly meaningful information, including questions, concerns, and suggestions (Tangirala and Ramanujam, 2008a). But should employee voice and silence be considered distinct constructs, or are they simply opposites with the presence of one implying the absence of the other? There has been some debate over this issue (see Morrison, 2011), but most scholars likely would admit that research specifically on silence has deepened our understanding of employees' willingness and unwillingness to speak up. From a behavioral standpoint, voice and silence may seem like the antithesis of each other. However, organizational situations and human relationships are complex and multifaceted. Employees may confront situations where they simultaneously want to speak up yet remain silent (for example, a person who witnesses an ethical transgression may want to speak up to be consistent with their core values, but also may feel compelled to remain silent due to fear of reprisal). However, the nature and implications of these opposing and potentially distinct forces for voice and silence is not well understood. It is likely that strong opposing forces for voice and silence could create considerable intrapsychic conflict, the psychological and behavioral implications of which may vary according to the nature and relative strengths of the distinct forces for voice and silence. In terms of Gestalt psychology (Kohler, 1992), voice related research has typically considered voice as figure and silence as ground, but in the case of silence the ground can have meaning too.

Another compelling reason to explicitly examine silence is that measures of voice behavior and voice related constructs do not necessarily reveal the extent or nature of intentional silence. Consider a person who is naturally outgoing. Others may rate them high on measures of voice, they may even rate themselves high on voice, but there could also be important situations in which they remain silent for a variety of different reasons. However, the extent or nature of their silence may not surface with assessments of voice or its antecedents. With this in mind there have been notable attempts to measure silence in organizations. For example, Vakola and Bouradas (2005) measured organizational silence by assessing climate factors such as employees' perception of management and supervisors' attitudes toward silence, communication opportunities, and extent of expressions of disagreement. Tangirala and Ramanujam (2008a) adapted items from Van Dyne et al.'s (2003) proposed measure of silence to assess the extent to which employees intentionally withheld ideas, concerns, questions, or information in their workgroup (that is, intentional silence behavior). Detert and Edmondson (2011) empirically assessed employees' taken-for-granted beliefs about when and why speaking up at work is risky or inappropriate (that is, implicit voice theories). Although these prior efforts have been helpful in deepening our understanding of silence in the workplace, none of these approaches enable the direct assessment of the extent and nature of different forms of intentional silence. In sum, investigating voice behavior and inferring employee silence is problematic because voice behavior is not necessarily equivalent to an absence of intentional silence. Assessing a general intention to remain silent, or the extent of intentional silence behavior, is a step in the right direction, but does not account for the potentially diverse meanings which may underlie silence (Pinder and Harlos, 2001; Van Dyne et al., 2003). The implicit voice theories approach developed by Detert and Edmondson (2011) is promising, but limits its discussion of silence to a response to the risks associated with speaking up.

A possible approach to the direct examination of silence could build upon the works of Pinder and Harlos (2001) and Van Dyne et al. (2003) on motives for employee silence. These authors proposed that it is the underlying motives that give meaning to the behavior of silence and distinguish it from simply an absence of voice. They also suggest that it is the motives that account for the phenomenological differences between different forms of silence. Hence, a variety of different motives have been proposed in the literature (for example, defensive, prosocial, quiescent, acquiescent, impression management, fear of managerial prerogative, employee resistance; Brinsfield, 2013; Donaghey et al., 2011; Pinder and Harlos, 2001; Premeaux and Bedeian, 2003). Developing measures of the different motives for silence could provide a means of directly assessing the different underlying forces for silence which employees may experience, but which cannot be discerned from an absence of voice behavior or from measures of intentional silence behavior. This also may serve as a catalyst toward investigating the nature and implications of the conflicting forces for voice and silence; forces which may be inherent in many situations employees face regarding whether or not to speak up.

Another prominent issue facing this field is the lack of an integrative framework for making sense of this extensive body of related literatures. This is not to say there has not been systematic development of new constructs; later constructs have frequently drawn on prior related ones. Rather, since many of these constructs have been of more or less interest to scholars in different areas of inquiry – who are interested in different questions – voice and silence researchers have not fully leveraged the diverse body of relevant knowledge. The need for better integration of research focused specifically on voice and silence has been acknowledged (see Morrison, 2011). However, better integration of the literature associated with the many other concepts discussed in the preceding overviews is also needed. Scholars contend there is still much we do not know about employees' willingness and unwillingness to speak up at work (Edwards and Greenberg, 2009). This may be true, but we may know more than we are aware of as a result of the substantial research which has been conducted on overlapping phenomena, but which has not been sufficiently integrated.

One approach to integrating these diverse literatures could build on the categorization scheme presented by Brinsfield et al. (2009) which illustrated many of these concepts according to voice or silence focus, target of communication (for example, upward, lateral, downward, internal, external), level of analysis (individual, group, organization), and the nature of the situation or event on which one would speak up or remain silent (for example, idea for improvement, ethical or fairness concern, response to dissatisfaction). In addition, many of these constructs implicitly or explicitly entail an underlying motive for the particular phenomenon. Using these types of factors and possibly others (for example, type of information conveyed, communication medium) as an organizing framework, researchers could investigate empirical findings across these different constructs with respect to common antecedents, moderators, and outcomes. Although a formal meta-analytical investigation may not be possible due to the diverse nature of the different constructs (an assumption which needs more scrutiny), a systematic review of empirical findings could reveal new insights and yield important theoretical synergies.

CONCLUSION

When people are unwilling to speak up about important issues and situations that they confront at work the human and economic costs can be staggering; critical assumptions remain unquestioned, fruitful ideas go unrealized, bad decisions are made, people's lives can even be lost. In this chapter I have provided an overview of some of the more notable constructs that have impacted the study of voice and silence in the field of organizational behavior. I have also presented a case for specifically examining both voice *and* silence, and how this can lead to a deeper understanding of situations where employees have something meaningful to say, but nonetheless feel compelled to remain silent. I then discussed the need for an integrative framework for making sense of the employee voice and silence literatures, as well as the need for more integration across a variety of other related constructs. And finally, I proposed one possible approach to organizing this extensive body of related literatures.

In addition to substantial research still being conducted on many of the constructs discussed in this overview, research is continually emerging across a wide range of academic disciplines which can bring valuable new perspectives to the study of voice and silence (for example, the effects of silence on forgetting; Stone et al., 2012). OB scholars need to stay abreast of relevant new research from a wide variety of sources. We also need to thoughtfully question our paradigmatic assumptions surrounding voice and silence which may unwittingly constrain our thinking. One of these assumptions is that managers and organizational leaders *want* employees to be willing to voice their concerns. However, as Donaghey et al. (2011) recently pointed out, this is not necessarily the case and management may even purposely perpetuate silence. Considering the wide ranging implications of voice and silence, as well as the potential to create synergies from a vast body of existing research and to conduct thought-provoking new research, it is indeed an exciting time to study voice and silence in organizational behavior.

REFERENCES

Allport, F. (1924), *Social Psychology*, Boston: Houghton Mifflin.
Arkin, R.M. and J.A. Shepperd (1989), 'Self-presentation styles in organizations', in R.A. Giacalone and P. Rosenfeld (eds), *Impression Management in the Organization*, Hillsdale, NJ: Erlbaum, pp. 125–39.
Ashford, S. J., N.P. Rothbard, S.K. Piderit and J.E. Dutton (1998), 'Out on a limb: the role of context and impression management in selling gender-equity issues', *Administrative Science Quarterly*, **43**, 23–57.
Baer, M. and M. Frese (2003), 'Innovation is not enough: climates for initiative and psychological safety, process innovations, and firm performance', *Journal of Organizational Behavior*, **24**, 45–68.
Barry, B. (1974), Review article: *Exit, Voice, and Loyalty*, British Journal of Political Science, **4**, 79–107.
Bateman, T.S. and D.W. Organ (1983), 'Job satisfaction and the good soldier: the relationship between affect and employee "citizenship"', *Academy of Management Journal*, **26**, 587–95.
Blader, S.L., and T.R. Tyler (2005), 'How can theories of organizational justice explain the effects of fairness?', in J. Greenberg and J.A. Colquitt (eds), *Handbook of Organizational Justice*, Mahwah, NJ: Lawrence Erlbaum Associates, pp. 329–54.

Boroff, K.E. and D. Lewin (1997), 'Loyalty, voice, and intent to exit a union firm: a conceptual and empirical analysis', *Industrial and Labor Relations Review*, **51**, 50–63.

Bowen, F. and K. Blackmon (2003), 'Spirals of silence: the dynamic effects of diversity on organizational voice', *Journal of Management Studies*, **40**, 1393–417.

Brinsfield, C.T. (2013), 'Employee silence motives: investigation of dimensionality and development of measures', *Journal of Organizational Behavior*, **34**, 671–97.

Brinsfield, C.T., M.S. Edwards and J. Greenberg (2009), 'Voice and silence in organizations: historical review and current conceptualizations', in J. Greenberg and M.S. Edwards (eds), *Voice and Silence in Organizations*, Bingley, UK: Emerald Group Publishing Limited, pp. 3–33.

Detert, J.R. and E.R. Burris (2007), 'Leadership behavior and employee voice: is the door really open?', *Academy of Management Journal*, **50**, 869–84.

Detert, J.R. and A.C. Edmondson (2011), 'Implicit voice theories: taken-for-granted rules of self-censorship at work', *Academy of Management Journal*, **54**, 461–88.

Donaghey, J., N. Cullinane, T. Dundon and A. Wilkinson (2011), 'Reconceptualising employee silence: problems and prognosis', *Work, Employment and Society*, **25**, 51–67.

Dutton, J. E. and S.J. Ashford (1993), 'Selling issues to top management', *Academy of Management Review*, **18**, 397–428.

Edmondson, A.C. (1999), 'Psychological safety and learning behavior in work teams', *Administrative Science Quarterly*, **44**, 350–83.

Edmondson, A.C. (2004), 'Psychological safety, trust, and learning in organizations: a group-level lens', in R.M. Kramer and K.S. Cook (eds), *Trust and Distrust in Organizations: Dilemmas and Approaches*, New York: Russell Sage Foundation, pp. 239–72.

Edwards, M.S. and J. Greenberg (2009), 'Sounding off on voice and silence', in J. Greenberg and M.S. Edwards (eds), *Voice and Silence in Organizations*, Bingley, UK: Emerald Group Publishing Limited, pp. 275–91.

Farrell, D. (1983), 'Exit, voice, loyalty, and neglect as responses to job dissatisfaction: a multidimensional scaling study', *Academy of Management Journal*, **26**, 596–607.

Goffman, E. (1959), *The Presentation of Self in Everyday Life*, New York: Doubleday.

Graham, J.W. (1986a), 'Organizational citizenship informed by political theory', paper presented at the Academy of Management meeting, Chicago, IL.

Graham, J.W. (1986b), 'Principled organizational dissent: a theoretical essay', in B.M. Staw and L.L. Cummings (eds), *Research in Organizational Behavior*, Vol. 8, Greenwich, CT: JAI Press, pp. 1–52.

Greenberg, J. and M.S. Edwards (eds) (2009), *Voice and Silence in Organizations*, Bingley, UK: Emerald Press.

Greenberg, J. and R. Folger (1983), ' Procedural justice, participation, and the fair process effect in groups and organizations,' in P.B. Paulus (ed.), *Basic Group Processes*, New York: Springer-Verlag, pp. 235–56.

Harlos, K.P. (2001), 'When organizational voice systems fail: More on the deaf-ear syndrome and frustration effects', *Journal of Applied Behavioral Science*, **37**, 324–42.

Harvey, J.B. (1974), 'The Abilene paradox: the management of agreement', *Organizational Dynamics*, **3**, 63–80.

Henriksen, K. and E. Dayton (2006), 'Organizational silence and hidden threats to patient safety', *Health Services Research*, **41**, 1539–54.

Hirschman, A.O. (1970), *Exit, Voice and Loyalty: Responses to Declines in Firms, Organizations and States*, Cambridge, MA: Harvard University Press.

Janis, I.L. (1972), *Groupthink: Psychological Studies of Policy Decisions and Fiascoes*, Boston: Houghton Mifflin.

Katz, D. (1964), 'The motivational basis of organizational behavior,' *Behavioral Science*, **9**, 131–46.

Katz, D., F. Allport and M.B. Jenness (1931), *Students' Attitudes: A Report of the Syracuse University Reaction Study*, Oxford: Craftsman Press.

Kish-Gephart, J., J.R. Detert, L.K. Trevino and A.C. Edmondson (2009), 'Silenced by fear: psychological, social, and evolutionary drivers of voice behavior at work,' in B.M. Staw and A.P. Brief (eds), *Research in Organizational Behavior*, Vol. 29, Greenwich, CT: JAI Press, pp. 163–93.

Kohler, W. (1992), *Gestalt Psychology*, New York: Liveright Publishing.

Kolarska, L. and H. Aldrich (1980), 'Exit, voice, and silence: consumers' and managers' responses to organizational decline', *Organization Studies*, **1**, 41–58.

Kowalski, R.M. (1996), 'Complaints and complaining: functions, antecedents, and consequences', *Psychological Bulletin*, **119**, 179–96.

Latané, B. and J.M. Darley (1968), 'Group inhibition of bystander intervention in emergencies', *Journal of Personality and Social Psychology*, **10**, 215–21.

LePine, J.A. and L. Van Dyne (1998), 'Predicting voice behavior in work groups', *Journal of Applied Psychology*, **83**, 853–68.

Miceli, M.P. and J.P. Near (1992), *Blowing the Whistle: The Organizational and Legal Implications for Companies and Employees*, New York: Lexington Books.

Milliken, F.J., E.W. Morrison and P.F. Hewlin (2003), 'An exploratory study of employee silence: issues that employees don't communicate upward and why', *Journal of Management Studies*, **40**, 1453–76.
Morrison, E.W. (2011), 'Employee voice behavior: integration and directions for future research', *Academy of Management Annals*, **5**, 373–412.
Morrison, E.W., and F.J. Milliken (2000), 'Organizational silence: a barrier to change and development in a pluralistic world', *Academy of Management Review*, **25**, 706–25.
Morrison, E.W., S.L. Wheeler-Smith and D. Kamdar (2011), 'Speaking up in groups: a cross-level study of group voice climate and voice', *Journal of Applied Psychology*, **96**, 183–91.
Near, J.P. and M.P. Miceli (1985), 'Organizational dissidence: the case of whistle-blowing', *Journal of Business Ethics*, **4**, 1–16.
Noelle-Neumann, E. (1974), 'The spiral of silence: a theory of public opinion', *Journal of Communication*, **24**, 43–51.
Noelle-Neumann, E. (1993), *The Spiral of Silence: Public Opinion – Our Social Skin*, Chicago, IL: University of Chicago Press.
Olson-Buchanan, J.B. and W.R. Boswell (2002), 'The role of employee loyalty and formality in voicing discontent', *Journal of Applied Psychology*, **87**, 1167–74.
Organ, D.W. (1988), *Organizational Citizenship Behavior: The Good Soldier Syndrome*, Lexington, MA: Lexington Books.
Organ, D.W. (1990), 'The motivational basis of organizational citizenship behavior', in L.L. Cummings and B.M. Staw (eds), *Research in Organizational Behavior*, Vol. 12, Greenwich, CT: JAI Press, pp. 43–72.
Peirce, E., C.A. Smolinski and B. Rosen (1998), 'Why sexual harassment complaints fall on deaf ears', *Academy of Management Executive*, **12**, 41–54.
Piderit, S.K. and S.J. Ashford (2003), 'Breaking silence: tactical choices women managers make in speaking up about gender-equity issues', *Journal of Management Studies*, **40**, 1477–502.
Pinder, C.C. and K.P. Harlos (2001), 'Employee silence: quiescence and acquiescence as response to perceived injustice', in G.R. Ferris (ed.), *Research in Personnel and Human Resources Management*, Vol. 20, Greenwich, CT: JAI Press, pp. 331–69.
Podsakoff, P.M., S.B. MacKenzie, J.B. Paine and D.G. Bachrach (2000), 'Organizational citizenship behaviors: a critical review of the theoretical and empirical literature and suggestions for future research', *Journal of Management*, **26**, 513–63.
Premeaux, S.F. and A.G. Bedeian (2003), 'Breaking the silence: the moderating effects of self-monitoring in predicting speaking up in the workplace', *Journal of Management Studies*, **40**, 1537–62.
Roberts, K.H. and C.A. O'Reilly (1974), 'Failures in upward communication in organizations: three possible culprits', *Academy of Management Journal*, **17**, 205–15.
Roethlisberger, F.J. (1941), *Management and Morale*, Cambridge, MA: Harvard University Press.
Rosen, S. and A. Tesser (1970), 'On reluctance to communicate undesirable information: the MUM effect', *Sociometry*, **33**, 253–63.
Rusbult, C.E., I.M. Zembrodt and L.K. Gunn (1982), 'Exit, voice, loyalty, and neglect: responses to dissatisfaction in romantic involvements', *Journal of Personality and Social Psychology*, **43**, 1230–42.
Rusbult, C.E., D. Farrell, G. Rogers and A.G. Mainous (1988), 'Impact of exchange variables on exit, voice, loyalty, and neglect: an integrative model of responses to declining job satisfaction', *Academy of Management Journal*, **31**, 599–627.
Spencer, D.G. (1986), 'Employee voice and employee retention', *Academy of Management Journal*, **29**, 488–502.
Stone, C.B., A. Coman, A.D. Brown, J. Koppel and W. Hirst (2012), 'Toward a science of silence: the consequences of leaving a memory unsaid', *Perspectives on Psychological Science*, **7**, 39–53.
Tangirala, S. and R. Ramanujam (2008a), 'Employee silence on critical work issues: the cross level effects of procedural justice climate', *Personnel Psychology*, **61**, 37–68.
Tangirala, S. and R. Ramanujam (2008b), 'Exploring nonlinearity in employee voice: the effects of personal control and organizational identification', *Academy of Management Journal*, **51**, 1189–203.
Tangirala, S. and R. Ramanujam (2009), 'The sound of loyalty: voice or silence', in J. Greenberg and M.S. Edwards (eds), *Voice and Silence in Organizations*, Bingley, UK: Emerald Group Publishing Limited, pp. 203–24.
Tedeschi, J.T., B.R. Schlenker and T.V. Bonoma (1971), 'Cognitive dissonance: private ratiocination or public spectacle?', *American Psychologist*, **26**, 685–95.
Thibaut, J. and L.Walker (1978), 'A theory of procedure', *California Law Review*, **66**, 541–66.
Turner, M.E. and A.R. Pratkanis (1998), 'Twenty-five years of groupthink theory and research: lessons from the evaluation of a theory', *Organizational Behavior and Human Decision Processes*, **73**, 105–15.
Vakola, M. and D. Bouradas (2005), 'Antecedents and consequences of organisational silence: an empirical investigation', *Employee Relations*, **27**, 441–58.

Van Dyne, L. and J.A. LePine (1998), 'Helping and voice extra-role behaviors: evidence of construct and predictive validity', *Academy of Management Journal*, **41**, 108–19.

Van Dyne, L., J.W. Graham and R.M. Dienesch (1994), 'Organizational citizenship behavior: construct redefinition, measurement, and validation', *Academy of Management Journal*, **37**, 765–802.

Van Dyne, L., L.L. Cummings and J.M. Parks (1995), 'Extra-role behaviors: in pursuit of construct and definitional clarity (a bridge over muddied waters)', in L.L. Cummings and B.M. Staw (eds), *Research in Organizational Behavior*, Vol. 17, Greenwich, CT: JAI Press, pp. 215–86.

Van Dyne, L., S. Ang and I.C. Botero (2003), 'Conceptualizing employee silence and employee voice as multidimensional constructs', *Journal of Management Studies*, **40**, 1359–92.

Whiting, S.W., P.M. Podsakoff and J.R. Pierce (2008), 'Effects of task performance, helping, voice, and organizational loyalty on performance appraisal ratings', *Journal of Applied Psychology*, **93**, 125–39.

PART II

ACTORS

9   Employers and voice
Peter Holland

INTRODUCTION

Despite the extensive research in recent times on the nature of employee voice, little attention has been given to the changing dynamics of voice from the employers' perspective. Considering employers are central to voice, set the agenda and develop and maintain the culture and values that surround voice, it seems unusual that this perspective has not received more attention. This chapter attempts to address this issue by exploring the developments of voice in the workplace from the employer perspective. The chapter begins with an exploration of the theoretical perspectives around participation from an employer point of view. The chapter then examines the contemporary workplace and provides an overview of the key changes that have taken place over the past three decades, including work deregulation, and the rise of human resource management strategies. This is followed by an analysis of the various types of voice that an employer can adopt and the potential benefits and drawbacks associated with each. Finally, the chapter analyses why a strategic fit between voice and management style is critical in the context of key employment indicators such as job satisfaction, turnover and trust. The features of organizations are also examined, including sector and size, country and regulations as key factors in influencing the style and structure of voice systems adopted by management. The chapter concludes with a brief analysis of future issues to consider in the development of efficient and effective voice systems.

THEORETICAL PERSPECTIVES ON PARTICIPATION IN THE CONTEMPORARY WORKPLACE: AN EMPLOYER PERSPECTIVE

There has been much theoretical debate around the nature and extent of workplace participation over the past three decades as the global economy has undergone radical change. Ramsay's (1983; 1977) cycles of control theory argues that management interest in employee representation is linked to the (perceived) strength, power and influence of labour (unions) within the workplace. As (perceived) union power increases, management will see alternative voice mechanisms as a means to dissipate or negate union influence. If union power is seen to be in decline, as is currently the case in Anglo-American countries, managerial interest in these alternative arrangements will dissipate. As such, management interest in participation is part of a management strategy to maintain control in the workplace, and only occurs when the legitimacy of management is threatened (Marchington, 1994). Under these conditions there is little change in the nature of decision-making in the workplace. Ramsay (1983; 1977) argued, therefore, that the accommodation of participation by management is superficial and temporary rather than a manifestation of employer commitment to greater employee participation.

Critics of the cycles of control thesis (for example, Marchington et al., 1993; Marchington 1992) argue that from the 1980s, labour and particularly trade union power declined around the world, yet interest in participation increased (Millward et al., 2000; Boxall and Purcell, 2011). The emergent theory was one based upon 'waves of intent' (after wave theory). Wave theory argues that there is not a set of common circumstances that initiate management interest in participation. Waves of participation can take a variety of forms and have varying impact and longevity (Marchington, 1994). The impetus for increased interest in participation from the 1980s, according to Marchington (2005), was increasing global competitiveness, which necessitated that management seek continuous improvements in products, services and work organization. In addition the shift from a manufacturing to a knowledge and service-based global economy has increased the focus on the key resource of human capital, and ways to engage these human resources (Boxall and Purcell, 2011). This imperative has led to the development of a variety of approaches by management seeking to motivate employees and harness their creativity and productivity through cooperative practices. Such practices include information-sharing, a variety of consultation processes, financial participation, decision-making involvement and new and more flexible patterns of work. Marchington (2005) argues that unlike cycles of control theory, wave theory is concentrated at the micro or organizational level. The focus on the enterprise level therefore explains the diversity and longevity of various forms of participation within organizations.

To take the analysis of participation beyond the seemingly intractable dichotomy of wave and cycle theories, Poole et al. (1999) developed the 'favourable conjunctures' model. This model posits that when a combination of favourable conditions occurs at both the macro and micro levels, increased participation will occur. Poole et al. (1999) isolated four major factors that explain the level of participation:

- macro conditions (economic conditions and culture);
- the strategic choices of actors (at the level of the firm);
- the power of actors (management and trade unions); and
- organizational structures and processes (linked to increased organizational de-layering and need for devolved expertise and decision-making within the organization).

At the macro level, increased competition and deregulation have led to greater attention being directed toward the link between firm performance and internal resources and relationships (Kepes and Delery, 2007; Lansbury and Wailes, 2003). Lindbeck and Snower (1996) note that since the mid-1980s, an increasing trend towards workplace restructuring, through a reduction in the division of labour (increased flexibility) and the breakdown of hierarchies through progressive de-layering of the workplace, has devolved decision-making throughout the organization. This situation is also linked to shifts in the global economy from a manufacturing base (focused on fixed assets) to a knowledge and service employment-based economy (focused on human resources). Blyton and Turnbull (1998) argue that these organizational changes also reflect increased levels of education and technological sophistication. As such, specialist knowledge is increasingly held away from the apex of the organization, requiring management to develop more cooperative approaches that secure increased commitment from skilled and essential employees to generate sustainable competitive advantage within their sector.

These favourable conjunctures for increased cooperation in the workplace are closely linked to the development of human resource management strategies, which emphasize direct communication and relationship building within the firm as having a considerable effect on the organization's sustained competitiveness (Boxall and Purcell, 2011; Holland et al., 2011). Within this context the approach to developing employee voice is critical in terms of engaging an increasingly sophisticated workforce. Consequently, Blyton and Turnbull (1998: 237) argue that the difference in the modern form of participation is a planned shift in focus away from power and control toward strategies that engage employees as a means to build commitment and sustainable competitive advantage.

It is important to note that increased competition has not only brought about a reassessment of the employment relationship and the value of participation by management. Trade unions have also changed their approach, with evidence (Holland et al., 2011; Pyman et al., 2009) indicating that the presence of trade unions may be conducive to the development of human resource management processes such as high performance work systems (HPWS), even if unions themselves are not involved. Thus, employee involvement and participation through alternative means is not necessarily overtly anti-union. Such strategies can in fact provide employees with increased security through the sustained economic performance of the firm. This scenario may go a long way to explaining the apparent paradox in the erosion of union power on the one hand, and increasing interest in participative workplace practices on the other (Boxall and Purcell, 2011).

The Importance of Context

The importance of management in shaping and encouraging voice channels in this changing landscape cannot be underestimated, and is reinforced by empirical research examining the rationale for employers' choices of voice regimes. Willman et al. (2006) argue that employers' adoption decisions are contingent upon their perceptions of the net benefits of voice to the firm. Until this point the focus has been on internal organizational factors, but theoretical and empirical work from an institutional perspective demonstrates the importance of external factors in influencing workplace processes and systems. In particular, the national employment relations context is critical in any understanding of the nature of voice (Hyman, 2004; Kaufman, 2004). Brewster et al. (2007) argue that organizational size and industrial sector as well as national systems are also key determinants of employers' choices. For example, Scandinavian countries and Germany are characterized by strong labour market institutions and governance systems while this is less so in other advanced market economies (AMEs), such as the Anglo-American economies of the USA, the UK and Australia. Further, UK evidence indicates that these external factors constrain and facilitate voice practices (Marginson et al., 2009). These studies illustrate the importance of management style, attitudes to the workplace and sectoral context in determining the nature and characteristics of employee voice arrangements, and are important factors in exploring the link between employee voice arrangements and the ways in which managers shape and construct voice for maximum impact. As Table 9.1 indicates there are many issues, situations and

Table 9.1   Factors influencing the adoption of voice systems

Factors shaping voice	Voice culture	
	Promoting voice	Impeding voice
Policy framework and financial system	Coordinated market economies	Liberal market economies
	Legislation supporting workers' rights and voice	Voluntarist approach to workers and voice
	Stakeholder perspective predominant	Shareholder perspective predominant
Product market	Oligopolistic and stable product markets	Highly competitive and unstable product markets
	Long-term partnership between organizations	Market driven by contracting culture/spot markets
Technology, skills and staffing levels	Capital-intensive systems	Labour intensive systems
	High staff to customer ratios	Low staff to customer ratios
Labour markets and industrial relations	High skill levels/workers hard to replace	Low skill levels/workers easy to replace
	Strong cooperative management–union relations	Hostile management–union relations or non-union organization
Supervisory skills and management style	Employer support for high-commitment HRM	Employer not interested in high-commitment HRM
	Supervisors trained in people management skills	Supervisors not trained in people management skills
Workers' interests	High levels of commitment from workers	High levels of apathy from workers
	Anticipation of long-term careers in organization	Fragmented work, little expectation of long-term career in organization

Source: Marchington (2007).

factors promoting and impeding voice arrangements. It is management's role to assess and develop the ideal voice framework for the greatest organizational impact.

VOICE AND THE CONTEMPORARY WORKPLACE

As noted, the industrial landscape across many countries has changed significantly in the past three decades. In many AMEs a combination of an increasingly hostile political and legal environment towards trade unions, declining union density, decentralized bargaining and the deregulation of labour markets has seen the traditional position of trade unions as the representatives of the workforce decline. In addition, the emergence of sophisticated human resource management (HRM) strategies with a focus on direct employer–employee relationships has major implications for communication strategies in the workplace. These changes have also had a significant effect on the structure of employment relations and more specifically on employee voice (Bryson, 2004), stimulating academic interest in the variety of types of voice emerging from this new landscape.

From a strategic perspective, employee voice arrangements are central to the development of employee involvement and participation and form part of an organization's human resource policies and practices (Tzafir et al., 2004). Employee voice arrangements, as part of a bundle of HR practices, have been linked to improved organizational performance (Boxall and Purcell, 2011). Lepak and Snell (2007) suggest that a strategic 'fit' between HRM policies and practices around key factors such as voice is necessary to ensure the development of a high quality relationship between employees and management. Therefore, it is seen as increasingly important for management to develop appropriate HRM policies to support voice practices if they want to engage employees, increase organizational commitment and performance, and effectively manage and develop the employment relationship (Marchington, 2005; Bryson, 2004).

A significant implication of these structural and attitudinal changes has been the marginalization of unions, the decline of the traditional voice model (Freeman and Medoff, 1984) and the emergence of alternative voice mechanisms. However, the need remains (and arguably has increased) for ongoing quality communication and relationship building between management and employees. With the shift of decision-making in the employment relationship to the workplace, and increased direct communications between employers and employees, attention is increasingly being given to the changing landscape of employee voice. Whilst much of the research has focused on the implications for employees in this changing environment, less attention has been focused on the implications for employers as new patterns of work and work organizations fundamentally recast the nature of employment and the employment relationship. Increasingly in this dynamic environment progressively based upon knowledge and knowledge management, employers need efficient and effective strategies to engage with and maintain a relationship with their key resources – human capital – to ensure they acquire and retain full commitment from these workers. In this context, whilst traditional voice mechanisms might be cast as the articulation of individual dissatisfaction, communication/ exchange or collective representation, a contemporary perspective would see voice in the context of the development of joint problem solving, engagement, contribution to management decision-making and as a demonstration of mutuality and cooperative relations (for example, Dundon et al., 2004; Wilkinson et al., 2004). It is therefore increasingly within management's charter and control to set the tenet, style and structures of voice in the workplace and effectively resource and manage this process within the employment relationship.

VOICE STRATEGIES: AN EMPLOYER PERSPECTIVE

What Voice?

The term 'voice' describes two-way communication between employers and employees. The contemporary focus takes the frame of reference from just raising concerns and expressing and advancing interests to facilitating employee engagement, contribution and commitment to participating in workplace decision-making and solving problems to achieve organizational goals. Employee voice is central to communication between employees and management. Traditionally 'voice' has been channelled through union recognition and representation, but this has never been the exclusive means of communication and influence at the workplace. For management, traditional voice provided a relatively stable structure where the union could be seen to represent the workforce and speak and negotiate on its behalf. However, the changing landscape of the workplace has markedly transformed the typology and structure of voice arrangements, and all have implications for management. The four categories of voice arrangements are direct, indirect union or non-union employee representation (NER) and hybrid channels. The latter are characterized by the presence of management-initiated voice arrangements and union representation (Holland et al., 2011; Bryson et al., 2007).

Direct voice

Direct voice is defined as unmediated two-way communication between employees and management. For management this provides an opportunity to develop a high commitment, consensual relationship through unmediated communication and employee involvement in workplace issues. For employees these channels of communication have the potential to increase managerial responsiveness (see Holland et al., 2011; Pyman et al., 2010; Bryson 2004). This is also important for management as it deals with the needs of an increasingly diverse workforce. As such, direct voice has the potential to allow management to engage more efficiently and effectively with employees in the absence of intermediaries, and therefore promote quality relationships between management and employees (Holland et al., 2012; Farndale et al., 2011a; Bryson 2004).

Indirect voice

Union voice is defined as communication between management and trade unions as the representative of the workforce as a whole. This is seen as the traditional approach to voice as unions provide a focus for employees. Union voice is seen as an 'independent' representative of employee interests and democratically accountable to its members (Charlwood and Terry, 2007; Wood and Fenton-O'Creevy, 2005). Unions also have at their disposal collective power or resources and sanctions for non-compliance by management, making them less susceptible to managerial influence and control (Charlwood and Terry, 2007; Wood and Fenton-O'Creevy, 2005; Wilkinson et al., 2004). It is argued therefore that union voice is potentially a superior form of voice, as unions are best placed to jointly regulate the employment relationship and to deliver procedural fairness and organizational justice (Tailby et al., 2007). Drawing on the concept of mutual gains, it has been argued that this is the most robust relationship as both parties to the employment relationship are independent and have (in theory) an equal voice. However, this does not mean they are of equal power. As Boxall and Purcell (2011) argue, this 'fostering' approach rather than a 'forcing' strategy means involving employees and/or their representatives in processes that may even result in downsizing or restructuring. Ideally, the long-term outcome is a positive-sum game. In practice this strategy needs ongoing maintenance, as Kaufman (2003) illustrated in his research on Delta Airlines, where the power imbalance was highlighted when management announced without consultation 'golden parachute' clauses for executives in the event of bankruptcy. The CEO acknowledged the negative backlash and apologized for stepping outside the process of consultation.

Non-union employee representation (NER) schemes can take a variety of forms and are generally initiated by the employer and/or the state and at a variety of levels within an organization (Tailby et al., 2007). The key features of NER are that management consult and negotiate with a group (for example, as a joint consultation committee) who represent fellow employees in dealing with management over issues of mutual concern. NER schemes are usually initiated by management, who set the agenda around employment-related issues. For employees, NER is expected to provide a platform for employee voice and to influence management decision-making. For management such a forum provides the opportunity to develop a consultative and cooperative process with employees and gauge the 'climate' of the workforce on issues that may cause friction between management and the employees (Taras and Kaufman, 2006).

Hybrid voice
Hybrid voice describes a situation where both direct and indirect (usually union) voice communication channels operate in parallel and have the potential to complement each other. Evidence of the complementarity of voice channels (see Boxall and Purcell, 2011; Wood and Fenton-O'Creevy, 2005; Bryson et al., 2004) raises the opportunity for the development of sophisticated human resource management strategies which emphasize the 'role and contribution of employees' and a platform (and potentially a revitalization strategy) for unions in the workplace, with management viewing unions as a complementary communication channel and partner, and as providing one element of a 'bundle' of unified voice mechanisms for the effective management of employee relations (Holland et al., 2011; Bryson, 2004).

Potential Problems and Pitfalls with Each Voice Strategy for Management

As has been established, voice is a central part of an organization's communication strategies and fundamental to the decision to implement a successful voice system is an understanding of the potential problems and pitfalls inherent within each approach. This knowledge allows management to better understand what resources it has to invest when determining which system to adopt. Getting the right voice system is also important when looking at the organization as whole, as Marchington (2007:142) argues:

> Voice is probably the area in HRM where tensions between the organisation and workers' goals and between shareholders' and stakeholders' views are the most apparent, because it connects with the question of managerial prerogatives and social legitimacy.

Direct voice appears best suited to a contemporary workplace. Management has a direct communication relationship with the workforce and can identify issues promptly and deal with them (Bryson, 2004). Equally, direct voice allows management to 'tap' into the workforce as a source of knowledge and therefore a source of competitive advantage (Boxall and Purcell, 2011). Underlying this is the emphasis on utilizing labour to its full capacity. However, this also means the development of a human resource management system that focuses on building and maintaining a high level of communication, commitment and engagement between the parties (Cox et al., 2006). To ensure an ongoing fit requires continued investment in the voice system. In other words, a direct voice system needs to be proactively managed and resourced. Underpinning this relationship is the development of shared mutual interest in ensuring that organizational goals are achieved

(Boxall and Purcell, 2011). A further challenge to the effectiveness of direct voice is that its capacity to transform the power relations in an organization is considerably weaker than union voice (Marchington, 2005). This is because direct voice systems lack sanctions for non-compliance, collective power and access to independent sources of advice or assistance (see Kaufman, 2003). These are also issues for NER systems and as research shows non-union voice mechanisms are more susceptible to managerial prerogative, influence and control (Terry, 1999; Wilkinson et al., 2004). This can potentially negate the benefits of direct voice and NER systems, as employees increasingly see a relationship that is not genuine but is built on rhetoric (Marchington, 2005). This can lead to direct voice becoming an opportunity for management to replace or substitute union voice. If this is the case, the effectiveness and the potential of direct voice will decline.

The substitution thesis is a major theme in the industrial relations and human resource management literature examining the incidence and superiority of different voice regimes. Research in the USA and UK often portrays non-union employee or direct voice representation as a union avoidance strategy, suggesting that such voice regimes are more likely to be found in non-union workplaces as part of a bundle of human resource management practices acting as a substitute for unionization and collective bargaining (Fiorito, 2001; Machin and Wood, 2005). In contrast, Bryson (2004) found that non-union voice was more effective than union voice in eliciting managerial responses to employee needs. This and other studies indicate that management attitudes, style and context become critical in determining the nature, characteristics and effectiveness of non-union voice at the level of the firm. Does management afford employees a genuine right to participate in organizational decision-making? Or as Charlwood and Terry (2007) suggest, does management use information provision as a fig leaf for concealing managerial unilateralism? These are key factors that management needs to examine and continually manage in order to develop an effective direct voice strategy.

While union voice is seen as the traditional approach to communications in the workplace, the decline of unions in many AMEs suggests that the importance of this voice system is in decline. While union voice systems may be seen as less favoured by management – a result of the conflict inherent in the relationship between unions and management – this system can nonetheless provide a bulwark against unfettered managerial prerogative. It is important that management has checks and balances in place to ensure they don't damage the employment relationship. It is argued, therefore, that unions are best placed to jointly regulate the employment relationship and to deliver procedural fairness and organizational justice (Tailby et al., 2007). Freeman and Medoff (1984) argued that unions have a positive effect on organizational performance by resolving grievances, which in turn promotes employee satisfaction and reduces labour turnover and absenteeism. Importantly, union voice mechanisms can also provide a means through which workers can suggest improvements to working practices in areas such as training and occupational health and safety (Freeman and Medoff, 1984). In other words where management develops a good relationship with unions it can be to the benefit of both parties. Equally, unions can ensure that management 'does the right thing' as they raise awareness of management inadequacies and the effects of these on workers (Garcia-Serrano, 2009; Guest and Conway, 1999).

As noted, union voice reduces turnover and absenteeism by encouraging dissatisfied employees to express a voice, which is less costly than their leaving the organization (Bryson, 2004). However, as Guest and Conway (2004) and Kochan (1979) argue, unions must sustain this role as a way to retain membership, as dissatisfaction in itself will not necessarily persuade employees to join unions. Explaining this approach to the role and impact of unions in the workplace, Renaud (2002) has developed the theory of reverse causation, which argues that union membership has an overall negative impact in the workplace. Several arguments have been put forward to explain this. The first is that employees with lower job satisfaction are more likely to join a union to improve their terms and conditions (Freeman and Medoff, 1984). The second and related point is that unionized workers are more likely to be dissatisfied, because unions raise awareness of management inadequacies, resulting in more negative evaluations of the workplace which can adversely affect employee relations and satisfaction with management (Guest and Conway, 1999; Gallie et al., 1998). A third argument is that unionized jobs tend to be less attractive in both content and context, and workers become primed to look for improvements (Hammer and Avgar, 2007). This leads to a fourth argument, which Bryson (2004) has advanced: that the union increases the quantity of dissatisfied employees in the workplace by encouraging them to express a voice through the union outlet as opposed to quitting. This expression of voice may then lead to a poorer industrial relations climate and employee dissatisfaction. A final argument is that unions, by their nature, protect jobs by restricting job classifications and maintaining demarcations therefore reducing autonomy and challenge, which are key determinants of job satisfaction (Hammer and Avgar, 2007).

A hybrid system or plurality of voice mechanisms may be seen to better reflect the heterogeneous nature and needs of the contemporary workforce, based on the view that multiple channels of communication are better able to give rise to more effective employee communication, involvement and participation across a diverse spectrum of workplace issues (Bryson, 2004), thus increasing the quality of relations between employees and management. Evidence from the 'social partnership' literature demonstrates that non-union representative and direct voice measures can coexist with union voice (Budd, 2004). This coexistence is clearly illustrated in practice through the operation of works council structures in Europe (Terry, 1999). There is increasing research on the operation and effectiveness of different combinations of voice mechanisms in practice. From the development of problem-solving practices (Kersley et al., 2006; Guest et al., 2003), to high involvement work system (HIWS) (Boxall et al., 2007) and self-managing teams (Poutsma et al., 2006), management is increasingly identifying complex and complementary voice systems as part of the process for sustained competitive advantage (Poutsma et al., 2006). In addition, Kim and Kim's (2004) comparison of union and non-union representation found that unionists were more satisfied than non-members, particularly in regard to distributive justice and employee advocacy issues.

However, hybrid voice arrangements require management to invest in employee communication strategies in parallel with union-based collective consultation and bargaining, based upon the notion of mutual gains (Boxall and Purcell, 2011: 178). This entails not only increased resource investment by management, but more significantly, that management accepts a new way of working, embracing dual authority and being prepared to share a certain level of power with trade unions and the requisite trust that comes with a hybrid voice arrangement (Bryson, 2004). This may be easier said than done; management at a variety of levels within the organization may find it difficult to accept sharing power in order to develop and maintain a high quality hybrid voice system (Pyman et al., 2013). Bryson (2004) also suggests that trade union effectiveness may increase under hybrid arrangements through the provision of additional information and influence. However, if different employee voice arrangements act as a replacement (Tailby et al., 2007), or conflict or compete with each other, this is likely to adversely affect the employment relationship. It is management's responses, cultural values, style, ability and resource allocation that are critical in determining the form and operation of hybrid voice arrangements and the overall (and ongoing) relationship between management, employees and unions. What is also clear is that employers need to understand the building blocks or architecture of genuine cooperation and mutual gains. Several key elements are outlined below.

THE ARCHITECTURE OF VOICE

It is clearly important for management to identify the appropriate voice system for the organization. As the research literature indicates, HR systems geared towards increased employee involvement can increase commitment (Lepak and Snell, 2007) and the potential for organizations to achieve sustainable competitive advantage (Boxall and Purcell, 2011). Employee voice is clearly one of these key HR sub-systems and the more integrated it is with other sub-systems the more effective it is likely to be. The following sections illustrate several key underlying issues that need to be considered by management in terms of developing an appropriate environment for effective voice systems. Whilst by no means exhaustive, the importance of these factors is that they are within the control of management to develop and maintain as the employee voice system evolves alongside the organization's strategic direction.

Industrial Relations Climate and Voice

From a management perspective the industrial relations climate of the organization has been identified as a key mediating factor in the link between high performance work systems, organizational performance, and effectiveness in achieving organizational goals (Buttigieg and Gahan, 2008). A 'mutual gains' approach with employees has been shown to have positive performance effects because it creates a more cooperative industrial relations climate, enhancing both the commitment and participation of employees in organizational decision-making (see Deery and Iverson, 2005). Other outcomes that have been found to be associated with a favourable industrial relations climate include positive perceptions of organizational prestige; positive attitudes toward supervisors; reduced absenteeism, turnover and conflict; and increased innovation, customer satisfaction and service/product quality (for example, Pyman, et al., 2009; Deery and Walsh, 1999). Such a climate can thus be seen as an intervening variable in HRM and organizational performance (Boxall and Purcell, 2011). In addition, Voos (1989) found that managerial attitudes were highly correlated with the quality of the industrial relations climate. In particular, cooperative labour–management relations were associated with certain managerial attitudes towards industrial relations practices. These practices included a willingness to communicate openly and fairly with unions, an acceptance of union involvement in decision-making, and a reluctance to use human resource management practices as a substitute for unionism.

Whilst research has explored industrial relations climates, consideration of the impact of employee voice on the industrial relations climate has been limited (see Holland et al., 2012; Pyman et al., 2006). As Bryson et al. (2007) note, voice regimes represent governance mechanisms for employment communication and employers' decisions to adopt various voice types and channels are primarily driven by managerial considerations. How employers deal with employee voice, including their attitudes to unions and other forms of representation, is inextricably linked to the working environment (Holland et al., 2012; Wood and Wall, 2007), placing the industrial relations climate at the centre of employers' voice adoption decisions. A cooperative climate and collaboration can only result when management constructively engages with employees and/or unions (for example, Holland et al., 2011). A key factor in this is developing and maintaining an employment relationship built on trust. Thus the responses, actions, attitudes and behaviour of management are critical in workplace governance, employees' experiences of the workplace and the effectiveness of voice mechanisms. This is because employees are continually assessing a variety of organizational indicators of management intent. The impact of cooperative union–management relations or 'social partnerships' in Europe and the UK (for example, Oxenbridge and Brown, 2004; Bryson, 2001) has shown that cooperative relations based on a (genuine) partnership between workers and their employers can improve both the working lives of employees and organizational outcomes, particularly firm performance (Guest, 1997). Cooperative union–management relations, or a mutual gains approach, have also been linked to enhanced organizational commitment (and union loyalty), where they are underpinned by trust, consultation, and information and communication sharing (Oxenbridge and Brown, 2004).

However, in order for such strategies to be successful there must be significant investment in the development of the appropriate culture (of trust) by management and, as the research indicates, multiple and complementary embedded channels of voice (Bryson, 2004; Holland et al., 2011). This is because evidence points to a range of negative outcomes where management fails to resource these approaches to participation, including little impact on employees' satisfaction or sense of attachment, heightened workplace stress, more negative evaluations of performance, and little evidence of genuine partnership in the form of information sharing and the sharing of power (Danford et al., 2008). These outcomes led Danford et al. (2008) to question the inevitability of mutual gains and the necessity of employer/union partnerships. As Spreitzer and Mishra (1999) point out, the paradox for management lies in giving up control without losing it. This is an important point as Boxall and Purcell (2011: 178) point out:

> There is plenty of evidence that voice arrangements are no more than 'bolt-ons' which become an additional burdens on line managers who fail to provide necessary support to make them effective.

This again reinforces the point made by Ichniowski et al. (1997) and others, that voice systems underpinned by trust are critical to supporting organization climate and effective participation.

Trust, Fit and Employee Voice Arrangements

Trust is an often overlooked, but critically important, element for management in maintaining and developing relationships with employees and their representatives (see Searle et al., 2011). Trust has been found to be positively associated with a range of desired employee attitudes (for example, job satisfaction and organizational commitment) and desired work behaviours, including organizational citizenship behaviours (OCB) (Boxall and Purcell, 2011). Consequently, trust has been identified as a critical variable affecting the efficiency and performance of organizations (Searle et al., 2011). As Kiffin-Peterson and Cordrey (2003) therefore note, the management of an organization can ill afford to ignore the influence of trust on employees' attitudes and their subsequent contributions to the organization. Trust enables cooperation, and is therefore a key element in judging how employees view their relationship with management (Searle et al., 2011).

Human resource policies and practices, in particular employee voice arrangements, constitute, *inter alia*, one of an organization's institutionalized processes and principles which can influence employees' perceptions of the trustworthiness of an organization's management or the organizational climate of trust (Searle et al., 2011; Tzafrir et al., 2004). The concept of trust in the employment relationship originates from social exchange theory (Blau, 1964). In an employment context, employees reciprocate the treatment they receive from management as the employment relationship unfolds (Boxall and Purcell, 2011; Farndale et al., 2011b). Trust is also influenced by past experiences of behaviour. Therefore, trust can be contextualized in the confidence that one party to the exchange will not exploit the other's vulnerabilities. This reflects the ongoing nature of the exchange upon which the employment relationship (and by default, employee voice arrangements) are based. As Lewicki et al. (1998) have argued, trust is the basis for quality relationships, cooperation and stability.

In a strategic human resource management context, the concept of trust is built upon the need for management to develop employee commitment to organizational goals to increase organizational performance (Nichols et al., 2009). As Farndale et al. (2011b: 6) note, this is often referred to as opening the black box between human resource management and performance. Because of the dynamic nature of the employment relationship, this reciprocity has both positives and negatives. As such, the actions of management towards employees are continually evaluated and assessed by both employees and their representatives. As Lewis and Welgert (1985) argue, the actions of others imply reciprocal trust. Those actions that violate trust can create an atmosphere of distrust and consequently employees and their representatives may be less willing to develop a committed relationship with management. As Nichols et al. (2009) and Tzafrir (2005) therefore point out, trust is a key outcome variable in the relationship between human resource practices and employee attitudes to management, and is likely to be influenced by communication channels, and the degree of involvement or participation of employees in organizational decisions. It is therefore logical that employee voice arrangements must also be underpinned by trust in order to be effective (Tzafir et al., 2004). The quality of communication between management and employees in an organization has been shown to be a key indicator of organizational effectiveness and trust in management (Boxall and Purcell, 2011). The ability to develop trust within the employment relationship is therefore an increasingly critical aspect of the 'voice' architecture for management to focus on, in order to create a sustainable and productive employment relationship (Boxall and Purcell, 2011; Guerrero and Herrbach, 2008).

Management's choice of information sharing processes, communication channels, employee involvement and participation mechanisms will be a direct reflection of its ideology and style, and consequently will influence the level of trust between employees and management (see Dietz, 2004). Indeed, empirical research confirms the importance of 'open' communication in positively influencing trust in the employment relationship, the role of organizational communication as a predictor of trust and the positive influence of a joint problem solving approach on trust between management and employees (Tzafir et al., 2004). With respect to trust and employee voice arrangements, Boxall and Purcell (2011: 187) have argued that the level of managerial sincerity and the degree of responsiveness that is generated are critical factors in the effectiveness of voice arrangements. Different types of employee voice arrangements will be underpinned by different levels of managerial sincerity and responsiveness due to their very nature and different management styles (Boxall and Purcell, 2011).

Embedded Voice

An important dimension to the nature of voice and its development in the workplace is proposed by Cox et al. (2006) in terms of how embedded voice is in the workplace. As Boxall and Purcell (2011) point out, the crucial variables in the success of voice arrangements are *how*, and to *what extent*, management and in particular line managers genuinely support employee involvement. In other words, simply deciding what voice is appropriate is only the first step. This point is reinforced by Marchington (2007), who argues that tension between employee and management views is most apparent in terms of the rhetoric and reality of how voice is implemented and maintained (see also Bowen and Ostroff, 2004). As Marchington (2007) argues, if employees are unwilling to use voice mechanisms because of the style of management and poor climate of trust or because suggestions are not implemented or are seen as challenging managerial prerogatives, then any advantage from such processes will be lost.

To help understand these factors, Cox et al. (2006) developed two measures of embeddedness – breadth and depth. Breadth describes the amount of participation systems in the workplace. Marchington (2005) makes the point that like the concept of 'bundles' or internal fit of human resource practice (see Boxall and Purcell, 2011), the more combinations of integrated and complementary practices there are in the work environment, the more effective the voice arrangements, as they reinforce each other. Depth is a measure of the embeddedness of the particular practice within the workplace, as determined by the regularity, significance, control and power accorded to employee voice. It is linked to the level of importance of the matters that employees can raise within these processes (Cox et al., 2006; Marchington, 2005). In combination these factors provide a more effective insight into the participatory and involvement practices within an organization (Cox et al., 2006; Marchington, 2005) and a useful insight or litmus test for management in terms of how effectively they manage and share power within the voice systems they develop and the industrial relations climate that emerges. Research (Holland et al., 2011; Purcell and Georgiadis, 2007; Bryson, 2004) increasingly shows that a combination of voice mechanisms working in harmony reduces conflict, increases managerial responsiveness and improves the operation of the organization (Lichen et al., 2004). These outcomes can have a significant impact upon the climate of the workplace, employee job satisfaction and trust, which are all factors in increasing employee commitment (Holland et al., 2012). From a broader HRM perspective, Marchington (2007: 241) notes that when considering the relationship between voice and the internal fit with other HRM policies and practices:

> . . . voice is an important and necessary component of HR systems, and that to be effective – in terms of employee perception and performance – it has to be embedded within the organisations and be visible to the workplace. This cannot be taken for granted because employers may be obsessed with cost reductions or restricting opportunities for workers to express their voice, in the belief that financial success can be achieved without committing themselves to an 'involving' culture (Goddard, 2004). Moreover, Cappelli and Neumark (2001) stress that because high-commitment HRM leads to increased costs, the lack of any immediate financial return could discourage employers from adopting voice regimes.

For management the important consideration is the appropriate depth and breadth of participation and timeframe. In this context, Marchington and Wilkinson (2000) have developed a useful scale to illustrate this 'escalator' of participation and provide management with a guide to the level of relationships within the workplace (see Figure 9.1).

Voice and Job Satisfaction

An important aspect of employee voice research from a management perspective is the relationship between employee voice arrangements and the individual's job satisfaction. Research indicates that employee voice is related to work behaviours, attitudes, job outcomes and organizational performance (Jones et al., 2009; Wood and Wall 2007).

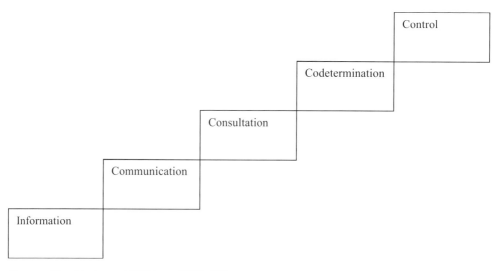

Source: Marchington and Wilkinson (2000: 343).

Figure 9.1   Escalator of participation

The relationship between job satisfaction and employee involvement is well established (Tsitsianis and Green, 2005), and job satisfaction is known to be a significant attitudinal variable associated with employee commitment and both job and organizational performance (Hammer and Avgar, 2007; Saari and Judge, 2004). Reviews of international research also reveal considerable meta-analytic evidence that job satisfaction reliably predicts a range of organizational-level outcomes such as productivity, employee turnover and absenteeism and financial performance (Jones et al., 2009). From an employee voice perspective, research indicates that workers who are empowered are more likely to have higher levels of job satisfaction, because empowerment generates intrinsic motivational factors. These same points are also defining features of employee voice, involvement and participation. Research by Holland et al. (2011) on employee voice and job satisfaction in Australia found that although the presence of both union and direct voice in the workplace is positively associated with job satisfaction, direct voice appears to be the significant voice mechanism underpinning employees' job satisfaction and the use of hybrid or multiple voice channels was not significant. As noted, this could be because these voice patterns raise managerial responsiveness.

Voice and Performance

Like all organizational investments, voice systems have to be evaluated. When attempting to assess the impact and effect on organizational performance or the business case (particularly financial), realistically it is hard to measure specific systems in isolation. As Marchington and Wilkinson (2005) point out, what are the appropriate measures – financial, attitudinal or level of cooperation? However, as Kaufman (2003: 183) notes, whilst the motivations for such systems may be varied, at the end of the day they have to affect the bottom line in 90 per cent of organizations or they are dead. To be effective voice needs to be involved in the 'core' business. In undertaking in-depth case study research of Delta Airlines, Kaufman (2003) identified several key outcomes – both positive and negative – including more effective but slower decision-making, (expensive) running costs and uncertain pay-offs. However, in terms of non-financial returns, Kaufman (2003) showed that these systems 'energized' employees, and that increased information and communication flows were seen as a major benefit that improved the decision-making process and forced management to be more effective. From an employee relations perspective these factors help reduce conflict. Underpinning this is what Kaufman identified as trust or mutual gains, where despite some setbacks management and employees have worked together and shared the rewards of cooperation.

Research by Dundon et al. (2004) found similar results with employee voice having three positive outcomes on the organization. First, valuing the contribution of employee involvement; second, evidence of improved performance measured as productivity, individual performance, lower absenteeism and the development of new business; third, an improvement in managerial systems through increased understanding, information and employee ideas. Although Wilkinson et al. (2004) do note that the relationship between voice and outcomes remains problematic in terms of isolating voice from other HR practices.

Exploring organizations through an analysis of tangible and intangible outcomes (or a balanced scorecard) is likely to provide a more in-depth and effective picture of the impact of voice systems. However, as Kaufman (2003) points out, whilst such systems provided a positive impact at Delta Airlines, these systems have to be assessed according to a case-by-case cost/benefit analysis in order to evaluate their suitability for each organization.

FUTURE ISSUES

The issues developed in this chapter have several implications for both management and researchers. Given the nature of the contemporary workforce and the centrality of voice in communication and engaging with this workforce, the appropriate voice 'fit' is fundamental to the quality of the employment relationship. What this highlights from a management perspective is the need for line managers and human resource managers, as the focal point for developing and maintaining voice arrangements, to support and encourage these processes. For senior management it is critical that the appropriate resources are allocated to developing and sustaining effective voice arrangements. For researchers, the deregulation of labour markets, globalization and the emergence of human resource management practices has provided a fertile area of research. Of particular interest in the future will be how effective the mutual gains philosophy will be and what will be the benefits and hindrances to the development of these practices. For example, whilst the development of hybrid voice mechanisms in Europe is supported by EU directives, in Australia, Holland et al. (2012) found no significant development of these work patterns and practices. This indicates that employers and HR managers may only consider the legitimacy of this form of arrangement where supported by legislation. Without such support, there appears limited vision by management on its own that a hybrid or dual voice strategy could form part of a sophisticated HRM strategy, providing for increased cooperation, reciprocity and trust in the employment relationship. The benefits of such a strategy may be manifest in a consensual relationship between unions and line managers, who typically deal with day-to-day employee relations and HRM issues. It may still be the case that both sides are too entrenched in the old models of conflict and/or that management (that is, HR managers and line managers) is not sophisticated enough to create a mutual investment employment relationship to maximize individual, team/group and organizational outcomes.

CONCLUSION

Managers must be increasingly cognizant of the fit between employee voice arrangements and management style as a means of building organizations that comprise committed, engaged and high-performing employees. The research across a wide range of aspects associated with employee voice arrangements including job satisfaction, trust, turnover and OCB, indicates a positive relationship where genuine and responsive voice arrangements have been developed. This is found to result in a more effective workplace and industrial relations climate. However, this can only be done through developing and building strategies and structures that allow employees to meaningfully and formally contribute to, and participate in, problem solving and workplace decision-making. In addition it also means management being prepared to invest resources in these voice arrangements and genuinely sharing some control and power with the workforce and their representatives (trade unions) to build a mutually supportive employment relationship. The danger is, as Charlwood and Terry (2007) point out, that if management does not afford employees a genuine right to participate in organizational decision-making, voice arrangements may just be seen as a fig leaf concealing managerial unilateralism, and will be seen by employees as no more than rhetoric. As Spreitzer and Mishra (1999) point out the paradox for management lies in giving up control without losing it. It is therefore important for management to develop building blocks of voice that are resourced and reviewed to ensure their relevance and effectiveness.

REFERENCES

Blau, M.P. (1964), *Exchange and Power in Social Life*, New York: Wiley.
Blyton, P. and P. Turnbull (1998), *The Dynamics of Employee Relations*, 2nd edn, Basingstoke: Palgrave Macmillan.
Bowen, D. and C. Ostroff (2004), 'Understanding HRM-firm performance linkages: the role of the "strength" of HRM systems', *Academy of Management Review*, **29**, 203–21.
Boxall, P. and J. Purcell (2011), *Strategy and Human Resource Management*, 3rd edn, Basingstoke: Palgrave Macmillan.
Boxall, P., J. Purcell and P. Wright (2007), *The Oxford Handbook of Human Resource Management*, Oxford: Oxford University Press.
Brewster, C., R. Croucher, G. Wood and M. Brookes (2007), 'Collective and individual voice: convergence in Europe?', *International Journal of Human Resource Management*, **18** (7), 1246–62.
Bryson, A. (2001), 'Union effects on managerial and employee perceptions of employee relations in Britain', Future of Trade Unions in Modern Britain Programme, Leverhulme Trust, Centre for Economic Performance, London School of Economics: London, April, pp. 1–59.
Bryson, A. (2004), 'Managerial responsiveness to union and non-union worker voice in Britain', *Industrial Relations*, **43** (1), 213–41.
Bryson, A. (2005), 'Union effects on employee relations in Britain', *Human Relations*, **58** (9), 1111–39.
Bryson, A., R. Gomez and P. Willman (2004), 'The end of the affair? The decline in employers' propensity to unionise', in J. Kelly and P. Willman (eds), *Union Organisation and Activity*, London: Routledge, pp. 129–49
Bryson, A., R. Gomez, T. Kretschmer and P. Willman (2007), 'The diffusion of workplace voice and high-commitment human resource management practices in Britain, 1984–1998', *Industrial and Corporate Change*, **16** (3), 394–426
Budd, J. (2004), *Employment with a Human Face: Balancing Efficiency, Equity, and Voice*, Ithaca: Cornell University Press.
Buttigieg, D. and P. Gahan (2008), 'High performance work systems and the social context of work: the role of workplace climate', *Labour and Industry*, **19** (1–2), 1–23.
Charlwood, A. and M. Terry (2007), '21st century models of employee representation: structures, processes and outcomes', *Industrial Relations Journal*, **38** (4), 320–37.
Cox, A., S. Zagelmeyer and M. Marchington (2006), 'Embedding employee involvement and participation at work', *Human Resource Management Journal*, **16** (3), 250–67.
Danford, A., M. Richardson, P. Stewart, S. Tailby and M. Upchurch (2008), 'Partnership, high performance work systems and quality of working life', *New Technology, Work and Employment*, **23** (3), 151–66.
Deery, S.J. and R.D. Iverson (2005), 'Labour–management cooperation and its impact on organizational performance', *Industrial and Labour Relations Review*, **58** (4) (July), 588–610.
Deery, S. and J. Walsh (1999), 'The character of individualised employment relations in Australia: a model of "hard" HRM', in S. Deery and R. Mitchell (eds), *Employment Relations: Individualisation and Union Exclusion*, Sydney: The Federation Press, pp. 115–28.
Dietz, G. (2004), 'Partnership and the development of trust in British workplaces', *Human Resource Management*, **14** (1), 5–24.
Dundon, T., A. Wilkinson, M. Marchington and P. Ackers (2004), 'The meanings and purpose of employee voice', *International Journal of Human Resource Management*, **15** (6), 1149–70.
Farndale, E., J. Van Ruiten, C. Keliher and V. Hope-Hailey (2011a), 'The influence of perceived employee

voice on organizational commitment; an exchange perspective', *Human Resource Management*, **50** (1), 113–29.

Farndale, E., V. Hope-Hailey and C. Kelliher (2011b), 'High commitment performance management: the role of justice and trust', *Personnel Review*, **10** (1), 5–23.

Fiorito, J. (2001), 'Human resource management practices and worker desires for union representation', *Journal of Labor Research*, **22**, 335–54.

Freeman, R.B. and J. Medoff (1984), *What Do Unions Do?*, New York: Basic Books.

Gallie, D., M. White, Y. Cheng and M. Tomlinson (1998), *Restructuring the Employment Relationship*, Oxford: Clarendon Press.

Garcia-Serrano, C. (2009), 'Job satisfaction, union membership and collective bargaining', *European Journal of Industrial Relations*, **15** (1), 91 111.

Guerrero, S. and O. Herrbach (2008), 'The affective underpinnings of psychological contract fulfilment', *Journal of Managerial Psychology*, **23** (1), 4–17.

Guest, D. (1997), 'Human resource management and performance: a review and research agenda', *International Human Resource Management*, **8** (3), 263–76.

Guest, D. and N. Conway (1999), 'Peering into the black hole: the downside of the new employment relations in the UK', *British Journal of Industrial Relations*, **37** (3), 367–89.

Guest, D. and N. Conway (2004), 'Exploring the paradox of unionised workers dissatisfaction', *Industrial Relations Journal*, **35** (2), 102–21.

Guest, D., J. Miche, N. Conway and M. Sheehan (2003), 'Human resource management and performance', *British Journal of Industrial Relations*, **41** (2), 291–314.

Hammer, T.H. and A. Avgar (2007), 'The impact of unions on job satisfaction, organizational commitment, and turnover', in J.T. Bennett and B.E. Kaufman (eds), *What Do Unions Do?*, New Brunswick: Transaction, pp. 346–72.

Holland, P., A. Pyman, B. Cooper and J. Teicher (2009), 'The development of alternate voice mechanisms in Australia: the case of joint consultation', *Economic and Industrial Democracy*, **30** (1), 67–92.

Holland, P., A. Pyman, J. Teicher and B. Cooper (2011), 'Employee voice and job satisfaction in Australian: the centrality of direct voice', *Human Resource Management*, **50** (1), 95–111

Holland, P., B. Cooper, A. Pyman and J. Teicher (2012), 'Trust in management: the role of employee voice arrangements and perceived managerial opposition to unions', *Human Resource Management Journal*, **22** (4), 377–91.

Hyman, R. (2004), 'Where next for partnership?', in M. Stuart and M. Martinez Lucio (eds), *Partnership and Modernization in Employment Relations*, London: Routledge, pp. 251–64.

Ichniowski, C., K. Shaw and G. Prennushi (1997), 'The effects of human resource management practices on productivity: a study of steel finishing lines', *American Economic Review*, **87** (3), 291–313.

Jones, M.K., R.J. Jones, P.L. Latreille and P.J. Sloane (2009), 'Training, job satisfaction and workplace performance in Britain: evidence from WERS 2004', *Labour*, **23** (1), 139–75.

Kaufman, B. (2003), 'High level employee involvement at Delta', *Human Resource Management*, **42** (2), 175–90.

Kaufman, B. (2004), *Theoretical Perspectives on Work and the Employment Relationship*, Champaign, IL: Industrial Relations Research Association.

Kepes, S. and J. Deler (2007), 'HRM systems and the problem of internal fit', in P. Boxall. J. Purcell and P. Wright (eds), *The Oxford Handbook of Human Resource Management*, Oxford: Oxford University Press, pp. 385–404.

Kersley, B., C. Alpin, J. Forth, A. Bryson, H. Bewley, G. Dix and S. Oxenbridge (2006), *Inside the Workplace: First Findings from the 2004 Workplace Employment Relations Survey*, London: Department of Trade and Industry.

Kiffin-Peterson, S. and J. Cordrey (2003), 'Trust, individualism and job characteristics as a predictor of employee preference for teamwork', *International Journal of Human Resource Management*, **14** (1), 93–116.

Kim, D. and H. Kim (2004), 'A comparison of the effectiveness of unions and non-union works councils in Korea: can non-union employee representation substitute for trade unionism?', *International Journal of Human Resource Management*, **15** (6), 1069–93.

Kochan, T.A. (1979), 'How American employees view labor unions', *Monthly Labor Review*, **102** (4), 23–31.

Lansbury, R. and N. Wailes (2003), 'The meaning of industrial democracy in an era of neo-liberalism,' in P. Gollan and G. Patmore (eds), *Partnership at Work: The Challenge of Employee Democracy*, Sydney: Pluto Press, pp. 37–46.

Lepak, D. and S. Snell (2007), 'Employment sub-system and the HR architecture', in P. Boxall, J. Purcell and P. Wright (eds), *The Oxford Handbook of Human Resource Management.* Oxford: Oxford University Press, pp. 210–30.

Lewicki, R., D. McAllister and R. Bies (1998), 'Trust and distrust: new relationships and realities', *Academy of Management*, **23** (3), 438–58.

Lewis, J. and A. Welgert (1985), 'Trust as a social reality', *Social Forces*, **63**, 65–79.

Liden, R.C., T.N. Bauer and B. Erdogan (2004), 'The role of leader-member exchange in the forming and dynamic relationship between employee and employer', in J. Coyle-Shapiro, L. Shore, S. Taylor and L. Tetrick (eds), *The Employment Relationship: Examining Psychological and Contextual Perspectives*, Oxford: Oxford University Press, pp. 226–50.

Lindbeck, A. and D. Snower (1996), 'The division of labour within firms', Institute of International Economic Studies, Stockholm University.

Machin, S. and S. Wood (2005), 'Human resource management as a substitute for trade unions in British workplaces', *Industrial and Labor Relations Review*, **58** (2), 201–18.

Marchington, M. (1992), 'Surveying the practice of joint consultation in Australia', *Journal of Industrial Relations*, **34** (4), 530–49.

Marchington, M. (1994), 'The dynamics of joint consultation', in K. Sisson (ed.), *Personnel Management*, Oxford: Blackwell, pp. 662–93.

Marchington, M. (2005), 'Employee involvement: patterns and explanation', in B. Harley, J. Hyman and P. Thompson (eds), *Participation and Democracy at Work*, Basingstoke: Palgrave Macmillan, pp. 20–37.

Marchington, M. (2007), 'Employee voice systems', in P. Boxall, J. Purcell and P. Wright (eds), *The Oxford Handbook of Human Resource Management*, Oxford: Oxford University Press, pp. 231–50.

Marchington, M. and A. Wilkinson (2000), 'Direct participation', in S. Bach. and K. Sisson (eds), *Personnel Management: A Comprehensive Guide to Theory and Practice*, Oxford: Blackwell, pp. 340–64.

Marchington, M. and A. Wilkinson (2005), 'Direct participation and involvement', in S. Bach (ed.), *Managing Human Resources*, Oxford: Blackwell, pp. 398–423.

Marchington, M., A. Wilkinson, P. Ackers and J. Goodman (1993), 'The influence of managerial relations on waves of employee involvement', *British Journal of Industrial Relations*, **31** (4), 553–76.

Marginson, P., P. Edwards, T. Edwards, A. Ferner and O. Tregaskis (2009), 'Employee representation and consultative voice in multinational companies operating in Britain', *British Journal of Industrial Relations*, **48** (1), 151–80.

Millward, N., A. Bryson and J. Forth (2000), *All Change at Work*, London: Routledge.

Nichols, T., A. Danford and A. Tasiran (2009), 'Trust, employer exposure and the employment relations', *Economic and Industrial Democracy*, **30** (2), 241–65.

Oxenbridge, S. and W. Brown (2004), 'Achieving a new equilibrium? The stability of cooperative employer–union relationships', *Industrial Relations Journal*, **35** (5), 388–402.

Poole, M., R. Lansbury and N. Wailes (1999), 'Participation and industrial democracy revisited: a theoretical perspective', in R, Markey, P. Gollan, A. Hodgkinson, A. Chouraqui and U. Veersma (eds), *Models of Employee Participation in a Changing Global Environment: Diversity and Interaction*, Aldershot: Ashgate, pp. 23–34.

Poutsma, E., P. Ligthart and U. Veersma (2006), 'The diffusion of calculative and collaborative HRM practices in European firms', *Industrial Relations*, **45** (4), 513–46.

Purcell, J. and K. Georgiadis (2007), 'Why should workers bother about employee voice?', in R.B. Freeman, P. Boxall and P. Haynes (eds), *What Workers Say: Employee Voice in the Anglo American Workplace*, Ithaca: Cornell University Press, pp. 181–97.

Pyman, A., B. Cooper, J. Teicher and P. Holland (2006), 'A comparison of the effectiveness of employee voice arrangements in Australia', *Industrial Relations Journal*, **37**, 543–59.

Pyman, A., J. Teicher, B. Cooper and P. Holland (2009), 'Union demand for unmet membership in Australia', *Journal of Industrial Relations*, **51** (1), 5–26.

Pyman, A., P. Holland, J. Teicher and B. Cooper (2010), 'Industrial relations climate, employee voice and managerial attitudes to unions: an Australian study', *British Journal of Industrial Relations*, **48**, 460–80.

Pyman, A., P. Holland, J. Teicher and B. Cooper (2013), 'The dynamics of employee voice in Australia', in J. Teicher, P. Holland and R. Gough (eds), *Australian Workplace Relations*, Cambridge: Cambridge University Press, pp. 118–36.

Ramsay, H. (1977), 'Cycles of control: participation in sociological and historical perspectives', *Sociology*, **11** (3), 481–506.

Ramsay, H. (1983), 'Evolution or cycle? Worker participation in the 1970s and 1980s', in C. Crouch and F. Heller (eds), *Organisational Democracy and Political Processes*, Chichester: John Wiley, pp. 203–25.

Renaud, S. (2002), 'Rethinking the union membership, job satisfaction relationship', *International Journal of Manpower*, **23** (2), 137–50.

Saari, L.M. and T.A. Judge (2004), 'Employee attitudes and job satisfaction', *Human Resource Management*, **43** (4), 395–407.

Searle, R., D.N. Den Hartog, A. Weibel, N. Gillespie, F. Six, T. Hatzakis and D. Skinner (2011), 'Trust in the employer: the role of high-involvement work practices and procedural justice in European organizations', *International Journal of Human Resource Management*, **22** (5), 1069–92.

Spreitzer, G. and A. Mishra (1999), 'Giving up without losing control: trust and its substitutes' effects on managers', *Group and Organization Management*, **24**, 155–87.

Tailby, S., M. Richardson, M. Upchurch, A. Danford and P. Stewart (2007), 'Partnership with and without trade unions in the UK financial services: filling or fuelling the gap?', *Industrial Relations Journal*, **38** (3), 210–28.

Taras, D. and B. Kaufman (2006), 'Non-union representation in North America: diversity, controversy and uncertain future', *Industrial Relations Journal*, **37**, 513–42.

Terry, M. (1999), 'Systems of collective representation in non-union firms in the UK', *Industrial Relations Journal*, **30** (1), 16–30.

Tsitsianis, N. and F. Green (2005), 'Can the changing nature of jobs account for national trends in job satisfaction?', *British Journal of Industrial Relations*, **43** (3), 401–29.

Tzafrir, S. (2005), 'The relationship between trust, HRM practices and firm performance', *International Journal of Human Resource Management*, **16** (9), 1600–1622.

Tzafrir, S., G. Harel, Y. Baruch and S. Dolan (2004), 'The consequences of emerging HRM practices for employees' trust in their managers', *Personnel Review*, **33** (4), 628–46.

Voos, P.B. (1989), 'The practices consonant with cooperative labour relations', *Labour Law Journal*, **40** (8), 483–90.

Wilkinson, A., T. Dundon, M. Marchington and P. Ackers (2004), 'Changing patterns of employee voice: case studies from the UK and Republic of Ireland', *Journal of Industrial Relations*, **46** (3), 298–322.

Willman, P., A. Bryson and R. Gomez (2006), 'The sound of silence: which employers choose no employee voice and why?', *Socio-Economic Review*, **4** (2), 283–99.

Wood, S.J. and M.P. Fenton-O'Creevy (2005), 'Direct involvement, representation and employee voice in UK multinationals in Europe', *European Journal of Industrial Relations*, **11** (1), 27–50.

Wood, S.J. and T.D. Wall (2007), 'Work enrichment and employee voice in human resource management-performance studies', *International Journal of Human Resource Management*, **18** (7), 1335–72.

10 The role of line managers in employee voice systems
Keith Townsend

INTRODUCTION

The notion of employee voice has been well established in the earlier chapters of this volume. Simply put, we are defining employee voice as the way employees are provided with an opportunity to have a 'say' over decisions that are made within organizations: this notion is central to most definitions (Marchington and Suter, 2013; Freeman et al., 2007) and goes beyond the simplest forms of participation which include managerial information sharing and communication. This chapter will use the term 'employee involvement' interchangeably with voice. Despite the broad body of literature written about works councils, joint consultative committees, worker participation and, more recently, a great deal of research on non-union forms of voice, questions and under-investigated areas remain (Wilkinson and Fay, 2011). One such under-investigated area concerns the role that line managers play within voice regimes.

The research suggesting that employee voice is important within organizations is well established; the argument goes that voice allows employees to have a productive inter-action with employers which results in a better understanding of what is expected from each party and, consequently, benefits will flow for either side. However, voice cannot be parachuted into an organization at an employer's whim. A culture whereby voice is embedded within the organization provides more effective, sustained results for all parties (Cox et al., 2006). Importantly, with the exception of small/medium enterprises, most employers rely upon line managers to capture and enact employee voice. Kaufman (2003: 188) argues that:

> Where the rubber really meets the road in employee involvement (EI), however, is at the middle and lower levels of management. These managers often see the least to gain and/or the most to lose from EI, so they remain non-committed or resistant. Many supervisors and middle managers can be won over to EI through strong encouragement from the top, revising performance evaluations to give weight to EI, and demonstrating that EI done the right way can benefit them too. Another portion will never abandon command and control methods and have to be replaced.

The people management decisions that are made within organizations must not be treated as 'incidental operational matters' or be left to the HR department (Storey, 1992: 26). Rather, line managers must understand their role as the link between the strategic direction of the organization and the management of staff members. Whether and how to give opportunities for voice and, equally importantly, 'hearing' that voice are key activities in organizations. Hence, while the HR department may play a vital role in developing the formal and informal mechanisms for voice, it is the managers who are closest to the employees; the line managers, who will play the critical role of facilitating voice in the organization.

The remainder of this chapter is organized as follows. First, it will outline who the line managers are and how they came to play such an important role in organizations. Second, it will recap some critical components of the employee voice debates. The third section offers an integrative review focusing on research that links line managers and employee voice as either core or peripheral to the work. Finally, we will outline areas that are under-investigated or of growing importance in relation to the study of line managers and employee voice.

LINE MANAGERS . . . WHO?

Most companies 'have a roughly similar management hierarchy' (Hamel, 2007: ix), yet within the broad body of literature, there is no consistent agreement on the role and experiences of line managers nor on how they achieve their results. Since the turn of the twenty-first century alone, numerous research articles have been published that refer to the line manager experience without offering an explicit definition of who the line manager might be (for example, Gibb, 2003; Larsen and Brewster, 2003; Cascon-Pereira et al., 2006; Perry and Kulik, 2008; Townsend et al., 2012b). However, other studies specify that the 'middle manager' is the focus of their research (for example, Conway and Monks, 2010; Fenton-O'Creevy, 2001; McCann et al., 2008). There is another body of research that explicitly states its focus on 'front-line managers' (for example, Hutchinson and Purcell, 2003; Chen and Wallace, 2011; Townsend et al., 2013). Front-line managers is a term we might assume is analogous with first-line manager (see for example, Hales, 2005) or first-tier managers (Martins, 2007; 2009), however, we need to be careful in ascertaining whether these roles are the same as, or different from, those of supervisors and team leaders (see for example, Down and Reveley, 2009; Kidd and Smewing, 2001; Yang et al., 2009; Mason, 2000; Townsend, 2004).

This chapter takes an inclusive approach to defining line managers, as suggested by Floyd and Wooldridge, which is that line managers are those who work between the strategic apex and the operating core of the organization (1999). However, this inclusive approach can be problematic if, as suggested above, researchers are not explicit and nuanced in their explanations. One would recognize quickly that multinational and transnational organizations would have a 'strategic apex' in existence in each of their operating countries, but within the larger, international organizational context these domestic strategists might not be considered the strategic apex. The context in which we speak of line management becomes very important. A manager of a multinational hotel might offer a good example. The organization has a strategic apex spanning the globe, while, for example, the Asia Pacific region will have another level of line managers that also represent a 'strategic apex'. At the workplace level, say for example the Hilton Hotel in Sydney, Australia, the hotel general manager would have a team of strategic managers to develop site-specific direction in marketing, management, finances and so on. Below them would be department heads (housekeeping, food and beverage, front office) and a series of front-line managers and supervisors. So we can see that a precise definition that goes beyond Floyd and Wooldridge's attempt is very context-specific and perhaps not useful. What would be more use is for researchers to explain precisely the role of their unit of analysis in publications.

The transition from isolated craft workers to employees herded into the modern factory is presented by Braverman (1974) as an important shift in people management. It also resulted in a substantial development of line managers. Once craft workers were brought together to perform their labour under one roof a variety of factors increased in importance, for example, enforcing regular hours and controlling the quality and the speed of the work that was being performed. There became a distinct division of labour between the devising and managing of work and the performance of the manual labour (Braverman, 1974). There are many who have provided us with an understanding of what 'management' means in theory and practice; however, for the purposes of understanding the intersection between line managers and employee voice, one writer laid the groundwork that best positions us to survey the field – Frederick Winslow Taylor.

Frederick Taylor is widely considered to be one of the most influential characters in the area of management throughout the twentieth century and it is his work that allows us to consider the role of the overseer, or in modern corporate parlance, the line manager. Taylor's view was that efficiency in the workplace came from 'knowing exactly what you want men to do, and then seeing that they do it in the best and cheapest way' (Taylor, 1911a: 21). It is this model, promoted by Taylor, that demonstrates the economic motivation of the worker, and Taylor's view was that management could become a science based on clearly defined laws and principles which would lead to the one best way to perform work tasks. In his classic work *The Principles of Scientific Management*, Taylor tells the story of Schmidt, the 'high-priced man' who was accompanied by a supervisor for his whole working day and given constant direction (Taylor, 1911b: 20–22). In fact, in his attempt to separate the planning and execution of tasks, the delegation of authority in the workplace was taken from the general manager to specialized, lower-level line managers (Wren, 1993).

Taylor's impact on the separation between the planning of tasks and the execution of tasks further reinforced the already developing tiered workforce. For some time the notion of a division of labour had been apparent (see for example Smith, 1976 [1776]; Babbage, 1835), and, indeed, a hierarchical division of labour was also well developed (Braverman, 1974). Taylor did not 'invent' or develop the science of management, but he synthesized ideas into an attempt to manage the work and the workers. While the experiments Taylor undertook at Bethlehem Steel and elsewhere have been argued to be of limited success (or worse), his system of 'scientific management' took hold in the psyche of management practitioners and theorists. Taylor advanced a line of thinking about the way people were managed that 'soon won him a strong following among capitalists and managers' (Braverman, 1974: 91). But did this new focus on the role of the supervisor have an impact on the opportunities for employee voice? In fact, most readings of Taylor's work would suggest the contrary. Taylor's legacy was to point to the motivation of the economic man, without any consideration of alternative motivations within a workforce – for example, having a say over objectionable circumstances, that is, employee voice. Taylor, it could be argued, did not provide workers with opportunities for voice; rather, his form of scientific management silenced the workers. Indeed, as Taylor tells Schmidt, the 'high-priced' man in *The Principles of Scientific Management* (Taylor, 1911b: 20–21):

> You know just as well as I do that a high-priced man has to do exactly as he's told from morning till night.

And:

> When he (the supervisor) tells you to pick up a pig and walk, you pick it up and you walk, and when he tells you to sit down and rest, you sit down. You do that right straight through the day. And what's more, no back talk. Now a high-priced man does just what he's told to do, and no back talk.

Clearly, in Taylor's view opportunities for voice with line managers were never acceptable. The presence and function of line managers has been a critical aspect of workplaces and people management for more than a century, yet the interaction of line managers and employee voice has not always been a comfortable mix.

RECENT DIRECTIONS IN LINE MANAGER RESEARCH

There is a substantial body of organizational psychology literature that examines line managers or supervisors through quantitative studies. Commonly framed according to social exchange theory (see Blau, 1964) and the norm of reciprocity (Gouldner, 1960), research has been used to explain the effects that 'leaders' have on employee attitudes to their work and positive employee behaviours or organizational citizenship behaviours. More recently, leader-member exchange (LMX) has been used to explain the quality of the exchange relationship between employees and their supervisors or line managers (Graen and Uhl-Bien, 1995). Within this broad body of work, the general consensus is that positive relationships between employees and their supervisors can have a positive impact upon job performance, job satisfaction, organizational commitment, organizational citizenship behaviours and safety (Gerstner and Day, 1997; Penley et al., 1991; Michael et al., 2006).

However, in the fields more relevant to this chapter, human resource management (HRM) and industrial relations (IR), there have been three broad themes in the recent research. Line manager research has been framed around the idea of: (1) workload intensification (typically without adequate support); (2) agency (the capacity for the LM to act independently); and (3) leverage (the LMs' capacity to leverage improved performance from their work group).

When we address the first theme of workload intensification, the development of the HRM paradigm has seen line managers taking a more central role in organizations. They are often viewed as the linchpin that enacts intended human resource management policies (Wright and Kehoe, 2008) and translates 'paper plans into operational reality' (Child and Partridge, 1982). Wall and Wood (2005) argue that line managers are at the crux of the HRM architecture and Hutchinson and Purcell (2003) suggest that effective line management is a means by which HR strategies can 'come to life' in organizations.

Yet one overwhelming image presented within the literature on line managers is that they are often the targets of organizational change through de-layering, restructuring, downsizing, heavier workloads, work intensification, broader spans of control, increased levels of performance monitoring, decreased promotion prospects and devolution of people management responsibilities from the HR or personnel department to the line manager (Balogun and Johnson, 2004; Burke and Cooper, 2000; Cameron et al., 1991; Cascio, 2002; Worrall et al., 2004; Hassard et al., 2011). Perhaps equally important is the role that line managers play as agents of change for the strategic levels of management (Huy, 2002; Gibb, 2003; Gilley et al., 2001). It is here that line managers inform employees of direction, but the way in which line managers listen to the employees is not adequately understood.

Typically, responsibilities for managing the HRM and employment or IR aspects of the organization have been directed from the executive level or HR department towards the lower level line managers (Guest and King, 2001). However, an increasing body of literature considers a shift of HR toward the line managers (see for example, Cunningham and Hyman, 1999; Cascon-Pereira et al., 2006; Hutchinson and Wood, 1995; McGovern et al., 1997, McConville and Holden, 1999; Renwick, 2003). The shift of HR responsibilities to line managers is often referred to as devolution and problems arise in organizations where there are tensions between the HR departments and the line managers. Underlying these tensions include the line managers' view that HR policies are fine in theory but hard in practice, and the discrepancy between the lack of immediacy by HR departments and the requirement of immediacy on the front line. Any resistance on the part of line managers to HR policy will undermine or at least dilute the translation of policy into effective practice (Thornhill and Saunders, 1998). Therefore, proponents of the devolution thesis suggest that being given more explicit responsibility for HRM will increase line managers' 'ownership' over these issues, hence increasing their commitment to integrating organizational HR approaches with workplace or workgroup HR practices (Marchington and Wilkinson, 2012). This body of work is not without its critics. As Renwick points out, much of the research that indicates positive outcomes when HR is shifted to line managers comes from 'excellent firms' which invest resources and support into their employees and where good outcomes are to be expected (Renwick, 2008: 234). Ownership over HR also means ownership over employee voice.

This brings us to some overlap with the second theme, that of line manager agency. Within the proponents of devolution camp, there is often an assumption that line managers will implement policies exactly in the ways intended by HR specialists or, as Marchington and Grugulis (2000) put it, act as 'robotic conformists'. As HRM is seen as a component of all managerial jobs (read: all 'line manager jobs'), it is one particular group of line managers – the front-line managers – who generally have the responsibility for the delivery of HRM to the greatest number of workers. Employees' perceptions of HRM, then, are of those practices that are typically applied by front-line managers (Purcell and Hutchinson, 2007). Our understanding of people in the workplace is sufficiently sophisticated for us to know that people are not always committed to 'one view' nor to 'one course of action'. Individuals promoted to line manager positions will still have minds of their own, free will and a capacity for decision-making in their own best interests. Line managers – just like their subordinate employees – maintain some ability to actively determine the level of engagement in their work.

Although HR issues remain the purview of HR departments, there are many shared responsibilities and HR policy can be different from the messages and practices that filter through to and are enacted on the shop floor (Townsend et al., 2012b). Line managers seem to think that they are most heavily involved in motivation and morale of staff, team briefings and communication, health and safety, identifying training needs, employee selection and performance appraisals (Watson et al., 2006). Commonly, senior managers and HR departments see lack of the requisite skills as one of the greatest problems for line managers. Perhaps not surprisingly line managers themselves less often identify their own lack of skill as a problem (Watson et al., 2006).

Despite the different perceptions held between senior managers, HR departments and line managers, we do have a strong body of evidence that demonstrates – not surprisingly – that different line managers perform differently. It is the way in which line managers implement HR practices that can lead to vastly different enactment of HR policy by the time it reaches the shop floor (Hall and Torrington, 1998; Thornhill and Saunders, 1998; Cunningham and Hyman, 1999; Townsend et al., 2012a). The skills that they hold, the motivation to act in a particular manner, and their capacity to influence differs between line managers both within and across organizations (Appelbaum et al., 2000; Delery and Shaw, 2001, Purcell and Hutchinson, 2007). Employee perceptions of the organization's approach to people management can be influenced by their line manager's approach. Gilbert et al. (2011) argue that the individual characteristics of the line manager are positively correlated with the employees' affective commitment to their organization. Clearly, there is plenty of scope for line managers to act in their own interests to minimize the information and knowledge that passes around them; and it becomes increasingly important to understand this agency at a time when line managers are being inundated with increased responsibilities without necessarily receiving a corresponding increase in power or authority, or adequate training and development.

Our final area of recent directions in research can be labelled as 'leverage'. If we consider a line manager as the fulcrum in a lever system, it is in the best interests of the organization that one line manager oversees the performance of many employees. To get a leverage result on a one-to-one basis is time consuming and costly, and generates nothing in terms of economies of management scale. Ideally, to meet organizational goals of profitability, efficiency and so on, the line manager leverages the best performance from subordinate employees; to invoke a term not commonly used in the HR departments of modern business schools – to generate surplus value. It is clear when surveying the literature that this is indeed what line managers – in theory at least – have the capacity to do.

Despite the current inadequacies in our knowledge of line managers as they perform their people management functions, there are some detailed studies examining aspects of what line managers 'do' across a broad range of HRM-related activities. These have incorporated studies of the line manager's involvement in handling sickness and disability cases (Cunningham et al., 2001), absence management (Dunn and Wilkinson, 2002), interpreting HR messages from senior management (Townsend et al, 2012b), information systems (Conway and Monks, 2010), performance management (Harris and Ogbonna, 2001) and discipline and grievance or dispute resolution (Teague and Roche, 2012; Rollinson et al., 1996). With such a long list of responsibilities it would be expected that a role in employee involvement is a certainty.

Wooldridge and Floyd (1990) and Wooldridge et al. (2008) suggest that mid-level line managers play an integral role in strategy formation (including people management strategy). In a similar vein, Ghoshal and Bartlett (1994) argue that mid-level line managers have a great deal of interaction and influence over front-line managers through mentoring and supporting entrepreneurial activities – the larger the organization, the wider the distribution of authority to middle and front-line managers. As an important addition for consideration in the area of mid-level line managers, Wooldridge et al. (2008) provide a synthesis of research that suggests that, in broad terms of strategy formation, middle managers play an important horizontal role (across departments) as well as the vertical role.

MacNeil (2003) presents evidence that within flatter organizations, and in particular knowledge management firms, the line manager can play a critical role in knowledge sharing within organizations. MacNeil suggests that the power that line managers hold within organizations is a result, not of their hierarchical position of authority, but from having 'specific knowledge that enables them to influence both strategic and operational organisational priorities' (2003: 294). In quite a positively framed view of what line managers do (and if they are not doing, could be doing) this research suggests the line manager can play a key role in developing a 'positive learning climate' (p. 301) and act as a facilitator of the 'important learning link for collective knowledge sharing in teams' (p. 302). The suggestion is that if line managers were performing these tasks better it 'could make a significant contribution to maximising the core competences of learning in the organisation' (p. 303). If this is the case, then it is reasonable to presume that information garnered through voice mechanisms can be shared between line managers and work groups. However, there remain questions over how much of this strategy is influenced by employee voice.

Gibb (2003) claims mixed results when considering the role of line manager involvement in learning and development in workplaces. That is to say, that learning and development is seen in some organizations to be an increasingly important part of what the line manager does, while it seems other organizations maintain the learning and development subset of HRM for specialist personnel. This research demonstrates the diversity and context-specific importance of the role line managers play in the skill development of their subordinates (see for example, Crampton et al., 1994). Nelson (1994) provides an analysis of the role that senior managers play in influencing line manager performance in occupational health and safety (OHS) results, suggesting that line managers clearly play an important role in OHS performance. Cunningham and James (2001) also focus on aspects of health and safety in their study which reveals that line managers are often unwilling to attend training to manage long-term sickness and disability cases. Within this body of work and specific to the realm of safety, the terminology 'upward safety communication' has been used to describe the 'freedom employees feel to discuss safety issues with their supervisors' (Kath et al., 2010: 643; see also Hofman and Morgeson, 1999; Hofman and Stetzer, 1998). This definition seems analogous with our definition of voice. Importantly, when employees feel they have freedom of 'upward safety communication' through their line manager or supervisor, injury rates decrease. This is a clear indication that while the paradigm and definitions might differ, employee voice through the line manager can have positive effects for both employees and the organization.

Some research has found that line managers played a critical role in controlling the escalation of industrial disputes (Anderson et al., 2009; Teague and Roche, 2012; Yarrington et al., 2007). That is to say, the more skilled line managers were in handling people management issues, the more likely they were to resolve problems that arose on the shop floor before the problems progressed through the managerial hierarchy and required union involvement. According to Anderson et al. (2009) it is the coaching and mentoring role of the line manager that assists in identifying where employees are facing problems and that can help resolve issues before escalation. According to the specialized conflict literature, conflict should be addressed as close as possible to the point of origin (Ury et al., 1989, cited in Teague and Roche, 2012) – the point of origin in most cases would be the line manager/employee interface. While somewhat limited, this research does provide enough evidence to warrant further investigation into the way line managers can mitigate or, alternatively, elevate industrial disputes.

With the increasingly evident shift of HR responsibilities from the centralized HR department to the line managers they also become critical intermediaries in shaping enterprise performance (Currie and Proctor, 2005). On this basis, Harney and Jordan (2008) suggest that it is the line managers' implementation of practices that directly impact on the abilities, motivation and opportunity (AMO) performance rubric (see also Boxall and Purcell, 2008: 5). Another useful way of thinking about what line managers do is the so-called 'black box' referred to in much of the high performance work systems and HR research, which attempts to link HR to business performance (see for example, Boselie et al., 2005; Delery and Doty, 1996; Huselid and Becker, 2009; Purcell and Kinnie, 2007; Purcell et al., 2008; Wright and Gardner, 2004; Wright et al., 2005). In short, the HR department's policies will step through numerous stages prior to the actualizing of practice and the behavioural outcomes on the shop floor. These stages are considered the black box of the HRM–performance causal chain and Purcell and Kinnie (2007) note that line managers are key personnel throughout each step of the chain. When we couple our knowledge of the role of line managers in the HR architecture with the recognition that employee voice is now a predominately management-led phenomenon as union-based schemes atrophy (Charlwood, 2006), it is reasonable to presume that line managers are likely to be playing a critical role in employee voice.

LINE MANAGERS AND VOICE LITERATURE

Marchington and Wilkinson (2012) argue that voice can be categorized in three key ways: direct communication, upward-problem solving and representative participation. Representative participation holds less relevance for this chapter as it is more likely to focus on the role of unions in works councils, joint consultative committees and collective bargaining. However, direct communication and upward-problem solving are by their very nature and intent likely to be channelled through at least one level of line manager. As has been pointed out though, implementation of HR policies by line managers can suffer as a result of the skilled practitioner being promoted to the role of people manager without adequate training or support (Townsend et al., 2012a). As a consequence, it is likely that research would find a shortfall in skills related to the successful capturing of voice and the determination of appropriate action on what has been heard.

Given that direct communication and upward problem solving are likely to take various forms across organizations, research must be designed to examine similarities and differences. Landau (2009: 47) suggests that there is no relationship between the number of voice mechanisms that exist and the propensity of employees to speak up at work. The author suggests that perhaps the presence of multiple alternative voice mechanisms is not required if the employee has a competent and approachable manager. Olson-Buchanan and Boswell (2002) agree, suggesting that regardless of the number of potential forums, an employee wishing to discuss a grievance is most likely to communicate directly with a supervisor. Some years ago Fenton-O'Creevy (1998: 68) noted: 'The most significant question to answer is no longer "what are the benefits of employee involvement?" Rather, it is "What makes the difference between effective employee involvement programs and those that fail to achieve their objectives?"' While line managers are likely to be central in the answer to this question, it is a question which the extant literature has not adequately answered.

While line managers have been 'named and shamed' in many studies of voice, their position within the work has generally been as a contributory factor in the success or otherwise of voice systems rather than as a focus of the research design. For example, Dundon et al. (2005) and Wilkinson et al. (2004) point to the barrier that line managers can set up in the implementation and effective use of voice mechanisms – a problem often attributed to a lack in requisite skills. Marchington et al. (2001) suggest that lower level line managers and supervisors might not implement voice schemes as they are designed and intended. This leads to inconsistencies across different organizational divisions. This was further developed by Marchington and Wilkinson in 2012, suggesting that differences in implementation and inconsistencies are likely to be a result of the line managers' performance appraisals, which very rarely include key performance indicators that relate to the implementation and development of successful voice mechanisms. Consequently, there is no apparent need for managers to involve their subordinates in organizational decision-making (Currie and Proctor, 2005). In essence, the line managers are pressed from both sides of the hierarchy and are often without sufficient training and experience in people management, hence they opt for the expedient and immediate pathway of people management. Managing the potential complexity of employee voice is not always expedient, nor immediate. Without the requisite skills and training, voice mechanisms will not be adequately embedded within the culture of the organization and, according to Cox et al. (2009), will diminish in their effectiveness and relevance over time.

With this more recent focus on the role of line managers in voice regimes, we must be careful not to overlook a substantial body of work from earlier decades regarding middle managers and participative programmes, for example, Quality of Working Life initiatives, which were popular in the 1970s, and the Quality Circles and Total Quality Management of the 1980s and 1990s. Each of these programmes relied on employee participation in decision-making (Bradley and Hill, 1987) – a definition at the higher end of the 'participation escalator' (Wilkinson et al., 2010). Levitan and Johnson (1983) for example, found that some programmes failed largely as a result of middle managers refusing to change their style of managing so that participative practices could succeed. In Bradley and Hill's (1987: 74) study, in some UK firms 'middle managers saw workers merely as the passive implements of managerial directives' and 'managers think the workforce exists simply to do their bidding'. Hespe and Wall (1976) offer an earlier study on the involvement of employees in participation and decision-making; however, this seemed to take place mostly at the department levels and participation was somewhat limited because of strategic (or distant) decision-making.

These articles represent only a small selection of the many studies that considered participation up to four decades ago, and times have changed and management styles have developed. Yet the results seem to show that the conclusions have not changed – line managers can still be a barrier to effective voice and participation and line managers remain underprepared in relation to the skills required to get the most out of voice schemes for either the organization or the employees. That said, in the context of modern HRM systems and more sophisticated management styles, the way that line managers at all levels throughout organizations use and abuse voice systems remains an area worthy of ongoing investigation.

Recent studies have considered the front line managers and supervisors as they contribute to a culture of informal voice in the workplace (Detert and Burris, 2007; Landau, 2009; Marchington and Suter, 2013; Townsend et al., 2013). Within this analytical paradigm, voice is not limited to the formal structures or procedures within the organization but is commonly seen as a 'discretionary provision of information intended to improve organisational functioning' (Detert and Burris, 2007: 222); it is also seen as improving the immediate and longer term state of affairs for employees (Townsend et al., 2013). What is clear throughout this body of work is that in most cases employees would prefer to speak directly to their immediate line manager when they have matters of concern. Further, when employees do speak (or attempt to speak) to their line manager and are not satisfied with the level of receptivity and responsiveness this dissatisfaction often determines an employee's willingness to speak up in the future, demonstrating the importance of the immediate line manager in employee voice systems, particularly when informality is relied upon (Wilkinson et al., 2013).

Informal voice exchanges between employees and managers are important in workplaces. Purcell and Georgiadis (2007) explain that employers need to acknowledge and maximize the value of face-to-face exchanges with employees. Bryson et al. (2006), Marchington and Suter (2013) and Townsend et al. (2013) all suggest that the best managers can capture employee views and use them to benefit both the organization and its employees. We are also aware that informal EIP (employee involvement and participation) tends to leave a number of issues untouched, for example, broader considerations around management decision-making, workload and representation in disputes. Furthermore, it is based on good relations existing between employees and managers. The employment relationship is one that is built around a social component and is always evolving. Consequently there is a fragility to the relationships; if the mix of managers and employees changes, the success of informal EIP can also change. What is important is the sustainability of reciprocal relationships between line managers and their employees. When successful, these relationships are often characterized by mutual respect, liking, trust and loyalty (Liden and Maslyn, 1998).

CONCLUSIONS

The intersection between line managers and employee voice is one that can draw on a number of bodies of literature for future directions, but the intersection itself is a topic worthy of its own focus. Based on what we already know, there are five key areas for future research. First, there must be a greater focus on the 'disaggregation' of the line manager. Line managers are not homogeneous and our research needs to be more nuanced in the way we understand the role of line managers based on their different hierarchical positions within an organization. We know that the responsibilities of front line managers differ from the responsibilities of managers higher in the organizational structure, but what does this mean for the way they engage with formal and informal voice processes?

Second, we need to recognize the differences between departments or work areas that might influence the way voice is performed. For example, front line managers in a surgical ward of a hospital are likely to face different challenges to the front line managers in a medical ward. The front line manager of a hotel's front office is likely to engage with employee voice systems in a different way from the housekeeping and kitchen managers whose interaction will be based primarily on the labour process in each area. This is a reasonable proposition to consider in any sector of the workforce. What do these differences and similarities mean for voice?

The third area for further consideration relates to the skills and experience of line managers. Townsend et al. (2012a) argued that front line managers in hospitals are often appointed to their role 'accidentally and unprepared' but that furthermore, they are not adequately supported when they are placed in a managerial role. Presuming that higher level managers in an organization face the same experience and that this experience is consistent across a range of sectors, research is required to understand what training and development is required for line managers in order that they should understand and perform their 'listening to voice' responsibilities *prior* to the point when they are thrust in to the role.

We know that there is a difference between voice and action. The fourth area that is worthy of a sustained research focus would benefit from a research methodology similar to the 'critical incident' approach to tracking individual incidents of voice. It is worth understanding how line managers hear employee voice, what mechanisms are used, how voice is recorded (if it is recorded), and how and when they might act upon what they have heard. Furthermore, and this seems important for employees, the final result of the employee's request can often be less important than the employee hearing directly from the line manager what the result was. That is to say – line managers must report back to employees for the employees to feel that their voice has been heard and not simply disregarded.

Finally, we see power as a critical component in deciding how employees are heard and how their views are used. Temporary workers, non-unionized workers, men and women, employees with different educational and cultural and ethnic backgrounds might all experience voice differently. We would suggest that the modern shift to increasing the role of line managers in managing the HR function will result in a greater level of informal employee involvement right at the point of production. This may in fact mean that there should be greater concern for a theoretical consideration of power as it affects informal EIP directly between line managers and employees. To this end, we must understand the relationship between formal and informal voice and ask if informal EIP is good, for whom is it good, and how does it become good?

REFERENCES

Anderson, V., C. Rayner and B. Schyns (2009), *Coaching at the Sharp End: The Role of Line Managers in Coaching at Work*, London: CIPD.
Appelbaum, E., T. Bailey, P. Berg and A. Kalleberg (2000), *Manufacturing Advantage: Why High-Performance Work Systems Pay Off*, Ithaca: ILR Press.
Babbage, C. (1835), *On the Economy of Machinery and Manufactures*, London: Charles Knight.
Balogun, J. and G. Johnson (2004), 'Organizational restructuring and middle manager sensemaking', *Academy of Management Journal*, **47** (4), 523–49.
Blau, P. (1964), *Exchange and Power in Social Life*, New York: Wiley.
Boselie, P., G. Dietz and C. Boon (2005), 'Commonalities and contradictions in HRM and performance research', *Human Resource Management Journal*, **15** (3), 67–94.
Boxall, J. and J. Purcell (2008), *Strategy and Human Resource Management*, Basingstoke: Palgrave Macmillan.
Bradley, K. and S. Hill (1987), 'Quality circles and managerial interests' *Industrial Relations*, **26** (1), 68–82.
Braverman, H. (1974), *Labour and Monopoly Capital: The Degradation of Work in the Twentieth Century*, New York: Monthly Review Press.
Bryson, A., A. Charlwood and J. Forth (2006), 'Worker voice, managerial response and labour productivity: an empirical investigation', *Industrial Relations Journal*, **37** (5), 438–55.
Burke, R. and C. Cooper (2000), 'The new organisational reality: transition and renewal', in R. Burke and C. Cooper (eds), *The Organisation in Crisis: Downsizing, Restructuring and Revitalisation*, Oxford: Blackwell, pp. 3–19.
Cameron, K., S. Freeman and A. Mishra (1991), 'Best practice in white-collar downsizing: managing contradictions', *Academy of Management Executive*, **5**, 57–73.
Cascio, W. (2002), 'Strategies for responsible restructuring', *Academy of Management Executive*, **16**, 80–91.
Cascon-Pereira, R., M. Valverde and G. Ryan (2006), 'Mapping out devolution: an exploration of the realities of devolution', *Journal of European Industrial Training*, **30** (2), 129–51.
Charlwood, A. (2006), 'What determined employer voice choice in Britain in the 20th century? A critique of the "Sound of Silence" model', *Socio-Economic Review*, **4** (2), 301–9.
Chen, L. and M. Wallace (2011), 'Multiskilling of frontline managers in the five star hotel industry in Taiwan', *Research and Practice in Human Resource Management*, **19** (1), 25–37.
Child, J. and B. Partridge (1982), *Lost Managers: Supervisors in Industry and Society*, Cambridge: Cambridge University Press.
Conway, E. and K. Monks (2010), 'Change from below: the role of middle managers in mediating paradoxical change', *Human Resource Management Journal*, **21** (2), 190–203.
Cox, A., S. Zagelmeyer and M. Marchington (2006), 'Embedding employee involvement and participation at work', *Human Resource Management Journal*, **16** (3), 250–67.
Cox, A., M. Marchington and J. Suter (2009), 'Employee involvement and participation: developing the concept of institutional embeddedness using WERS2004', *International Journal of Human Resource Management*, **20** (10), 2150–68.
Crampton, S.M., J.W. Hodge and J.G. Motwani (1994), 'Diversity and career development issues in the 90s', *Supervision*, **55** (6), 6–9.
Cunningham, I. and J. Hyman (1999), 'Devolving human resource responsibilities to the line: beginning of the end or a new beginning for personnel?', *Personnel Review*, **28** (1), 9–27.
Cunningham, I. and I. James (2001), 'Line managers as people managers: prioritising the needs of the long-term sick and those with disabilities', British Academy of Management Conference Paper, Cardiff University.
Currie, G. and S. Procter (2005), 'The antecedents of middle managers' strategic contribution: the case of a professional bureaucracy', *Journal of Management Studies*, **42** (7), 1325–56.
Delery, J. and D. Doty (1996), 'Modes of theorizing in strategic human resource management: tests of universalistic, contingent and configurational performance predictions', *Academy of Management Journal*, **39** (4), 802–35.
Delery, J. and J. Shaw (2001), 'The strategic management of people in work organisations: review, synthesis and extension', *Research in Personnel and Human Resource Management*, **20**, 165–97.
Detert, J.R. and E.R. Burris (2007), 'Leadership behavior and employee voice: is the door really open?', *Academy of Management Journal*, **50** (4), 869–84.
Down, S. and J. Reveley (2009), 'Between narration and interaction: situating first line supervisor identity work', *Human Relations*, **62** (3), 379–401.
Dundon, T., A. Wilkinson, M. Marchington and P. Ackers (2005), 'The management of voice in non-union organisations: managers' perspectives', *Employee Relations*, **27** (3), 307–20.
Dunn, C. and A. Wilkinson (2002), 'Wish you were here: managing absence', *Personnel Review*, **31** (2), 228–46.

Fenton-O'Creevy, M. (1998), 'Employee involvement and the middle manager: evidence from a survey of organisations', *Journal of Organizational Behavior*, **19** (1), 67–84.

Fenton-O'Creevy, M. (2001), 'Employee involvement and the middle manager: saboteur or scapegoat?', *Human Resource Management Journal*, **11** (1), 24–40.

Floyd, S. and B. Wooldridge (1999), 'Knowledge creation and social networks in corporate entrepreneurship: the renewal of organisational capability', *Entrepreneurship Theory and Practice*, **23** (3), 123–44.

Freeman, R.B., P. Boxall and P. Haynes (eds) (2007), *What Workers Say: Employee Voice in the Anglo-American Workplace*, Ithaca, NY: Cornell University Press.

Gerstner, C. and D. Day (1997), 'Meta-analytic review of leader–member exchange theory: correlates and construct issues', *Journal of Applied Psychology*, **82** (6), 827–44.

Ghoshal, S. and C. Bartlett (1994), 'Linking organizational context and managerial action: the dimensions of quality of management', *Strategic Management Journal*, **15**, 91–112.

Gibb, S. (2003),'Line managers' involvement in learning and development: small beer or big deal?', *Employee Relations*, **25** (3), 281–93.

Gilbert, C., S. de Winne and L. Sels (2011), 'The influence of line managers and HR Departments on employees' affective commitment', *International Journal of Human Resource Management*, **22** (8), 1618–37.

Gilley, J., S. Quatro, E. Hoekstra, D. Whittle and A. Maycunich (2001), *The Manager as a Change Agent: A Practical Guide to Developing High Performance People Organisations*, Cambridge: Perseus.

Gouldner, A. (1960), 'The norm of reciprocity: a preliminary statement', *American Sociological Review*, **25**, 161–78.

Graen, G. and M. Uhl-Bien (1995), 'Relationship-based approach to leadership: development of leader–member exchange (LMX) theory over 25 years: applying a multi-level multi-domain perspective', *Leadership Quarterly*, **6**, 219–47.

Guest, D. and Z. King (2001), 'HR and the bottom line', *People Management*, 27 September, 29–34.

Hales, C. (2005), 'Rooted in supervision, branching into management: continuity and change in the role of first-line manager', *Journal of Management Studies*, **42** (3), 471–506.

Hall, L. and D. Torrington (1998), 'Letting go or holding on: the devolution of operational personnel activities', *Human Resource Management Journal*, **8**, 41–55.

Hamel, G. (2007), *The Future of Management*, Cambridge, MA: Harvard Business School Press.

Harney, B. and C. Jordan (2008), 'Unlocking the black box: line managers and HRM performance in a call centre context', *International Journal of Productivity and Performance Management*, **57** (4), 275–96.

Harris, L. and E. Ogbonna (2001), 'Strategic human resource management, market orientation, and organizational performance', *Journal of Business Research*, **51** (2) (February), 157–66.

Hassard, J., L. McCann and J. Morris (2011), 'Employment relations and managerial work: an international perspective', in K. Townsend and A. Wilkinson (eds), *Research Handbook on the Future of Work and Employment Relations*, Cheltenham, UK and Northampton, MA, USA: Edward Elgar, pp. 150–66.

Hespe, G. and T. Wall (1976), 'The demand for participation among employees', *Human Relations*, **29** (5), 411–28.

Hofman, D. and F. Morgeson (1999), 'Safety-related behaviour as a social exchange: the role of perceived organisational support and leader–member exchange', *Journal of Applied Psychology*, **84** (2), 286–96.

Hofman, D. and A. Stetzer (1998), 'The role of safety climate and communication in accident interpretation: implications for learning from negative events', *Academy of Management Journal*, **41** (6), 644–57.

Huselid, M. and B. Becker (2009), 'Strategic human resource management: where do we go from here?', in A. Wilkinson, N. Bacon,T. Redman and S. Snell (eds), *Sage Handbook of Human Resource Management*, London: Sage, pp. 351–76.

Hutchinson, S. and J. Purcell (2003), *Bringing Policies to Life: The Vital Role of Front Line Managers in People Management*, London: Chartered Institute of Personnel and Development.

Hutchinson, S. and S. Wood (1995), *Personnel and the Line: Developing a New Relationship*, London: Institute of Personnel Management.

Huy, Q. (2002), 'Emotional balancing or organisational continuity and radical change: the contribution of middle managers', *Administrative Science Quarterly*, **47** (1), 31–69.

Kath, L., K. Marks and J. Ranney (2010), 'Safety climate dimensions, leader–member exchange, and organisational support as predictors of upward safety communication in a sample of rail industry workers', *Safety Science*, **48**, 643–50.

Kaufman, B.E. (2003), 'High-lvel employee involvement at Delta Airlines', *Human Resource Management*, **42** (2), 175–90.

Kidd, J. and C. Smewing (2001), 'The role of supervisor in career and organizational commitment', *European Journal of Work and Organizational Psychology*, **10** (1), 25–40.

Landau, J. (2009), 'To speak or not to speak: predictors of voice propensity', *Journal of Organizational Culture, Communication and Conflict*, **13** (1), 35–55.

Larsen, H. and C. Brewster (2003), 'Line management responsibility for HRM: what is happening in Europe?', *Employee Relations*, **25** (3), 228–44.
Levitan, S. and C. Johnson (1983), 'Labour and management: the illusion of cooperation', *Harvard Business Review*, **LXIII**, 65–71.
Liden, R.C. and J.M. Maslyn (1998), 'Multidimensionality of leader–member exchange: an empirical assessment through scale development', *Journal of Management*, **24** (1), 43–72.
MacNeil, C. (2003), 'Line managers: facilitators of knowledge sharing in teams', *Employee Relations*, **25** (3), 294–307.
Marchington, M. and I. Grugulis (2000), '"Best practice" human resource management: perfect opportunity or dangerous illusion?', *International Journal of Human Resource Management*, **11** (6), 1104–24.
Marchington, M. and J. Suter (2013), 'Why informality matters: patterns of employee involvement and participation in a non-union firm', *Industrial Relations*, **51** (S1), 284–313.
Marchington, M. and A. Wilkinson (2012), *Human Resource Management at Work*, 5th edn, London: Chartered Institute of Personnel and Development.
Marchington, M., A. Wilkinson, P. Ackers and T. Dundon (2001), *Management Choice and Employee Voice*, London: CIPD.
Martins, L.-P. (2007), 'A holistic framework for the strategic management of first tier managers', *Management Decision*, **45** (3), 616–41.
Martins, L.-P., (2009), 'The nature of the changing role of first-tier managers: a long cycle approach', *Journal of Organisational Change Management*, **22** (1), 92–123.
Mason, G. (2000), 'Production supervisors in Britain, Germany and the United States: back from the dead again?', *Work, Employment and Society*, **14** (4), 625–45.
McCann, L., J. Morris and J. Hassard (2008), 'Normalised intensity: the new labour process of middle management', *Journal of Management Studies*, **45** (2), 343–71.
McConville, T. and L. Holden (1999), 'The filling in the sandwich: managers in the health sector', *Personnel Review*, **28** (516), 406–24.
McGovern, F., L. Gratton, V. Hope-Hailey, P. Stiles and C. Truss (1997), 'Human resource management on the line?', *Human Resource Management Journal*, **7** (4), 12–29.
Michael, J., Z. Guo, J. Wiedenbeck and C. Ray (2006), 'Production supervisor impacts on subordinates' safety outcomes: an investigation of leader–member exchange and safety communication', *Journal of Safety Research*, **37**, 469–77.
Nelson, L. (1994), 'Managing managers in occupational health and safety', *Asia Pacific Journal of Human Resources*, **32** (1), 13–28.
Olson-Buchanan, J.B. and W.R. Boswell (2002), 'The role of employee loyalty and formality in voicing discontent', *Journal of Applied Psychology*, **87** (6), 1167–74.
Penley, L., E. Alexander, I. Jernigan and C. Henwood (1991), 'Communication abilities of managers: the relationship to performance', *Journal of Management*, **17** (1), 57–76.
Perry, E. and C. Kulik (2008), 'The devolution of HR to the line: implications for perceptions of people management effectiveness', *International Journal of Human Resource Management*, **19** (2), 262–73.
Purcell, J. and K. Georgiadis (2007), 'Why should employers bother with worker voice?', in R.B. Freeman, P. Boxall and P. Haynes (eds), *What Workers Say: Employee Voice in the Anglo American Workplace*, Ithaca: Cornell University Press, pp. 181–97.
Purcell, J. and S. Hutchinson (2007), 'Front-line managers as agents in the HRM–performance causal chain: theory, analysis and evidence', *Human Resource Management Journal*, **17**, 3–20.
Purcell, J. and N. Kinnie (2007), 'HRM and business performance', in P. Boxall, J. Purcell and P. Wright (eds), *The Oxford Handbook of Human Resource Management*, New York: Oxford University Press, pp. 533–51.
Purcell, J., N. Kinnie, J. Swart, B. Rayton and S. Hutchinson (2008), *People Management and Performance*, London: Taylor and Francis.
Renwick, D. (2003), 'Line manager involvement in HRM: an inside view' *Employee Relations*, **25** (3), 262–80.
Renwick, D. (2008), 'Line managers', in T. Redman and A. Wilkinson (eds), *Contemporary Human Resource Management: Text and Cases*, London: Prentice Hall, pp. 225–42.
Rollinson, D., C. Hook, M. Foot and J. Handley (1996), 'Supervisor and manager styles in handling discipline and grievance: part two – approaches to handling discipline and grievance', *Personnel Review*, **25** (4), 38–55.
Smith, A. (1976 [1776]), *The Wealth of Nations*, ed. R.H. Campbell and A.S. Skinner, The Glasgow edition of the Works and Correspondence of Adam Smith, vol. 2a, Indianapolis: Liberty Fund.
Storey, J. (1992), *Developments in the Management of Human Resources*, Oxford: Blackwell.
Taylor, F. (1911a), *Shop Management*, New York: Harper and Brothers Publishers.
Taylor, F. (1911b), *The Principles of Scientific Management*, New York: Harper and Brothers Publishers.
Teague, P. and B. Roche (2012), 'Line managers and the management of workplace conflict: evidence from Ireland', *Human Resource Management Journal*, **22** (3), 235–51.

Thornhill, A. and M. Saunders (1998), 'What if line managers don't realise they're responsible for HR? Lessons from an organisation experiencing rapid change', *Personnel Review*, **27** (6), 460–76.

Townsend, K. (2004), 'When the LOST found teams: a consideration of teams in the individualised call centre environment', *Labour and Industry*, **14** (3), 111–26.

Townsend, K., A. Wilkinson, C. Allan and G. Bamber (2012a), 'Accidental, unprepared and unsupported: the ward manager's journey', *International Journal of Human Resource Management*, **23** (1), 204–20.

Townsend, K., A. Wilkinson, G. Bamber and C. Allan (2012b), 'Mixed signals in human resources management: the HRM role of hospital line managers', *Human Resource Management Journal*, **22** (3), 267–82.

Townsend, K., A. Wilkinson and J. Burgess (2013), 'Filling the gaps: patterns of formal and informal participation', *Economic and Industrial Democracy*, **34** (2), 337–54.

Wall, T. and S. Wood (2005), 'The romance of human resource management and business performance, and the case for big science', *Human Relations*, **58** (4), 429–62.

Watson, S., G.A. Maxwell and L. Farquharson (2006), 'Line managers' views on adopting human resource roles: the case of Hilton (UK) hotels', *Employee Relations*, **29** (1), 30–49.

Wilkinson, A. and C. Fay (2011), 'New times for employee voice?', *Human Resource Management*, **50** (1), 65–74.

Wilkinson, A., T. Dundon, M. Marchington and P. Ackers (2004), 'Changing patterns of employee voice', *Journal of Industrial Relations*, **46** (3), 298–322.

Wilkinson, A., P. Gollan, M. Marchington and D. Lewin (2010), 'Conceptualising employee participation in organisations', in A. Wilkinson, P. Gollan, M. Marchington, and D. Lewin (eds), *The Oxford Handbook of Participation in Organizations*, Oxford: Oxford University Press, pp. 4–25.

Wilkinson, A., K. Townsend and J. Burgess (2013), 'Reassessing employee involvement and participation: atrophy, reinvigoration and patchwork in Australian workplaces', *Journal of Industrial Relations*, **55** (3), 583–600.

Wooldridge, B. and S. Floyd (1990), 'The strategy process, middle management involvement, and organisational performance', *Strategic Management Journal*, **11**, 231–41.

Wooldridge, B., T. Schmid and S.W. Floyd (2008), 'The middle management perspective on strategy process: contributions, synthesis, and future research', *Journal of Management*, **34**, 1190–221.

Worral, L., C. Parkes and C. Cooper (2004), 'The impact of organisational change on the perceptions of UK managers', *European Journal of Work and Organisational Psychology*, **13**, 139–63.

Wren, D. (1993), *The Evolution of Management Thought*, New York: John Wiley and Sons.

Wright, P. and T. Gardner (2004), 'The human resource–firm performance relationship: methodological and theoretical challenges', in D. Holman, T. Wall, C. Clegg, P. Sparrow and A. Howard (eds), *The New Workplace: A Guide to the Human Impact of Modern Work Practices*, London: John Wiley, pp. 311–30.

Wright, P. and R. Kehoe (2008), 'Human resource practices and organisational commitment: a deeper examination', *Asia Pacific Journal of Human Resources*, **46**, 6–20.

Wright, P., T. Gardner, L. Moynihan and M. Allen (2005), 'The HR–performance relationship: examining causal direction', *Personnel Psychology*, **58**, 409–46.

Yang, J., K.W. Mossholder and T.K. Peng (2009), 'Supervisory procedural justice effects: the mediating roles of cognitive and affective trust', *Leadership Quarterly*, **20** (2), 143–54.

Yarrington, L., K. Townsend and K. Brown (2007), 'Models of engagement: union management relations for the 21st century', in *Diverging Employment Relations Patterns in Australia and New Zealand*, proceedings of the AIRAANZ conference, Auckland, New Zealand.

11 Union voice
Sarah Kaine

This chapter will consider the purpose and form of union voice. It will chart the development of 'voice' as a means of describing union representation and explore the implications of changes to both labour market structures and the nature of the employment relationship for union voice. It will then examine the various levels at which union voice is expressed, and in doing so highlight the key differences between union voice and other forms of worker voice. Finally, it offers some observations about the possible future of union voice.

INTRODUCTION

The classic definition of a trade union provided by Sidney and Beatrice Webb (Webb and Webb, 1920: 1) as 'a continuous association of wage-earners for the purposes of improving the conditions of their working lives' still succinctly captures the essence of union representation. Hyman (1997: 310) further clarifies this purpose by explaining that 'When we speak of employee representation, by implication we refer to the representation of *interests*.' However, in attempting to more fully understand the role of unions as a vehicle for the advancement of the interests of workers, it is also necessary to consider not only their aim but also their methods of representation. The Webbs endeavoured to do this in *Industrial Democracy* (1914), where they set out the various representative roles performed by unions. They differentiated between the aspirations of unions to 'elevate the social position of . . . members' (Webb and Webb, 1914: 146) and the 'everyday action' of union members, with particular emphasis on the role of unions as regulators. The Webbs described this regulatory role as the setting of rules and the enforcement of them by methods of 'mutual insurance, collective bargaining and legal enactment' (1914: 150).

Despite radical changes to the labour market and the global economy, such that these are almost beyond recognition since the Webbs' time, each of these methods remains evident in the practices of modern unions. Many unions maintain a 'mutual insurance' role (Cliffe, 2013), providing the means of access to unemployment benefits. Collective bargaining is a fundamental activity of unions around the world, and unions often still attempt to influence the legal regulation of the labour market. Indeed, for much of the twentieth century industrial relations scholars have continued to explore the representative methods and strategies of unions. One of the most significant works in this area was that of Freeman and Medoff, who in 1984 wrote a book *What Do Unions Do?* which sought to articulate the role of unions, to quantify the effect of unions on productivity and to highlight the advocacy role which unions enact, stating 'unions are an important voice for some of our society's weakest and most vulnerable groups, as well as for their own members' (1984: 5).

Most significantly for the discussion in this chapter, Freeman and Medoff describe 'voice' as 'discussing with an employer conditions that ought to be changed, rather than quitting the job' and that 'a trade union is the vehicle for collective voice – that is, for providing workers as a group with a means of communicating with management' (1984: 8). While this is the definition of union voice which will be used in the following discussion, the dramatic decline in unionization rates across the developed world since the 1980s has prompted a reconsideration of the capacity of unions to effectively express this 'voice' even for their own members let alone more broadly. This chapter will examine the concept of union voice in more depth, analysing the methods and configurations of union voice, and its continuing relevance in an increasingly fragmented global labour market.

WHAT IS 'UNION VOICE' AND DOES IT MATTER?

The concept of union voice gained currency following Freeman and Medoff's (1984) seminal work *What Do Unions Do?* Essentially, Freeman and Medoff differentiated between two main functions of unions which they referred to as the two 'faces' of unionism – the monopoly face and the collective voice/institutional response face (Freeman and Medoff, 1984: 6). The monopoly face refers to the ability of unions to raise wages beyond market rates. It references neoclassical economic theory which presumes unions have the capacity, through their 'monopoly power' over labour supply, to set wages. Freeman and Medoff challenge this assumption, arguing that 'wages obtained by unions must be viewed as the joint responsibility of management and labor' (1984: 6). They also argue that unions have another important representational face – the 'collective voice face' – which has the potential to provide improvements in workplace productivity. The 'collective voice face' is influenced by Hirschman's (1970) 'voice' or 'exit' thesis (see Allen, Chapter 3). This argument posits that there are two ways of addressing problems in a social or economic context – 'exit', where individuals choose to exercise choice by leaving a situation or relationship (when applied to the workplace context this means 'quitting' a job) or 'voice', which 'refers to the use of direct communication to bring actual and desired conditions closer together' (Freeman and Medoff, 1984: 8). In other words, Freeman and Medoff suggest that the representative role of unions, or the 'collective voice' role of unions 'channels worker discontent' (Blanchflower and Bryson, 2004). Thus collective voice provides a productive alternative to an 'exit' scenario, and in so doing increases productivity and reduces turnover.

Unionization rates have been in decline in many industrialized countries since Freeman and Medoff's influential publication of 1984. At that time unionization rates across the OECD averaged close to 30 per cent. By 2011 this figure had decreased by almost half, to 17.5 per cent (OECD, 2013). While these aggregated statistics do mask variations in the extent of the decline between countries, the general trend is significant and has been particularly pronounced in Western Europe, the United Kingdom and Australia. The United States has also experienced declining rates of unionization, but started from a lower base of just over 18 per cent in 1984, dropping to 11.3 per cent in 2011 (OECD, 2013). This decline has resulted in what has come to be known as the 'representation gap' which Towers (1997: 2) measured by examining whether workers had 'access to the independent representation of their individual and collective interests'. In light of this gap and in the absence of effective union representation, recent research has focused on alternative non-union employee representation (NER) (see Dobbins and Dundon, Chapter 21). Given the proliferation of other vehicles for worker voice and the decline in union density, it is pertinent to ask whether union voice remains a relevant concept in the current international debate.

While not dismissing the potential for NER to provide some legitimate opportunities for worker involvement in decision-making at work, there is evidence to suggest that the declining influence of union voice has had serious implications for a worsening social inequality. In its 2012/2013 *Global Wages Report* the International Labour Organization (ILO) considered the impact of union density on the wages share of national income across developed countries. It cites OECD research which found that in 26 out of 30 developed countries there was a decline in the average wages share of GDP between 1990 and 2009 (ILO, 2013). It estimates that changes in union density (combined with changes in government consumption) contributed 25 per cent to the fall in wages share of income (ILO, 2013: 51). Similarly, Heery (2010: 551) highlights the 'generally redistributive effect of unions' in the UK, noting that as unions have declined 'so British society has become more unequal'.

While the neo-liberal influence on business and political discourse and decision-making has advocated for worker voice to be contained at the firm or workplace level (Thelen, 2001) the changing structure of work and pressing market realities have impelled unions to engage in 'voicing' concerns at different scales in order to adequately represent their members. As work has moved away from the traditional full-time, direct employment relationship between an employee and one employer to a multiplicity of forms from agency, to contract, to casual, the implication in some quarters is that there should be corresponding 'multi-form trade unions' (Heery, 2009b: 439), capable of representing workers for whom the 'workplace' is not static or a constant. OECD statistics mirror this rapidly shifting nature of the workplace, and its effects on collective bargaining. Levels of collective bargaining in all but Finland and Norway have declined markedly, notably in Australia and New Zealand, Portugal and the UK as a result of labour reforms (ILO, 2012: 137). Associated with the decline in collective bargaining and rise in inequality is the redistribution of economic risk from employers to employees. As traditional employment based on a full-time, direct and continuing relationship between employers and employees has been replaced with more contingent and precarious arrangements (Standing, 2011), this change has entailed a challenge to established notions of union voice and to practices of union representation. Heery (2009b) argues that collective bargaining may not be the most effective method of voice for many categories of workers. Echoing earlier work by Hyman (1997) examining levels of representation, Heery (2009b) suggests that collective bargaining provides a limited arena for union voice, and that scale affords a better instrument to harness and conceptualize effective union voice.

Specifically, where collective bargaining at the workplace is recognized as a key component of union voice (Hyman, 1997), we should ask what these changes to the very concept of work and workplace mean for the ongoing relevance of union representation? This question has prompted much soul-searching from unions globally and a proliferation of research exploring options for union revitalization. The revitalization literature has examined strategies pursued by unions to overcome decline, including, most commonly, a return to grassroots organizing techniques, union–management partnership and union–community coalitions (Dufour et al., 2010; Hickey, 2004; Hyman and Gumbrell-McCormick, 2010; Levesque and Murray, 2010; Turner, 2005). An alternative strand of scholarship has considered the role of unions in providing a variety of regulatory opportunities outside extant labour law. This may extend the regulatory role of union voice to formulate activities beyond the bounds of traditional employment configurations (Arup et al., 2006; Johnstone et al., 2012) and beyond the remit of collective bargaining. In particular, this approach explores the potential for unions to be agents of regulation in the context of complex and fragmented supply chains. It suggests that while collective bargaining may be assumed to be the most obvious manifestation of union voice (see Chapter 12 Doellgast and Benassi), unions are exploring a variety of methods for voice and representation.

The remainder of the chapter examines the purpose of union voice in more detail, and the different scales of union voice, from the workplace through to industry, national and supra-national level. It concludes by contemplating the future of union voice.

FREEMAN AND MEDOFF REVISITED

In addition to identifying the organizational efficiencies and productivity gains enabled by worker voice, Freeman and Medoff (1984) strongly advocated for unions as the appropriate vehicle for the expression of such voice. Specifically, they outlined four main reasons why collective rather than individual voice is preferable at the workplace. The first two of these, in their own words, are that:

> many important aspects of an industrial setting are 'public goods' and that as a consequence without some collective organisation these shared goods or benefits – such as safety and other issues related to the workplace environment or policies on remuneration or promotion – are unlikely to be pursued by individuals. Second, collective representation is necessary because workers are unlikely to truly voice their opinions to their employer for fear of retribution of some kind. (Freeman and Medoff, 1984: 8–9)

The third point is that in a non-union environment 'where exit-and-entry is the predominant form of adjustment' firms are likely to respond to the types of workers who are 'marginal'; that is, those workers who are more ready and willing to leave rather than those workers who, for a variety of reasons including, age, skill and non-transferable rights and entitlements may be 'effectively immobile' (Freeman and Medoff, 1984: 9, 10). In contrast, union presence is more likely to ensure that the desires of all workers are heard, even those who are unlikely to leave the organization. Finally, Freeman and Medoff note (like many sociologists from Marx onwards) that the exercise of collective voice through unions 'fundamentally alter[s] the social relations of the workplace' (1984: 10). As unions provide a counter to managerial power, workers are less prone to engage in individual actions (such as shirking or sabotage) in response to perceived unfair treatment. Further, union presence promotes the security of labour contracts, and the likelihood that they will be improved and enforced.

A number of criticisms have been levelled at Freeman and Medoff, the most serious of which is that the monopoly/voice dichotomy is ambiguous (Hirsch, 2004). Specifically,

Turnbull notes that effective voice in the workplace '*depends on* some degree of union monopoly power' (Turnbull, 2003: 499). In addition, the exact mechanisms through which the 'collective voice face' results in improvements in productivity remain unclear (Turnbull, 2003). Subsequent research by Boroff and Lewin (1997) also questioned the notion that workers with 'unvoiced' grievances are more likely to exit an organization. They found that those employees who register a grievance were more likely to leave an organization and that 'loyal employees who experienced unfair treatment were more likely to respond by suffering in silence' (Dundon et al., 2004: 1151). Furthermore, there is an implicit assumption in Freeman and Medoff's discussion of the benefits of union representation that unions represent all workers equally. This ignores the chequered history of unions in representing the interests of workers outside the traditional mainstream of the labour movement – for example, women, particular racial groups and ethnic minorities and those employed on non-standard contracts (Agnone, 2010; Bertone et al., 1995). While Freeman and Medoff (1984) were eloquent in their articulation of the collective voice/institutional response face of unions and incisive in identifying the undervalued potential for union voice to contribute to improvements in productivity (Turnbull, 2003), their imagined worker is abstract and disembodied. They did not explicitly consider gender as a variable that may affect voice, following a long tradition of gender-blindness in industrial relations scholarship (Holgate et al., 2006). While union membership has traditionally been male dominated, an increasing proportion of public sector unionism compared to the private sector signals a shift in the union heartland (Briggs et al., 2002) away from male-dominated blue-collar occupations to female dominated areas, a trend which has only increased in recent years (Visser, cited in Scheuer, 2011: 66). Recent OECD statistics reveal the dominance of public sector unionism in which women are well represented. In the UK 64.5 per cent of public services are covered by collective agreements, compared with 14 per cent in private enterprise; in the USA 37 per cent of public servants are covered, compared with only 6.9 per cent of the private sector (OECD, 2013: 163). In addition to sector, other factors strongly influence unionism, namely country, age, size of workplace and attitudes to unionism and collective bargaining (Scheuer, 2011).

Combined with the changes to the structure of the labour market and the employment relationship itself, this spectacular decline in unionization rates – witnessed across the OECD – might reasonably lead to an assessment that union voice at the workplace has passed its prime. Even in the public sector, which has become the union heartland in many countries (Buchanan and Callus, 1993; Bureau of Labor Statistics, 2012), the pressures of the global financial crisis have wrought havoc for collective bargaining frameworks. Many national and regional governments have pursued radical workplace reform and an aggressive cost-cutting agenda. In NSW, the most populous state in Australia, the O'Farrell government intervened in the operation of the state's industrial tribunal, effectively compromising the separation of judicial and executive powers. This intervention worked to limit both the scope of collective bargaining for public servants and for wage outcomes (Bennett et al., 2012). This echoes the actions of the Wisconsin legislature, which in 2011 worked to deny collective bargaining rights to workers in the public sector (Bennett et al., 2012; Cliffe, 2013; Davey and Greenhouse, 2011; Marley, 2011; Prideaux, 2013; Wisconsin, 2012).

Diminishing unionization rates and the wane of collective bargaining seem to suggest that unions are becoming less relevant in the expression of voice on behalf of workers. However, this would only be true if union voice were limited to collective bargaining at a workplace level. If the measure of effective representation is the 'capacity to regulate terms and conditions of employment through an independent institution' (Heery, 2009a: 326) then the other ways in which unions regulate conditions of employment also need to be examined. Additionally, as previously stated, any consideration of the method of voice needs to be supplemented by attention to the various methods and levels at which union voice is exercised (Heery 2009b). What follows is an overview of the methods and the various levels of voice used by unions in their representation of workers.

LEVELS AND METHODS OF UNION VOICE

Table 11.1 provides an overview of the different levels and methods of union voice and some examples of the regulatory outcomes that might be achieved through these.

While unions do provide representation at the individual level, a fundamental feature of union representation is that it is based on the collective. It should also be noted that providing voice for individual grievances frequently requires unions to call on the collective power of their membership, at a workplace (or occasionally higher) level. This highlights the fact that although it is useful to differentiate between the scales of union voice, the levels are not mutually exclusive and that, being multi-scalar, union voice is a richly textured phenomenon. This echoes Heery's explanation that 'regulation itself is often developed in complex systems of "multi-level" governance . . . that encompass action at sub-national, national and supra-national levels' (2009b: 549). Workplace collective bargaining is comprehensively dealt with by Doellgast and Benassi in Chapter 14 of this volume. The industry, national and supra-national scales listed in Table 11.1 are discussed below.

Voice Beyond Collective Bargaining at the Industry Scale

In recognition that collective bargaining is not an option available to all workers, unions have developed methods of voice beyond collective bargaining. These are not limited to the 'information and consultation' (Hyman, 1997) function characteristic of many NERs (see Table 21.1 in Dobbins and Dundon's chapter). Heery (2009b) specifically investigates the options for union representation of workers deemed to be contingent or precarious. Workers in this category have employment contracts that are non-standard, non-permanent and unpredictable (Standing, 2011).[1] Given these characteristics, traditional avenues of union representation do not serve these workers. Their predicament is exacerbated by the diversity among this group, which includes those 'directly employed, temporary workers, agency staff . . . and the self-employed' (Heery 2009b: 429). Workplace based unionism is particularly ill-suited to the representative needs of these workers. Hence, unions have had to adapt and develop methods of regulating conditions of employment not based on the workplace. These methods have included attempts by unions to negotiate recognition agreements with labour hire agencies, the setting of standard fees or the issuing of model contracts. In an increasing number of cases, unions have sought not only to 'upscale' (Heery, 2009b) their representative efforts, but have

Table 11.1   Overview of union voice levels, methods and potential outcomes

Level	Examples of method	Examples of outcomes
Individual	Grievance advocacy	Resolution and potential adaptation of company policy
Workplace	Collective bargaining	Collective contracts/agreements
Industry	Collective bargaining	Collective contracts/agreements
	Leveraging of commercial pressure and organizational reputation in supply chains	• Industry specific legislation: For example the Australian *Road Safety Remuneration Act 2012*
		• Joint employer-union enforcement mechanisms (see JfJ case discussed below)
	Use of law other than labour law	• Environmental regulation – see US Teamsters case discussed below)
	Political lobbying about industry policy	• Public investment in the industry, industry specific labour market initiatives
		• Industry specific labour market initiatives
National	Political affiliations	Social pacts
	Test cases	Changes to labour law
	Living wage campaigns	Changes to the social wage
Supra-national	Global union federations	International framework agreements
	Participation in multilateral forums such as the ILO and EU committees	EU directives
		ILO conventions

Source: Levels adapted from Heery (2009b).

also engaged in forms of regulation that could be considered to be outside the bounds of conventional labour law.

As unions grapple with the complexities of representing workers in precarious employment, examples from around the world are emerging which demonstrate an increasing willingness by unions to experiment with innovative regulatory techniques. In the USA, the best-known example is that of the 'Justice for Janitors' (JfJ) campaign initiated by the Service Employees International Union (SEIU) in the late 1980s. JfJ attempted to leverage the logic of service supply chains to achieve better wages and conditions for cleaners of commercial properties in Los Angeles and other US cities. In essence, JfJ sought to take wages out of competition in the awarding of contracts. It used the economic power of building owners to pressure commercial cleaning companies into providing better wages and conditions for workers. The campaign focused on leveraging the reputational risk of building owners by exposing them to public embarrassment (Waldinger et al., 1998). The difficulties experienced by the SEIU in organizing the entire commercial cleaning market in Los Angeles combined with ineffectual enforcement of labour law by state agencies inspired innovation. The SEIU partnered with large unionized employers to fund activities in 1999 aimed at abolishing 'illegal and unfair business practices in the janitorial industry' (MCTF, 2009).

The lessons learnt from the JfJ campaign about alternative means of deploying union voice to expose the economic power relations in service supply chains have found global application. In the UK a joint union/civil society organization campaign in the commercial cleaning sector mirrored the JfJ strategy. They targeted the lead firms that engage contract cleaning firms, rather than the contract cleaning firms themselves (Wills, 2008; Wright and Brown, 2013). Likewise in 2006, the Australian union 'United Voice', representing contract cleaners, launched its 'CleanStart' campaign (United Voice, 2011). This adopted a similar approach to both the UK and US campaigns, leveraging power in the cleaning supply chain to exercise that influence to benefit workers at the bottom of the chain.

These examples highlight experiments with methods of union voice outside the traditional collective bargaining role. However, they also underline the importance of scale. These are situations in which the interests of workers could not be effectively voiced at a workplace level. They required the unions to move their representative efforts up a level to be industry-wide (as per Heery's (2009b) suggestion, mentioned above). Indeed, union efforts in exercising voice for workers enmeshed in complex employment relationships within supply chains have extended to a variety of industries. In Australia, and to a lesser extent in the USA, road transport unions have been pursuing the interests of so-called 'independent contractors' through regulatory mechanisms outside the remit of labour law. In Australia, these efforts have centred on the campaign to secure regulation through 'safe rates' for independent contractors and employee drivers in the road transport industry. 'Safe rates' describes a pay 'rate high enough to prevent . . . drivers from accepting inadequate pay which may lead them to engage in activities which pose safety risks' (Kaine and Rawling, 2010: 196). The 'safe rates' campaign was aimed at making lead contractors accountable for unsafe work practices. These unsafe practices were the result of pressure applied to those lower in the contracting chain to provide their labour and vehicle more cheaply. This campaign culminated in legislation being enacted that specifically regulates the wages and safety of road transport workers by holding all participants in the transport supply chain responsible for the wages and safety of those that labour within it. An important feature of the legislation with regard to union voice is that it provides mechanisms for the union to insert itself into the regulatory architecture of the road transport industry. It achieves this by allowing the union to initiate enforcement proceedings in relation to suspected breaches and through exercising powers of inspection for suspected contraventions (Rawling and Kaine, 2012).

In the USA the same types of contracting chains seen in Australia have structured the road transport industry. Direct employees have increasingly been replaced by owner-drivers (who often lease trucks from the larger transport companies) since the deregulation of the sector in the 1980s. Independent contractors such as owner-drivers are not permitted to join unions, providing an obvious barrier to effective collective representation. In order to overcome this barrier, the International Brotherhood of Teamsters has been conducting a 'clean rates' campaign in the country's biggest ports. It has been working with environmentalists and local community groups since 2008 to have 'clean air' regulations introduced to improve air quality around the ports. Such regulations would require that trucking companies purchase new vehicles and that truck drivers previously engaged as 'owner-drivers' be deemed to be employees of the companies, resulting in 'clean' pay rates rather than the contracting rates previously earned by the truck drivers (Greenhouse, 2010). To date the union and its community allies have only been partially successful. In late 2011 an attempt to use port regulation (rather than labour law) to ban the use of owner-drivers was lost in the US Court of Appeals (Mongelluzzo,

2012). Clearly, this setback is disappointing and further time and distance are required to assess the effectiveness of these representations. However, what they do demonstrate are efforts by unions to extend their repertoires of voice to accommodate non-standard employment relationships and changing (sometimes seemingly amorphous) business structures. Of course, these examples are only illustrative and it must be noted that significant variation will occur in the types of voice pursued by unions in different economic and political contexts with varying levels of effectiveness.

Measuring the efficacy of voice

While unions may engage in similar voice activities across national and regional boundaries, the efficacy of voice may vary. As Hyman notes, there is no simple

> objective measure of the success of union officials and other employee representatives; not only does the overall evaluation of material outcomes require qualitative judgement, but achievements must be viewed as relative to what is potentially attainable – which is always in an important sense hypothetical. (Hyman, 1997: 311)

Indeed, measures that would seem instinctively to correlate with the capacity of unions to effectively represent workers (for example, union density) are not necessarily corroborated in reality. For example, while union membership in France has been historically low compared to other OECD countries and now sits at around 8 per cent (OECD, 2013), coverage of collective agreements is now close to 90 per cent. This is the result of regulatory mechanisms that allow for the extension of agreements across industries or even regions. These mechanisms can also allow for the collective agreements to be extended by the government even across companies that have not signed an agreement themselves (EIRO online, 2010). If effectiveness is measured by breadth, then French unions could be viewed as effective, although with membership so low an obvious issue to consider is the depth of the bargaining or representation that takes place (Hyman, 1997). This prompts the more general questions: how much involvement do workers have, via their unions, in decision-making processes in their workplaces (that is, how deep are the representative structures and opportunities) and does greater depth equal better outcomes? Moreover, union voice is exercised at various levels indicating that its scope extends beyond immediate and local issues such as pay to broader issues which may need addressing at industry or national levels, such as skill development and training or pension entitlements.

Voice at the National Scale

In many OECD countries the decline in unionization and the increasing difficulty in engaging in workplace collective bargaining has also prompted unions to reconsider options for representing workers at the national level through involvement in politics and policymaking. This section considers such options but explicitly acknowledges that union strategies regarding voice are heavily influenced by their own national contexts.

While unions around the world are being challenged by the 'mega trends of socioeconomic transformation such as globalization, deindustrialization and the digital revolution' (Lee and Lansbury, 2012: 434), there are crucial differences in how these are manifested across regions. It has long been recognized that the national regulatory context within which unions (and other parties) operate influences strategy and action (Frege and Kelly, 2003; Whitley, 1999); the same contextual factors influence the expression of union voice. Indeed, 'varieties of unionism' (VoU) should be expected. The 'varieties of capitalism' (VoC) framework classifies developed economies as either liberal market economies (LMEs) or coordinated market economies (CMEs) depending on their different institutional configurations. The institutional variations arising from these ascriptions provide the source of potential comparative advantage (Hall and Soskice, 2001). Contributing to VoC scholarship, Thelen (in Hall and Soskice, 2001) cogently argues that the key difference faced by unions in LMEs and CMEs is that of employer strategy. She suggests that in LMEs (for example, the USA, UK and Australia), particularly since the 1980s, employers have striven for flexibility at the workplace level and have pursued the restoration of 'managerial freedom' (Thelen, 2001: 72). In contrast, while employers in CMEs (for example Germany, Sweden) have also sought flexibility at the workplace level, these have not been achieved at the expense of strong national institutions. Consequently, unions in advanced economies have generally had to contend with employers' pursuit of 'firm level concerns with productivity and efficiency' to the detriment of the broader 'distributional agendas' of unions (Thelen, 2001: 71).

Despite the privileging of workplace level bargaining by employers, unions have prioritized their representative efforts depending, at least in part, on the national business system within which they operate (Frege and Kelly, 2003). That is, while most unions have by necessity devoted increased efforts to representation at a local level, some unions in particular contexts have focused more on the industry level (see examples above) and others on the national level (Hamann et al., 2012; Hamann and Kelly, 2007). Still others have concluded that the influence of global capital – often more economically powerful than states themselves (Levitt, 1983; Scholte, 1997) – requires them to extend their representation efforts to a supra-national level (Cotton and Gumbrell-McCormick, 2012; Helfen and Fichter, 2013).

The VoC distinction between LMEs and CMEs has been subject to criticism. In particular, some argue that it does not allow for variations over time (Schneider and Paunescu, 2012) and that such a loose dichotomy does not adequately capture the subtlety of differences between countries (Crouch, 2005). Still others note that such terms do not address the particular histories and institutional complementarities of some countries (Donaghey and Teague, 2009). They note, 'in Ireland, there is an ongoing debate about whether Ireland is closer to Boston or Berlin, whether it is a liberal or co-ordinated economy. The conclusion from this analysis is that it is neither: it represents an idiosyncratic mixture of the two models' (2009: 74). Subsequent scholarship has sought to take account of institutional change (Hall and Thelen, 2009), but a more serious limitation for the purpose of understanding varieties of union voice is that this perspective is primarily based on the situation and experiences of unions in the developed Western countries. Thus, it is debatable whether either the VoU or VoC perspectives can be applied to the different contexts of developing countries and state-led economies (Lee and Lansbury, 2012: 435).

This is significant, particularly so given the size and importance of the economies omitted in the VoC perspective. China in particular poses a challenge to any attempt at a neat categorization of union voice. Chinese unions, in common with others in communist countries, face the organizational dilemma of being both an instrument of the state and (at least notionally) the representatives of workers (Chan and Hui, 2012). This duality means that representing the interests of workers by Chinese unions is constrained by the imperative to cater to the interests of the state. In general, any tension between these two identities is settled in favour of the state. However, in recent years Chinese unions (through the All-China Federation of Trade Unions – ACTFU) have engaged in grass-roots organizing and have been more active in the protection of workers' rights. Chinese trade unions are also legally entitled to participate in collective bargaining at the workplace level (Cheng et al., 2011). Chinese state-dominated unions, at least formally, share some of the voice mechanisms of their democratic counterparts – again begging the question of the relative efficacy of voice in different contexts.

The expression of voice by unions at a national level resonates with a more socio-logical analysis of the role of unions. Its consideration prompts a question that is the philosophical counterpart of that posed by Freeman and Medoff: not what do unions do but what *should* unions do? Historically, the answer to this question has been answered broadly in one of two ways. The first interpretation is the more radical, emphasizing the revolutionary potential of unions to challenge the capitalist system (Hyman, 1971).[2] The second interpretation suggests that the role of unions is fundamentally to regulate the 'conditions of employment in such a way as to ward off from the manual-working producers the evil effects of industrial competition' (Webb and Webb, 1914: 805). With the decline of socialist regimes from the 1980s onwards, it has been argued that unions have become less ideologically driven and have increasingly pursued what Hyman (1997: 319) calls the 'bread and butter' approach. However, this focus on the so-called 'bread and butter' issues of nominal wages and workplace conditions should not lead to an assumption that these matters can only be prosecuted at a local level. These issues can be pursued beyond the workplace and through means other than collective bargaining. Unions routinely participate in national test cases and campaigns for the protection or development of a 'living wage'. Recent examples include the British Trade Union Congress (TUC) campaign for contingent workers (Heery, 2009b), the equivalent campaign by the Australian Council of Trade Unions (ACTU, 2013) and the response of unions in continental Europe to austerity measures imposed as a condition of EU assistance (Kitsantonis, 2013; Minder, 2012). These examples suggest that although the appetite of workers for revolutionary change may be questionable, it does not automati-cally follow that workers are 'simply concerned with their nominal wages'.[3] Rather they are also interested in real wages and the '"social wage" constituted by the welfare state' (Hyman and Gumbrell-McCormick, 2010: 317).

Politics and voice
A more instrumental analysis of the involvement of unions on a national level reveals that, particularly post-Cold War, unions have often pursued representative methods that have been less about revolutionary change and more about the 'method of legal enforcement' described by the Webbs in *Industrial Democracy*. The Webbs allude to the variable appetite of unions to pursue legal enforcement through Acts of Parliament and note that 'the fervour with which they [unions] believed in the particular Method, and the extent to which they have been able to employ it have varied according to the political circumstances of the time' (Webb and Webb, 1914: 247). While the Webbs were referring to union action in the context of nineteenth century Britain, the tendency for unions to

participate in the political process has been constant over time, if to varying degrees. One of the most common methods of political participation in the European context in recent years has been the negotiation of social pacts. Social pacts are 'bi- or tripartite national-level agreements including wage and/or nonwage issues' (Hamann and Kelly, 2007: 972). The past two decades have seen the proliferation of such arrangements across Europe with almost every Western European country (except the UK) being involved in some kind of social pact during that time (Hamann et al., 2012). Hamann and Kelly (2007) and Hamann et al. (2012) consider the motivations for governments to pursue social pacts. They suggest that pacts are an electoral strategy deployed by political parties seeking government (or to maintain government); to this end, pacts are utilized to legitimize contentious policies and, by incorporating unions, political parties circumvent large and public protests. Given this potential motivation it is reasonable to ask whether social pacts provide a legitimate avenue for union voice. Still others (Donaghey and Teague, 2005) find pacts a 'pragmatic adaptation to the trilemma of reconciling market integration, intergovernmentalism and democratic accountability' and point to the considerable social and economic gains in governance enabled by social pacts in the EU, including reform to welfare systems and facilitating conditions for enterprise agreements (Donaghey and Teague, 2005: 491). In the context of European pacts however, they too, ask the question 'how much commitment should European labour have to social pacts, particularly as they represent a weakening of corporatist deals of the past?' (Donaghey and Teague, 2005: 479).

Despite the political expedience behind the use of pacts by governments (and would-be governments) which theoretically undermines the integrity of engagement within the pact, there is still an underlying logic (and practical purpose?) to the continuing engagement of unions in the political process. Hyman (2001, cited in Hyman and Gumbrell-McCormick, 2010) notes that the regulation of the labour market is itself imbued with politics. The state, either actively or by default, 'underwrites a particular (im)balance between different participants in market relations' (Hyman and Gumbrell-McCormick, 2010: 316). Accordingly unions recognize that they need to 'influence the ways in which the state shapes the rules of the game in the labour market, including their own right to exist, to bargain collectively and to mobilize collective action' (2010: 316–17).

It is impossible to discuss the political engagement of unions without explicitly referencing the formal relationships that many unions have with particular political parties. As Dufour et al. (2010: 293) note, the 'history of most trade union movements is intertwined with political parties . . . [and the] evolution of this relationship is not merely an artefact of history but a living and often unconscious heritage on which contemporary union action has been constructed'. Formal affiliations of unions to political parties are coming under increasing scrutiny. In a number of countries, long-standing political ties between the industrial and political wings of the labour movement are coming under strain. In the UK, the re-positioning of labour as 'New Labour' in the 1990s was largely predicated on the party moving away from its union connections (McIlroy, 1998; Smith and Morton, 2006) The Australian Labor Party likewise has been engaged in a fierce internal debate about the level of influence that unions exert within the party. On the one hand, a former leader of the Parliamentary Labor party urges a move away from what he sees as 'union dominance' (Peatling, 2013); on the other, the current vice president of the party (who is a prominent union leader) argues that the current woes of Australian

Labor lie in its institutional drift from core labour values enshrined in the union move-ment (Van Onselen, 2013). European scholarship also notes the need for unions to balance their political actions and collective bargaining with service based activities (Scheuer, 2011). Particularly in Western Europe, post-Cold War politics, secularization and the decline in traditional 'working-class' industries, have resulted in an 'ideological blurring' (Pasture, 1996: 380, cited in Hyman and Gumbrell-McCormick, 2010: 321) which has affected the very identity of unions as political actors (Hyman and Gumbrell-McCormick, 2010).

This severing or loosening of traditional political ties at the national level provides at least a partial explanation of the burgeoning of union voice at a supra-national level, and of the deepening of relationships with non-traditional partners of labour, such as NGOs. The next sections consider whether representation at a supra-national level and in col-laboration with other civil society organizations (CSOs) might shed light on the future of union voice.

Supra-National Voice

The political influence of unions is being challenged on a number of fronts. Not only are traditional allegiances to political parties under scrutiny, but the proliferation of multi-lateral trade agreements determining regulatory frameworks elevates the scale at which decisions that impact on labour markets are made. In addition, such multilateral trade agreements commonly favour market regulation over social regulation such as labour standards (Elliott, 2003; Grandi, 2009; Krueger, 1996). This means that conventional union practices of lobbying for legislative change at a national level are, in and of them-selves, increasingly inadequate for shaping the regulation of labour standards. The situa-tion represents a paradox for union voice: on the one hand, the issues of union members can be seen as very localized – wages and conditions, workplace grievances; on the other, the factors impacting on those issues are often global. For example, decisions by multi-national corporations about how and where to invest present an even greater challenge for unions, particularly given that there is competition between countries to attract such investment, and that labour costs are a key consideration within that investment decision (IMF, 2007; Pain, 2007).

The influence of context on actors and regulatory outcomes has long been the subject of industrial relations scholarship. Dunlop's (1958) systems approach highlighted the various contextual pressures that are exerted on industrial relations systems and the actors within them. More recent scholarship in the area accounts for these contexts to be 'above the level' of the nation. This allows for the consideration of the impact of develop-ments in the global economy (Bray et al., 2011).

With globalization, the ubiquitous term used as short-hand for the transformation of the international economy away from the nation-state towards global markets and com-petition (Levitt, 1983), has come a shift in importance away from the local environment/context towards the global one.[4] For unions, this has resulted in greater interest in devel-oping more robust representative structures and regulatory instruments on an interna-tional scale (Helfen and Fichter, 2013). Examples of such instruments are international framework agreements (IFAs), also known as global framework agreements (GFAs). GFAs are transnational agreements negotiated by global union federations (GUFs) with transnational corporations. By the end of 2012 there were 88 such agreements in operation (Helfen and Fichter, 2013). Helfen and Fichter (2013: 2) argue that GFAs ideally create 'a transnational arena of labour relations by defining the content, selecting the actors, delineating the processes and setting the scope of labour-management interaction'. They also highlight the importance of these global agreements in enabling unions to exercise voice at a local level, albeit described in terms of 'creating space at the local level for organizing and strengthening unions' (2013: 5). Union representation at the supra-national level is not without complication. Language barriers, differences between cultures, political and legal systems, organizational forms and resource constraints pose ongoing and serial challenges for international union cooperation (Larsson, 2012). A further obstacle for the ongoing participation of unions at this level is the distance of these instruments and activities from individual union members. This distance can obscure the potential benefits of cooperation and may be exacerbated by the 'diffuse reciprocity' upon which such cooperation is based – meaning that while members of the GUF may expect equal advantages from involvement, these will be 'in the aggregate and over the long term, rather than short-term pay-offs' (Cotton and Gumbrell-McCormick, 2012: 720). Despite these limitations and attendant criticisms that GFAs have not managed to slow union decline, their effective reach into the governance issues associated with subcontractors and suppliers (where their capacity exceeds the boundaries of transnational corporations) suggests that GFAs may ultimately prove to be an important component of union voice in complex global production networks (Helfen and Fichter, 2013).

Supplementing union voice at a supra-national level is collaboration between unions and CSOs with an interest in labour issues. CSOs have been prominent partners in transnational labour struggles with companies such as Nike (Bair and Palpacuer, 2012) and Foxconn (*The Economist*, 2012). Heery et al. cite a number of UK-led initiatives, namely Amnesty International UK, Daycare Trust and Public Concern at Work (2012: 146).

Such collaborations are evident at other scales. The campaigns in the commercial cleaning sector and the 'safe rates' and 'clean rates' campaigns all featured the involvement of community groups. Their social justice platform addressed a diverse audience and in so doing harnessed broader community support. Literature on these collaborations is usually couched in terms of community unionism, often discussed as one facet of union revitalization (Tattersall, 2005). Alternatively, Heery (2010) reflects upon CSOs in relation to the particular voice functions they provide for workers. Many pursue issues such as the living wage and quality of work with a strong emphasis on equality and diversity. They also 'enjoy high legitimacy, are regarded as experts in the particular issues with which they deal and are effective campaigning organizations, especially within the political process' (Heery, 2012: 554). There are some obvious limitations to the representation that CSOs can provide at the workplace level. For instance, many depend financially upon the state and/or corporations for their survival. However, coalitions with unions that harness the specific characteristics and strengths of CSO representation can amplify union voice. Despite some tensions between unions and CSOs (Fine, 2007) it is likely that union–community coalitions will become a louder part of the worker voice chorus as unions continue to search for ways to revitalize and rebuild membership and representative power (Heery, 2010).

CONCLUSION

With union density continuing to decline internationally, the future of union representation and, by association, union voice is by no means certain. Changes in the organization of global capital and product markets are proving a challenge to traditional notions of union representation and organization. Thus, the capacity of collective bargaining to provide regulatory outcomes favourable to workers is being undermined. In order for unions to maintain legitimacy and voice, they have been required to embrace diversity beyond the bounds of their traditional male-dominated blue-collar base, to engage in innovative regulatory methods and increasingly to invest in representative efforts at different scales. This multi-scalarity highlights the difference and potential advantage of union voice over NERs in representing the interests of workers. NERs tend to be pre-occupied by 'consultation and information' (Hyman, 1997) while union representation extends to distributive issues. More importantly unions can, and do, pursue these issues beyond the workplace or industry. Indeed, given the reduction in the coverage of collective bargaining, the very survival of union voice may lie in attempts by unions to build representation and achieve labour market regulation at national and supra-national levels (Heery, 2009b). Furthermore, in considering their future, specifically how to amplify their voice, unions will need to anticipate and respond to the activities of global capital. In so doing unions grapple with the question of whether to keep singing solo or, with CSOs, to become part of a larger concert calling for better outcomes for workers globally.

NOTES

1. This type of employment arrangement has proliferated over the past two decades (ILO, 2012) as these forms of work are synonymous with the rhetoric of flexibility which has dominated debate about labour market policy (Johnstone et al., 2012).
2. The radical perspective is obviously more nuanced than this and in *Marxism and the Sociology of Trade Unionism*, Hyman (1971: 3–4) divides this socialist perspective into two categories, 'those approaches which discern significant revolutionary potential in trade union activity: and those which argue that such activity does not itself facilitate . . . the revolutionary transformation of capitalist society' and details both the 'optimistic' and 'pessimistic' traditions.
3. While not necessarily looking to overthrow capitalism itself, many of the Arab spring protests began with strikes and protests by unions (Fahim and Kirkpatrick, 2011; Faiola, 2011; Lee and Lansbury, 2012).
4. Although it should be noted that arguments about globalization and the downward pressure exerted on labour costs by competition between countries were used by early proponents of international unionism in the 1920s and that antecedents of international union organizations were evident as far back as the late nineteenth century and have existed in some form ever since (Cotton and Gumbrell-McCormick, 2012).

REFERENCES

ACTU (2013), 'Secure jobs: better future', accessed 7 April 2013 at http://www.securejobs.org.au/Home/Campaigns/Secure-Jobs-Better-Future.aspx.
Agnone, Jon-Jason M. (2010), 'Racial inequality in wealth: do labor unions matter?', PhD dissertation, University of Washington, Washington.
Arup, Christopher, Peter Gahan, John Howe, Richard Johnstone, Richard, Mitchell and Anthony O'Donnell

(2006), *Labour Law and Labour Market Regulation: Essays on the Construction, Constitution and Regulation of Labour Markets and Work Relationships*, Sydney: Federation Press.

Bair, J. and F. Palpacuer (2012), 'From varieties of capitalism to varieties of activism: the antisweatshop movement in comparative perspective', *Social Problems*, **59**, 522–43.

Bennett, James T., L. Jones and M. Godfrey (2012), 'Public service pay cuts needed: O'Farrell', *The Australian*, 29 August, accessed 5 November 2013 at http://www.theaustralian.com.au/news/breaking-news/psa-accuses-nsw-govt-of-disgraceful-attack/story-fn3dxiwe-1226460442349.

Bertone, S., G. Griffin and R.D. Iverson (1995), 'Immigrant workers and Australian trade unions: participation and attitudes', *International Migration Review*, **29** (3), 722–44.

Blanchflower, D. and A. Bryson (2004), 'What effect do unions have on wages now and would Freeman and Medoff be surprised?', *Journal of Labor Research*, **25** (3), 383–414.

Boroff, K. and D. Lewin (1997), 'Loyalty, voice and intent to exit a union firm: a conceptual and empirical analysis', *Industrial & Labour Relations Review*, **51** (1), 50–63.

Bray, Mark, Peter Waring and Rae Cooper (2011), *Employment Relations: Theory and Practice*, 2nd edn, Sydney: McGraw-Hill.

Briggs, C., M. Cole and J. Buchanan (2002), 'Where are the non-members? Challenges and opportunities in the heartlands for union organising', *International Journal of Employment Studies*, **10** (2), 1–23.

Buchanan, J. and R. Callus (1993), 'Efficiency and equity at work: the need for labour market regulation in Australia', *Journal of Industrial Relations*, **35** (4), 515–37.

Bureau of Labor Statistics (2012), 'Union members 2012', accessed 29 March 2013 at http://www.bls.gov/news.release/pdf/union2.pdf.

Chan, C. and E. Hui (2012), 'The dynamics and dilemma of workplace trade union reform in China: the case of the Honda workers' strike', *Journal of Industrial Relations*, **54** (5), 653–68.

Cheng, J.Y., K.I. Ngok and Y. Huang (2011), 'Multinational corporations, global civil society and Chinese labour: workers' solidarity in China in the era of globalization', *Economic and Industrial Democracy*, **33** (3), 379-401. doi: 10.1177/0143831x11411325.

Cliffe, Jeremy (2013), 'Unions are in trouble. But some are learning new tricks – from the bosses', *The Economist*, 6 April, available at: http://www.economist.com/news/international/21575752-unions-are-trouble-some-are-learning-new-tricksfrom-bosses-unions-inc (accessed 5 November 2013).

Cotton, E. and R. Gumbrell-McCormick (2012), 'Global unions as imperfect multilateral organizations: an international relations perspective', *Economic and Industrial Democracy*, **33** (4), 707–28. doi: 10.1177/0143831x12436616.

Crouch, C. (2005), 'Models of capitalism', *New Political Economy*, **10**, 439–56.

Cullinane, N., J. Donaghey, T. Dundon and T. Dobbins (2012), 'Different voices, different rooms: double-breasting and the managerial agenda', *International Journal of Human Resource Management*, **23** (2), 368–84.

Davey, M. and S. Greenhouse (2011), 'Angry demonstrations in Wisconsin as cuts loom', *New York Times*, February 16.

Donaghey, J. and P. Teague (2005), 'The persistence of social pacts in Europe', *Industrial Relations Journal*, **36** (6), 478–93.

Dufour, C., G. Murray, D. Peetz and C. Yates (2010), 'Rethinking collective representation: introduction', *Transfer: European Review of Labour and Research*, **16** (3), 291–7. doi: 10.1177/1024258910374276.

Dundon, T., A.Wilkinson, M. Marchington and P. Ackers (2004), 'The meanings and purpose of employee voice', *International Journal of Human Resource Management*, **15** (6), 1149–70.

Dunlop, John T. (1958), *Industrial Relations Systems*, New York: Holt.

The Economist (2012), 'When workers dream of life beyond the factory gates', 15 December, available at: http://www.economist.com/news/business/21568384-can-foxconn-worlds-largest-contract-manufacturer-keep-growing-and-improve-its-margins-now (accessed 22 January 2013).

EIRO online (2010), 'France: industrial relations profile', accessed 6 April 2013 at http://www.eurofound.europa.eu/eiro/country/france_4.htm.

Elliott, Kimberley Ann and Richard B. Freeman (2003), *Can Labor Standards Improve Under Globalization?*, Washington, DC: Peterson Institute for International Economics.

Fahim, Kareem and David D. Kirkpatrick (2011), 'Labor actions in Egypt boost protests', *The New York Times*, 9 February, accessed 5 November 2013 at http://www.nytimes.com/2011/02/10/world/middleeast/10egypt.html.

Faiola, Anthony (2011), 'Egypt's labor movement blooms in Arab spring', *Washington Post*, 25 September, accessed 5 November 2013 at http://articles.washingtonpost.com/2011-09-25/world/35275505_1_labor-unrest-labor-leaders-interim-government.

Fine, J. (2007), 'A marriage made in heaven? Mismatches and misunderstandings between worker centres and unions', *British Journal of Industrial Relations*, **45** (2), 335–60.

Freeman, R.B. and J. Medoff (1984), *What Do Unions Do?*, New York: Basic Books.

Frege, C. and J. Kelly (2003), 'Union revitalization strategies in comparative perspective', *European Journal of Industrial Relations*, **9** (1), 7–24.

Grandi, Pablo Lazo (2009), 'Trade agreements and their relation to labour standards: the current situation', ICTSD Programme on EPAs and Regionalism, Issues Paper No. 3, International Centre for Trade and Sustainable Development (ICTSD), Geneva.

Greenhouse, S. (2010), 'Clearing the air at American ports', *New York Times*, 26 February.

Hall, P. and D. Soskice (2001), *Varieties of Capitalism: The Institutional Foundations of Competitive Advantage*, Oxford: Oxford University Press.

Hall, Peter A. and Kathleen Thelen (2009), 'Institutional change in varieties of capitalism', *Socio-Economic Review*, **7** (1), 7–34. doi: 10.1093/ser/mwn020.

Hamann, K., A. Johnstone and J. Kelly (2012), 'Unions against governments: explaining general strikes in Western Europe, 1980–2006', *Comparative Political Studies*. doi: 10.1177/0010414012463894.

Hamann, K. and J. Kelly (2007), 'Party politics and the reemergence of social pacts in Western Europe', *Comparative Political Studies*, **40** (8), 971–94. doi: 10.1177/0010414006294818.

Heery, E. (2009a), 'The representation gap and the future of worker representation', *Industrial Relations Journal*, **40** (4), 324–36.

Heery, E. (2009b), 'Trade unions and contingent labour: scale and method', *Cambridge Journal of Regions, Economy and Society*, **2** (3), 429–42. doi: 10.1093/cjres/rsp020.

Heery, E. (2010), 'Worker representation in a multiform system: a framework for evaluation', *Journal of Industrial Relations*, **52** (5), 543–59. doi: 10.1177/0022185610381565.

Heery, E., S. Williams and B. Abbott (2012), 'Civil society organizations and trade unions: cooperation, conflict and indifference', *Work, Employment and Society*, **26** (1), 145–60.

Helfen, Markus and Michael Fichter (2013), 'Building transnational union networks across global production networks: conceptualising a new arena of labour-management relations', *British Journal of Industrial Relations*. doi: 10.1111/bjir.12016.

Hickey, Robert (2004), 'Preserving the pattern: membership mobilization and union revitalization at PACE Local 4-227', *Labor Studies Journal*, **29** (1), 1–20.

Hirsch, Barry T. (2004), 'What do unions do for economic performance?', *Journal of Labor Research*, **25** (3), 415–55.

Hirschman, A. (1970), *Exit, Voice, Loyalty: Response to Decline in Firms, Organizations and States*, Cambridge, MA: Harvard University Press.

Holgate, J., G. Hebson and A. McBride (2006), 'Why gender and "difference" matters; a critical appraisal of industrial relations research', *Industrial Relations Journal*, **37** (4), 310–28.

Hyman, R. (1971), *Marxism and the Sociology of Trade Unionism*, London: Pluto Press.

Hyman, R. (1997), 'The future of employee representation', *British Journal of Industrial Relations*, **35** (3), 309–36.

Hyman, R. and R. Gumbrell-McCormick (2010), 'Trade unions, politics and parties: is a new configuration possible?', *Transfer: European Review of Labour and Research*, **16** (3), 315–31. doi: 10.1177/1024258910373863.

International Labour Organization (2012), 'World of Work Report 2012: better jobs for a better economy', Geneva: International Institute for Labour Studies.

International Labour Organization (2013), 'Global Wage Report 2012/13: wages and equitable growth', Geneva: International Labour Office.

International Monetary Fund (2007), 'World economic outlook: globalization and inequality', IMF Occasional Paper, Washington DC.

Johnstone, R., S. McCrystal, I. Nossar, M. Rawling and J. Riley (2012), *Beyond Employment: The Legal Regulaton of Work Relationships*, Sydney: The Federation Press.

Kaine, S. and M. Rawling (2010), 'Comprehensive campaigning in the NSW transport industry: bridging the divide between regulation and union organizing', *Journal of Industrial Relations*, **52** (2), 183–200.

Kitsantonis, N. (2013), 'Greek workers walk out in fresh austerity protest', accessed 7 April 2013 at http://www.nytimes.com/2013/02/21/world/europe/greek-unions-walk-out-in-austerity-protest.html?_r=0.

Krueger, Alan B. (1996), 'Observations in international labor standards and trade', NBER Working Paper Series, National Bureau of Economic Research, Cambridge MA.

Larsson, Bengt (2012), 'Obstacles to transnational trade union cooperation in Europe: results from a European survey', *Industrial Relations Journal*, **43** (2), 152–70.

Lee, B. and R. Lansbury (2012), 'Refining varieties of labour movements: perspectives from the Asia-Pacific region', *Journal of Industrial Relations*, **54** (4), 433–42.

Levesque, C. and G. Murray (2010), 'Trade union cross-border alliances within MNCs: disentangling union dynamics at the local, national and international levels', *Industrial Relations Journal*, **41** (4), 312–32.

Levitt, T. (1983), 'Globalisation of markets', *Harvard Business Review*, May-June, 92–102.

Marley, Patric (2011), 'New poll relflects divide on bargaining limits', *JS Online*, accessed 17 April 2013 at http://www.jsonline.com/news/statepolitics/130173963.html.

McIlroy, J. (1998), 'The enduring alliance? Trade unions and the making of New Labour, 1994–1997', *British Journal of Industrial Relations*, **36** (4), 537–64.

MCTF (2009), 'Cleaning up the cleaning industry', available at: http://www.janitorialwatch.org/ (accessed 9 December 2012).

Minder, R. (2012), 'Workers across Europe synchronise protests', *New York Times*, 14 November, accessed 7 April 2013 at http://www.nytimes.com/2012/11/15/world/europe/workers-in-southern-europe-synchronize-anti-austerity-strikes.html.

Mongelluzzo, B. (2012), 'The Teamsters refuse to quit', accessed 4 April 2013 at http://www.laane.org/whats-new/2012/02/02/how-independent-are-owner-operators/.

OECD (2013), OECD StatExtracts, Trade Union Density, accessed 21 March 2013 at http://stats.oecd.org/Index.aspx?DatasetCode=UN_DEN.

Pain, Nigel and Isabell Koske (2007), 'The effects of globalisation on labour markets, productivity and inflation', in OECD (ed.), *Meeting of Heads of National Economic Research Organisations at OECD Headquarters*, Paris: OECD.

Peatling, Stephanie (2013), 'Latham: Labour must lead on issues', *Sydney Morning Herald*, 11 March, accessed 5 November 2013 at http://www.smh.com.au/opinion/political-news/latham-labor-must-lead-on-issues-20130310-2fu7d.html.

Prideaux, J. (2013), 'Interview with Jeremy Cliffe. Unions are in trouble. But some are learning new tricks - from the bosses', *The Economist* 6 April, available at: http://www.economist.com/news/international/21575752-unions-are-trouble-some-are-learning-new-tricksfrom-bosses-unions-inc (accessed 28 November 2013).

Rawling, M. and S. Kaine (2012), 'Regulating supply chains to provide a safe rate for road transport workers', *Australian Journal of Labour Law*, **25**, 237–57.

Scheuer, Steen (2011), 'Union membership variation in Europe: a ten-country comparative analysis', *European Journal of Industrial Relations*, **17** (1), 57–73.

Schneider, Martin R. and Mihai Paunescu (2012), 'Changing varieties of capitalism and revealed comparative advantages from 1990 to 2005: a test of the Hall and Soskice claims', *Socio-Economic Review*. doi: 10.1093/ser/mwr038.

Smith, P. and G. Morton (2006), 'Nine years of New Labour: neoliberalism and workers' rights', *British Journal of Industrial Relations*, **44** (4), 401–20.

Standing, G. (2011), *The Precariat: The New Dangerous Class*, New York: Bloomsbury Academic.

Tattersall, A. (2005), 'There is power in coalition: a framework for assessing how and when union-community coalitions are effective and enhance union power', *Labour and Industry*, **16** (2), 97–112.

Thelen, K. (2001), 'Varieties of labor politics in the developed democracies', in P. Hall and D. Soskice (eds), *Varieties of Capitalism: The Institutional Foundations of Comparative Advantage*, Oxford: Oxford University Press, pp. 71–103.

Towers, B. (1997), *The Representation Gap: Change and Refrom in the British and American Workplace*, Oxford: Oxford University Press.

Turnbull, Peter (2003), 'What do unions do now?', *Journal of Labor Research*, **24** (3), 491–527.

Turner, L. (2005), 'From transformation to revitalization: a new research agenda for a contested global economy', *Work and Occupations*, **32**, 383–99.

United Voice (2011), 'CleanStart: fair deal for cleaners', accessed 3 April 2013 at http://www.cleanstart.org.au/about.

Van Onselen, P. (2013), 'ALP facing moral crisis, says party vice-president Tony Sheldon', *The Australian*, 2 February, accessed 5 November 2013 at http://www.theaustralian.com.au/national-affairs/alp-facing-moral-crisis-says-party-vice-president-tony-sheldon/story-fn59niix-1226567132990.

Waldinger, R., C. Erickson, R. Milkman, D. Mitchell, A.Valenzuela, K. Wong and M. Zeitlin (1998), 'Helots no more: a case study of the Justice for Janitors Campaign in Los Angeles', in K. Bronfenbrenner, S. Friedman, R. Hurd, R. Oswald and R. Seeber (eds), *Organizing to Win*, New York: Cornell University Press, pp. 102–20.

Webb, S. and B. Webb (1914), *Industrial Democracy*, London: Longman, Green and Co.

Webb, S. and B. Webb (1920), *The History of Trade Unionism*, revised edn, New York: Longman, Green and Co.

Whitley, R. (1999), *Divergent Capitalisms: The Societal Structuring and Change of Buisness Systems*, Oxford: Oxford University Press.

Wills, J. (2008), 'Making class poltitics possible: organizing contract cleaners in London', *International Journal of Urban and Regional Research*, **32** (2), 305–23.

Wisconsin (2012), Union Voice: State Employee Council Newsletter, Wisonsin: AFT Wisconsin.

Wright, C. and W. Brown (2013), 'The effectiveness of socially sustainable sourcing mechanisms: assessing the prospects of a new form of joint regulation', *Industrial Relations Journal*, **44** (1), 20–37.

12 The missing employee in employee voice research
Dionne M. Pohler and Andrew A. Luchak

INTRODUCTION

The purpose of this review is to discuss employee voice from the perspective of the employee. However, employee voice is not a uniform concept with a broadly agreed upon definition. Employee experiences with voice differ across different voice regimes and also greatly depend on the underlying purpose or motivation behind its use. Given this, we felt it appropriate to develop a matrix to allow for the broad categorization of the seemingly disparate literatures on employee voice. Our matrix is based on two dimensions: the normative intention or purpose of voice and the phenomenon of interest under study. Based on this classification system, we briefly review the key developments in each of these literatures. We then take stock of this research by highlighting how the various literatures examining employee voice have all fallen somewhat short in explicitly integrating the perspective and interests of employees. We conclude by proposing avenues for future research. In particular, we argue that increased integration between disciplines that examine voice and participation in the workplace would better serve not only employees, but also unions, employers, policy-makers and researchers.

DEFINITIONS OF EMPLOYEE VOICE

The meaning of employee voice is highly contested (Dundon et al., 2004). Although it falls under different labels (citizenship behavior, participation, involvement, engagement, empowerment, and so on), employee voice has been studied extensively across a broad range of social science and management disciplines including, but not necessarily limited to, industrial and labor relations, political science, law, human resource management, organizational behavior, and economics. Whether justified by and/or understood through notions of industrial democracy and citizenship (Ackers et al., 2004; Clegg, 1960; Freeman and Medoff, 1984; Webb and Webb, 1902), efficiency (Freeman and Medoff, 1984), equity (Budd, 2004), human rights (Adams, 2001), procedural justice (Greenberg, 1987; Thibault and Walker, 1975), retribution (Detert and Burris, 2007; Turnley and Feldman, 1999), pro-organizational involvement and engagement (Morrison, 2011), or responses to dissatisfaction (Farrell and Rusbult, 1992; Rusbult et al., 1988; Withey and Cooper, 1989), employee voice is without a doubt one of only a few concepts that has been studied so extensively across such a wide range of disciplines. However, the majority of this research to date has been performed in silos within the respective fields, often separated by differing normative assumptions surrounding the intention or purpose of voice, and/or an examination of voice as either a behavior or a system. Although the relative contributions in each of these fields are notable in their own right, the lack of integration has hindered a deeper and more comprehensive understanding of the purpose, antecedents, processes, and consequences of employee voice for both individuals and organizations.

The problem begins with the narrow manner in which employee voice is conceptualized in most disciplines, defining it a priori in terms of both its normative purpose and form. For instance, a recent 'integrated' conceptualization of voice in the organizational behavior literature defined voice as the 'discretionary communication of ideas, suggestions, concerns, or opinions about work-related issues *with the intent to improve organizational or unit functioning*' (Morrison, 2011: 375, italics added). This definition in effect excludes any employee voice that is reactive, formal, collective, representative, non-discretionary, and may not be primarily intended to improve organizational functioning (that is, whistle-blowing, grievance filing, and so on). And although culture and climate have recently been integrated into the examination of employee voice behavior in this literature (Morrison et al., 2011), research following this or similar definitions still ignores the ways in which different voice systems (for example, high involvement work systems, unions, and so on) influence perceptions of psychological safety with expressing voice and the overall voice climate in the organization, both of which have been shown to have a direct impact on employee behavior (Moss and Sanchez, 2004). On the opposite end of the spectrum in the industrial relations literature, the predominant focus in the study of employee voice has been on understanding the outcomes of formal and often representative voice systems (unions, works councils, and so on). However, research on voice systems in this literature rarely takes into account individual differences, employee desires for more cooperative and direct forms of voice, and employee motivations to help improve the efficient and effective functioning of the organization.

DIMENSIONS OF EMPLOYEE VOICE

Based on an extensive, though not completely exhaustive, review of the voice research, we propose that a broad categorization of the seemingly disparate literatures on employee voice can be developed based on two dimensions: the normative intention or purpose of voice (that is, promotive or remedial) and the phenomena under study (that is, human behavior or system impact). With regard to the first dimension relating to intention or purpose, our definition of promotive voice can be linked very closely to Morrison's (2011) definition of voice mentioned above in that it has the primary intention of improving organizational or unit functioning. In a broader sense then, promotive voice is any type of voice that assumes a priori a unity of interest between the employee and the organization with regard to the purpose of voicing behavior as being beneficial for both. Remedial voice, on the other hand, encompasses conceptualizations of voice as both justice-oriented, which is defined as voice with a 'focus on achieving restitution for perceived mistreatment and/or restoring justice via seeking retribution for wrong-doing' (Olson-Buchanan and Boswell, 2008; compare Klaas et al., 2012: 327), and problem-focused, which is defined as a focus on stopping or preventing harm (Morrison, 2011). However, unlike these previous definitions, we also include under our definition of remedial any voice which is focused on ensuring the establishment, protection and oversight of employee rights and interests vis-à-vis the organization. As such, our definition of remedial includes any type of employee voice which assumes a priori that there is *potential* for conflict between the interests of the employee and the interests of the organization.

The second dimension encompasses phenomena under study and the categorizations include voice as a behavior and voice as a system. Voice as a behavior is primarily concerned with the antecedents and consequences of employee choice with regard to using voice. Voice as a system is primarily concerned with individual and organizational outcomes under different voice systems or arrangements (Marchington, 2007). While previous attempts to categorize employee voice have focused on other dimensions such as formal/informal (Klaas et al., 2012), anonymous/identifiable (Klaas et al., 2012), direct/representative (Luchak, 2003), and union/non-union (Marsden, 2013), unlike previous conceptualizations, our dimensions allow us to cut across traditional silos in employee voice research.

Cross-classifying our two dimensions leads to the typology of research contributions shown in Figure 12.1. Each item in the matrix will be discussed briefly in turn, with the exception of litigation and worker ownership/directors, as we limit our focus to voice behaviors and systems that exist within the context of a traditional employment relationship, though we include them in our typology to show its extension to research on voice outside this primary context.

REVIEW OF KEY DEVELOPMENTS IN EMPLOYEE VOICE RESEARCH

Pro-Social Voice

Pro-social voice is meant to refer to discretionary communication of ideas, suggestions or opinions with the intent of improving organizational functioning (Burris et al., 2008; Detert and Burris, 2007; Detert and Trevino, 2010; Klaas et al., 2012; LePine and Van

	Voice behavior	Voice system
Promotive	Pro-social voice	High involvement work systems Non-union employee representation *Worker ownership/directors*
Remedial	Grievance filing Whistle-blowing *Litigation*	Collective bargaining/unions Works councils Alternative dispute resolution

Figure 12.1   A typology of employee voice research

Dyne, 1998; Morrison 2011; Tangirala and Ramanujam, 2008; Van Dyne et al., 2003; Van Dyne and LePine, 1998). Guided by a belief in its value for employees and organizations alike, considerable organizational behavior research has been focused on understanding the antecedents and consequences of individuals engaging in pro-social voice, largely as an organizational citizenship behavior.

An important theme underlying this research is to understand what factors contribute to or detract from the willingness of employees to provide (or withhold) helpful information to the organization. Employees who engage in pro-social voice are believed to be motivated by two underlying concerns: a *utility motive* centered on the question of whether they think speaking up will be successful or effective; and a *self-preservation motive* centered on the question of whether they think speaking up will be safe in the sense of not drawing unwelcome attention to themselves as trouble-makers or complainers (Morrison, 2011). A wide variety of contextual and individual factors has been considered in the research.

Contextual factors can convey important information to employees about whether voice will make a difference or not, as well as whether it can be harmful to one's image or career. Consistent with these arguments, contexts that encourage upward or lateral communication flow such as less bureaucratic or hierarchical structures (Glauser, 1984) or cultures (Stamper and Van Dyne, 2001) have been found to encourage voice while a lack of formal upward feedback channels has been found to contribute to a climate of silence (Morrison and Miliken, 2000). Thematic of the voice-enhancing effects of contexts that make it easier and less intimidating to speak out, work group voice has been found to be more common in groups that are smaller (Islam and Zyphur, 2005; LePine and Van Dyne, 1998), self-managed (LePine and Van Dyne, 1998), where they adopt egalitarian practices (Erez et al., 2002), where group members are more satisfied (LePine and Van Dyne, 1998), and where the group shares a belief in the safety and utility of voice (Morrison et al., 2011).

More open and supportive supervisory relationships have also been found to encourage voice (Milliken et al., 2003), perhaps because these characteristics cue employees that it is worthwhile and safe to voice. Consistent with this line of research, higher quality leader-member exchange relationships (Burris et al., 2008), the commitment enhancing effects of transformational leadership (Detert and Burris, 2007; Liu et al., 2010), and the more trusting environment created by ethical leadership (Walumbwa and Schaubroeck, 2009) have all been found to enhance voice.

Regardless of context, some individuals may be more likely to voice than others and so antecedent research has also focused on the personal characteristics of voicers. Early work emphasized attitudes towards jobs or organizations, showing that individuals with higher levels of job satisfaction and organizational commitment are more likely to voice (Rusbult et al., 1988; Withy and Cooper, 1989), presumably because they are more motivated to offer constructive input to resolve sources of dissatisfaction. Research on dispositional factors has shown that employees higher in traits such as conscientiousness and extraversion are more willing to speak up and help whereas those higher on neuroticism and agreeableness will be less likely to risk challenging the status quo (LePine and Van Dyne, 2001).

Considerable research suggests that pro-social voice can have important benefits for organizations, work groups, and individuals. At the organizational level, voice has been shown to increase the effectiveness of organizational decision-making and to improve error detection (Morrison and Milliken, 2000). Within cross-functional teams, voice has been argued (LePine and Van Dyne, 1998) and shown (Edmondson, 2003) to contribute to better decision-making and encourage implementation of best practices. However, the effects of voice on individuals are somewhat mixed. On the one hand, voice may enhance control, which has been shown to improve employee satisfaction and motivation as well as to reduce stress (Greenberger and Strasser, 1986; Parker, 1993). The opportunity to express one's views itself may contribute to more positive attitudes (Morrison and Milliken, 2000) such as increased job satisfaction and organizational commitment (Vakola and Bourades, 2005). On the other hand, voicers can face image loss (for example, being seen as trouble-makers) or be formally sanctioned through the reward structure (for example, through lower performance evaluations; see Seibert et al., 2001). In an attempt to reconcile debate over the individual consequences, Burris et al. (2013) suggest the effects will depend on the consensus shared between the employee and supervisor on the value of voice being offered, with positive outcomes where they agree the employee is contributing high quality voice and negative outcomes where employees overestimate the value of their contributions. This line of reasoning is consistent with the utility and self-preservation motives underlying employee voice with supervisory cues informing employees' assessments about whether to voice or not.

High Involvement Work Systems

As promotive voice is also a central concept in such employment systems as high involvement (Lawler, 1986), mutual gains enterprises (Kochan and Osterman, 1994), and high performance work systems (Applebaum et al., 2000; Benson and Lawler, 2003; Cappelli and Neumark, 2001), considerable research has also focused on how promotive voice systems impact employees and organizations. Though conceptualized in different ways, high involvement management systems are meant to offer employees the opportunity to be involved and to participate in decisions affecting their work role and in broader issues of organizational governance (Wood, 2010). Two streams of research on the consequences of high involvement systems have emerged in the literature.

The first, primarily examined within the organizational behavior or human resource management fields, views organizations, and by extension employees, as benefiting from these interventions. This research views high involvement as satisfying employees' intrinsic need to be involved in decisions regarding their work role and the broader organization. Having their social and psychological needs met by involvement, employees are believed to experience greater well-being with positive consequences for their interest in contributing to the success of the organization through greater in-role and extra-role behaviors. Consistent with this line of research, high involvement systems have been connected to higher levels of job satisfaction (Macky and Boxall, 2007; Wu and Chaturvedi, 2009), organizational commitment (Macky and Boxall, 2007; Sanders et al., 2008; Takeuchi et al., 2007), lower turnover (Gould-Williams, 2004; Wright and Kehoe, 2008), and higher extra-role performance (Wright and Kehoe, 2008).

The second stream of research derives from the labor-process and industrial relations literatures and sees high involvement systems as intensifying work with negative consequences for worker well-being (Thompson and Harley, 2007). Though perspectives vary, the essence of this argument is that organizations will not completely reciprocate workers with improved job security, wage increases or even development opportunities (Thompson, 2011) for the greater demands placed on them through expectations of higher involvement. As a result, employees will be more likely to experience high involvement as a form of work intensification that lowers job satisfaction, increases stress and fatigue, and contributes to emotional exhaustion (Macky and Boxall, 2008; Godard, 2010; Wood et al., 2012). High job demands or intensification pressures appear to be important boundary conditions for determining whether workers experience high involvement positively or negatively (Kroon et al., 2009; Macky and Boxall, 2008).

Non-Union Employee Representation

Another type of promotive voice system includes non-union employee representation (NER). NER has been defined as one or more employees acting in a representative capacity in dealing with management over workplace issues (Taras and Kaufman, 2006). Although in Britain scholars began discussing NER systems much earlier (Marchington et al., 1992), with few exceptions (for example, Lewin and Mitchell, 1992), research on NER systems in North America really only exploded the following decade, with the publication of a book dedicated to NER (Kaufman and Taras, 2000). Preceding this, most of the research on NER in North America focused on historical studies of company unions and debates in legal/policy circles over sections of the National Labor Relations Act in the United States banning NER committees in the workplace (Kaufman and Taras, 2000).

Since then, there has been a growing interest in NER systems around the world. However, with a few exceptions (for example, Bryson et al., 2006; Lipset and Meltz, 2000), the majority of the growing international research has been conducted as case studies at individual organizations (for example, Benson, 2000; Gollan, 2007; Pyman et al., 2006; Gospel and Willman, 2005; Morishima and Tsuru, 2000; Kim and Kim, 2004). The motives for adopting NER systems vary, resulting in a very diverse set of systems between companies (Gollan, 2007; Kaufman and Taras, 2000; Terry, 1999), and consequently, a diverse set of outcomes (Kaufman and Taras, 2010). Though the motives and structures vary, the ultimate goals of most NER systems include either an improvement in business performance and/or an attempt to substitute for trade unions (Kaufman and Taras, 2010). The vast majority of empirical research focuses on the forms, functions, purposes, and structures of NER systems, and the few studies that have examined employee outcomes under NER have often concluded that these systems fall short with regard to meaningful representation of employees' interests or engagement in distributive bargaining (Terry, 1999), as employees lack any real leverage over the company. On the other hand, qualitative case study research has shown that it is too simplistic to completely dismiss voice in non-union organizations as ineffective (Dundon et al., 2005) and some quantitative research has shown NER systems to increase productivity and wages and reduce turnover (Addison et al., 2000; Batt et al., 2002; Pencavel, 2006), as well as having a greater positive impact on employee perceptions of managerial responsiveness to voice than in unionized organizations (Bryson, 2004). Furthermore, in cases where employees perceive a breach of commitments or opportunism on the part of the employer (Gollan, 2006; Moriguchi, 2005; Taras and Copping, 1998; Upchurch et al., 2006; Watling and Snook, 2003), NER leaders have been found to utilize (threats of) unionization in an instrumental manner in order to force management to take their concerns seriously (Timur et al., 2012).

Unions

When one discusses employee voice in the industrial relations literature, the first thought that comes to mind is a system of representative and collective voice as defined by unionization (Freeman and Medoff, 1984). Notwithstanding the fact that the purpose behind collective bargaining systems differs between countries (that is, in the EU, collective bargaining is seen as a component of human rights and in the USA, collective bargaining is seen as a vehicle for minimizing economic disruption: Block and Berg, 2010), unions and collective bargaining can be broadly classified as a remedial voice system due to the recognition that there are potentially competing interests between employees and organizations. The debate surrounding the impact of unions on both individual and organizational outcomes has received a substantial amount of attention in the USA, in particular since 1984, following the publication of Freeman and Medoff's theory of collective voice/ institutional response (CVIR) introduced in their seminal book entitled *What Do Unions Do?*, while until more recently in Europe (for example, Bryson et al., 2005), research on union impact focused on addressing power imbalances (Block et al., 2004; Kelly, 2004) and generating consensus in a pluralistic society (Kerr et al., 1964). CVIR posited that unions have both a monopoly and voice face. The monopoly view portrayed unions as encouraging an organization's workforce to withhold effort or engage in costly conflict through such means as restrictive work practices, strikes, grievances, and other forms of industrial action in pursuit of objectives such as above-average wage and benefit settlements (Booth, 1995; Hirsch and Addison, 1986; Lewis, 1986). The voice view built on the work of Hirschman (1970), and portrayed unions as providing their members with an alternative to exit in response to workplace problems, instead seeking resolution by institutionalizing voice practices, and offering security against employer retribution for speaking up (Kaufman, 2004). Rather than withhold effort, the voice face created incentives for employees to resolve sources of conflict, reducing worker turnover and increasing positive attitudes and discretionary behaviors, while at the same time allowing a continuous improvement mentality to pervade the workforce (Addison and Belfield, 2004).

Since the publication of these ideas, individual level research studies have not provided a clear and convincing endorsement of CVIR for employee outcomes, particularly with regard to the voice face of unions, a not insignificant problem given that policy support for collective bargaining in most countries is predicated on the potential for unions to do more good than harm for providing employees with voice. For instance, although the research is clear that unionized employees are less likely to quit (Cotton and Tuttle, 1986), they have also been found to exhibit more of a continuance rather than affective form of commitment to the organization (Luchak, 2003). These two forms of commitment distinguish people whose motives for remaining in an organizational setting emanate from feelings of 'having' rather than 'wanting' to stay, only the latter being positively related to individual well-being and such pro-social outcomes as higher in-role and extra-role performance (Meyer et al., 2002). Lastly, unionized workers often exhibit lower overall levels of job satisfaction (Hammer and Avgar, 2005), and have higher rates of absenteeism than non-unionized employees (Allen, 1984; Mefford, 1986) leading to questions about whether unions might only encourage a reactive, un-engaged form of attachment to most organizations today (Addison and Belfield, 2004). This may be one reason why collective voice as embodied by the representational function of trade unionism has been declining in many liberal market countries around the world (Kaufman 2008; Wilkinson et al., 2004).

Works Councils

Another remedial voice system is the works councils that are highly prevalent in continental Western Europe. Works councils have been defined as 'institutionalized bodies for representative communication between a single employer and the employees of a single plant or enterprise' (Rogers and Streeck, 1995: 6). However, works councils differ from NER in the sense that works councils are mostly enshrined in legislation, and exist independently of management voluntarism (Gumbrell-McCormick and Hyman, 2010). Works councils generally have broad jurisdiction over employment-related issues, though there are almost as many different forms and structures as there are countries that possess them.

Research on works councils has focused on the relationship between representatives (for example, works councilors) and those they represent (Regalia, 1988), questioning the extent to which works councilors adequately represent the interests of the workforce due to increasing professionalization of the role (Muller-Jentsch, 1995) and increasing bureaucratization (Teulings, 1989). Evidence from Germany in 2005 demonstrated the existence of bribery and corruption of works councilors in order to achieve agreement over restructuring plans (Gumbrell-McCormick and Hyman, 2010). There has also been research on the extent to which works councils, which are dominated by older, highly-skilled males, adequately represent a diversity of employee interests (Engelen, 2004), for example, tending to neglect the interests of traditionally marginalized groups such as women, younger workers, ethnic minorities, and part-time workers, even though these groups make up a large proportion of the workforce. Some countries have attempted to rectify this through legislation, though this is not always successful (Gumbrell-McCormick and Hyman, 2010). The foregoing research would support the contention of some that the effectiveness of representation goes beyond access to formal and legislated rights to voice in the workplace, and that increasing globalization and changes in the traditional employment relationship require a re-thinking of whether works councils are effective voice mechanisms for employees (Gumbrell-McCormick and Hyman, 2010).

Alternative Dispute Resolution

Although alternative dispute resolution (ADR) encompasses a wide variety of procedures and forms (for example, mediation, arbitration, ombudspersons, peer review, and so on), and ADR can also exist within a unionized organization (Colvin et al., 2006), it is increasingly used to refer to an alternative to unionized representation and/or litigation to resolve employment-related disputes (Lewin, 2010). As such it can be considered similar to NER in the sense that NER systems are also alternatives to unionized representation, and both are voluntarily adopted and determined by management. However, ADR differs from NER in that the focus of the majority of previous research has been on the efficiency and effectiveness of ADR for resolving conflict and competing interests (Colvin et al., 2006; Ewing, 1989; Feuille and Delaney, 1992; Feuille and Chachere, 1995; Colvin, 2003a), whereas the focus of NER research has been on how it improves organizational functioning and avoids unionization (Kaufman and Taras, 2010). ADR also differs from NER in that it is a direct, rather than representative, system of employee voice, and ADR is also more often adopted to avoid litigation. On the other hand, some NER systems may adopt ADR systems as part of the broader voice system (Colvin et al., 2006).

According to a study conducted in 2006 by Lewin (2010), 63 percent of organizations in a sample of 1150 business units of US-based publicly traded companies had some type of ADR system. Of these organizations, almost 70 percent used arbitration as part of their dispute resolution process. Furthermore, the formal complaint/grievance filing rate was 13.5 percent, an incidence of grievances higher than those usually found in unionized organizations (Lewin, 2010).

Research on the consequences of using ADR systems is more recent, and still relatively limited, particularly when it comes to research on employee outcomes. Peer review procedures in ADR systems increase the potential for objectivity and fairness in decision-making (Wilensky and Jones, 1994; Payson, 1998), and have also been shown to improve win rates for employees with regard to disciplinary decisions (Colvin, 2003b). Peer review systems create positive employee perceptions of the organization's attractiveness (Colvin et al., 2006), while at the same time potential applicants are less likely to perceive an organization as attractive in the presence of mandatory and binding employment arbitration (Richey et al., 2001; Mahony et al., 2005), though the presence of clear due process and just-cause protections in the procedures can mitigate negative employee perceptions of these systems (Mahony et al., 2005).

With regard to win rates, employers have been shown to be more successful when the grievance proceeds to employment arbitration, winning between 60–67 percent of cases (Colvin et al., 2006; Wheeler et al., 2004). However, research has also shown that win rates vary depending on the nature of the case (Wheeler et al., 2004), and there is a growing literature on the attributions made by decision-makers in determining awards based on the underlying nature of the individual cases (see Colvin et al., 2006 for a review). In contrast to ADR, although win rates also vary depending on the nature of the case in labor arbitration (Haber et al., 1997), the aggregate win rates are more likely to be evenly split between employers and unions (Dilts and Dietsch, 1989; Wheeler et al., 2004).

Grievance Filing

Although grievance filing generally exists under the context of a remedial voice system (for example, either unions or ADR), the nature of the research on understanding the antecedents and consequences of employee choices surrounding whether or not to file a dispute, complaint or grievance and the consequences arising from that decision, means that the literature in this area is most appropriately categorized as a remedial voice behavior.

Research on the antecedents of grievance filing that examines demographic character-istics as predictors has been mixed, although some research has found grievance filing to be greater among women and minorities under certain aversive workplace conditions (Bamberger et al., 2008). Contextual factors that increase the cost or reduce the availabil-ity of alternative options for employees, such as above average wages or labor market conditions, have been found to increase the likelihood of filing a grievance (Bacharach and Bamberger, 2004; Cappelli and Chauvin, 1991; Lewin and Peterson, 1988). Supportive leadership behaviors and programs aimed at reducing labor–management conflict have been shown to reduce grievances (Bemmels, 1994; Bemmels et al., 1991; Katz et al., 1983). Research on the consequences of using grievance procedures has shown that unionized grievance filers face potential retribution by management (Lewin, 1999). It has been proposed that many committed and loyal employees may avoid griev-ance filing (Olson-Buchanan and Boswell, 2002) by 'suffering in silence' (Boroff and Lewin, 1997), and that grievance filing is more common among dissatisfied employees (Allen and Keaveny, 1985) or those whose commitment to the organization derives from a feeling of 'having' rather than 'wanting' to belong (Luchak, 2003). However, there is generally a negative relationship between grievance filing and turnover (Peterson and Lewin, 2000; Rees, 1991).

Contrary to the unionized literature surrounding the relationship between grievance procedures and reduced turnover, research on non-union grievance procedures has gen-erally shown these procedures to have weak or no relationships with turnover (Batt et al., 2002). Experimental research has shown grievance filers to be more likely to engage in withdrawal behavior (Olson-Buchanan, 1996). One of the proposed reasons that union-ized grievance procedures are thought to have better outcomes is that unions legitimize and institutionalize grievance procedures, while at the same time providing due process protections (Colvin et al., 2006). Consistent with this interpretation, employee usage of non-union grievance procedures has been shown to result in managerial retribution against grievance filers in the form of lower performance evaluations (Lewin, 1990), though as previously mentioned, retaliation behavior has also been shown in the union-ized sector (Lewin, 1999; Lewin and Peterson, 1999).

Whistle-Blowing

Whistle-blowing is also a remedial voice behavior, and generally involves exposing illegal or unethical practices to relevant stakeholders outside the organization (Morrison, 2011). In light of the increasing number of corporate scandals that have been exposed by whistle-blowers (Vinten, 1994) and the presence and enactment of legislation protect-ing whistle-blowers (Paul and Townsend, 1996), there has been a growing interest in academic research surrounding this form of employee voice (Miceli et al., 2008). With regard to employee outcomes, whistle-blowers may face retaliation (Morrison, 2011), and though the rate and severity of retaliation reported in news outlets is generally thought to be overstated (Near and Miceli, 1996), if whistle-blowers fear retaliation for speaking up, they will be less likely to do so (Casal and Bogui, 2008). Furthermore, employees have still been shown to engage in this voicing behavior when they perceive that they will actually be able to effect change (Miceli and Near, 1992) and/or when there is perceived support for whistle-blowing through either formal channels in the organization (Perry,

1993) or supportive leadership (Miceli et al., 2008). Whistle-blowing is more likely in the presence of legislation to support and protect whistle-blowers (Miceli and Near, 1989; Miceli et al., 1999; Near et al., 1993) and when whistle-blowing systems are anonymous (Elliston, 1982).

TAKING STOCK OF EMPLOYEE VOICE RESEARCH

Though we attempted to focus on the employee in our review, there is a surprising paucity of research on employee outcomes of voice, and this is consistent across all of the various literatures. The majority of studies focus on the antecedents of pro-social voice behavior in the organizational behavior literature (Morrison, 2011; Klaas et al., 2012) or organizational outcomes under different voice systems in the human resource management (Wood, 2010) and industrial relations literatures (Addison and Belfield, 2004). The missing employee in research on employee voice likely reflects the increasing need to create a 'business case' for employee voice and participation in light of the decline in unionization and revamping of labor legislation in many countries, and the subsequent increase in management-driven voice initiatives that give employees voice only if it serves organizational interests. However, it is important to understand that from the employee's perspective, there are different purposes behind voicing behaviors that do not first and foremost benefit the organization. Indeed, these behaviors may actually be viewed by the organization as counterproductive and have elsewhere been termed the potential 'dark side' of voice (Klaas, et al., 2012). Furthermore, across each of the literatures, there are assumptions made about the 'best' form of voice behavior or system for meeting employee needs; however, employee needs for voice and meaningful input into workplace decision-making are far from being met in organizations today (Budd, 2004; Freeman et al., 2007).

What appears to be common across the voice literatures is that considerations surrounding 'instrumentality' and 'safety' underlie employee motivations in using both promotive and remedial voice. We see this in the research on pro-social voice as employees are unwilling to engage in other-regarding behavior on behalf of the organization (for example, providing cost-saving suggestions) where they fear being made to look foolish by suggesting an unworkable idea. Similarly, employees will not file grievances and challenge the authority structure of the organization where they fear retaliation by their supervisors. Regardless of whether there is a promotive or a remedial purpose for voicing behavior, in both cases the instrumentality or utility motive must override the safety or self-preservation motive in order for voice to find expression. Given these common motives for employee voice to find expression in whatever form it takes, we thus propose that the distinctions made in the literature between pro-social voice meant to help the organization and remedial voice meant to rectify potential conflicts between employees and the organization cease, as they only serve to hinder our ability to develop a complete understanding of voice behavior. These common motives of the employee in engaging in either promotive or remedial voice behaviors provide a natural point of intersection for studying the two purposes of voice simultaneously.

However, though the voice motives of employees appear well understood in the voice as a behavior literature, they are often only assumed in the voice as a system research. Thus, the vast majority of OB/HR research studies examining high involvement work practices as a source of competitive advantage assume this advantage extends to the employed workforce by virtue of lower turnover rates in such organizations, something critics of such systems in industrial relations have increasingly started to challenge. Similarly, union impact studies predominantly focused on organizational outcomes assume the union wage or benefit premium and potential for a productivity advantage ensures employees' interests and participation are well served through the representation role of the union, something adherents of the union's monopoly face have long disputed. These normative assumptions cut both ways in most voice research and as long as they remain unchallenged in the respective disciplines, the more progress in this research domain will be inhibited.

Implications for Theory and Research

The research reviewed in this chapter supports the contention that different voice regimes are better for addressing certain employee needs than others, and as such, multiple forms of voice systems should exist within organizations (Freeman et al., 2007). What employees desire with regard to meaningful representation at work and their experiences under different voice systems would be better understood through integrating research across the disparate literatures. These arguments also imply the need for researchers to adopt a multi-channel, multi-stakeholder approach to the study of voice. For the voice research informed by OB/HR this implies examining how third-party institutions such as trade unions or works councils might not only contribute to competitive advantage for employers, but would also benefit employees and their representatives. For voice researchers informed by IR, this implies examining how more direct forms of employee voice and involvement can complement union representation and increase employee well-being.

Mixed effects and hierarchical linear modeling would help in determining the relative effects of systems, culture, group-level norms, motives, and individual differences when it comes to understanding why employees may or may not choose to voice, and it would be beneficial to collect systematic data on each of these variables in the same study. It would also be beneficial to begin thinking about the seemingly disparate literatures on employee voice as complementing each other's current weaknesses in developing a more comprehensive understanding of employee voice, rather than viewing the separate literatures as focusing on completely different phenomena, and as irrelevant to the important questions in the different literatures. In this regard, further integration across traditional disciplinary silos is key.

There is also a need for an understanding of the antecedents and consequences of employee voice in organizations that possess multiple channels, and some current research has begun to examine this by looking at direct and representative forms of voice across unionized and non-unionized firms (Marsden, 2013) and synergies created between individual and collective forms of voice (Pohler and Luchak, forthcoming). Future research on voice should recognize that most voice behavior is likely to have dual purposes (for example, both remedial and promotive: Klaas, et al., 2012), and that employee needs may be better satisfied by having access to different channels within organizations (Freeman et al., 2007). It is also important that both academics and practitioners explicitly acknowledge that there is a potential for conflicts of interest between the organization and the employee at times (though this may not always be the case), but that even remedial voice may benefit the organization in the long run, even if not in the short term.

The research on silence in the workplace has at times been conducted alongside research on employee voice, and thus silence is often considered the absence of voice (Morrison, 2011). However, we still have a weak understanding of silence in organizations, particularly of the ways in which systems interact with individual differences in determining whether or not an employee will choose voice or silence. Given the antecedents and outcomes that have been examined with regard to employee voice, we believe that, *ceteris paribus*, both fear of voicing and employee silence are likely to be present to a greater extent when employees contemplate engaging in remedial voice rather than in promotive voice. Some very recent research has begun to validate scales measuring different types of voice (Liang et al., 2013) and examine how employee outcomes may differ when engaging in one form of voice over the other (Burris, 2012); however, this research is still in its infancy.

The dearth of research on employee outcomes of voice certainly suggests a ripe opportunity for future research. First, voice is not a unidimensional construct with the 'promotive' and 'remedial' purposes primarily serving the respective interests of the employer and employee. This type of thinking perpetuates the silo approach that has characterized voice research to date. As evidenced, however, by the countervailing research results in our review of employee outcomes in every voice quadrant, future research can ill afford to treat these two purposes in isolation from one another. That is, employees covered by promotive voice systems are subject to intensification pressures that demand remedial protection that direct voice alone appears unable to regulate. Conversely, employees covered by remedial voice systems are assumed to be content with a representative form of voice that appears ill-equipped to satisfy demands for more direct, proactive forms of employee involvement. Work focused on developing a multidimensional measure of voice that reflects both its promotive and remedial purposes will require researchers to take a more systemic view of voice in the workplace, forcing researchers to consider how different voice practices serve or fail to serve these two purposes, and serve or do not serve the interests of employees, unions, and employers.

Second, and related to the first point, researchers need to avoid conceptualizing voice as an organizational 'practice' or 'system' with an anticipated homogeneous effect on employees. A dummy variable reflecting the presence or absence of an ADR program or of a union is a case in point. It is well documented that employees in the same organization covered by the same workplace practices experience them idiosyncratically (Bowen and Ostroff, 2004), something a dummy variable is ill equipped to reveal. Thus, rather than relying on easy to use measures of whether a voice practice or union is present or absent in an employee's workplace, research should examine how employees experience that practice or union's representational function directly. Such measures would be used directly in individual level studies or aggregated across all employees for organizational level studies of the antecedents or consequences of employee voice (Takeuchi et al., 2007).

Implications for Policy and Practice

Though unions were once considered synonymous with employee voice, their precipitous decline over the past two decades in most developed countries calls this statement into question. In these same countries, however, many more workers desire formal channels of voice than have access to them, a sentiment that is especially prevalent among workers who are the most vulnerable or who face major sources of discontent in their workplaces (Freeman et al., 2007). In their analysis of voice across six Anglo-American countries, Freeman et al. (2007) draw three other important conclusions. First, employee needs for voice in the workplace vary, and no single mode or channel for voice can satisfy or fit all employee needs. Second, there has been a rapid expansion of management-driven initiatives supporting voice, and employees appear to prefer more cooperative styles of voice to more adversarial approaches. Finally, the most successful approach to creating public policy surrounding employee representation in the workplace is to encourage diversity and complementarity between and within voice systems. Based on our review of the employee voice research, we would agree with these assertions.

We would also argue that the most important policy implication related to the issues surrounding employee voice includes a necessity for policymakers to make a commitment to the fundamental democratic principle that employees should have some say in the decisions that affect their working lives, recognizing that voice is not only a means to achieve a balance between efficiency and equity in the employment relationship, but also that voice is an end in itself (Budd, 2004, 2005). If this basic principle is accepted, the role of all democratic governments is to develop legislative frameworks or 'rules of the game' that allow for an approximate equalization of power to be achieved between employees and managers. The framework of research we are advocating should encourage the development of diverse and complementary systems that are negotiated between the parties, as innovative context-specific solutions are more likely to arise when legislators defer to the parties, so long as there is not a major imbalance of power. Previous approaches that give primacy to one form or type of voice system over others are unlikely to result in outcomes that benefit employees or any of the relevant stakeholders.

REFERENCES

Ackers, P., M. Marchington, A. Wilkinson and T. Dundon (2004), 'Partnership and voice, with or without trade unions: changing UK management approaches to organisational participation', in M. Stuart and M. Martinez Lucio (eds), *Partnership and Modernisation in Employment Relations*, London: Routledge, pp. 23–45.
Adams, R. (2001), 'Choice or voice? Rethinking American labor policy in light of the international human rights consensus', *Employee Rights and Employment Policy Journal*, **5**, 521–48.
Addison, John, and Clive Belfield (2004), 'Union voice', *Journal of Labor Research*, **25**, 563–96.
Addison, J., C. Schnabel and J. Wagner (2000), 'Nonunion employee representation in Germany', in B. Kaufman and D. Taras (eds), *Nonunion Employee Representation: History, Contemporary Practice, and Policy*, Armonk, NY: M.E. Sharpe, pp. 365–85.
Allen, R.E. and T.J. Keaveny (1985), 'Factors differentiating grievants and nongrievants', *Human Relations*, **38** (6), 519–34.
Allen, Steven (1984), 'Trade unions, absenteeism, and exit-voice', *Industrial and Labor Relations Review*, **37**, 331–45.
Appelbaum, E., T. Bailey, P. Berg and A.L. Kalleberg (2000), *Manufacturing Advantage: Why High Performance Work Systems Pay Off*, Ithaca, NY: Cornell University Press.
Bacharach, S. and P. Bamberger (2004), 'The power of labor to grieve: the impact of the workplace, labor market, and power-dependence on employee grievance filing', *Industrial and Labor Relations Review*, **57**, 518–29.
Bamberger, P., E. Kohn and I. Nahum-Shani (2008), 'Aversive workplace conditions and employee grievance filing: the moderating effects of gender and ethnicity', *Industrial Relations*, **47**, 229–59.

Batt, Rosemary, Alexander Colvin and Jeffrey Keefe (2002), 'Employee voice, human resource practices, and employee quit rates: evidence from the telecommunications industry', *Industrial and Labor Relations Review*, **55**, 573–94.

Bemmels, B. (1994), 'The determinants of grievance initiation', *Industrial and Labor Relations Review*, **47**, 285–301.

Bemmels, B., Y. Reshef and K. Stratton-Devine (1991), 'The roles of supervisors, employees, and stewards in grievance initiation', *Industrial and Labor Relations Review*, **45** (1), 15–30.

Benson, G.S. and E.E. Lawler III (2003), 'Employee involvement: utilization, impacts and future prospects', in D. Holman, T. Wall, C. Clegg, P. Sparrow and A. Howard (eds), *The Essentials of the New Workplace*, London: Wiley, pp. 155–73.

Benson, J. (2000), 'Employee voice in union and non-union Australian workplaces', *British Journal of Industrial Relations*, **38** (3), 453–9.

Block, R. and P. Berg (2010), 'Collective bargaining as a form of employee participation', in A. Wilkinson, P. Gollan, M. Marchington and D. Lewin (eds), *Participation in Organizations*, New York: Oxford University Press, pp. 186–211.

Block, R., P. Berg and D. Belman (2004), 'The economic dimension of the employment relationship', in J. Coyle-Shapiro, L.M. Shore, M.S. Taylor and L.E. Tetrick (eds), *The Employment Relationship: Examining Psychological and Contextual Perspectives*, Oxford: Oxford University Press, pp. 94–118.

Booth, Alison (1995), *The Economics of the Trade Union*, New York: Cambridge University Press.

Boroff, Karen, and David Lewin (1997), 'Loyalty, voice, and intent to exit a union firm: a conceptual and empirical analysis', *Industrial and Labor Relations Review*, **51**, 50–63.

Bowen, D.E. and C. Ostroff (2004), 'Understanding HRM–firm performance linkages: the role of "strength" of the HR system', *Academy of Management Review*, **29** (2), 203–21.

Bryson, A. (2004), 'Managerial responsiveness to union and non-union voice', *Industrial Relations*, **43**, 213–41.

Bryson, A., J. Forth and S. Kirby (2005), 'High-involvement management practices, trade union representation and workplace performance in Britain', *Scottish Journal of Political Economy*, **52**, 451–91.

Bryson, A., A. Charlwood and J. Forth (2006), 'Worker voice, managerial responsiveness and labour productivity: an empirical investigation', *Industrial Relations Journal*, **37** (5), 438–56.

Budd, John (2004), *Employment with a Human Face: Balancing Efficiency, Equity, and Voice*, Ithaca, NY: Cornell University Press.

Budd, John (2005), 'Employment with a human face: the author responds', *Employee Responsibilities and Rights Journal*, **17** (3), 191–9.

Burris, E. (2012), 'The risks and rewards of speaking up: managerial responses to employee voice', *Academy of Management Journal*, **55** (4), 851–75.

Burris, E.R., J.R. Detert and D.S. Chiaburu (2008), 'Quitting before leaving: the mediating effects of psychological attachment and detachment on voice', *Journal of Applied Psychology*, **93**, 912–22.

Burris, E.R., J.R. Detert and A. Romney (2013), 'Speaking up versus being heard: the disagreement around and outcomes of employee voice', *Organization Science*, **24** (1), 22–38.

Cappelli, P. and K. Chauvin (1991), 'A test of an efficiency model of grievance activity', *Industrial and Labor Relations Review*, **45** (1), 3–14.

Cappelli, P. and D. Neumark (2001), 'Do "high performance" work practices improve establishment level outcomes?', *Industrial and Labor Relations Review*, **54** (4), 737–75.

Casal, J.C. and F.B. Bogui (2008), 'Predictors of responses to organizational wrongdoing: a study of intentions of management accountants', *Psychological Reports*, **103** (1), 121–33.

Clegg, H. (1960), *A New Approach to Industrial Democracy*, Oxford: Blackwell.

Colvin, Alexander (2003a), 'Institutional pressures, human resource strategies, and the rise of nonunion dispute resolution', *Industrial and Labor Relations Review*, **56**, 375–92.

Colvin, Alexander (2003b), 'The dual transformation of workplace dispute resolution', *Industrial Relations*, **42**, 712–35.

Colvin, A., B. Klaas and D. Mahony (2006), 'Research on alternative dispute resolution procedures', in David Lewin (ed.), *Contemporary Issues in Employment Relations*, Champaign, IL: Labor and Employment Relations Association, pp. 103–47.

Cotton, John, and Jeffrey Tuttle (1986), 'Employee turnover: a meta-analysis and review with implications for research', *Academy of Management Review*, **11**, 55–70.

Detert, J.R. and E.R. Burris (2007), 'Leadership behavior and employee voice: is the door really open?', *Academy of Management Journal*, **50**, 869–84.

Detert, J.R. and L.K. Trevino (2010), 'Speaking up to higher ups: how supervisor and skip-level leaders influence employee voice', *Organization Science*, **21**, 241–70.

Dilts, D. and C. Dietsch (1989), 'Arbitration win/loss rates as a measure of arbitrator neutrality', *Arbitration Journal*, **44** (3), 42–7.

Dundon, T., A. Wilkinson, M. Marchington and P. Ackers (2004), 'The meanings and purpose of employee voice', *International Journal of Human Resource Management*, **15** (6), 1149–70.

Dundon, T., A. Wilkinson, M. Marchington and P. Ackers (2005), 'The management of voice in non-union organisations: managers' perspectives', *Employee Relations*, **27** (3), 307–19.

Edmondson, A.C. (2003), 'Speaking up in the operating room: how team leaders promote learning in interdisciplinary action teams', *Journal of Management Studies*, **40**, 1419–52.

Elliston, F.A. (1982), 'Anonymity and whistleblowing', *Journal of Business Ethics*, **1** (3), 167–77.

Engelen, E. (2004), 'Problems of descriptive representation in Dutch works councils', *Political Studies*, **52** (3), 491–507.

Erez, A., J.A. LePine and H. Elms (2002), 'Effects of rotated leadership and peer evaluation on the functioning and effectiveness of self-managed teams: a quasi-experiment', *Personnel Psychology*, **55**, 929–48.

Ewing, D. (1989), *Justice on the Job: Resolving Grievances in the Nonunion Workplace*, Boston, MA: Harvard Business School Press.

Farrell, D. and C. Rusbult (1992), 'Exploring the exit, voice, loyalty and neglect typology', *Employee Responsibilities and Rights Journal*, **5**, 201–18.

Feuille, P. and D. Chachere (1995), ' Looking fair or being fair: remedial voice procedures in nonunion workplaces', *Journal of Management*, **21** (1), 27–42.

Feuille, P. and J. Delaney (1992), 'The individual pursuit of organizational justice: grievance procedures in nonunion workplaces', in G.R. Ferris and K.M. Rowland (eds), *Research in Personnel and Human Resource Management*, Stamford, CT: JAI Press, pp. 187–232.

Freeman, Richard B. and James Medoff (1984), *What Do Unions Do?*, New York: Basic Books.

Freeman, Richard B., Peter Boxall and Peter Haynes (2007), *What Workers Say*, Ithaca, NY: Cornell University Press.

Glauser, M.J. (1984), 'Upward information flow in organizations: review and conceptual analysis', *Human Relations*, **37**, 613–43.

Godard, John (2010), 'What is best for workers? The implications of workplace and human resource management practices revisited', *Industrial Relations*, **49**, 466–88.

Gollan, P. (2006), 'Twin tracks – employee representation at Eurotunnel revisited', *Industrial Relations*, **45** (4), 606–49.

Gollan, P. (2007), *Employee Representation in Non-Union Firms*, London: Sage.

Gospel, H. and P. Willman (2005), 'Statutory information disclosure for consultation and bargaining in Germany, France, and the UK', in J. Storey (ed.), *Adding Value through Information and Consultation*, Basingstoke: Palgrave Macmillan, pp. 219–39.

Gould-Williams, J. (2004), 'The effects of "high commitment" HRM practices on employee attitude: the views of public sector workers', *Public Administration*, **82** (1), 63–81.

Greenberg, J. (1987), 'A taxonomy of organizational justice theories', *Academy of Management Review*, **12**, 9–22.

Greenberger, D.B. and S. Strasser (1986), 'The development and application of a model of personal control in organizations', *Academy of Management Review*, **11**, 164–77.

Gumbrell-McCormick, R. and R. Hyman (2010), 'Works councils: the European model of industrial democracy?', in A. Wilkinson, P. Gollan, M. Marchington and D. Lewin (eds), *Participation in Organizations*, New York: Oxford University Press, pp. 286–314.

Haber, L., A. Karim and J.D. Johnson (1997), 'A survey of published, private-sector arbitral decisions', *Labor Law Journal*, **48** (7), 431–6.

Hammer, Tove, and Ariel Avgar (2005), 'The impact of unions on job satisfaction, organizational commitment and turnover', *Journal of Labor Research*, **26**, 241–66.

Hirsch, Barry, and John Addison (1986), *The Economic Analysis of Unions*, Boston, MA: Allen and Unwin.

Hirschman, Albert (1970), *Exit, Voice, and Loyalty*, Cambridge, MA: Harvard University Press.

Islam, G. and M.J. Zyphur (2005), 'Power, voice, and hierarchy: exploring the antecedents of speaking up in groups', *Group Dynamics: Theory, Research, and Practice*, **9**, 93–103.

Katz, H.C., T.A. Kochan and K.R. Gobeille (1983), 'Industrial relations performance, economic performance, and QWL programs: an interplant analysis', *Industrial and Labor Relations Review*, **37** (1), 3–17.

Kaufman, B. (2004), 'What unions do: insights from economic theory', *Journal of Labor Research*, **25** (3), 351–82.

Kaufman, B. (2008), 'Paradigms in industrial relations: original, modern and versions in-between', *British Journal of Industrial Relations*, **46** (2), 314–39.

Kaufman, B. and D. Taras (2000), *Non-Union Employee Representation: History, Contemporary Practice, and Policy*, Armonk, NY: M.E. Sharpe.

Kaufman, B. and D. Taras (2010), 'Employee participation through non-union forms of employee representation', in A. Wilkinson, P. Gollan, M. Marchington and D. Lewin (eds), *Participation in Organizations*, New York: Oxford University Press, pp. 167–285.

Kelly, J. (2004), 'Industrial relations approaches to the employment relationship', in J. Coyle-Shapiro, L.M. Shore, M.S. Taylor and L.E. Tetrick (eds), *The Employment Relationship: Examining Psychological and Contextual Perspectives*, Oxford: Oxford University Press, pp. 48–64.

Kerr, C., J. Dunlop, F. Harbison and A. Myers (1964), *Industrialism and Industrial Man*, New York: Oxford University Press.

Kim, D. and H. Kim (2004), 'A comparison of the effectiveness of unions and non-union works councils in Korea: can non-union employee representation substitute for trade unionism?', *International Journal of Human Resource Management*, **15** (6), 1069–93.

Klaas, B., J. Olson-Buchanan and A. Ward (2012), 'The determinants of alternative forms of workplace voice: an integrative perspective', *Journal of Management*, **38**, 314–45.

Kochan, T.A. and P. Osterman (1994), *The Mutual Gains Enterprise*, Cambridge, MA: Harvard Business School Press.

Kroon, B., K. Van Voorde and M. Van Veldhoven (2009), 'Cross-level effects of high-performance work practices on burnout', *Personnel Review*, **38** (5), 509–25.

Lawler, E. (1986), *High Involvement Management*, San Francisco, CA: Jossey-Bass.

LePine, Jeffrey, and Linn Van Dyne (1998), 'Predicting voice, behavior in work groups', *Journal of Applied Psychology*, **83**, 853–68.

LePine, Jeffrey, and Linn Van Dyne (2001), 'Voice and cooperative behavior as contrasting forms of contextual performance: evidence of differential relationships with big five personality characteristics and cognitive ability', *Journal of Applied Psychology*, **86**, 326–36.

Lewin, D. (1990), 'Grievance procedures in nonunion workplaces: an empirical analysis of usage, dynamics, and outcomes', *Chicago-Kent Law Review*, **66** (3), 823–44.

Lewin, D. (1999), 'Theoretical and empirical research on the grievance procedure and arbitration: a critical review', in Adrienne Eaton and Jeffrey Keefe (eds), *Employment Dispute Resolution and Worker Rights in the Changing Workplace*, Madison, WI: Industrial Relations Research Association, pp. 137–86.

Lewin, D. (2010), 'Employee voice and mutual gains', in A. Wilkinson, P. Gollan, M. Marchington and D. Lewin (eds), *Participation in Organizations*, New York: Oxford University Press, pp. 427–52.

Lewin, D. and D. Mitchell (1992), 'Systems of employee voice: theoretical and empirical perspectives', *California Management Review*, **35**, 95–111.

Lewin, D. and R.B. Peterson (1988), *The Modern Grievance Procedure in the United States: A Theoretical and Empirical Analysis*, Westport, CT: Quorum.

Lewin, D. and R. Peterson (1999), 'Behavioral outcomes of grievance activity', *Industrial Relations*, **38** (4), 554–76.

Lewis, H. Gregg (1986), *Union Relative Wage Effects: A Survey*, Chicago: University of Chicago Press.

Liang, J., C. Fahr and L. Fahr (2013), 'Psychological antecedents of promotive and prohibitive voice: a two-wave examination, *Academy of Management Journal*, **55** (1), 71–92.

Lipset, S. and N. Meltz (2000), 'Estimates of nonunion employee representation in the United States and Canada: how different are the two countries?', in B. Kaufman and D. Taras (eds), *Nonunion Employee Representation: History, Contemporary Practice, and Policy*, Armonk, NY: M.E. Sharpe, pp. 223–30.

Liu, W., R. Zhu and Y. Yang (2010), 'I warn you because I like you: voice behavior, employee identifications, and transformational leadership', *Leadership Quarterly*, **21**, 189–202.

Luchak, Andrew (2003), 'What kind of voice do loyal employees use?', *British Journal of Industrial Relations*, **41**, 115–34.

Macky, K. and P. Boxall (2007), 'The relationship between "high performance work practices" and employee attitudes: an investigation of additive and interaction effects', *International Journal of Human Resource Management*, **18** (4), 537–67.

Macky, K. and P. Boxall (2008), 'High-involvement work processes, work intensification and employee well-being: a study of New Zealand worker experiences', *Asia Pacific Journal of Human Resources*, **46** (1), 38–55.

Mahony, D., B. Klaas, J. McClendon and A. Varma (2005), 'The effects of mandatory employment arbitration systems on applicants' attraction to organizations', *Human Resource Management*, **44** (4), 449–70.

Marchington, M. (2007), 'Employee voice systems', in P. Boxall, J. Purcell and P. Wright (eds), *Oxford Handbook of Human Resource Management*, New York: Oxford University Press, pp. 231–50.

Marchington, M., J. Goodman, A. Wilkinson and P. Ackers (1992), 'New developments in employee involvement', Employment Department Research Series no. 2, HMSO, London.

Marsden, D. (2013), 'Individual voice in employment relationships: a comparison under different forms of workplace representation' *Industrial Relations*, **52** (S1), 221–58.

Mefford, Robert (1986), 'The effect of unions on productivity in a multinational manufacturing firm', *Industrial and Labor Relations Review*, 40, 105–14.

Meyer, John, David Stanley, Lynne Herscovitch and Laryssa Topolnytsky (2002), 'Affective continuance and normative commitment to the organization: a meta-analysis of antecedents, correlates and consequences', *Journal of Vocational Behavior*, **61** (1): 20–52.

Miceli, M. and J. Near (1989), 'The incidence of wrongdoing, whistle-blowing, and retaliation: results of a natural occurring field experiment', *Employee Responsibilities and Rights Journal*, **2**, 91–108.

Miceli, M.P. and J.P. Near (1992), *Blowing the Whistle*, New York: Lexington Books.

Miceli, M.P., M. Rehg, J.P. Near and K.C. Ryan (1999), 'Can laws protect whistleblowers?', *Work and Occupations*, **26** (1), 129–51.

Miceli, M.P., J.P. Near and T.M. Dworkin (2008), *Whistleblowing in Organizations*, New York: Routledge.

Milliken, F.J., E.W. Morrison and P. Hewlin (2003), 'An exploratory study of employee silence: issues that employees don't communicate upward and why', *Journal of Management Studies*, **40**, 1453–76.

Moriguchi, C. (2005), 'Did American welfare capitalists breach their implicit contracts during the great depression? Preliminary findings from company-level data', *Industrial and Labor Relations Review*, **59** (1), 51–81.

Morishima, M. and T. Tsuru (2000), 'Nonunion employee representation in Japan', in B. Kaufman and D. Taras (eds), *Nonunion Employee Representation: History, Contemporary Practice, and Policy*, Armonk, NY: M.E. Sharpe, pp. 386–409.

Morrison, E. (2011), 'Employee voice behavior: integration and directions for future research', *Academy of Management Annals*, **5**, 373–412.

Morrison, E.W. and F.J. Milliken (2000), 'Organizational silence: a barrier to change and development in a pluralistic world', *Academy of Management Review*, **25**, 706–25.

Morrison, E.W., S. Wheeler-Smith and D. Kamdar (2011), 'Speaking up in groups: a cross-level study of group voice climate', *Journal of Applied Psychology*, **96**, 183–91.

Moss, S. and J. Sanchez (2004), 'Are your employees avoiding you? Managerial strategies for closing the feedback gap', *Academy of Management Executive*, **18** (1), 32–44.

Muller-Jentsch, W. (1995), 'Germany: from collective voice to co-management', in J. Rogers and W. Streeck (eds), *Works Councils: Consultation, Representation and Cooperation in Industrial Relations*, Chicago: University of Chicago Press, pp. 53–78.

Near, J. and M. Miceli (1996), 'Whistle-blowing: myth and reality', *Journal of Management*, **22** (3), 507–26.

Near, J.P., T.M. Dworkin and M.P. Miceli (1993), 'Explaining the whistle-blowing process: suggestions from power theory and justice theory', *Organization Science*, **4**, 393–411.

Olson-Buchanan, J. (1996), 'Voicing discontent: what happens to the grievance filer after the grievance?', *Journal of Applied Psychology*, **81**, 52–63.

Olson-Buchanan, Julie and Wendy Boswell (2002), 'The role of employee loyalty and formality in voicing discontent', *Journal of Applied Psychology*, **87**, 1167–74.

Olson-Buchanan, Julie and Wendy Boswell (2008), 'An integrative model of experiencing and responding to mistreatment at work', *Academy of Management Review*, **33**, 76–96.

Parker, L.E. (1993), 'When to fix it and when to leave: relationships among perceived control, self efficacy, dissent, and exit', *Journal of Applied Psychology*, **78**, 949–59.

Paul, R. and J. Townsend (1996), 'Don't kill the messenger! Whistle-blowing in America – a review with recommendations', *Employee Responsibilities and Rights Journal*, **9** (2), 149–61.

Payson, M. (1998), 'A jury of peers', *Industry Week*, **247** (3), 71.

Pencavel, J. (2006), 'Company unions, wages, and work hours', *Advances in Industrial and Labor Relations*, **12**, 7–38.

Perry, J. (1993), 'Whistleblowing, organizational performance, and organizational control', in H. George Frederickson (ed.), *Ethics and Public Administration*, Armonk, NY: M.E. Sharpe, pp. 79–99.

Peterson, R. and D. Lewin (2000), 'Research on unionized grievance procedures: management issues and recommendations', *Human Resource Management*, **39**, 395–407.

Pohler, D. and A. Luchak (forthcoming), 'Balancing efficiency, equity and voice: the impact of unions and high involvement work practices on work outcomes', *Industrial and Labour Relations Review*.

Pyman, A., B. Cooper, J. Teicher and P. Holland (2006), 'A comparison of the effectiveness of employee voice arrangements in Australia', *Industrial Relations Journal*, **37** (6), 543–59.

Rees, D. (1991), 'Grievance procedure strength and teacher quits', *Industrial and Labor Relations Review*, **45**, 31–43.

Regalia, I. (1988), 'Democracy and unions: towards a critical appraisal', *Economic and Industrial Democracy*, **9** (3), 345–71.

Richey, B., J. Bernardin, C. Tyler and N. McKinney (2001), 'The effect of arbitration program characteristics on applicants' intentions toward potential employers', *Journal of Applied Psychology*, **86** (5), 1006–13.

Rogers, J. and W. Streeck (1995), 'The study of works councils: concepts and problems', in J. Rogers and W. Streeck (eds), *Works Councils: Consultation, Representation and Cooperation in Industrial Relations*, Chicago: University of Chicago Press, pp. 3–26.

Rusbult, C.E., D. Farrell, G. Rogers and A.G. Mainous III (1988), 'Impact of exchange variables on exit, voice, loyalty, and neglect: an integrative model of responses to declining job satisfaction', *Academy of Management Journal*, **31**, 599–627.

Sanders, K., L. Dorenbosch and R. de Reuver (2008), 'The impact of individual and shared employee perceptions of HRM on affective commitment: considering climate strength', *Personnel Review*, **37** (4), 412–25.

Siebert, S.E., M.L. Kraimer and J.M. Crant (2001), 'What do proactive people do? A longitudinal model linking proactive personality and career success', *Personnel Psychology*, **54**, 845–74.

Stamper, C. and L. Van Dyne (2001), 'Work status and organizational citizenship behavior: a field study of restaurant employees', *Journal of Organizational Behavior*, **22**, 517–36.

Takeuchi, R., D.P. Lepak, H. Wang and K. Takeuchi (2007), 'An empirical examination of the mechanisms mediating between high performance work systems and the performance of Japanese organizations', *Journal of Applied Psychology*, **92** (4), 1069–83.

Tangirala, S. and R. Ramanujam (2008), 'Exploring nonlinearity in employee voice: the effects of personal control and organizational identification', *Academy of Management Journal*, **51**, 1189–203.

Taras, D. and J. Copping (1998), 'The transition from formal nonunion representation to unionization: a contemporary case', *Industrial and Labor Relations Review*, **52** (1): 22–44.

Taras, D. and B. Kaufman (2006), 'Non-union employee representation in North America: diversity, controversy, and uncertain future', *Industrial Relations Journal*, **37** (5), 513–42.

Terry, M. (1999), 'Systems of collective employee representation in non-union firms in the UK', *Industrial Relations Journal*, **30** (1), 16–30.

Teulings, A. (1989), 'A political bargaining theory of codetermination', in G. Szell, P. Blyton and C. Cornforth (eds), *The State, Trade Unions and Self-Management*, Berlin: de Gruyter, pp. 75–101.

Thibault, J. and L. Walker (1975), *Procedural Justice: A Psychological Analysis*, Hillsdale, NJ: Lawrence Erlbaum.

Thompson, P. (2011), 'The trouble with HRM', *Human Resource Management Journal*, **21** (4), 355–67.

Thompson, P. and B. Harley (2007), 'HRM and the worker: labor process perspectives', in P. Boxall, J. Purcell and P. Wright (eds), *The Oxford Handbook of Human Resource Management*, Oxford and New York: Oxford University Press, pp. 147–65.

Timur, A.T., D. Taras and A. Ponak (2012), 'Shopping for voice: do pre-existing non-union representation plans matter when employees unionize?', *British Journal of Industrial Relations*, **50** (2), 214–38.

Turnley, W.H. and D.C. Feldman (1999), 'The impact of psychological contract violations on exit, voice, loyalty, and neglect', *Human Relations*, **52**, 895–922.

Upchurch, M., M. Richardson and P. Stewart (2006), 'Employee representation and partnership in the non-union sector: a paradox of intentions', *Human Resource Management Journal*, **16** (4), 393–410.

Vakola, M. and D. Bourades (2005), 'Antecedents and consequences of organizational silence: an empirical investigation', *Employee Relations*, **27**, 441–58.

Van Dyne, L. and J.A. LePine (1998), 'Helping and voice extra-role behavior: evidence of construct and predictive validity', *Academy of Management Journal*, **41**, 108–19.

Van Dyne, L., S. Ang and I. Botero (2003), 'Conceptualizing employee silence and employee voice as multidimensional constructs', *Journal of Management Studies*, **40**, 1359–92.

Vinten, G. (1994), 'Whistleblowing – fact and fiction: an introductory discussion', in G. Vinten (ed.), *Whistleblowing: Subversion or Corporate Citizenship*, New York: St Martin's Press, pp. 1–20.

Walumbwa, F.O. and J. Schaubroeck (2009), 'Leader personality traits and employee voice behavior: mediating roles of ethical leadership and work group psychological safety', *Journal of Applied Psychology*, **94**, 1275–86.

Watling, D. and J. Snook (2003), 'Works council and trade unions: complementary or competitive: the case of SAGCo', *Industrial Relations Journal*, **34** (3), 260–270.

Webb, Sydney, and Beatrice Webb (1902), *Industrial Democracy*, New York: Augustus M. Kelley.

Wheeler, H., B. Klaas and D. Mahony (2004), *Workplace Justice without Unions*, Kalamazoo, MI: Upjohn Institute.

Wilensky, R. and K. Jones (1994), 'Quick response key to resolving complaints', *HR Magazine*, **39** (3), 42–47.

Wilkinson, A., T. Dundon, M. Marchington and P. Ackers (2004), 'The changing patterns of employee voice: case studies from the UK and Republic of Ireland', *Journal of Industrial Relations*, **46** (3), 298–323.

Withey, M.J. and W.H. Cooper (1989), 'Predicting exit, voice, loyalty, and neglect', *Administrative Science Quarterly*, **34**, 521–39.

Wood, S. (2010), 'High involvement management and performance', in A. Wilkinson, P. Gollan, M. Marchington and D. Lewin (eds), *Participation in Organizations*, New York: Oxford University Press, pp. 407–26.

Wood, S., M. Van Veldhoven, M. Croon and L. de Menezes (2012), 'Enriched job design, high involvement management and organizational performance: the mediating roles of job satisfaction and well-being', *Human Relations*, **65**, 419–45.

Wright, P.M. and R.R. Kehoe (2008), 'Human resource practices and organizational commitment: a deeper examination', *Asia Pacific Journal of Human Resources*, **468** (1), 6–20.

Wu, P.C. and S. Chaturvedi (2009), 'The role of procedural justice and power distance in the relationship between high performance work systems and employee attitudes: a multilevel perspective', *Journal of Management*, **35** (5), 1228–47.

13 Civil society organizations and employee voice
Edmund Heery, Brian Abbott and Steve Williams

INTRODUCTION

In this chapter we examine the form of employee voice developed by civil society organizations, institutions that have become the focus of considerable research attention by employment relations scholars in recent years, particularly in the USA and UK. By civil society organizations (CSOs) we mean non-union and non-profit seeking organizations that are formally independent of the state and which develop campaigns, services, programmes or other initiatives designed to advance the interests of working people. Generally, organizations of this type are not concerned solely with the workaday selves of the people they represent and are quite diverse in their structure and patterns of activity. Most of those that provide voice to workers, however, fall into one of three overlapping categories: advocacy organizations that provide information, advisory and representation services, identity-based organizations that promote the interests of working women and minorities and issue-based organizations that run campaigns relating to the workplace.

An example of the first type is the UK's Citizens Advice, a voluntary organization that provides advice on a broad range of issues, including employment, through a network of walk-in centres spread across the country (Abbott 2004). Examples of prominent identity-based organizations, also from the UK, that have an employment role are Stonewall, the main gay rights organization, Age UK, which campaigns on behalf of older people, and the Fawcett Society, a long-established campaigning organization on women's rights (Williams et al. 2011b). Many disability organizations also fall into this category. Equivalent institutions can be readily identified in other countries (Jamieson 2008; Osterman et al. 2001). Issue-based organizations include community campaigns advocating the Living Wage, American Worker Centers that seek to represent casual workers, organizations of carers promoting work-life balance, and the multitude of organizations concerned with labour standards, human rights, working poverty, health and safety, whistleblowing, homeworking and the protection of migrants (Fine 2006, 2007; Freeman 2005; Heery et al. 2012; Holgate and Wills 2007; Luce 2004; Osterman 2006).

In examining the form of voice provided to employees by CSOs we have chosen to focus on five aspects of their role. The first is the identity of those within the working population that they aspire to represent. Most representative institutions of workers necessarily select particular constituencies, which may be broadly or narrowly framed. For trade unions, the principles of selection encompass occupation, enterprise, industry, sector and in some countries, religion, ideology, geography and ethnicity (Fiorito and Jarley 2008). Our first objective is to map the equivalent selection principles that guide worker representation through CSOs. The second aspect relates to the substantive interests of the worker constituents that CSOs choose to represent. Once again, the principle of selection necessarily applies. There is a vast array of potential interests that might be expressed through systems of employee voice and these can be classified in a variety of ways. One distinction, drawn by Hyman (1997a), lies between workers' 'quantitative' interest in improving the material return from the employment relationship and 'qualitative' interests that relate to the experience of work, but it is also possible to distinguish between individual and collective interests and workplace interests and those that relate to the wider economy and society. Our second objective is to identify the choices of CSOs within this range of possibilities.

The remaining three aspects relate to the methods CSOs use. A central issue in this regard is the manner in which CSOs relate to their worker constituents. Are they 'non-worker organizations' as Freeman (2005) has suggested, acting on behalf of workers but affording them no opportunity to participate in governance, or do they involve workers in their own representation? And to what extent do CSOs seek to collectivize and mobilize workers or rely on workplace activism and organization to advance interests in the manner of trade unions? Another issue concerns the relationship of CSOs to employers. The classic methods of trade unionism are collective bargaining and grievance-handling. Is it the case that CSOs form analogous relationships, or does the expression of voice in their case take place without significant interaction with employers? The final question of method concerns the state and the degree and manner in which CSOs seek to provide employee voice through participation in the political process or via legal action. The 'logic of collective action' for trade unions within liberal democratic societies has drawn them very substantially into the process of political governance (Crouch 1982). Our aim is to establish whether this is equally true for CSOs.

In examining these five aspects of employee voice through CSOs, we want at each stage to draw a comparison with trade union representation. Of course, the representative strategies of trade unions are both complex and variable, reflecting the different characteristics of union members, different union structures and identities, the institutional context in which unions operate and the strategic choices of their leaders (Fiorito and Jarley 2008). Nevertheless, it is possible to identify predominant patterns and to use these as a basis for comparison. By making use of the comparative method, we hope to throw CSOs into relief and highlight their distinctive attributes and their morphology as institutions of worker representation.

CONSTITUENCIES

The worker constituencies for which CSOs provide voice vary greatly in scope. In some cases CSOs define their constituency extremely broadly, encompassing the generality of working people (Williams at al. 2011). Advocacy CSOs, for example, may provide a generally available service and, while unorganized workers and those in peripheral labour market positions may be more likely to use this service (Abbott 1998), it is in principle open to all. In addition, many policy CSOs seek to intervene across the full range of issues that affect working people. In this they resemble trade union confederations, which speak for a general 'labour interest' within the public sphere. The UK's Citizens Advice is an example of an organization that performs both roles. It responds to 400,000 employment inquiries from the general public per year and lobbies actively on a broad range of employment law and labour market policy.

A second type of constituency is those composed of identity or equity-seeking groups: women, the disabled, ethnic minorities, older workers, workers of faith and belief and lesbian and gay workers. Clearly, the emergence of CSOs as institutions of employee voice reflects the rise of new social movements and a shift in the 'axes of social mobilization' from economic identities to identities formed in the wider society (Piore and Safford 2006). In this regard, it seems that CSOs can be sharply differentiated from trade unions, which classically are rooted in occupation, industry, enterprise and class. The distinction is not absolute, however, as the non-work identities that are expressed through CSOs are also expressed through trade unions. One of the most striking changes in trade unions, visible across countries, is the emergence of gender, ethnicity, disability, age, belief and sexual orientation as union categories; identities that are recognized in systems of union government and articulated both through collective bargaining and union political action (Cobble 2007; Foley and Baker 2009). The expression of these newly assertive identities has run through trade unions as well as non-union institutions of worker representation.

A third group who are represented by CSOs are carers, those who seek to combine paid work with involvement in childcare, care for those with disabilities and eldercare. CSOs with this constituency include dedicated organizations of carers, such as Carers UK, Working Families, the Daycare Trust and Counsel and Care in Britain and the National Partnership for Women and Families, Catalyst, Work Family Directions and the Families and Work Institute in the United States (Kochan 2005; Osterman et al. 2001; Williams et al. 2011a). Once again, this is evidence of CSOs defining their constituency in terms of a non-work identity that is nonetheless attached to particular workplace interests. It is also the case that carers' interests have come to be expressed through trade unions (Gregory and Milner 2009). Indeed, this coincidence of CSO–union priorities has provided the basis for joint working between the two types of representative institution.

A fourth type of constituency consists of workers who are vulnerable and exposed to exploitation whether as a consequence of their status or their work situation. In the USA, workers of this type have been a major focus of CSO activity, including living wage campaigns and the creation of Worker Centers for day labourers and others in marginal employment (Fine 2006, 2007; Luce 2004, 2007; Meléndez et al. 2008; Theodore et al. 2008). A similar pattern can be seen in the UK, where migrant workers in London have become the focus of a living wage campaign, modelled on those in the USA (Holgate and Wills 2007; Tapia 2013). One reason for CSOs targeting constituents of this type is that typically they are unorganized and fall below the protection of the trade union movement. To be sure, unions have sought to organize migrant and low-paid workers and lobby government on their behalf, but the primary constituency of unions is often core workers in relatively favourable employment (Hyman 1997b). This pattern of representation has presented CSOs with a representative opportunity to act on behalf of those outside labour's ranks.

A final type of employee constituency for which CSOs provide voice is defined by 'workplace identities' grounded in contractual status, industry and occupation (Williams et al. 2011a). At first sight this workplace focus suggests that CSOs are reproducing principles of constituency selection long adhered to by trade unions but this conclusion is probably unwarranted. CSOs seek to represent part-time and temporary workers primarily because these categories are gendered, linked to caring responsibilities and characterized by vulnerability. They may represent workers within the bounds of a particular sector or occupation but usually on the basis of a prior, more significant identity. Thus, in the UK, Women and Manual Trades is an organization of women construction workers but it emerged from the feminist movement, while the Gay Police Association and the Armed Forces Lesbian and Gay Association are primarily organizations of sexual minorities that happen to work in uniformed public services.

The answer to the question who is it that CSOs represent therefore is that they define their constituencies in three main ways. Many operate with a very broad definition of their constituency as composed of worker-citizens, a conception that is akin to that of central union confederations. The function of CSOs with regard to this broadly-defined constituency is to expand the framework of legal protection and ensure that existing rights are given genuine effect through advice and advocacy. Many CSOs also seek to represent quite narrowly defined constituencies, which are of two main types. On the one hand, CSOs represent identities formed beyond but relevant to the workplace, while on the other they represent workers in vulnerable positions who often lie beyond the bounds of the formal labour movement. Here again the form of interest representation developed by CSOs is distinctive and differs from that offered by unions. This difference is only one of degree however as unions have also embraced identity groups and carers and those in secondary labour market positions (Fitzgerald and Hardy 2010; Heery 2006). There is convergence as well as difference in the forms of employee voice offered by the two types of institution.

INTERESTS

Our second question concerns the substantive interests that become the subject of CSO voice. One possibility that has been suggested is that CSOs prioritize 'qualitative' interests, relating to the treatment of workers and their subjective experience of work (Piore and Safford 2006), and that this differentiates CSOs from trade unions. Trade unions, it has been suggested, express an instrumental logic on behalf of their constituents, whereas CSOs often have an expressive purpose, celebrating feminist, gay, lesbian, senior or disabled identities regardless of instrumental benefit. In fact, many CSOs prioritize the material well-being of their constituents, reflecting the disadvantage and discrimination they often face. In the UK, there are CSOs dedicated to raising low wages (for example, Citizens UK, Scottish Low Pay Unit), equal pay remains an abiding concern of women's organizations in all countries, and for disability CSOs a key objective is to ensure that their constituents secure and retain paid employment. It is certainly the case that many CSOs are concerned with how workers are treated and with promulgating an agenda of dignity and respect at work but most CSOs do not pursue an exclusively 'post-material' agenda.

Another possible choice for CSOs is between the pursuit of individual and collective interests. The main choice of trade unions is to pursue collective interests. Through collective bargaining unions display commitment to the device of the 'common rule', collective agreements that standardize employment conditions for workers across a bargaining unit. CSOs also seek to standardize employment conditions, though typically not through collective bargaining as we will explore below. Nevertheless, many CSOs also prioritize individual interests and in many cases their commitment to diversity leads to calls for the flexibilization of standard employment rules. Trade unions also act in these ways but the weight attached to individual and diverse interests amongst CSOs is arguably greater and in these ways their form of interest representation is distinctive.

Many CSOs are servicing organizations catering to the labour market and workplace needs of their individual constituents. This servicing assumes a number of forms (Williams et al. 2011a). A common form is for CSOs to provide information, advisory and advocacy services to workers in need of employment protection, to help in dealing with workplace problems and disputes. Another form is for CSOs to offer services that cater to the development interests of workers, including the provision of training and opportunities to network with other workers with the same interests and experiences. It is relatively common for women's, ethnic minority and lesbian and gay organizations to operate mentoring schemes and help constituents build careers. A third form of servicing is to support workers in finding and maintaining employment, catering to the labour market interests of constituents. An important feature of Worker Centers in the USA is the provision of job placement for casual workers (Fine 2006), while Working Today, the main freelancers' organization in the USA, provides an equivalent service for higher skilled contingent workers (Osterman et al. 2001). Working Today also supports freelance careers through the provision of portable benefits, healthcare and insurance. A different type of support for continuing employment is offered by many disability CSOs. In this case support can include therapies that allow people to keep working, grants and other material provisions and help to ensure that employers make reasonable adjustments to the work environment.

The latter is an example of CSOs seeking the adaptation of standard employment arrangements to meet the needs of their constituents. Action of this kind is common and as a group CSOs are major proponents of diversity management. The UK disability charity Arthritis Care, for instance, makes the case for flexible employment schedules because many muscular-skeletal conditions fluctuate in intensity. Women's and carers' organizations make an equivalent case for flexible working time policies, while faith and ethnic organizations make the case for flexible leave and uniform policies to accommodate religious observance and cultural differences. To repeat, unions also press for diversity and seek to negotiate 'positive flexibility' (Heery 2006) but it is the centrality of the diversity agenda to the employment mission of many CSOs that makes it distinctive. Their aim is to make the employment system adapt to the diverse and differentiated interests of the groups they represent.

A final distinction that can be drawn is between those interests that are manifest at the workplace and those which are expressed at higher levels or beyond the employment relationship altogether. For UK and US trade unions and increasingly for unions in other countries, the workplace is typically the primary locus of representation: unions protect workers and advance their economic interests at the place of work through a decentralized system of representation and bargaining. CSOs are also concerned with workplace interests. They campaign to improve legal protections for people at work, to improve material conditions – especially for vulnerable workers – to counter discrimination and harassment and to seek the flexibilization of employment practice to accommodate diverse needs. Again, however, their form of interest representation is distinctive. Most CSOs have a tenuous foothold at best within the workplace and are not in a position to provide the ongoing representation of workers' interests in the manner of trade unions. Instead, much of their activity is directed beyond the workplace and seeks to advance the labour market interests of constituents. This has already been alluded to. In the United Kingdom CSOs are major providers of work-related training and education, often under contract to the state (Davies 2008), and also provide career advice and support and help with finding employment, through job boards, networking and partnerships with employers. In certain respects, CSOs function as labour market intermediaries and in this regard are perhaps closer to the trade unionism of contingent workers than they are to the union mainstream (Heery et al. 2004).

CSOs also represent the non-work interests of their constituents. For most CSOs representing the employment interests of constituents sits alongside representation in the fields of welfare, human rights, housing, education, criminal justice or the home. Thus, many disability organizations are just as concerned with the question of the conditionality of welfare benefits as they are with ensuring access to paid work; CSOs of carers are as concerned with the quality of child and eldercare as they are with flexible working; and lesbian and gay organizations give as much priority to discrimination in the provision of goods and services as they do to discrimination at work. As these examples illustrate, the function of CSOs is often to connect workplace interests to those that arise in other institutional spheres. They straddle the boundary of the system of employment relations and in so doing diminish the latter's character as a self-contained institutional sub-system.

PARTICIPATION

In considering the involvement of workers in the activities of CSOs two questions are paramount. The first concerns democratic governance and the degree to which worker-constituents are also members of the organizations that promote their interests, with rights to elect leaders, hold them to account and participate in the formulation of policy. The second concerns participation in the ongoing, operational activities of CSOs and the degree to which they rely upon the activism and collective organization to perform the task of representation. For trade unions both forms of participation are strongly evident. While systems of union government vary they are invariably characterized by democratic participation and the constituencies of unions, those they represent, coincide to a very large degree with the dues-paying membership. It is to this membership that the leadership of unions is formally accountable. Moreover, unions in many countries have a long tradition of workplace activism and rely heavily on shop stewards to recruit, organize and service the membership.

Formal systems of governance among CSOs are much more variable than those of trade unions and so too are the opportunities they afford for worker-constituents to participate. For example, many CSOs are membership organizations but that membership may not coincide with the constituency of CSOs to any great degree. It can include supporters of the organization and the family members and carers of the young, disabled or older people the CSO exists to represent. A different pattern can be seen in American Worker Centers, in which membership is restricted to leaders or activists with the broad mass of constituents remaining beyond the formal bounds of the organization (Fine 2007). It is also common for the membership of CSOs to consist solely or in part of other organizations. A substantial proportion of CSOs are umbrella bodies that bring together other CSOs in a particular campaigning or lobbying organization. British examples include the Age and Employment Network, the Equality and Diversity Forum and the Migrants' Rights Network. In other cases, CSOs operate forms of corporate membership alongside individual membership, in which other CSOs, civic organizations, employers and trade unions affiliate to and support the organization. Reflecting this mixed pattern of membership, only a minority of CSOs rely upon a democratic system of governance. Most are not controlled formally by their members through mechanisms such as the election of leaders or the existence of a sovereign conference or assembly. There are CSOs which closely resemble trade unions in their governance arrangements, in that constituents are members and members govern the organization through a system of representative democracy. But in most cases CSOs depart from this pattern and in this regard are described accurately by Freeman (2005) as 'non-worker organizations'.

However, this assessment of CSOs needs qualifying in two ways. First, there is a trend to strengthen the representativeness of CSOs that is especially apparent amongst disability organizations. Among the latter there is a common desire to shed their earlier status as charitable foundations acting on behalf of disabled people and to become organizations controlled by disabled people themselves, an expression of the disability movement. The Royal National Institute of Blind People (RNIB), for example, one of the oldest and most established of UK disability organizations, recreated itself as a membership organization in 2002 with a governing assembly partly elected by its membership and partly drawn from 'stakeholder' organizations. Other disability organizations have a requirement that a majority of trustees must be drawn from their constituency and seek to recruit disabled people to officer posts. Second, even in non-membership CSOs mechanisms often exist to consult constituents and develop policy in line with their needs and preferences. This can be done through market research. Thus, Stonewall has developed its employment programme on the basis of survey research of its own supporter basis and commissioned research into the workplace experiences of the wider gay community. Carers UK consulted its membership on the UK government's carers' strategy through a survey, regional seminars and a national summit of 250 delegates. Other CSOs use focus groups and standing panels to help develop services and comment on policy proposals. Trade unions have also made extensive use of these forms of consultation (Heery and Kelly 1994) and the use of market research does not distinguish CSOs. For organizations lacking the membership-based systems of governance characteristic of trade unions, however, its relative importance in guiding policy and practice is probably greater.

It is also the case that many CSOs seek to involve their constituents in their ongoing work of providing voice. There are both individual and collective aspects to this involvement. With regard to the former, many CSOs catering to a client group emphasize self-help, the empowerment of individuals to resolve their own problems. Again, this is particularly a feature of disability CSOs. Macmillan Cancer Support, for example, the main organization of cancer sufferers in the UK, conceives of its mission as helping those with cancer manage their condition, including negotiating leave and work arrangements with employers. Although many CSOs are servicing organizations, therefore providing a direct service to worker-constituents, this is often conceived of in terms of empowerment, rather than action on behalf of a dependent and passive client group. In this specific sense there is widespread commitment to involving workers in their own representation.

For at least a proportion of CSOs there is also a collective dimension to ongoing provision of voice. Amongst a minority there is sometimes a very strong commitment to volunteer activism and to mobilizing constituents in protest and other forms of collective action. Citizens UK is committed to the principle of citizen activism within local communities and seeks actively to develop community leaders, including those engaged in the living wage and union organizing campaigns (Holgate 2009). It has a strong record of mobilizing its worker-constituents. These commitments reflect its affiliation to the similarly activist-based Industrial Areas Foundation in the USA (Osterman 2006). Worker Centers provide another example, and like living wage organizations, frequently mobilize clients and supporters in demonstrations, pickets, public protests and web-based actions. According to Tapia (2013), CSOs are often very successful when using mobilizing tactics of this kind and have a greater capacity in this regard than do trade unions, owing to the value- rather than instrumental-based orientation of their members and supporters.

Where the difference with trade unions is most striking is in the almost complete absence of attempts to develop workplace organization amongst CSOs. Where there is an initiative of this kind it tends to take the form of the creation of identity or issue-based networks within organizations, typically with employer support. Stonewall seeks to develop networks of this kind both to provide mutual support and mentoring and to create a representative structure that can enter a dialogue with managers (Colgan et al. 2007). Networks of this type have become an increasingly common feature of employment relations within the UK and USA and probably of other countries (Healy and Oikelome 2007; Scully and Segal 2002) but active attempts to promote their development are confined to only a minority of CSOs.

Rather more common are attempts to develop networks and other forms of organization amongst constituents who are not confined to an employing enterprise. In some cases CSOs have well-developed local branch structures, made up of supporters, members and constituents. British examples include Amnesty International UK, Arthritis Care, the Fawcett Society and Carers UK. In others, there is a looser form of organization, a network that may coordinate campaigning activity but which also in many cases offers mentoring and support. As we have already noted, networks of this kind may help with job placement and career development and reflect the orientation of CSOs towards the labour market, rather than towards the workplace interests of their constituents.

EMPLOYERS

Central to the form of employee voice developed by trade unions is interaction with employers. Unions engage both with associations of employers and the managers of individual enterprises through collective bargaining and are involved extensively in individual representation, protecting the interests of members facing discipline, redundancy and other problems. Two other features of union interaction with employers are also immediately notable. First, the relationship is frequently adversarial, not so much because unions engage in open conflict with employers but because unions typically assume that the interests of workers and employers conflict to a very large degree and scrutinize, challenge and critique employer behaviour as a result. Second, unions are formally independent of employers – unlike the identity and issue-based networks mentioned above. To be sure, many unions receive indirect subsidy from employers through facilities agreements (Willman et al. 1993) but unions are financially independent, employ their own bureaucracy and allow no role for employers in their systems of governance.

Interaction with employers is not a feature of interest representation for many CSOs; they provide support to their constituents and lobby government with little or no direct contact with business. When there is contact it frequently takes the form of employer support for CSOs. It is quite common for CSOs to accept donations from employers, operate a business membership scheme or sell consultancy services. In some cases CSOs have created separate membership organizations for employers: Stonewall has created a Diversity Champions programme to which more than 600 mainly large UK employers have affiliated (Williams et al. 2011b). To be sure, a minority of CSOs decline funding from employers but the emphasis on formal independence, which is such a pronounced feature of trade union–employer relations, is not characteristic of CSOs. Even radical CSOs, such as Citizens UK, which campaigns aggressively against employers that fail to pay the living wage, formally accredits businesses that do and seeks employer endorsements.

The explanation for this reduced emphasis on independence is that many CSOs operate with the assumption that they share common interests with employers. Thus, Age UK markets its training and job location services to employers on the basis that they will enhance workforce quality, while Public Concern at Work, a whistleblowing charity, argues that all parties to the employment relationship – employers, workers and consumers – can benefit if businesses introduce public interest disclosure procedures. To help diffuse this message of common interests and recruit employers to their programmes, many CSOs also seek contact with employers' and management organizations. Macmillan Cancer Support, for instance, has run a joint campaign with the Chartered Institute of Personnel and Development, the organization of HR professionals in the UK, to encourage improvements in the employment retention rates of cancer sufferers. In the USA, CSOs campaigning for public policy on work–life issues have entered a formal coalition with Corporate Voices for Working Families, a business membership organization with the same broad objective (Kochan 2005).

While this orientation differentiates many CSOs from unions, it is important to qualify this judgement. There has been a trend amongst unions in several countries in recent years to conclude formal partnership agreements with employers that seek to develop common interests and encourage integrative bargaining (Bacon and Samuel 2009; Kochan et al. 2009). The reasons for this development are partly the same as those that encourage CSOs to seek partnerships with employers and accentuate the business case. It reflects both the power of employers and the need for other institutional actors to win their support (Kelly 2004) and the role of government in promoting a partnership orientation to employment relations (McIlroy 2009).

It is also important to note that not all CSOs espouse partnership and that, even if they do, this does not preclude anti-business campaigning. Advocacy CSOs, seeking the strengthening of employment law, human rights organizations, CSOs concerned with international labour standards, and health and safety organizations are particularly likely to adopt this stance. Another group of CSOs which campaigns vigorously against employers are US Worker Centers, which expose employer abuses, such as non-payment of wages, and frequently run campaigns against individual businesses (Kochan 2005; Fine 2006). Integral to the anti-employer stance of Worker Centers is the sponsorship of legal cases, often initiated to recover unpaid wages, while many CSOs launch 'impact' legal cases, designed to test the law or expose egregious business malpractice (Fine 2006). Activity of this kind is analogous to the grievance-handling of trade unions, with the notable difference that it is located in the formal legal system, beyond the workplace, and not within internal, employer-based procedures. Another resource that CSOs may deploy against targeted employers is consumer boycotts and associated campaigns that seek to tarnish the brands of employers operating poor labour standards. This method is particularly though not exclusively associated with campaigns against multinational companies, such as Nike, with outsourced supply chains in the Global South (Freeman 2005; Locke et al. 2007). Once again, it is notable that this is a form of pressure that is directed from beyond the enterprise.

Many of the organizations that adopt a militant orientation to employers have strong links to the trade union movement and may be regarded as 'labour movement' CSOs. When not born directly out of the labour movement, they have been created by activists who share many of labour's assumptions and ways of thinking. This is true of safety campaigning organizations and many US Worker Centers. Proximity to the labour movement fosters the adversarial orientation to employers that is found routinely within trade unions. The provenance of many other CSOs is very different, however, and this partly accounts for differences in the orientation to employers. Public Concern at Work emanates from the consumer movement, while many disability organizations are long-established charitable foundations with strong connections to social elites. The relations that CSOs develop with employers reflect their point of origin and appear often to be path dependent.

Where CSO relations with employers depart most sharply from those of trade unions is with regard to collective bargaining. CSOs do not strike collective agreements with employers or develop joint regulation. Indeed, Kolins Givan (2007) labels CSOs, 'non-bargaining actors'. They often seek to shape employer practice but this tends to be through the development of what is known as 'civil regulation' (Hutter and O'Mahoney 2004) or 'non-governmental regulation' (O'Rourke 2003). CSOs unilaterally formulate standards or codes of practice for employers that they seek to have adopted through persuasion, advancing the business case, or through an implicit threat that failure to comply will expose employers to the risk of legal action. Trade unions may also act in this way. Unions of freelance workers, for instance, issue draft contracts, codes and fee sheets (Heery et al. 2004) but for the labour movement as a whole unilateral regulation of the employment relationship is now a marginal activity. For many CSOs it is central and seems to be growing in importance.

The component elements of civil regulation of the employment relationship by CSOs have become institutionalized as best practice, which has diffused across CSOs and across national boundaries. They comprise offering training and advice to employers, issuing standards, reinforcing these standards through surveys and benchmarking and operating an award scheme to recognize good practice (Heery et al. 2012). A number of CSOs have self-auditing tools for employers on their websites. Participation in these systems of voluntary regulation is often initiated by employers themselves. Of course, not all CSOs dealing with employers engage in civil regulation and benchmarking, and award schemes are confined to a minority of larger organizations with formal workplace programmes. Nevertheless, for CSOs that are involved it can be a high priority and become quite elaborate. Stonewall's Diversity Champions programme, for instance, is based on a series of employment standards and practices, including workforce monitoring and the development of a lesbian and gay network. These are implemented through ongoing consultancy that involves repeat visits to the employer, monitored through an annual benchmarking survey and supported through an award scheme that is reported in the business and national press. Stonewall has created a specialist department to manage its workplace activities and is distinctive in terms of its level of investment and the scale of its programme (Williams et al. 2011b). Other UK CSOs which have developed similar initiatives include Age UK, Andrea Adams Trust, Carers UK, Chwarae Teg, Macmillan Cancer Support, Migrant Workers North West, Public Concern at Work and the Royal Society for the Prevention of Accidents. The development of unilateral, civil regulation of the employment relationship is one of the most distinctive features of CSO interaction with employers and of their form of employee voice per se.

THE STATE

The state and the wider political and legal system constitute a primary terrain upon which unions express employee voice. This has been done in a variety of ways that differ both according to national state traditions and the political character of incumbent governments. However, it is possible to identify a common repertoire of union political action. Central to this repertoire has been the classical method through which unions have sought political representation for their members, through affiliation to labour and social democratic political parties. Equally classic has been the prime function of this affiliation: to secure favourable collective labour law that permits unions to form effective bargaining relationships with employers. Other methods upon which unions have relied include acting as lobbyists and pressure groups to promote or block policy and assuming the role of social partner, a trusted and authoritative representative that works cooperatively with government and representatives of business to regulate the economy and formulate public policy. What is striking about the use of all of these methods in the recent past is that they have been deployed to press for the strengthening of individual as well as collective employment law. Even in the UK, where unions have traditionally been resistant to statutory regulation of employment contracts, they have become primary institutions pressing for new individual rights and *inter alia* their influence has helped secure the introduction of minimum wage and working time legislation and new rights for contingent workers and carers (Hamann and Kelly 2003).

Union involvement in the creation of law has been accompanied by attempts to give effect to new rights at work. Unions play an important role in ensuring laws are translated into policy and practice within employing organizations (Brown et al. 2000) and offer representation to workers seeking to enforce their rights. The latter includes the sponsorship of test cases to clarify and extend the law, which in turn provides leverage to unions in dealing with employers. Collective bargaining in the UK often uses statute and case law as a reference point, with precedents set at court being diffused across the economy through collective agreements (Heery and Conley 2007). Unions have also been used by the state in recent years to implement aspects of labour market policy, most notably in the UK through funds to promote workplace learning (McIlroy 2009). Initiatives of this kind represent the recruitment of unions as subaltern partners in the 'decentred' state (Marinetto 2007).

How does this pattern of involvement in political and legal processes compare with that of CSOs? The first thing to note is that the state is a central focus of activity for most CSOs. Influencing government policy is a major priority and a greater proportion of CSOs seek to influence government than target employers (Heery et al. 2012). CSOs engage with international government organizations, the institutions of the European Union, national governments and regional and local authorities. Living wage campaigns, one of the most striking expressions of CSO intervention in employment relations, have largely been conducted at a local level (Luce 2004). Despite this political orientation, however, the majority of CSOs espouse a formal position of political neutrality and are not associated formally with political parties. This reflects the charitable status of many CSOs and is a feature that differentiates them sharply from trade unions.

In other respects the activities of CSOs at state level correspond closely to those of trade unions. Like unions they function as pressure groups within a pluralist political system seeking to initiate or deflect changes in employment law and associated public policy, albeit without the union preoccupation with collective law. Indeed, CSOs are often part of the same policy networks as unions, working jointly with them to review and influence government policy (Heery et al. 2012; Kochan 2005). It is common for CSOs to respond to government consultation and use research evidence, elected representatives and ongoing contact with ministries as instruments to acquire influence. Many report that they have drafted employment legislation and that they are represented on government bodies (Heery et al. 2012). In this regard, CSOs act as 'insiders' that rely upon expertise, representativeness and legitimacy to exert political influence, an aspect of their role which corresponds to that of central union confederations (McIlroy 2000).

Acting as authoritative insiders may be common but does not encompass all forms of political action used by CSOs. Even those which operate deep within government may also campaign against the state. CSOs frequently expose failings of public policy that affect working people and many organize demonstrations and use other forms of direct action to influence state policy. In the USA, a particularly striking example was the successful mobilization in 2006 of millions of protestors against changes to law that would penalize immigrants, including in their role as employees, and in favour of the extension of citizenship rights to those who are undocumented (Kolins Givan 2007). Unions also participated in this mobilization and the pattern of ongoing engagement in lobbying and other insider activities alongside occasional protest – acting as an 'outsider' – is also seen within trade unionism. The organization of public protests against austerity, a feature of labour politics in many countries since the financial crisis, provides a case in point.

In addition to formulating policy, CSOs are involved in its implementation and here again there are parallels with trade unionism. CSOs play an important part in 'mediating' employment law; that is they seek to ensure that statutory rights are given genuine effect (Dickens 1989). The provision of information and advice to individual workers about their rights is one form of mediation, while representing workers before labour and other courts is another. The latter can include the sponsorship of test cases – the kind of 'impact' cases referred to above. A striking recent example is Age UK's challenge to mandatory retirement, which was taken to the European Court and stimulated a review of law in this area. Trade unions effectively use legal rights as levers or platforms, seeking to build on statutory entitlements through collective bargaining. CSO mediation of employment law has a similar aspect though in their case law is used as a lever to develop civil regulation. The codes of practice and other advice that many CSOs seek to have adopted by employers often go beyond legal minima but nevertheless rest on the platform of law. Stonewall's Diversity Champions programme, for instance, has successfully diffused across UK business on the back of a European directive that outlaws discrimination on the basis of sexual orientation (Williams et al. 2010).

Stonewall, Age UK and other CSOs have on occasion been contracted by the state to help educate both workers and their employers about their rights under newly passed legislation. They have worked as sub-contractors to implement public policy. A small percentage of CSOs have a deliberate policy of declining state funding but the vast majority receive grants from national, local and international government agencies. They are largely grant-funded (Freeman 2005). The provision of employment training and job placement services to those seeking work has been an area in which sub-contracting has been particularly marked in the UK and which has led to tension with trade unions over the transfer of work from the public to the voluntary sector (Davies 2008). But, as we have seen, trade unions have also been in receipt of substantial state funds to deliver services in the adjacent field of workplace learning and this is another element of CSO activity that corresponds to the contemporary trade union role. Both institutions have been drawn into a 'decentred' form of governance, in which non-state actors assume responsibility for policymaking and implementation.

CONCLUSION

The purpose of this chapter has been to sketch the form of voice offered to workers by civil society organizations, a significant 'new actor' in the industrial relations of the United Kingdom and many other countries. It has examined the who, what and how of CSO representation at the same time drawing a comparison with trade unions, traditionally the dominant institution of employee voice. Table 13.1 summarizes the findings, setting out the morphology of CSO representation and accentuating the contrast with trade unions. Compared with the latter, CSOs define their constituencies in terms of political (citizenship) or social identities and prioritize individual interests and the flexibilization of job rules at the expense of the 'common rule'. They also prioritize labour market interests and link interests within employment to a wider representation agenda that encompasses the domestic sphere, human rights and welfare. Other distinctive attributes include the emphasis on unilateral civil regulation and partnership-working in their relations with employers, and the pattern of pressure group activity, with its focus on individual employment law, seen in their relations with the state.

Emphasis on the distinctiveness of CSO voice and its difference to trade unionism has been a recurrent feature of academic discussion (for example, Piore and Safford 2006). It is often linked with two other substantive claims. The first is that the increasing prominence of non-union representation and its distinctive form arise from deep-seated shifts

Table 13.1   Interest representation through trade unions and CSOs

	Trade unions	CSOs
Constituency	Economic identities (class, occupation and industry); focus on core workers	Political (citizenship) and social identities; focus on marginal workers
Interests	Collective interests pursued through common rule; focus on workplace interests	Individual and diverse interests pursued through flexibilization; focus on labour market interests
Relationship to workers	Worker organizations with formal democracy; workplace organization	Non-worker organizations with market research and empowerment; labour market organization
Relationship to employers	Adversarial orientation; collective bargaining	Partnership orientation; civil regulation
Relationship to the state	Party politics; reform of collective employment law	Pressure-group politics; reform of individual employment law

in the nature of industrial society. Thus, Piore and Safford link the emergence of CSOs as significant actors to the juridification of the employment relationship, which in turn is rooted in the new social movements of gender, race, age and sexuality. The second is that trade unions are less well suited to this new context and that their primary method of interest representation through collective bargaining will therefore increasingly yield to the methods deployed by CSOs. Identification of a distinctive form of interest representation therefore is connected to an argument about union replacement; CSOs, this argument goes, are the wave of the future while unions are a relic of the past.

One problem with this argument is that although CSOs are distinctive their pattern of interest representation shares many characteristics with that provided by unions. In particular, both have been shaped by forces of social change emanating from within the working population and by changes in forms of state intervention emanating from above. With regard to the former it is notable that while the feminization of the workforce and the increasing assertiveness of minority groups have led to the formation of CSOs that engage with work and employment, they have also powerfully influenced trade unionism. A concern with diversity, the flexibilization of employment rules and the need to link workplace to non-work interests, which are characteristic of much representation through CSOs, are trends just as apparent within trade unions. The juridification of the employment relationship, and the stress on partnership and sub-contracting within decentred forms of governance have also shaped both types of institution. Once the classic repositories of voluntarism, trade unions now work in coalition with CSOs to create individual employment law and both now routinely use the law to influence the behaviour of employers. Moreover, both CSOs and unions are frequently drawn into a consultative relationship with the state over policy development and are used as hired instruments of policy implementation.

The implication of this shared experience is that trade unions may not yield to alternative and better adapted forms of interest representation. On the contrary, there is perhaps room for both in a multiform system of worker representation, in which trade unions and CSOs perform different but frequently overlapping roles and work together in coalition.

REFERENCES

Abbott, Brian (1998), 'The emergence of a new industrial relations actor – the role of the Citizens' Advice Bureaux', *Industrial Relations Journal*, **29** (4), 257–69.
Abbott, Brian (2004), 'Worker representation through the Citizens' Advice Bureaux', in Geraldine Healy, Edmund Heery, Phil Taylor and William Brown (eds), *The Future of Worker Representation*, Basingstoke: Palgrave Macmillan, pp. 245–63.
Bacon, Nicolas, and Peter Samuel (2009), 'Partnership agreement adoption and survival in the British private and public sectors', *Work, Employment and Society*, **23** (2), 231–48.
Brown, William, Simon Deakin, David Nash and Sarah Oxenbridge (2000), 'The employment contract: from collective procedures to individual rights', *British Journal of Industrial Relations*, **38** (4), 611–29.
Cobble, Dorothy Sue (ed.) (2007), *The Sex of Class: Women Transforming American Labor*, Ithaca, NY: ILR Press.
Colgan, Fiona, Chris Creegan, Aidan McKearney and Tessa Wright (2007), 'Equality and diversity policies and practices at work: lesbian, gay, and bisexual workers', *Equal Opportunities International*, **26** (3), 590–609.
Crouch, Colin (1982), *Trade Unions: the Logic of Collective Action*, Glasgow: Fontana.
Davies, Steve (2008), 'Contracting out of employment services to the third and private sectors: a critique', *Critical Social Policy*, **28** (2), 136–64.
Dickens, Linda (1989), 'Women – a rediscovered resource?', *Industrial Relations Journal*, **20** (3), 167–75.
Fine, Janice (2006), *Worker Centers: Organizing Communities at the Edge of the Dream*, Ithaca, NY: ILR Press.
Fine, Janice (2007), 'Worker centers and immigrant women', in Dorothy Sue Cobble (ed.) *The Sex of Class: Women Transforming American Labor*, Ithaca NY: Cornell University Press, pp. 211–30.
Fiorito, Jack, and Paul Jarley (2008), 'Trade union morphology', in Paul Blyton, Nick Bacon, Jack Fiorito and Edmund Heery (eds), *The Sage Handbook of Industrial Relations*, Los Angeles, CA: Sage, pp. 189–208.
Fitzgerald, Ian and Jane Hardy (2010), 'Thinking outside the box? Trade union organizing strategies and Polish migrant workers in the United Kingdom', *British Journal of Industrial Relations*, **48** (1), 131–50.
Foley, Janice R. and Patricia L. Baker (eds) (2009), *Unions, Equity and the Path to Renewal*, Vancouver, BC: UBC Press.
Freeman, Richard B. (2005), 'Fighting for other folks' wages: the logic and illogic of living wage campaigns', *Industrial Relations*, **44** (1), 14–31.
Gregory, Abigail, and Susan Milner (2009), 'Trade unions and work–life balance: changing times in France and the UK?', *British Journal of Industrial Relations*, **47** (1), 122–46.
Hamann, Kerstin, and John Kelly (2003), 'The domestic sources of differences in labour market policy', *British Journal of Industrial Relations*, **41** (4), 639–63.
Healy, Geraldine, and Franklin Oikelome (2007), 'Equality and diversity actors: a challenge to traditional industrial relations?', *Equal Opportunities International*, **26** (1), 44–65.
Heery, Edmund (2006), 'Bargaining for balance: union policy on work–life issues in the United Kingdom', in Paul Blyton, Betsy Blundon, Ken Reed and Ali Dastmalchian (eds), *Work–Life Integration: International Perspectives on the Balancing of Multiple Roles*, Basingstoke: Palgrave Macmillan, pp. 42–62.
Heery, Edmund, and Hazel Conley (2007), 'Frame extension in a mature social movement: British trade unions and part-time work, 1976–2002', *Journal of Industrial Relations*, **49** (1), 445–72.
Heery, Edmund and John Kelly (1994), 'Professional, participative and managerial unionism: an interpretation of change in trade unions', *Work, Employment and Society*, **8** (1), 1–21.
Heery, Edmund, Hazel Conley, Rick Delbridge and Paul Stewart (2004), 'Beyond the enterprise: trade union representation of freelances in the United Kingdom', *Human Resource Management Journal*, **14** (2), 20–35.
Heery, Edmund, Brian Abbott and Steve Williams (2012), 'The involvement of civil society organizations in British industrial relations: extent, origins and significance', *British Journal of Industrial Relations*, **50** (1), 47–72.
Holgate, Jane (2009), 'Contested terrain: London's living wage campaign and the tensions between community and union organizing', in Jo McBride and Ian Greenwood (eds), *Community Unionism: A Comparative Analysis of Concepts and Contexts*, Basingstoke: Palgrave Macmillan, pp.49–74.
Holgate, Jane, and Jane Wills (2007), 'Organizing labor in London: lessons from the campaign for a living

wage', in Lowell Turner and Daniel B. Cornfield (eds), *Labor in the New Urban Battlegrounds*, Ithaca, NY: ILR Press, pp. 211–23.

Hutter, Bridget M., and Joan O'Mahony (2004), 'The role of civil society organisations in regulating business', Discussion Paper No.26, ESRC Centre for Analysis of Risk and Regulation, London.

Hyman, Richard (1997a), 'The future of employee representation', *British Journal of Industrial Relations*, **35** (3), 309–36.

Hyman, Richard (1997b), 'Trade unions and interest representation in the context of globalization', *Transfer*, **3** (4), 515–33.

Jamieson, Suzanne (2008), 'The National Pay Equity Coalition: the role of women's groups in employment relations', in Grant Michelson, Suzanne Jamieson and John Burgess (eds), *New Employment Actors: Developments from Australia*, Bern: Peter Lang, pp. 135–52.

Kelly, John (2004), 'Social partnership agreements in Britain: labor cooperation and compliance', *Industrial Relations*, **43** (1), 267–92.

Kochan, Thomas A. (2005), *Restoring the American Dream*, Cambridge, MA: MIT Press.

Kochan, Thomas A., Adrienne E. Eaton, Robert B. McKersie and Paul S. Adler (2009), *Healing Together: The Labor–Management Partnership at Kaiser-Permanente*, Ithaca, NY: Cornell University Press.

Kolins Givan, Rebecca (2007), 'Side by side we battle onward? Representing workers in contemporary America', *British Journal of Industrial Relations*, **45** (4), 829–55.

Locke, Richard M., Fei Qin and Alberto Brause (2007), 'Does monitoring improve labor standards: lessons from Nike', *Industrial and Labor Relations Review*, **61** (1), 3–31.

Luce, Stephanie (2004), *Fighting for a Living Wage*, Ithaca, NY: ILR Press.

Luce, Stephanie (2007), 'The US living wage movement: building coalitions from the local level in a global economy', in Lowell Turner and Daniel B. Cornfield (eds), *Labor in the New Urban Battlegrounds*, Ithaca and London: ILR Press, pp. 21–34.

Marinetto, Michael (2007), *Social Theory, the State and Modern Society: The State in Contemporary Social Thought*, Buckingham: Open University Press.

McIlroy, John (2000), 'The new politics of pressure – the Trades Union Congress and New Labour in government', *Industrial Relations Journal*, **31** (1), 2–16.

McIlroy, John (2009), 'A brief history of British trade unions and neo–liberalism in the age of New Labour', in Gary Daniels and John McIlroy (eds), *Trade Unions in a Neoliberal World*, London: Routledge, pp. 63–97.

Meléndez, Edwin, Nik Theodore and Abel Valenzuela Jr (2008), 'Day Labor Worker Centers: new approaches to protecting labor standards in the informal economy', Working Paper, Institute for Research on Labor and Employment, Los Angeles, CA.

O'Rourke, Dara (2003), 'Outsourcing regulation: nongovernmental systems of labor standards and monitoring', *Policy Studies Journal*, **31** (1), 1–29.

Osterman, Paul (2006), 'Community organizing and employee representation', *British Journal of Industrial Relations*, **44** (4), 629–49.

Osterman, Paul, Thomas A. Kochan, Richard M. Locke and Michael J. Piore (2001), *Working in America: A Blueprint for the New Labor Market*, Cambridge, MA: MIT Press.

Piore, Michael J. and Sean Safford (2006), 'Changing regimes of workplace governance: shifting axes of social mobilization and the challenges to industrial relations theory', *Industrial Relations*, **45** (3), 299–325.

Scully, Maureen, and Amy Segal (2002), 'Passion with an umbrella: grassroots activists in the workplace', in Michael Lounsbury and Marc J. Ventresca (eds), *Social Structure and Organizations Revisited*, Oxford: Elsevier Science Limited, pp. 125–68.

Tapia, Maite (2013), 'Marching to different tunes: commitment and culture as mobilizing mechanisms of trade unions and community organizations', *British Journal of Industrial Relations*, **51** (4), 666–88.

Theodore, Nik, Edwin Meléndez, Abel Valenzuela Jr and Ana Luz Gonzalez (2008), 'Day labor and workplace abuses in the residential construction industry', in Annette Bernhardt, Heather Boushey, Laura Dresser and Chris Tilly (eds), *The Gloves-Off Economy: Workplace Standards at the Bottom of America's Labor Market*, Champaign, IL: Labor and Employment Relations Association, pp. 91–110.

Williams, Steve, Edmund Heery and Brian Abbott (2010), 'Mediating equality at work through civil society organizations', *Equality, Diversity and Inclusion*, **29** (6), 627–38.

Williams, Steve, Brian Abbott and Edmund Heery (2011a), 'Non-union worker representation through civil society organizations', *Industrial Relations Journal*, **42** (1), 69–85.

Williams, Steve, Edmund Heery and Brian Abbott (2011b), 'The emerging regime of civil regulation in work and employment relations', *Human Relations*, **64** (7), 951–70.

Willman, Paul, Tim Morris and Beverley Aston (1993), *Union Business: Trade Union Organization and Financial Reform in the Thatcher Years*, Cambridge: Cambridge University Press.

PART III

FORMS

14 Collective bargaining
Virginia Doellgast and Chiara Benassi

INTRODUCTION

The term 'collective bargaining' was first used in 1891 by Beatrice Webb, an economic theorist and one of the founders of the industrial relations field in the UK. She and her partner Sidney Webb described collective bargaining as a process through which workers come together and send representatives to negotiate over their terms and conditions of employment. It was seen as a collective alternative to individual bargaining – or 'one of the methods used by trade unions to further their basic purpose "of maintaining or improving the conditions of their [members'] working lives"' (Webb and Webb 1920: 1, cited in Flanders 1968: 1–2).

The Webbs' definition emphasizes the importance of collective action on the part of workers in establishing and negotiating formal agreements. Other scholars have defined collective bargaining more broadly as a process of negotiation, joint decision-making, or joint regulation between groups who represent both employer and employee interests; and which implies the 'negotiation and continuous application of an agreed set of rules to govern the substantive and procedural terms of the employment relationship' (Windmuller et al. 1987, cited in Traxler 1994: 168). It is distinct from consultation or joint problem-solving, in that it results in formal, bargained agreements or contracts to which both parties are obliged to adhere during an agreed upon period.

Collective bargaining can be viewed as the most developed form of representative or collective voice, as it is typically carried out within a framework of rules, procedures, and rights set out in national and international law. It can involve the different actors discussed in other chapters in this volume: the state, trade unions, works councils, employers, middle managers, and employees. However, the role played by each of these actors in the bargaining system varies considerably across countries, depending on the bargaining structure and rights accorded to them through law and practice.

Scholarship on collective bargaining has examined its impact on a range of outcomes for firms, workers, economies, and societies. Collective bargaining can involve partnership and can be complementary to direct forms of voice, such as individual or team-based worker involvement. This kind of integrative or 'mutual gains' bargaining can reduce shop-floor conflict, promoting trust, facilitating restructuring, and reducing employee turnover. At the national level, organized or coordinated collective bargaining models typical of northern and central Europe have been associated with reduced strike rates, high productivity, and wage moderation. Collective bargaining also plays an important role in shaping distributional outcomes within firms and societies. Collective agreements and collective bargaining institutions affect how productivity gains and risks are allocated between different stakeholder groups. For this reason, collective bargaining is often characterized by conflict. Employers and unions engage in 'zero-sum' or distributive bargaining on many issues and use strikes, pickets, and lock-outs as common means to demonstrate or exercise countervailing power.

The distinctiveness of collective bargaining lies in this role as an institution that involves formal negotiations between two organizations representing employer and worker interests, and holding different forms of political and economic power. As unions and bargaining institutions have come under pressure in the last twenty years, a debate has arisen over whether bargaining remains a viable form of voice – if it is perhaps being replaced by human resource management, direct participation, and government regulation through individual employment rights. How researchers interpret the causes of these changes and their implications for workers and society varies according to the emphasis they place on the integrative or distributive aspects of the bargaining system.

In this chapter, we first present an overview of different forms of collective bargaining, looking at how institutions and models differ across countries. This is the basis for a review of research examining the integrative or efficiency-enhancing role of collective bargaining – which typically emphasizes strategic choice and mutual gains, and studies focusing on the distributional consequences of these institutions – which place more emphasis on the role of power and conflict in shaping bargaining processes and outcomes. We argue that research focusing on performance outcomes provides a useful but incomplete set of tools to analyze the form and consequences of collective bargaining institutions. These institutions have historically played a central role in redistributing political and economic power within workplaces, industries, and societies. Attention to contemporary changes in labor power can help to explain why and how this distinctive form of employee voice has been weakened within different national contexts.

COLLECTIVE BARGAINING FORMS AND STRUCTURES

Collective bargaining institutions vary across countries as a result of differences in the legal framework, as well as the distinctive traditions and organizational structure of employers and labor unions. One important institutional difference is whether governments protect employees' right to join unions and to engage in industrial action, or instead intervene to obstruct collective bargaining. Although the right to collective bargaining is a core labor standard as defined by the International Labor Organization (ILO), workers continue to lack these basic rights in many countries (ILO 2008).[1] The International Trade Union Confederation (2012) reports that in 2011 at least 76 workers were murdered worldwide as a direct result of union activities, while repressions of strike action and organizing activities resulted in a reported 3508 arrests and 15 860 dismissals.

In countries with developed industrial relations institutions, collective bargaining can take different forms. In 'single-employer bargaining', individual employers negotiate agreements at the company or workplace level with labor unions or other worker representatives with legal rights, such as works councils. In 'multi-employer bargaining', one or more unions or union confederations negotiate agreements with one or more employers' associations (Jackson 2005). These agreements can cover the workforce in a particular industry or occupation; or can cover a range of sectors at the national level – often with the involvement of government agencies through 'tripartite' arrangements.

Countries also differ in the degree of bargaining centralization. 'Centralized bargaining' implies that national or industry agreements are the dominant form for regulating terms and conditions of employment; while 'decentralized bargaining' implies that company or establishment-level agreements predominate.[2] Bargaining often takes place at multiple levels. In many European countries, multi-employer collective bargaining between employers' associations and labor unions establishes minimum wage levels or overall wage increases at the industry or national level; but individual employers negotiate supplementary agreements with unions and/or works councils at the company and establishment levels. For example, in Sweden wage increases are agreed centrally, but are distributed at the local level based on company-level negotiations, allowing substantial pay individualization.

Countries with multi-level bargaining systems further differ in the degree of coordination between levels. Bargaining coordination can be defined as the extent to which 'minor players' (such as managers or union representatives at the company level) follow or adhere to agreements reached by 'major players' (such as peak associations) (Soskice 1990; Hall and Gingerich 2004). There are different ways to achieve coordination in wage bargaining: through direct means, as an explicit goal of peak business and labor associations or through state intervention; or through more informal means, such as pattern agreements led by bargaining agents at large firms or in leading industries. Countries with company or establishment-level bargaining, such as the USA and Canada, are typically viewed as having uncoordinated systems. Informal coordination is common in countries with sectoral bargaining systems, such as Germany, in which peak associations are weaker and employer associations at the industry level negotiate agreements with industry-based unions. Coordination in this case relies on strong and relatively encompassing associations that are able to exert control over their members. Overt or direct coordination takes different forms. For example, in Belgium economy-wide agreements are negotiated between the main employer and union confederations at the national level, which then establish a framework for negotiations at industry and cross-industry levels. In other countries, such as Spain and Portugal, national accords between peak associations and the government have been important at different periods in standardizing wage increases and ensuring member organizations do not deviate from those agreements. In Japan, the main union confederations set minimum objectives for the annual spring bargaining round, and unions adjust their company-level demands based on negotiation outcomes in the biggest companies.

Most countries have experienced change over time in dominant collective bargaining levels, as well as in the degree of coordination between levels. In general, there has been a trend toward increased company or establishment-level bargaining, even where sectoral agreements remain dominant (Katz 1993; OECD 2012: 139–42). Sweden exemplifies this trend: it had a centralized and coordinated bargaining system, but following an employer offensive in the 1990s, it moved to sectoral and company bargaining with weaker coordination (Swenson and Pontusson 2000). At the same time, other countries have experienced a shift toward increased bargaining centralization and coordination. In Italy, union confederations became involved in tripartite negotiations in the 1990s through social pacts aimed at controlling wage inflation (Baccaro 2002).

These patterns are shaped in part by the history, traditions, and strategies of major actors. However, they are also strongly influenced by the legal framework within which collective bargaining takes place. Laws establish union recognition procedures, rights to strike, and rights to engage in secondary boycotts; as well as what actions constitute 'unfair' or illegal practices by employers, such as their rights to lock out striking workers or dismiss workers for participating in union activities. Even among the OECD and EU member states, 24 percent of countries are reported to have minor or major restrictions on collective bargaining rights in the market sector, while 44 percent have restrictions on the right to strike (Visser 2011). Labor laws and policies can make a substantial difference to union power and strategies. For example, sympathy strikes or secondary boycotts are typically illegal, but continue to be a viable tool of industrial action in Nordic countries – which unions have used to maintain bargaining coverage in industries characterized by a high degree of subcontracting, such as construction (Lillie and Greer 2007).

Participation rights, which define those areas in which workers have a right to negotiate collective agreements and participate in management decision-making, also vary across countries. One difference concerns the bargaining subjects on which employers are legally required to negotiate or come to agreement with worker representatives. In the USA, if a union has been certified as a bargaining partner, employers are required to bargain 'in good faith' over certain 'mandatory' subjects, defined as wages, hours, and other terms and conditions of employment. However, they are not required to discuss other subjects defined as 'permissive', including reorganization decisions or evaluation criteria. In Germany, works councils hold strong 'co-determination rights', which give them not only the right to negotiate but also effective veto power over a wider range of decisions concerning, for example, the design of variable pay or the use of monitoring (See Chapter 15 on works councils). Countries may also have different forms of board-level participation rights, which require large companies to include worker representatives in consultation or decision-making bodies, such as supervisory boards.[3]

Another area in which the legal framework differs across countries concerns the mandatory extension of collective agreements through public law. This can be important for ensuring broad application of bargaining agreements to more poorly organized firms or economic sectors. Table 14.1 lists those OECD countries that have widely available and regularly applied legal provisions for mandatory extension of agreements; those with provisions that are available but not widely used; and those where extension provisions are not available.

These legal provisions take different forms. In some countries, such as Germany, legal

Table 14.1   Legal provision for mandatory extension in OECD countries

Legal provision for mandatory extension	Countries
Available, regularly applied, and affecting a significant share of the workforce (>10%)	Austria, Belgium, France, Finland, Greece, Hungary, Luxembourg, Portugal, Slovenia, Spain
Available, but not regularly or widely used (<10%)	Australia, Chili, Czech Republic, Germany, Estonia, Israel, Korea, Netherlands, New Zealand, Poland, Slovakia
Not available	China, Canada, Denmark, Ireland, Italy, Japan, Mexico, Norway, Sweden, UK, USA

Source: ICTWSS Database (Visser 2011).

extension of agreements is dependent on the bargaining parties covering a certain percentage of the workforce in a particular industry or occupation, and typically requires both parties to request an extension. In other countries, such as France, the government directly intervenes to declare agreements generally binding to all firms in the relevant sector and/or region. In Austria, membership in employers' associations is mandatory, and all members are required to apply the relevant collective agreement. There are alternatives to legal extension by the state that can also ensure broad adherence to collective agreements. In Denmark, high union density and social pressure traditionally have ensured that a majority of firms follow agreements. Institutions providing for legal extension are strongly influenced by government policy, and can thus change rapidly. In Australia, a conservative government passed major labor law reform in 2005, eliminating a system of national arbitration that had allowed pay and conditions negotiated in unionized workplaces to be applied across the workforce. These reforms were only partially reversed in 2009 under a Labor government.

The different bargaining arrangements and legal frameworks discussed above have an impact on bargaining coverage (the proportion of the workforce covered by collective agreements) as well as on union density (the proportion of the workforce who are union members). Figures 14.1 and 14.2 illustrate the variation in both measures across OECD countries.

For the OECD as a whole, over 60 percent of the workforce is covered by collective agreements. Coverage is over 70 percent in most of Western Europe – with over 90 percent coverage in Austria, Belgium, Sweden, Finland, and France. Union density rates are significantly lower in most countries, and are not always correlated with bargaining coverage. A comparison of bargaining coverage and union density shows three patterns. One group of countries has high bargaining coverage and high union density. Most of these are Nordic (for example, Finland, Denmark, and Sweden). They typically rely on high union membership rates to secure high coverage and bargaining power, and have other institutions, such as union involvement in social insurance provision, that provide additional incentives for membership. A second group of countries has low union membership density and low bargaining coverage, including the Anglo-American countries, most of central and eastern Europe, Japan, and Mexico. In these countries, bargaining is relatively decentralized and there are no or weak legal provisions for extension of agreements. A third group of countries has high bargaining coverage and low union membership rates. This group includes, among others, Austria, Spain, and the Netherlands. France is the most extreme example, with 7.6 percent union density and 90 percent bargaining coverage. This pattern is most common where there are strong legal provisions for extension of agreements, but weaker or more fragmented union presence at company and establishment level.

Figures 14.1 and 14.2 also show that both bargaining coverage and trade union density have declined in most OECD countries over the past two decades. Between 1990 and 2011, coverage fell most dramatically in countries that experienced major changes to labor laws affecting recognition and extension procedures, including Australia and New Zealand, and to a lesser extent the UK and Portugal. However, it is also notable that coverage has remained stable or increased in many countries, including most of the Nordic countries, Belgium, Austria, Spain, and the Netherlands. In contrast, union density has decreased – although by varying degrees – in most OECD countries.

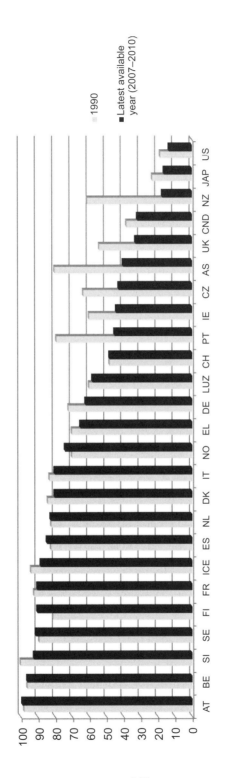

Source: ICTWSS Database (Visser 2011).

Figure 14.1 Collective bargaining coverage in OECD countries

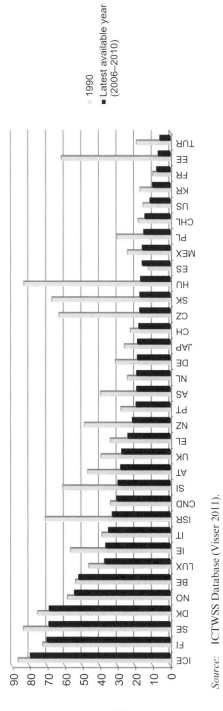

Source: ICTWSS Database (Visser 2011).

Figure 14.2   Union membership density in OECD countries

These comparative statistics demonstrate the continued importance of collective bargaining institutions in determining wages and working conditions. They also provide further evidence of the large variation in the structure of and changes in these institutions. In the following sections, we review the literature on outcomes from these different institutional configurations, and discuss the implications for the future of collective bargaining.

ECONOMIC AND SOCIAL EFFECTS OF COLLECTIVE BARGAINING

Neoclassical economic models are typically the starting point for debates concerning the economic and social effects of collective bargaining. According to these models, efficient or 'equilibrium' wage and employment levels are derived from variation in the supply of and demand for labor in perfect markets. Collective bargaining institutions are theorized to introduce inefficiencies into labor markets, as unions create 'cartels' and force firms to employ labor at above market rates. In the long run, firms with these institutions should only be able to compete when they are themselves in a monopoly position, allowing them to share their monopoly rents with unions. Alternatively, employers may seek to create their own cartel arrangements by joining employers' associations and bargaining at industry level to take wages out of competition. Where they are not able to exercise monopoly power, firms may seek to remain competitive through introducing labor-saving technology – although unions often resist these changes. All of these alternatives are viewed as efficiency-destroying, through driving up labor costs and restricting employment growth.

According to the insider-outsider framework, unions also exacerbate inequality through seeking to advance the immediate interests of 'labor market insiders' at the expense of 'outsider' groups such as women, young people, and immigrants, or workers in more poorly organized sectors and workplaces. Collective agreements are thus argued to secure a wage premium and job security for union members, while creating negative externalities in regard to lower levels of overall employment, unequal wage distribution, and higher job insecurity for non-members (Lindbeck and Snower 1986; Rueda 2007). Friedrich Hayek famously observed along these lines that British unions were 'the biggest obstacle to raising the living standards of the working class . . . The chief cause of the unnecessarily big differences between the best and worst-paid workers . . . the prime source of unemployment . . . and the main reason for the decline of the British economy in general' (Hayek 1984: 52).[4] Following from these arguments, neoclassical theorists often conclude that the state has the obligation to curb union power in order to promote society's welfare, both in terms of economic growth and equity. Their ideas influenced the labor market policies and labor law reforms of Ronald Reagan in the USA and Margaret Thatcher in the UK in the 1980s, and have become dominant in microeconomic models estimating the impact of collective bargaining institutions on wage and employment levels.

Neoclassical models of the labor market described above have been criticized on both theoretical and empirical grounds. Some of the most influential criticism derives from the institutional economists who founded the industrial relations discipline in the USA and UK, including Commons (1934) and the Webbs (1920). These scholars argued that labor markets were both imperfect and different from other factor markets, and thus to understand their operation it was necessary to analyze the wider legal, political, social, and economic relations in which they were embedded. On the economic side, unions were shown to have more ambiguous effects on efficient wage and employment levels. Labor markets were not fully competitive, due to the monopsony power of large firms, and the difficulty of specifying labor contracts and overseeing labor effort meant that assumptions of zero transaction costs and complete contracts could not be applied.

The institutional economists also outlined a broader series of arguments for the positive social or distributional role of collective bargaining. Underlying this was an ethical concern that labor should be treated differently from other factor inputs, as it was embodied in human beings and thus subject to 'uniquely human concerns and considerations' (Kaufman 2007: 11). Commons observes that in neoclassical theory, workers are treated 'as commodities to be bought and sold according to demand and supply' while in the institutional perspective 'they are treated as citizens with rights against others on account of their value to the nation as a whole' (cited in Kaufman 2007: 19). One substantial obstacle to the exercise of citizenship rights was employers' disproportionate power to unilaterally determine terms and conditions of employment. Legislation and collective bargaining were thus needed to correct not only market imperfections, but also to remedy the unequal balance of power in the employment relationship by redistributing and redefining property rights.

These two concerns of the early institutional economists – with labor unions' role in enhancing economic performance and improving equity in the distribution of power and resources in a society – have continued to be central in scholarship on outcomes from alternative collective bargaining arrangements. We review this literature below.

Collective Bargaining and Economic Performance

One stream of research on outcomes from collective bargaining has focused on its contribution to efficiency, productivity, and macroeconomic performance.

There are several ways in which firms can benefit from collective bargaining institutions. At the establishment, company, or industry level, collective bargaining can enhance social peace, helping to reduce conflict through providing a formal structure for labor–management cooperation. Strikes have been found to be less frequent in countries with high union density and a centralized and unified labor movement as unions can more effectively push their demands with employers and the government in the institutional arenas (Korpi and Shalev 1979; Lehmbruch 1984). Collective agreements can help to correct inefficiencies associated with information asymmetries, underinvestment in human capital, and arbitrary management. They can be a means for establishing transparent administrative rules and procedures, such as internal labor markets, which can encourage firm-specific investments in training and reduce employee turnover (Doeringer and Piore 1971; Osterman and Burton 2006). Collective bargaining also provides workers with the opportunity to exercise 'collective voice' in decisions concerning work organization or pay-setting (Freeman and Medoff 1984). This can reduce hiring and training costs associated with quits (Doellgast 2008) and provide worker input on changes in production that may stimulate increased efficiency (Addison et al. 2001; Huebler and Jirjahn 2003).

A large body of research has examined the role of collective bargaining institutions in facilitating productivity-enhancing work reorganization. One group of studies in the USA and UK has focused on union participation in implementing 'high involvement' or 'high performance' work systems (see Chapter 6). Case studies of firms such as Saturn (Rubinstein 2000) and Kaiser Permanente (Kochan, Eaton et al. 2009), as well as reviews of partnership initiatives (for example, Kochan and Osterman 1994; Appelbaum et al. 2000; Bamber et al. 2009), have shown that union involvement in work reorganization can help to enhance trust and lead to 'mutual gains' in terms of improved working conditions and increased productivity. However, these outcomes depend on the organizational strength and strategy of unions. Comparative studies have found that labor–management cooperation over restructuring is more widespread (Turner 1991) and more often associated with productivity improvements (Addison et al. 2000; Zwick 2004) in countries with high bargaining coverage and strong participation rights. One argument holds that because unions in these settings enjoy institutional security, they are more willing to cooperate with measures to introduce new technology or efficiency-enhancing work reorganization strategies (Katz and Sabel 1985). Managers are also more likely to cooperate with worker representatives where they have less opportunity and incentive to exit costly agreements (Doellgast 2012). These institutions thus put 'productive constraints' on firms through encouraging the adoption of measures that improve organizational performance while ensuring that gains from these improvements are more equitably shared with workers (Dore 1973; Streeck 1996).

Multi-employer bargaining has also been found to benefit firms through improving predictability and overcoming market failures. Sectoral agreements can take wages out of competition, reducing incentives for poaching. Studies have found a lower union wage premium in those countries with more centralized bargaining systems (Blau and Kahn 1999). Alternatively, a high-wage policy by unions at the national level may be used to encourage firms to invest in productivity improvements or to trigger a shift of labor to higher productivity firms and sectors. This was an explicit goal, for example, of the solidaristic wage policies pursued by Scandinavian unions in the 1980s, following the Rehn-Meidner model (Meidner and Rehn 1953). Industry-level bargaining systems can also encourage collective solutions to problems such as underinvestment in occupational skills and support inter-firm cooperation in R&D (Iversen and Soskice 2001; Amable 2003: 87). The resulting higher levels of skills in an economy and the improved capacity of firms to use these skills are believed to promote industrial upgrading and innovation.

Centralized or tripartite bargaining arrangements have been widely studied to assess the distinctive advantages they provide for firms and national economies. Neo-corporatist theories argued that tripartite bargaining encouraged the division of productivity gains between the social partners and promoted wage restraint (Schmitter and Lehmbruch 1979). More recently, the literature on 'social pacts' has examined the conditions under which unions overcome past conflicts to negotiate tripartite agreements aimed at supporting economic competitiveness and controlling inflation through wage moderation (Regini 2000; Rhodes 2001; Molina and Rhodes 2002). Research has shown that these pacts tend to emerge in situations of economic crisis or stress, weak governments, and intermediately centralized unions (Avdagic et al. 2011).

A comparison of responses to the 2008 financial crisis provides a contemporary example of how corporatist forms of collective bargaining continue to help employers and economies adjust to economic shocks (Glassner and Galgòczi 2009). In Germany, short-time working policies allowed companies to reduce working hours during the economic downturn without having to lay off employees – thus assuring retention of skilled labor. These policies were supported by unions and backed by direct subsidies at the national level, but were also negotiated as part of concessionary packages by unions and works councils at the sector and workplace levels (Dribbusch 2009). Another example is the success of the Danish economy in the 2000s, which has been attributed to a strong tradition of labor cooperation and to 'flexicurity' policies that combined reduced employment protections with a high level of unemployment insurance and government investment in retraining (Madsen 2002).

A number of quantitative studies have analyzed the relationship between bargaining structure and macroeconomic performance. Some scholars have examined the degree of bargaining centralization, testing the neo-corporatist thesis that more centralized systems are better able to control inflation and weather economic shocks. Calmfors and Driffill (1988) showed that macroeconomic performance was strongest in countries with either highly centralized systems characterized by national bargaining, such as the Nordic countries, where encompassing unions were more likely to support wage moderation, or highly decentralized systems, such as the USA, where unions had little power over wage structures. Others argued that the degree of bargaining coordination was a better measure for predicting wage moderation, as it accounts for the ability of central actors to control local pay-setting (Soskice 1990; Kenworthy 2003). Recent studies demonstrate that the performance of different bargaining structures is dependent on a range of factors, including monetary policy and central bank independence (Cukierman and Lippi 1999; Coricelli et al. 2006), productivity differentials between exposed and sheltered sectors (Traxler and Brandl 2011), the extent of economic stability or change (Aidt and Tzannatos 2008), and internal governance processes in trade union confederations (Baccaro and Simoni 2010).

This large body of theory and research has demonstrated that collective bargaining can contribute to improving the productivity of individual firms or workplaces, and encourage economic competitiveness at the industry or national level. However, these studies also necessarily highlight the inefficiencies associated with collective bargaining institutions that lack certain structural or strategic characteristics. While in some countries these institutions promote wage moderation, in others they contribute to wage inflation. While unions may form 'productivity coalitions' with management and contribute to joint problem solving, they can also obstruct restructuring measures aimed at reducing labor costs and generate additional costs associated with industrial action.

In addition, while there is a large body of evidence establishing the positive macroeconomic effects of certain configurations of collective bargaining institutions, studies seeking to establish the impact of collective bargaining on organizational performance report mixed findings. For example, a recent series of cross-national studies looking at multiple industries and multinational firms found significant national differences in the labor practices of establishments, but report only modest productivity effects of those differences (Freeman and Shaw 2009). This suggests that while collective bargaining can play a productivity-enhancing or market-correcting role, a focus on these outcomes provides only a partial explanation for the form that these institutions take and justification for policies supporting labor's organizing and bargaining rights.

Collective Bargaining, Power, and Inequality

Collective bargaining institutions have also been widely studied for their distributional effects. These include the distribution of economic gains from productivity improvements, the distribution of risks resulting from fluctuations in the business cycle, and the broader distribution of economic and political power within workplaces or in society. Researchers focusing on distributional outcomes typically start from the premise that collective bargaining involves correcting a basic power imbalance in the employment relationship through legal intervention and collective action, with the goal of improving workers' access to enhanced industrial or workplace democracy.

Of central concern in this literature are the ways in which institutions channel or subvert conflict within organizations and societies. One source of conflict concerns the degree of worker control over pay and working conditions. Labor market segmentation theorists argue that the structure of internal labor markets is the result of a struggle between employers and unions over the control of work – for example, over technologies and skill demarcations (Rubery 1978; Grimshaw and Rubery 1998), and often serves as a successful strategy by employers to control or marginalize union control on the shop-floor (Stone 1974). Thus, while performance may be improved under cooperative workplace initiatives, this is argued to be at the expense of worker power, associated with reduced job security, work intensification, and increased 'capture' of gains from productivity improvements by management and owners (Parker and Slaughter 1988; Kelly 2004).

Comparative research suggests that unions' success in advancing worker interests in improved pay and working conditions depends on bargaining rights and structures. In most liberal or Anglo-American countries, collective bargaining is associated with a union wage premium and stronger job security for union members (Shaw et al. 1998; Cully et al. 1999) but has been found to have little effect on practices that affect direct worker control over working pace and methods, such as teamwork, discretion, and monitoring (Wood 1996; Doellgast et al. 2009).

Worker representatives have been found to have more influence over pay structures and work design in countries with stronger participation rights and more encompassing bargaining institutions. In northern and central Europe, where these institutions are strongest, unions have most successfully promoted models of work organization that incorporate high levels of worker control and discretion. The 'quality of working life' movements in the 1970s and 1980s are the best-known examples of these initiatives (Gustavsen et al. 1996). Comparative studies have found that Nordic countries have particularly high levels of worker control, with better opportunities for participation (Gallie, 2003), higher influence over work tasks (Gallie, 2009), higher worker autonomy (Esser and Olsen, 2012), more 'learning-oriented' forms of work organization (Gustavsen, 2007), and a stronger use of negotiated or cooperative approaches to restructuring (Brandt et al., 2008) compared to other European countries. This has been attributed in part to union strength at the workplace and industry levels (Sørensen and Weinkopf 2009).

Collective bargaining institutions may also influence which groups of workers have access to jobs with good pay and working conditions – including patterns of wage or income inequality, and availability of permanent and secure (non-contingent) employment. Research has shown that centralized bargaining institutions with broad coverage (Traxler and Brandl 2011), high union density (Rueda and Pontusson 2000), and high minimum wage levels (Koeniger et al. 2006) are the factors most strongly associated with lower levels of pay dispersion. These institutions have also been found to positively affect the gender wage gap (Arulampalam et al. 2007), to reduce labor market segmentation or 'dualization', and to encourage the adoption of welfare policies serving the interests of marginal workforce groups (Thelen 2009; Bosch et al. 2010).

Again, the Nordic countries most clearly typify this ideal of coordinated and inclusive bargaining. They also share a tradition of 'solidaristic bargaining', which relied on groups with stronger labor market power accepting reductions in wage demands, encouraging redistribution from more strongly organized segments of the economy or workforce to weaker segments (Erixon 2008: 51). This has resulted in relatively homogeneous wages and working conditions between standard and contingent workers, high replacement ratios (Aiginger 2008; Thelen 2009), and a high 'labor share', measured as the share of labor compensation, in terms of wages and benefits, in the national income (ILO 2010: 26). These institutions provide unions with a framework that allows them to bargain and enforce agreements for a broad workforce domain, making it more difficult for employers to exit agreements or to employ workers on sub-standard terms through, for example, subcontracting and non-standard work arrangement (Doellgast et al. 2009; Bosch et al. 2010).

The findings of these studies suggest that collective or representative voice through collective bargaining can improve worker outcomes across different dimensions: pay, job security, and control or discretion, as well as patterns of pay inequality and the distribution of risk. However, these relationships differ across countries and can change over time. In the next section, we examine how different research traditions have interpreted recent changes in bargaining institutions and outcomes associated with these changes.

Explaining Changes in Collective Bargaining and its Effects

As discussed above, union density and collective bargaining coverage have declined in most countries. Collective bargaining has become increasingly decentralized, with more bargaining taking place at the workplace and firm levels, and is increasingly 'disorganized', with less coordination between labor and employer representatives at different levels. These trends have been accompanied by a growth in inequality, expansion of low wage and insecure employment, and declining labor share within many advanced economies – particularly in continental or 'social' Europe. In OECD countries, the median labor share dropped from 66.1 percent at the beginning of the 1990s to 61.7 percent in the late 2000s, while the income of the top 1 percent of earners increased by 20 percent over the same period (OECD 2012: 110). Moreover, the concentration of capital income increased by 9 percent between 1995 and 2005. Those workforce groups who are in a weaker position in the labor market have been the most affected by these trends, such as low-skilled, women, migrant, and atypical workers (Appelbaum et al. 2010; Kalina and Weinkopf 2012).

Theorists focusing on the role of collective bargaining institutions in enhancing productivity and efficiency have broadly interpreted the shrinking coverage of these institutions as the consequence of their declining economic returns – at least in certain segments of national economies. According to the 'varieties of capitalism' framework, firms in countries characterized by non-market forms of coordination between business, labor, and the state derived distinctive 'comparative institutional advantages' in global markets – allowing them to successfully compete in industries and market segments requiring high skill levels and long-term investment strategies (Hall and Soskice 2001; Hancké et al. 2007).[5] The coordinated economies of continental Europe thus experienced the (relative) resilience of strong unions and multi-employer arrangements in the 1980s and 1990s because these institutions complemented the business strategies of leading firms, while unions declined in 'liberal market economies' because collective bargaining conflicted with employer interests in labor market flexibility (Thelen 2001).

Recent literature in this area has argued that strong collective bargaining institutions continue to support economic competitiveness in coordinated market economies, but their value is increasingly limited to core economic sectors, where a cross-class coalition between management and labor supports them. Meanwhile, deregulation has been allowed to occur in more peripheral sectors and workplaces, where employers stand to benefit more from low costs and labor market flexibility (Höpner 2007; Palier and Thelen 2010).

An alternative approach to explaining national differences in collective bargaining institutions is derived from power resource theory. These theorists argue that structures and outcomes of labor market institutions are explained by variation in the power of labor relative to employers, mediated through the state (Korpi 1983; Esping-Andersen and Korpi 1984). Differences in unions' access to 'power resources' – including their organizational strength, level of coordination, and participation rights – influence their ability to promote worker interests in redistribution and control over their work.

This suggests that coordinated forms of collective bargaining are not primarily established and maintained by employers seeking to resolve their own coordination problems, but instead are the product of the conflict between societal attempts to regulate the market through collective institutions and employer attempts to pursue individual economic advantage through undermining or escaping those institutions (Streeck 2009: 4). Market internationalization and liberalization have allowed employers to exit collective agreements, while the increased threat of exit has made it more difficult for unions to negotiate strong agreements or resist concessions (Bosch et al. 2010). Cross-country differences in patterns of inequality and dualism are the result of the resilience of institutions like collective bargaining, which redistribute risk and bargaining power in some national contexts, as well as the strategies of civil society actors, unions, and policymakers to establish and maintain these institutions in the face of business pressure (Emmenegger et al. 2012). This suggests that unions are not necessarily complicit in the growth of peripheral jobs: they may also seek to represent new groups of workers, developing and using different 'power resources' as their traditional sources of bargaining power decline.

The difference between these two approaches can be illustrated by comparing alternative explanations for recent changes in German industrial relations. Germany has experienced a large decline in bargaining coverage, dropping from 72 percent in 1990 to 59 percent in 2011. The proportion of workers in low-wage work also grew over the same period, from 14.4 percent in 1995 to 23.1 percent in 2010 – levels close to those in the USA and UK (see Bosch et al. 2010: 36). This expanding group is made up of a disproportionate number of women and non-standard workers (Kalina and Weinkopf 2012).

Scholars adopting the varieties of capitalism perspective have argued that these trends are the result of a growing gap between the interests of different employer groups. Coordinated bargaining continues to support the competitive strategies of large manufacturing firms in Germany, and so has been relatively stable in these companies. According to this view, employer exit from collective agreements and wage concessions is occurring primarily in small firms and service sector industries – and the expansion of these kinds of activities helps to explain declining bargaining coverage and growing inequality (Palier and Thelen 2010; Hassel 2011).

In contrast, scholars adopting a power resources perspective have argued that a substantial, structural shift in bargaining power provides a more compelling explanation for the magnitude of recent changes in bargaining structures and outcomes in Germany. Research evidence suggests that large German employers have not on the whole cooperated with unions, but instead have demanded concessions from their own workforce while directly pursuing strategies that have increased inequality across their production chain. These strategies include shifting work to lower-cost, non-union subcontractors and hiring temporary workers at lower wages (Greer 2008a; Holst et al. 2009). They have been able to do this because unions' traditional sources of institutionalized bargaining power have progressively weakened. Changing government policies have allowed companies to pay temporary workers lower wages, and employers' associations and lead employers within those associations have been unable or unwilling to extend agreements to smaller firms. German unions have organized campaigns aimed at mobilizing members in poorly organized industries and workplaces, but have had limited success in reversing these trends (Doellgast and Greer 2007; Greer 2008b; Turner 2009).

The above comparison further illustrates the limitations of analyses that seek to explain the existence of and contemporary changes in collective bargaining institutions based on their performance effects. Recent trends of 'institutional erosion' have been strongly shaped by a power shift in favor of management as a result of market internationalization and government-led deregulation. Declining bargaining power, in turn, reduces unions' capacity to pursue distributive goals within national economies. This suggests that policies aimed at reducing economic and social inequality require governments, unions, and civil society to develop innovative strategies that seek to redress the growing imbalance in bargaining power.

CONCLUSIONS AND FUTURE RESEARCH

This chapter has reviewed the different forms that collective bargaining takes, national differences in these institutions, and their effects on organizational, economic, and societal outcomes. A key area of disagreement in the literature was shown to be how scholars conceptualize cross-national variation in collective bargaining and outcomes associated with these institutions. Researchers focusing on the performance effects of collective bargaining emphasize the advantages to firms and economies of cooperation between management and labor, and seek to explain the conditions under which cooperation is supported or enhanced. Those focusing on the distributional consequences of collective bargaining place more emphasis on diverging interests and on the role of power in the employment relationship. They view the bargaining power of labor unions as a key factor explaining differences in these institutions across countries, as well as their labor market effects.

Research on the economic consequences of collective bargaining has shown that strong unions, high bargaining coverage, and organized or 'coordinated' bargaining institutions are often resources for employers and their associations, rather than simply obstacles to implementing efficient or rational strategic choices. More generally, collective bargaining can help to resolve class conflict or channel it in more socially efficient and productive ways. However, analyses sensitive to distributional outcomes have provided distinctive insights into contemporary changes in collective bargaining institutions and their labor market effects. These scholars have shown that the declining power of labor relative to business interests has contributed to the erosion of coordinated collective bargaining in many countries and reduced the capacity of unions to pursue distributional goals. They also suggest that these trends are not inevitable, but influenced by policy and politics: governments, unions, and other groups in civil society can develop new strategies aimed at redressing power imbalances and extending these institutions to poorly represented industry segments and employee groups.

Future research on structures of and outcomes from collective bargaining should seek to integrate these perspectives. One broad research question concerns how collective voice institutions can be maintained or strengthened under conditions in which companies are able to restructure production across national borders and make wide use of subcontractors and atypical contracts. Studies should combine comparisons of legal and institutional bargaining structures with analyses of strategies that allow workers to negotiate and enforce agreements. As production structures and workforce composition change, the form and the content of workers' collective responses are transforming as well. Actors are developing new policies and strategies aimed at rebuilding bargaining power in production networks within and across national borders. These measures involve standard-setting and policymaking by international organizations and governments, but also consumer boycotts and worker mobilization through unions and other civil society actors. These innovative strategies often operate outside traditional collective bargaining institutions. More research is required to understand their impact on the balance of power within organizations and societies.

NOTES

1. According to the ILO, Belarus, Cambodia, Colombia, Eritrea, Myanmar, and the Philippines have among the worst records of regular government obstruction of collective bargaining (ILO 2008).
2. According to Visser (2011), only three OECD countries, Belgium, Germany, and Ireland, were characterized by national or central bargaining in 2010, complemented by sectoral and local or company bargaining. Other continental European countries, together with Australia and Israel, had predominantly sectoral bargaining; while local or company bargaining was dominant in the Anglo-American countries, several central and eastern European countries (Slovakia, Poland, and Estonia), and the Asian and Latin American countries, Japan, Korea, Mexico, and Chile. However, these broad categories show considerable diversity: for example, 'centralized' bargaining in Ireland was based on tripartite social partnership agreements, which collapsed in 2010.
3. Among OECD countries, Austria, Denmark, Germany, Norway, and Sweden have the strongest legal rights to board-level representation; while the Anglo-American countries, Japan, South Korea, and Switzerland have no rights (Jackson 2005).
4. Friedman (1962: 123–4) observed along more general lines that 'Unions have . . . not only harmed the

public at large and workers as a whole by distorting the use of labor; they have also made the incomes of the working class more unequal by reducing the opportunities available to the most disadvantaged workers.'

5. There have been a range of other typologies describing 'national models' of capitalism, including, for example, the national business systems approach (Whitley 1999), the theory of employment systems (Marsden 1999), and the social systems of production literature (Hollingsworth and Boyer 1997).

REFERENCES

Addison, J., S. Siebert, J. Wagner and X. Wei (2000), 'Worker participation and firm performance: evidence from Germany and Britain', *British Journal of Industrial Relations*, **38** (1), 7–48.

Addison, J.T., C. Schnabel and J. Wagner (2001), 'Works councils in Germany: their effects on establishment performance', *Oxford Economic Papers*, **53** (4), 659–94.

Aidt, T.S. and Z. Tzannatos (2008), 'Trade unions, collective bargaining and macroeconomic performance: a review', *Industrial Relations Journal*, **39** (4), 258–95.

Aiginger, K. (2008), 'Performance differences in Europe: tentative hypotheses on the role of institutions', WIFO Working Paper, REPEC/IDEAS, University of Connecticut.

Amable, B. (2003), *The Diversity of Modern Capitalism*, Oxford: Oxford University Press.

Appelbaum, E., T. Bailey, P. Berg and A.L. Kalleberg (2000), *Manufacturing Advantage: Why High Performance Work Systems Pay Off*, Ithaca, NY: Cornell University Press.

Appelbaum, E., G. Bosch, J. Gautie, G. Mason, K. Mayhew, W. Salverda, J. Schmitt and N. Westergard-Nielsen (2010), 'Introduction and overview', in J. Gautié and J. Schmitt (eds), *Low Wage in the Wealthy World*, New York: Russell Sage Foundation, pp. 1–32.

Arulampalam, W., A.L. Booth and M.L. Bryan (2007), 'Is there a glass ceiling over Europe? Exploring the gender pay gap across the wage distribution', *Industrial and Labor Relations Review*, **60** (2), 163–86.

Avdagic, S., M. Rhodes and J. Visser (2011), *Social Pacts in Europe: Emergence, Evolution, and Institutionalization*, Oxford: Oxford University Press.

Baccaro, L. (2002), 'The construction of "democratic" corporatism in Italy', *Politics and Society*, **30** (2), 327–57.

Baccaro, L. and M. Simoni (2010), 'Organizational determinants of wage moderations', *World Politics*, **62** (4), 594–635.

Bamber, G., J.H. Gittell, T. Kochan and A. Von Nordenflycht (2009), *Up in the Air: How Airlines Can Improve Performance by Engaging Their Employees*, Ithaca, NY: ILR Press.

Blau, F.D. and L.M. Kahn (1999), 'Institutions and laws in the labor market', in C.A. Orley and C. David (eds), *Handbook of Labor Economics*, Vol. 3, Amsterdan: Elsevier, pp. 1399–461.

Bosch, G., K. Mayhew and J. Gautié (2010), 'Industrial relations, legal regulations and wage setting', in J. Gautié and J. Schmitt (eds), *Low Wage in the Wealthy World*, New York: Russell Sage Foundation, pp. 91–146.

Brandt, T., T. Schulten, G. Sterkel and J. Wiedemuth (eds) (2008), *Europa im Ausverkauf: Liberalisierung und Privatisierung öffentlicher Dienstleistungen und ihre Folgen für die Tarifpolitik*, Hamburg: VSA-Verlag.

Calmfors, L. and J. Driffill (1988), 'Bargaining structure, corporatism and macroeconomic performance', *Economic Policy*, **3** (6), 13–61.

Commons, J.R. (1934), *Institutional Economics: Its Place in Political Economy*, New York: Macmillan.

Coricelli, F., A. Cukierman and A. Dalmazzo (2006), 'Monetary institutions, monopolistic competition, unionized labor markets and economic performance', *Scandinavian Journal of Economics*, **108** (1), 39–63.

Cukierman, A. and F. Lippi (1999), 'Central bank independence, centralization of wage bargaining, inflation and unemployment: theory and some evidence', *European Economic Review*, **43** (7), 1395–434.

Cully, M., S. Woodland and A.D.G. O'Reilly (1999), *Britain at Work: As Depicted by the 1998 Workplace Employee Relations Survey*, London: Routledge.

Doellgast, V. (2008), 'National industrial relations and local bargaining power in the US and German telecommunication industries', *European Journal of Industrial Relations*, **14** (3), 265–87.

Doellgast, V. (2012), *Disintegrating Democracy at Work. Labor Unions and the Future of Good Jobs in the Service Economy*, Ithaca, NY: ILR Press.

Doellgast, V. and I. Greer (2007), 'Vertical disintegration and the disorganization of German industrial relations', *British Journal of Industrial Relations*, **45** (1), 55–76.

Doellgast, V., H. Nohara and R. Tchobanian (2009), 'Institutional change and the restructuring of service work in the French and German telecommunication industry', *European Journal of Industrial Relations*, **15** (4), 373–94.

Doeringer, P.J. and M. Piore (1971), *Internal Labor Markets and Manpower Analysis*, Lexington, MA: Heath Lexington Books.

Dore, R.P. (1973), *British Factory, Japanese Factory: The Origins of National Diversity in Industrial Relations*, Berkeley/Los Angeles/Oxford: University of California Press.

Dribbusch, H. (2009), 'Working time accounts and short-time work used to maintain employment', *European Industrial Relations Observatory*, accessed 27 August 2012 at http://www.eurofound.europa.eu/eiro/2009/12/articles/de0912059i.htm.

Emmenegger, P., S. Hausermann, B. Palier and M. Selaib-Kaiser (2012), *The Age of Dualization: The Changing Face of Inequality in Deindustrialising Societies*, Oxford: Oxford University Press.

Erixon, L. (2008), 'The Rehn-Meidner model in Sweden: its rise, challenges and survival', *Journal of Economic Issues*, **44** (3), 677–715.

Esping-Andersen, G. and W. Korpi (1984), 'Social policy as class politics in post-war capitalism: Scandinavia, Austria, and Germany', in J.H. Goldthorpe (ed.), *Order and Conflict in Contemporary Capitalism: Studies in the Political Economy of Western European Nations*, Oxford: Oxford University Press, pp. 179–208.

Esser, I. and K.M. Olsen (2012), 'Perceived job quality: autonomy and job security within a multi-level framework', *European Sociological Review*, **28** (4), 443–54.

Flanders, A. (1968), 'Collective bargaining: "a theoretical analysis"', *British Journal of Industrial Relations*, **6** (1), 1–26.

Freeman, Richard B. and James Medoff (1984), *What Do Unions Do?*, New York: Basic Books.

Freeman, Richard B. and Kathryn L. Shaw (eds) (2009), *International Differences in the Business Practices and Productivity of Firms*, Chicago: University of Chicago Press.

Friedman, M. (1962), *Capitalism and Freedom*, Chicago: Chicago University Press.

Gallie, D. (2003), 'The quality of working life: is Scandinavia different?', *European Sociological Review*, **19** (1), 61–79.

Gallie, D. (2009), 'Institutional regimes and employee influence at work: a European comparison', *Cambridge Journal of Regions, Economy and Society*, **2**, 379–93.

Glassner, V. and B. Galgòczi (2009), 'Plant-level responses to the economic crisis in Europe', working paper, European Trade Union Institute.

Greer, I. (2008a), 'Organized industrial relations in the information economy: the German automotive sector as a test case', *New Technology, Work and Employment*, **23** (3), 181–96.

Greer, I. (2008b), 'Social movement unionism and social partnership in Germany', *Industrial Relations*, **47** (4), 602–24.

Grimshaw, D. and J. Rubery (1998), 'Integrating the internal and external labour markets', *Cambridge Journal of Economics*, **22** (2), 199–220.

Gustavsen, Bjørn (2007), 'Work organization and "the Scandinavian model"', *Economic and Industrial Democracy*, **28** (4), 650–71.

Gustavsen, B., B. Hofmaier, M.E. Philips and A. Wilkman (1996), *Concept-Driven Development and the Organization of the Process of Change: An Evaluation of the Swedish Work Life Fund*, Amsterdam/Philadelphia: John Benjamins Publishing Co.

Hall, P.A. and D. Gingerich (2004), 'Varieties of capitalism and institutional complementarities in the macro-economy', Discussion Paper 04/5, Cologne, Max Planck Institute for the Study of Societies.

Hall, P.A. and D. Soskice (2001), *Varieties of Capitalism: The Institutional Foundations of Comparative Advantage*, Oxford/New York: Oxford University Press.

Hancké, B., M. Rhodes and M. Thatcher (2007), 'Introduction: beyond varieties of capitalism', in B. Hancké, M. Rhodes and M. Thatcher (eds), *Beyond Varieties of Capitalism: Conflict, Contradictions, and Complementarities in the European Economy*, Oxford: Oxford University Press, pp. 3–38.

Hassel, A. (2011), 'The paradox of liberalization: understanding dualism and the recovery of the German political economy', DOI:10.2139/ssrn.1863928 (accessed 3 December 2013).

Hayek, F.A. (1984), *Money, Capital and Fluctuations: Early Essays*, London, Melbourne and Henley: Routledge & Kegan Paul.

Herrigel, G. (2010), *Manufacturing Possibilities: Creative Action and Industrial Recomposition in the United States, Germany, and Japan*, Oxford/New York: Oxford University Press.

Hollingsworth, J.R. and R. Boyer (1997), *Contemporary Capitalism: The Embeddedness of Institutions*, Cambridge and New York: Cambridge University Press.

Holst, H., O. Nachtwey and K. Dörre (2009), *Funktionswandel von Leiharbeit. Neue Nutzungsstrategien und ihre arbeits- und mitbestimmungspolitischen Folgen. Eine Studie im Auftrag der Otto Brenner Stiftung*, Frankfurt/Main, OBS–Arbeitsheft 61.

Höpner, M. (2007), 'Coordination and organization: the two dimensions of nonliberal capitalism', MPIfG Discussion Paper 07/12, Max Planck Institute for the Study of Societies, Cologne.

Huebler, O. and U. Jirjahn (2003), 'Works councils and collective bargaining in Germany: the impact on productivity and wages', *Scottish Journal of Political Economy*, **50** (4), 471–91.

ILO (2008), 'Freedom of association in practice: lessons learned', Global Report under the follow-up to the ILO Declaration on Fundamental Principles and Rights at Work, International Labour Conference 97th Session, Geneva.

ILO (2010), *Global Wage Report 2010/11*, Geneva: International Labour Office.

International Trade Union Confederation (2012), 'Annual survey 2012: statistics per region', available at: http://survey.ituc-csi.org/spip.php?page=generalgraphs (accessed 10 November 2013).

Iversen, T. and D. Soskice (2001), 'An asset theory of social policy preferences', *American Political Science Review*, **95** (4), 875–93.

Jackson, G. (2005), 'Contested boundaries. ambiguity and creativity in the evolution of German coordination', in W. Streeck and K. Thelen (eds), *Beyond Continuity. Institutional Change in Advanced Political Economies*, New York: Oxford University Press, pp. 229–54.

Kalina, T. and C. Weinkopf (2012), 'Niedriglohnbeschäftigung 2010: Fast jede/r Vierte arbeitet für Niedriglohn', Aktuelle Forschungsergebnisse aus dem Institut Arbeit und Qualifikation [Institute for Work, Skills and Training] University Essen/Duisburg.

Katz, H.C. (1993), 'The decentralization of collective bargaining: a literature review and comparative analysis', *Industrial and Labor Relations Review*, **47**(1), 3–22.

Katz, H.C. and C. Sabel (1985), 'Industrial relations and industrial adjustment in the car industry', *Industrial Relations*, **24** (3), 295–315.

Kaufman, B.E. (2007), 'The institutional economics of John R. Commons: complement and substitute for neoclassical economic theory', *Socio-Economic Review*, **5** (1), 3–45.

Kelly, J. (2004), 'Social partnership agreements in Britain: Labor cooperation and compliance', *Industrial Relations*, **43** (1), 267–97.

Kenworthy, L. (2003), 'Quantitative indicators of corporatism', *International Journal of Sociology*, **33** (3), 10–44.

Kochan, T. and P. Osterman (1994), *The Mutual Gains Enterprise*, Boston, MA: Harvard Business School Press.

Kochan, T.A., A.E. Eaton, R. McKersie and P. Adler (2009), *Healing Together: The Labor–Management Partnership at Kaiser Permanente*, Ithaca, NY: ILR Press.

Koeniger, W., M. Leonardi and L. Nunziata (2006), 'Labor market institutions and wage inequality', *Industrial and Labor Relations Review*, **60** (3), 340–56.

Korpi, W. (1983), *The Democratic Class Struggle*, London: Routledge and Kegan Paul.

Korpi, W. and M. Shalev (1979), 'Strikes, industrial relations and class conflict in capitalist societies', *British Journal of Sociology*, **30** (2), 164–87.

Lehmbruch, G. (1984), 'Concertation and the structure of corporatist networks', in J.H. Goldthorpe (ed.), *Order and Conflict in Contemporary Capitalism*, Oxford: Oxford University Press, pp. 60–80.

Lillie, N. and I. Greer (2007), 'Industrial relations, migration, and neoliberal politics: the case of the European construction sector', *Politics and Society*, **35** (4), 551–81.

Lindbeck, A. and D. Snower (1986), 'Wage setting, unemployment, and insider–outsider relations', *American Economic Review*, **76** (2), 235–9.

Madsen, P.K. (2002), 'The Danish model of flexicurity: A paradise – with some snakes', in H. Sarfati and G. Bonoli (eds), *Labour Market and Social Protections Reforms in International Perspective: Parallel or Converging Tracks?*, Aldershot: Ashgate, pp. 243–56.

Marsden, D. (1999), *A Theory of Employment Systems: Micro-Foundations of Societal Diversity*, Oxford: Oxford University Press.

Meidner, R. and G. Rehn (1953), 'Trade unions and full employment', report to the LO Congress 1951, the Swedish Confederation of Trade Unions, Stockholm (first published in Swedish in 1951).

Molina, O. and M. Rhodes (2002), 'Corporatism: the past, present, and future of a concept', *Annual Review of Political Science*, **5** (1), 305–31.

OECD (2012), *OECD Employment Outlook*, Paris: OECD.

Osterman, P. and D. Burton (2006), 'Ports and ladders: the nature and relevnce of internal labor markets in a changing world', in S. Ackroyd, R. Batt and P. Thompson (eds), *The Oxford Handbook of Work and Organization*, Oxford/New York: Oxford University Press, pp. 425–44.

Palier, B. and K. Thelen (2010), 'Institutionalizing dualism: complementarities and change in France and Germany', *Politics and Society*, **38** (1), 119–48.

Parker, M. and J. Slaughter (1988), *Choosing Sides: Unions and the Team Concept*, Boston: South End Press.

Regini, M. (2000), 'Between deregulation and social pacts: the responses of European economies to globalization', *Politics and Society*, **28** (1), 5–34.

Rhodes, M. (2001), 'The political economy of social pacts: competitive corporatism and European welfare reform', in P. Pierson (ed.), *The New Politics of the Welfare State*, Oxford: Oxford University Press, pp. 165–94.

Rubery, J. (1978), 'Structured labour markets, worker organisation and low pay', *Cambridge Journal of Economics*, **2** (1), 17–36.

Rubinstein, S. (2000), 'The impact of co-management on quality performance: the case of the Saturn Corporation', *Industrial and Labor Relations Review*, **53** (January), 197–218.

Rueda, D. (2007), *Social Democracy Inside Out. Partisanship and Labor Market Policy in Advanced Industrialized Democracies*, Oxford/New York: Oxford University Press.

Rueda, D. and J. Pontusson (2000), 'Wage inequality and varieties of capitalism', *World Politics*, **52** (3), 350–83.

Schmitter, P.C. and G. Lehmbruch (1979), *Trends toward Corporatist Intermediation*, Beverly Hills: Sage.

Shaw, J.D., J.E. Delery and D. Jenkins (1998), 'An organization-level analysis of voluntary and involuntary turnover', *Academy of Management Journal*, **41** (5), 511–25.

Sørensen, O.H. and C. Weinkopf (2009), 'Pay and working conditions in finance and utility call centres in Denmark and Germany', *European Journal of Industrial Relations*, **15** (4), 395–416.

Soskice, D. (1990), 'Wage determination: the changing role of institutions in advanced industrialized countries', *Oxford Review of Economic Policy*, **6** (4), 36–61.

Stone, K. (1974), 'The origins of job structures in the steel industry', *Review of Radical Political Economics*, **6**, 61–97.

Streeck, W. (1996), 'Lean production in the German automobile industry: a test case for convergence theory', in S. Berger and R. Dore (eds), *National Diversity and Global Capitalism*, Ithaca, NY: Cornell University Press, pp. 138–70.

Streeck, W. (2009), *Re-Forming Capitalism: Institutional Change in the German Political Economy*, Oxford: Oxford University Press.

Swenson, P. and J. Pontusson (2000), 'The Swedish employer offensive against centralized wage bargaining', in T. Iversen, J. Pontusson and D. Soskice (eds), *Unions, Employers, and Central Banks: Macroeconomic Coordination and Institutional Change in Social Market Economies*, Cambridge: Cambridge University Press, pp. 77–106.

Thelen, K. (2001), 'Varieties of labour politics in the developed democracies', in P.A. Hall and D. Soskice (eds), *Varieties of Capitalism: The Institutional Foundations of Comparative Advantage*, Oxford: Oxford University Press, pp. 71–103.

Thelen, K. (2009), 'Institutional change in advanced political economies', *British Journal of Industrial Relations*, **47** (3), 471–98.

Traxler, F. (1994), 'Collective bargaining: levels and coverage', in *OECD Employment Outlook*, Paris: OECD, pp. 167–94.

Traxler, F. and B. Brandl (2011), 'The economic impact of collective bargaining coverage', in S. Hayter (ed.), *The Role of Collective Bargaining in the Global Economy: Negotiating for Social Justice*, Cheltenham/Geneva, Edward Elgar/International Labour Office, pp. 227–53.

Turner, L. (1991), *Democracy at Work: Changing World Markets and the Future of Labor Unions*, Ithaca, NY: Cornell University Press.

Turner, L. (2009), 'Institutions and activism: crisis and opportunity for a German labor movement in decline', *Industrial and Labor Relations Review*, **62** (3), 294–312.

Visser, J. (2011), 'ICTWSS: Database on institutional characteristics of trade unions, wage setting, state intervention and social pacts in 34 countries between1960 and 2007 (updated until 2011)', Advanced Institute for Advanced Labour Studies, Amsterdam.

Webb, S. and B. Webb (1920), *The History of Trade Unionism 1666–1920*, London: Longmans.

Whitley, R. (1999), *Divergent Capitalisms: The Social Structuring and Change of Business Systems*, Oxford: Oxford University Press.

Wood, S. (1996), 'High commitment management and unionization in the UK', *International Journal of Human Resource Management*, **7** (1), 41–58.

Zwick, T. (2004), 'Employee participation and productivity', *Labour Economics*, **11**, 715–40.

15 Works councils
Werner Nienhüser

INTRODUCTION

Works councils are an instrument with which to represent employee interests to management and a means for furthering industrial and societal democracy. For a long time, these functions were at the forefront of the academic debate. Today, the debate is receiving fresh impetus, partly because in many countries we find a growing representation gap through decreasing union density and works councils are being discussed as a possible means of compensating the diminished power of employee representation (Buchanan and Briggs, 2002: 69). At the same time, however, a relatively new element has joined the debate. Employee 'voice' is increasingly being seen as a factor of growing importance from the perspective of efficiency and management interests (Markey, 2007: 188). It is assumed that participation, also in the form of a works council, involves employees in reorganization processes, which in turn raises commitment and ultimately economic efficiency.

Two hypotheses on the effects of participation in general and also of works councils come under discussion particularly frequently. The debate is informed to a very great extent by economic theories (compare, in summary, Dilger, 2002; Keller, 2006; see also Addison et al., 2004), which were initially applied to the functions assumed by unions (Freeman and Medoff, 1984) and later (Freeman and Lazear, 1995) to the effects of works councils. The first hypothesis states that if employees have the opportunity for a 'collective voice' (that is, the chance to have their demands heard through a works council) then the quit rate is lower and employees are more likely to invest in their human capital and pass on their knowledge. Such effects can be economically beneficial – the effect of a works council is therefore rent-producing, it enhances the size of the pie. A second hypothesis emphasizes the cost of institutionalized participation, particularly to shareholders. The central mechanism consists in the employees being able, through the works council, to aggregate the labour supply (at the firm level) and restrict competition, thereby achieving higher wages and benefits than would be possible under competitive conditions. This effect is known as rent-seeking. A trade-off becomes possible between generating and distributing the surplus: on the one hand, the existence of a works council influences the size of the joint surplus. On the other, the increased bargaining power has an effect on the distribution of the surplus in the form of higher wages and/or a higher proportion of the value added. If the value added distributed to the employees on account of participation is greater than that created by increased commitment and more voice, participation becomes unattractive to the employer because the company runs the risk of losing competitiveness. From this economic perspective, the power granted to employees must not be too great (Addison and Belfield, 2004: 8).

In summary, the debate has turned away from seeing works councils as a means for democratizing work and society to a perspective that focuses on economic effects at firm level and ignores societal effects. But what effects works councils have at different levels is only one of the questions addressed in this chapter. It also explains what I mean by the term 'works council' and how widespread these bodies are. Thus the questions we consider in this chapter are: what does the term 'works council' mean? What forms of works council can be distinguished between empirically? How widespread are works councils and why do differences exist – in the extent to which they are found in firms – within and between countries? What effects do works councils have on employees, firms and society? And what are the main limitations of current research and what should be done to overcome them?

DEFINITION AND TYPES OF WORKS COUNCIL

Definition

The term works council is used to describe some very different forms of employee representation. It is therefore important that we clarify how we define the term. Most definitions take works councils to mean an institutionalized, representative body – one that represents the interests of all employees of a company to its management (Rogers and Streeck, 1995: 6). As such, the term does not cover forms of individual, direct participation or employee codetermination on supervisory boards. Similarly, European works councils are excluded from our definition, since they operate above establishment level. It also makes sense to define as works councils only those institutions that may be established independently of or against the will of the management. For this reason, non-mandatory, voluntary bodies that are established on the initiative of management, and may be dissolved again by management, are not defined as works councils. A third distinction is the breadth of issues subject to participation by the works council (Gumbrell-McCormick and Hyman, 2010: 286). 'Health and safety committees' for example are not classed as works councils because of their limited scope.

Two further criteria are occasionally used in the literature to distinguish between works councils and non-works councils, although, arguably it is more appropriate to make the essential distinctions as outlined above and draw on the following two criteria to distinguish between different types of works councils. The first of these is whether a works council is purely an employee body or whether the employer may also be a member. Markey (2007: 188) suggests the term 'joint consultative committee' rather than works council for such a construction. However, such bodies will also be included in the discussion here under the term works council, provided they meet the aforementioned criteria. The second consideration is that some authors regard independence from unions as a precondition for definition as a works council (Kaufman and Taras, 2010). By contrast, Visser (2012) joins other authors (Bryson et al., 2012; Fulton, 2011; Gumbrell-McCormick and Hyman, 2010) in considering union representations at establishment level as works councils. This is reasonable as long as the other requirements outlined above are also satisfied. This implies that were a body of representation to represent only the interests of union members or only to be elected by union members, the term works council would not be appropriate.

If the basic defining terms as outlined are used, 'works councils are almost exclusively a phenomenon of continental Western Europe' (Gumbrell-McCormick and Hyman,

Table 15.1   Rights of works councils in different countries

Rights of works council	Countries
No or only information rights	Estonia, United Kingdom
Social rights only	Czech Republic, Spain, Italy, Poland
Economic and social rights – consultation (advice) only	Belgium, Denmark, Finland, France, Hungary, Luxembourg, Norway, Sweden, Slovenia, Slovakia
Economic and social rights, including codetermination rights on some issues	Austria, Germany, Netherlands

Source: Data from ICTWSS data base (Visser, 2012; see also Fulton, 2011; Bryson et al., 2012, pp. 71–2); compiled by the author.

2010: 286). This definition excludes non-mandatory, voluntary bodies which are of particular importance in countries without legislated works councils (for example, in Australia, Great Britain, and the USA). I will treat these forms of employee interest representation as works council-like bodies and not as a different type of works council. Not only works councils in a strict sense, but also works council-like bodies could have important effects for employees, management, unions and wider society. Thus I will also summarize the main results of research in this area.

In the following section I will initially provide a brief overview of three types of works councils and then discuss works council-like bodies.

Different Types of Works Council: Examples from Three Countries

In his ICTWSS database, Jelle Visser (2012) compiled information on works councils in a total of 36 countries. In five of the countries (Australia, Brazil, Canada, New Zealand, the USA) there are no provisions relating to any kind of works council. In the remaining 31 countries we find very different forms of works councils. Table 15.1 shows that works councils are most typically a European institution.

Primarily those 17 countries in which the existence and the rights of works councils are mandated by law or by basic agreements have been taken into account in this chapter. Estonia and the UK have been excluded as these countries only guarantee information rights, and works councils are in fact empirically insignificant (Fulton, 2011).

Important criteria for differentiating between works councils are the number and importance of issues they are entitled to participate in, and the strength of their rights (Visser, 2012 interconnects these dimensions, see Table 15.1). These extend from simple information rights to consultation rights and all the way up to codetermination at the other end of the scale. A works council has strong rights of codetermination if it is able to block corporate decisions by its rejection or non-agreement or to initiate management decisions itself. A distinction is often made between social and economic issues. Social issues include health and safety, start and end of working time, overtime, general principles on holidays and fringe benefits, principles and methods of remuneration. Economic issues may include, for example, investment decisions. Even in countries where the works councils enjoy strong codetermination rights (in particular Austria, Germany and the Netherlands), it is essentially the 'social' consequences of company decisions that are subject to codetermination, not the decisions themselves. A works council may have strong codetermination rights in relation to the consequences of a plant closure but not in relation to the actual decision to close the plant.

Major variations within Europe are apparent in other areas, too. Legislation in the countries with works councils does not generally require works councils to be established in all companies. An important condition relates to the size of an establishment necessary legally to initiate works council representation: this varies between one employee in Portugal and Sweden, five in Germany, the Czech Republic, Austria and Latvia, and up to 50 employees in Hungary (Toth, 1997), Poland and France, or 100 in Belgium (Bryson et al., 2012: 71–2).

In addition to the rights issue, an important distinction can also be made between works councils on whether they are embedded in a single-channel or dual-channel structure. Single- and dual-channel refers to the form of employee representation at establishment level. Single-channel means that there is only one form of employee interest representation (works council or a trade union representation body as a functional equivalent of a works council). In the case of a dual-channel structure there are both forms (trade union and works council) (Aumayr et al., 2011: 10–11). We find typical single-channel structures of representation in works councils in Germany, but also in Austria, Luxembourg and the Netherlands. Single-channel structures with the trade unions being the sole representation body at establishment level are typical of Sweden (Gumbrell-McCormick and Hyman, 2010). A dual-channel structure of representation, where both types of employee representation exist, can be found in France.

If we move the single-channel versus dual-channel structure criterion into the foreground, we can distinguish between three forms or types (Table 15.2). I will outline the details of each type using the example of a country that best represents it.

One has to add that the differentiation between a single- and dual-channel structure strongly refers to the *de jure* situation and not so much to the *de facto* situation. In Germany, for instance, the works council is formally independent of the unions at establishment level. In fact, works councils and trade unions work closely together and most works councillors are union members. Nevertheless the works council is the dominating body at the establishment level, so that we speak of a single-channel structure for Germany.

Type 1   Single-channel employee representation by a non-union body: Germany
German works councils are categorized as a single-channel system. At the establishment level, the works council is the single or at least strongly dominant body of inter-

Table 15.2   Types of works council (single-channel versus dual-channel structure)

Type	Structure at establishment level	Typical example
1	Single channel of representation (works council is the dominating, non-union body at establishment level)	Germany
2	Single channel of representation (trade union is the sole body of employee representation)	Sweden
3	Dual-channel (union and non-union body of employee representation coexist at establishment level)	France

est representation (Aumayr et al., 2011; see, for the following, in particular Keller and Kirsch, 2011; Müller-Jentsch, 2008). Works councils are – as in other countries too – the result of a compromise in the struggle between capital and labour and have a relatively long history in Germany. Workers' or factory committees, precursors of the present institution of the works council, could already be found towards the end of the nineteenth century. They became compulsory for the mining industry in 1905. During the First World War, this was extended to include companies in industries significant to the war effort. After 1920, companies with 20 or more employees were required by law to establish a works council. In the political climate of the Weimar Republic, there was little opportunity for the effects of the law to unfold (Müller-Jentsch, 1995: 53), and it was revoked in 1933. In 1952 a Works Constitution Act (*Betriebsverfassungsgesetz*) was passed by the parliament. In 1972 the law was redrafted and extended the rights of the works council. With the exception of some minor amendments (in 2001), the Works Constitution Act is still valid to this day. A similar law, the Federal Staff Representation Act (*Personalvertretungsgesetz*), applies to the public sector and is specified by the *Länder* Staff Representation Acts (Weiss and Schmidt, 2000: 209–10). These acts prescribe the establishment of staff councils, which are comparable to works councils (Keller, 2005), but are not considered in greater detail here.

The 1972 Works Constitution Act stipulates that works councils may be established in companies with at least five employees. Three employees or a union represented in a company by at least one member must take the initiative and call a meeting at which an election board is established to hold elections to the works council. The members of the works council are elected by all a firm's employees for a term of four years and represent its entire workforce. Only employees who are classed by law and in legal practice as executive staff (*Leitende Angestellte*) are not represented by the works council.

A key feature of the German labour relations system is its single-channel structure. The works council is the only body of employee representation that is formally independent of the unions at establishment level. The responsibilities of the unions and the works council are strictly separate in terms of their content and bargaining arena or level. The methods of resolving conflicts also differ (Müller-Jentsch, 1995): wage negotiation takes place on an industry-wide (that is to say, external to the firm) level between employers' associations and unions. In this case, industrial action may be used to put forward employee interests. The outcomes of negotiations are set down in collective agreements, which are then applied to all firms belonging to the organization concluding the agreement. In addition, a collective agreement may under certain conditions be extended by the state to include non-member companies in the same sector. At establishment level, by contrast, the works council is not permitted to negotiate on issues that are actually or usually covered by collective agreements, unless a collective agreement explicitly provides for exemption clauses *(Öffnungsklauseln)*. For issues not covered by a collective agreement works councils are allowed to conclude what are called works agreements (*Betriebsvereinbarungen*) with the management, in particular on 'social matters', for instance on the beginning and termination of daily working time.

Legally, the separation between the two channels of employee representation (unions on an industry-wide or external level, works councils at establishment level) is strict. Practically, there is in fact close cooperation between unions and works councils. The majority of works council members are union members (Aumayr et al., 2011). Unions provide support, for example with information and training. Unions in return require the support of the works councils, particularly in winning new members and concluding, implementing and overseeing compliance with collective agreements (Keller and Kirsch, 2011: 206). The works council is under a legal obligation of 'trustful cooperation' (*Vertrauensvolle Zusammenarbeit*). This means that works councils and management are obliged to constructively seek a solution before any conflict is sent to arbitration for resolution. It also means that the works council may not call for industrial action.

The rights of the works council extend from pure information rights all the way to genuine codetermination in an area referred to as 'social matters'. This includes some rights of veto, albeit relating more to the implementation and the consequences of corporate action than to the actual decisions themselves. To put it in simple terms, the more economic and strategic the decisions are, the weaker the works council's rights of participation. One of its most powerful rights is the right to force a company to draw up a social plan (*Sozialplan*). A social plan is designed to compensate for and alleviate the economic disadvantages suffered by company employees, particularly in the event of mass redundancies. The works council may, for example, demand an agreement with the employer on severance pay. If agreement cannot be reached with the employer, what is known as the arbitration committee (*Einigungsstelle*) rules on the social plan, whereby its decision must take the interests of the employee and the economic viability for the company into account. The arbitration committee comprises an equal number of employee and employer representatives. It is presided over by a neutral individual, who does not initially take part in voting but holds the casting vote in the event of a stalemate.

Since election of a works council is dependent on employee initiative, works councils in Germany are not that widespread. In 2011, 10 per cent of companies in western Germany (with more than 5 employees) had a works council and 9 per cent in eastern Germany. Accordingly, 44 per cent (west) and 36 per cent (east) of employees in the private sector are represented by a works council (Ellguth and Kohaut, 2012: 301).

The functioning of German works councils can hardly be understood without taking employee representation on the supervisory board into account. Employee representatives on the supervisory board have the same rights as those members representing the owners (Weiss and Schmidt, 2000: 218–19). In most cases the employee representatives are also works council members (and members of a trade union as well). Thus there is close cooperation between works council, employee representatives on the supervisory board and the trade unions. This kind of embeddedness is also relevant to other countries and systems.

Type 2   Single-channel employee representation by a union body: Sweden
By contrast with the first type, employee representation in Sweden takes place through a union body. Unions are also responsible for representing interests at establishment level in Cyprus and Finland. The Swedish system of employee representation at establishment level is characterized by comparatively extensive rights.

In 1946 a central agreement was reached between the largest union and the employers' associations on the establishment of joint works councils (*företagsnämnderna*). The employee representatives were elected by union members only (Gumbrell-McCormick and Hyman, 2010: 300). This agreement was later revoked, when the law of codetermination (*Medbestämmandelagen*, MBL) passed in 1976 obliged employers to bargain with unions at establishment level on all labour relations issues, including those normally covered by collective negotiations (Fulton, 2011). The works council is elected by all employees and represents the entire workforce of a company. This was not the case in Sweden for a long time. In 2005 the law had to be amended to comply with the EU Directive (2002/14/EC), with the result that the union bodies of representation now also represent non-members and include employees in companies where the unions have reached no such agreements on employee representation.

Many of the issues that in other countries – such as Germany – have a legal basis are negotiated in Sweden at local level between the employer and the unions (Kjellberg, 1998). With a 71 per cent level of organization (Fulton, 2011), the unions have a strong bargaining position.

Employers are required to negotiate on questions of work organization, technical developments and economic issues. There is a necessity for negotiation, but not for agreement. Ultimately, the employer – as in the other types and/or countries – is free to make fundamental business decisions. Negotiation is possible in several ways and on several levels: union representatives can negotiate directly with the responsible manager, management and unions can hold negotiations at establishment level, and a joint committee comprising union and employer representatives may also be used (Fulton, 2011). The union has powers of veto in one area: it may prevent a company from awarding contracts to subcontractors unless for special types of task or short-term assignments (Fulton, 2011).

According to the European Company Survey 2009 (Aumayr et al., 2011: 18), around 63 per cent of Swedish companies had a works council, representing 80 per cent of employees. It is important to note that there is no threshold regarding the size of a firm for electing a works council.

Type 3   Dual-channel employee representation: France
In the dual-channel structure of France, union representation exists alongside non-union representation at company level (Goetschy and Jobert, 2011; Zagelmeyer, 2011). Firstly there are employee delegates (*délégués du personnel*, DP), who are formally independent of the unions (Gumbrell-McCormick and Hyman, 2010: 297). DPs must be elected in all companies with more than 10 employees. They are responsible for voicing complaints to the management and are concerned with the implementation and observance of laws and collective agreements. This body of employee representation was legally instituted in 1936. Secondly, employee interests are represented by a works council (*comité d'entreprise*, CE). A works council is compulsory in establishments with more than 50 employees. An employee delegate (DP) can also be a member of the works council (Fulton, 2011). In companies with fewer than 200 employees, the employer may decide to replace these two bodies with a single one known as the unique delegation (*délégation unique du personnel*, DUP). One particular feature that sets France apart from Germany and Sweden is that the works council is not made up purely of employees; the employer is also a member and presides over it. Thirdly, the unions may appoint union delegates (*délégués syndicaux*, DS) in companies, on the condition that the company has more than 50 employees and the union is representative, that is, supported by at least 10 per cent of the workforce. If a union is not representative, it is, only entitled to appoint one representative of the union section, who has lesser rights. Union delegates and works councils may coexist in French establishments (Fairris and Askenazy, 2010).

The election or appointment procedures for members of the three bodies differ. The union delegates are appointed by the regional or national union. By contrast, members of both the DP and the works council are elected by all members of the workforce. The unions nevertheless have a considerable influence on this process, as only the unions may put forward candidate lists in the first ballot. If the union list does not win at least half of the votes in the first round, a second ballot is held in which non-union employees may also be nominated (Fulton, 2011).

The rights of the DP, the works council and the union delegates differ in their strength and content. As in Germany, there is some kind of formal division of labour between the employee representation bodies, but in practice they work closely together (Gumbrell-McCormick and Hyman, 2010). The DPs tend to deal with complaints and ensure that the legal or negotiated rights of the employees are upheld. The works council has more far-reaching rights of information and consultation. It has the right to be informed on economic and social developments of the establishment, as well as on the introduction of new technologies. It has consultation rights regarding redundancies and vocational training. The works council may also be responsible for running social and cultural activities for employees, such as libraries, canteens, holiday homes or sports clubs (Fulton, 2011). True rights of codetermination in the sense of withholding agreement or initiating decisions are not held by either DPs or works councils.

Neither the DP nor the works council has bargaining rights. Only the union delegates have the right to bargain with the employer. However, the industry level is more important for bargaining than the establishment level (Fulton, 2011).

In 2004/2005, 87 per cent of all workplaces with at least 50 employees had employee delegates or a DUP, 81 per cent had a works council or a combined body, and 63 per cent had at least one union delegate. In larger companies these figures are above 95 per cent (Fulton 2011). On average, the coverage rate is much higher than in Germany. One reason is that, in contrast to Germany, a works council must be established independently of the employees' will.

Similarities and differences

There are significant differences between the three countries in the incidence of works councils. Virtually all large companies have a works council, while the majority of small firms do not. Differences in the incidence of works councils are partly attributable to the minimum number of employees required to establish one (Bryson et al., 2012: 71f.). More significant, however, is the fact that in France as opposed to Germany, the appointment of a works council is prescribed by law. Similarities are apparent in a number of areas: economic decisions on the use of capital (for example investments) and revenue (dividends to shareholders) are subject to participation to a minor extent. Even in the use of 'human capital', for example in mass redundancies, rights are restricted to consultation. Only the consequences of redundancies for the employees – as with the social plan in Germany – are subject to codetermination by the works councils.

Works council-like bodies

Works council-like bodies exist in countries without mandated works councils, for example, in Australia, the UK and the USA. But we also find such bodies in Germany, predominantly in establishments without an elected works council. The incidence is by no means low. In the USA and in Canada, about 20 per cent of employees have a form of non-union employee representation at their workplace (Campolieti et al., 2013: 380). In the UK the proportion of workplaces with non-union on-site employee representatives is 16 per cent (Bryson et al., 2013, the data refer to 2004). Even in Germany, non-statutory forms of employee representation exist in 5 to 20 per cent of all establishments (Hertwig, 2011: 531).

EVOLUTION AND CAUSES OF WORKS COUNCILS

What causes works councils to evolve? This question can be addressed both at country and at establishment level. The first question is why we find provisions permitting or even prescribing the establishment of works councils in some countries and not in others. The second question is why in one country not all companies satisfying the formal requirements for establishing a works council actually have one.

There are two strands of literature dealing with the evolution and establishment of works councils. The first strand is historically oriented and takes a sociological and macro-level perspective in considering the social embeddedness of institutions. The second strand is characterized by a more micro-level perspective concentrating on the establishment level and taking a short-term view. Typical of this kind of research are econometric studies at the firm level, trying to identify causes of the establishment of works councils in cross-sectional analyses.

From the first perspective, works councils are generally seen as an institutional compromise between capital and labour (Knudsen, 1995; Müller-Jentsch, 1995). This is particularly evident in German history. At the beginning of the nineteenth century and particularly in historically favourable phases for the labour movement, capital and government feared that political forces calling, amongst other things, for socialization of key industries could gain power. By institutionalizing works councils, they saw a way of averting such demands (Müller-Jentsch, 1995).

From a macro-level view, we find differences between coordinated and liberal market economies (Hall and Soskice, 2001). Works councils are generally found more in countries of the first type and may be seen as an element of the co-evolution of social structures; they have not evolved in isolation but with other institutions, such as the collective bargaining system and labour law, and with political ideologies. Works councils are seen as a 'fitting' element of CMEs. Organized negotiations between collective actors in these economies are the central mechanism for determining action: coordination by cooperation and less by prices and competition. In CMEs, labour is assumed to be in an inferior position of power to that of capital, a situation institutions such as laws to protect employees and legally underpinned employee interest representation are designed to alleviate. In LMEs, by contrast, markets and prices are the main coordination mechanisms. Collective negotiations in contexts regulated by standards and norms play a lesser role here. The imbalance of power between capital and labour is seen less as a problem, which goes hand in hand with the view that there is less demand for power-balancing institutions such as works councils. It appears that historically a kind of institutional structure emerges that also includes the allocation of responsibilities and the power of the relevant actors on the different levels of regulation. We therefore find works councils more in countries in which the unions play a lesser role in firms and wage negotiations are more centralized, that is, these functions primarily take place at sectoral, national or regional level. Germany, the Netherlands and Austria as typical CMEs are characterized by relatively strong codetermination rights and a formal separation between unions and works councils. In the countries in which wages are bargained more at establishment level, unions also play a major role in employee representation at this level, and works councils are less significant. Typical cases are the USA, where we find no works councils, and Great Britain, where at best we find the rough outlines of such an institution (Bryson et al., 2012: 37).

In the countries with provisions for establishing works councils, why do not all companies actually have a works council, and under what conditions do works councils come into being? This question applies primarily to countries in which establishment of a works council is conditional upon the will of the employees, even in companies satisfying conditions such as the minimum size. A typical example of this, once again, is Germany. Here the employees or a union represented in the firm must actively initiate election of a works council.

Empirical studies which can be subsumed under the second, more micro-level oriented strand of literature have shown that works council presence and also the introduction of new works councils is positively related to establishment size, collective agreement coverage, the proportion of blue-collar and shift workers and whether a company belongs to the manufacturing industry. Upcoming reorganization also makes establishment of a works council more likely (Mohrenweiser et al., 2012). A negative statistical relationship exists between the proportion of female and part-time employees, the profit situation and status as a family-owned business (Addison et al., 1997; Frick, 1996; Jirjahn, 2010). Interpretation of some variables is not without its difficulties. Variables such as the proportions of blue-collar workers, shift workers, females and employees working part-time are understood as reflecting the employees' preferences for collective representation (Addison et al., 2003). But it remains unclear whether such variables actually measure preferences or some other quantity.

Management preferences for or against employee representation could also play a role in the establishment and maintenance of works councils. In the literature, in particular from the field of business administration, we find on the one hand the suggestion that participation can be a means of achieving the goals of management and shareholders. Employee participation is seen as a 'productivity factor' (Markey, 2007: 188f.). But very often this argument is limited to voluntary forms of participation and does not refer to mandatory representative participation by works councils. On the other hand, one might assume that management has a negative opinion of works councils if it does not expect or need the positive effects of participation, such as commitment, or considers that the 'price' for such effects is too high. There is a lot of evidence that works council busting is quite common: management activities trying to hinder the election of works council work are well documented in case study-like reports (Behrens and Dribbusch, 2012; Bormann, 2008).

EFFECTS OF WORKS COUNCILS

The following, interrelated effects of works councils are at the core of the discussion (see Addison et al., 2004; Frege, 2002; Jirjahn, 2010; Kaufman and Taras, 2010; Keller, 2006). Firstly, effects on the mental disposition and behaviour of employees are examined, including work motivation, communication, or inclination to leave the company. Such studies do not generally refer to works councils, but to participation in general, and mostly to participation at the workplace level. Secondly, there are many studies on the effects of the existence of works councils on economically relevant processes and the market success of a company. They analyse such things as effects on innovation, wage levels, productivity or profits. A third group of studies looks into the social consequences of works councils. They deal with the regulatory functions fulfilled by works councils (such as monitoring and control in relation to health and safety) and their effects on democratizing economy and society. Most frequently, studies are on the economic effects at the firm level, while there has been considerably less empirical examination of the effects of works councils on society.

In the literature we find again two very different strands of studies on works councils. There are studies analysing the work and the problems of works councils, their reactions to changes such as new technologies, and the social relationship between works council and employees, trade unions and management. Most of these studies are more or less qualitative case studies based on expert interviews. Economic effects (from a management standpoint) are in the background in these works, whereas democratization and employee interests are in the foreground (for an overview see Frege, 2002; Greifenstein and Kißler, 2010). Conversely, especially in the past 20 years and above all in Germany, numerous quantitative large-scale studies have examined the effects of works councils on performance econometrically (compare, in summary, Addison et al., 1993; Dilger, 2002; Jirjahn, 2010). In this currently influential economic view, the focus is very much on effects that are relevant to shareholders. Many studies consider the effects of works councils on factors such as productivity, profits and wages, but also concern themselves with closures or innovative behaviour. In contrast, little attention is paid to the effects on employee interests.

In the following sections, the essential findings on the effects of works councils at the establishment level are examined, and the starting points for empirical studies on effects over and above that level are briefly outlined. Most of these studies refer to Germany (regarding the economic effects, the comprehensive overview by Jirjahn, 2010 is referred to). In other countries, however, studies are few and far between, and above all there is a lack of quantitative analysis. An early study on works councils in South Korea was made by Kleiner and Lee (1997), although the study does not include companies without works councils. For the Netherlands there is only one quantitative study on the effect of works councils, because the relevant data were not available (van den Berg et al., 2011: 498). The situation is similar in France, and Fairris and Askenazy (2010: 212) point out that their study is the first quantitative analysis on the economic effects of works councils. The following overview is restricted primarily to quantitative studies, as most of the work on effects is quantitative and it is difficult to compare and generalize results of qualitative analyses. This brings with it the problem of a one-sided, shareholder-oriented view inherent in most economic studies. Thus, the restrictions and one-sidedness of these studies will be briefly discussed in the final section.

Effects at the Establishment Level

For Germany, the earlier studies based on smaller datasets predominantly point towards the negative effects of works councils on firm performance (for example, FitzRoy and Kraft, 1987). The findings of more recent studies with larger sets of data suggest positive rather than negative economic effects (Jirjahn, 2010). Research is currently engaged in the search for moderator variables or interaction effects – an attempt to identify the contextual conditions under which positive or negative effects occur. In the language of economic theory, the conditions under which rent-producing or rent-seeking effects prevail.

Effects on value creation, productivity, profits and innovation
Many studies suggest that the existence of a works council leads to higher value added (for example, Frick and Möller, 2003) and higher productivity (for a summary see Looise et al., 2010). However, contextual effects appear to play a role – the positive effects cannot be observed equally under all conditions. Jirjahn (2010: 11) argues that profit sharing and collective bargaining coverage alleviate distribution conflicts and that, under such conditions, productivity-enhancing effects such as increased motivation and improved communication predominate, and resource consumption caused by conflicts is less apparent. Generally speaking, it is fair to say in summing up the findings that the existence of a works council does not reduce company performance and, under certain conditions, has a productivity-enhancing or value-added-enhancing effect.

Alongside productivity, a company's profits are an important indicator of its success. The statistical relationship between the existence of a works council and profits depends on whether profits are based on the subjective assessments of those questioned or measured objectively. The effect of a works council is generally negative based on subjective measurements, but positive if outcomes are measured by objective means (Jirjahn, 2010: 19; Mueller, 2011). Regarding innovation, the present findings show that works councils at least do not have a negative influence on company innovation (Jirjahn, 2010: 21–2).

Effects on wages and employment strategies
According to the collective voice hypothesis, in companies with a works council, wages and, more generally, human resource management practices should be more in tune with the preferences of the workforce (Jirjahn, 2010). This assumption is by and large confirmed. Firstly, there is considerable evidence that the wage level is positively influenced by the existence of a works council (Addison et al., 2010; Jirjahn, 2010: 11). Secondly, companies with works councils are more likely to have a family-friendly human resources policy (Heywood and Jirjahn, 2009) and company-financed training (Zwick, 2005). Thirdly, the extent of personnel turnover is lower (Frick, 1996). Overall, companies with a works council are more committed to a long-term employment strategy and make greater use of the internal labour market (Jirjahn, 2010: 25).

All in all, there is strong empirical evidence to confirm the assumption that works councils have positive economic effects at the establishment level. By contrast, little evidence is available to support the negative effects hypothesis.

Consequences in the Broader Social and Economic Context

The majority of econometric studies concentrate on the establishment level and pay little attention to the wider effects of works councils. By contrast, sociologists and political scientists take a broader view (for instance, Rogers and Streeck, 1994). Firstly, works councils contribute to social peace – a public good in which individual companies have an interest but invest too little (free-riding behaviour). Secondly, works councils fulfil regulatory functions which would otherwise have to be assumed by state or other institutions. These include tasks such as monitoring work safety, compliance with health and safety laws, collective agreements and so on (Rogers and Streeck, 1995). Thirdly, works councils are institutions of social learning (Müller-Jentsch, 2008), they also play a democratizing role for business and society – this is democracy at work in a firm. Such emergence effects, which occur as a result of the interplay between various elements of an industrial relations system, are excluded from studies that concentrate purely on the establishment level. However, economic and other general social effects can hardly be reduced to the results of microeconomic efficiency. They are about processes of creating social stability and the ability to adapt.

Effects of Works Council-Like Bodies

Because the form and context of voluntary bodies representing employees' interests vary considerably between countries and also firms, a summarizing overview on the effects is difficult to provide. In the literature, first and foremost discussed are the following questions (see, for example, Kaufman and Taras, 2010: 270–73): do works council-like bodies avoid or substitute for the influence of unions or, particularly with regard to Germany, are these forms a substitute for mandated works councils? Or are works council-like bodies complementary to existing institutions of interest representation or even a station on the way to mandated workers' participation? Campolieti et al. (2013), for instance, find for the USA and Canada that the existence of non-union employee representation reduces the demand for unionization, that is, the preference of the employees to belong to a union, and also the observed union membership. On the other hand, their results show that the strength of the effects is considerably different between the two countries, that is, the effects seem to be dependent on the form of the respective bodies and the legal and institutional context.

Currently I would draw only a very general conclusion based on research on works council-like bodies and in particular on employee representation bodies established on a voluntary basis. The more the existence of a representative body depends on the will of the management, the stronger is, all other things being equal, the power disadvantage for the employees in the exchange relationship with management. And this creates differences in the outcomes of negotiations compared to non-voluntary works councils.

CONCLUSION

Research to date has made a number of distinctive points, but some research questions are still unanswered. Firstly, the picture is dominated by studies from Germany on

German works councils. We need more studies comparing different countries and systematically taking the national context into account.

Secondly, econometric studies have dominated for several years. It is noticeable that many of the studies are by the same authors, who repeatedly refer back to one another and work with the same sets of data. It would be worth asking to what extent the findings stand up if other samples and other surveying methods are used.

Thirdly, the relationship between the causes and effects of works councils is still conceptually unclear. The cause and effect variables are difficult to separate, which econometrists refer to as an endogeneity problem. If the causes of the establishment of works councils also influence their effects, the relevant effects must be isolated from one another. One example is the influence of the economic situation, such as a cyclical downturn in demand. If a firm finds itself in such an unfavourable economic situation, establishment of a works council becomes more likely. At the same time, recession has an influence on its economic performance. In other words, companies that are in an unfavourable economic situation will more often have a works council and at the same time lower performance, but that performance is not necessarily attributable to the existence of the works council. Interestingly, the existing studies indicate that the positive effects of the works council on company productivity become more apparent if the endogeneity problem is addressed statistically (see, in particular, Müller, 2009). At the same time, the contextual conditions under which works councils can have different effects require more detailed analysis. For Germany it has become clear since Kotthoff's study (1981) at the latest that the effects of works councils can differ according to the nature of the social relationship between works council and management.

Research would benefit from deeper theoretical and empirical explanation of the causal relationships. This is where economic theory and a view that dismisses social processes – such as interaction and learning – to the black box reach their limits. Elaborating the statistical methods alone will not help to advance research. The black box needs to be broken open and social interaction processes between management and works councils (and also works council-like forms), perceptions, power structures and processes as well as contextual conditions given greater consideration. Studies on the differential effects of the types of works councils indicate that there is little point in analysing the effects of the existence versus non-existence of a works council on their own. More causal and longer-term case studies considering different forms of works councils, works council-like bodies and country- and company-specific structural context (for example, labour law and the entire bargaining and industrial system) would be useful.

Finally, in many studies it is impossible to overlook a normative position of economic research for or against institutionalized employee representation. Above all, there is a predisposition against legally mandated and non-voluntary forms of interest representation. This is evident from efforts to prove its negative effects or an absence of positive consequences. At the same time, certain effects are considered positive (desirable) or negative (undesirable) without further debate: a productivity-enhancing effect is always seen as positive, no matter what it means for time pressure or stress, for example. By contrast, the wage-enhancing effects of works councils are usually regarded as negative, although this assessment should differ from the point of view of the workforce and/or works council (Keller, 2006). If a normative bias is effectively part and parcel of the theory, this may influence the interpretation of empirical findings, particularly if they are not conclusive. The problem is not that the discussion is value-loaded, but that the value judgements are not addressed as a subject in themselves. Differences between them are inevitable, the diverging interests of capital and labour make works councils contested terrain. For that reason, the debate will always be a controversial one.

ACKNOWLEDGEMENT

I thank Berndt Keller and the editors for their valuable comments on an earlier version of this chapter and Amanda Dixon for helping me with the translation.

REFERENCES

Addison, J.T. and C.R. Belfield (2004), 'Union voice', *Journal of Labor Research*, **25** (4), 563–97.
Addison, J.T., K. Kraft and J. Wagner (1993), 'German works councils and firm performance', in B.E. Kaufman and M.M. Kleiner (eds), *Employee Representation: Alternatives and Future Directions*, Wisconsin: Industrial Relations Research Association, pp. 305–38.
Addison, J.T., C. Schnabel and J. Wagner (1997), 'On the determinants of mandatory works councils in Germany', *Industrial Relations*, **36** (4), 419–45.
Addison, J.T., L. Bellmann, C. Schnabel and J. Wagner (2003), 'German works councils old and new: incidence, coverage and determinants', *Schmollers Jahrbuch*, **123**, 339–58.
Addison, J.T., C. Schnabel and J. Wagner (2004), 'The course of research into the economic consequences of German works councils', *British Journal of Industrial Relations*, **42** (2), 255–81.
Addison, J.T., P. Teixeira and T. Zwick (2010), 'Works councils and the anatomy of wages', *Industrial and Labor Relations Review*, **63**, 250–74.
Aumayr, C., S. Demetriades, D. Foden, V. Scepanovics and F. Wolf (2011), *Employee Representation at Establishment Level in Europe. European Company Survey 2009*, European Foundation for the Improvement of Living and Working Conditions, Dublin.
Behrens, M. and H. Dribbusch (2012), 'Wie man Betriebsräte abblitzen lässt. WSI-Befragung', *Mitbestimmung*, **6**, 16–19.
Bormann, S. (2008), 'Unternehmenshandeln gegen Betriebsratsgründungen – Der Fall Schlecker', *WSI-Mitteilungen*, **1**, 45–50.
Bryson, A., J. Forth and A. George (2012), *Workplace Employee Representation in Europe*, European Foundation for the Improvement of Living and Working Conditions, Dublin.
Bryson, A., P. Willman, R. Gomez and T. Kretschmer (2013), 'The comparative advantage of non-union voice in Britain, 1980–2004', *Industrial Relations*, **52**, 194–220.
Buchanan, J. and C. Briggs (2002), 'Works councils and inequality at work in contemporary Australia', in P.J. Gollan, R. Markey, and I. Ross (eds), *Works Councils in Australia*, Annandale, NSW: The Federation Press, pp. 48–73.
Campolieti, M., R. Gomez and M. Gunderson (2013), 'Does non-union employee representation act as a complement or substitute to union voice? Evidence from Canada and the United States', *Industrial Relations*, **52**, 378–96.
Dilger, A. (2002), *Ökonomik betrieblicher Mitbestimmung*, Munich and Mering: Rainer Hampp Verlag.
Ellguth, P. and S. Kohaut (2012), 'Tarifbindung und betriebliche Interessenvertretung – aktuelle Ergebnisse aus dem IAB-Betriebspanel 2011,' *WSI-Mitteilungen*, **65** (4), 297–305.
Fairris, D. and P. Askenazy (2010), 'Works councils and firm productivity in France', *Journal of Labor Research*, **31** (3), 209–29.
FitzRoy, F. and K. Kraft (1987), 'Efficiency and internal organization: works councils in West German firms', *Economica*, **54**, 493–504.
Freeman, R.B. and E. Lazear (1995), 'An economic analysis of works councils', in J. Rogers and W. Streeck (eds), *Works Councils: Consultation, Representation and Cooperation in Industrial Relations*, Chicago: University of Chicago Press, pp. 27–52.
Freeman, R.B. and J.L. Medoff (1984), *What Do Unions Do?*, New York: Basic Books.
Frege, C. (2002), 'A critical assessment of the theoretical and empirical research on German works councils', *British Journal of Industrial Relations*, **40**, 221–48.

Frick, B. (1996), 'Codetermination and personnel turnover: the German experience', *Labour*, **10**, 407–30.

Frick, B. and I. Möller (2003), 'Mandated works councils and firm performance: labor productivity and personnel turnover in German establishments', *Schmollers Jahrbuch*, **123**, 423–54.

Fulton, L. (2011), 'Worker representation in Europe', accessed 11 November 2013 at http://www.worker-participation.eu/layout/set/print/content/view/full/779.

Goetschy, J. and A. Jobert (2011), 'Employment relations in France', in G. Bamber, R. Lansbury, and N. Wailes (eds), *International and Comparative Employment Relations: Globalisation and Change*, 5th edn, Sydney: Allen and Unwin, pp. 169–95.

Greifenstein, R. and L. Kißler (2010), *Mitbestimmung im Spiegel der Forschung: Eine Bilanz der empirischen Untersuchungen 1952–2010*, Berlin: Edition Sigma.

Gumbrell-McCormick, R. and R. Hyman (2010), 'Works councils: the European model of industrial relations', in A. Wilkinson, P. J. Gollan, M. Marchington and D. Lewin (eds), *The Oxford Handbook of Participation in Organizations*, Oxford: Oxford University Press, pp. 286–314.

Hall, P.A. and D. Soskice (eds) (2001), *Varieties of Capitalism: The Institutional Foundations of Comparative Advantage*, Oxford: Oxford University Press.

Hertwig, M. (2011), 'Patterns, ideologies and strategies of non-statutory employee representation in German private sector companies', *Industrial Relations Journal*, **42** (6), 530–46.

Heywood, J. and U. Jirjahn (2009), 'Family friendly practices and worker representation: German evidence', *Industrial Relations*, **48**, 121–45.

Jirjahn, U. (2010), '*Ökonomische Wirkungen der Mitbestimmung in Deutschland: Ein Update*', Working Paper No. 186, Hans-Böckler-Stiftung, Düsseldorf.

Kaufman, B. and D. Taras (2010), 'Non-union employee representation,' in A. Wilkinson, P. J. Gollan, M. Marchington and D. Lewin (eds), *The Oxford Handbook of Participation in Organizations*, Oxford: Oxford University Press, pp. 258–85.

Keller, B. (2005), 'Changing employment relations in the public sector', *European Industrial Relations Review*, **376**, 27–30.

Keller, B. (2006), 'Mitbestimmung: Aktuelle Forderungen im Licht empirischer Daten', *Sozialer Fortschritt*, **55** (2–3), 41–50.

Keller, B. and A. Kirsch (2011), 'Employment relations in Germany', in G. Bamber, R. Lansbury and N. Wailes (eds), *International and Comparative Employment Relations: Globalisation and Change*, 5th edn, Sydney: Allen and Unwin, pp. 196–223.

Kjellberg, A. (1998), 'Sweden: restoring the model?', in A. Ferner and R. Hyman (eds), *Changing Industrial Relations in Europe*, Oxford: Blackwell, pp. 74–117.

Kleiner, M.M. and Y.-M. Lee (1997), 'Works councils and unionization: lessons from South Korea', *Industrial Relations*, **36** (1), 1–16.

Knudsen, H. (1995), *Employee Participation in Europe*, London: SAGE

Kotthoff, H. (1981), *Betriebsräte und betriebliche Herrschaft: eine Typologie von Partizipationsmustern im Industriebetrieb*, Frankfurt/M.: Campus.

Looise, J.K., N. Torka and J.E. Wigboldus (2010), 'Participation and organizational performance', in F. Garibaldo and V. Telljohann (eds), *The Ambivalent Character of Participation*, Frankfurt/M.: Peter Lang, pp. 327–39.

Markey, R. (2007), 'Non-union employee representation in Australia: a case study of the Suncorp Metway Employee Council Inc. (SMEC)', *Journal of Industrial Relations*, **49** (2), 187–209.

Mohrenweiser, J., P. Marginson and U. Backes-Gellner (2012), 'What triggers the establishment of a works council?', *Economic and Industrial Democracy*, **33** (2), 295–316.

Mueller, S. (2011), 'Works councils and firm profits revisited', *British Journal of Industrial Relations*, **49**, 27–43.

Müller, S. (2009), 'The productivity effect of non-union representation', BGPE Discussion (No. 74), Erlangen-Nürnberg.

Müller-Jentsch, W. (1995), 'Germany: from collective voice to co-management', in J. Rogers and W. Streeck (eds), *Works Councils: Consultation, Representation and Cooperation in Industrial Relations*, Chicago: University of Chicago Press, pp. 53–78.

Müller-Jentsch, W. (2008), 'Industrial democracy: historical development and current challenges', *Management Revue*, **19** (4), 260–73.

Rogers, J. and W. Streeck (1994), 'Workplace representation overseas: the works council story', in R.B. Freeman (ed.), *Working under Different Rules*, New York: Russell Sage Foundation, pp. 97–156.

Rogers, J. and W. Streeck (1995), 'The study of works councils: concepts and problems', in J. Rogers and W. Streeck (eds), *Works Councils: Consultation, Representation and Cooperation in Industrial Relations*, Chicago: University of Chicago Press, pp. 3–26.

Toth, A. (1997), 'The invention of works councils in Hungary', *European Journal of Industrial Relations*, **3** (2), 161–81.

Van den Berg, A., Y. Grift and A van Witteloostuijn (2011), 'Managerial Perceptions of Works Councils' Effectiveness in the Netherlands', *Industrial Relations: A Journal of Economy and Society*, **50** (3), 497–513.

Visser, J. (2012), 'ICTWSS – data base on institutional characteristics of trade unions, wage setting, state intervention and social pacts, 1960–2010 (ICTWSS): version 3.0 May 2011', Amsterdam Institute for Advanced Labour Studies AIAS, University of Amsterdam.

Weiss, M. and M. Schmidt (2000), *Labour Law and Industrial Relations in Germany*, The Hague: Kluwer Law International.

Zagelmeyer, S. (2011), 'Employment relations in France and Germany', in M. Barry and A. Wilkinson (eds), *Research Handbook of Comparative Employment Relations*, Cheltenham, UK, and Northampton, MA, USA: Edward Elgar, pp. 322–56.

Zwick, T. (2005), 'Continuing vocational training forms and establishment productivity in Germany', *German Economic Review*, **6**, 155–84.

16 Joint consultative committees
Amanda Pyman

INTRODUCTION

Employee voice takes many forms. Joint consultative committees are one mechanism for the provision of indirect employee voice and have been a durable form of participation in many countries for most of the twentieth century (Beaumont and Deaton 1981; Cregan and Brown 2010). Marchington et al. (1992: 11) define 'joint consultation' as a mechanism for managers and employee representatives to meet on a regular basis in order to exchange views, to utilize members' knowledge and expertise, and to deal with matters of common interest which are not subject to collective bargaining. The distinctive features of joint consultation are that a cross-section of employees and managers come together to solve complex problems jointly and on an ongoing basis, and that consultation is indirect and exercised through workforce representatives (Marchington 1992a, 1992b; Kessler and Purcell 1996).

Flowing from the definition of joint consultation, 'joint consultative committees' (JCCs) are a representative structure (management and employee representatives) dealing with collective concerns regarding work organization, and, in some instances, the employment contract (Brewster et al. 2007: 52). JCCs serve to promote cooperation and mutuality and in practice, representative and productivist purposes (Haynes et al. 2005). JCCs are distinct from joint advisory committees or joint decision-making committees, yet nevertheless represent a formal, as opposed to informal, consultative structure (Lansbury and Marchington 1994). They are therefore a forum whereby employees seek to indirectly influence organizational decision-making through labour representatives (Morishima 1992).

This brief introduction sets the scene for this chapter, which provides a nuanced analysis of JCCs as a form of employee voice. The first section of the chapter discusses joint consultation in a historical perspective. This background context is followed by a critical analysis of the seminal theoretical and empirical contributions on JCCs. It is argued that there are three key issues pertaining to JCCs and joint consultation more broadly: structure, processes and practices and outcomes. The penultimate section analyses future issues in joint consultation and proposes a research agenda to address these questions. The final section of the chapter concludes, drawing together the key ideas presented and the core contribution of this chapter, that is, the argument that it is important to understand the conditions under which joint consultation and JCCs are an effective form of voice, including questions of power or control, whether the goal of employee voice is humanistic or organizational effectiveness. Employee voice must be substantive not merely procedural and it must be embedded within the entire network of actors to the employment relationship (longevity) in order to ensure that employees have a genuine influence on organizational decision-making.

HISTORICAL CONTEXT AND BACKGROUND

Beaumont and Deaton (1981) argue that the intellectual origins of JCCs lie in the human relations school of thought which placed a high premium on the importance of communication between management and employees as a way of removing industrial relations difficulties and resolving problems which grew out of workers' distrust and suspicion of management's aims and objectives. According to more contemporary, strategic, high performance, human resource management (HRM) perspectives, joint consultation is a form of employee voice which constitutes part of a sophisticated HRM stratagem designed to generate employee engagement, motivation, commitment and loyalty in a globally competitive marketplace (Gollan et al. 2006; Cregan and Brown 2010). Enhanced two-way communication is a means for improving economic efficiency and competitiveness, thus lowering organizations' transaction costs (Willman et al. 2006). In this light, joint consultation may also be viewed as an element of the mutual gains organization, whereby the benefits of employee voice accrue to all stakeholders, enhancing trust, cooperation and team working, and in turn, resulting in improved organizational decision-making (Kochan and Osterman 1994; Johnstone et al. 2009; Dietz and Fortin 2007). The variety of influences and perspectives on joint consultation reinforce Marchington's (1994: 689) argument regarding the inadequacies of any attempt to analyse joint consultation with reference to one all-embracing theory.

In Britain, the USA and Australia, the extensiveness of joint consultation has waxed and waned since the 1940s (Marchington 1992b; for a comprehensive overview of the history of joint consultation in Britain, see Marchington 1994). JCCs were important in all three countries in facilitating post-war productivity and efficiency during periods of reconstruction (Lansbury and Marchington 1994). JCCs have also been utilized extensively in Japanese workplace relations (Nitta 1984). The historical development of JCCs in Anglophone and European countries has been shaped by institutions, regulatory rules, laws and workplace changes, such as the introduction of enterprise-based productivity bargaining in Australia and the historical voluntarist employment relations context in Britain and Ireland (for example, Lansbury and Marchington 1994; McGraw and Palmer 1995; Morehead et al. 1997; Mitchell et al. 1997; Forsyth et al. 2008; Dobbins 2010). In fact, the degree of legal support for joint consultation is a key factor distinguishing the nature and power of JCCs, as each country's participation arrangements are embedded as a system, in a society, with its social institutions and varying interdependent complementarities (Gollan et al. 2006; Markey 2007). The theme of national variation is therefore an important one. For example, in Britain and Australia, JCCs have little or no legal support, whereas in Germany, works councils are embedded in a wider institutional system through both detailed laws and established practice (Brewster et al. 2007; see also Chapter 15 above for a detailed discussion of works councils). In Europe, employees' generalized statutory rights to information and consultation are widespread, despite disagreement between unions and employers in the European Community on the precise legal forms which joint consultation should take (Lansbury and Marchington 1994).

It is apparent that internationally, laws and norms support workplace consultative bodies to varying degrees. These different industrial relations systems (political and economic climates) affect not only the structure of JCCs, in terms of their defined responsibilities and powers, but also influence their processes, practices and outcomes (Brewster et al. 2007; Markey 2007). It is also important to recognize that formally pre-scribed consultation (*de jure*) and actual consultation (*de facto*) are far from perfectly correlated (Heller et al. 1998). In the absence of legal regulation, the voice adoption choices of employers (Willman et al. 2006) and managerial attitudes to joint consultation become critically important in shaping the structure, processes and outcomes of JCCs at the workplace level (Marchington 1994; Forsyth et al. 2008; Dobbins 2010).

As Fox (1985) also recognized, the historical, structural and institutional context in which management find themselves also influences the extent and degree of cooperation between the parties to the employment relationship. In this context, it is important to note that unilateral management authority to make decisions is a cultural managerialist mindset that is characteristic of liberal market economies (LMEs), whereas institutional complementarities promote a mindset of cooperation and longer-term collaborative relations between employers, employees and their representatives in coordinated market economies (CMEs) (Godard 2004; Dobbins 2010). As Markey (2007) has argued, JCCs in the Anglophone countries, and particularly Australia, are an exemplar of liberal market economies. Such committees are products of unilateral management initiatives, rather than of statute, and therefore vary considerably in terms of composition, jurisdic-tion, powers and organizational levels of operation.

As a consequence of the significant variation in the purpose, powers and impact of JCCs, trade unions in many countries hold ambivalent attitudes to, or are wary of, joint consultation (Lansbury and Marchington 1994; Kelly 1995; Dietz and Fortin 2007; Cregan and Brown 2010). The most common response of unions to JCCs has been described as 'cautious skepticism' (Kochan et al. 1984: 155–7). This response arises from a fear that such employee voice channels do not comprise a wholly separate domain from trade union-based collective voice and that they have the potential to encroach upon, and undermine, trade union activities; thus reducing union influence and power and limiting workers' input (Beaumont and Deaton 1981; Fantasia et al. 1988; Lansbury and Marchington 1994; Cregan and Brown 2010). As a consequence, unions are likely to resist joint consultation, especially when employee representatives are elected from the larger workforce, including non-union members, thus potentially eroding collective bargaining arrangements (Brewster et al. 2007; Cregan and Brown 2010). In non-union workplaces, worker participation programmes can promote and inculcate manage-rial attitudes, while either supplanting or preventing unionism (Fantasia et al. 1988). However, unions may in fact benefit from a decentralized, enterprise-based system of industrial relations which emphasizes employee involvement in decision-making, using such structures to strengthen their role and presence at the workplace level (Lansbury and Marchington 1994).

The growth in the heterogeneity of employee voice practices has also influenced the incidence and nature of JCCs (Holland et al. 2009; Forsyth et al. 2008). Labour market deregulation, the global decline of organized labour, increased technological sophisti-cation, increased educational levels, widespread industry restructuring and the spread of neo-liberal ideologies have created a favourable environment for the weakening of collective voice and the subsequent diffusion of direct and non-union voice, with an emphasis on enhancing productivity and employee commitment rather than on promot-ing industrial democracy (Morishima 1992; Brewster et al. 2007; Bryson 2004; Dundon et al. 2004; Blyton and Turnbull 1998; Wilkinson et al. 2004). As a consequence, in many of the Anglophone countries (LMEs), over many years there has been a shift away from negotiation to consultation (Johnstone et al. 2010).

LITERATURE REVIEW

Potential predictors of joint consultation can be gleaned from theories of workplace participation. Ramsay's (1977, 1983) cycles of control theory argues from a Marxist perspective that management interest in employee participation is dependent on the power of trade unions in the workplace. Where unions are stronger, management will use alternative voice regimes such as joint consultation to marginalize union involvement and influence, subsequently diminishing their power. In contrast, Marchington et al.'s (1992) waves thesis focuses on micro- rather than macro-level factors. Marchington et al. (1992) identify a paradox of participation: an increase in employee participation in a period of declining organized labour – which they attribute to increasing global competitiveness – and, consequently, a variety of demands upon managers to seek continuous improvements in work organization to enhance productivity and efficiency through cooperative practices. Such practices may include financial involvement, information-sharing and workplace flexibility. Marchington et al. (1992), in contrast to Ramsay (1977), recognize that a multiplicity of factors may drive the development and effectiveness of joint consultation and that these factors may not necessarily lie within the realm of managerial control. Poole et al. (1999) advocate a similar argument, identifying four primary factors that explain employee participation: macroeconomic conditions, the strategic choices of actors, the power of actors and organizational structures and processes. It is therefore the mediation and combination of internal and external contextual conditions and each organization's unique circumstances that shape employment relations practices and joint consultation at the workplace level (Dobbins 2010).

The broad range of antecedents of employee voice and participation means that there is enormous potential for diversity in the nature of joint consultative structures, their processes and outcomes across contexts (for example, Kessler and Purcell 1996). Determinants of variation and predictors of the incidence and nature of joint consultation which have been demonstrated empirically include organizational size and operational structure, union presence, that is the relative bargaining power of a union and managerial attitudes to unions, employee skill levels, technology, sector, industry, the prevailing industrial relations climate, and bargaining structures and the balance of power between the parties to the employment relationship (Ackers et al. 2005; Beaumont and Deaton 1981; Haynes et al. 2005; Heller et al. 1998; Marchington 1992a, 1992b; Morishima 1992; Lansbury and Marchington 1994; Forsyth et al. 2008; Brewster et al. 2007; Holland et al. 2009; Dobbins 2010). Problems in gathering statistical evidence on consultation through company level surveys have however been recognized as a long-standing problem in the industrial relations discipline, since factual questions about the existence, remit, coverage and/or effectiveness of a JCC are ambiguous notions, depending on the way the question is framed and to whom it is addressed (MacInnes 1985).

Empirical research also validates theoretical approaches to workplace participation and confirms widespread variation in practice. For example, in Australia, Marchington

(1992b) found that models of consultation were linked with the degree and strength of unionization at the workplace. Industries with traditionally powerful unions such as mining and construction demonstrated a greater incidence of JCCs than those less-unionized industries, such as retail trade and financial and business services. Management objectives for joint consultation, the frequency with which JCCs meet, their composition, the means by which employee representatives are selected and the subject matter within the remit of JCCs have also been the subject of empirical research. Significant variation across each of these issues has been demonstrated (for example, Haynes et al. 2005; Marchington 1992a, 1992b; Lansbury and Marchington 1994; Morehead et al. 1997; Mitchell et al. 1997; Forsyth et al. 2008). Much of this variation is attributable to whether or not joint consultation is sanctioned by law. In the absence of legal regulation, managers have far greater prerogative with respect to the operation and dynamics of JCCs and often adopt, and indeed favour, organizational-specific arrangements (for example, Morishima 1992; Dobbins 2010). Moreover, in Australia, legislated mechanisms for consultation do not exist as they do in Europe (Combet 2003).

McGraw and Palmer (1995: 98) categorize managerial motivations for introducing JCCs into four models, which focus on questions concerning the relationship between joint consultation and collective bargaining and employee involvement and trade unions that are also seminal in the joint consultation and employee voice literatures (for example, Marchington 1994; Ackers et al. 2005). In the first, *non-union model*, JCCs are used by management to demonstrate a concern for employee welfare and to negate the idea that belonging to a union will be in the workers' best interests. In the *competitive model*, management aims to increase employees' levels of awareness, morale and trust, as a means to increase productivity, product quality and the firm's competitive position. An increase in consultation downgrades the importance of collective bargaining, whether implicitly or explicitly. In the *adjunct model*, joint consultation sits alongside collective bargaining. Wages and working conditions are the remit of bargaining, whilst other organizational issues are the domain of JCCs. Consultation may play a preliminary role in the bargaining process in this model, acting as a precursor to the negotiation of wages and conditions, whereby union representatives are often members of both committees. In the final model, the *marginal model*, the agenda of JCCs is limited to trivial issues – commonly framed as 'tea, towels and toilets' (McGraw and Palmer 1995). Such committees often have a short lifespan. McGraw and Palmer (1995) recognize that these four models are not mutually exclusive and that managerial motivations for the establishment of JCCs may encompass multifarious intentions. Managerial motivations will of course also be influenced by economic, institutional and operational conditions (Morishima 1992; Dobbins 2010).

Evidence from Japan reinforces the above models and categorizations of managerial intentions in practice (Nitta 1984; Sugeno and Koshiro 1987; Tokunaga 1983; Morishima 1992). On the one hand, JCCs have been used strategically by Japanese employers as an institutional mechanism to engage in continuous information sharing, as a means to obtain labour's consent and cooperation in potentially conflictual situations (disputes), and/or to moderate and pre-empt labour militancy (adjunct model) (Morishima 1992). On the other hand, JCCs have also been used as a management device for union co-optation (Morishima 1992). Against a backdrop of centralized coordination of wage bargaining in the 1970s and 1980s and high wage increases, Japanese employers in large firms have also used JCCs for firm-level negotiations of wages and benefits, as a means to generate bargaining outcomes that reflect conditions specific to the firm (adjunct model) (Morishima 1992). In sum, Morishima (1992: 419) found that the factors that influence employers' use of JCCs differ, depending on whether JCCs are used to develop integrative labour relations (information sharing) or a means to prepare for wage bargaining and discussions.

In light of the importance of national variation, trade union attitudes to joint consultation and managerial attitudes to and intentions for joint consultation, the chapter now considers three major issues pertaining to JCCs: their structure, processes and practices, and outcomes.

Structure

One key issue with respect to the structure of JCCs is whether they are pure or hybrid forms of employee voice (Marchington 1992a, 1992b; Morehead et al. 1997). A pure structure could be taken to mean a body that is comprised of a single type of workplace representative. A hybrid structure comprises different types of workplace representatives. The obvious example is union versus non-union representatives. Since trade unions preceded JCC structures as the dominant form of employee voice in most Anglophone countries (LMEs), representative positions on JCCs have typically been dominated by union members and delegates (Lansbury and Marchington 1994; Morehead et al. 1997; Brewster et al. 2007). However, growth in different types of participatory structures has induced hybrid forms, that is, JCCs comprised of both union affiliated representatives and non-union representatives (for example, Marchington 1992a, 1992b). Hybrid structures can potentially lead to tensions and difficulties of interest aggregation between the two types of representatives (Brewster et al. 2007). However, non-union representative consultative structures can also provide an alternative to union channels of employee voice, creating competition. Therefore, one of the key theoretical issues identified in the literature is the extent to which hybrid JCCs, that is, committees comprised of union and non-union representatives, act as a substitute for unionization, threatening their independent collective bargaining role and therefore leading to union exclusion and the marginalization of union power (Beaumont and Deaton 1981; Terry 1983; French 2001; Hyman 1999). In part, the extent of union substitution will be determined by management's intentions for and use of joint consultation.

The degree to which JCCs assist or harm trade unions depends in part on whether such bodies are for the purpose of negotiation and/or consultation; that is, whether they operate separately from collective bargaining (Biagi 1992). Consultation means that management solicits the opinion of employee representatives on specific issues without being bound to take their views on board: a unitarist form of joint consultation (Brewster et al. 2007; Cregan and Brown 2010). Participation implies that workers themselves gain a more direct and active role in decision-making (Brewster et al. 2007). If JCCs blur the boundaries between negotiation and consultation, they may indeed undermine union activity (Cully et al. 1999). In many European countries for example, works councils are required to represent the interests of all employees, including non-union members, which can potentially lead to the erosion of collective bargaining arrangements (Müller-Jentsch 1997).

In an empirical examination of works councils and JCCs across sixteen European countries, Brewster et al. (2007) found that both types of consultative bodies were mutually supportive of trade unions rather than mutually antagonistic, irrespective of the national business system in operation. Similarly, Cregan and Brown (2010), in a study of one company-based JCC in an Australian public sector organization, concluded that union members did not perceive joint consultation as a separate domain from union-based collective voice. Similar results can be seen in the 2007 Australian Worker Representation and Participation Survey (AWRPS) (Teicher et al. 2007). Utilizing this data, Holland et al. (2009) found that the incidence of joint consultation was higher in unionized workplaces and that there was a positive relationship between favourable management attitudes to unions and the presence of joint consultation. Other, more general, empirical research on employee voice in Europe, Australia and the UK has also questioned the union substitution thesis, following findings that reveal that direct and indirect forms of voice can coexist and complement one another (for example, Sako 1998; Pyman et al. 2006; Charlwood and Terry 2007).

Alongside the type of representatives on a JCC, a related structural issue is the method of selection of representatives to JCCs and whether these mandate union and/or non-union representation *de jure*. In Australia for example, in the absence of legal regulation, the most common methods of selection of employees (representatives) to JCCs are via elections or the use of unelected volunteers (Holland et al. 2009). The issue of *effective representation* is a generic problem that plagues all forms of employee participation, and it is important that JCCs are constituted in such a way that staff are aware of how to gain access to representation on committees (McGraw and Palmer 1995). Empirically, in Britain, union representation on JCCs has been found to improve the likelihood of their success (Beaumont and Deaton 1981). Similarly, in the USA, using data from a national sample of the American labour force from the Quality of Employment Survey, Fenwick and Olson (1986) found that support for worker participation was strongest among union members.

Additional evidence from the USA and Britain has also suggested that union-supported consultation is most effective in achieving performance effects and securing jobs (Cooke 1990a, 1990b; Marchington 1994). More recently, Cregan and Brown (2010: 344), in a study of 1456 employees in a large Australian public sector organization, found that the more union members expected the JCC to result in instrumental outcomes, and the more they believed that management should seek the views of workers about HRM issues outside collective bargaining, the more willing they were to participate. Members were less willing to participate in a company-based JCC the more they believed that workers should be involved in discussions about issues normally dealt with in union-based negotiations. Non-union members were more willing to participate the more they expected the JCC to result in democratic representation; suggesting that non-union members viewed the JCC as an alternative form of representation that was free from sectional interests, costs, conflict and victimization.

Processes and Practices

Whilst the meaning and structure of consultative mechanisms have been explored in depth (for example, Dundon et al. 2004; Gollan 2001; Marchington 1987; Marchington et al. 2001; Trevor 1988; Wilkinson and Ackers 1995), comparatively little attention has been paid to the processes and practices (conditions) that make JCCs more or less successful (Kessler and Purcell 1996; Dietz and Fortin 2007). Dietz and Fortin (2007) suggest that there are five phases of the JCC process: pre-voice history, design of the JCC, preparations, first meeting, and subsequent meetings. These phases mirror many of the determinants and associated processual dynamics of JCCs that have been empirically substantiated in the literature, such as managerial attitudes to unions, management culture, managerial involvement and responsiveness, the provision of adequate resources, the provision of training for representatives, facilitation of communication, the presence of a union and the gaining of union support for JCCs (for example, Beaumont and Deaton 1981; Marchington 1994; McGraw and Palmer 1995; Gollan et al. 2006; Holland et al. 2009).

Empirical research has also demonstrated the importance of trust and justice (distributive and procedural justice) in the processes of initiating, designing, establishing and maintaining JCCs; reflecting the 'social exchange' that characterizes and underpins the employment relationship (Kessler and Purcell 1996; Driscoll 1978; Dietz and Fortin 2007; Dobbins 2010). As Fox (1974) noted in his seminal book, *Beyond Contract*, trust between management and the workforce lies at the heart of cooperative industrial relations behaviour. In fact, numerous studies of highly developed participation practices suggest that a consensual relationship based on a high level of trust between management and employees is a critical underpinning (Gollan et al. 2006). Similarly, where employers breach workplace bargains, employees' trust in management will be restricted (Streeck 1997). Trust acts as a springboard for the achievement of mutual gains from employee voice (Dobbins 2010).

Given the importance of trust in the employment relationship, the tone of the industrial relations climate and the organization's cultural and historical attitude toward employee consultation and representation are also pivotal in shaping the process of joint consultation and the dynamics of the exchange relationship between management, unions and employees (Lansbury and Marchington 1994; Morishima 1992; Marchington et al. 2001; Pyman et al. 2010; Dietz and Fortin 2007). By way of example, evidence from Australia and America has demonstrated a strong correlation between best practice in workplace productivity and performance and the degree (intensity) of consultation and collaboration between management and employees (for example, Lansbury and Marchington 1994; Cooke 1989, 1990a, 1990b; Cutcher-Gershenfeld 1991; Kochan et al. 1986). Biagi (1992) argued that in Japan the extensive arrangements that exist for consultation between managers and employees (often through their union) were one of the keys to Japanese success in technological innovation and rationalization, the transformation of management methods and the development of cooperation and understanding between management and unions.

Such *a priori* evidence must be carefully considered when weighed against more recent general evidence from the 2004 British Workplace Employment Relations Survey (WERS). Findings from the 2004 WERS reveal that unionized workplaces are characterized by lower trust relations, whilst non-union workplaces are characterized by higher trust and an increased quality of employee relationships (Kersley et al. 2005). This disparity may be explained by the fact that the existence of a mechanism for employee voice, such as joint consultation, in the form of a JCC, is not a sufficient condition for effective representation of employee interests. Indeed, in the case of a unionized work-place, much of the strength of voice is dependent upon the legitimacy and effectiveness of trade unions in representing employees' interests and working with JCCs (Gollan et al. 2006). In non-unionized workplaces, the strength and responsiveness of management to employee interests through JCCs is a critical determinant of effectiveness.

Outcomes

A myriad of potential and actual outcomes of JCCs have been examined in the litera-ture (for example, Driscoll 1978; Palmer and McGraw 1995; Kessler and Purcell 1996; Holland et al. 2009). Potentially positive outcomes that can result from JCCs include enhancing worker voice and input to maximize the use of human capital and increase democratic representation, increased trust and cooperation, improved information and communication flows within organizations, and diffusion of best practices and encour-agement of industrial upgrading (Brewster et al. 2007; Beaumont and Deaton 1981). Potential benefits can also be viewed through the prism of mutual gains, whereby the outcomes of joint consultation benefit the individual, the committee and the organiza-tion, acting as an effective way to organize and regulate work and the labour market (Johnstone et al. 2004). Employee involvement in problem-solving and decision-making is indeed a central feature of the mutual gains enterprise (Kochan and Osterman 1994) and is assumed to create high commitment, high involvement workplaces, leading to an increase in motivation and loyalty, and in turn, improved organizational performance (Walton 1985; Lawler 1986; Hammer 2000; Cregan and Brown 2010). The incidence of joint consultation in Australia for example has been positively correlated with higher levels of productivity (Lansbury and Marchington 1994).

Irrespective of the potential benefits of joint consultation, an evaluation of actual outcomes is dependent on the purpose of JCCs and whose perspective is examined. Actual outcomes are therefore subject to differing interpretations along the dimen-sions of control and cooperation, depending upon whose interests are being served in a JCC (Morishima 1992). As Dietz and Fortin (2007) further elucidate, there is a risk in assuming joint responsibility for decision-making outcomes forged in a JCC. Both managers and employee representatives face a fundamental social dilemma, wherein gains are expected to come from collaborating, but collaboration also entails risks of vulnerability (Dietz and Fortin 2007). Dobbins (2010) similarly argues that workplace cooperation is predicated on a reciprocal bargain that employees and their representa-tives share responsibility for company competitiveness in exchange for employers pro-moting employee voice, fairness and employment security. On this basis, Heller et al. (1998) suggest that the requirements for participative success are manifold: support from organizational stakeholders, association with appropriate human resources policies, a favourable organizational context, a favourable environmental infrastructure and an ability to survive.

One key theme that dominates the literature on JCC outcomes is the degree to which such structures are embedded in the workplace: that is, the extent to which a JCC fades out or becomes institutionalized – their longevity (Beaumont and Deaton 1981; Dietz and Fortin 2007). Key determinants of the embeddedness of JCCs are the remit and action of these bodies in practice. In cases where JCCs are designed to support a managerial rhetoric of empowerment and are not institutionalized, they may actually do little more than burden employees with increased responsibilities (work intensification), against a backdrop of increasing managerial power (Brewster et al. 2007; Godard 2004), acting as a fig leaf for managerial unilateralism (Charlwood and Terry 2007). Depending on the balance of power between management and labour in the employment relationship, participation programmes may be structured by management to weaken the power of workers. In America, Fantasia et al. (1988) argued that worker participation programmes, as constituted over the last two decades, were not an expression of workplace democracy, but rather one component of a larger managerial offensive to increase capital's power in the workplace and weaken or replace foundations for worker power in the form of unions. In Australia, Forsyth et al. (2008), basing their research on an empirical analysis of federal and state certified agreements, drew comparable conclusions. They argued that despite the growth in the provision for JCCs in enterprise agreements over the period 1991–2004, and despite the fact that productivity, flexibility and other issues of strategic importance to businesses were prominent among the matters JCCs were authorized to discuss, employees were generally not empowered with decision-making rights over the *a priori* issues (Forsyth et al. 2008). They therefore concluded that JCCs were not acting as a significant mechanism for the extension of employee power (Forsyth et al. 2008).

Empirical evidence has shown that the more embedded employee voice structures are, the better the outcomes achieved (Cox et al. 2006). Similarly, in a study of joint labour management committees in Japan, Kato (2006) found that the extent of participation in such committees deepens with age. That is, labour and management share more information, management consults labour more frequently and information is shared more widely with all employees over time. This systematic evidence of organizational learning and the development of participatory practices over time is of critical account when considering performance effects and outcomes (Gollan et al. 2006).

Factors that influence the extent to which JCCs are embedded in the workplace include the agency of the actors (managers and employees) and how they utilize this agency in the employment relationship exchange, and the institutional environment, that is, the legislative, political and social context shaping workplaces and industrial relations systems more generally (Blau 1964; Hyman 2005). As Hyman (2005) eloquently argued, employee voice is only one feature of the broader regulation of the employment relationship: the relative efficacy and sustainability of voice is intertwined with other social and economic features. The factors influencing the embeddedness of JCCs are consistent with the various frameworks in the literature discussed at the beginning of this chapter, which identify the importance of both endogenous and exogenous factors influencing employee voice and participation more broadly (for example, Marchington 1992b; Poole et al. 1999; Cox et al. 2006).

A second key theme pertaining to the outcomes of JCCs is their effectiveness. Whilst there is no simple, objective measure of effectiveness (Hyman 1997; Heller et al. 1998) and it is difficult to measure the tangible effects of JCCs on the workplace, it is important to examine the objectives the parties had when establishing JCCs (Lansbury and Marchington 1994). As a consequence, organizational and structural procedures, processes and interpersonal conduct, from the perspective of employers, employees and trade unions are significant determinants of effectiveness (Beaumont and Deaton

1981; Granovetter 1985; Lansbury and Marchington 1994; Marchington 1994; Kessler and Purcell 1996; Hyman 1997; Strauss 2006; Dietz and Fortin 2007). In Australia for example, Holland et al. (2009) found that employees reported high levels of effectiveness of JCCs. Although this finding is limited by the survey measure of effectiveness (not operationalized), it does reinforce Marchington's (1992b) earlier findings derived from the 1990 Australian Workplace Industrial Relations Survey, which also showed that the parties were highly satisfied with the operation of JCCs.

A key issue with respect to assessments of effectiveness is whether joint consultation results in a change in the nature of decision-making within organizations. Indeed, it is reasonable to question whether much of what appears to be consultation is part of a process whereby organizations develop and entrench a culture of cooperation and commitment through 'pseudo-participation' (Teicher 1992), that is, a feeling of influence (passive involvement) rather than actual influence (Strauss 2006). In this vein, outcomes may equate to processual benefits, such as improved communication and input into decision-making, vis-à-vis the achievement of substantive outcomes such as improved productivity, quality, turnover, efficiency, satisfaction or health and safety (Lansbury and Marchington 1994; Strauss 2006). A related issue that it is important to consider when evaluating the outcomes of JCCs and joint consultation more broadly is the potential for employer behaviour to be counterproductive. That is, employer defections from cooperative bargains with employees can actually lead to employees questioning management, diluting any positive effects of cooperation (Streeck 1997).

Empirical analyses of the efficacy of employee voice have produced inconsistent results. However, the findings from these studies can largely be summarized according to three perspectives which are not mutually exclusive and are pertinent to JCCs and an evaluation of their effectiveness (outcomes). The first perspective identifies union presence as a prerequisite of effective voice (Charlwood and Terry 2007), leading to increased employee satisfaction on distributive justice and employee advocacy issues (Holland et al. 2009; Kim and Kim 2004). The assumption that union voice is a requirement for effective workplace-based forms of participation and consultation is consistent with the relationship between unionization and HRM under high performance work systems or mutual gains approaches. Such approaches have been empirically supported in the literature (White 2005). The second perspective argues that non-union voice can fill the void or 'representation gap' that has arisen as a result of the ongoing decline of organized labour, and that non-union voice is not only effective in eliciting managerial responsiveness to employee needs, but more effective than union voice (Holland et al. 2009; Bryson 2004). The third perspective argues that hybrid voice arrangements, whereby union, non-union and direct channels coexist, are the most effective for employers and employees (Sako 1998), for instance in reducing wage dispersion and increasing procedural fairness and productivity (Charlwood and Terry 2007), and in increasing managerial responsiveness to employee needs, job control and influence over job rewards (Pyman et al. 2006). Empirical validation of the use of a plurality of employee voice arrangements contradicts the union substitution thesis (Fiorito 2001), which argues that non-union and direct employee voice practices act as a substitute for unionization and collective bargaining. Evidence of hybrid voice arrangements also supports the strategic HRM literature, and in particular the notion that, in order to have a lasting impact, participative schemes should be 'bundled' with other high performance oriented HRM practices such as training and job security (Heller et al. 1998; Strauss 2006).

FUTURE ISSUES AND RESEARCH AGENDA

Despite the enduring nature of joint consultation in both Anglophone and European countries, there is a dearth of research that examines the use and outcomes of joint consultation in a unionized environment. Extant research has tended simply to focus on the incidence of joint consultation in a unionized environment. Whilst a shift from indirect to direct participation in many of the Anglophone countries has been accompanied by a continuing decline in trade union representation, there is merit in investigating how hybrid forms of joint consultation can deliver outcomes for employees, management and trade unions. Future empirical research should investigate the extent to which joint consultation can be used in tandem with a union presence at the workplace and organizational level, as part of a meaningful, collaborative, strategic approach to HRM and high performing work systems, in order to deliver job security, organizational survival and effective outcomes on issues of important mutual interest for all stakeholders (Gooderham et al. 1999; Gollan et al. 2006). As Strauss (2006) argues, the main question is not whether employee voice can work, but how to make it work. In LMEs where management values are focused on the short term, including cost minimization and the primacy of shareholder value, long-term investments in employee voice are inimical to joint consultation (Ackers et al. 2005; Strauss 2006). Moreover, employee voice requires management to share power and this opposes dominant unitarist ideologies (Strauss 2006), a notion reminiscent of McCarthy's (1966) thesis and insights into the contradictory nature of consultation and its relationship to managerial prerogative. However, whilst it cannot be assumed that for all managers, joint consultation is driven by a power calculus (Haynes et al. 2005), this view does raise wider questions of power and control which are essential considerations in any debate on joint consultation and JCCs.

A second important issue for future research and one that is the subject of ongoing debate in practice is the degree to which rights to joint consultation should be, or need to be, enshrined in legislation (for example, Markey 2004; Dobbins 2010). Because JCCs are established with diverse settings along the dimensions of control and cooperation, in part as a result of differing institutional environments and legislative supports, there is considerable divergence in their structure, scope, processes, practices and outcomes in workplaces. Evidence shows, more often than not, in the Anglophone countries (LMEs), that in the absence of a legislative framework for the operation of joint consultation, JCCs have little meaningful impact on mainstream industrial relations and employee voice (Lansbury and Marchington 1994; Freeman and Lazear 1995). Left to their own devices and prerogative, many employers will simply introduce weak forms of voice that employees are sceptical of. By way of example, using two case studies of workplace cooperation in Ireland, Dobbins (2010: 497) found that such cooperation was rare. He largely attributed this finding to Ireland's permissive voluntarist institutional and employment relations context, characterized by limited institutional coordination linking national and workplace governance. In sum, the contextual conditions (derived from the institutional environment) promoting workplace cooperation were weaker than the conditions hindering it.

An important question then, in many of the Anglophone countries (LMEs), is whether there is a case for the introduction of beneficial constraints on employer choice to balance gains in employee voice. Beneficial constraints are state-sponsored institutional and regulatory measures promoting workplace consensus (Streeck 1997). In countries like Australia, Britain, the USA and Ireland for example, where voluntarism, a system of industrial relations based on voluntary settlements between employers, employees and their representatives (rather than legal regulation) has been dominant, is there a case for the introduction of beneficial constraints (through policy intervention) as a means to institutionalize and generalize workplace pluralism and create robust mutual gains arrangements which provide employee representatives with a meaningful voice in company governance (Dobbins 2010)? Given evidence that the adoption of high performance work systems in LMEs has been limited and piecemeal, and that the performance outcomes of such systems are debatable, it could be argued that high performance work systems on their own are not sufficient; state supported rights to employee representation/participation are also required (Dobbins 2010).

Is there merit then in the Anglophone countries (LMEs) following the approaches of northern European countries (CMEs) such as Germany, Sweden, Denmark and Finland, where institutional frameworks with beneficial constraints support quality competition and workplace consensus? Indeed, in these CMEs, joint governance is the process whereby management and labour share joint decision-making authority on matters of mutual concern. Does such an approach afford organizations in LMEs the opportunity to achieve higher value added performance? What additional skills and training do management, unions and employees need in order to adopt such a collaborative approach? Such questions need to be investigated further, empirically, and international comparisons drawn. As Dobbins (2010: 498) notes, we do not know enough about either the contextual conditions that promote or hinder cooperation and consultation or the links between national industrial relations institutions and workplace level structures, processes, practices and outcomes. What is clear is that the institutional conditions in LMEs such as the UK, Australia and the USA have historically encouraged adversarial relations, cost competition and managerial prerogative, rather than quality competition and workplace collaboration (Dobbins 2010). In the absence of beneficial constraints which provide for meaningful employee voice, joint consultation and JCCs in these LMEs are unlikely to 'deliver' the mutual gains that are possible in practice (Dobbins 2010).

CONCLUSION

As one form of employee voice, JCCs can lead to many benefits, reducing power imbalances in organizations, satisfying human skills and contributing to organizational effectiveness (Strauss 2006). In both Anglophone and European countries, JCCs have been an enduring form of employee voice, established as part of a trend towards greater participation in enterprise level decision-making as a means to enhance productivity (Lansbury and Marchington 1994). Empirical data, however, signify a decline in the presence and utilization of JCCs since the 1980s, particularly in the Anglophone countries, in favour of more direct employee voice mechanisms (Gollan et al. 2006; Brewster et al. 2007; Charlwood and Terry 2007; Teicher et al. 2007; Holland et al. 2009, 2011). Interestingly, European countries have also experienced a growth in the incidence of direct participation, but this has not necessarily been at the expense of other forms (Gollan et al. 2006).

Despite the replacement of indirect forms of participation, including JCCs, with direct forms in many of the Anglophone countries, management-initiated JCCs have traditionally been one of the primary means for ongoing consultation with employees over matters important to their working lives, particularly in large organizations. Indeed, JCCs remain part of the employee voice mix. Nevertheless, the nature, power, status and influence of JCCs are complex and varied. In the absence of institutional supports and regulation (beneficial constraints), and therefore under the dominance of managerial prerogative and unilateralism, JCCs have generally not acted or proved a significant determinant for the extension of employee power in LMEs where consultation rights are not enshrined in law (Lansbury and Marchington 1994; Forsyth et al. 2008).

A key issue in theory and in practice, then, is whether JCCs are, on the one hand, 'talking shops on trivial issues such as tea, towels and toilets' (Palmer and McGraw 1995: 97), or, on the other hand, a forum for the articulation of employee voice which enables a significant extension of employee power through participation in workplace and organizational decision-making. These issues have often been framed in historical terms as a contentious relationship between consultation and managerial decision-making. In a globalized world and in twenty-first-century organizations, JCCs and joint consultation, if they are successfully to enhance efficiency and equity and deliver genuine employee voice (Budd 2004), must be seen as a *means of employee voice and participation in decision-making rather than an end in themselves* (Fantasia et al. 1988). An employee's ability to participate in decision-making at work, regardless of the form of employee voice, is arguably as critical to their citizenship in a democracy as is the right to vote (Combet 2003). Successful and effective joint consultation and JCCs will not transpire if viewed as merely rhetoric or a gimmick – success requires changes in organizational relationships and values among employers, employees and trade unions, and a 'fit' with both the national and the organizational context (Heller et al. 1998).

REFERENCES

Ackers, P., M. Marchington, A. Wilkinson and T. Dundon (2005), 'Partnership and voice, with or without trade unions – changing UK management approaches to organisational participation', in M. Stuart and M. Martinez–Lucio (eds), *Partnership and Modernisation in Employment Relations*, London: Routledge, pp. 23–45.

Beaumont, P.B. and D.R. Deaton (1981), 'The extent and determinants of joint consultative arrangements in Britain', *Journal of Management Studies*, **18** (1), 49–71.

Biagi, M. (1992), 'Employee representation in small and medium sized enterprises: a comparative overview', *Comparative Labour Law Journal*, **13** (3), 257–72.

Blau, P.M. (1964), *Exchange and Power in Social Life*, New York: Wiley.

Blyton, P. and P. Turnbull (1998), *The Dynamics of Employee Relations*, 2nd edn, Basingstoke: Palgrave Macmillan.

Brewster, C., G. Wood, R. Croucher and M. Brookes (2007), 'Are works councils and joint consultative committees a threat to trade unions? A comparative analysis', *Economic and Industrial Democracy*, **28** (1), 49–77.

Bryson, A. (2004), 'Managerial responsiveness to union and non–union worker voice in Britain', *Industrial Relations*, **43** (1), 213–41.

Budd, J. (2004), *Employment with a Human Face: Balancing Efficiency, Equity and Voice*, Ithaca, NY: Cornell University Press.
Charlwood, A. and M. Terry (2007), '21st century models of employee representation: structures, processes and outcomes', *Industrial Relations Journal*, **38** (4), 320–37.
Combet, G. (2003), 'Employee consultation in an Australian context: the works council debate and trade unions', in P. Gollan and G. Patmore (eds), *Partnership at Work: The Challenge of Employee Democracy*, Pluto Press: Sydney, pp. 134–9.
Cooke, W.N. (1989), 'Improving productivity and quality through collaboration', *Industrial Relations*, **28** (2), 219–31.
Cooke, W. (1990a), *Labor-Management Cooperation: New Partnerships or Going in Circles*, Michigan: Upjohn Institute for Employment Research.
Cooke, W.N. (1990b), 'Factors influencing the effect of joint union–management programs on employee–supervisor relations', *Industrial and Labor Relations Review*, **43** (5), 587–603.
Cox, A., S. Zagelmeyer and M. Marchington (2006), 'Embedding employee involvement and participation at work', *Human Resource Management Journal*, **16** (3), 250–67.
Cregan, C. and M. Brown (2010), 'The influence of union membership status on workers' willingness to participate in joint consultation', *Human Relations*, **63** (3), 331–48.
Cully, M., S. Woodland, A. O'Reilly and G. Dix (1999), *Britain at Work*, London: Routledge.
Cutcher-Gershenfeld, J. (1991), 'The impact on economic performance of a transformation in industrial relations', *Industrial and Labor Relations Review*, **44** (1), 241–60.
Dietz, G. and M. Fortin (2007), 'Trust and justice in the formation of joint consultative committees', *International Journal of Human Resource Management*, **18** (7), 1159–81.
Dobbins, T. (2010), 'The case for "beneficial constraints": why permissive voluntarism impedes workplace cooperation in Ireland', *Economic and Industrial Democracy*, **31** (4), 497–519.
Driscoll, J.W. (1978), 'Trust and participation in organizational decision-making as predictors of satisfaction', *Academy of Management Journal*, **21** (1), 44–56.
Dundon, T., A. Wilkinson, M. Marchington and P. Ackers (2004), 'The meanings and purpose of employee voice', *International Journal of Human Resource Management*, **15**, 1149–70.
Fantasia, R., D. Clawson and G. Graham (1988), 'A critical view of worker participation in American industry', *Work and Occupations*, **15** (4), 468–88.
Fenwick, R. and J. Olson (1986), 'Support for worker participation: attitudes among union and non-union workers', *American Sociological Review*, **51** (August), 505–22.
Fiorito, J. (2001), 'Human resource management practices and worker desires for union representation', *Journal of Labor Research*, **22** (2), 335–54.
Forsyth, A., S. Korman and S. Marshall (2008), 'Joint consultative committees in Australia: an empirical update', *International Journal of Employment Studies*, **16** (1), 99–130.
Fox, A. (1974), *Beyond Contract: Work, Power and Industrial Relations*, London: Faber and Faber.
Fox, A. (1985), *Man Mismanagement*, London: Hutchison.
Freeman, R.B. and E. Lazear (1995), 'An economic analysis of works councils', in J. Rogers and W. Streeck (eds), *Works Councils: Consultation, Representation and Cooperation in Industrial Relations*, Chicago, IL: University of Chicago Press, pp. 27–52.
French, S. (2001), Works councils in united Germany: still loyal to the trade unions', *International Journal of Manpower*, **22** (6), 560–78.
Godard, J. (2004), 'A critical assessment of the high-performance paradigm', *British Journal of Industrial Relations*, **42** (2), 349–78.
Gollan, P. (2001), 'Tunnel vision: non-union employee representation at Eurotunnel', *Employee Relations*, **23**, 376–400.
Gollan, P., E. Poutsma and U. Veersma (2006), 'Editor's introduction: new roads in organizational participation?', *Industrial Relations*, **45** (4), 499–512.
Gooderham, P.N., O. Nordhaug and K. Ringdal (1999), 'Institutional and rational determinants of organizational practices: human resource management in European firms', *Administrative Science Quarterly*, **44**, 507–31.
Granovetter, M. (1985), 'Economic action and social structure: a theory of embeddedness', *American Journal of Sociology*, **91**, 481–510.
Hammer, T.H. (2000), 'Non-union representational forms: an organisational behaviour perspective', in B. Kaufman, D. Taras and X. Mitchell (eds), *Non-Union Employee Representation: History, Contemporary Practice and Policy*, Armonk, NY: M.E. Sharpe, pp. 176–95.
Haynes, P., P. Boxall and K. Macky (2005), 'Non–union voice and the effectiveness of joint consultation in New Zealand', *Economic and Industrial Democracy*, **26** (2), 229–56.
Heller, F., E. Pusić, G.Strauss and B. Wilpert (1998), *Organizational Participation: Myth and Reality*, Oxford: Oxford University Press.

Holland, P., A. Pyman, B.K. Cooper and J. Teicher (2009), 'The development of alternative voice mechanisms in Australia: the case of joint consultation', *Economic and Industrial Democracy*, **30** (1), 67–92.
Holland, P., A. Pyman, B.K. Cooper and J. Teicher (2011), 'Employee voice and job satisfaction in Australia: the centrality of direct voice', *Human Resource Management*, **50** (1), 95–111.
Hyman, R. (1997), 'The future of employee representation', *British Journal of Industrial Relations*, **35** (3), 309–36.
Hyman, R. (1999), 'Imagined solidarities: can trade unions resist globalization?', in P. Leisink (ed.), *Globalization and Labour Relations*, Cheltenham, UK and Northampton, MA, USA, Edward Elgar, pp. 94–115.
Hyman, R. (2005), 'Whose (social) partnership', in M. Stuart and M. Martinez Lucio (eds), *Partnership and Modernization in Employment Relations*, London: Routledge, pp. 251–65.
Johnstone, S., A. Wilkinson and P. Ackers (2004), 'Partnership paradoxes: a case study of an energy company', *Employee Relations*, **26** (4), 353–76.
Johnstone, S., P. Ackers and A. Wilkinson (2009), 'The British partnership phenomenon: a ten year review', *Human Resource Management Journal*, **19** (3), 260–79.
Johnstone, S., A. Wilkinson and P. Ackers (2010), 'Critical incidents of partnership: five years' experience at NatBank', *Industrial Relations Journal*, **41** (4), 382–98.
Kato, T. (2006), 'Determinants of the extent of participatory employment practices: evidence from Japan', *Industrial Relations*, **45** (4), 579–605.
Kelly, R. (1995), 'Total quality management: industrial democracy of another form of managerial control?', *Labour and Industry*, **6**, 119.
Kersley, B., C. Alpin, J. Forth, A. Bryson, H. Bewley, G. Dix and S. Oxenbridge (2006), *Inside the Workplace: Findings from the Workplace Employment Relations Survey* (WERS), London: Routledge.
Kessler, I. and J. Purcell (1996), 'The value of joint working parties', *Work, Employment and Society*, **10** (4), 663–82.
Kim, D. and H. Kim (2004), 'A comparison of the effectiveness of unions and non-union works councils in Korea: can non-union employee representation substitute for trade unionism?', *International Journal of Human Resource Management*, **15** (6), 1069–93.
Kochan, T.A. and P. Osterman (1994), *The Mutual Gains Enterprise: Forging a Winning Partnership Among Labour, Management and Government*, Boston, MA: Harvard University Press.
Kochan, T.A., H.C. Katz and N.R. Mower (1984), *Worker Participation and American Unions: Threat or Opportunity?*, Kalamazoo, MI: Upjohn.
Kochan, T.A., H.C. Katz and R.B. McKersie (1986), *The Transformation of American Industrial Relations*, New York: Basic Books.
Lansbury, R. and M. Marchington (1994), 'Joint consultation and industrial relations: experience from Australia and overseas', *Asia Pacific Journal of Human Resources*, **31**, 62–82.
Lawler, E.E. (1986), *High Involvement Management*, San Francisco: Jossey-Bass.
MacInnes, J. (1985), 'Conjuring up consultation: the role and extent of joint consultation in post-war private manufacturing industry', *British Journal of Industrial Relations*, **23** (1), 93–113.
Marchington, M. (1987), 'A review and critique of research on developments in joint consultation', *British Journal of Industrial Relations*, **25**, 340–52.
Marchington, M. (1992a), 'The practice of joint consultation in Australia: a preliminary analysis of the AWIRS data', ACIRRT Working Paper, No. 21, ACIRRT. Sydney.
Marchington, M. (1992b), 'Surveying the practice of joint consultation in Australia', *Journal of Industrial Relations*, **34** (4), 530–49.
Marchington, M. (1994), 'The dynamics of joint consultation', in K. Sisson (ed.), *Personnel Management*, 2nd edn, Oxford: Blackwell, pp. 662–93.
Marchington, M., J. Goodman, A. Wilkinson and P. Ackers (1992), 'New developments in employee involvement', Department of Employment Research Series, No. 2, HMSO, London.
Marchington, M., A. Wilkinson, P. Ackers and T. Dundon (2001), 'Management choice and employee voice', Research Report, CIPD, London.
Markey, R. (2004), 'The state of representative participation in Australia: where to next?', *International Journal of Comparative Labour Law and Industrial Relations*, **20** (4), 533–61.
Markey, R. (2007), 'Non-union employee representation in Australia: a case study of the Suncorp Metway Council Inc', *Journal of Industrial Relations*, **49** (2), 187–209.
McCarthy, W.E.J. (1966), 'The role of shop stewards in British industrial relations', Royal Commission on Trade Unions and Employers' Associations, Research Paper No. 1, HMSO, London
McGraw, P. and I. Palmer (1995), 'Beyond tea, towels and toilets? Lessons from a top 500 company in using joint consultative committees for enterprise bargaining', *Asia Pacific Journal of Human Resources*, **32** (3), 97–104.
Mitchell, R., R. Naughton and R. Sorensen (1997), 'The law and employee participation – evidence from the federal enterprise agreements process', *Journal of Industrial Relations*, **39** (2), 196–217.

Morehead, A., M. Steele, M. Alexander, K. Stephen and L. Duffin (1997), *Change at Work: The 1995 Australian Workplace Industrial Relations Survey*, South Melbourne: Longman.

Morishima, M. (1992), 'Use of joint consultation committees by large Japanese firms', *British Journal of Industrial Relations*, **30** (3), 405–24.

Müller-Jentsch, W. (1997), *Soziologie der Industrielle Beziehungen: eine Einführung*. Frankfurt am Main and New York: Campus.

Nitta, M. (1984), 'Conflict resolution in the steel industry: collective bargaining and workers' consultation in a steel plant', in T. Hanami and R. Blanpain (eds), *Industrial Conflict Resolution in Market Economies: A Study of Australia, the Federal Republic of Germany, Italy, Japan and the USA*, Antwerp: Kluwer, pp. 233–47.

Palmer, I. and P. McGraw (1995), 'A new era for joint consultation? Human resources managers' perceptions of JCCs and enterprise bargaining', *International Journal of Employment Studies*, **3** (1), 17–33.

Poole, M., R. Lansbury and N. Wailes (1999), 'Participation and industrial democracy revisited: a theoretical perspective', in R. Markey, P. Gollan, A. Hodgkinson, A. Chouraqui and U. Veersma (eds), *Models of Employee Participation in a Changing Global Environment: Diversity and Interaction*, Aldershot: Ashgate, pp. 23–34.

Pyman, A., B. Cooper, J. Teicher and P. Holland (2006), 'A comparison of the effectiveness of employee voice arrangements in Australia', *Industrial Relations Journal*, **37**, 543–59.

Pyman, A., P. Holland, J. Teicher and B.K. Cooper (2010), 'Industrial relations climate, employee voice and managerial attitudes to unions: an Australian study', *British Journal of Industrial Relations*, **48** (2), 460–80.

Ramsay, H. (1977), 'Cycles of control', *Sociology*, **11** (3), 481–506.

Ramsay, H. (1983), 'Evolution or cycle? Worker participation in the 1970s and 1980s', in C. Crouch and F. Heller (eds), *Organizational Democracy and Political Processes*, London: Wiley, pp. 203–26.

Sako, M. (1998), 'The nature and impact of employee "voice" in the European car components industry', *Human Resource Management Journal*, **9** (1), 5–13.

Strauss, G. (2006), 'Worker participation – some under-considered issues', *Industrial Relations*, **45** (4) (October), 778–803.

Streeck, R. (1997), 'Beneficial constraints: on the economic limits of rational voluntarism', in J. Hollingsworth, J. Rogers and R. Boyer (eds), *Contemporary Capitalism: The Embeddedness of Institutions*, Cambridge: Cambridge University Press, pp. 197–219.

Sugeno, K. and K. Koshiro (1987), 'The role of neutrals in the resolution of shopfloor disputes: a twelve nation study – Japan', *Comparative Labor Law Journal*, **9**, 129–63.

Teicher, J. (1992), 'Theories of employee participation and industrial democracy: towards an analytical framework', in B. Dabscheck, G. Griffin and J. Teicher (eds), *Contemporary Australian Industrial Relations*, Melbourne: Longman Cheshire, pp. 476–94.

Teicher, J., P. Holland, A. Pyman and B. Cooper (2007), 'Employee voice in Australia', in R.B. Freeman, P. Boxall and P. Haynes (eds), *What Workers Say: Employee Voice in the Anglo-American World*, Ithaca, NY: ILR Press, pp. 125–44.

Terry, M. (1983), 'Shop stewards through expansion and recession, *Industrial Relations Journal*, **44** (3), 49–58.

Tokunaga, S. (1983), 'A Marxist interpretation of Japanese industrial relations, with special reference to large private enterprises', in T. Shirai (ed.), *Contemporary Industrial Relations in Japan*, Madison, WI: University of Wisconsin Press, pp. 313–29.

Trevor, M. (1988), *Toshiba's New British Company: Competitiveness through Innovation in Industry*, London: Policy Studies Institute.

Walton, R. (1985), 'From control to commitment in the workplace', *Harvard Business Review*, **63** (2), 77–85.

White, M. (2005), 'Cooperative unionism and employee welfare', *Industrial Relations Journal*, **36** (5), 348–66.

Wilkinson, A. and P. Ackers (1995), 'When two cultures meet: new industrial relations at Japanco', *International Journal of Human Resource Management*, **6**, 849–71.

Wilkinson, A., T. Dundon, M. Marchington and P. Ackers (2004), 'Changing patterns of employee voice: case studies from the UK and Republic of Ireland', *Journal of Industrial Relations*, **46** (3), 298–322.

Willman, P., A. Bryson and R. Gomez (2006), 'The sound of silence: which employers choose no voice and why?', *Socio-Economic Review*, **4**, 283–99.

17 Individual voice: grievance and other procedures
David Lewin

INTRODUCTION

The concept of an employee exercising voice in an employment relationship is of relatively recent origin. For much of recorded history, those who performed work did so in a serf, slavery or indentured servitude context during which survival was the ultimate objective. Later, as medievalism became supplanted by mercantilism, industrialization and eventually market capitalism, the concept of employment emerged and became widespread to the point where, today, most people in advanced and developing nations earn their living through such employment (Tawney, 1926; Smith, 1776; Ashton, 1948).

In an employment relationship, an individual employee performs labor services in exchange for compensation. From a microeconomic theory perspective on this relationship, labor is a factor of production and an employer will add labor to the point where the marginal cost from doing so equals the marginal revenue (obtained) from doing so (Kaufman, 2010). In this rudimentary labor market exchange, nothing else is in play; there is no bonus pay, fringe benefit, payroll tax or collective behavior, such as unionization. There is also no place for individual employee voice in this factor of production-based view of employment.

In the real world of labor markets and employment, by contrast, numerous institutional arrangements prevail and influence the quantity of employment as well as terms and conditions of employment. These include unemployment insurance, minimum wage, overtime, workplace health and safety, maternity-paternity leave and anti-discrimination laws; company personnel/human resource management policies and practices; union representation and grievance procedures; non-union grievance and grievance-like procedures; and individual employment contracts. Laws offer employees potential external voice regarding certain aspects of their employment relationships, whereas company personnel/human resource management policies and practices, unionization, non-union grievance procedures and individual employment contracts provide employees with potential internal voice in their employment relationships.

This chapter focuses on individual employee exercise of voice, both informally and formally, through two of these internal channels, namely, unionized and non-union grievance procedures. The specific institutional arrangements – mechanisms – through which such voice is exercised are examined, followed by analysis of actual use of such mechanisms. Attention then turns to the consequences of employee use of voice or, in other words, post-employment dispute resolution outcomes. The chapter concludes with some recommendations for new research on individual employee exercise of voice.

FORMAL AND INFORMAL VOICE IN UNIONIZED AND NON-UNION CONTEXTS

In a unionized context, the potential for employee exercise of voice in the employment relationship is embodied in a grievance procedure that forms part of a collective bargaining agreement negotiated between a company's management and a union representing the company's employees. Perhaps more than any other provision of a collective bargaining agreement, a grievance procedure reflects the tempering of management's authority unilaterally to manage employees and impose discipline on them. The grievance procedure also enables labor and management to resolve disputes that might otherwise fester, go unresolved, and lead to work slowdowns, strikes and lockouts that would disrupt the production of goods and services. Generations of industrial relations scholars have celebrated unionized grievance procedures in terms of their contribution to maintaining production and work, preserving industrial peace and, most fundamentally, promoting industrial democracy (Budd, 2010; Chamberlain and Kuhn, 1965). Some empirical evidence and case examples support this favorable perspective on unionized grievance procedures (Katz and Kochan, 1999; Lewin, 1999), but other empirical evidence and case examples paint a more mixed picture of such procedures (Lewin, 2008a; Bemmels and Foley, 1996; Lewin and Boroff, 1996).

Until relatively recently, grievance procedures prevailed largely, if not exclusively, in unionized companies. Over the last quarter-century or so, and especially during the early twenty-first century, grievance procedures and variants thereof have spread widely among non-union companies. Recent studies estimate that a majority, perhaps two-thirds, of publicly traded non-union US companies and a majority of British workplaces have adopted such procedures (Lewin, 2008a; Colvin et al., 2006; Bryson et al., 2013). In the USA, these procedures are sometimes referred to as alternative dispute resolution (ADR), meaning that they are an alternative to litigation. In the USA and especially in other countries, they are also sometimes referred to as non-union employee representation (NER), meaning that they are an alternative to unionization (Gollan and Lewin, 2013; Campolieti et al., 2013). Whatever their label or acronym, non-union grievance procedures are celebrated by some scholars who regard them as a component of strategically oriented high-involvement human resource management practices that, as a set or bundle, have positive effects on organizational performance (for example, Huselid, 1995; Bryson et al., 2013). Other scholars, however, regard non-union grievance procedures as union avoidance and/or litigation avoidance devices (Colvin, 2013, 2003), and as being too one-sided in favoring company management (Colvin et al., 2006).

When a unionized or non-union employee files a grievance, it indicates that the employer must have taken some action with which the employee disagrees. Following Hirschman (1970), such disagreement signals deterioration of the employment relationship. By filing a grievance, the aggrieved employee challenges the employer's decision – exercises voice – and thereby seeks to redress the deterioration at hand. Again following Hirschman, the alternative to such exercise of voice is exit, meaning that a dissatisfied employee may quit his/her job and search for work elsewhere. Also from this theoretical perspective, the more loyal the employee the more likely he/she is to exercise voice and the less likely he/she is to exit. In other words, employee loyalty is hypothesized to be positively correlated with voice and negatively correlated with exit.

Most employment relationship conflicts, however, don't result in the filing of written grievances. Rather, such conflicts are informally discussed by the aggrieved employees and their immediate supervisors (or managers) and are usually resolved without ever entering the formal grievance procedure. One study of unionized grievance procedures estimated that approximately twelve grievances are settled informally for every one grievance that is settled through the formal grievance procedure (Lewin and Peterson, 1988). There is little reason to believe that this estimate would be significantly different in non-union settings with NER procedures. In both unionized and non-union settings, however, the incidence of informal grievance settlement may be substantially greater if high involvement type HRM (featuring, for example, workplace teams and employee consultation) is practiced. Further, a recent study by Marsden (2013) found that in Britain and France informal grievance resolution through direct access to management was significantly positively associated with individual employee exercise of voice. In sum, this reasoning together with available evidence indicates that informal employee voice is far more commonly exercised than formal employee voice and, therefore, that formal grievance filing and settlement activity is only a partial measure of the extent of employment relationship conflict.

In exercising informal voice, employees have a wide range of options. A unionized employee may discuss his/her grievance with a family member, a friend, a peer, a union representative, a labor relations or human resource management staff specialist, a supervisor or combinations thereof. A non-union employee may do the same except that a union representative will, by definition, not be available. These informal discussions of grievances can be quick and perfunctory or sustained and deep. Analytically, such informal discussions potentially invoke a network of contacts through which an aggrieved employee assesses his/her conflict issue and ultimately decides whether or not formally to exercise voice by filing a written grievance. This, in turn, involves such considerations as the seriousness of the grievance, the risk to the employee of filing a formal grievance in terms of potential retaliation for doing so, and the likelihood of having the grievance issue resolved in his/her favor. Further in this regard, the presence of high involvement type HRM practices is likely to be negatively associated with formal grievance filing because such practices are in part aimed at identifying potential or actual workplace conflict issues and resolving them before they deepen to the point where employees initiate formal grievances (Colvin, 2013).

If an aggrieved employee decides to file a formal grievance, that event will be known and the grievance will make its way through the grievance handling process. If an employee decides not to file a formal grievance, then the employee has in effect chosen to be silent. Following this reasoning, silence or, as some researchers label it, neglect, must be added to voice and exit as potential responses to employment relationship deterioration (Rusbelt et al., 1988). How does employee loyalty affect these differential responses to employment relationship deterioration? In both unionized and non-union contexts, empirical studies indicate that, controlling for exit, employee loyalty is significantly negatively correlated with the exercise of voice (Boroff and Lewin, 1997; Lewin and Boroff, 1996). In one of these studies, the analysis was limited to unionized employees who indicated that they had experienced one or more episodes of employment relationship deterioration, meaning that the more loyal the employee the more likely he/she was to be silent rather than exercise voice even in the face of such deterioration. In another of these studies, which involved both unionized and non-union employees and also controlled for employee exit, similar negative relationships were found between employee loyalty and the exercise of voice. In addition, among non-union employees fear of retaliation for filing a grievance was significantly negatively related to grievance filing, that is, the exercise of voice, meaning once again that aggrieved employees chose to be silent despite having experienced employment relationship conflict (that is, deterioration).

Grievance Filing Issues and Settlement in Unionized and Non-Union Contexts

When employees file formal grievances, most of them are settled at the first step of the grievance procedure and the bulk of remaining grievances are settled at the second step. Relatively few grievances make their way to the final step of the grievance procedure, which in unionized contexts and a rising proportion of non-union contexts is third-party arbitration (Lewin, 2010). More specifically, about 60 percent of unionized employee grievances are settled at the first procedural step, about 30 percent at the second step, about 7 percent at the third step, and about 3 percent at the final (arbitration) step (Lewin and Peterson, 1988). Roughly similar step settlement percentages occur in non-union grievance procedures, although the number and type of steps in such procedures vary considerably more then they do in unionized grievance procedures (Lewin, 2008b, 1997). To illustrate, some non-union grievance procedures incorporate two steps, others three steps, and still others four steps. Some of these procedures feature peer review of individual employee grievances, usually at the second or third step. Others feature a senior human resource officer or a top management committee to review individual employee grievances and recommend settlement decisions, typically at the third step. A few of these procedures require a chief operating officer (COO) or even a chief executive officer (CEO) to review individual employee grievances and make settlement decisions, almost always at the last step of the procedure. Increasingly, however, arbitration is the final step in non-union grievance procedures, just as it is in unionized grievance procedures.

That most formal grievances filed by unionized and non-union employees are settled at the early (that is, first and second) steps of grievance procedures can be interpreted to mean that most employment relationship conflicts are resolved relatively close to their sources of origin, which comports with a longstanding principle of effective employment conflict resolution (Katz and Kochan, 1999; Chamberlain and Kuhn, 1965). The fact that most grievances are settled through informal discussions and never enter the formal grievance procedure strengthens this conclusion. Alternatively, this evidence can be interpreted to mean that the costs of grievance processing and settlement to employee-grievants and to management rise rapidly as grievances are pursued through higher steps of the procedure. Hence, employee-grievants and management settle for suboptimal, that is, second- or third-best, solutions.

Both unionized and non-union employees are particularly prone to filing grievances over discipline, which ranges from relatively minor docking of pay for occasional or persistent lateness in reporting for work and unauthorized absenteeism to termination for violation of a company policy concerning, as examples, theft or accessing pornographic websites on company computers during work time. In the United States and some other nations, ' termination for cause' basically means that an employee has broken the rules and is therefore ineligible to receive unemployment insurance payments (which are provided to employees laid off for economic reasons). The typical unionized and non-union grievance procedure also reflects the principle of progressive discipline whereby discipline imposed for employee violations of company policies and practices becomes more severe for repeat offenses (Jacoby, 1986). This internal discipline and due process system closely resembles that of the external judicial system, which is why it is sometimes referred to as a system of industrial justice (Budd, 2010).

Empirical studies of grievance procedure usage in both unionized and non-union settings find that grievances are most often filed over issues regarding pay, work assignments, working conditions (such as safety) and supervision. Men are more likely than women to file grievances over these types of issues, as are younger workers compared to older workers. Further, women are relatively more likely than men to file grievances over (lack of) access to training for current and higher level jobs, whereas older workers are relatively more likely than younger workers to file grievances over (lack of) promotions and performance evaluations (Lewin and Peterson, 1988). Women are somewhat more likely than men to file grievances over gender discrimination, including sexual harassment, but are far more likely than men to file lawsuits alleging gender discrimination at work. Extant evidence also indicates that Asians and Latinos are significantly less likely than Anglos to file grievances over virtually any issue, and that African-American grievance filing rates are roughly similar to those of Anglos (Boswell and Olson-Buchanan, 2004; Lewin, 2010).

An important difference between unionized and non-union grievance procedures concerns the scope of job/occupational coverage. In a unionized grievance procedure, only employees who are represented by the union and are thus part of the bargaining unit may file grievances under the procedure specified in the collective bargaining agreement. In the USA, all such bargaining units exclude supervisors and managers, meaning that none of these higher job/occupational level employees may exercise voice through the grievance procedure. In a non-union grievance procedure, there is no bargaining unit and the procedure may be quite wide in its scope of job/occupational coverage. This means that it may include first-line supervisors, foremen, lower-level managers and mid-level managers, especially if the procedure is cast as an internal organizational governance mechanism. In light of the decline of unionism and collectively bargained grievance procedures and the growth of non-union grievance procedures in the USA and elsewhere, far more employees are covered by and eligible to use non-union than unionized grievance procedures or, in other words, to exercise voice in the employment relationship. Nonetheless, such coverage and eligibility does not necessarily mean that higher-level non-union employees will actually file formal grievances. In this regard, empirical studies of non-union employment dispute resolution find that job/occupational ranking is inversely correlated with grievance filing and that lower and middle-management personnel in particular fear retaliation for filing grievances, preferring to remain silent even when experiencing employment relationship deterioration (Lewin, 2004; Lewin and Boroff, 1996).

In Europe, lower level and mid-level supervisors and managers are 'represented' through works councils and thereby exercise voice in their employment relationships. The scope of issues over which such voice is exercised – as examples, plant closings and relocation, new product introduction, product pricing, mergers and acquisitions – is considerably wider than the scope of issues over which unionized US employees exercise voice, which is limited to the 'terms and conditions of employment' specified in collective bargaining agreements and the grievance procedures contained therein. The scope of issues covered by works councils is also typically wider than the scope of issues covered by high involvement type HRM practices, both in Europe and the USA. In this regard, Marsden (2013) found that in Britain and France management-led forms of voice, including through high involvement type HRM, were insignificantly associated with individual employee exercise of voice.

Grievance Procedure Dynamics

When a unionized employee files a written grievance, a shop steward or union grievance committee member usually assists him/her. When a non-union employee files a grievance, a peer, a human resource staff specialist, or occasionally an attorney, may assist him/her. Submitting a grievance in writing is a significant act because it puts the employee on record as challenging a management decision. For industrial relations scholars, formal grievance filing constitutes the premier expression of voice in the employment relationship and, more fundamentally, the main evidence of why and how unionization provides workers with a mechanism to exercise such voice (Lewin, 2005). In a non-union employment relationship, formal grievance filing also represents the expression of voice but with no comparable, independent institutional support mechanism.

Once a grievance is filed, management must respond. At the first step of the grievance procedure, the employee's direct supervisor or another supervisor or front-line manager typically meets with the employee to discuss the substance of the grievance. This occurs in both unionized and non-union contexts. Following this discussion and consistent with the provisions of a collective bargaining agreement or a non-union grievance procedure, the employee-grievant receives a written response from management that contains proposed terms of settlement. If the employee-grievant accepts those terms, the grievance is closed (that is, ended). As indicated earlier, about 60 percent of all grievances filed by unionized and non-union employees are settled at the first step of the procedure.

If an employee-grievant rejects management's proposed settlement at the first grievance step, the grievance moves to the next step. At this step in unionized and non-union grievance procedures, a second-level supervisor, manager, labor relations or human resource specialist typically represents management. In a unionized context, a shop steward or union grievance committee official represents the employee. In a non-union context, a peer or outside counsel (that is, attorney) may represent the employee. When these representatives meet to discuss the substance of the grievance, the employee-grievant and his/her immediate supervisor typically are not present. Following this discussion, the employee-grievant receives a written response from management that contains proposed terms of settlement. If the employee-grievant accepts those terms, the grievance is closed. As indicated earlier, about 30 percent of all grievances filed by unionized and non-union employees are settled at the second step of the procedure.

If an employee-grievant rejects management's proposed settlement at the second grievance step, the grievance moves to the next step. At this step in a unionized grievance procedure, a senior management official and a top-level union grievance committee member or union official represent the employer and the employee-grievant, respectively. These representatives then meet to discuss the content of the grievance, sometimes doing so with the employee grievant or his/her immediate supervisor being present and sometimes not. Following this meeting, the employee-grievant receives a written response from management containing proposed terms of settlement. If the employee-grievant accepts those terms, the grievance is closed. In a non-union grievance procedure, this step usually features a senior human resource management officer or a senior management committee to represent the employer, but sometimes features a senior line management official such as a COO or CEO. If this is the final step of the non-union grievance procedure, the employee-grievant typically is not present or represented and the management representative renders a final decision. If it is the next-to-last step of the procedure, the employee-grievant may be present and/or represented by a peer or outside counsel or, alternatively, not be present or represented. In either case, the management representative recommends terms of settlement. As indicated earlier, about 7 percent of all grievances filed by unionized employees are settled at the third step of the procedure. For non-union employees, between 5 and 10 percent of all grievances are settled at the third step of the procedure depending upon whether this is the penultimate or final step of the grievance procedure.

If the employee-grievant rejects management's proposed settlement at the third grievance step, the grievance moves to the next or final step, which in virtually all instances involving unionized employees and a majority of instances involving non-union employees is third-party arbitration. This step is substantially more formal then the preceding steps. To illustrate, the arbitrator holds a hearing at which management and employee-grievant representatives are present; these representatives as well as witnesses for each party give sworn testimony that is transcribed by a professional transcriptionist; and each party provides the arbitrator with supporting documents and exhibits. In some instances, audio and video recordings of the arbitration hearing are made. Further, an arbitrator may require the parties to submit post-hearing briefs. As indicated earlier, about 3 percent of all grievances filed by unionized employees are settled at the final (arbitration) step of the procedure. A similar percentage of grievances involving non-union employees are settled at this step if it is the final step of the grievance procedure (Lewin, 2008b, 2004).

Grievance Arbitration

When unionized employee grievances reach the arbitration stage, management and union representatives jointly select the arbitrator and each party pays half the costs of arbitration. Grievance procedure provisions of collective bargaining agreements typically spell out the method of arbitrator selection. For example, this type of provision may specify that the parties will request a list of several potential arbitrators from the American Arbitration Association (AAA), the National Academy of Arbitrators (NAA), the Judicial Arbitration and Mediation Services (JAMS) or some other organization specializing in employment dispute resolution. Once received, the parties review the list of arbitrators and each side may strike the names of individual arbitrators it deems unacceptable. If one or more of the listed arbitrators are acceptable to both sides, the parties will rank order these arbitrators and request that the top ranked arbitrator be assigned to the grievance case. If that arbitrator is unavailable, the parties will request the next highest ranked arbitrator. If none of the arbitrators on the original list are acceptable to one or the other party or are otherwise unable to serve, a second list of potential arbitrators will be requested and the selection process proceeds in exactly the same way as with the original list until an arbitrator is chosen and assigned to the grievance case.

When non-union employee grievances reach the arbitration stage, either management alone selects the arbitrator or management and the employee or employee's representative together select the arbitrator. When management alone selects the arbitrator, it is likely that this process will be perceived by employees as relatively unjust compared to a process in which both management and the employee or employee's representative select the arbitrator (Colvin et al., 2006). In either instance, however, management alone pays the arbitration costs. This aspect of the non-union grievance procedure is not necessarily perceived by employees to be unjust, but is perhaps the main reason why some scholars regard the arbitration of non-union employment disputes as being overly one-sided, that is, as favoring the employer (Blancero et al., 2010).

Following completion of the arbitration hearing and the parties' submission of post-hearing briefs, the arbitrator renders a written decision and transmits it to the parties. In both unionized and non-union contexts, an arbitrator's decision is final and binding. In the case of unionized employees, this decision standard is spelled out in the grievance procedure provisions of a collective bargaining agreement – an agreement that presumably has been voluntarily negotiated by management and union representatives on behalf of their respective organizations and constituents. In the case of non-union employees, this decision standard is spelled out either in company policy statements (often included in an employee handbook) or in individual employment contracts that employees presumably have willingly agreed to and signed as a condition of employment. While management or an employee may be dissatisfied with an arbitrator's decision to the point where it wants to challenge that decision in a court, the US Supreme Court has consistently ruled that where collective bargaining agreements contain grievance procedures culminating in binding arbitration and where individual employment contracts contain provisions requiring the arbitration of employment relationship disputes, any grievances that arise thereunder must be settled via arbitration and cannot be appealed to or reviewed by the courts (Lewin, 2014 (forthcoming); Colvin, 2013; Chamberlain and Kuhn, 1965). This deferral to arbitration doctrine has clearly strengthened the decision-making power of arbitrators in employment relationship conflicts involving unionized and non-union employees.

Expedited Arbitration

Because arbitration is the final step of unionized grievance procedures and is the most formal component of such procedures, a substantial amount of time – as much as one year – may lapse between the initial filing of a grievance and an arbitrated grievance decision. In other words, there is a negative correlation between the speed of grievance settlement and the number of grievance procedure steps used to resolve grievances. For the employee-grievant, this may mean that (industrial) justice delayed is (industrial) justice denied. It also may mean that management experiences a prolonged period of uncertainty about the resolution of the grievance issue at hand. For these reasons some unionized grievance procedures permit the use of expedited arbitration, which basically means skipping certain steps of the procedure, typically the second and/or third steps. When expedited arbitration occurs, the amount of time between initial grievance filing and an arbitration decision is substantially reduced, specifically by between 40 and 50 percent (Lewin, 1997). This, in turn, implies that perceived procedural justice will be greater when unionized employee grievances that proceed past the first step of the procedure are ultimately settled through expedited arbitration rather than conventional arbitration.

While the speedier justice and uncertainty reduction rationales for expedited arbitration imply that this type of arbitration will be widely used in unionized settings, the evidence suggests otherwise. By skipping intermediate steps of the grievance procedure, the parties forgo opportunities for grievance settlement at lower steps of the procedure (recall that about 37 percent of unionized employee grievances are settled at the second and third steps). Such lower step settlements also avoid the costs associated with arbitration. Further, the binding nature of arbitrator decisions may set precedents for handling certain employment relationship disputes that limit the flexibility that management and union representatives may prefer to retain in dealing with similar future disputes.

In non-union grievance procedures that culminate in arbitration, it is likely that grievance settlements occur more quickly than in unionized grievance procedures. This is because, on average, non-union grievance procedures have fewer steps than unionized grievance procedures, relatively more stringent time limits on management responses to employee-grievants at each procedural step, and relatively less use of employee representation during the grievance handling process. Further, in some non-union employment relationship disputes, arbitration is invoked quite quickly because it is the only grievance settlement step after grievances are filed. A case in point is the securities industry. In that industry, the New York Stock Exchange (NYSE) and later the National Association of Securities Dealers (NASD) adopted policies and programs requiring the use of arbitration to settle any disputes arising between brokers and brokers' firms. In 2007, these policies and programs were merged under the Financial Industry Regulatory Authority (FINRA). Thousands of arbitration awards have been issued in this industry over the last quarter-century (Lipsky et al., 2013). Irrespective of which party prevailed in these awards, the FINRA program represents a leading example of expedited arbitration, meaning that grievance cases are settled relatively quickly and therefore employees don't have to wait long to know the results of their exercise of voice.

Most grievance procedure provisions of collective bargaining agreements limit the type of infractions and the discipline associated with such infractions for which expedited arbitration may be invoked. To illustrate, grievances challenging discipline for drunkenness at work may not be subject to expedited arbitration whereas grievances challenging discipline for theft at work may be subject to expedited arbitration. In another example, grievances challenging termination may be subject to expedited arbitration whereas grievances challenging suspension from work may not be subject to expedited arbitration. Hence, the benefit of speedier grievance settlement that is associated with the use of expedited arbitration must be balanced against the behavioral and procedural limitations on the use of expedited arbitration.

Scope of Issues

The scope of issues over which unionized employees may file grievances is defined by and limited to those terms and conditions of employment specified in a collective bargaining agreement. Such terms and conditions typically cover pay (for example, regular pay, overtime pay, shift pay), fringe benefits (for example, retirement plans, health care plans, vacations, sick leave), job classifications, work shifts, supervision, layoffs, discipline and due process. Unionized employees may file grievances involving any of these terms and conditions of employment and over discipline imposed for violating company policies and practices pertaining to these terms and conditions. They may not file grievances over other company policies and practices even if those policies and practices impact certain aspects of employment and employment relationships (Budd, 2010).

The scope of issues over which non-union employees may file grievances is by definition not determined through a collective bargaining agreement but, instead, by a company's management. The aforementioned variation in types of non-union dispute resolution procedures also applies to the scope of issues covered by the procedures. In some instance, the scope may be quite wide and in other instances quite narrow. Further, some non-union dispute resolution procedures are very specific in this regard, while others are very general. On balance, non-union employees may have a wider scope of issues over which they can file grievances than unionized employees because non-union dispute resolution procedures often apply to most or all of the terms and conditions of employment specified in a company's employee handbook, whereas unionized dispute resolution procedures apply only to those terms and conditions of employment spelled out in the collective bargaining agreement.

In the USA and many other nations, the concept of private property is dominant. This means that business owners and the management hired by these owners retain the right to lead and manage the businesses as they see fit subject only to certain regulations and to contractual arrangements they may reach with employees and others – for example, customers, suppliers, shareholders and community groups. This is known as the doctrine of management's reserved rights and means that even when a company's employees are unionized and a collective bargaining agreement is in place, those employees may not file grievances over any company policy or practice or any term and condition of employment not covered by the collective bargaining agreement (Chamberlain and Kuhn, 1965). It also means that grievance arbitration does not apply to these company policies, practices and non-covered terms and conditions of employment.

The same reasoning applies and even stronger conclusions emerge with respect to non-union dispute resolution procedures. A non-union company decides whether or not to adopt a grievance or grievance-like procedure, which may be labeled ADR or NER. If it adopts such a procedure, it then determines the scope of issues over which non-union employees can invoke the procedure. As noted earlier, this scope may be wide or narrow but employees do not participate – have a voice – in making this determination. Once again, management's reserved rights are in play. In light of the continuing experimentation by non-union firms in determining the scope of issues covered by their dispute resolution procedures, however, this scope is more elastic than in unionized firms where collective bargaining agreements in effect set an upper bound on the scope of issues over which unionized employees can file grievances. Nonetheless and as elaborated below, in both unionized and non-union settings, the scope of issues over which employees may raise and seek the redress of grievances can be influenced – expanded – through management's adoption of high involvement type HRM practices.

Reactive and Proactive Employee Voice

In both unionized and non-union contexts, grievance and grievance-like procedures enable employee voice to be exercised ex post, that is, after management makes decisions with which employees disagree; this can be labeled 'reactive employee voice.' By doing so, however, the question arises, 'Is there proactive employee voice?' For those who favor what is variously known as high involvement, high participation or high performance type human resource management practices, the answer to this question is yes. To illustrate, strategic human resource management (SHRM) theory posits that high involvement human resource management practices enhance organizational performance, especially when these practices are sustained (Colvin, 2003; Pfeffer, 1998). Examples of such practices include self-managed or self-directed work teams, consultation committees, targeted training, performance-based pay, and business information sharing, which are aimed at building employee trust in management and commitment to the company (or other type of organization). In this type of high involvement human resource management system, work-related issues that might otherwise become the subject of employee grievances surface early on and can potentially be nipped in the bud, thereby providing an ex ante approach to employment dispute resolution. Empirical support for this proposition is provided by several studies (for example, Ichniowski, 1992), including one that found a significant negative association between an index of high involvement human resource management practices and the employee grievance filing rate in telecommunications companies (Colvin, 2013).

As noted earlier, however, a high involvement human resource management system may also include a grievance or grievance-like procedure. The conceptual basis for such inclusion rests on principles of due process, procedural justice and/or employee voice, each of which can be invoked to claim that employee trust in management and commitment to the organization will be enhanced by having a grievance procedure in place (Lipsky et al., 2003; Kaminski, 1999). While this positivist strategic orientation may guide some firms in their adoption of non-union grievance and grievance-like procedures, other firms adopt these procedures to defend against the threat of employee unionization and/or the threat of employment dispute litigation. In any case, empirical evidence shows a significant positive association between the presence of a grievance procedure as a component of a high involvement human resource management system and the employee grievance filing rate (Colvin, 2013). One interpretation of this finding is that when a grievance or grievance-like procedure is available to non-union employees, it generates employee demand for use of the procedure. In sum, a high involvement human resource management system enables employee voice to be heard relatively early on or proactively in organizational decision-making processes. When a formal employment dispute resolution process accompanies a high involvement human resource management system, however, employee voice is heard relatively later on, that is, reactively, which is quite similar to what occurs under traditional unionized grievance procedures.

POST-DISPUTE RESOLUTION OUTCOMES

Most of the literature on unionized and non-union grievance procedures focuses on the antecedents of grievance filing, the dynamics of grievance processing, and the outcomes of grievance settlement, especially the parties' relative win-loss rates. A small portion of this literature, however, focuses on post-dispute resolution outcomes or, in question form, 'What happens after grievances are settled?' This question derives from an industrial relations-based conceptualization of the grievance procedure as a mechanism for reversing an employee's deteriorated relationship with an employer, and from an organizational behavior-based conceptualization of the grievance procedure as a mechanism for providing restorative justice (Boroff and Lewin, 1997; Hirschman, 1970; Goodstein and Aquino, 2010).

The clearest answer to this question comes from studies that use a quasi-experimental research design to select a sample of a company's unionized or non-union employees who file grievances (grievants) and an accompanying sample of unionized or non-unionized employees who did not file grievances (non-grievants). In this design, the sample of grievants is the treatment group and the sample of non-grievants is the control group (other variables, such as job content, are also controlled). These two groups are then compared with respect to job performance, promotions and work attendance before grievances are filed (by the first group), during the grievance-processing period, and after grievances are settled. They are also compared with respect to turnover after grievances are settled. Some provocative findings have emerged from studies that use this type of research design (Lewin, 2008b; Lewin and Peterson, 1999; Lewin and Peterson, 1988; Lewin, 1987).

In particular, prior to grievance filing, grievants and non-grievants do not differ significantly with respect to job performance ratings, promotion rates and work attendance rates. The two groups also do not differ significantly on any of these measures during the grievance filing and settlement period. During the one-to-three-year period following the settlement and closure of grievance cases, however, grievants have significantly lower job performance ratings and promotion rates, insignificantly lower work attendance rates, and significantly higher voluntary (and insignificantly higher involuntary) turnover rates than non-grievants. These findings, which have been replicated in a variety of unionized and non-union settings as well as in laboratory studies conducted by psychologists (Klaas and DeNisi, 1989; Olson-Buchanan, 1996), suggest that employment relationship deterioration is not reversed and restorative justice is not achieved through the unionized grievance procedure.

Additional support for these conclusions comes from a subset of studies in which company-specific samples of supervisors of grievants are compared with company-specific samples of supervisors of non-grievants in terms of the same sequence: prior to grievance filing, during the filing and settlement period and after grievances are settled (Lewin, 2007, 1987; Lewin and Peterson, 1988). The findings indicate that prior to employee grievance filing and during the grievance filing and settlement period there are no significant differences between the supervisors of grievants and the supervisors of non-grievants with respect to job performance ratings, promotion rates and work attendance. By contrast, during the one-to-three-year period following grievance settlement, supervisors of grievants have significantly lower job performance ratings and promotion rates, insignificantly lower work attendance rates, and significantly higher turnover rates, especially involuntary turnover rates, than supervisors of non-grievants. These findings have also been replicated in a variety of unionized and non-union settings and provide further evidence of the reactive nature of the grievance procedure (Lewin and Peterson, 1999; Lewin, 1987).

But they do more than this. That employee-grievants and their supervisors have higher involuntary turnover rates (significantly higher in the case of supervisors) than non-grievants and their supervisors during the period following grievance settlement implies that management retaliates against employees who exercise voice and even more so against those who supervise employee-grievants (Boroff and Lewin, 1997; Lewin and Boroff, 1996). Such retaliation is also implied by grievants' and supervisors of grievants' significantly lower post-grievance settlement job performance ratings and promotion rates compared to non-grievants and supervisors of non-grievants, especially because neither of the treatment groups differed significantly from the control groups on these measures either prior to or during the period of grievance filing and settlement. Such retaliation also appears to be at odds with strategic human resource management (SHRM) theory and practice, particularly when a grievance or grievance-like procedure is included in a set of high involvement type human resource management practices intended to enhance organizational performance.

Apart from retaliation, there is another explanation of why grievants and their supervisors fare more poorly than non-grievants and their supervisors after grievances are settled. This is the ' revealed performance' explanation and refers to a company's discovery after the fact of grievance filing and settlement that employees who file grievances and their supervisors are poorer performers than employees who don't file grievances and their supervisors (Lewin, 2007; Lewin and Peterson, 1999). For this explanation to hold, grievance activity must shock management into paying closer attention to employee performance measurement and management.

Two contrasting examples support this alternative explanation. First, in litigation over employment disputes, especially in the case of layoffs involving claims of age, gender and race discrimination (that is, disparate impact), employee performance appraisal data produced by companies in defending themselves against such claims typically show no statistically significant differences between laid off employees and retained employees (Cascio and Bernardin, 1981). Consequently and especially when defendants lose such cases, companies will take steps to improve their performance appraisal practices by providing more supervisor/manager training and sometimes by requiring a forced distribution of employee performance appraisal ratings. Hence, this employment litigation experience shocks management into paying closer attention to performance management.

Second, when employees unionize and negotiate a collective bargaining agreement with a company, management usually reexamines its operating practices and winds up changing some, perhaps many, of them. Such changes may affect workflow, work scheduling, inventory control, record keeping, job design, job assignments, performance evaluation and, especially, supervision. These changes, in turn, lead to increased productivity and efficiency. This dynamic is known as 'union shock' theory and is used to explain why unionized and non-union companies can coexist in the same industry or sector (Lewin, 2005; Freeman and Medoff, 1984; Rees, 1977; Chamberlain, 1948). Under collective bargaining, pay and benefits – costs – will be higher in unionized than in non-union firms but productivity will also be higher, meaning that unit labor costs will be (approximately) the same in these firms. Therefore, both the litigation shock and union shock examples support a revealed performance explanation of differential post-grievance settlement outcomes between grievants and their supervisors and non-grievants and their supervisors.

In related research, Bryson et al. (2013) found that in Britain union-only voice and dual-channel (that is, union and non-union) voice were significantly negatively associated with employee quit rates, non-union voice was significantly positively associated with workplace climate, and non-union only voice was significantly positively associated with (estimated) company financial performance. In a US-based study set in the telecommunications industry, Colvin (2003) found that high involvement type HRM practices were significantly negatively associated with employee discipline, including dismissal, and with employee grievance filing and grievance appeal rates, suggesting that workplace conflict is lower under high involvement HRM practices compared to other practices. In a study of a British non-union restaurant company, Marchington and Suter (2013) found that compared to formal employee involvement and participation (EIP) practices, informal EIP practices were significantly positively correlated with employee job satisfaction, manager job satisfaction, employee commitment to the organization and employee commitment to the (employee's) manager, thereby confirming the authors' hypothesis that employees and managers prefer informal EIP over formal EIP.

RESEARCH RECOMMENDATIONS

The grievance procedure has long been regarded as the main mechanism through which unionized employees exercise voice in the employment relationship, perhaps implying that non-union employees cannot exercise voice in their employment relationships. But the rise of grievance and grievance-like procedures in non-union companies in various countries and industries suggests otherwise, at least in so far as the availability of such voice mechanisms is concerned. Given this development together with the decline of private sector unionism and collective bargaining in most nations, it is likely that many more non-union than unionized employees are covered by grievance and grievance-like procedures. Nonetheless, it would be helpful in this regard if researchers conducted new studies aimed at more precisely determining the extent to which non-union employees are covered by grievance procedures and other voice mechanisms.

Similarly, the extent to which unionized and especially non-union employees in the modern economy actually use grievance procedures – exercise formal voice – is not well known. In the case of unionized employees, estimates of such use are contained in relatively older studies. In the case of non-union employees, estimates of such use are largely based on particular company examples and case studies. Here, again, researchers could enhance our knowledge of employee exercise of voice by conducting new, deeper studies focusing in particular on grievance filing by non-union employees at different job/occupational levels in organizations and on the specific issues over which such grievances are filed.

In both unionized and non-union settings, empirical evidence indicates that grievants fare more poorly than non-grievants after grievances are settled and that the same is true of the supervisors of grievants relative to the supervisors of non-grievants. Whether this occurs because of retaliation or because of revealed performance is uncertain. Researchers could help sort out this conundrum by conducting more in-depth, longitudinal studies of post-employment dispute resolution outcomes, especially by selecting and comparing samples of non-union companies in which strategic human resource management, union avoidance and litigation avoidance rationales, respectively, underlie these companies' adoption of grievance procedures.

New research on employee voice could also focus on voice exercised by customers, vendors and shareholders. In this regard, Hirschman's original (1970) formulation of the exit-voice-loyalty framework didn't focus on employees. Rather, it focused on customers and, most broadly, on citizens, proposing that dissatisfied customers could either exercise voice or exit to other firms and that dissatisfied citizens could either exercise voice or exit to other political jurisdictions or even nations. In both instances and following the microeconomic principle of marginal analysis, only some customers and some citizens have to exhibit voice-exercising behavior to validate the exit-voice-loyalty framework. Similar reasoning can be applied to vendors and shareholders, especially from an organizational constituency management perspective. More specifically, it would be helpful to know if the extent of voice exercised by one constituency, such as employees, is matched by or is significantly different from the extent of voice exercised by customers, vendors and/or shareholders. Pursuing this type of research question would signal that employment relationship conflict scholars can break out of their relatively narrow research silo to consider broader, deeper organizational constituency relationship conflict.

Finally, the question of whether or not employee voice can be exercised more proactively or ex ante rather than reactively or ex post merits new research attention. In both unionized and non-union settings, employees who file grievances do so after the fact, that is, after they experience employment relationship deterioration or dissatisfaction. Recall that the extant literature indicates that grievance procedure availability is significantly positively associated with organizational performance, whereas grievance procedure usage is significantly negatively associated with organizational performance. In other words and with respect to organizational performance, the best grievance procedure – employee voice mechanism – apparently is one that is available but not used! In this regard, it would be especially helpful to have new research concerning if, how and to what extent high involvement type human resource management practices elicit ex ante informal and formal employee voice and thereby provide a relatively more proactive approach to employment dispute resolution. All of this proposed new research would enhance our knowledge even more if it was conducted in cross-national settings, that is, in a global context.

REFERENCES

Ashton, T.S. (1948), *The Industrial Revolution, 1760–1830*, Oxford: Oxford University Press.
Bemmels, B. and J. Foley (1996), 'Grievance procedure research: a review and theoretical recommendations', *Journal of Management*, **22**, 359–84.
Blancero, D.M., R.G. DelCampo and G.F. Marron (2010), 'Just tell me! Making alternative dispute resolution systems fair', *Industrial and Labor Relations Review*, **49**, 524–43.
Boroff, K.E. and D. Lewin (1997), 'Loyalty, voice, and intent to exit a union firm: a conceptual and empirical analysis', *Industrial and Labor Relations Review*, **51**, 50–63.
Boswell, W.R. and J.B. Olson-Buchanan (2004), 'experiencing mistreatment at work: the role of grievance-filing, nature of mistreatment, and employee withdrawal', *Academy of Management Journal*, **47**, 129–40.
Bryson, A., P. Willman, R. Gomez and T. Kretschmer (2013), 'The comparative advantage of non–union voice in Britain, 1980–2004', *Industrial Relations*, **52**, 194–220.
Budd. J.W. (2010), *Labor Relations: Striking a Balance*, 3rd edn, New York: McGraw-Hill/Irwin.
Chamberlain, N.W. (1948), *The Union Challenge to Management Control*, New York: Harper.

Chamberlain, N.W. and J.W. Kuhn (1965), *Collective Bargaining*, 2nd edn, New York: McGraw-Hill.
Campolieti, M., R. Gomez and M. Gunderson (2013), 'Does non-union employee representation act as a complement or substitute to union voice? Evidence from Canada and the United States', *Industrial Relations*, **52**, 378–96.
Cascio, W.F. and H.J. Bernardin (1981), 'Implications of performance appraisal litigation for personnel decisions', *Personnel Psychology*, **34**, 211–26.
Colvin, A.J.S. (2003), 'Institutional pressures, human resource strategies, and the rise of nonunion dispute resolution procedures', *Industrial and Labor Relations Review*, **56**, 375–92.
Colvin, A.J.S. (2013), 'Participation versus procedures in non-union dispute resolution', *Industrial Relations*, **52**, 259–83.
Colvin, A.J.S., B. Klaas and D. Mahoney (2006), 'Research on alternative dispute resolution procedures', in D. Lewin (ed.), *Contemporary Issues in Employment Relations*, Champaign, IL: Labor and Employment Relations Association, pp. 103–47.
Freeman, R.B. and J.L. Medoff (1984), *What Do Unions Do?*, New York: Basic Books.
Gollan, P.J. and D. Lewin (2013), 'Employee representation in non-union firms: an overview', *Industrial Relations*, **52**, 173–93.
Goodstein, J. and K. Aquino (2010), 'And restorative justice for all: redemption, forgiveness, and reintegration in organizations', *Journal of Organizational Behavior*, **31**, 624–8.
Hirschman, A.O. (1970), *Exit, Voice and Loyalty*, Cambridge, MA: Harvard University Press.
Huselid, M. (1995), 'The impact of human resource management practices on turnover, productivity, and corporate financial performance', *Academy of Management Journal*, **38**, 635–72.
Ichniowski, Casey (1992), 'Human resource practices and productive labor–management relations', in D. Lewin, O.S. Mitchell and P.D. Sherer (eds), *Research Frontiers in Industrial Relations and Human Resources*, Madison, WI: Industrial Relations Research Association, pp. 239–72.
Jacoby, S.M. (1986), 'Progressive discipline in American industry: its origins, development and consequences', in D.B. Lipsky and D. Lewin (eds), *Advances in Industrial and Labor Relations*, Vol. 3, Greenwich, CT: JAI Press, pp. 213–60.
Kaminski, M. (1999), 'New forms of work organization and their impact on the grievance procedure', in A.E. Eaton and J.H. Keefe (eds), *Employment Dispute Resolution and Worker Rights in the Changing Workplace*, Champaign, IL: Industrial Relations Research Association, pp. 219–46.
Katz, H.C. and T.A. Kochan (1999), *Introduction to Collective Bargaining and Industrial Relations*, 2nd edn, Homewood, IL: Irwin.
Kaufman, B.E. (2010), 'The theoretical foundation of industrial relations and its implications for labor economics and human resource management', *Industrial and Labor Relations Review*, **64**, 817–51.
Klaas, B.S. and A.S. DeNisi (1989), 'Managerial reactions to employee dissent: the impact of grievance activity on performance Ratings', *Academy of Management Journal*, **32**, 705–17.
Lewin, D. (1987), 'Dispute resolution in the nonunion firm: a theoretical and empirical analysis', *Journal of Conflict Resolution*, **3**, 465–502.
Lewin, D. (1997), 'Workplace dispute resolution', in D. Lewin, D.J.B. Mitchell and M. Zaidi (eds), *The Human Resource Management Handbook*, Part II, Greenwich, CT: JAI Press, pp. 197–218.
Lewin, D. (1999), 'Theoretical and empirical research on the grievance procedure and arbitration: a critical review', in A.E. Eaton and J.H. Keefe (eds), *Employment Dispute Resolution and Worker Rights in the Changing Workplace*, Champaign, IL: Industrial Relations Research Association, pp. 137–86.
Lewin, D. (2004), 'Dispute resolution in nonunion organizations: key empirical findings', in S. Estreicher and D. Sherwin (eds), *Alternative Dispute Resolution in the Employment Arena*, New York: Kluwer, pp. 379–403.
Lewin, D. (2005), 'Unionism and employment conflict resolution: rethinking collective voice and its consequences', *Journal of Labor Research*, **26**, 209–39.
Lewin, D. (2007), 'Management responses to nonunion dispute resolution outcomes: a political analysis', *Proceedings of the 59th Annual Meeting*, Labor and Employment Relations Association, Champaign, IL: LERA, pp. 85–103.
Lewin, D. (2008a), 'Resolving conflict', in P. Blyton, N. Bacon, J. Fiorito and E. Heery (eds), *The Sage Handbook of Industrial Relations*, London: Sage, pp. 447–68.
Lewin, D. (2008b), 'Workplace ADR: what's new and what matters?', in S.E. Befort and P. Halter (eds), *Workplace Justice for a Changing Environment: Proceedings of the Sixtieth Annual Meeting, National Academy of Arbitrators*, Washington, DC: Bureau of National Affairs, pp. 23–9.
Lewin, D. (2010), 'Mutual gains', in A. Wilkinson, P.J. Gollan, M. Marchington and D. Lewin (eds), *The Oxford Handbook of Participation in Organizations*, Oxford: Oxford University Press, pp. 427–52.
Lewin, D. (2014), 'Collective bargaining and grievance procedures', in William K. Roche, Paul Teague and Alex Colvin (eds), *Oxford Handbook of Conflict Management in Organizations*, Oxford: Oxford University Press, forthcoming.
Lewin, D. and K.E. Boroff (1996), 'The role of loyalty in exit and voice: a conceptual and empirical analysis',

in D. Lewin and B.E. Kaufman (eds), *Advances in Industrial and Labor Relations*, Vol. 7, Greenwich, CT: JAI Press, pp. 69–96.

Lewin, D. and R.B. Peterson (1988), *The Modern Grievance Procedure in the United States*, Westport, CT: Quorum.

Lewin, D. and R.B. Peterson (1999), 'Behavioral outcomes of grievance activity', *Industrial Relations*, **38**, 554–79.

Lipsky, D.B., R.L. Seeber and R.D. Fincher (2003), *Emerging Systems for Managing Workplace Conflict*, San Francisco, CA: Jossey-Bass.

Lipsky, D.B., J.R. Lamare and A. Gupta (2013), 'The effects of gender on awards in employment arbitration cases: the experience in the securities industry', *Industrial Relations*, **52** (S1), 314–42.

Marchington, M. and J. Suter (2013), 'Where informality really matters: patterns of employee involvement and participation (EIP) in a non-union firm', *Industrial Relations*, **52**, 284–313.

Marsden, D. (2013), 'Individual voice in employment relationships: a comparison under different forms of workplace representation', *Industrial Relations*, **52**, 221–58.

Olson-Buchanan, J.B. (1996), 'Voicing discontent: what happens to the grievance filer after the grievance?', *Journal of Applied Psychology*, **81**, 1–11.

Pfeffer, J. (1998), *The Human Equation: Building Profits by Putting People First*, Boston, MA: Harvard Business School Press.

Rees, A. (1977), *The Economics of Trade Unions*, revised edn, Chicago: University of Chicago Press.

Rusbelt, C.E., D. Farrell, G. Rogers and A.G. Mainous, III (1988), 'Impact of variables on exit, voice, loyalty and neglect: an integrative model of responses to declining job satisfaction', *Academy of Management Journal*, **31**, 599–627.

Smith, A. (1776), *The Wealth of Nations: An Inquiry into the Nature and Causes of the Wealth of Nations*, London: Strahan and Caddell.

Tawney, R.H. (1926), *Religion and the Rise of Capitalism*, London: John Murray.

18 Task-based voice: teamworking, autonomy and performance
Stephen Procter and Jos Benders

INTRODUCTION

In this chapter we look at how the idea of voice can be applied to the actual work that employees do. In other words, how much say do employees have in deciding what tasks they perform and how they perform them? We shall see in the first main section of the chapter how current trends in the restructuring of work – particularly the development of team-based systems – are, on the face of it, consistent with, and to some degree actually based on, the enhancement of employee voice (or, as we shall also call it, autonomy or discretion). A full picture, however, requires that we take a number of qualifying considerations into account. In the next section we look at how issues of autonomy play out in work systems based on 'lean' principles, in which task-based voice appears to be largely absent. We then address the implications for management of giving employees a greater say in how their work is conducted, before looking at the relationship between employee voice at an individual and at a team level and, finally, at the relationship between task-based voice and organizational performance. We conclude the chapter by drawing together these various threads and, in doing so, we try to identify the areas in which organizational practice and academic research might most usefully be focused.

TASK-BASED VOICE IN (SEMI-)AUTONOMOUS WORKING GROUPS

Any examination of the contemporary restructuring of work organization shows the development of team-based systems to be at its core (Benders, 2005). Such systems are often based explicitly on the benefits that are claimed to arise from giving employees a greater say in how the day-to-day work of their organization is carried out. According to Sinclair (1992: 613), 'team theorists almost inexorably end up looking for decision-making as the predominant group work indicator'. We can thus see teamworking as part of the broader movement towards the greater direct involvement of employees in organizational decision-making. Whether we call this direct participation (Marchington and Wilkinson, 2000; Benders, 2005), employee involvement (Marchington, 2000), empowerment (Wilkinson, 1998) or voice (Marchington, 2007), the key argument is that the increasing volatility of markets and the acceleration of technological change make necessary an enhanced role for employees in decisions about how their work is organized. Increasingly this has meant a greater degree of autonomy at the level of the team. Marchington (2000), for example, explicitly considers teamworking as an extension of existing forms of employee involvement; while in Wilkinson's (1998) classification of forms of empowerment, 'task autonomy' is expected to involve the restructuring of work around semi-autonomous teams.

Teamworking and autonomy can also be seen as important parts of high performance work systems (HPWSs) (see Harley, Chapter 6 above). For Boxall and Purcell (2003: 103), attempts to foster employee commitment through these new systems are 'most usually achieved through the extensive adoption of teamworking as the fundamental building block of the organization'. Similarly, Appelbaum and Batt (1994) identify 'American Team Production' as one of the two major types of HPWS, its chief distinguishing characteristic being its emphasis on worker participation in decision-making.

The theoretical underpinnings of the association between teamworking and voice can be found in sociotechnical systems (STS) theory, and, in particular, in its concept of the autonomous work group (AWG). As Manz (1992: 1121) argues, the 'joint optimization' of the social and technical aspects of the organization of work usually involves a 'shift in focus from individual to group methods'. Underlying this is 'the view that a group can more effectively apply its resources to address work condition variances within the group than can individual employees working separately' (1992: 1121).

These ideas provide us with a theoretical understanding of teamworking, but this is not the same thing as saying that teamworking in practice is always the result of their application. Certainly – although the linkage may sometimes be no more than superficial (Thompson and Wallace, 1996) – we can see cases in which STS theory has played a direct role in the introduction of teamworking (Benders and Van Hootegem, 1999), but there are a number of sources from which the rationale for teamworking might emerge. Buchanan (2000) shows how the early development of STS theory in the 1950s was itself based on pre-existing arrangements of work which had emerged spontaneously in such settings as coal mines and textile mills. The move towards autonomous teams has taken place under a variety of labels. In the UK, for example, cellular manufacturing was one of the most important channels through which teamworking was introduced in the 1980s and 1990s (Benders and Van Hootegem, 1999). We have also seen customer- or product-focused teams emerging as part of such developments as 'business process reengineering' (Hammer and Champy, 1993) and 'strategic segmentation' (Batt, 2000). In the same vein, Mueller et al. (2000) identify a number of discrete 'trajectories' for teamworking, amongst which STS theory lines up alongside 'humanization of work' and 'employee involvement'.

Under whatever label we use, what we have at first sight is a broad, positive alignment. We can see the restructuring of work around teams, on the one hand, and the extension of autonomy or voice, on the other, both as good things in themselves; even better, therefore, that we can see them so closely linked together. A deeper examination, however, reveals that the picture is not quite so simple.

THE ISSUE OF AUTONOMY: EMPLOYEE VOICE UNDER 'LEAN' PRINCIPLES

A first concern arises when we consider one of the main headings under which work and organizations are being restructured. We have seen in recent years the widespread application of 'lean' principles, particularly in healthcare and the public sector. Leading examples in healthcare can be found in the USA, Australia and the UK (Radnor et al., 2012). Some commentators have seen in lean a way of transforming the operation and performance of organizations (for example, Fillingham, 2007). At the other extreme are those such as Carter et al. (2011), who argue that lean is effective only to the extent that it degrades work and removes from employees any discretion they had been able to exercise.

While current developments are focused on healthcare and the public sector, the principles of lean are rooted in the Japanese automotive industry and, in particular, in the way these were captured in the 1990 book, *The Machine that Changed the World* (Womack et al., 1990; see Holweg, 2006). Although based largely on the just-in-time (JIT) principles of operations management under the Toyota production system (TPS), Womack et al. argued that the essence of lean production lay in the way that employees are organized and managed: 'in the end', they say (1990: 99), 'it is the dynamic work team that emerges as the heart of the lean factory'.

These 'lean' teams, however, appear to be something very different to the kind of teams identified in the previous section of this chapter. The expression of voice which characterizes the AWG appears here to be almost wholly absent. At one level this raises questions about how we define a team or teamworking: what Benders and Van Hootegem (1999) call the 'issue of autonomy' (see also Procter and Currie, 2004). The issue is that if we rely on the exercise of voice or autonomy to define what teamworking is, then this means that some forms of work organization, especially the lean teams, cannot be considered to be teams at all.

There are a number of ways in which this issue can be approached. One line of argument is that we should include within a team's autonomy the discretion exercised by the team leader (Benders and Van Hootegem, 1999; see also Delbridge et al., 2000). Although this allows the lean teams to be considered autonomous, it does so only by stretching the conception of autonomy almost to breaking point. We shall return later in this chapter to look specifically at issues of management and supervision. Another possibility is to 'solve the issue of autonomy by considering it as a variable rather than as a defining characteristic' (Benders and Van Hootegem, 1999: 618). This is the position taken by, for example, Mueller (1994: 383–4). Even if we treat autonomy as a variable, we still have a situation in which groups with greater degrees of autonomy are seen as being stronger or more pure forms of team than those in which autonomy is more limited. Koch and Buhl (2001), for example, distinguish between 'strong' and 'weak' teams, with the latter characterized by 'little development of autonomy and decision latitude' (2001: 165).

For the purposes of this chapter we do not need to be so concerned with this particular 'issue of autonomy'. Instead we can identify and compare the different forms that autonomy takes in the two approaches to teamworking that we have looked at above. A major difference between lean or Japanese production and sociotechnical ideas concerns standardization by means of standard operating procedures (SOPs). If work is to be done in a standard way, what should this standard way be and, more importantly, who should decide it? Whereas SOPs are emphasized as the basis for continuous improvement by a number of Japanese authors (for example, Ohno, 1988), they are criticized by Berggren (1993) as an impediment to worker autonomy. From a technical viewpoint, SOPs can be seen as being at odds with the sociotechnical principle of 'minimal critical specification' (Cherns, 1987: 155), which holds that one should not specify what does not need to be specified. This principle came to be formulated as a reaction against the Tayloristic prescription of having engineers formulate SOPs, leaving workers merely to execute them. Operating in this way can be very inefficient, it is argued, especially in turbulent production environments. Thus, rather than waste time waiting for an engineer to arrive, workers should be given the authority to intervene themselves.

The autonomy enjoyed by employees is, in a sense, taken a stage further under lean systems. SOPs were embraced in Japan as a learning mechanism and as a basis for continuous improvement (*kaizen*): it was stressed that workers themselves rather than engineers should design the SOPs. This can be seen as an important factor in Japanese companies gaining a competitive edge in repetitive manufacturing industries such as electronics and cars (Young, 1992). Sociotechnical theorists have discarded SOPs altogether as being at odds with minimal critical specification and local autonomy. Unfortunately, although sociotechnical systems design (STSD) supports the generic notion of continuous improvement (Van Amelsvoort and Scholtes, 1993) it has no clear view on how to achieve this.

Indeed, in the Toyota production system workers are not only given the opportunity but are even expected to question the prevailing SOP. This has been labelled 'democratic Taylorism' (Adler and Cole, 1993) and is seen as a major source of employee involvement: through suggesting changes workers may influence their own working situation. From a sociotechnical point of view it could be argued that this involvement is very limited: workers may suggest changes to the norm, but may not change the norm on their own authority. Against this, it could in turn be countered that the employee's position at the heart of the production process makes their suggestions more influential than is implied by the formal decision-making process.

GIVING EMPLOYEES VOICE: THE IMPLICATIONS FOR MANAGEMENT

As well as looking at the different forms that an enhanced employee voice or autonomy might take, we need to look at its implications for those in the organizational hierarchy. What does a greater say for employees imply for those who currently determine how work is done? At one level this is an issue of broad management style. Giving employees greater voice might seem to necessitate a move away from 'command and control' and towards a more open and participative style. The problems involved in doing so can be seen when we look at the way in which the extension of voice is planned and introduced. Again we can draw on the principles of sociotechnical design, the first one being that '[the] process of design must be compatible with its objectives' (Cherns, 1976: 785). Using Fox's (1974) terminology, we can say that because teamworking assumes all the characteristics of a high-discretion syndrome, its introduction as well as its operation requires the use of high-trust management. Procter et al.'s (1995) study of the introduction of team-based cellular working in two parts of a large engineering concern shows how its failure in one of these was associated with a closed and uncommunicative style of management. Relationships between employees can also be an issue. In Ezzamel and Willmott's (1998) study of a clothing manufacturer, for example, the idea of workers supervising each other was frustrated, with some employees being unwilling to take on managerial responsibility for those they saw as fellow workers.

The implications for management might in any case be felt most acutely at the first-line or supervisory level. Townsend (Chapter 10 above) shows how management at this level can be important in the informal aspects of the operation of employee voice. Gittell (2009) also points to the dangers of simply assuming that the removal of first-line managers will lead to 'empowered' workers and better decisions. Especially when work is structured on a highly interdependent basis, she argues, there might be benefit in investing in closer and more proactive supervision. If we are looking at the extension of voice through the development of team-based systems of work, then these considerations form part of a more specific question: what is or should be the role of the team leader? In looking at this question we are faced immediately with Manz and Sims's (1986) 'paradox': if the essential characteristic of teams is their self-management, what role is there for the external management of teams? Manz and Sims's (1987) own research suggested that a legitimate role exists in getting the team to manage itself, and they identified a number of 'leader behaviours' – such as the encouragement of self-observation and self-evaluation – which form part of this. On their own admission they provide no evidence of a link between this role and team performance, and Cohen et al.'s (1996) study was also unable to provide evidence of its effectiveness.

Despite this, there is a widespread belief that the transition from supervisor to team leader involves a change of style – from 'cop' to 'coach', as it is sometimes expressed. In practice, however, this might be very difficult to achieve. This is in part because of the difficulties in finding people to fill the team leader role (Procter et al., 1995). If operations are reorganized along team-based lines, the obvious people to fill the new roles are those who were previously working as supervisors. In some cases these may be considered to be exactly the wrong people to take on the new position, schooled as they are in a very different tradition. At the same time it may be difficult to develop team leaders from members of the team; while bringing in team leaders from outside can be the cause of resentment amongst existing staff.

In parallel to the previous section, we can draw a distinction between different traditions. While STS theory would prescribe the leaderless group implied by Manz and Sims's (1986) paradox, lean or Japanese-influenced teams are characterized by the presence of a strong leader – and indeed have been described as leader-guided teams (LGTs) to distinguish them from AWGs (autonomous work groups). This can give rise to problems for the aggregation level to which the notion of 'autonomy' is applied. In the LGT decision-making is concentrated with the leader, so that the unit as a whole may have a large autonomy while individual team members have little formal decision-making power (Delbridge et al., 2000). Within the AWG decisions are to be taken jointly, although a certain horizontal differentiation can exist and may also be recommended (Van Eijnatten, 1993).

As Townsend (see Chapter 10 above) demonstrates, it is not just at the level of the team leader that we need to consider the relationship between employee voice and management. Those in middle management positions are also likely to face their own particular set of pressures. Their active involvement in the process might be essential for the successful enhancement of employee voice; yet the same enhancement of voice might be a threat to their own position. From a senior management point of view, the issue is whether their middle-level colleagues have the ability to effect change; for the middle managers themselves, it is more a question of whether they have the power to resist. Batt (2004) goes so far as to place these issues of management at the heart of our understanding of the rationale for, and impact of, extending employee voice through the restructuring of work. In her account of a US telecoms company she shows how consideration needs to be given to the effect on all occupational groups, not just those who are members of the new teams. Those in middle management positions felt their positions to be under pressure: the proposed self-managing teams were seen as a direct threat to their authority. Their ability to resist change, moreover, argues Batt, provides an alternative explanation for the failure of teamworking to diffuse quickly across the US economy. Rather than this being the result of economically rational decisions, Batt claims that an explicitly political perspective provides a much better explanation.

INDIVIDUAL EMPLOYEE VOICE AND TEAM VOICE

What the discussion of different first-line management roles also points up is that autonomy can exist at a number of different levels. When we talk about autonomy it is all too easy to collapse these levels into one, and thus either ignore any distinctions or – to the extent that distinctions are recognized – simply assume that greater autonomy on the part of the team, say, is associated with greater autonomy on the part of the individual team member. A more complex picture emerges when we relax this assumption and address the issue in a direct way.

One focus of research has been the relationship between team autonomy and individual autonomy. Van Mierlo et al. (2006), for example, found that there was a broadly positive relationship between the two forms of autonomy, with the degree of social support acting as an important moderating variable. A study of four Danish organizations undertaken by Jonsson and Jeppesen (2013) followed up on this. They also found a broadly positive relationship, but one for which they were unable to identify any moderating variables.

Indeed, that a distinction can and should be made between team autonomy and individual autonomy is one way of understanding a critical perspective on the impact of work restructuring. From this perspective, teamworking results not in autonomy but in a change in the nature of control: individuals are now controlled by the team rather than being controlled directly by management. In Barker's (1993) account of change in a US manufacturing company, for example, teamworking involves a move away from a rational, bureaucratic form of management control, and, in its place, the emergence of 'concertive' control, in which team members' actions are controlled by normative rules which they themselves establish. Enhanced voice in this case was thus seen to lead to a 'tightening [of] the iron cage', the control exercised by the team being all the more effective because of its lack of visibility. Sewell (1998) reinforced this interpretation on the basis of a similar workplace study. In addition to the 'concertive control' identified by Barker, he stressed the 'panoptical' or all-seeing aspects of the team-based system.

The relationship between team and individual autonomy has also been used to understand the link between teamworking and organizational performance. Kirkman and Rosen's (1999) study of 'empowered' and 'autonomous' teams concluded that 'what is needed most now in the team effectiveness literature is research that examines empower-ment at the individual and team levels simultaneously' (1999: 70).

Taking up this theme, and drawing on large-scale UK workplace data, Harley (2001) found that employees who work in autonomous teams did not report a significantly more positive experience of work than those who were not working in any kind of team. In particular, they reported no greater a level of discretion. For Harley, this called into question '[both] the assumption . . . that teamwork enhances discretion and the extension of that assumption to the belief that it is via discretion that other positive outcomes arise' (2001: 735). Harley's findings need also to be seen within the broader question of the link between employee voice and organizational performance, and it is to this question that we now turn.

VOICE AND ORGANIZATIONAL PERFORMANCE

We look finally at the question of organizational performance. In trying to establish the existence and nature of any link between teamworking (or work restructuring more widely) and organizational performance, we are, of course, faced with a host of conceptual and empirical issues. The most basic of these is the question of what pre-cisely we mean by performance. In the wider context of high performance work systems (HPWS), this question has received a good deal of explicit attention (see Procter, 2008). As Ichniowski et al. (1996) point out, while the use of financial measures of performance might be preferred on the grounds that this is what decisions about work are often aimed at affecting, the effect of any particular change is likely to be difficult to isolate. Operational performance measures (for example, Appelbaum et al., 2000), on the other hand, while possibly having a more direct link with changes in work, might be expected to be more varied across sectors, thus making it more difficult to make comparisons between different settings. In the context of teamworking, Delarue et al.'s (2008) review of survey-based research on the link with performance showed that, in fact, the same positive association was found in both studies using financial measures and those using operational ones.

Beyond the question of what we mean by performance, Harley (Chapter 6 above) points to the inherent difficulties involved in determining whether or not any relation-ship exists between performance and workplace change. In particular, he argues, most studies rely on a cross-sectional design which makes causality very difficult to establish. Most studies of the impact of high performance work systems, moreover, do not allow for the identification of the impact of particular voice mechanisms or other individual 'high performance' practices. If we focus on teamworking as a form of employee voice whose impact is easier to isolate, however, there are a number of reasons why we might expect a relationship to exist with organizational performance. As we have seen, the sociotechnical systems theory (STS) view of autonomous work groups is not just that these provide a better experience for employees, but that 'a group can more effectively apply its resources to address work condition variances within the group than can indi-vidual employees working separately' (Manz, 1992: 1121). Other perspectives simply tend to confine their attention to the motivational impact of the kinds of jobs associated with teamworking. In this view, self-managing teams are characterized by 'Work high in task variety, autonomy, identity, significance, and feedback [which] foster[s] internal work motivation, which in turn leads to high performance and satisfaction' (Cohen and Ledford, 1994: 14).

This association between, on the one hand, the organization of work on the basis of autonomous teams and, on the other, the type of jobs individuals have within these teams, is one that raises important conceptual issues. As Cohen and Ledford (1994) point out, the type of work undertaken by individuals under teamworking is very similar to that recommended by the job characteristics model (JCM) of Hackman and Oldham (1980). Because the JCM is applicable to the design of individual jobs, it can be difficult to isolate the effects that teamworking in itself might have. This means that it can be hard to identify a single channel through which the extension of autonomy is of influence on performance. The similarities in what STS theory and the JCM imply for job design have led to calls for them to be brought together in a single approach (Cohen and Ledford, 1994). Even if this was done, it would still make sense to try and differentiate between, on one side, the effect the introduction of teamworking might have through the redesign of individual jobs and, on the other, its effect through the redesign of work structures at an organizational level.

Empirical evidence is mixed regarding the proposition that autonomy provides the link between enhanced employee voice and performance. Bacon and Blyton's (2000) study of teamworking in the UK steel industry distinguishes between what they call 'high-road' and 'low-road' teamworking with the 'high road' including teams whose work was characterized by such things as task variety, identification with team tasks and the power to make decisions. Across a range of outcomes the high-road teams were found to outperform their low-road counterparts. Cohen and Ledford (1994), however, found that while the introduction of self-managed teams in a US telecommunications company resulted in significant improvements, this was restricted to those aspects of performance to which the intervention was most directly related.

Procter and Burridge (2008) used the UK's Workplace Employment Relations Survey (WERS) to address this teamworking–performance relationship. Their conclusions were, first, that a positive association did exist between performance and the *extent* of teamworking within the workplace, and, second, that there was also a relationship between performance and the *intensity* of teamworking. Once teamworking was established, in other words, there seemed to be some additional benefit from giving these teams a greater degree of autonomy or voice.

These findings need to be considered alongside the studies of Ramsay et al. (2000) and Harley (2001). Ramsay et al.'s (2000) analysis of the same WERS data established the existence of an association between performance and the existence of a 'high perform-ance' work system. The problem for Ramsay et al. was that this association could not be explained in terms of a more positive experience of work on the part of those working under such systems. As we have already seen, Harley (2001), on the other hand, found that members of the more autonomous teams did not themselves report higher levels of discretion than employees in other workplaces who were not members of teams of any sort. On the face of it, this is inconsistent with Procter and Burridge's (2008) finding that differences in performance between workplaces can in part be explained by differences in the degree of autonomy possessed by the type of team in operation. To reconcile these two things it seems that we must return to the distinction between individual and team voice. There must be some distinction between what individuals experience as discretion and what teams exercise as autonomy. An employee might well feel that they have as little individual discretion when decisions are made at a team level, as they do when they are made at the level of the workplace.

More broadly, Procter and Burridge's (2008) study might also allow us to say something about the 'transmission mechanism' through which voice has an impact on performance. Harley's (2001: 722–5) discussion of 'competing accounts' of team-based forms of operation distinguishes between the 'positive' and the 'critical'. Both, he concludes, 'may have overstated the impact' of teamworking (2001: 739), but it is specifically the former, he argues, that is undermined by his findings on employee discretion. Included in what Hayley characterizes as the 'positive' account are, *inter alia*, both the sociotechnical systems (STS) theory and the job characteristics model (JCM). While it might be accepted that the JCM implies that teamworking works in the way that Harley describes, the same is not true of STS theory. As we have seen, the emphasis in the latter is on the organizational flexibility facilitated by teamworking rather than the motivational impact of the design of individual jobs. The apparent inconsistency between Harley's findings and those of Procter and Burridge does at least suggest that STS theory should be given more serious consideration in attempts to understand the relationship between employee voice and organizational performance.

CONCLUSIONS

From our review we can see the importance of direct, task-based forms of employee voice. While the concept of voice is often associated with more indirect, representative forms of employee involvement or participation, the impact on employees is likely to be more keenly felt as a result of the degree and nature of control they have over the work they do. As we have seen, the appeal of systems of work based on autonomous teams is not difficult to understand in this context. They appear to offer both better work for employees and better performance for employers.

Further investigation, of course, reveals a more complex picture. If we look at 'lean' as the most prominent current manifestation of team-based working, then we have a form of teamworking in which autonomy appears largely to be absent. There are a number of ways in which this 'issue of autonomy' can be addressed, perhaps the most fruitful of which is to look at the different forms that autonomy can take. Under 'lean', therefore, an employee, or even a team, might have little direct discretion in how they do their own job, but they might have a significant, though indirect, say in how employees as a whole perform their work.

In looking at the enhancement of voice, we need to look also at its effects on management. For the forms of work organization we are concerned with here, this is in part a question of what is implied in the role of team leader, but there are implications as well for middle-level managers as a whole. For these 'linchpins' of the organization, teamworking is very much a double-edged sword: although central to the successful implementation of organizational change, middle managers might at the same time see their own positions as under threat.

As all these discussions imply, employee voice in the form of 'autonomy' or 'discretion' is itself a far from unproblematic concept. As we have seen, an important issue here is the relationship between individual discretion and team autonomy. Rather than the two things going hand-in-hand, we can see from both a conceptual and an empirical viewpoint how the latter might be enhanced at the expense of the former.

This, in turn, leads us to the question of how, if at all, employee voice is linked to organizational performance. Even if there is a body of evidence to suggest that a positive relationship does exist between the two things, there are two reasons why we need to treat it with caution. First, we need to be much clearer on *why* such a relationship exists. In particular, does any effect come through the simple aggregation of increased effort on the part of individual employees, or is the more important factor the structural properties of teams? Second, we need to establish *where* such a relationship exists. More specifically we need to guard against the inference that just because a positive relationship has been established between voice and performance, the enhancement of voice will cause performance to improve in any circumstances. Not only does this give to predominantly cross-sectional, quantitative analysis a quite unwarranted degree of predictive power, it takes no account of why voice might not be well developed in the first place.

Looking forward, where might research effort best be placed? Our review of existing work in this area suggests four related sets of questions:

- What do current manifestations of team-based working imply for employee voice? In particular, in what ways does current 'lean' differ in its implications from the automotive-sector-based ideas of 'lean production'?
- Is it possible to distinguish between a number of different 'transmission mechanisms' through which voice might be of effect on organizational performance? If so, which are the most important and what is the implication of this for our conceptual understanding?
- What is the relationship between individual voice and team voice? Again, what are the implications of this for our understanding of voice?
- How can we explain the limited rate of 'diffusion' of work systems based on enhanced employee autonomy or voice? In particular, following Batt (2004), do we need to understand this in a political as well as an economic context?

REFERENCES

Adler, P. and R. Cole (1993), 'Designed for learning: a tale of two auto plants', *California Management Review*, **36** (1), 85–94.

Appelbaum, E. and R. Batt (1994), *The New American Workplace*, Ithaca, NY: ILR Press.

Appelbaum, E., T. Bailey, P. Berg and A. Kalleberg (2000), *Manufacturing Advantage: Why High Performance Work Systems Pay Off*, Ithaca NY: ILR Press.

Bacon, N. and P. Blyton (2000), 'High road and low road teamworking: perceptions of management rationales and organizational and human resource outcomes', *Human Relations*, **53**, 1425–58.

Barker, J. (1993), 'Tightening the iron cage: concertive control in self-managing teams', *Administrative Science Quarterly*, **38**, 408–37.

Batt, R. (2000), 'Strategic segmentation in front-line services: matching customers, employees and human resource systems', *International Journal of Human Resource Management*, **11** (3), 540–61.

Batt, R. (2004), 'Who benefits from teams? Comparing workers, supervisors and managers', *Industrial Relations*, **43** (1), 183–212.

Benders, J. (2005), 'Team working: a tale of partial participation', in B. Harley, J. Hyman and P. Thompson (eds), *Participation and Democracy at Work*, Basingstoke: Palgrave Macmillan, pp. 55–74.

Benders, J. and Van Hootegem, G. (1999), 'Teams and their context: moving the team discussion beyond existing dichotomies', *Journal of Management Studies*, **36** (5), 609–28.

Berggren, C. (1993), *The Volvo Experience: Alternatives to Lean Production in the Swedish Auto Industry*, London: Macmillan.

Boxall, P. and J. Purcell (2003), *Strategy and Human Resource Management*, Basingstoke: Palgrave Macmillan.

Buchanan, D. (2000), 'An eager and enduring embrace: the ongoing rediscovery of teamworking as a management idea', in S. Procter and F. Mueller (eds), *Teamworking*, London: Macmillan, pp. 25–42.

Carter, B., A. Danford, D. Howcroft, H. Richardson, A. Smith and P. Taylor (2011), 'Lean and mean in the civil service: the case of processing in HMRC', *Public Money and Management*, **31** (2), 115–22.

Cherns, A. (1976), 'The principles of sociotechnical design', *Human Relations*, **29** (8), 783–92.

Cherns, A. (1987), 'Principles of sociotechnical design revisited', *Human Relations*, **40** (3), 153–62.

Cohen, S. and G. Ledford (1994), 'The effectiveness of self-managing teams: a quasi-experiment', *Human Relations*, **47** (1), 13–42.

Cohen, S., G. Ledford and G. Spreitzer (1996), 'A predictive model of self-managing work team effectiveness', *Human Relations*, **49** (5), 643–76.

Delarue, A., G. Van Hootegem, S. Procter and M. Burridge (2008), 'Teamworking and organizational performance: a review of survey-based research', *International Journal of Management Reviews*, **10** (2), 127–48.

Delbridge, R., J. Lowe and N. Oliver (2000), 'Worker autonomy in lean teams: evidence from the world automotive components industry', in S. Procter and F. Mueller (eds), *Teamworking*, London: Macmillan, pp. 125–42.

Ezzamel, M. and H. Willmott (1998), 'Accounting for teamwork: a critical study of group-based systems of organizational control', *Administrative Science Quarterly*, **43**, 358–96.

Fillingham, D. (2007), 'Can lean save lives?', *Leadership in Health Services*, **20** (4), 231–41.

Fox, A. (1974), *Beyond Contract: Work, Power and Trust Relations*, London: Faber & Faber.

Gittell, J. (2009), *High Performance Healthcare: Using the Power of Relationships to Achieve Quality, Efficiency and Resilience*, New York: McGraw Hill.

Hammer, M. and J. Champy (1993), *Reengineering the Corporation: A Manifesto for Business Revolution*, London: Nicholas Brealey.

Harley, B. (2001), 'Team membership and the experience of work in Britain: an analysis of the WERS98 data', *Work, Employment and Society*, **15**, 721–42.

Holweg, M. (2006), 'The genealogy of lean production', *Journal of Operations Management*, **25**, 420–37.

Hackman, J. and G. Oldham (1980), *Work Redesign*, Reading, MA: Addison-Wesley.

Ichniowski, C., T. Kochan, D. Levine, C. Olson and G. Strauss (1996), 'What works at work: overview and assessment', *Industrial Relations*, **35** (3), 299–333.

Jonsson, T. and H. Jeppesen (2013), 'Under the influence of the team? An investigation of the relationships between team autonomy, individual autonomy and social influence within teams', *International Journal of Human Resource Management*, **24** (1), 78–93.

Kirkman, B. and B. Rosen (1999), 'Beyond self-management: antecedents and consequences of team empowerment', *Academy of Management Journal*, **42**, 58–74.

Koch, C. and H. Buhl (2001), 'ERP-supported teamworking in Danish manufacturing?', *New Technology, Work and Employment*, **16** (3), 164–77.

Manz, C. (1992), 'Self-leading work teams: moving beyond self-management myths', *Human Relations*, **45** (11), 1119–40.

Manz, C. and H. Sims (1986), 'Leading self-managed groups: a conceptual analysis of a paradox', *Economic and Industrial Democracy*, **7**, 141–65.

Manz, C. and H. Sims (1987), 'Leading workers to lead themselves: the external leadership of self-managing work teams', *Administrative Science Quarterly*, **32** (1), 106–28.

Marchington, M. (2000), 'Teamworking and employee involvement: terminology, evaluation and context', in S. Procter and F. Mueller (eds), *Teamworking*, London: Macmillan, pp. 60–80.

Marchington, M. (2007), 'Employee voice systems', in P. Boxall, J. Purcell and P. Wright (eds), *Oxford Handbook of Human Resource Management*, Oxford: Oxford University Press, pp. 231–50.

Marchington, M. and A. Wilkinson (2000), 'Direct participation', in S. Bach and K. Sisson (eds), *Personnel Management: A Comprehensive Guide to Theory and Practice*, 3rd edn, Oxford: Blackwell, pp. 340–64.

Mueller, F. (1994), 'Teams between hierarchy and commitment: change strategies and the "internal environment"', *Journal of Management Studies*, **31** (3), 383–404.

Mueller, F., S. Procter and D. Buchanan (2000), 'Teamworking in its context(s), antecedents, nature and dimensions', *Human Relations*, **53** (11), 1387–424.

Ohno, T. (1988) *Toyota Production System: Beyond Large-Scale Production*, Cambridge: Productivity Press.

Procter, S. (2008), 'New forms of work and the high performance paradigm', in P. Blyton, N. Bacon, J. Fiorito and E. Heery (eds), *SAGE Handbook of Industrial Relations*, London: Sage, pp. 149–69.

Procter, S. and M. Burridge (2008), 'Teamworking and performance: the extent and intensity of teamworking in the 1998 UK Workplace Employee Relations Survey (WERS98)', *International Journal of Human Resource Management*, **19** (1), 153–68.

Procter, S. and G. Currie (2004), 'Target-based teamworking: groups, work and interdependence in the UK civil service', *Human Relations*, **57** (12), 1547–72.

Procter, S., J. Hassard and M. Rowlinson (1995), 'Introducing cellular manufacturing: operations, human resources and high-trust dynamics', *Human Resource Management Journal*, **5** (2), 46–64.

Radnor, Z., M. Holweg and J. Waring (2012), 'Lean in healthcare: the unfilled promise?', *Social Science and Medicine*, **74**, 364–71.

Ramsay, H., D. Scholarios and B. Harley (2000), 'Employees and high-performance work systems: testing inside the black box', *British Journal of Industrial Relations*, **38**, 501–31.

Sewell, G. (1998), 'The discipline of teams: the control of team-based industrial work through electronic and peer surveillance', *Administrative Science Quarterly*, **43** (2), 397–428.

Sinclair, A. (1992), 'The tyranny of a team ideology', *Organization Studies*, **13** (4), 611–26.

Thompson, P. and T. Wallace (1996), 'Redesigning production through teamworking: case studies from the Volvo Truck Corporation', *International Journal of Operations and Production Management*, **16** (2), 103–18.

Van Amelsvoort, P. and G. Scholtes (1993), *Zelfsturende Teams; Ontwerpen, Invoeren en Begeleiden*, Oss: ST-groep.

Van Eijnatten, F. (1993), *The Paradigm that Changed the Work Place*, Stockholm/Assen: Arbetslivscentrum/van Gorcum.

Van Mierlo, H., C. Rutte, J. Vermunt, M. Kompier and J. Doorewaard (2006), 'Individual autonomy in work teams: the role of team autonomy, self-efficacy, and social support', *European Journal of Work and Organizational Psychology*, **15** (3), 281–99.

Wilkinson, A. (1998), 'Empowerment: theory and practice', *Personnel Review*, **27** (1), 40–56.

Womack, J., D. Jones and D. Roos (1990), *The Machine That Changed the World*, New York: Rawson Associates.

Young, S. (1992), 'A framework for successful adoption and performance of Japanese manufacturing practices in the United States', *Academy of Management Review*, **17** (4), 677–700.

19 Workplace partnership
Stewart Johnstone

INTRODUCTION

This chapter explores one of the most topical debates concerning representative forms of voice of the last two decades: the notion of 'workplace partnership'. In simple terms, the notion of workplace partnership is concerned with developing collaborative relationships between employment relations actors, especially between trade unions and employers, as part of a quest for mutual gains outcomes (Kochan and Osterman, 1994). The surge of academic and policy interest in partnership can be related to earlier debates regarding employee representation, and in particular the potential benefits and costs of trade unions as a form of governance in organizations (Freeman and Medoff, 1984). While trade unions can be viewed as negative forces that distort labour market outcomes, they can also be viewed as institutions that can positively influence both productivity and equality outcomes in organizations (Freeman and Medoff, 1984). From this perspective, trade unions are about much more than determining economic (wage) outcomes; they are also concerned with organizational processes such as the expression of worker voice, and can potentially make positive contributions to organizations, as well as to the functioning of the broader economic and social system (Johnstone and Wilkinson, 2013).

This chapter comprises four main sections. The first section explores the meaning of partnership, as the term has become contested and conceptually ambiguous, despite widespread usage internationally in both academic and policy circles. It then presents some theoretical perspectives on partnership, and suggests that partnership can be interpreted in very different ways and that the frames of reference developed by Fox (1966) remain useful in this respect. It also helps illustrate how the notion of workplace partnership draws upon both continental European traditions of employee representation and US-influenced debates regarding HRM generally and in particular the 'high performance' variant. The second section considers the case for and against partnership, and outlines some of the main controversies. The third section then maps some international experiences with partnership, looking at the UK, Ireland, Australia and New Zealand. The fourth section reviews some of the evidence on the outcomes of partnership, focusing particularly on the experiences of the UK and Ireland, while the final section draws some conclusions and assesses the future of partnership as a form of employee voice.

WHAT IS WORKPLACE PARTNERSHIP?

Defining Workplace Partnership

Over the last two decades, the term 'workplace partnership' has become ubiquitous in both policy and practice circles and has also attracted a significant amount of academic research. Yet despite the intensity of debates, the term has remained conceptually ambiguous and contested. It is important at the outset, given the loose and fluid nature of the term, that we evaluate some of the interpretations of 'partnership'. However, before we do this, it is useful to briefly consider broader developments regarding employee participation. 'Participation' is often used as an umbrella term for a heterogeneous array of practices associated with employee voice and employee representation that acknowledge the various contradictions and strategic tensions that characterize the management of work and people (Boxall and Purcell, 2008). As a result of these tensions, the employment relationship is essentially 'contested' (Edwards, 2003), balancing dual demands from employers for both 'control and commitment' (Walton, 1985) and 'control and consent' (Hyman, 1987). Managing these tensions has long been a priority of employers, and the search for cooperation has a long history regarding the regulation of the employment relationship. Clearly, there are a wide range of options available to employers regarding how they choose to manage the sometimes contradictory tensions which characterize the employment relationship.

Thirty years ago, Purcell and Sisson (1983) devised a typology of five management styles based on the extent to which unitarism and pluralism were emphasized. They suggest that a unitarist management style could either be authoritarian in character, with workers excluded from decision-making, or paternalistic, characterized by a more sophisticated but individualistic approach to HRM. Alternatively, from a pluralist perspective, there could be a greater emphasis on collective employment relations, normally involving trade unions. Union–management relations could be either arm's length and adversarial, which they term the 'sophisticated modern constitutional' approach, or based on a more flexible and problem-solving approach, which they termed the 'sophisticated modern consultative' approach. In many ways, it is the latter that best represents contemporary debates about workplace 'partnership' as a form of employee voice.

Yet while the idea of cooperative union–management relations is far from new, the exact meaning of workplace partnership in modern workplaces has remained both ambiguous and contested, and a commonly accepted definition has remained somewhat elusive. Partnership has thus been described as 'an idea with which almost anyone can agree without having any clear idea of what they are agreeing about' (Guest and Peccei, 2001: 207). The ambiguity and fluidity of the term probably explains in part why the partnership concept has been both popular and controversial.

Nevertheless, several key aspects can be discerned from the literature on partnership. Firstly, and in contrast to some of the more unitarist and individualistic HRM literatures, the notion of workplace partnership returns to a focus upon understanding the collective dimensions of the employment relationship. In voice terms, partnership returns the focus to the importance and value of representative forms of employee voice. Partnership is also concerned less with micro-level HR techniques, and more with improving the overall quality of the employment relationship and workplace relations. The emphasis is on reducing conflict and increasing collaboration between stakeholders. Secondly, and again in contrast to some unitarist HRM debates, an analysis of the partnership literature reveals a concern with 'reciprocity', 'respect', 'legitimacy' and 'mutual gains'. Indeed, a core component of partnership is a dual concern with balancing the tensions of economic efficiency and competitiveness on the one hand, with ethical and fair employment conditions on the other (Martinez Lucio and Stuart, 2002).

While such a philosophy might be considered to be far from novel in many continental European nations, such as Germany (Frege and Kelly, 2004), the notion only gained traction in several Anglo-Saxon economies in the 1990s, inspired in part by approaches to employee participation and employment relations in Europe. However, the emphasis was less upon the societally-embedded, national-level social partnerships characteristic of more coordinated Germanic and Nordic economies. At a macro-level, social partnerships represent a particular and distinctive political and economic approach, with important implications for employment relations issues such as skills and training, and employee participation and representation. Such approaches are also underpinned by legislation and strong institutional supports, as well as established European traditions of industrial democracy and social dialogue.

Workplace partnership, however, is concerned more with employment relations at a workplace level. In the UK, two influential policy definitions were offered in the 1990s by the Trades Union Congress (TUC, 1999) and the Involvement and Participation Association (IPA, 1997), both of which defined partnership in terms of a particular set of principles and commitments regarding the conduct of workplace relations. The TUC definition included:

- Commitment to the success of the enterprise
- Recognizing legitimate interests
- Commitment to employment security
- Focus on the quality of working life
- Transparency
- Win-win.

The IPA definition included:

- Joint commitment to the success of the organization
- Joint recognition of each other's legitimate interests
- Joint commitment to employment security
- Joint focus on the quality of working life
- Joint commitment to operating in a transparent manner
- Joint commitment to adding value to the arrangement.

Academic definitions, however, tend to define workplace partnership in terms of a particular approach to organizational governance. Teague and Hann (2010) define partnership as:

> A method of governing an organisation so that corporate strategies incorporate the interests of both management and employees – the notion of mutual gains . . . fostering new forms of collaboration and joint action between management and employees. (Teague and Hann, 2010, 101)

It has been suggested that a more useful definition of partnership would also identify the association of practices and processes with partnership (Johnstone et al., 2009). In terms of practices, employee voice is central to all definitions, and this may involve a mix of direct participation, representative participation and financial involvement. However, most policy definitions identify representative voice as a central pillar of partnership. Often, independent trade unions are assumed to be the most appropriate vehicle for representative voice, though more inclusive definitions, such as those used by the UK government, the IPA and the Confederation of British Industry (CBI), have also allowed for the possibility of partnership in non-union contexts. In addition, workplace partnership as used in this sense is distinctive from the use of 'partnership' as a term to describe a particular model of ownership and organizational structure, such as that of the John Lewis Partnership in the UK. This does not preclude John Lewis from also having a partnership employment relations model, characterized by collaboration between employers and employees (see Cathcart, 2014 for a discussion). Besides (representative) employee voice, complementary HR practices often include mechanisms to support communication, flexibility and job security.

It is noteworthy that many of the complementary HR practices are similar to those normally identified as part of a 'high performance work system' or 'high commitment' approach to HRM, where the aim is to increase productivity by raising levels of employee commitment, and indeed some commentators draw parallels between partnership and a HPWS approach (for example, Appelbaum et al., 2000; Danford et al., 2005; Glover and Butler, 2012). Inclusive definitions inevitably mean the boundaries between partnership and other HRM approaches are blurred. Other commentators, therefore, offer narrower definitions that limit partnership to situations where a formal collective agreement, committed to enhancing cooperation between employers and independent trade unions and staff associations, is signed by an employer and an independent representative body (Bacon and Samuel, 2009: 232). They thus exclude the possibility of non-union forms of workplace partnership, in part reflecting a long-running suspicion of the motives and effectiveness of non-union participation in industrial relations. However, it is perhaps limiting to assume that partnership cannot occur in non-union contexts without first examining the empirical evidence (Ackers et al., 2005; Johnstone et al., 2010). Narrow definitions also exclude the possibility of 'informal partnerships' as part of what might be termed 'good industrial relations' or 'sophisticated HRM'. A potential limitation of such a tight definition, however, is that in most Anglo-Saxon economies workplace partnership is a voluntary agreement rather than a legislative requirement, and state regulation or inducement of partnership may be weak or non-existent (Macneil et al., 2011). It may therefore be preferable to allow for the possibility of informal partnerships and collaborative workplace relations which rely upon 'informal relationships', 'shared understandings' and 'cultural norms' (Dietz, 2004). More inclusive definitions of partnership would include not only formal *de jure* partnerships but also *de facto* partnerships which might have many similar characteristics, but without expressly engaging with the politicized language of partnership.

In terms of processes, decision-making processes and the nature of actor relationships are crucial. Partnership rejects autocratic management styles; decision-making processes are expected to be highly participative with extensive dialogue and consultation between management, employees and their representatives at an early stage. Actor relationships thus require high levels of trust, openness and transparency, as well as an overall commitment to joint problem-solving in a way that is constructive and ultimately supportive of business success. Arm's length adversarialism is believed to be counter to the partnership ethos and the aim is shifting collective employment relations towards a problem-solving approach (Bacon and Storey, 2000).

Finally, partnership is often associated with particular employment relations outcomes, such as 'adding value' or 'sharing success'. Other outcomes typically cited in the partnership literature include job security, employee satisfaction, work-life balance and improved organizational performance. Nevertheless, these must be thought of as aspirations that can be explored and tested empirically, rather than components of the partnership process. Partnership may concern an attempt to attain these outcomes, irrespective of whether or not they are achieved (Johnstone et al., 2009; 2011). Despite this caveat, a key part of the partnership ethos is the notion that partnership practices and processes will lead to mutually beneficial employment relations outcomes.

Theoretical Perspectives on Partnership

Clearly, the notion of workplace cooperation is not new, but draws upon a long history and various attempts at 'enlightened' employment relations whose aim has been to reconcile the tensions between conflict and cooperation. Yet, as outlined above, workplace partnership – as a particular form of collaborative employment relations and as a form of employee voice – still lacks a commonly accepted definition. Given this inherent ambiguity, and in order to make some progress, we must return to some fundamental assumptions about the nature of organizational life and the characteristics of the employment relationship. It is useful to turn to the work of Alan Fox in this respect, as 'frames of reference' (Fox, 1966), can have important implications regarding the desirability and feasibility of workplace partnership.

Unitarism emphasizes the common goals of an enterprise, with employees regarded as team members united by loyalty to their employer around a common goal of business success. For unitarists, conflict is counterproductive and unnecessary and is usually the result of poor management communication, bad outside influences or aberrant employee behaviour. Cooperation is viewed as the natural state of employment relations. Thus there is no inherent governance challenge to manage or other 'interest' to develop a 'partnership' with. The regulation of employment is best left either to the external 'invisible hand' of the market or some version of 'sophisticated human relations' which aims to integrate employer and employee interests and maximize employee commitment and involvement (Purcell and Sisson, 1983). Financial involvement and shared ownership is one possible option in this regard, as is direct employee participation in day-to-day job-related issues. Decision-making power, however, is left in management hands, meaning that as far as 'partnership' goes, it is a rather one-sided arrangement (Guest and Peccei, 2001). Similar arguments can be made regarding debate on high performance work systems or, more recently, employee engagement, which tends to focus on the relationships employees have with organizations as individuals (see for example Harley, Chapter 6 above, and Gruman and Saks, Chapter 28 below). In short, while aspects of unitarism might hold true for some employers who are ambivalent or even suspicious of employee collective representation and trade unions, most IR scholars reject this view of organizational life as unrealistic (Johnstone and Ackers, 2014 forthcoming).

Pluralism, on the other hand, views organizations as 'miniature democratic states composed of sectional groups with divergent interests' (Fox, 1966: 2). Organizations are characterized by complex tensions which need to be managed in order to reconcile different opinions and keep conflict within accepted bounds. A key challenge is the regulation of employment and the representation of competing interests. Different interests are believed to be both inevitable and legitimate; the focus is therefore upon developing channels through which conflict can be channelled, expressed and institutionalized. Classical IR pluralists saw trade unions and collective bargaining as the single-channel solution to these problems (see Ackers, 2012 for a discussion). A pluralist perspective on partnership draws upon continental European industrial democracy and a perceived need to address the imbalance of power between capital and labour. Legislative intervention is believed to be required to address such an imbalance, resulting in commitments to co-determination, consultation and communication. Robust employee representation is a central feature of this model of worker participation (Guest and Peccei, 2001). A limitation, perhaps, is that traditionally pluralism has assumed that collective bargaining and trade union activity inevitably occur within a conflict-oriented system characterized by arm's length adversarialism and bargaining over distributive issues. A broader view of pluralism, however, includes the possibility of operating within the more collaborative joint problem-solving framework emphasized by workplace partnership.

In reality, in the context of the Anglo-Saxon economies partnership involves a blend of unitarist and pluralist assumptions that could be described as *unitarist/pluralist hybrid*. Conceptually, many of the aspirations of partnership appear unitarist in tone, for example commitment to the success of the organization, and notions of harmony, cooperation and 'win–win'. Partnership can in part be viewed as an evolution of the 'employee involvement' and 'soft HRM' debates of the 1980s. Nevertheless, when partnership is operationalized as an employment relations process it is generally founded upon pluralist assumptions (Kinge, 2014), such as joint recognition of each party's interests, and commitments to managing the tension between the employer's desire for workforce flexibility and the employees' desire for job security. Inspiration is taken from countries with embedded systems of societal-level social partnerships between labour and business interests, and where trade unions are influential. Again, in practice it is also likely that a workplace partnership will form one component of an overarching HR system, coexisting with various direct employee involvement and HRM techniques. Indeed, one of the most influential articulations of such a hybrid approach comes from Kochan and Osterman (1994) and their conceptualization of the 'mutual gains enterprise' in the context of the USA.

Central to the work of Kochan and Osterman is the need for integration of an employment relations system within the overall workplace HR system. Drawing on developments from the 1980s 'strategic choice school', partnership can be viewed as a particular model of organizational governance which can constitute part of a mutually beneficial high performance work system. The idea is that such a system means overall performance and productivity can be increased, which in turn means greater gains, which can subsequently be distributed. However, Kochan and Osterman (1994) deliberately avoid the term 'high performance work system' stating that:

> [mutual gains] conveys a key message: achieving and sustaining competitive advantage from human resources requires the strong support of multiple stakeholders ... employees must commit their energies to meeting the economic objectives of the enterprise. In return, owners must share the economic returns with employees and invest those returns in such a way as promotes the long-run economic security of the workforce. (Kochan and Osterman, 1994: 46)

THE CASE FOR AND AGAINST WORKPLACE PARTNERSHIP

Given these different perspectives and conceptualizations of partnership, it is perhaps inevitable that the partnership debate has resulted in a strongly contested case both for and against the potential for workplace partnership to deliver mutual gains for all organizational actors. It is to this debate that we now turn.

The Case for Partnership

The case for partnership has two main strands. Firstly, it is suggested that partnership is in the best interests of employers, employees, unions and governments. Much has focused upon partnership as the only option for revitalizing the beleaguered trade union movement in many liberal market economies (Ackers and Payne, 1998). Within a voluntarist environment where employers have significant latitude over their preferred approach to the conduct of employment relations generally, and employee voice specifically, it is argued that trade unions can use partnership as a way of achieving much needed buy-in from employers. Trade unions can thus be viewed, as both Tony Blair and Barack Obama have stated, as part of the solution to employment relations and business challenges (Spillius, 2009). Partnership can be viewed as compatible with – and even supportive of – business success, and as such the only form of unionism likely to attract much-needed state support. Employer support is also believed to be essential, and working in partnership to achieve business success is believed to be the only option for winning this. Partnership is thus a potentially shrewd strategy in terms of revitalizing the labour movement and repositioning trade unions as a legitimate and even desirable form of employee voice in contemporary workplaces. It has been suggested that cooperative labour–management approaches are desired by most workers. Employees have become disaffected with adversarial industrial relations and unions can revitalize themselves (in the eyes of members) by adopting a more cooperative and collaborative approach to employment relations (Kochan, 2000). In the UK, for example, it has been suggested that there is simply no appetite among most workers to return the adversarialism and divisiveness of the 1970s and 1980s (Brown, 2011).

   The second argument in favour of partnership is that it will deliver mutual gains which can in turn be shared between the actors (see Avgar and Owens, Chapter 20 below). The mutual gains thesis is based upon the proposition that collaboration affords the opportunity to expand the 'size of the pie' whereas the focus of a more adversarial model might just be on dividing the (same size) pie (Cooke, 1990; Freeman and Medoff, 1984); in other words a shift from zero-sum to positive-sum relations. In some of the earlier US writings, it has been suggested that the potential benefits of labour–management cooperation include enhanced union capacity to represent member interests and, in turn, greater employee commitment to and support of unions. Employees also benefit from higher levels of job satisfaction, greater voice, improved work-life balance, less stress and greater autonomy. Finally, employers stand to benefit from improved firm performance, stronger employee commitment, less conflict, improved productivity, better staff retention and higher quality employment relations (Cooke, 1990; Kochan and Osterman, 1994).

The Case against Partnership

The case against partnership is primarily underpinned by a view that the achievement of mutual gains is illusory at best and damaging at worst, with potentially detrimental consequences for trade unions, their members, and the regulation of work and employment in general (Gall, 2008; Kelly, 2004; Thompson, 2003; Upchurch et al., 2008). Mutual gains are believed to be illusory for several reasons. Firstly, at the micro- (firm) level, it is suggested that many firms compete on the basis of a 'low-road' strategy based on cost-minimization and low pay, despite the rhetoric of shifts towards a more sophisticated and potentially enlightened high performance HRM. Kochan (2012) notes how in the USA, the very birthplace of HRM, the reality is a 'human capital paradox' where HR often remains a low priority relative to financial and shareholder considerations. The preponderance of such strategies at the firm level is arguably incompatible with the diffusion of workplace partnership, which leads to the question of why employers would want to engage in partnership (Terry, 2003), or, as Kelly (1996: 88) puts it, 'it's difficult, if not impossible, to achieve a partnership with a party who would prefer that you didn't exist'. Secondly, at a macro- (political economy) level, structures of corporate governance and employer dominance mean a short-term focus on financial performance is inevitably prioritized despite the rhetoric of stakeholding (Deakin et al., 2005; Heery, 2002). Partnership notions such as balancing flexibility with security are therefore naive at best. The shift from managerial to financial capitalism, it is argued, means that contrary to best intentions, even the most enlightened employers will be unable to keep promises to share either the gains or pains experienced; as such, mutual gains are unattainable (Thompson, 2003, 2011). Management will always have the upper hand and as a result any notion of balance is inevitably false. Further, unscrupulous employers might seek to exploit the advantageous position that partnership affords. Even more critical is the suggestion that partnership could actually act as a facade for the further exploitation of ordinary labour by employers (Claydon, 1998; Taylor and Ramsey, 1998). In short, partnership cannot deliver for trade unions, and might actually mean they are unable to effectively represent their members, further undermining their legitimacy. Within lightly regulated employment regimes, the resultant imbalance of power means strategies such as organizing or militancy are thus more appropriate strategies for revitalizing trade unions (Kelly, 2004). Genuine partnership would require a degree of labour parity, which liberal market economies such as the Anglo-Saxon nations do not and cannot offer.

An Ideological Divide

In trying to understand these seemingly contradictory perspectives, it is useful to return briefly to notions of frames of reference (Fox, 1966). Most commentators broadly in support of the case for partnership subscribe to a pluralist view of organizations. Ackers (2002, 2012) has taken this a step further in his conceptualization of a particular brand of pluralism, which he terms 'neo-pluralism'. He argues that while classical IR pluralism came to be associated with an over-reliance on trade unions and collective bargaining, a narrow emphasis on relations within the organization, and a rather passive tolerance of damaging levels of conflict or arm's length adversarialism, neo-pluralism retains the core sense of a collective tension in the employment relationship, but stresses the potential to bridge this through proactive partnership solutions. Workers and management can construct high levels of cooperation, sometimes termed, 'productivity coalitions'. Shared values around specific projects can give a normative momentum to collaboration. Unions are usually central to this, but so are other forms of employee involvement and stakeholder relationships that go beyond wages and conditions to wider issues of work–life quality and balance. A neo-pluralist perspective sees a potential for conflict between employer and employees over both the processes of employment regulation and the distribution of economic outcomes (Ackers, 2012). The challenge is to develop institutions of workplace governance and regulation which pre-empt and resolve conflict, while actively promoting cooperation. In many ways this resonates with the shift from constitutional pluralism to consultative pluralism (Purcell and Sisson, 1983).

Most critical commentators of partnership, on the other hand, subscribe to a more radical perspective of the employment relationship and argue almost the exact opposite. Influenced by Marxism, IR radicals stress the inevitability of workplace conflict, linked to societal class strife arising from inequalities of power inherent in the entire economic, social, political and legal structure. Capitalism creates fundamental inequalities and leaves little potential for constructive bargaining processes. Corporate governance within neo-liberal systems that prioritize shareholder returns, combined with management opportunism, makes voluntarism a high risk strategy. Streeck (1998) suggests that within a 'rational voluntarist' model it is easy for parties to withdraw and defect from approaches that might be in the best long-term interests of the partners, as opposed to responding to short-term expediencies (see also Thompson, 2003). Attempts at partnership could actually mask and reinforce inequalities behind a veneer of cooperation, while seeking to re-balance the employment relationship through regulation is likely to be futile. Kelly (1996) suggests that the growing hostility of employers to any form of union and the meagre achievements of partnership underline this clash of interests, and therefore, in the absence of strong macro-level supports, militant union opposition to management is considered to be a better approach.

INTERNATIONAL EXPERIENCES OF PARTNERSHIP

United Kingdom

In the UK, the recent interest in workplace partnership can be traced to the early 1990s, and builds upon a long history of employee participation and interest in labour–management cooperation. The turning point towards workplace partnership is typically attributed to the election of New Labour and the Blair government in 1997. The Blair government followed almost 20 years of Conservative government which had, following the industrial relations crises of 1970s Britain, sought to limit the power of trade unions and to de-emphasize the collective dimension of employment relations. Trade unions have long been significant benefactors to the Labour Party and made significant financial contributions to the 1997 election campaign. 'New' Labour attempted to strike a difficult balance between being perceived as too 'business friendly' by trade union interests and too 'union friendly' by business interests. However, the Trade Union

Congress and Confederation of British Industry had also been, to some extent, sidelined by the Conservative government. While government interest in European-style national level social partnership was limited, there was some evidence of increased engagement between government and other stakeholders. TUC leader John Monks's 'New Unionism' was broadly supportive of the need for unions to work together with organizations in the public and private sector to improve their competitiveness, a stance also taken by his successor Brendan Barber (Brown, 2011). The context was also one of union decline, which was arguably as much about the changing economic environment and the intensification of global competition as it was to do with the unsympathetic government policies of Thatcher (Brown, 2011). Economically, the 1997 election followed a decade of growth, and New Labour's 'Fairness at Work' agenda aimed both to improve economic performance and to 'modernize' employment relations (DTI, 1998). The rhetoric was of fostering a model of trade unionism that provided services to members but that also helped firms to become more competitive (Howell, 2005). Practical and financial support to promote partnership was made available through the government-funded 'Partnership at Work' programme.

At a workplace level, partnerships often arose as a response to crises. Partnership agreements were signed between a range of high-profile British employers – such as Tesco and Barclays Bank – and their recognized trade unions. Reflecting higher union density, a large proportion of agreements were also signed in the public sector. However, formal workplace partnership has not become the dominant form of employment relations in Britain. A useful analysis of the spread of partnership has been conducted by Bacon and Samuel (2009). Their findings reveal that 248 formal partnership agreements were signed in the period 1990–2007, with the highest proportions signed in health and social work (34 per cent), public administration (19 per cent) and manufacturing (15 per cent). In 2007, partnership agreements in the UK covered one-third of employees in the public sector but only 4 per cent of workers in the private sector. Overall, this suggests that around 10 per cent of all UK employees are employed in a workplace covered by a partnership agreement. While this might sound small, only ten years earlier the figure was 1 per cent. Importantly, most appear to be robust with over 80 per cent 'surviving', and few employers have simply reneged upon a partnership agreement. Where partnership agreements have ended, common causes are mergers and acquisitions or changes of business ownership. However, unlike some more pessimistic commentators, Bacon and Samuel (2009: 261) reject the notion that partnership is 'fading from the British industrial relations agenda'. Survival of partnership in particular contexts might be interpreted either in optimistic terms – that is, partnerships survive because the actors continue to perceive overall benefits – or in more pragmatic terms, in situations where perhaps unions and employers consider partnership to be better than other alternatives.

Ireland

Ireland, in contrast to the UK, developed a centralized bargaining system as part of a national-level social partnership between 1987 and 2009. This was concerned with the alignment of wage determination processes with state macroeconomic priorities, and the launch of various social and economic initiatives, involving unions, employers, government and community/voluntary organizations (Rittau and Dundon, 2010). As in the

UK, collective bargaining has traditionally been conducted within a broadly voluntarist framework. However, in the 1990s, there was increasing recognition of a disconnect between national-level social partnerships and the conduct of employment relations at the workplace level (Teague and Hann, 2010). There was subsequent interest in the concept of partnership at the micro- (workplace) level, especially after 1997, and promotion of workplace partnership become more explicit in the document 'Partnership 2000'. This provided a framework for partnership and encouraged a broad shift towards cooperative employment relations in private and public as well as unionized and non-unionized contexts. A National Centre for Partnership, later renamed the National Centre for Partnership and Performance (NCPP; dissolved in 2010), was also established in 2000 to support partnership (Roche and Teague, 2014), as was the Workplace Innovation Fund (Dobbins, 2010). The Irish Congress of Trade Unions and the Irish Business and Employers Federation also developed partnership principles in a similar way to their UK equivalents. However, the approach to partnership promotion has been soft, with a reluctance to engage in regulation that it is believed might have compromised Ireland as an attractive place for foreign direct investment (Dobbins, 2010). Nevertheless, several high profile organizations – such as Aer Rianta and Waterford Crystal – embraced the partnership approach at the workplace level (Teague and Hann, 2010), although the adoption of partnership has not been widespread. Rittau and Dundon (2010) suggested that the diffusion of partnership has been low with around 25 per cent of organizations reporting some form of workplace partnership agreement. However, when this is restricted to those with formal workplace agreements – excluding informal partnerships – the figure falls to only 4.3 per cent (Rittau and Dundon, 2010).

Australia and New Zealand

In Australia and New Zealand, interest in partnership can be traced to government initiatives to improve workplace employment relations and performance in the 1990s and 2000s respectively. As in the UK and Ireland, the aim was to use 'soft' regulation to encourage management and unions to shift towards a 'high-road' approach to the conduct of employment relations (Macneil et al., 2011). However, Australia and New Zealand have traditionally differed from other Anglo-Saxon liberal market economies such as the UK and the USA. Prior to the 1980s both countries were described as having 'moderately coordinated economies', given the level of regulation and intervention of business and employment policy. However, since the 1980s the trend in both nations has been towards greater economic deregulation, decentralization, and individualization of the employment relationship, bringing the two nations increasingly into line with other liberal market Anglo-Saxon economies (Macneil et al., 2011: 3815). Similarly, both nations have had instances of social democratic governments utilizing 'soft' rather than 'hard' regulation to promote a more 'partnership' approach to employment relations, reflecting in part a trajectory towards increasing economic liberalization, but also reacting to possible actor preferences for voluntary participation in labour–management partnership initiatives. Examples of specific initiatives include the Partnership Resource Centre (PRC) in New Zealand and the Workplace Productivity and Partnership Pilot in Queensland, Australia.

In Australia, labour management cooperation was promoted as part of 'best practice' through the Australian Best Practice Demonstration Program established by the Labour government in the early 1990s, at a time when, like many other countries, the nation was entering economic recession. This was bolstered by various other government programmes to support training, export, innovation and workplace restructuring and cooperation. From this perspective, partnership could be viewed as a component of other 'best practice' and organizational change initiatives, which were influential at the time. However, when the Howard government took office in 1996, the approach to employment relations changed, and the administration took a less sympathetic stance to trade unions. The government terminated the best practice programme and interest in best practice quickly evaporated. The notion of partnership subsequently reappeared under the Gillard government (Macneil et al., 2011).

In New Zealand, when the Labour Party came to power after 15 years of Conservative government, it was also interested in devising means of managing which balanced economic performance and workplace reform. In part the impetus came from concerns about low productivity in New Zealand compared to other small nations such as Finland, Denmark and Singapore. Partnership was supported by the PRC which was created in 2005 and offered support in moving towards a partnership approach. However, given the relatively low levels of union recognition in the New Zealand private sector, the impact was mainly in the public sector (Macneil et al, 2011). It has been argued that outside the New Zealand Public Service Association, formal partnership relations between management and unions at workplace level remain 'virtually unknown' (Haynes et al., 2006: 225).

OUTCOMES OF PARTNERSHIP

International workplace partnerships have attracted a high level of interest from academic researchers, providing a strong body of evidence regarding the outcomes of partnership in achieving their espoused goals. Rich empirical evidence now exists in relation to the experience of partnership in the UK and Ireland. Three main perspectives dominate the literature: the 'pessimistic perspective', the 'constrained mutuality' perspective and the 'contingency perspective'. We now explore each of these.

The pessimistic perspective suggests that workers and trade unions do not stand to gain much, if anything, from workplace partnership. Evidence of this perspective is probably most apparent in the partnership critiques in the British literature. John Kelly (1996, 2004) is arguably the most vocal proponent of this perspective. In a study of matched partnership and non-partnership firms, Kelly (2004) found that while employers appeared to benefit from partnership, there were negligible gains for workers or trade unions when evaluated against criteria such as wages, hours worked, holidays or job losses. Employee gains were only found to be achieved where unions were strong, and where the firm was performing well. His findings in terms of factors such as wage levels, influence in the company and employment security were negative. Gall (2008) also represents this critical perspective, and suggests that in some cases partnership has actually weakened unions and worker influence over issues such as the terms and conditions of employment, with limited endorsement of partnership from union members. Critical studies thus reject the mutual gains thesis, and suggest that a range of negative outcomes for labour are actually more likely. These include difficulties demonstrating union effectiveness, greater distance between unions and their members, work intensification, job insecurity and labour outcomes that are no better than those achieved in non-partnership firms (Kelly, 2004; Upchurch et al., 2008).

On the other hand, several British studies have revealed some benefits of partnership, including stronger union organization at the workplace-level, greater employee support for unions, improved consultation and enhanced union access to senior decision-makers (Wills, 2004; Samuel, 2007). This is not to say, however, that this more optimistic perspective portrays some kind of mutual gains nirvana; mutuality is often 'constrained' (Guest and Peccei, 2001). The 'constrained mutuality' perspective suggests that employees may well stand to benefit from partnership, but typically the 'balance of advantage' will be tipped in favour of the employer, with the focus on issues such as employee responsibilities and productivity rather than employee welfare (Guest and Peccei, 2001). Nevertheless, to be sustainable, partnership cannot be completely lop-sided, for 'positive organisational outcomes of interest to employers depend for their achievement upon the prior achievement of outcomes likely to be relevant to employees and their representatives' (Guest and Peccei, 2001: 1321). In other words, when partnership is perceived to be serving primarily or even exclusively the interests of employers, the potential for these gains will be short lived.

Positive outcomes of workplace partnership have also been identified in the Irish context (Roche and Geary, 2002, 2006; Geary and Trif, 2011; Rittau and Dundon, 2010; Roche, 2009; Dobbins, 2010; Dobbins and Gunnigle, 2009). For employers the gains identified have included improved productivity, support for change, greater flexibility, higher levels of trust, better communications, fewer disputes, better employment relations climate, employee commitment, reduced absenteeism and labour turnover, and higher levels of innovation. For employees, positive outcomes identified include greater job satisfaction and sense of fairness, better communications, information provision, pay and working hours, and influence over the job. Finally, perceived benefits of workplace partnership for Irish trade unions include greater influence and involvement, higher membership and the ability to better represent members.

In some ways this suggests that partnership outcomes are contingent upon a range of conditions that determine the favourability of the context to partnership working. Firstly, at a macro-level, the national legislative environment is believed to be significant. In the context of the UK, Samuel and Bacon (2010) suggest that perhaps it is expecting too much for employers and unions to recast employment relations towards an 'enlightened' approach without the coercion found in other northern continental European countries. They highlight the limitations of a non-statutory approach to diffusing partnership employment relations, with arm's length and low trust approaches to employment relations still common in many British workplaces (Samuel and Bacon, 2010). Similarly, in Ireland it has been argued that workplace cooperation goes against the grain of voluntarist regimes which prioritize shareholder value and short-term results, and that despite a macro-level social partnership, the use of law in promoting workplace partnership has been avoided with national social partnership largely disconnected from workplace employment relations strategies (Dobbins, 2010).

However, where partnerships have been forged, they have often been driven by workplace-level factors, such as business crises, organizational change or a need to address poor employment relations. It could be argued that organizations which have voluntarily and proactively entered into partnerships might provide fertile ground for the development of cooperative employment relations precisely because the decision has been made voluntarily rather than resembling an arranged marriage imposed by legislation. It could also be argued that if we simply accept that 'employers cannot keep their promises' (Thompson, 2003), we risk becoming locked into a position of economic determinism. Evans et al., (2012) suggest that besides (macro-) political economy factors, we should also consider features of the industry (meso-) or micro-context that might support mutual gains. Increasingly the research evidence lends support to a more nuanced and contingent perspective, suggesting several factors that are believed to be supportive of partnership, including, for example, a buoyant economic climate, a quality-driven business strategy, management support, union support, strong actor relationships, trust, high union density and integration with supportive HR practices (see for example, Belanger and Edwards, 2007; Dobbins, 2010; Geary and Trif, 2011). The fact that many flagship British partnership agreements still appear to be robust (Bacon and Samuel, 2009) further calls into question some of the more deterministic arguments (Thompson, 2003).

CONCLUSION

To conclude, a strong ideological dimension to partnership remains when considering the *a priori* conceptual case for and against workplace partnership (McBride and Stirling, 2002). Partnership appears to be more acceptable to IR pluralists, while radicals remain sceptical as a result of their beliefs that political economy and corporate governance undermine any serious attempt at 'partnership' (Kelly, 2004; Thompson, 2003). Pluralists, on the other hand, argue that mutual gains can be achieved within a context of 'permissive voluntarism' (Dobbins, 2010), but that both the effectiveness of the process and the balance of gains depend upon the favourability of contextual factors such as the rationale for partnership, product and labour markets, technology and competitive strategy. It could be argued that many of these factors determine the extent to which governments and employers are convinced that a 'business case' for partnership is believed to exist, for example, as a voice regime supportive of an organization pursuing a high performance work system approach to HRM, where management believe labour–management cooperation is essential for productivity and competitiveness (Butler et al., 2011).

These conceptual and theoretical debates also influence the way in which we interpret the empirical evidence on partnership, and in particular the extent to which such analyses focus upon interpreting the evidence as 'partial success' or 'partial failure'. What constitutes success is highly problematic (Geary and Trif, 2011), in part because radicals focus upon 'hard' substantive outcomes, while pluralists also value 'soft' outcomes such as the quality of relationships and fairness of organizational processes and procedures (Evans et al., 2012; see also the distinction by Cooke, 1990 between extrinsic versus intrinsic costs and benefits). To add to this complexity, different organizational actors may place different weights upon the perceived balance of these outcomes (Geary and Trif, 2011). Of course partnership must do more than simply improve the quality of relationships and must also generate tangible hard outcomes (Kochan et al., 2008) but the former may even be a precondition for the achievement of the latter (Evans et al., 2012).

We need to transcend simplistic 'who wins/who loses' debates, and continue to develop a richer understanding of the context, processes, meaning and outcomes of partnership, as well as the contextual conditions associated with both positive and negative evaluations of workplace partnership (Johnstone et al., 2009). Some thirty years after Purcell and Sisson (1983) outlined a 'sophisticated modern (consultative)' variant in their typology of management styles, it could be argued that we have limited evidence of such a model becoming dominant in employment relations in most Anglo-Saxon nations. Partnership appears to remain a relatively rare model of employment relations, and it is easy to dismiss such approaches on the grounds that they have failed to 'modernize' employment relations (Wilkinson et al., 2014). However, the pressure remains to identify and develop forms of governance and voice that can manage the strategic tensions between the economic and social imperatives that characterize the management of work and employment. The quest for workplace cooperation, mutual gains and collaboration is unlikely to go away (Boxall, 1996, 2013), whatever the process is called (Brown, 2011).

REFERENCES

Ackers, P. (2002), 'Reframing employment relations: the case for neo-pluralism', *Industrial Relations Journal*, **33** (1), 2–19.

Ackers, P. (2012), 'Rethinking the employment relationship: a neo-pluralist critique of British industrial relations orthodoxy', *International Journal of Human Resource Management*, (July), 1–18.

Ackers, P. and J. Payne (1998), 'British trade unions and social partnership: rhetoric, reality and strategy', *International Journal of Human Resource Management*, **9** (3), 529–50.

Ackers, P., M. Marchington, A. Wilkinson and T. Dundon (2005), 'Partnership and voice, with or without trade unions: changing UK management approaches to organisational participation', in M. Stuart and M. Martinez-Lucio (eds), *Partnership and Modernisation in Employment Relations*, London: Routledge, pp. 23–45.

Appelbaum, E., T. Bailey, P. Berg and A.L. Kalleberg (2000), *Manufacturing Advantage: Why High-Performance Systems Pay Off*, Ithaca, NY: Cornell University Press.

Bacon, N. and P. Samuel (2009), 'Partnership agreement adoption and survival in the British private and public sectors', *Work, Employment and Society*, **23** (2), 231–48.

Bacon, N. and J. Storey (2000), 'New employee relations strategies in Britain: towards individualism or partnership?', *British Journal of Industrial Relations*, **38** (3) (September), 407–27.

Belanger, J. and P. Edwards (2007), 'The conditions promoting compromise in the workplace', *British Journal of Industrial Relations*, **45** (4), 713–34

Boxall, P. (1996), 'The strategic HRM debate and the resource-based view of the firm', *Human Resource Management Journal*, **6** (3), 59–75.

Boxall, P. (2013), 'Mutuality in the management of human resources: assessing the quality of alignment in employment relationships', *Human Resource Management Journal*, **23** (1), 3–17.

Boxall, P. and J. Purcell (2008), *Strategy and Human Resource Management*, Basingstoke: Palgrave.

Brown, W. (2011), 'International review: industrial relations in Britain under New Labour, 1997–2010: a post mortem', *Journal of Industrial Relations*, **53** (3), 402–13.

Butler, P., L. Glover and O. Tregaskis (2011), '"When the going gets tough . . . ": recession and the resilience of workplace partnership', *British Journal of Industrial Relations*, **49** (4), 666–87.

Cathcart, A. (2014), 'Paradoxes of participation: non-union workplace partnership in John Lewis', *International Journal of Human Resource Management*, **25** (6), 762–80.

Claydon, T. (1998), 'Problematising partnership: the prospects for a co-operative bargaining agenda', in P. Sparrow and M. Marchington (eds), *Human Resource Management: The New Agenda*, London: Pitman, pp. 180–91.

Cooke, W.N. (1990), *Labor–Management Cooperation: New Partnerships or Going in Circles?*, Kalamazoo, MI: W.E. Upjohn Institute.

Danford, A. (2005), 'Workplace partnership and employee voice in the UK: comparative case studies of union strategy and worker experience', *Economic and Industrial Democracy*, **26** (4), 593–620.

Danford, A., M. Richardson, P. Stewart, S. Tailby and M. Upchurch (2005), 'Workplace partnership and employee voice in the UK: comparative case studies of union strategy and worker experience', *Economic and Industrial Democracy*, **26** (4), 593–620.

Deakin, S., R. Hobbs, S. Konzelmann and F. Wilkinson (2005), 'Working corporations: corporate governance and innovation in labour-management partnerships in Britain', in M. Stuart and M. Martinez-Lucio (eds), *Partnership and Modernisation in Employment Relations*, London: Routledge, pp. 63–82.

Dietz, G. (2004), 'Partnership and the development of trust in British workplaces', *Human Resource Management Journal*, **14** (1), 5–24.

Dobbins, A. (2010), 'The case for "beneficial constraints": why permissive voluntarism impedes workplace cooperation in Ireland', *Economic and Industrial Democracy*, **31** (4), 497–519.

Dobbins, A. and P. Gunnigle (2009), 'Can voluntary workplace partnership deliver sustainable mutual gains?', *British Journal of Industrial Relations*, **47** (3), 546–70.

DTI (1998), 'Fairness at Work', Cm3698, Department of Trade and Industry, London.

Edwards, P. (2003), 'The employment relationship and the field of industrial relations', in P. Edwards (ed.), *Industrial Relations: Theory and Practice in Britain*, Oxford: Blackwell, pp. 1–48.

Evans, C., G. Harvey and P. Turnbull (2012), 'When partnerships don't "match-up": an evaluation of labour-management partnerships in the automotive components and civil aviation industries', *Human Resource Management Journal*, **22** (1), 60–75.

Fox. A. (1966), 'Industrial relations and industrial sociology', Research Paper 3, Royal Commission on the Trade Unions and Employers Associations, HMSO, London.

Freeman, R.B. and R. Medoff (1984), *What Do Unions Do?*, New York: Basic Books.

Frege, C. and J. Kelly (eds) (2004), *Varieties of Unionism: Strategies for Union Revitalization in a Globalizing Economy*, Oxford: Oxford University Press.

Gall, G. (2008), *Labour Unionism in the Financial Services Sector*, Farnham: Ashgate.

Geary, J. and A.Trif (2011), 'Workplace partnership and the balance of advantage: a critical case analysis', *British Journal of Industrial Relations*, **49** (s1), s44–s69.

Glover, L. and P. Butler (2012), 'High-performance work systems, partnership and the working lives of HR professionals', *Human Resource Management Journal*, **22** (2), 199–215.

Guest, D. and R. Peccei (2001), 'Partnership at work: mutuality and the balance of advantage', *British Journal of Industrial Relations*, **39** (2), 207–36.

Haynes, P., M. Marchington and P. Boxall (2006), 'Workplace union–management partnership: prospects for diffusion of contemporary British approaches in New Zealand', *Asia Pacific Business Review*, **12** (2), 225–41.

Heery, E. (2002), 'Partnership versus organizing: alternative futures for British trade unionism', *Industrial Relations Journal*, **33** (1), 20–35.

Howell, C. (2005), *Trade Unions and the State: The Construction of Industrial Relations Institutions in Britain, 1890–2000*, Princeton, NJ: Princeton University Press.

Hyman, R. (1987), 'Strategy or structure', *Work, Employment and Society*, **1** (1), 25–56.

IPA (1997), *Towards Industrial Partnership*. London: IPA.

Johnstone, S. and P. Ackers (2014 forthcoming), 'Partnership and mutual gains', in D.E. Guest and D. Needle (eds), *Encyclopedia of Human Resource Management*, 3rd edn, Wiley: London.

Johnstone, S. and A. Wilkinson (2013), 'Employee voice, partnership and performance', in G. Saridakis and C. Cooper (eds), *How Can HR Drive Growth?*, Cheltenham, UK and Northampton, MA, USA: Edward Elgar, pp. 141–69.

Johnstone, S., P. Ackers and A. Wilkinson (2009), 'The British partnership phenomenon: a ten year review', *Human Resource Management Journal*, **19** (3), 260–79.

Johnstone, S., P. Ackers and A. Wilkinson (2010), 'Better than nothing? Is non-union partnership a contradiction in terms?', *Journal of Industrial Relations*, **52** (2), 151–68.

Johnstone, S., A. Wilkinson and P. Ackers (2011), 'Applying Budd's model to partnership', *Economic and Industrial Democracy*, **32** (2), 307–28.

Kelly, J. (1996), 'Union militancy and social partnership', in P. Ackers, C. Smith and P. Smith (eds), *The New Workplace and Trade Unionism*, London, Routledge, pp. 77–109.

Kelly, J. (2004), 'Social partnership agreements in Britain: Labor cooperation and compliance', *Industrial Relations: A Journal of Economy and Society*, **43** (1), 267–92.

Kinge, J. (2014), 'Testing times: the development and sustainability of partnership relationships', *International Journal of Human Resource Management*, **25** (6), 852–78.

Kochan, T. (2000), 'On the paradigm guiding industrial relations theory and research: comment on John Godard and John T. Delaney, "Reflections on the 'High Performance' Paradigm's Implications for Industrial Relations as a Field"', *Industrial and Labor Relations Review*, **53** (July 2000), 704–11.

Kochan, T. (2012), 'America's human capital paradox', Upjohn Institute Working Paper, 12-180, W.E. Upjohn Institute for Employment Research, Kalamazoo, MI.

Kochan, T. and P. Osterman (1994), *The Mutual Gains Enterprise: Forging a Winning Partnership Among Labor, Management, and Government*, Cambridge, MA: Harvard Business School Press.

Kochan, T., P.S. Adler, R.B. McKersie, A.E. Eaton, P. Segal and P. Gerhart (2008), 'The potential and precariousness of partnership: the case of the Kaiser Permanente labor management partnership', *Industrial Relations: A Journal of Economy and Society*, **47** (1), 36–65.

Macneil, J., N. Haworth and E. Rasmussen (2011), 'Addressing the productivity challenge? Government-sponsored partnership programs in Australia and New Zealand', *International Journal of Human Resource Management*, **22** (18), 3813–29.

Martinez Lucio, M. and M. Stuart (2002), 'Assessing partnership: the prospects for, and challenges of, modernisation', *Employee Relations*, **24** (3), 252–61.

McBride, J. and J. Stirling (2002), 'Partnership and process in the maritime construction industry', *Employee Relations*, **24** (3), 290–304.

Purcell, J. and Sisson, K. (1983), Strategies and practice in the management of industrial relations. In G. S. Bain (ed.), Industrial Relations in Britain. Oxford: Blackwell.

Rittau, Y. and T. Dundon (2010), 'The roles and functions of shop stewards in workplace partnership: evidence from the Republic of Ireland', *Employee Relations*, **32** (1), 10–27.

Roche, W.K. (2009), 'Who gains from workplace partnership?', *The International Journal of Human Resource Management*, **20** (1), 1–33.

Roche, W.K. and J. Geary (2002), 'Advocates, critics and union involvement in workplace partnership: Irish airports', *British Journal of Industrial Relations*, **40** (4 December), 659–88.

Roche, W.K. and P. Teague (2014), 'Successful but unappealing: fifteen years of workplace partnership in Ireland', *International Journal of Human Resource Management*, **25** (6), 781–94.

Samuel, P. (2007), 'Partnership consultation and employer domination in two British life and pensions firms', *Work, Employment and Society*, **21** (3), 459–77.

Samuel, P. and N. Bacon (2010), 'The contents of partnership agreements in Britain 1990–2007', *Work, Employment and Society*, **24** (3), 430–48.

Spillius (2009), 'Barack Obama welcomes union leaders to the White House', *Telegraph*, 30 January.

Streeck, W. (1998), 'Beneficial constraints: on the economic limits of rational voluntarism', in J.R. Hollingsworth and R. Boyer (eds), *Contemporary Capitalism: The Embededdness of Institutions*, Cambridge: Cambridge University Press, pp. 197–219.

Taylor, P. and H. Ramsey (1998), 'Unions partnership and HRM: sleeping with the enemy?', *International Journal of Employment Studies*, **6** (2), 115–43.

Teague, P. and D. Hann (2010), 'Problems with partnership at work: lessons from an Irish case study', *Human Resource Management Journal*, **20** (1), 100–114.

Terry, M. (2003), 'Can "partnership" reverse the decline of British trade unions?', *Work, Employment and Society*, **17** (3), 459–72.

Thompson, P. (2003), 'Disconnected capitalism: or why employers can't keep their side of the bargain', *Work, Employment and Society*, **17** (2), 359–78.

Thompson, P. (2011), 'The trouble with HRM', *Human Resource Management Journal*, **21** (4), 355–67.

TUC (1999), *Partners for Progress: Next Steps for the New Unionism*, London: TUC.

Upchurch, M., A. Danford, S. Tailby and M. Richardson (2008), *The Realities of Partnership at Work*, Basingstoke: Palgrave Macmillan.

Walton, R.E. (1985), 'From control to commitment in the workplace', *Harvard Business Review*, **85** (2), 77–85.

Wills, J. (2004), 'Trade unionism and partnership in practice : evidence from the Barclays – Unifi agreement', *Industrial Relations Journal*, **35** (4), 329–43.

Wilkinson, A., T. Dundon, J. Donaghey and K. Townsend (2014), 'Partnership, collaboration and mutual gains: evaluating context, interests and legitimacy', *International Journal of Human Resource Management*, **25** (6), 737–47.

20 Voice in the mutual gains organization
Ariel C. Avgar and Stacey Owens

THE RISE OF THE MUTUAL GAINS ENTERPRISE: A VOICE AND INVOLVEMENT-CENTERED INDUSTRIAL RELATIONS MODEL

From its infancy as a discipline, industrial relations scholarship has been founded on the core proposition that conflict and fundamental divergences of interests stand at the heart of the employment relationship (Lewin 2001; Godard and Delaney 2000; Barbash 1984; Commons 1935; Webb and Webb 1897). These inherent conflicts give rise to the need for institutional actors, such as unions and governments, who can mitigate potential negative consequences for employees (Commons 1935; see also Lewin 2001). As such, industrial relations scholarship has developed an acute sensitivity over the past century to the divergence of interests and the tensions that are inextricably linked to labor and employment dynamics in the workplace (see, for example, Barbash 1984; for a discussion, see Lewin 2001; Godard and Delaney 2000). Industrial relations has set itself apart from other disciplines by, among other things, identifying and exposing the implications associated with this foundational assumption about conflict and its central role in organizations (Barbash 1984). This lens, applied to the study of the workplace, has highlighted the adversarial dimensions inherent in the employment relationship and obscured much of the potential for partnership and collaboration between these actors (Walton and McKersie 1965).

A second major theme inherent in the study of industrial relations, which is inextricably linked to the dominant focus on conflicts between actors, is the centrality of employee voice as an essential workplace mechanism with the potential to positively contribute to both employee and employer outcomes. Beginning with Hirschman's (1970) seminal work on the tradeoff between voice and exit, workplace scholars have expanded on the organizational and individual level potential inherent to voice at work. Freeman and Medoff (1984) applied Hirschman's voice/exit framework to the collective voice provided by unions. Freeman and Medoff explained the significantly lower levels of turnover in union settings as the byproduct of the institutionalized forms of collective voice inherent to labor–management relations.

Although a large body of research has since examined different individual and collective forms of voice and their implications for multiple stakeholders, industrial relations scholarship has been dominated by a focus on union related voice (Wilkinson and Fay 2011; Dundon et al. 2004). Given the traditional focus on inherent conflicts of interest between labor and management, much of the conceptualization of voice has been predominately based on mechanisms through which unions can combat, or at the very least safeguard against, managerial unilateral actions.

It is against this disciplinary backdrop that research on the potential for a mutual gains enterprise emerged in the 1980s and 1990s. The mutual gains model is based on an alternative view of the workplace and the fundamental dynamics between core actors; one in which conflicts of interest do not necessarily dominate relationships and interactions between employers and their employees. As such, the rise of the mutual gains perspective challenged traditional industrial relations assumptions regarding the roles of conflict and voice in the workplace. The mutual gains firm represents a dramatic departure from well-established industrial relations doctrine and, central to the focus of this volume, the conceptualization of employee voice. This paradigm challenged the claim that key employer and employee interests are, to a large extent, incompatible (Masters et al. 2006; Martinez Lucio and Stuart 2004; Cooke 1990). Employers and their employees, alongside their representatives, can negotiate work arrangements, practices, and processes, including new voice-related mechanisms that allow both parties to advance their core interests in a mutually beneficial manner (Guest and Peccei 2001; Kochan and Osterman 1994).

Employee voice, according to this perspective, should not be viewed merely as a combative tool in a long war of attrition between employees and employers or labor and management (Danford et al. 2004). Rather, it is a vehicle through which mutual interests and their associated gains can be explored and capitalized upon. Central to the ability to restructure the workplace in a manner that focused on mutuality, the mutual gains paradigm was one of the first attempts to introduce employee voice in a new guise – one that was not inextricably linked to traditional collective bargaining institutions (Wilkinson and Fay 2011; Tailby et al. 2007; Dundon et al. 2004). This is not to say that collective voice is not accounted for in mutual gains research. Rather, mutual gains scholars called for a complementary focus on other outlets for employee voice (for a review of alternative voice options, see Wilkinson and Fay 2011; Budd et al. 2010). Mutual gains scholars, such as Kochan and Osterman (1994), broadened the scope of employee voice and included informal and individual vehicles for providing input.

Employee input, discretion, and voice are essential components of the mutual gains paradigm, which has sought to redefine the very contours of how work is organized and how employees, their representatives, and employers interact (for a similar discussion, see Geary 2008; Teague 2005). If voice in the traditional conceptualization of the employment relationship is formal and used as a means of combating employer unilateral actions and resisting managerial control, according to the mutual gains paradigm, it is informal and focused on ways in which employee input and involvement can advance the interests of the organization and its multiple stakeholders (for a discussion of different types of voice and distinctions between formal and informal mechanisms, see Dundon et al. 2004).

In their seminal book, *The Mutual Gains Enterprise*, Kochan and Osterman (1994) argue that organizations can attain a competitive advantage by rearranging the manner in which the workforce is managed and the conditions under which management engages the workforce. Furthermore, the authors maintain that in doing so, organizations can deliver gains that are distributed to multiple stakeholders. This is not to say that conflicts and divergences of interest between employers and employees are not a common workplace phenomenon, even according to the mutual gains conceptualization of organizations. Rather, mutual gains proponents argue that this well-established pattern of interactions does not have to dominate the employment relationship in a cooperative industrial relations context (Cutcher-Gershenfeld 1991).

   Kochan and Osterman (1994) maintain that alongside the reorganization of work in a manner that increases employee voice, input, and participation, the mutual gains framework also requires the presence of a strong formal mechanism for collaborative dynamics between employers, employees, and their representatives (for a similar discussion, see Butler et al. 2011; Geary and Trif 2011; Eaton and Rubinstein 2006; Guest and Peccei 2001; Rubinstein and Kochan 2001; Cooke 1994). Thus, labor–management partnership is commonly viewed as an integral, although not always present, dimension of the mutual gains organization (Butler et al. 2011). This chapter will review the dominant features of the mutual gains paradigm and the implications these have for employee voice. In doing so, we hope to highlight both the potential associated with the mutual gains organization and the limitations it may have for the type of employee voice it promotes in the workplace.

THE MUTUAL GAINS ENTERPRISE IN CONTEXT: A CHANGING INDUSTRIAL RELATIONS AND ORGANIZATIONAL LANDSCAPE

The rise of the mutual gains paradigm was not solely the product of a conceptual or normative departure from the traditional, and predominately adversarial, industrial relations approach. Rather, this new paradigm was, in many ways, born out of real and dramatic changes in the organizational and industrial relations landscape beginning in the late 1970s and early 1980s. More specifically, the past three decades have been associated with a comprehensive transformation in the structure and design of many organizations (Appelbaum et al. 2000; Heckscher and Donnellon 1994; Kochan et al. 1994). As the result of a variety of both external and internal pressures, organizations have been restructuring their traditional bureaucratic models in search of alternatives that can, among other things, increase their competitive viability (Appelbaum et al. 2000; Osterman 2000; Appelbaum and Batt 1994: 3; Kochan and Osterman 1994). Alongside this general restructuring, employment and work practices in many organizations in developed countries have also undergone drastic alterations. In the quest for increased competitiveness, organizations have been shedding their traditional rigid rule-based practices. As an alternative, flexible, 'innovative' and dynamic structures in which employees have increased discretion and voice have been implemented in a growing number of organizations (Osterman 2000). In fact, individual employee voice stands at the heart of the overarching logic of the mutual gains firm. The promise of delivering gains to employers and employees, rests, to a large extent, on a comprehensive shift in the role that frontline employees play and in the input they provide (Appelbaum et al. 2000).
   The mutual gains paradigm is based on the argument set forth by a stream of industrial relations research that maintains that these new organizational structures and innovative work practices have the potential for reducing or even eliminating conflict in the workplace (see, generally, Appelbaum et al. 2000; Kochan and Osterman 1994; Cutcher-Gershenfeld 1991; for empirical evidence partially supporting this claim, see Colvin 2004). According to this claim, the dismantling of traditional hierarchies and work practices and the facilitation of increased employee voice, discretion, and involvement allows for the fulfillment of enhanced organizational potential for both employers

and employees (Teague 2005; Kochan and Osterman 1994; Cooke 1990). Expanding the proverbial 'pie' in this manner creates the foundation for a 'win-win' employment relationship in which conflicts of interest play a much less dominant role than they did in the past. The mutual gains paradigm, therefore, challenges the axiomatic foundation set forth by Commons (1935) and a long line of industrial relations scholars that conflict and divergence of interest stand at the heart of industrial relations activity.

The mutual gains enterprise is, in many ways, an organizational form that stands in contrast to the traditional bureaucratic firm. Thus, understanding the rise of the mutual gains enterprise requires an assessment of the perceived shortcomings associated with the well-established and longstanding bureaucratic model. As with any organizational archetype, the bureaucratic organizational characteristics have both advantages and disadvantages. On the one hand, the intense level of specification and rule rigidity allows for increased certainty and efficiency, particularly in large organizations. Management and employees have a clear understanding of the organizational delineation and of the manner in which they must function in order to maintain routine operation (see Hirschhorn and Gilmore 1992: 105).

On the other hand, bureaucratic organizational design has also been deemed by some scholars as less appropriate in periods of uncertainty and change (Heckscher 1994; Starkey et al. 1991; Lawrence and Lorsch 1967). Bureaucracies are claimed to be slow to recognize the need for change and even then have a hard time adapting to change without undergoing comprehensive restructuring, as a result of their formal rules and procedures (Heckscher 1994). One of the arguments made early on by organizational scholars is that bureaucracies are ill-equipped in terms of their innovative capacity and their general ability to deal with environmental complexity (Adler and Borys 1996; Thompson 1965; Burns and Stalker 1961).

Among the many disadvantages perceived to be associated with the bureaucratic organizational form is the claim that it stifles employee involvement and, by extension, voice. Supporters of a mutual gains model of industrial relations maintain that confining employees to narrowly defined job categories and responsibilities and the enforcement of rigid rules are counterproductive and inhibit employee creativity, voice, and input (Cappelli et al. 1997). This is due, in part, to the fact that it does not allow for the fulfillment of existing employee potential, such as tacit knowledge and creativity and broad organizational commitment (Child and McGrath 2001; Kochan and Rubinstein 2000; Appelbaum et al. 2000; Heckscher 1994). This claim is absolutely central in the development of emerging innovative work practices, and the availability of voice, in particular, which set out to tap into previously underutilized employee abilities and knowledge and to enhance organizational commitment (Adler and Borys 1996). The key link between the mutual gains model of work organizations and the ability to advance employer and employee needs rests, therefore, on the very ability to capture new 'hidden' value through voice.

Furthermore, bureaucratic organizations create a well-defined formal structure, yet have great difficulty in taming and utilizing the informal structures and systems of communication and voice that develop in the workplace (Heckscher 1994). Thus, it has been claimed that informal organizational practices develop in bureaucracies in order to bypass the rigid constraints that are imposed by the emphasis on formal and dictated modes of operation. Bureaucratic organizations are ill-equipped to identify these practices and do not make appropriate use of the alternative informal forces that act within the organization (see, for example, Burawoy 1979). This also explains the limited and constrained efforts to enhance or promote individual voice in bureaucratic organizations. The removal of the bureaucratic organizational shackles in the mutual gains firm, therefore, also removes institutional barriers to employee voice.

Osterman (1999) analyzes some of the core pressures that may have pushed organizations to restructure and depart from the longstanding traditional bureaucratic design. First, international competition has increased substantially since the late 1970s–early 1980s. Deregulation in certain industries such as telecommunications, airlines, and banking and the opening of international trade can account for much of this increased competition (Osterman 1999; also see Heckscher 1994; Hammer and Champy 1993). One of the primary manifestations of this competition is the increasingly short period within which firms are able to maintain a given competitive advantage (Volberda 1996). Increased competition also led to a growing emphasis on product and service quality (Mazzeo 2003). Some scholars have argued that it was this increased attention to quality that pushed organizations to seek out mechanisms to provide employees with greater say and involvement (Appelbaum 2002; Kochan and Rubinstein, 2000; Kling 1995). Thus, in many ways, the centrality of individual employee voice emerged as a necessary response to external environmental pressures and their implications for the strategies employed by firms reacting to these intensely competitive market conditions.

Alongside dramatic changes to organizational structure, a number of central industrial relations shifts have also contributed toward the context under which the mutual gain paradigm evolved. Over the past three decades, industrial relations in general and employment systems and their employment practices in particular have also been the subject of comprehensive transformation (Kochan et al. 1994). The drivers of this transformation are diverse. However, the economic conditions and competitive pressures discussed above in reference to general organizational change have also had a substantial effect on the search for new forms of innovative employment patterns (Appelbaum and Batt 1994).

Like the organizational transformation, this change is also characterized by its shift away from the traditional hierarchical rule-based and adversarial approaches to the employment relationship toward labor–management partnership and increasingly cooperative, participatory, and discretionary work practices (Kochan et al. 1994; Cooke 1990). The restructuring of the workplace represents a fundamental dismantling of some of the key features of work organization and industrial relations that were in place for over half a century. First and foremost, at the macro industrial relations level and as has been well documented, the hegemony and strength of the unionized employment setting has been drastically weakened (Cutcher-Gershenfeld and Kochan 2004).

Second, many industrial relations systems have experienced an erosion of collectivist forms of action (Ridley-Duff and Bennett 2011; Doellgast 2010; Brewster et al. 2007). As such, collective bargaining has lost its perceived position as the 'cornerstone' of labor–management interactions (Johnstone et al. 2010; Godard and Delaney, 2000; Kochan et al. 1994). This trend is of crucial importance since the breakdown of the formal system of rule-making created a vacuum that required the erection of a new industrial relations model. Third and related to the first two shifts, as the non-union sector grew, many non-union firms attempted to develop human resource practices that could enhance organizational performance through the improvement of employee satisfaction and engagement (Kochan et al. 1994; Appelbaum and Batt 1994). Experimentation in the non-union sector diffused in many cases to union settings seeking to enhance employee and labor participation. In many cases, this shift preceded the experimentation with innovative work practices and set the stage for their conceptual evolution.

In the shift toward 'sophisticated' human resource practices in both the union and non-union settings, organizations have been shifting their industrial relations focus from a contractual rule-based one to an individual psychological one (Kochan et al. 1994; Appelbaum and Batt 1994). The implication of this shift is that the manner in which power and control are negotiated between employers and employees has drastically changed. These developments are central to understanding the changes that took place at the workplace level and to the development of a mutual gains approach to the employment relationship. Much of the experimentation with and use of new forms of employment practices grew out of the need to adjust to the changing macro industrial relations reality in many developed countries. A reality in which the traditional certainty associated with a sound system of conflict management and rule-making provided by collective bargaining and well-developed grievance procedures is no longer a given (Lipsky et al. 2003; Godard and Delaney 2000).

PARTICIPATION, VOICE, AND DISCRETION: EMPLOYEE INPUT IN THE MUTUAL GAINS WORKPLACE

The mutual gains workplace is characterized by a shift from clear and defined management supervisory roles versus employee tasks to increased cooperation and dialog between management, employees and, where present, labor. This leads to a blurring of the traditional division of power and control that is manifested in greater employee involvement, autonomy, voice, and decision-making prerogatives. Furthermore, many mutual gains organizations take employee involvement beyond the shop floor. A number of leading mutual gains organizations in the United States, such as Xerox, Saturn, and Kaiser Permanente, involve employees and their representatives, through the use of joint committees, in non-production issues such as human resource policies and strategic planning, thereby providing new avenues for collective and individual voice (Avgar and Kuruvilla 2011; Kochan et al. 2008; Rubinstein and Kochan 2001; Kochan et al. 1994; Appelbaum and Batt 1994; Cutcher-Gershenfeld 1991).

Many innovative organizations set up problem-solving groups comprised of employees and managers from different units that are designed to discuss and debate a wide range of production and non-production-related issues, giving new meaning to the role of voice in the workplace (Cappelli et al. 1997: 92; Kochan and Osterman 1994). The Saturn Corporation had been labeled as having developed one of the boldest work systems in this regard. Employees and their union were involved in the majority of managerial decisions from issues of overtime to questions concerning product orders and so on (Rubinstein and Kochan 2001). It is important and interesting to note that Saturn is no longer in existence and was shut down in 2010.

The shift toward increased employee participation, discretion, and voice stems, among other things, from the economic pressures that instigated workplace transformation in the first place (Osterman 1999; Kochan and Osterman 1994). Seeking new methods of achieving economic competitiveness, employers have been paying closer attention to the potential vested in their employees. Employee knowledge and know-how are viewed as a powerful source of competitive advantage and must, therefore, be tapped into via new methods of employee voice, involvement, and participation (Kochan and Rubinstein 2000; Cooke 1994). In an effort to elicit this potential, the mutual gains firm is designed to provide employees with the opportunity to participate and the empowerment to execute this opportunity (Appelbaum et al. 2000; Kochan and Osterman 1994; Bahrami 1992). As noted above, alongside potential performance gains, the mutual gains focus on employee voice and involvement is also founded on the notion that employees themselves prefer to work in settings that provide greater opportunities to participate in a meaningful manner (Geary 2008; Kochan 1995; Kochan and Osterman 1994). Thus, the mutual gains paradigm is founded on the proposition that employers and employees have a mutual interest in organizational structures and practices that provide for new voice and input avenues in the workplace.

Employee participation in production and non-production issues fundamentally alters the manner in which work is organized. In order to allow for employees to properly participate, organizations must restructure communication channels, employee skills and knowledge, job classifications, labor–management negotiations, conflict resolution, and management–employee dynamics in general (Rubinstein and Kochan 2001; Appelbaum et al. 2000). The Saturn example described in detail by Rubinstein and Kochan (2001) is a good case in point. In other words, delivering on the promise of new forms of employee voice requires the creation of new organizational foundations. The creation of a high level of lateral communication and interaction between the United Auto Workers and management throughout the different organizational entities created a network organization (Rubinstein and Kochan 2001; Rubinstein 2000). Participation can therefore be seen as the employment system's adaptation to the post-bureaucratic organization and the dismantling of traditional hierarchical patterns.

Some researchers maintain that a well-implemented system of employee voice and participation is strongly linked to improved organizational performance (Rubinstein and Kochan 2001; Appelbaum et al. 2000; Ichniowski et al. 1997; Kochan and Osterman 1994; Heckscher 1994). Scholars and practitioners maintain that broadening the span of employees' autonomous control and associated voice increases their contribution to the firm (Mills and Ungson 2003). As an example of partnership at a strategic level, Kaiser Permanente, a national healthcare provider and insurer, linked partnership goals with its business strategy (Kochan et al. 2008). The partnership focused on improving its services, maintaining competitive performance, expanding current and new markets, consulting and advocating on public policy issues, and engaging in typical partnership behaviors that create a better working environment for its employees (that is, working conditions, training, employment and income security), allowing employees greater business control and collective voice than traditional collective bargaining (Kochan et al. 2008).

Stemming from both the push for greater levels of employee involvement and from increased flexibility, the mutual gains enterprise is also characterized by a new type of reliance on trust and commitment driven by mutuality of purpose. In contrast to the adversarial nature of the traditional employment pattern, the mutual gains firm is founded upon the assumption that the parties can engage in a trusting relationship beyond any contractually defined rights and obligations (Appelbaum et al. 2000; Kochan and Osterman, 1994; Lorenz 1992), which can yield joint benefits (Dobbins and Gunnigle 2009; Frost 2001). Employers are encouraged to trust their employees to utilize discretion for the improvement of organizational outcomes; employees are encouraged to trust their employers in delivering enhanced employment and work-life improvement. Employees and employers are expected to abandon their mutual suspicion and instead trust that mutual gains from this new relationship will be realized (Martinez Lucio and Stuart 2002).

EMPLOYEE VOICE IMPLICATIONS IN THE MUTUAL GAINS ENTERPRISE

One of the central questions related to the mutual gains model is the extent to which employees are afforded real and meaningful access to voice and whether this form of organizational input and influence can be translated into concrete gains beyond firm performance. With the recent increase in alternative non-union methods of delivering voice, this question has become increasingly dominant (for a recent review see Budd et al. 2010).Voice can take on a number of different forms with drastically different implications for employees and employers (Wilkinson and Fay 2011). Employee voice varies, among other factors, in the extent to which it provides employees with genuine influence and power in the workplace. Voice scholars have distinguished between voice with and without muscle (for a recent review see Wilkinson and Fay 2011).

As such, voice can serve multiple objectives, including, but not limited to, countering managerial power, improving working conditions and employee well-being, and increasing organizational participation and involvement. Voice associated with the mutual gains enterprise is unique in that it is designed, in theory, to meet a number of these objectives. Nevertheless, the extent to which this voice distributes benefits to employees and employers is, to a large extent, still an open question. What is the nature of the mutual gains voice and who stands to benefit from it? In what follows we consider three possible pitfalls associated with participation and voice in the mutual gains model.

Voice for What Purpose? From Working Conditions to Organizational Performance

As previously discussed, the mutual gains enterprise was created, for the most part, as a means for obtaining a sustained competitive advantage. The overarching assumption made by scholars and practitioners is that organizational changes designed to increase performance are also likely to improve employee working conditions and associated attitudes and perceptions. Greater access to voice and influence in the workplace are likely, it was assumed, to create the foundation for organizational roles that are more rewarding and satisfying. In particular, scholars have examined the extent to which these roles are associated with greater levels of job security. For example, leading mutual gains organizations such as Kaiser Permanente, Saturn, and Xerox went to great lengths to integrate employment security as a part of their high performance work design (Kochan et al. 2008; Kochan et al. 1994; Appelbaum and Batt 1994; Cutcher-Gershenfeld 1991). Based on the innovative workplace demands for increased employee participation and effort, it would be expected that the innovative workplace within the mutual gains enterprise would maintain a commitment to working conditions such as job security, compensation and benefits, and work–life quality. A look at comparative innovative systems, such as Japanese lean production, demonstrates, in fact, the link between employee commitment to the firm and employment security (Appelbaum and Batt 1994).

Nevertheless, voice in the mutual gains firm is, for the most part, not designed to address issues related to working conditions (that is, job intensity and burnout; Godard 2001) or job security in particular (Osterman 2000, 1999). In other words, this voice is, largely, lacking real muscle. In the absence of this type of voice, how do employees fare in the mutual gains firm? Alongside evidence from well-known case studies, there is a body of evidence that suggests that the mutual gains organization and its performance-focused voice do not, in fact, safeguard employee working conditions. The new mutual gains workplace, some argue, has dismantled the traditional institutions that helped secure long-term employment. This has created the potential for substantially reduced employment security (Stone 2004; Cappelli 1999; Cappelli et al. 1997). The mutual gains organization, which blurs both internal and external boundaries, is claimed to have altered its policies regarding internal mobility and employment longevity (Heckscher 1994). Osterman (2000, 1999) has provided empirical evidence that supports the positive relationship between innovative high performance practices and layoffs, and thus a reduced level of job security. Additional research has also shown that workplace restructuring in general has been associated with substantial downsizing and high layoff rates (Osterman et al. 2001; Cappelli et al. 1997). There is also some evidence that suggests that the labor–management partnership dimension associated with the mutual gains model in the unionized setting is also associated with job insecurity (O'Dowd and Roche 2009; Danford et al. 2005; Gittell et al. 2004; Martinez Lucio and Stuart 2002).

As with job security, there are also concerns that wages and benefits and work–life quality are secondary to organizational success in the mutual gains firm. There is some empirical evidence that indicates that despite the use of pay for performance schemes, wages in organizations that use innovative high performance practices have not increased (Cappelli and Neumark 2004; Osterman 2000; for contradictory evidence on earnings inequality, see Osterman 2006; Appelbaum et al. 2000; Appelbaum and Batt 1994). Additionally, wage outcomes documented for labor–management partnership are also mixed, with some studies showing partnership associated gains and others documenting wage deterioration (Geary and Trif 2011; Gittell et al. 2004; Oxenbridge and Brown 2002). Furthermore, partnerships have been associated with diminishing work–life quality and increasing work intensity (Danford et al. 2004; Martinez Lucio and Stuart 2002).

One way to explain these negative implications associated with the mutual gains firm is based on the substitution of traditional collective voice, which is directed towards the safeguarding of employment conditions. Focusing on individual voice may, in fact, produce organizational gains, but it is not necessarily an effective means of ensuring that these gains are being distributed to employees. If this is the case, it points to a fundamental paradox in the mutual gains model, namely that the core foundational characteristic upon which it is erected – individual employee voice – weakens the ability to secure mutuality of gains, supposedly its defining feature.

Voice for Whom? The Gap between High-Skilled and Low-Skilled Employees

Collective forms of voice are, by their very nature, designed to provide access across a diverse set of employee groups. Since voice is intended to provide employees with an institutionalized vehicle to raise questions and concerns regarding employment and working conditions, there are very few barriers to use. The fundamental rationale for providing employees with voice in the mutual gains model is very different. Voice, as noted, is seen, first and foremost as a mechanism through which employees can better contribute to the performance of the firm, with the expectation that these gains will then be distributed across stakeholders. As such, there is less of an incentive to provide unrestricted access to voice. Specifically, it is likely that voice in the mutual gains firm will be directed towards specific categories of employees, with a particular focus on those who are highly skilled. As such, the mutual gains firm is likely to create voice-related differentiation as a function of skill levels, which is a central resource in this new industrial relations model. This potential pattern is exacerbated by the implications that the mutual gains firm has for employee skills and knowledge and associated job security.

The mutual gains workplace has two potentially contradictory influences on skills and training. On the one hand, employee positions are increasingly complex and uncertain. Employees are required to perform a wider range of tasks and to contribute more of themselves to their work and to the organization. This facet of the innovative workplace requires that employees receive greater training and attain enhanced skills (Osterman et al. 2001; Appelbaum et al. 2000; Cappelli et al. 1997; Osterman 1995). This facet is also compatible with the notion of employability security. On the other hand, the same institutions that increased job security, namely internal advancement ladders, which are no longer central in the high performance organization, were also important in the development of employee skills (Stone 2004). In their absence, companies may risk the erosion of the skills upon which the innovative workplace is founded (Cappelli 1999; Cappelli et al. 1997). In addition, the structural changes in the mutual gains organization reduce the incentives for internal training. The flattening of the organization limits the positions to which workers can advance by decreasing the need to train a large proportion of employees. The reduction in supervisory roles also decreases opportunities for on-the-job training (Cappelli 1999).

One of the ways in which organizations have been resolving this tension is by hiring employees with greater skill levels to begin with (Osterman et al. 2001). In accordance with the 'boundaryless career' model, employees move across organizations and many enter firms with existing high skill levels. This approach has led to what is referred to as 'employee poaching' (Cappelli 1999), which creates an entirely new set of organizational complexities and negative incentives for providing internal training. A second option is to create new opportunities and forums for skill acquisition through networking and cross-organization fertilization (Stone 2004). Finally, some employers who seek to maintain an internal training apparatus have been searching for ways to share the cost of training with their employees (Cappelli et al. 1997).

Thus, the effects of mutual gains restructuring on skills and training are mixed (Cappelli et al. 1997). First, organizations vary in the manner in which they strike the balance between the need for skills and the search for flexibility (Cappelli 1999). Second, the new workplace offers different outcomes to different categories of workers

(Osterman 1995). For highly skilled and well educated employees, the new emphasis on already trained employees increases their leverage and provides for greater opportunities within and across organizations. However, for lower skilled employees, this new reality leads to reduced opportunities to acquire on-the-job skills, which therefore negatively affects access to voice. This gap is characteristic of the new workplace's process of individualization and the growing inequality between high and low-skilled employees. This division is then reinforced by the likely differentiation in access to voice across this skill-based divide. Since individual voice is an increasingly important resource in the mutual gains firm, its disproportionate availability to highly skilled employees is likely to exacerbate this growing inequality. Voice in the mutual gains firm, may, therefore, become a currency that symbolizes and cements status and skill differences in the workplace.

Voice in the Absence of Hierarchy

In a study of alternative work practices associated with high performance work practices, Godard (2001) found that these were not consistently associated with positive employee outcomes. When adopted at high rates, these practices were associated with more difficult working conditions and the relationship with empowerment, commitment, and job satisfaction was weak and statistically insignificant (for similar evidence regarding partnership, see Danford et al. 2004; Johnstone et al. 2004; Martinez Lucio and Stuart 2002). Furthermore, Godard found that team voice-related practices such as autonomy and responsibility were also not associated with positive outcomes. In attempting to explain this evidence, which contradicts much of the mainstream literature on high performance work practices, Godard (2001: 798) proposes, 'It is possible that, in the absence of an immediate supervisor there is greater uncertainty and opportunity for disagreement over how to allocate and perform tasks, increasing individual insecurities and resulting in intra-group conflicts' (see also Sinclair 1992). Building on Godard's claim, it is possible that the characteristics of the new mutual gains workplace discussed above, the uncertainty associated with the reduction of rules and the broadening of roles and boundaries, may constrain the benefits associated with employee voice.

The mutual gains organization replaces the vertical hierarchical structure with a flattened horizontal one. On the one hand, this structural change reduces the level of authoritative power-based relations in the organization, allowing for greater employee voice, input, and autonomy. As mentioned above, power and authority are replaced by influence. However, this transformation creates the potential for increased tension within and between organizational units. In the absence of formal hierarchical control, teams, which are the prevalent production unit in many of these organizations, are required to become self-regulating. Despite the widespread assumptions that this form of regulation reduces the use of control and the subsequent development of conflict, critical research has provided evidence that undermines this relationship. Researchers such as Barker (1993) and Godard (2001) have found that self-regulated teams develop new mechanisms of concerted control that are no less repressive than the traditional top-down ones (for similar evidence see Ezzamel and Willmott 1998; Sewell 1998; Sinclair 1992). Additionally, joint committees have been associated with power struggles and cooperation breakdowns (Johnstone et al. 2004; Preuss and Frost 2003).

In the absence of clear responsibilities and division of labor and in the presence of greater levels of potential peer-to-peer conflict, increased levels of employee voice may serve as a double-edged sword. In other words, greater levels of input and voice in agile and flexible organizations are also likely to be associated with the potential for negative individual and team-level consequences as a result of the complexities inherent in their use.

CONCLUSIONS

The mutual gains firm arose in the 1980s and 1990s as a means of addressing growing competitive pressures and the increasing inadequacies inherent in the bureaucratic organizational form. The mutual gains model garnered a great deal of support among scholars and practitioners excited by the paradigmatic shift that it represented. Specifically, proponents highlighted the departure from a conflict-centered model of employment relations. The promise of this new model was based on the argument that in the absence of structurally created conflicts of interests between employees and employers, this new industrial relations pattern could deliver gains to both parties. As such, this model challenged many core assumptions regarding organizational structure and employment relations. In particular, the mutual gains model reimagined the very contours of employee voice and the role that it could play in organizations. In contrast to its traditional grievance and collective bargaining focus, voice was conceptualized as a vehicle through which employees could engage in a meaningful and value added manner. Voice in the mutual gains firm provides employees with the opportunity for real input and involvement in production and service delivery-related decisions.

Alongside its clear potential, there are a number of important questions about the extent to which the mutual gains organization can, in fact, deliver on its well-articulated promise. Specifically, it is unclear whether the shift from collective to individual voice allows for a long-term commitment to the distribution of gains to employees. Collective voice has proven to be an effective means of improving and safeguarding employment conditions. Individual voice, on the other hand, has proven to be an effective means of advancing performance-related gains. Can the organizations deliver on the promise of mutuality of gains in the absence of both forms of voice? In addition, linking voice to expected performance gains – as opposed to employment gains – may create segmentation in accessibility to voice. If voice is seen primarily as a means of facilitating employee input and involvement in an effort to enhance performance, it is possible that its availability will be limited to certain employee groups and categories. Can the mutual gains organization deliver on its promise when voice is seen as a resource allocated on the basis of perceived skill levels? Finally, restructuring associated with the mutual gains firm has created a number of complexities that may challenge employees' abilities to make use of their increased access to voice and input. Specifically, the collapsing of organizational hierarchies and the flattening of organizational design both have the potential for creating new forms of uncertainty and ambiguity. Exercising voice in this context may be more difficult than mutual gains proponents acknowledge.

The mutual gains framework and its associated employment systems sparked a renewed interest in the power associated with employee voice and its potential to bypass some of the longstanding employment relations challenges prevalent in traditional industrial relations models. While there is a large body of research suggesting that this academic and practitioner interest and excitement have been warranted, there are also a number of empirically-based questions that support a more nuanced and mixed portrait associated with the mutual gains model. Industrial relations researchers will, it is likely, continue to debate the viability of such new employment models and the implications they have for employee voice.

REFERENCES

Adler, P.S. and B. Borys (1996), 'Two types of bureaucracy: enabling and coercive', *Administrative Science Quarterly*, **41**, 61–89.

Appelbaum, E. (2002), 'The impact of new forms of work organisation on workers', in G. Murray, J. Bélanger and A. Giles (eds), *Work and Employment Relations in the High-Performance Workplace*, London: Continuum, pp. 120–49.

Appelbaum, E. and R. Batt (1994), *The New American Workplace: Transforming Work Systems in the United States*, Ithaca, NY: Cornell University/ILR Press.

Appelbaum, E., T. Bailey, P. Berg and A.L. Kalleberg (2000), *Manufacturing Advantage: Why High-Performance Work Systems Pay Off*, Ithaca, NY: Cornell University Press, pp. 1–46.

Avgar, A. and S. Kuruvilla (2011), 'Dual alignment of industrial relations activity: from strategic choice to mutual gains', in David Lewin, Bruce E. Kaufman and Paul J. Gollan (eds), *Advances in Industrial and Labor Relations*, Vol. 18, Bingley: Emerald Publishing, pp. 1–39.

Bahrami, H. (1992), 'The emerging flexible organization: perspectives from Silicon Valley', *California Management Review*, Summer, 35–52.

Barbash, J. (1984), *Elements of Industrial Relations*, Madison, WI: University of Wisconsin Press.

Barker, J.R. (1993), 'Tightening the iron cage: concertive control in self-managing teams', *Administrative Science Quarterly*, **38** (3), 408–38.

Brewster, C., R. Croucher, G. Wood and M. Brookes (2007), 'Collective and individual voice: convergence in Europe?', *International Journal of Human Resource Management*, **18** (7), 1246–62.

Budd, J., P. Gollan and A. Wilkinson (2010), 'New approaches to employee voice and participation', *Human Relations*, **63** (3), 1–8.

Burawoy, M. (1979), *Manufacturing Consent: Changes in the Labor Process under Monopoly Capitalism*, Chicago, IL: University of Chicago Press.

Burns, T. and G.M. Stalker (1961), *The Management of Innovation*, London: Tavistock Publications.

Butler, P.A., O. Tregaskis and L.A. Glover (2011), 'Workplace partnership and employee involvement – contradictions and synergies: evidence from a heavy engineering case study', *Economic and Industrial Democracy*, **34** (1), 5–24.

Cappelli, P. (1999), *The New Deal at Work: Managing the Market-Driven Workforce*, Boston MA: Harvard Business School Press.

Cappelli, P. and D. Neumark (2004), 'External churning and internal flexibility: evidence on the functional flexibility and core-periphery hypotheses', *Industrial Relations*, **43** (1), 148–82.

Cappelli, P., L. Bassi, H. Katz, D. Knoke, P. Osterman and M. Useem, M. (1997), *Change at Work*, New York: Oxford University Press.

Child, J. and R.G. McGrath (2001), 'Organizations unfettered: organizational form in an information-intensive economy', *Academy of Management Journal*, **44** (6), 1135–48.

Colvin, A.J.S. (2004), 'The relationship between employee involvement and workplace dispute resolution', *Relations Industrielles/Industrial Relations*, **59** (4), 681–704.

Commons, J.R. (1935), *History of Labour in the United States*, Vol. 1, New York: Macmillan.

Cooke, W.N. (1990), *Labour–Management Cooperation: New Partnerships or Going in Circles?*, Kalamazoo, MI: Upjohn Institute for Employment Research.

Cooke, W.N. (1994), 'Employee participation programs, group-based incentives, and company performance: A union–nonunion comparison', *Industrial and Labor Relations Review*, **47** (4), 594–609.

Cutcher-Gershenfeld, J. (1991), 'The impact of economic performance on a transformation in workplace relations', *Industrial and Labor Relations Review*, **44** (2), 241–60.

Cutcher-Gershenfeld, J. and T. Kochan (2004), 'Taking stock: collective bargaining at the turn of the century', *Industrial and Labor Relations Review*, **58** (1), 3–26.

Danford, A., M. Richardson, P. Stewart, S. Tailby and M. Upchurch (2004), 'High performance work systems and workplace partnership: a case study of aerospace workers', *New Technology, Work and Employment*, **19** (1), 14–29.

Danford, A.J., M. Richardson, P. Stewart, M. Upchurch and S. Tailby (2005), *Partnership and the High Performance Workplace: Work and Employment Relations in the Aerospace Industry*, Basingstoke: Palgrave Macmillan.

Dobbins, A. and P. Gunnigle (2009), 'Can voluntary workplace partnership deliver sustainable mutual gains?', *British Journal of Industrial Relations*, **47** (3), 546–70.

Doellgast, V. (2010), 'Collective voice under decentralized bargaining: a comparative study of work and reorganization in US and German call centers', *British Journal of Industrial Relations*, **48** (2), 375–99.

Dundon, T., A. Wilkinson, M. Marchington and P. Ackers (2004), 'The meanings and purpose of employee voice', *International Journal of Human Resource Management*, **15** (6), 1149–70.

Eaton, A.E. and S.A. Rubinstein (2006), 'Tracking local unions involved in managerial decision-making', *Labor Studies Journal*, **31** (2), 1–29.

Ezzamel, M. and H. Willmott (1998), 'Accounting for teamwork: a critical study of group-based systems of organizational control', *Administrative Science Quarterly*, **43** (2), 353–96.

Freeman, R.B. and J.L. Medoff (1984), *What Do Unions Do?*, New York: Basic Books.

Frost, A.C. (2001), 'Reconceptualizing local union responses to workplace restructuring in North America', *British Journal of Industrial Relations*, **39** (4), 539–64.

Geary, J. (2008), 'Do unions benefit from working in partnership with employers? Evidence from Ireland', *Industrial Relations: A Journal of Economy and Society*, **47** (4), 530–68.

Geary, J. and A. Trif (2011), 'Workplace partnership and the balance of advantage: a critical case analysis', *British Journal of Industrial Relations*, **49** (S1), s44–s69.

Gittell, J.H., A.V. von Nordenflycht and T.A. Kochan (2004), 'Mutual gains or zero sum? Labor relations and firm performance in the airline industry', *Industrial and Labor Relations Review*, **57** (2), 163–79.

Godard, J. (2001), 'High performance and transformation of work? The implications of alternative work practices for the experience and outcomes of work', *Industrial and Labor Relations Review*, **54** (4), 776–806.

Godard, J. and J.T. Delaney (2000), 'Reflections on the "high performance" paradigm's implications for industrial relations as a field', *Industrial and Labor Relations Review*, **53** (3), 482–502.

Guest, D.E. and R. Peccei (2001), 'Partnership at work: mutuality and the balance of advantage', *British Journal of Industrial Relations*, **39** (2), 207–36.

Hammer, M. and J. Champy (1993), *Reengineering the Corporation: A Manifesto for Business Revolution*, New York: Harper Business.

Heckscher, C. (1994), 'Defining the post-bureaucratic type', in Charles Heckscher and Anne Donnellon (eds), *The Post-Bureaucratic Organization: New Perspectives on Organizational Change*, Thousand Oaks, CA: Sage, pp. 14–62.

Heckscher, C. and A. Donnellon (1994), *The Post-Bureaucratic Organization: New Perspectives on Organizational Change*, Thousand Oaks, CA: Sage.

Hirschhorn, L. and T. Gilmore (1992), 'The new boundaries of the "boundaryless" company', *Harvard Business Review*, **70** (3), 104–15.

Hirschman, A.O. (1970), *Exit, Voice, and Loyalty: Responses to Decline in Firms, Organizations, and States*, Cambridge, MA: Harvard University Press.

Ichniowski, C., K. Shaw and G. Prennushi (1997), 'The effects of human resource management practices on productivity: a study of steel finishing lines', *American Economic Review*, **87** (3), 291–313.

Johnstone, S., A. Wilkinson and P. Ackers (2004), 'Partnership paradoxes: a case study of an energy company', *Employee Relations*, **26** (4), 353–76.

Johnstone, S., P. Ackers and A. Wilkinson (2010), 'Better than nothing? Is non-union partnership a contradiction in terms?', *Journal of Industrial Relations*, **52** (2), 151–68.

Kling, J. (1995), 'High performance work systems and firm performance', *Monthly Labor Review*, May, 29–36.

Kochan, T.A. (1995), 'Using the Dunlop report to achieve mutual gains', *Industrial Relations*, **34** (3), 350–66.

Kochan, T.A. and P. Osterman (1994), *The Mutual Gains Enterprise: Forging a Winning Partnership among Labor, Management, and Government*, Boston, MA: Harvard Business School Press.

Kochan, T.A. and S.A. Rubinstein (2000), 'Toward a stakeholder theory of the firm: the Saturn partnership', *Organization Science*, **11** (4), 367–86.

Kochan, A.T., C.H. Katz and R.B. McKersie (1994), *The Transformation of American Industrial Relations*, Ithaca, NY: ILR Press.

Kochan, T.A., P.S. Adler, R.B. McKersie, A.E. Eaton, P. Segal and P. Gerhart (2008), 'The potential and precariousness of partnership: the case of the Kaiser Permanente labor management partnership', *Industrial Relations: A Journal of Economy and Society*, **47** (1), 36–65.

Lawrence, P.R. and J.W. Lorsch (1967), *Organization and Environment*, Boston, MA: Harvard Business School Press.

Lewin, D. (2001), 'IR and HR perspective on workplace conflict: what can each learn from the other?', *Human Resource Management Review*, **11** (4), 453–85.

Lipsky, D.B., R.L. Seeber and R.D. Fincher (2003), *Emerging Systems for Managing Workplace Conflict: Lessons from American Corporations for Managers and Dispute Resolution Professionals*, San Francisco, CA: Jossey-Bass.

Lorenz, E.H. (1992), 'Trust and the flexible firm: international comparisons', *Industrial Relations*, **31** (3), 455–70.

Masters, M.F., R.R. Albright and D. Epilion (2006), 'What did partnerships do? Evidence from the federal sector', *Industrial and Labor Relations Review*, **59** (3), 367–85.

Martinez Lucio, M. and M. Stuart (2002), 'Assessing the principles of partnership: workplace trade union representatives' attitudes and experiences', *Employee Relations*, **24** (3), 305–20.

Martinez Lucio, M. and M. Stuart (2004), 'Swimming against the tide: social partnership, mutual gains and the revival of "tired" HRM', *International Journal of Human Resource Management*, **15** (2), 410–24.

Mazzeo, M.J. (2003), 'Competition and service quality in the U.S. airline industry', *Review of Industrial Organization*, **22** (4), 275–96.

Mills, P.K. and G.R. Ungson (2003), 'Reassessing the limits of structural empowerment: organizational constitution and trust as controls', *Academy of Management Review*, **28** (1), 143–53.

O'Dowd, J. and W.K. Roche (2009), 'Partnership structures and agendas and managers' assessments of stakeholder outcomes', *Industrial Relations Journal*, **40** (1), 17–39.

Osterman, P. (1995), 'Skill training and work organization in American establishments', *Industrial Relations*, **34** (2), 125–46.

Osterman, P. (1999), *Securing Prosperity: The American Labor Market: How it has Changed and what to do about it*, Princeton, NJ: Princeton University Press.

Osterman, P. (2000), 'Work reorganization in an era of restructuring: trends in diffusion and effects on employee welfare', *Industrial and Labor Relations Review*, **53** (2), 179–96.

Osterman, P. (2006), 'The wage effects of high performance work organization in manufacturing', *Industrial and Labor Relations Review*, **52** (2), 187–204.

Osterman, P., T.A. Kochan, R.M. Locke and M.J. Piore (2001), *Working in America: A Blueprint for the New Labor Market*, Cambridge, MA: MIT Press.

Oxenbridge, S. and W. Brown (2002), 'The two faces of partnership? An assessment of partnership and cooperative employer/trade union relationships', *Employee Relations*, **24** (3), 262–76.

Preuss, G.A. and A.C. Frost (2003), 'The rise and decline of labor–management cooperation: lessons from health care in the twin cities', *California Management Review*, **45** (2), 85–106.

Ridley-Duff, R. and A. Bennett (2011), 'Towards mediation: developing a theoretical framework to understand alternate dispute resolution', *Industrial Relations Journal*, **42** (2), 106–23.

Rubinstein, S.A. (2000), 'The impact of co-management on quality performance: the case of the Saturn Corporation', *Industrial and Labor Relations Review*, **53** (2), 197–218.

Rubinstein, S.A. and T.A. Kochan (2001), *Learning from Saturn*, Ithaca, NY: ILR Press.

Sewell, G. (1998), 'The discipline of teams: the control of team-based industrial work through electronic and peer surveillance', *Administrative Science Quarterly*, **43** (2), 397–428.

Sinclair, A. (1992), 'The tyranny of a team ideology', *Organization Studies*, **13** (4), 611–27.

Starkey, K., M. Wright and S. Thompson (1991), 'Flexibility, hierarchy, markets', *British Journal of Management*, **2** (3), 165–76.

Stone, V.W.K. (2004), *From Widgets to Digits: Employment Regulation for the Changing Workplace*, Cambridge: Cambridge University Press.

Tailby, S., M. Richardson, M. Upchurch, A. Danford and P. Stewart (2007), 'Partnership with and without trade unions in the UK financial services: filling or fueling the representation gap?', *Industrial Relations Journal*, **38** (3), 210–28.

Teague, P. (2005), 'What is enterprise partnership?', *Organization*, **12** (4), 567–89.

Thompson, V.A. (1965), 'Bureaucracy and innovation', *Administrative Science Quarterly*, **10** (1), 1–20.

Volberda, H.W. (1996), 'Toward the flexible form: how to remain vital in hypercompetitive environments', *Organization Science*, **7** (4), 359–74.

Walton, R.E. and R.B. McKersie (1965), *A Behavioral Theory of Labor Negotiations: An Analysis of a Social Interaction System*, New York: McGraw-Hill.

Webb, Sidney and Beatrice Webb (1897), *Industrial Democracy*, London: Longmans.

Wilkinson, A. and C. Fay (2011), 'New times for employee voice?', *Human Resource Management*, **50** (1), 65–74.

21 Non-union employee representation
Tony Dobbins and Tony Dundon

INTRODUCTION

In recent decades employers and policymakers in most westernized economies have shown increased interest and sponsorship towards company specific forms of non-union employee representation (NER). The attractiveness of NER to both employers and policymakers has materialized against a backdrop of competitive pressures allied to emerging legal developments. Regulations such as the European Information and Consultation Directive enable employers, should they wish, to introduce NER as a new voice right for employees (but not necessarily unions) to receive information and be consulted on a range of employment and business matters. However, the evidence to date in the UK and Ireland suggests that employers have rarely used this directive to implement new forms of NER, more often than not opting to preserve direct individualized voice channels (Hall et al., 2011; Dundon and Collings, 2011). Evidently, legal arrangements influencing NER differ widely across Europe, with the likes of the UK and Ireland favouring direct channels while other parts of Europe, such as Germany, prefer indirect collective structures of worker engagement. Declining trade union density has also fed into rising interest in alternatives to union-only collective forms of voice delivery (Gomez et al., 2010). For example, protest and anger about spiralling corporate executive pay has sparked calls by the High Pay Commission in the UK for employee representatives to be consulted on such matters and placed on company remuneration boards (High Pay Commission, 2012). Non-union representation is rare in Britain but has increased among larger private sector employers, rising from 6 per cent in the 2004 Workplace Employment Relations Survey (WERS) to 13 per cent in 2011 (van Wanrooy et al., 2013: 15). Overall, around 7 per cent of all workplaces reported the presence of a non-union-only employee representative system (van Wanrooy et al., 2013: 15).

Given the prevailing changes and the fragmentation of traditional patterns of single-channel union representation, scholars continue to subject NER to greater scrutiny (Gollan, 2010; Willman et al., 2006; Dundon and Gollan, 2007; Lavelle et al., 2010; Gomez et al., 2010; Kaufman and Taras, 2010; Lewin, 2010; Wilkinson et al., 2010). Two broad strands of NER literature are evident: the first of these discusses NER as simply a union avoidance tactic and the second considers the possibilities of employers displaying various or multiple motives and rationales for adopting NER, including delivering employee voice as part of a sophisticated mutual gains work regime. The first strand focuses heavily on debates around management using NER as a mechanism for union avoidance (Gall, 2004; Kelly, 2004; Upchurch et al., 2006; Gunnigle et al., 2009). There are similarities in this union avoidance literature with Ramsey's (1977) 'cycles of control' thesis; the central argument being that management introduces NER arrangements when they perceive that their power and authority are under challenge by the agency of labour. The second strand of contemporary research has sought to move beyond this by arguing that employers may have a range of rationales and objectives when implementing NER (Dundon and Rollinson, 2004; Butler, 2009a, 2009b; Cullinane et al., 2012; Kaufman, 2013). For example, NER may provide a mechanism for delivering positive mutual gains for both employers and employees. This is an important issue given the contemporary prevalence of non-union firms across the globe. While existing literature has focused on the processes and outcomes of management–union collaboration under unionized partnership regimes (Kochan et al., 2008; Dobbins and Gunnigle, 2009; Butler et al., 2011; Evans et al., 2012), more understanding is required about whether or not NERs can deliver mutual gains style relations in non-union or partially unionized firms. Important also are the contextual factors affecting NER mutuality: external macro pressures such as changing regulatory and market conditions, and internal micro-organizational dimensions shaping employee voice, notably management strategy and choice over the adoption of NERs (Dundon and Gollan, 2007). A number of questions arise in this regard: can employer-sponsored non-union employee representation deliver positive-sum mutual gains? What are the contextual conditions that support or obstruct effective NER voice? Is NER voice sustained over time in non-union or partially unionized workplace regimes?

These issues are addressed as follows. First, we review the definitions of NER, describing what they are, what they are not, and the forms they take. We then consider the extent of NER arrangements while a subsequent section focuses on the purpose and utility of NER in some detail. This is followed by a section exploring the contextual conditions shaping NER and its longevity. The concluding section summarizes some implications that can be extracted to provide greater understanding of NER as a vehicle of employer-driven voice.

WHAT IS NER? DEFINITION, FORM AND FUNCTIONALITY

NER is, broadly speaking, a company-specific forum of some sort that provides opportunities for non-union employee representative voice (Donaghey et al., 2012). A general definition of NERs is outlined by Taras and Kaufman (2006: 515), who also refer to a possible mutual gains agency function:

> . . . one or more employees . . . act in an agency function for other employees in dealings with management over issues of mutual concern, including the terms and conditions under which people work . . . In setting up such plans management expects that the plans will encourage cooperative, advisory and consultative modes of interaction so that friction points between management and workers can be lessened or eliminated. In taking on a representational function, workers expect that NER will provide a meaningful form of employee voice, a capacity to influence management decision-making, and recognition by managers that workers have a right to respectful treatment.

Gollan (2000) identifies five core features of NER. First, membership of NER forums is restricted to individuals employed by and within the organization. In other words, there is no formal recognition of an outside trade union official. Second, there are likely to be only limited formal linkages to trade unions or other external representative organizations, or none at all. In this regard there has been a reported increase in the prominence of external civil society organizations (CSOs) providing a representative or advocacy function for employees, for example, CSOs promoting rights at the workplace for families or people with disabilities (see Williams et al., 2011). In short, there are non-union forums external to the organization which provide a representative role for some employees in certain situations. A third key feature to NER voice is that the firm often provides the resources to enable the employee representative forum to function and exist. Fourth is that NER bodies are essentially indirect in nature, providing a more 'representative' function for employee interests than that offered by more direct mechanisms of individual employee involvement. Finally, according to Gollan (2000), such structures tend to represent all employees at the establishment or workplace level, although this need not be the case in practice. For example, the presence of non-union forms of employee representation does not mean that there are no trade union members within a company. Managers may consult with a union in respect of certain parts of the workforce, while avoiding union recognition for other employees. With the rise in NER, scholars have reported a growth in the phenomenon of 'double-breasting' voice, defined as the practice where an employer recognizes a union at one plant, while operating alternative non-union voice at another company location (Gunnigle et al., 2009; Lavelle et al., 2010; Cullinane et al., 2012).

NER can encompass a multitude of indirect collective mechanisms that often go under different names in different countries: works councils, joint consultative committees, staff associations, partnership forums, health and safety committees, quality and productivity committees, or the inclusion of employee representatives on company boards (among others). The range of choices open to employers, in terms of enterprise-specific mechanisms of NER voice, is heightened in the context of the increasingly permissive and fragmented voluntarist industrial relations systems now characteristic of liberal market regimes (Dobbins, 2010). The variety of forms, their primary functions and other associated characteristics, is summarized in Table 21.1.

The first column in Table 21.1 is about the *form* of NER. By form is meant the various practices that can be used to enable and facilitate NER voice, ranging from the structured committees dealing with matters such as health and safety, to facilitating a role on the company board of directors for non-union employee representatives. There is also a *function* to each of the different forms of NER arrangements (column 2 in Table 21.1). For example, a non-union grievance panel may function to rectify problems raised by individual employees; while the use of a plant production committee or company-wide communication forums may serve to avoid unionization (Dundon et al., 2004). In reality form and function are likely to be related to *level* (column 3), ranging from small work groups (formal or informal) to company or even transnational divisions through non-union European Works Councils (EWCs). Column 4 identifies the *scope* (or topics) of NER coverage. Scope is often connected to level. For example, issues to do with work process or technical matters may be considered at team or work group level, while quality matters may be decided at a higher level or plant-wide forum. Likewise, higher order issues such as pay or terms and conditions of employment may be the subject of representative dialogue through more senior advisory and representative committees. An example is at the 'BritCo' case reported by Cullinane et al. (2012). The NER forum at 'BritCo' initially met to resolve employee concerns over parity of redundancy terms at different company locations. While this involved a substantive issue – redundancy terms

Table 21.1 Form and functionality of NER arrangements

Form	Function	Level	Scope	Mode of representation	Power resources	Temporal features of NER
Grievance panel or committee	Rectify a problem	Work-group; team; department; function	Working conditions; employee–manager relationships	Internal. Appointed by management/supervisor	Informal and relational	Permanency, but ad hoc and informal across different levels
Joint health, safety and employee well-being committee	Maintain and review protocols for safe working conditions and standards	Department; function; division; plant	Health, safety, welfare, well-being concerns	Internal. Elected by peers in ballot. External. Some external role through state H&S agencies (depending on country)	Varies by scope and level, from narrow to broad	Time-bound depending on scope/topic/issue
Profit-share /gain-share focus group	Distribution of profit or bonus plans / agreements	Cost-centre unit (function or division)	Bonus payments; recognition awards	Internal. Selected by management/supervisor	Minimal and advisory	Disbandable; formal; infrequent
Quality forum	Employee input to improve product design / service delivery	Team; department	Quality of products/ service; standards	Internal. Selected by management External. Some external expertise on technical matters/issues (if appropriate)	Minimal and advisory	Informal, regular and relational-based at lower levels
Plant production committee	Production scheduling; union avoidance communications	Function; division; plant	Targets; pace of work; supervisor concerns	Internal. Elected by peers and/or appointed by management	Varies by scope, level and function, from distributive to integrative agenda	Temporary; crisis or issue-driven initially. Can establish degree of stability over time
Equal opportunity dialogue forum	Support and encourage equality and diversity culture	Division; plant, including senior management team	Employee rights; promotion; work attendance issues for women or older employees	Internal. Selected by management. External. Some advocacy support (e.g. CSO charity for some employee groups, such as working families or disabilities)	Informal and formal. Can influence agenda-setting of other forums/committees	Temporary; crisis or issue-driven initially. Can establish degree of stability over time

Table 21.1 (continued)

Form	Function	Level	Scope	Mode of representation	Power resources	Temporal features of NER
Company-wide communication forum/works committee	Engender commitment from employees by avoiding union channels of voice	Plant; division, including HR and/or senior management team	Terms and conditions; pay, potential for distributive bargaining topics	Internal. Elected by peers and/or appointed by management	Formal bargaining capacity. Informal consensus-building agenda (range depends on scope and level)	Temporary; Crisis or issue-driven initially. Can establish degree of stability over time
European Works Council	Legal compliance and/or transnational consultation	Transnational division, including senior managers across countries (if relevant)	Information-sharing and consultation; corporate strategy topics	Internal. Elected by peers and/or selected by management. External. (For example, employee advisor permissible under EWC regulations)	Formal information-sharing. Minimal or no bargaining. Distribution of minutes	Mandated stability over time (annual). Voluntary EWC uncommon
Employee reps on board of directors	Union substitution	Plant; company-wide; transnational	Information-sharing and consultation; corporate strategy topics	Internal. Selected by and from among existing employee representatives cohort	Decision-making role; although power can be marginalized on board	Formal; limited permanency

Sources: Adapted from Kaufman and Taras (2010: 265–6) and from Dundon et al. (2004: 1152).

– employee representatives on the NER forum explained that once management felt the issue was resolved and the threat of workers joining a trade union receded, the scope of issues presented to the NER forum narrowed.

The fifth column in Table 21.1 illustrates the variable *modes of representation* across different NER-type practices, which are mostly internal to the firm, although external advocacy is not unknown in certain contexts. Employee representatives may be elected by their peers, appointed by management or, as Williams et al. (2011) have found, CSO-type bodies may influence management policy concerning the rights of some groups of workers in a firm (disabled or older workers, for instance). In the sixth column, as Kaufman and Taras (2010: 267) note, the *power resource* is perhaps the most contested issue in much of the NER literature. Most managers have a definite preference for communicating and involving workers without the outside interference of a trade union. To a large degree, NER bodies are conceived, at least in the eyes of company owners, as a system to avoid and replace an adversarial or 'them and us' attitude through the ideal of mutuality and shared interests. Critics argue that NER bodies are essentially a hollow shell owing to a lack of independent power resources to challenge management decisions (Kelly, 2004; Upchurch et al., 2006). These issues will be discussed more fully later, as it has also been posited that NER may complement or add value rather than existing merely as forums to diminish worker power (Willman et al., 2006; Dundon and Gollan, 2007; Butler, 2009a). The *temporal features* of NER bodies are listed in the final column of Table 21.1, ranging from short-term or ad hoc structures that may have been created to deal with specific issues at a moment in time to those that have been designed as a permanent strategic means to engage employees. The issue of permanence over temporary presence is a contentious one. Scholars have reported that in practice NER bodies tend to be established in response to a crisis, to emerge because of certain regulatory or legal mandates in certain countries, or to be based on long-term strategies dependent on managerial philosophies of inclusion and engagement (Kaufman and Taras, 2010; Cullinane et al., 2012). In any event, an NER system with a high degree of permanency can be shallow or strong, weak or narrow, depending on its scope, level and primary function.

THE EXTENT OF NER

There has been a decline in union-only voice arrangements in many countries, with managerial strategies increasingly gravitating towards voice arrangements that do not involve unions (Kersley et al., 2006; Bryson et al., 2012; van Wanrooy et al., 2013). NER in one guise or another appears to be quite common across countries, although much less so than direct forms of employee involvement (Wilkinson et al., 2010; Bryson et al. 2012). According to the British WERS data, only 7 per cent of all workplaces have 'stand-alone' non-union employee representatives, with an increased presence of non-union reps found among 13 per cent of larger private sector employers (van Wanrooy et al., 2013: 15). It appears, as Charlwood and Terry (2007) observed, that union representation is not being replaced by non-union voice, as NER channels have not replaced union representation in many traditional sectors of the economy. The WERS data paints an uneven and variable pattern of indirect voice, illustrated in Table 21.2 below. It confirms that there is no employee access to *any* form of indirect representation, union or non-union,

Table 21.2   Patterns of employee representative arrangements in British workplaces

Representative pattern	All workplaces		Private sector		Public sector	
	Firms (%)	Workers (%)	Firms (%)	Workers (%)	Firms (%)	Workers (%)
No representation	75	49	83	60	21	11
Non-union	5	10	6	13	0.3	9
Union recognition	18	34	10	20	72	79
Dual-channel	1.5	7	1	6	6	0.5
n	224		1681		543	

Notes: Weighted based: workplaces with five or more employees. Percentages rounded for simplicity.

Sources: Adapted from Charlwood and Terry (2007: 324). See also van Wanrooy et al. (2013: 15) for 2011 updates.

in most UK organizations. Overall, Table 21.2 indicates that around half of all *workers* have no access to any sort of employee representation, and there is no employee representation in 75 per cent of *firms* (Charlwood and Terry, 2007; van Wanrooy et al, 2013).

However, given the strong association between workplace size and incidence of representation, it is still the case that a slight majority of employees overall (51 per cent) work in organizations where some form of employee representation exists. In most of these cases representation solely involves unions (18 per cent of workplaces and 34 per cent of employees). A key finding for the purpose of this chapter, shown in Table 21.2, is the incidence of non-union-only employee representation, which exists in 5 per cent of workplaces and covers 10 per cent of employees (13 per cent of private sector employees) in workplaces where representation is provided solely through non-union channels. In addition, just over 1.5 per cent of workplaces have dual-channel or hybrid representation structures (covering 7 per cent of employees in the UK) where, generally, some employees are represented by union representatives and some or all of the rest by non-union representatives. Charlwood and Terry (2007: 335) conclude that the WERS data illustrates the increasing heterogeneity of patterns of employee representation across British workplaces 'and their inaccessibility to many employees'. While 75 per cent of workplaces have no form of representation whatsoever (if employees in workplaces with fewer than five employees are included), this does not mean little is happening. In WERS 2011, among the most common issues that involved non-union employee representatives were discipline and grievance (77 per cent), health and safety (66 per cent), rates of pay (62 per cent), pension entitlements (55 per cent) and staffing levels (van Wanrooy et al., 2013:17). The time that NER reps devoted to these issues was consistently higher than the time union shop stewards spent on same issues. In this regard the data conforms to the emergence of a diverse pattern of employee representation noted by Charlwood and Terry (2007: 335), with the continuing viability of the coexistence within workplaces of 'hybrid' union and non-union institutions.

As noted, comprehensive survey data on the extent of NER is less common in other countries than the UK. A national survey of NER in the USA and Canada discovered that while approximately 50 per cent of employees in non-union companies were involved in some form of collaborative work group, only about 20 per cent were covered by some form of NER (Lipset and Meltz, 2000). Comparative Europe-wide data on

NER is provided by the European Company Survey (ECS) (2009) carried out by the European Foundation for the Improvement of Living and Working Conditions (see also Hall and Purcell, 2011; Bryson et al., 2012). The survey enquired about the presence of legally established or institutional forms of employee representation at establishment and company level, which can be trade union representation and/or a general works council/ NER type structure (works council was broadly defined in ECS (2009), influenced by country variation, but included many of the NER forms discussed above, including works councils, joint consultative committees and staff associations). Table 21.3 summarizes ECS estimates of the proportion of workplaces with 10 or more employees that have a union and/or a general works council representing some or all employees. The second column shows the percentage of employees covered by these arrangements.

Examining the findings of the ECS, Bryson et al. (2012) identify considerable variation

Table 21.3   Incidence and coverage of institutional forms of employee representation

Country	Establishments/companies (%)	Employees covered (%)
EU27	37	63
Sweden	73	85
Denmark	72	88
Finland	68	90
Belgium	64	83
Spain	58	71
France	56	81
Luxembourg	53	83
Romania	52	77
Netherlands	49	77
Slovenia	43	68
Slovakia	43	60
Latvia	39	48
Cyprus	38	47
Poland	38	65
Italy	38	65
Bulgaria	36	50
Ireland	33	69
Hungary	29	49
Germany	28	59
Lithuania	26	49
UK	24	45
Estonia	23	39
Austria	22	59
Czech Republic	19	43
Malta	15	33
Greece	4	17
Portugal	3	15

Note: The table shows the incidence and coverage of legally established or institutional forms of employee representation at establishment and company level, which can be trade union representation and/or a works council/NER. Ad hoc and health and safety arrangements are excluded.

Sources: European Company Survey (2009), Hall and Purcell (2011).

between countries regarding the percentage of workplaces with either or both union-based or works council/NER forms of employee representation. The overall rate is above 55 per cent in Denmark, Sweden and Finland, but below 20 per cent in five countries, most notably Portugal and Greece, where less than 5 per cent of workplaces have either form of employee representation. The average level of employee representation across all workplaces in the sample is 34 per cent. Likewise, extensive variation exists across countries regarding the percentage of workplaces with trade union or works council type representation. For instance, trade union representation is the only form observed in ECS 2009 in countries like Sweden (73 per cent of workplaces), Cyprus (38 per cent) and Turkey (16 per cent). Meanwhile, works council/NER representation is the only form observed in countries like Spain (58 per cent), Germany (28 per cent) and Austria (22 per cent) at workplace level. In most countries, both representational types are found, but there is significant variation in the balance between the two. For selected countries with workplaces that have a mixture of representation models, the approximate breakdown in each is as follows: Denmark – union only (20 per cent), works council only (8 per cent), both (over 40 per cent); France – union only (5 per cent), works council only (26 per cent), both (25 per cent); Ireland – union only (13 per cent), works council only (13 per cent), both (7 per cent); Netherlands – union only (3 per cent), works council only (38 per cent), both (8 per cent); Italy – union only (4 per cent), works council only (6 per cent), both (28 per cent).

THE PURPOSE AND UTILITY OF NER

Notwithstanding oversimplification and to reiterate the point made above, the extant literature often posits two competing interpretations of employer motives and rationales for NER voice. The first is 'union avoidance', in which the primary objective is to design and implement various NER voice mechanisms in order to stave off the incursion of an external union into management affairs by demanding forms of union representation. The second interpretation, while not necessarily dismissing the first, argues that employers can have other motives in addition to or 'beyond the union avoidance' thesis. Here it is argued, for example, that NER arrangements may complement union structures, rather than replacing or competing with them per se. These will briefly be discussed next.

Union Avoidance

Many accounts of NER in the literature are premised on the argument that a seemingly omnipotent management is intent on avoiding or substituting unions (Gall, 2004; Kelly, 2004; Upchurch et al., 2006; O'Sullivan and Gunnigle, 2009). For authors like Kelly (2004), NER bodies are merely a means through which management can maintain their organization's non-union status or, in circumstances of weakened or de-recognized unions, consolidate the shift to non-unionism. Avoidance of unions through various non-union voice arrangements has been depicted in either/or terms of union 'suppression' or union 'substitution' (Dundon and Gollan, 2007). On the one hand, companies such as IBM, Hewlett Packard or Marks & Spencer are cited as exemplars of good human relations practice that serves as a 'substitute' for unionization. It assumes employers create an alternative form of employee representation that employees will prefer to a union (Dundon, 2002; Dundon and Rollinson, 2004). This form of union substitution can operate in two ways. First, at workplace level, NER arrangements can be subverted to serve a union avoidance strategy as a captive audience of employees allows management to instil anti-union propaganda or to socially engineer the employment relations climate as seen 'through management eyes' (Taras and Kaufman, 1999: 19). Second, at a more institutional level, NER avoids unions by marginalizing worker activism and diminishing network mobilizations of such activism from firm to firm. At the far end of this union avoidance typology is the sweatshop or exploitative firm that 'suppresses' union demands (McLoughlin and Gourlay, 1994).

The significance of suppression and substitution is such that typologies can depict situations where organizations can establish a particular non-union voice channel to reduce the likelihood of outside involvement by unions, ensuring that voice processes are contained within the organization. There is a strong body of international literature supporting union avoidance perspectives. A range of studies have illustrated how NERs are frequently used in the midst of union organizing campaigns in liberal market economies (van den Broek, 1997; Peetz, 2002; Gall, 2004; D'Art and Turner, 2005; Logan, 2006). According to this interpretation, NERs are introduced to supplant or suppress the union role by showing that the union is unnecessary through offering mechanisms for resolving grievances and giving expression to non-union voice. Dundon (2002) shows how management promote internal forms of employee involvement – company councils and semi-autonomous work teams – as a tactic to replace unions. In two cases, worker participation schemes were implemented to counter claims for collective representation. In a study of Irish employer opposition to union recognition, D'Art and Turner (2005: 130) observe that the creation of NERs was the second most typical response used by companies after 'captive audience' dissuasion of union membership (Peetz, 2002; Logan, 2006).

One problem with the union avoidance literature though is that 'either/or' categories of union avoidance tend to oversimplify and polarize practices that can also be diverse and nuanced. Indeed, there is evidence to suggest that the dimensions that comprise 'substitution' and 'suppression' are not mutually exclusive but can in fact overlap and coexist, even within the same organization (Dundon and Gollan, 2007). Most significantly, however, union avoidance perspectives only offer a partial picture of management intent with regard to NER. As discussed below, management may have multiple rationales and motives for implementing NER, which may or may not include union avoidance.

Beyond Union Avoidance: Alternative Faces of Voice

A second strand of literature has emerged that challenges the notion that management introduces NER with the sole purpose of avoiding unions (Taras and Kaufman, 1999, 2006; Dundon and Rollinson, 2004; Butler, 2009a, 2009b; Gollan, 2010; Kaufman and Taras, 2010). Kaufman and Taras (2010: 270) describe NER as 'a tangled web' consisting of four possible 'faces' that can potentially coexist. First is the *evolutionary* face of NER, premised on a continuum. At one extreme can be imagined a Dickensian-type sweatshop devoid of any voice or employment regulation. As capitalism moves through different phases of social accumulation, a degree of humanistic or welfare paternalism evolves, although business leaders still prefer to engage with workers in the absence of a trade union. However, should non-unionism be regarded as having diminished utility by workers, then NER arrangements may come under threat by the forces of organized labour at the opposite end of the continuum. Second is the *unity interest* face of NERs. In this perspective employers see NER as source of competitive advantage and as promoting an agenda of shared interests; a view compatible with the high performance work system paradigm. HR systems and practices are integrated with NERs becoming more embedded and part of a performance-focused outcome approach. The third face is that of *union avoidance*, in which NERs are designed and implemented primarily with the objective of keeping unions out, as discussed above. Kaufman and Taras's (2010) final face is a *complementary* one. In this view, NER arrangements do not replace but complement and support other forms of voice: this can help explain to some extent the emergence of double-breasting voice where an employer recognizes a union at one company plant but opts for non-union voice systems at another location.

Recognizing that NER may evolve into different forms or overlap with other complementary arrangements with multiple faces, helps to move the debate beyond the exclusivity of union avoidance as the primary employer rationale. Dundon and Gollan (2007) argue that managerial strategies are often complex, uneven and ad hoc but ultimately shaped by multiple factors and objectives. While some firms choosing NER may do so to avoid a trade union, studies also show alternative rationales for 'making' voice (Willman et al., 2006). Gollan (2010) identifies a number of general influences on management NER choices including, for example, that such arrangements can act as a safety valve in the absence of an active union presence; non-union voice may help facilitate the process of organizational change by enabling management to highlight issues of concern early, thus reducing the potential for disruption come implementation; non-union voice may be introduced to enhance organizational performance by providing a forum whereby employees can input new ideas; and finally, non-union voice may be seen as an alternative to negotiation in situations where there is little active union or collective bargaining presence.

In moving beyond the union avoidance thesis, Willman et al. (2003, 2006) see the emergence of different voice arrangements as linked to a transactional contracting problem: whether to 'make' voice arrangements internally, or to 'buy' voice from an external third party, such as a trade union or possibly some other CSO (Willman et al., 2003: 3; Heery, 2011). Willman et al. (2003) suggest that the probability of 'buying' union voice is dependent on three variables: employee propensity to join a union, union propensity to organize a workplace and employer willingness to deal with a union. These multiple or competing variables affecting NER are likely to include a variety of potential factors with varied outcomes. For example, employees may become active around a grievance or set of grievances and seek to join a union. A union may focus its organizing activity within a particular workplace or industry and try to force the employer to recognize it. Or an employer may pre-emptively recognize a union by choosing one that it prefers to do business with. Willman et al. (2003) add that while employer preferences may change as the result of a number of factors (legislation, union campaigns, employee dissatisfaction, conflict and so on), there is a degree of 'stickiness' to the eventual choice of voice based on the associated transaction cost of switching (Willman et al., 2003: 4). From an employer perspective, the choice of whether to 'buy', 'make' or adopt 'hybrid' (dual or double-breasted) voice will be dependent on a number of influences. Importantly, where risks are high for both the 'make' or 'buy' option, employers may opt for a 'hybrid' channel of union and non-union voice. The 'hybrid' bet is the highest cost option overall, although the one with the lowest risk. Willman et al. (2003: 11) suggest that firms wishing to change existing arrangements are more likely to switch from wholly union or wholly non-union to a dual channel, rather than switching from wholly union to wholly non-union single channels (or the reverse). They argue that if one channel is unsatisfactory (because the union is weak or too militant) or too costly (because of the need for in-house personnel specialists), then hedging to a dual channel arrangement is more likely than the abandonment of sunk costs.

A further argument that takes us beyond the union avoidance debate is that while union resistance may in some circumstances provide the initial impetus behind the establishment of NERs, employers may subsequently instil non-union voice institutions with a functional purpose and utility aimed at generating positive outcomes for workers and delivering elements of positive sum mutual gains (Taras and Kaufman, 2006; Dundon and Gollan, 2007; Butler, 2009a, 2009b; Kaufman and Taras, 2010; Lewin, 2010). With this in mind, managerial strategies towards NERs may be directed towards delivering an effective employee voice that gives employees scope to develop their knowledge and skills and affords them an input into decisions normally the sole preserve of management prerogative (Gollan, 2006b). Kaufman (2013) has also explored how formalization of voice through NER mechanisms can provide employers with an opportunity to test and fine-tune managerial messages and thereby attempt to bring added legitimacy to non-union arrangements. Evidence shows that line managers find it necessary in certain circumstances to engage in informal dialogue with employees and their representatives to ensure an efficient level of production continuity, thereby highlighting the relevance of informal patterns of social exchange as well as formal voice (Detert and Burris, 2007). NER in this context is not exclusively viewed through the prism of formal procedures and institutions, but can be affected by informal views and opinions on the part of the employee. According to Detert and Burris (2007: 222), voice is the 'discretionary provision of information intended to improve organizational functioning . . . even though such information may challenge and upset the status quo of the organization and its power holders'.

Taras and Kaufman (1999: 14) have inserted the cautionary observation that NER arrangements are 'no easy substitute for unions and that employers who believe they can use NER for this purpose are seriously deluding themselves'. Heery (2011: 547) argues that workers have a hierarchy of interests, from preserving the status quo and seeking modest incremental improvement in working conditions to challenging managerial authority and social order. Importantly, employees have interests that both coalesce with and oppose those of their employer: what Edwards (2003: 16) describes as 'embedded antagonism'. Importantly, evidence indicates that unless non-union forums hold a satisfactory utility for employees, one outcome may be a heightening of their attachment to trade unions (Broad, 1994; Taras and Copping, 1998; Dundon et al., 2005). Broad's (1994) research into employment relations in a Japanese firm illustrates the point that managerial strategies with union avoidance intent may provoke counter mobilization and resistance by groups of workers. In his case, a company employee council was used as an alternative voice channel to suppress unionization. When workers realized that the mechanism advanced management interests over employee concerns, they eventually supported the idea of unionization. An important finding in Taras and Copping's (1998: 39) research into non-union voice arrangements at Imperial Oil in Canada was that the company allowed perceptions of 'worker power and influence to develop', and representatives 'over-estimated their capacity to halt corporate-level initiatives'. This can lead to widened expectations which foment frustrations among employees, with a renewed impetus for union representation as the result.

According to Kaufman and Taras (2010), there may be an incentive for some employers to see NER move beyond any initial purpose and utility of union avoidance to evolve into institutions that can potentially deliver positive-sum mutual gains outcomes. There is also the observation that NER which effectively complements and supports other HR policies and generates a mutually beneficial collaborative exchange between employer and employee can potentially render traditional trade union representation obsolete (Gollan and Davis, 1999; Dundon and Gollan, 2007). This notion is based on the premise that employees do not necessarily desire or need an independent protective agency (since this emphasizes the conflict-distributive element of the employment relationship) so long as their basic interests are satisfied. From a management perspective, the common purpose and utility here of non-union voice is to encourage and foster an integrative partnership style alignment of interests between employer and employees (Walton et al., 1994; McKersie et al., 2008). Kaufman's (2013) research at Delta Air Lines suggests that if the motive and purpose of non-union voice arrangements is to foster cooperative mutual gains, then employees may feel satisfied with their jobs and express commitment to the company. A further scenario is when traditional trade union structures and non-union voice 'complement' each other, dovetailing in terms of form and function, as in the case of German works councils and/or certain 'double-breasting' situations in large organizations (Taras, 1997; Heery, 2011; Cullinane et al., 2012).

But for NERs to endure, management needs to move beyond a union avoidance approach and align employee voice mechanisms with broader HR strategy. However, many studies remain sceptical of the viability of NER to achieve a deep or meaningful mutual gains outcome (for example, see Ramsay's (1977) aforementioned 'cycles' of control thesis). In short, there is no simple or clear-cut pattern of employee behaviour or management rationale towards NER adoption and implementation. Nor are there any definitive or predictable voice outcomes. Research indicates that just as employer motives for introducing NER are diverse, it is evident that NER does not generate simple or neatly packaged outcomes for either employer or employee. Much of the reasoning for this is because a multitude of scenarios may be played out in reality and these scenarios are often shaped by different contexts. It is to the issue of contextual influence that we turn next in evaluating NER voice arrangements.

THE CONTEXT OF NER: DIVERSE PATTERNS OF VOICE

Context matters to the eventual systems of worker voice, including the pattern of NER arrangements. Both external macro factors and internal micro-organizational influences can shape the choices and attendant outcomes relating to NER voice. While external factors such as market pressures and regulatory factors are important, the interplay of these sources with internal managerial decisions and power-related dynamics is a crucial determinant in the processes and outcomes of NER (Dundon and Gollan, 2007). Ultimately, therefore, employee voice in non-union environments has to be contextualized against a broader set of managerial strategies, worker responses and external forces. The dynamic interplay between external factors and internal micro influences points to a complex picture regarding choice of voice options and whether or not NERs can deliver mutual gains type arrangements that can last (Marchington, 2005; Donaghey et al., 2012).

Marchington et al. (2001) critique the idea of a simple model of management strategy for employee voice with predictable patterns and outcomes. Dundon and Gollan (2007) similarly observe that several contextual factors impinge upon employer choice over voice arrangements. Regulatory laws may encourage certain behaviours that otherwise would not have occurred, and which can benefit both employees and employers (Marchington, 2005). Other influences may also be at play, such as a particular management ideology that seeks to constrain certain choices; for example, by excluding trade unions in favour of an NER forum. Employee behaviour and actions may also influence the characteristics of consultation, particularly when occupational identities lead to strong workforce solidarity and possible counter mobilizations against management plans for non-union voice. While not widespread, Van den Broek and Dundon (2012) report, for example, that non-union employees can and do actively challenge management plans through forms of protest, misbehaviour and collectively-orchestrated resistance even when unions are absent. Finally, organizational culture and historical legacies relating to employee consultation and representation may also be contributory factors.

Donaghey et al. (2012) suggest that while the potential for NER to generate enduring positive-sum mutual gains cannot be rejected altogether, this is likely to be quite rare in a context of voluntarism with few if any restrictions on management prerogative. Arguably, embedded or successful NER patterns are likely to be dependent upon extensive employer resources and the requisite skills of non-union employee representatives, as well as institutional support mechanisms outside the firm. Crucially, such patterns of non-union voice would need to encourage conflict in order for effective cooperation to be sustainable in terms both of enhancing productivity and addressing worker concerns. The existence of NER in voluntarist regimes does not automatically undermine its potential capacity to deliver mutual gains. But, importantly, effective NER within voluntarist contexts probably requires a degree of independence from management. However, as Streeck (2004) argues, non-union workplace voice is unlikely to be meaningful unless supported by hard regulatory constraints. This is because when left to their own devices many employers introduce shallow forms of employee voice of which workers may be sceptical. Management tend to limit the workplace governance reforms required to enable a distribution of power necessary for genuine participation as they seek to preserve their managerial prerogative. On the other hand, workers may demand more influence than deemed acceptable by employers. Additionally, under voluntarism, and in the absence of regulatory constraints, it tends to be quite easy for employers to breach or exit NER arrangements in liberal market economic contexts (Thompson, 2011).

In this context of liberal voluntarism, NER may often fall short of what is 'said on the tin', imbuing employee voice with too little power and independence from management, and functioning as a poor relation to union-based collective representation (Gollan,

2006a, 2006b; Lloyd, 2001; Kaufman and Taras, 2010). It has been argued that NER can fail to deliver lasting outcomes under four contextual situations (Kaufman and Taras (2010: 277): the first is when it is used for union avoidance; the second is when firms engage in substantial cost cutting that undermines NER; the third is where management injects NER with insufficient power for genuine employee voice and, meanwhile, continues to act unilaterally on major workplace decisions; and the fourth is where management takes decisions (or fails to take decisions) that workers perceive as a breach of trust or a broken promise. Ultimately these situations or context-specific variations can be linked to the overarching issues of 'power' and 'independence' and NERs are often seen to lack both (Gollan, 2002; Butler, 2009a): they typically do not have direct access to legal or unionized resources that offer independent sanction against an employer; and they are often dependent upon management-sponsored systems that tend to be perceived as relatively weak by employees themselves. These contextual situations tend to render NER voice regimes unstable and short-lived in liberal market economies, where employers' competitive postures are often geared towards cost reduction rather than quality competition (Godard, 2004).

CONCLUSION

The decline of the traditional single channel of trade union representation in most countries, and especially liberal market economies like the UK, Ireland, the USA and Australia, has left a representation gap for the majority of workers across the Anglo-Saxon world, if not also further afield (Freeman et al., 2007). Research survey evidence suggests that this representation gap is not necessarily being filled on a wide-ranging basis by NER arrangements, despite increased employer experimentation with these non-union voice methods (Kersley et al., 2006; Charlwood and Terry, 2007; Cullinane et al., 2012; Bryson et al., 2012). In the UK, for instance, a rather stark finding is that over 80 per cent of workplaces have no form of representative voice whatsoever (if employees in workplaces with fewer than five employees are included) (Charlwood and Terry, 2007).

This chapter has noted that employer-sponsored NER has attracted growing interest among human resource management practitioners, policymakers and scholars. Two contrasting streams of academic thought have emerged on the subject of NER. First, NER is premised as a union avoidance strategy by employers implementing such arrangements. The second stream of thought reviewed in this chapter argues that rather than being driven exclusively by union avoidance tactics many employers have multiple motives for implementing NERs. These motives may include union avoidance, but can also revolve around searching for mutual gains style outcomes or responding to global or local market competitiveness.

We have argued that while there are likely to be circumstances where employers use NER as a means to avoid unionization, such a response does not negate the possibility that there can also be a complex array of motives for establishing non-union voice. Related to this is the fact that NER can also take a variety of forms with multiple purposes and divergent outcomes, all of which can evolve and change over time and across a range of contexts. In short, NER may have a number of different 'faces' even within a single workplace (Kaufman and Taras, 2010: 270). Whereas some radical theorists traditionally collapsed all employee participation schemes under the umbrella of management seeking to quell employee resistance (Ramsay, 1977), others have highlighted the ways in which employee voice regimes can be introduced by employers for diffuse motives, adding that non-union based representation cannot be simply categorized under one pattern. Rather, different methods employed in different contexts can diverge greatly in terms of substantive content and in what they deliver for workers (Marchington, 2005; Wilkinson et al., 2010).

Overall, however, research indicates that contextual conditions in liberal market economies, especially where cost competition is dominant, are not conducive to enduring mutual gains through NER arrangements. This is because employers inject NER with insufficient power and independence to enable employees to experience robust voice and non-union worker representatives lack the resources and skills to engage in joint problem-solving (Gollan, 2002; Freeman et al., 2007; Donaghey et al., 2012). In the absence of hard regulation or union mobilization, NER arrangements tend to be too weak to address workplace issues owing to disconnected capitalism and models of HRM that render meaningful voice unstable and potentially prone to breakdown. This situation has intensified in an era of 'financialization' (Thompson, 2011).

In light of the arguments reviewed in this chapter, it remains to be fully tested empirically whether NER is another form of union avoidance based on strategic employer choice, a means of attempting to construct positive-sum mutual gains outcomes, or something else. To what extent are robust and enduring NER bodies feasible in the context of voluntarist industrial relations systems, particularly in a recessionary economic climate when many employers are focused on retrenchment and cutting costs and financialization has heightened instability? The challenge for researchers is to advance our understanding by finding empirically grounded answers to these matters in different contexts in liberal market economies.

REFERENCES

Broad, G. (1994), 'Japan in Britain: the dynamics of joint consultation', *Industrial Relations Journal*, **25** (1), 126–38.

Bryson, A., J. Forth and A. George (2012), *Workplace Employee Representation in Europe*, Dublin: European Foundation for the Improvement in Living and Working Conditions.

Butler, P. (2009a), 'Non-union employee representation: exploring the riddle of management strategy', *Industrial Relations Journal*, **40** (3), 198–214.

Butler, P. (2009b), 'Riding along the crest of a wave: tracking the shifting rationale for non-union consultation at FinanceCo', *Human Resource Management Journal*, **19** (2), 176–92.

Butler, P., L. Glover and O. Tregaskis (2011), 'When the Going Gets Tough . . . Recession and the Resilience of Workplace Partnership', *British Journal of Industrial Relations*, **49** (4), 666–87.

Charlwood, A. and M. Terry (2007), '21st century models of employee representation: structures, processes and outcomes', *Industrial Relations Journal*, **38** (4), 320–37.

Cullinane, N., J. Donaghey, T. Dundon and T. Dobbins (2012), 'Different voices, different rooms: double-breasting and the managerial agenda', *International Journal of Human Resource Management*, **23**, 368–84.

D'Art, D. and T. Turner (2005), 'Union recognition and partnership at work', *Industrial Relations Journal*, **36** (2), 121–39.

Detert, J. and E. Burris (2007), 'Leadership behavior and employee voice: is the door really open?', *Academy of Management Journal*, **50** (4), 869–84.

Dobbins, T. (2010), 'The case for beneficial constraints: why permissive voluntarism impedes workplace cooperation in Ireland', *Economic and Industrial Democracy*, **31** (4), 497–519.

Dobbins, T. and P. Gunnigle (2009), 'Can voluntary workplace partnership deliver sustainable mutual gains?', *British Journal of Industrial Relations*, **47** (3), 546–70.

Donaghey, J., N. Cullinane, T. Dundon and T. Dobbins (2012), 'Non-union representation, union avoidance and the managerial agenda: a case study', *Economic and Industrial Democracy*, **33** (2), 163–83.

Dundon, T. (2002), 'Employer hostility to union organising in the UK', *Industrial Relations Journal*, **33** (3), 234–45.

Dundon, T. and D. Collings (2011), 'Employment relations in the United Kingdom and Republic of Ireland', in M. Barry and A. Wilkinson (eds), *Research Handbook of Comparative Employment Relations*, Cheltenham, UK and Northampton, MA, USA: Edward Elgar, pp. 214–38.

Dundon, T. and P. Gollan (2007), 'Re-conceptualising voice in the non-union workplace', *International Journal of Human Resource Management*, **18** (7), 1182–98.

Dundon, T. and D. Rollinson (2004), *Employment Relations in Non-Union Firms*, London: Routledge.

Dundon, T., A. Wilkinson, M. Marchington and P. Ackers (2004), 'The meanings and purpose of employee voice', *International Journal of Human Resource Management*, **15** (6), 1149–70.

Dundon, T., A. Wilkinson, M. Marchington and P. Ackers (2005), 'The management of voice in non-union organisations: managers' perspectives', *Employee Relations*, **27** (3), 307–19.

Edwards, P.K. (2003), *Industrial Relations Theory and Practice*, 2nd edn, Oxford: Blackwell Publishing.

European Company Survey (2009), European Foundation for the Improvement of Living and Working Conditions, Dublin.

Evans, C., G. Harvey and P. Turnbull (2012), 'When partnerships don't "match-up": an evaluation of labour–management partnerships in the automotive components and civil aviation industries', *Human Resource Management Journal*, **22** (1), 60–75.

Freeman, R.B., P. Boxall and P. Haynes (eds) (2007), *What Workers Say: Employee Voice in the Anglo-American Workplace*, Ithaca: Cornell University Press.

Gall, G. (2004), 'British employer resistance to trade union recognition', *Human Resource Management Journal*, **14** (2), 36–53.

Godard, J. (2004), 'A critical assessment of the high-performance paradigm', *British Journal of Industrial Relations*, **42** (2), 349–78.

Gollan P.J. (2000), 'Non-union forms of employee representation in the United Kingdom and Australia', in B. Kaufman and D.G. Taras (eds), *Non-Union Employee Representation: History, Contemporary Practice and Policy*, New York: M.E. Sharpe, pp. 410–49.

Gollan P.J. (2002), 'So what's the news? Management strategies towards non-union employee representation at News International', *Industrial Relations Journal*, **33** (4), 316–31.

Gollan, P.J. (2006a), *Employee Representation in Non-Union Firms*, London: Sage.

Gollan, P.J. (2006b), 'Twin tracks: employee representation at Eurotunnel revisited', *Industrial Relations*, **46** (4), 606–49.

Gollan, P.J. (2010), 'Employer strategies towards non-union collective voice', in A. Wilkinson, P. Gollan, M. Marchington and D. Lewin (eds), *The Oxford Handbook of Participation in Organizations*, Oxford Handbooks in Business and Management, Oxford: Oxford University Press, pp. 212–36.

Gollan, P.J. and E. Davis (1999), 'High involvement management and organizational change: beyond rhetoric', *Asia Pacific Journal of Human Resources*, **37** (3), 69–91.

Gomez, R., A. Bryson and P. Willman (2010), 'Voice in the wilderness? The shift from union to non-union voice in the workplace', in A. Wilkinson, P. Gollan, M. Marchington and D. Lewin (eds), *The Oxford Handbook of Participation in Organizations*, Oxford Handbooks in Business and Management, Oxford: Oxford University Press, pp. 383–406.

Gunnigle, P., J. Lavelle and A. McDonnell (2009), 'Subtle but deadly? Union avoidance through "double breasting" among multinational companies', *Advances in Industrial and Labor Relations*, **16**, 51–73.

Hall, M. and J. Purcell (2011), 'Information and consultation practice across Europe five years after the EU Directive', European Foundation for the Improvement of Living and Working Conditions, Dublin.

Hall, M., S. Hutchinson, J. Purcell, M. Terry and J. Parker (2011), 'Promoting effective consultation? Assessing the impact of the ICE regulations', *British Journal of Industrial Relations*, available at: doi: 10.1111/j.1467-8543.2011.00870.x (accessed 19 November 2013).

Heery, E. (2011), 'Worker representation in a multiform system: a framework for evaluation', *Journal of Industrial Relations*, **52** (5), 543–59.

High Pay Commission (2012), 'Cheques with balances: why tackling high pay is in the national interest', final report of the High Pay Commission.

Kaufman, B.E. (2013), 'Keeping the commitment model in the air during turbulent times: employee involvement at Delta Airlines', *Industrial Relations*, **52** (S1), 343–77.

Kaufman, B. and D.G. Taras (2010), 'Employee participation through non-union forms of employee representation'. in A. Wilkinson, P. Gollan, M. Marchington and D. Lewin (eds), *The Oxford Handbook of Participation in Organizations*, Oxford Handbooks in Business and Management, Oxford: Oxford University Press, pp. 258–85.

Kelly, J. (2004), 'Social partnership agreements in Britain: labor cooperation and compliance', *Industrial Relations*, **43** (1), 267–92.

Kersley, B., C. Alpin, J. Forth, A. Bryson and H. Bewley (2006), *Inside the Workplace: First Findings from the 2004 Workplace Employment Relations Survey*, London: Department of Trade and Industry.

Kochan, T., P. Adler, R. McKersie, A. Eaton, P. Segal and P. Gerhart (2008), 'The potential and precariousness of partnership: the case of the Kaiser Permanente labour management partnership', *Industrial Relations*, **47** (1), 36–66.

Lavelle, J., P. Gunnigle and A. McDonnell (2010), 'Patterning employee voice in multinational companies', *Human Relations*, **63**, 395–418.

Lewin, D. (2010), 'Employee voice and mutual gains', in A. Wilkinson, P.J. Gollan, M. Marchington and D. Lewin (eds.), *The Oxford Handbook of Participation in Organizations*, Oxford: Oxford University Press, 427–52.

Lipset, S. and N. Meltz (2000), 'Estimates of non-union employee representation in the United States and Canada: how different are the two countries?', in B. Kaufman and D. Taras (eds), *Non-Uuion Employee Representation: History, Contemporary Practice, and Policy*, Armonk, NY: M.E. Sharpe, 223–30.

Lloyd, C. (2001), 'What do employee councils do? The impact of non-union forms of representation on trade union organisation', *Industrial Relations Journal*, **32** (4), 313–27.

Logan, J. (2006), 'The union avoidance industry in the United States', *British Journal of Industrial Relations*, **44** (4), 651–75.

Marchington, M. (2005), 'Employee involvement: patterns and explanations', in B. Harley, J. Hyman and P. Thompson (eds), *Participation and Democracy at Work: Essays in Honour of Harvie Ramsay*, Basingstoke: Palgrave Macmillan.

Marchington, M., A. Wilkinson, P. Ackers and T. Dundon (2001), 'Management choice and employee voice', research report, CIPD, London.

McKersie, R.B., T. Sharpe, T.A. Kochan, A.E. Eaton, G. Strauss and M. Morgenstern (2008), 'Bargaining theory meets interest-based negotiations', *Industrial Relations*, **47** (1), 66–96.

McLoughlin, I. and S. Gourlay (1994), *Enterprise without Unions: Industrial Relations in the Non-Union Firm*, Buckingham: Open University Press.

O'Sullivan, M. and P. Gunnigle (2009), 'Bearing all the hallmarks of oppression: union avoidance in Europe's largest low cost airline', *Labor Studies Journal*, **34** (2), 252–70.

Peetz, D. (2002), 'Decollectivist strategies in Oceania', *Industrial Relations*, **57** (2), 252–78.

Ramsay, H. (1977), 'Cycles of control: worker participation in sociological and historical perspective', *Sociology*, **11** (3), 481–506.

Streeck, W. (2004), 'Educating capitalists: a rejoinder to Wright and Tsakalotos', *Socio-Economic Review*, **2** (3), 425–37.

Taras, D.G. (1997), 'Managerial intentions and wage determination in the Canadian petroleum industry,' *Industrial Relations*, **36** (2), 178–205.

Taras, D.G. and J. Copping (1998), 'The transition from formal non-union representation to unionization: a contemporary case', *Industrial and Labor Relations Review*, **52** (1), 22–44.

Taras, D.G. and B.E. Kaufman (1999), 'What do non-unions do? What should we do about them?', MIT Task Force Working Paper #WP14, prepared for the May 25–26, conference 'Symposium on Changing Employment Relations and new Institutions of Representation', Washington, DC.

Taras, D.G. and B. Kaufman (2006), 'Non-union employee representation in North America: diversity, controversy and uncertain future', *Industrial Relations Journal*, **37** (5), 513–42.

Thompson, P. (2011), 'The trouble with HRM', *Human Resource Management Journal*, **21** (4), 355–67.

Upchurch, M., M. Richardson, S. Tailby, A. Danford and P. Stewart (2006), 'Employee representation in the non-union sector: a paradox of intention?', *Human Resource Management Journal*, **16** (4), 393–410.

van den Broek, D. (1997), 'Human resource management, cultural control and union avoidance: an Australian case study', *Journal of Industrial Relations*, **3** (3), 332–48.

van den Broek, D. and T. Dundon (2012), '(Still) up to no good: reconfiguring the boundaries of worker resistance and misbehaviour in an increasingly non-union world', *Relations Industrielles/Industrial Relations*, **67** (1), 97–121.

van Wanrooy, B., H. Bewley, A. Bryson, J. Forth, S. Freeth, L. Stokes and S. Wood (2013), 'The 2011 Employment Relations Study: first findings', Department for Business Innovation and Skills, London, available at: https://www.gov.uk/government/organisations/department-for-business-innovation-skills (accessed 19 November 2013).

Walton, R., J. Cutcher-Gershenfeld and R. McKersie (1994), *Strategic Negotiations: A Theory of Change in Labor–Management Relations*, Boston: Harvard Business School Press.

Wilkinson, A., P. Gollan, M. Marchington and D. Lewin (eds) (2010), *The Oxford Handbook of Participation in Organizations*, Oxford Handbooks in Business and Management, Oxford: Oxford University Press.

Williams, S., E. Heery and B. Abbott (2011), 'The emerging regime of civil regulation in work and employment relations', *Human Relations*, **64** (7), 951–70.
Willman, P., A. Bryson and R. Gomez (2003), 'Why do voice regimes differ?', Centre for Economic Performance, Working Paper No CEPDP0591, November, London School of Economics.
Willman, P., A. Bryson and R. Gomez (2006), 'The sound of silence: which employers choose no employee voice and why', *Socio-Economic Review*, **4** (2), 283–99.

PART IV

EVALUATING VOICE

22 Regulation of employee voice
*Paul J. Gollan, Glenn Patmore and Ying Xu**

INTRODUCTION

Employee voice is profoundly influenced by the law. The law determines the forms of voice that are permitted or encouraged, the structure of workplace institutions, and the relationship between management and employees. Yet there is a 'relative absence' of legal perspectives in the industrial relations (IR) literature on employee voice (Novitz and Bogg 2011: 3). The lack of research linking legal provisions to workplace practices and outcomes (see also Bogg and Novitz 2012) is an important oversight in the existing scholarship. This is especially so since legal regulation is a key determinant of workplace democracy, organizational efficiency and employee well-being (see, for example, Bogg and Novitz 2012; Gollan and Patmore 2006; Kaine 2012; Perrett 2007). This chapter addresses the lacuna in the literature by providing an overview of the existing and emerging research regarding legal regulation of employee voice in the USA and Australia, with a particular focus on the regulation of collective bargaining. We compare the progenitor of labour law reform in Anglo countries, the *National Labor Relations Act* 29 USC §§ 151–69 (hereafter NLRA, also known as the Wagner Act (1935)), with the most recent form of such regulation, the Australian *Fair Work Act 2009* (Cth) (herein FWA). There has been relatively little recent research comparing these two countries since the enactment of the FWA in 2009 (Forsyth 2012). Our comparison highlights the fact that there are varieties of national legislation regulating employee voice. In addition, the chapter examines key workplace factors that interact with the legal regulation of employee involvement and participation at the workplace.

We begin by defining the meaning of employee voice regulation. Regulation of employee voice refers to laws establishing structures, processes and rights for employees to express their views through direct and representative means. According to Patmore (2010) there are three broad categories of employee voice regulation (see also Fudge 2008: 4; Lee 2004: 31). First, there is market-based regulation which occurs on the enterprise level and encompasses agreements between employers and employees either on an individual or collective basis. The former happens through face-to-face consultation, participation in team meetings and so on while the latter may occur through employee representative committees. The second form of regulation, according to Patmore (2010), includes negotiated collective agreements at the enterprise or industry level. Trade unions have primarily been responsible for representing employees in such collective agreements and negotiating on wages and working conditions. Third, employee voice is regulated through state interventions via statutes or Acts of Parliament which define the employment conditions that apply across the labour market. Such conditions typically protect employees from the imbalance of power in the employment relationship. For instance, employee involvement and participation is protected by prohibiting unfair dismissal based solely on union membership.

Workplace health and safety (WHS) legislation provides another example of state-based regulation. The rationale for health and safety representation is explained by Harris et al. (2012) who maintain that participation is the cornerstone of systematic occupational health and safety (OHS) management because 'managers simply do not know or control the production base of OHS in enough detail to do without the experience, competence and motivation of workers to detect and abate hazards' (Walters and Frick 2000: 44). Research on WHS is underpinned by relevant country-specific legislation; however, according to Markey and Patmore (2011), the literature of WHS as a form of representative voice faces similar challenges to the literature on non-union employee representation (NER), in that it is still in a developing phase. While WHS representatives and committees are a form of legally mandated representative employee participation in Anglo-Saxon countries, they lie outside the scope of this chapter.

The three different forms of regulation may coexist, but one form often dominates. In Europe, for example, legislative initiatives have become prominent. The Information and Consultation of Employees Directive (2002) (ICE) provided a general framework for informing and consulting employees. This directive requires medium-sized and large enterprises to inform and consult their employees in good time about issues directly affecting work organization, job security and employment contracts regarding terms and conditions of employment (Directive 2002/14/EC). European Union directives are a form of European law that must be implemented in national legislation. The ICE directive is therefore implemented through state-based legislation. The consultation is normally done via employee representatives, defined according to national law and practice, illustrating the co-existence of both legislative and market-based regulation (Directive 2002/14/EC). Moreover, dominant forms of regulation may change over time (Fudge 2008: 3). Prior to the 2002 European directive, Germany and other continental European countries legally mandated employee representative committees or works councils that must be consulted regarding topics such as redundancies, threats to employment or transfers of the business (Patmore 2010). The existing works council legislation satisfied the implementation requirement of the ICE directive. The ICE directive has provided more extensive legislative requirements for employee voice than in some non-EU countries. European examples are critical in understanding the diverse ways in which the law affects employee voice, and highlight the interaction between different forms of regulation. While they remain outside the scope of this chapter they are discussed in more detail in other chapters in this volume. Legislation regulating information and consultation of employees also exists in Australia and the United States but unlike most European laws, the legislative requirements are implemented principally through negotiated collective agreements at the enterprise level.[1] The laws regulating collective bargaining in each jurisdiction are examined in this chapter.

Finally, legally prescribed rules and voluntary and customary standards (known as norms) operate side by side in a system of regulation (Patmore 2010; Fudge 2008: 3). Some customary norms establishing employee voice are derived from collective bargains (Fudge 2008: 3). The diversity of regulation arrangements highlights the critical role that the law plays in the employment relationship and the need to incorporate legal perspectives to enhance the existing industrial relations literature.

Hereinafter the chapter is structured as follows: first, we compare collective bargaining required by labour law in the USA and Australia with particular emphasis on the bargaining partners, their rights and the way in which an agreement is brought to fruition; second, we explore research on employee voice regulations in the workplace context in each legal system; and finally, we discuss the limits of employee voice regulation, as well as other implications and directions for future research.

LABOUR LAW REQUIREMENTS FOR COLLECTIVE BARGAINING AND TRADE UNION REPRESENTATION IN THE USA AND AUSTRALIA

Legal regulation of indirect participation through trade union representation has developed over many years. Trade unions emerged during periods of industrialization (Cox et al. 2011: 6; Creighton and Stewart 2010: 22; Bamber and Sheldon 2007: 590) and have traditionally acted as the representatives of all employees. Today, the law provides a framework for trade union participation in workplace decisions, principally as representatives of their members and as bargaining partners.

Negotiation between an employer and a trade union over terms and conditions of employment is known as collective bargaining in the United States and enterprise bargaining in Australia. For the parties, the aim of collective bargaining is 'to reach an agreement that will regulate terms and conditions of employment' (Bamber and Sheldon 2007: 588). For society, the purposes of collective negotiations are to help deliver growth in real incomes, to enhance productivity and to act as a 'countervailing power' to 'otherwise overwhelming business domination' (Rogers 1995: 376; FWA s 3). Another vital purpose of collective bargaining is to address the conflict between management and labour over the proper remuneration of workers, working hours and other conditions. While the aim of the firm is to generate wealth for its shareholders, the aim of the trade union is to seek, amongst other things, appropriate remuneration for the contribution of labour in generating that revenue. However, the greater the redistribution of company profits, the lower the return for shareholders. How then does the law address the conflict between management and labour? The law's response to this conflict is to provide rules that govern the bargaining process. As Cox et al. (2011: 42) explain, when the law simply permitted collective bargaining, as occurred in the 1930s and 1940s in the United States, collective negotiation was characterized by voluntarism. Ultimately, it was 'economic force' that determined whether or not an employer would recognize the trade union for the purposes of collective bargaining, what subjects would be discussed, how bargaining would take place, and what industrial action or corporate responses would occur outside the formal negotiations (Cox et al. 2011: 313).

Legislation profoundly changed this form of bargaining. No longer did 'economic force' determine the bargaining relationship between the employer and the trade union. Employers were compelled to recognize trade unions for the purposes of collective bargaining in the United States in 1935 (Cox et al. 2011: 313). The NLRA established a union recognition procedure that has become the dominant bargaining model, influencing developments in Canada, the United Kingdom and Australia (Bogg 2012). Nonetheless, as this chapter will demonstrate, the legal regulation of bargaining operates very differently in Australia and the United States. Only since the early 1990s has the legislature in Australia introduced statutory recognition of trade unions for the purposes of enterprise bargaining (Creighton and Stewart 2010).[2] Australia's enterprise bargaining system was also comprehensively reformed when the Federal Labour government enacted the *Fair Work Act 2009* (Cth).

In the following section, we analyse employee voice at the workplace through the lens of collective bargaining and consultation, drawing upon the legal scholarship. We provide an overview of the legal rights of employee representatives in the bargaining process in the United States and Australia. This comparison will show how each country's legal regulation both supports and limits employee voice. Each jurisdiction's laws reflect a variety of sometimes conflicting social norms, including compulsion and voluntarism in each country, plurality in Australia, and exclusivity in the United States (see Table 22.1). This chapter adds to the comparative literature by arguing that plurality in Australia extends beyond the selection of bargaining representatives to influence the bargaining process itself (Buchanan and van Wanrooy 2009; Forsyth 2012).

The Bargaining Representatives

In both the USA and Australia, legislation provides a procedure for recognition of employee representatives, and then grants these representatives bargaining rights over wages, hours and other terms and conditions of employment (Bogg 2012). In both countries, the bargaining representatives must be independent of management (Fair Work Regulations 2009 (FW Regs) reg 2.06; NLRA s 7; Rogers 1995: 376). Independence and the freedom from external control or constraint from an employer guarantees genuine voice for labour at the workplace and provides a countervailing power to management in negotiating over employment conditions. Management representatives may voluntarily negotiate with representatives of their workforce; if they cannot reach agreement, legislation compels recognition of bargaining representatives to provide voice for labour at the workplace (Mundlak 2012). In the United States, the NLRA provides exclusive union bargaining rights over listed topics (NLRA s 9(a)). Exclusivity – cutting out other bargaining organizations – provides a guarantee of a single collective voice (Rogers 1995: 399). Employers must recognize a trade union 'designated or selected by a majority of its employees in an appropriate bargaining unit' (NLRA ss 8(a)(5) and 9(a); Cox et al. 2011: 313).

By contrast, in Australia, employers and employees are free to choose their own representatives, whether the choice be a trade union or another representative nominated by an employee; an employee can also nominate themselves or a non-trade union member as a representative (FWA s 176). Plurality – free choice of representatives – guarantees that all voices are heard. Hence, management may have to negotiate with multiple employee representatives over an enterprise agreement (Creighton and Stewart 2010: 726–7). Indeed employers must 'inform their employees of their right to be represented in bargaining' (FWA s 173). However, the FWA privileges trade union representation, as a trade union is the bargaining representative of its members, unless a member revokes that authorization or chooses another representative (FWA ss 176(1)(b), 176(3), 178A(2)). If an employer refuses to bargain, they can be compelled to recognize bargaining representatives if a majority of employees want to negotiate a single agreement for an enterprise (FWA s 236).[3] Ultimately, in Australia, having a single agreement requires a collective accord between labour and management.

Table 22.1   Exclusivity and plurality in representative negotiation and consultation

	United States (exclusivity)	Australia (plurality)
The bargaining representatives	Exclusive union representation. Union exclusivity guarantees a single representative voice for labour in the workplace. Duty to collectively bargain confers exclusive bargaining rights on trade unions.	Plurality of bargaining representatives provides opportunities for all voices to be represented (including union, non-union and individuals). The duty to act in good faith is imposed on all bargaining representatives.
Scope of bargaining and consultation (union and non-union consultation)	*Negotiation* Union and management negotiations mandatory on listed statutory terms (pay, hours and other conditions of employment). Exclusive bargaining over listed topics is limited by a broader conception of managerial prerogative compared to Australia. *Consultation* Representative consultation over major workplace change affecting statutory terms is legally permitted only with a trade union, or not at all.	*Negotiation* Bargaining partners negotiate over permitted topics pertaining to the employment relationship and making of workplace agreements. Bargaining is limited by a narrower conception of managerial prerogative compared to the United States. *Consultation* Consultation over major workplace change is legally required with either trade union or non-trade union representatives.
The collective bargaining process		
How collective bargaining works	The threats of economic sanctions and long negotiations make collective bargaining work.	The threats of economic sanctions and long negotiations make collective bargaining operate.
Protection of bargaining representatives by quasi-judicial tribunals	Weak remedies mean the protections are limited.	Numerous remedies result in strong protection.
Extent of collective bargaining and the limits of legal regulation	Union exclusivity over bargaining has not guaranteed extensive coverage of collective bargains. The existence of employer/ employee representation committees undermines the principle of exclusivity of union representation.	Plurality in bargaining coexists with significant coverage of collective bargains through union and non-union agreements. Representative consultation over major workplace change in agreements promotes the principle of plurality of representation. The mandatory consultation term in agreements promotes joint consultative committees and other forms of representation at workplaces.

Once the bargaining partners have been recognized, they are subject to an obligation to bargain. The rationale for compelling the parties to bargain is explained by UK labour lawyer Gwyneth Pitt. There is an 'important difference [between] the employer who is involved in voluntary collective bargaining [who] is already prepared to engage in negotiation, which will not be the case with an employer who has been forced to recognise a union' (Pitt 2009: 155). Thus employers and employees who have been compelled to bargain are subject to procedural requirements.

In the United States, section 8(d) of the NLRA states that the duty to bargain collectively is 'the performance of the mutual obligation of the employer and the representative of the employees to meet at reasonable times and confer in good faith with respect to wages, hours, and other terms and conditions of employment, or the negotiation of an agreement, or any question arising thereunder'. In Australia, similar good faith requirements are imposed on bargaining representatives for a proposed enterprise agreement (s 228(1) FWA).[4] The good faith obligations in both countries consist of compulsory and voluntary requirements. It is the content, rather than the process of making an agreement, that must be reached through voluntary bargaining. Section 8(d) of the NLRA, like the Australian provisions, explicitly compels representatives to confer but they are not compelled to agree, nor to make a concession.[5] Thus either party may walk away from the negotiations leaving arrangements as they are, or have recourse to the 'economic weapons' of the strike or the lockout, or in Australia they may jointly ask the Fair Work Commission (FWC) to arbitrate their differences of opinion (FWA Part 6-2).

Overall, the good faith requirements in Australia and the duty to bargain collectively in the United States are ambivalent.[6] As Chief Justice Vinson explains, the theory of the NLRA is: 'that the making of voluntary labor agreements is encouraged by protecting employees' rights to organize for collective bargaining and by imposing on labor and management the mutual obligation to bargain collectively'.[7] However, the parties do have antagonistic interests[8] and negotiations may be brought to an end by economic power. As we shall see, this ambivalence promotes collective agreements. Legislation regulates not only the quality of the process of making agreements, but also its terms.

Scope of Bargaining and Consultation

In the United States, bargaining topics fall into three categories: mandatory, permissive or illegal (Cox et al. 2011: 379). Employers and trade unions in the United States are under an obligation to bargain on the listed statutory topics of 'pay, hours and "other conditions of employment"' contained in section 8(d) of the NLRA. There is no obligation to bargain about non-listed legal topics, but it is permitted (Cox et al. 2011: 379, 388).[9] Each party may, however, refuse to discuss these topics. Some topics may not be discussed because they are illegal: for instance, it is unlawful for the parties to agree to only hire union members (NLRA s 8). The role of the union as a bargaining partner is limited. The US Supreme Court has explained the role of the bargaining partners in light of managerial prerogative under the Act by reference to legislative intent: 'Congress had no expectation that the elected union representative would become an equal partner in the running of the business enterprise in which the union's members are employed.'[10] Clearly, management may only be compelled to bargain over particular aspects of the employment relationship and the activities of the trade union. Overall, the NLRA has been interpreted as subordinating labour's interests to those of capital and preserving an exclusive discretion for management.

In Australia, the FWA provides an alternative scheme for the regulation of what terms are negotiated in an enterprise agreement. The bargaining partners may negotiate over permitted matters – including mandatory terms – but if an 'unlawful term' is included in a single enterprise agreement, that term has no effect.[11] Plurality is fostered, since bargaining is permitted on unlisted topics pertaining to the employment relationship and making of workplace agreements. Subsection 172(1)(a) of the FWA is the most important provision regarding topics of negotiation in enterprise agreements. The phrase 'a matter pertaining to the employment relationship' in that section has been used in various pieces of employment legislation over a long period of time in Australia (see EM para 669, for example). The wording of this phrase has changed from time to time. The alternative legislative phrase referred to an 'industrial matter'.

For the first 80 years of the twentieth century such terms were narrowly interpreted by industrial tribunals and the courts. They traditionally treated managerial prerogative as sacrosanct outside areas narrowly defined as 'industrial issues' (essentially wages and hours) (Markey 1987). In the 1980s the High Court narrowed the scope of this managerial prerogative doctrine, stating that the principle:

> probably echoes in some respects what was received doctrine at an earlier time; that it was the prerogative of management to decide how a business enterprise should operate and whom it should employ, without the workforce having any stake in the making of such decisions . . . Over the years that climate of opinion has changed quite radically . . . No doubt our traditional system of industrial conciliation and arbitration has itself contributed to a growing recognition that management and labour have a mutual interest in many aspects of the operation of a business enterprise. (*Re Cram*: 125)[12]

The High Court reinforced this view by broadly defining the meaning of an 'industrial matter' to include management decisions that directly affect the employment relationship, such as levels of employment and modes of recruitment. While the High Court has not consistently applied such a broad interpretation (Creighton and Stewart 2010), the FWA does appear to cohere substantially to the more restrictive interpretation of managerial prerogative, as espoused by the court in *Re Cram*.

Today, the meaning of 'a matter pertaining to an employment relationship' will depend on the construction of each term (EM para 671). For some terms this will be obvious: for example, those relating to pay and hours of employment (EM para 671). The EM also provides examples of terms which are and are not intended to be within the employment relationship (EM paras 672–3). For instance, the permitting of negotiations over staffing levels highlights the mutual accommodation of interests in the operation of the enterprise, which implicitly echoes the views of the court in *Re Cram*.

Nonetheless, the legislation removes core managerial decisions from the bargaining process. An agreement may not generally restrict who management can employ or where management may source their products. There are some matters which are exclusively the province of the employer. In addition, the parties' discretion in bargaining is limited by a small number of unlawful[13] and mandatory terms.[14]

Union and Non-Union Consultation

The mandatory requirement for consultation over major workplace change in Australia illustrates how a mandatory restriction is imposed on managerial prerogative; its aim is a mutual accommodation of employer and employee interests in the organization of the business.[15] 'Major workplace change' is defined as change that would have a significant impact on employees, and includes changes to production, programme, organization, structure or technology (FW Regs Schedule 2.3(1)). The FWA requires consultation of representatives about major workplace change to be a term of an enterprise agreement (FWA s 205). If an enterprise agreement does not include such a term, determined by the parties, the model term is taken to be part of the agreement. The model term is pre-scribed in the regulations: it requires that information be provided to employees, and consultation of relevant employees or appointment of an employee representative (FW Regs Schedule 2.3). Thus the representative can be a union or non-union member. The use of non-union representation in relation to major workplace change is regulated very differently under the NLRA.

In the United States, non-union representative consultation is severely curtailed, although not totally eliminated (Gollan 2007).[16] Employee representation plans, or company unions, were used to avoid independent trade unions, so they were largely prohibited as unfair labour practices by the NLRA.[17] Employee representation plans included committees of employee representatives supported by an employer. The NLRA restricts the activities of company unions and employee representation plans by defin-ing them as labour organizations (s 2(5)) and then prohibits employer support of them (s 8(a)). Thus, a non-union employee committee discussing major workplace change which touched on the traditional subjects of collective bargaining listed in s 2(5) would be illegal. Employees' interests in pay, hours and other working conditions may only be represented by a trade union. Accordingly, managers and trade unions are permitted to establish a union–management information and consultation committee through the process of collective bargaining.

In Australia, plurality in choice of representatives means employees may be repre-sented by both trade union and non-trade union representatives. Employees may appoint union or non-union representatives for the purposes of bargaining and consultation. The US requirement for exclusive representation or no representation at all limits the choice of representatives. There is a difference in philosophy between the United States and Australia in relation to negotiation and discussion of topics mandated by legislation. In the United States, the legislature and courts defer to exclusive managerial preroga-tive to a greater extent than in Australia. The US courts are of the view that unions are not equal partners in the running of businesses. Thus, the principle of exclusivity may confine discussion of topics within workplace relations. By contrast, the Australian High Court has recognized that there is an interdependence between employers and employee representatives. Industrial matters have been defined broadly and include recognition of a mutual accommodation of interests in many aspects of the operation of a busi-ness, such as consultation of major workplace change. Hence, these principles reinforce pluralism in discussions within workplace relations.

The Collective Bargaining Process

How then does collective bargaining work? The prevailing view is that agreements are reached through trade-offs and the threat of economic power. To bring about an agreement a union may hold a strike and an employer may lock out their employees. Cox et al. (2011: 438) explain that it is the threat rather than the strike itself that provides the impetus for agreement: 'the strike or the fear of a strike is the motive power that makes collective bargaining operate'. They further explain, from an American perspective, how the process operates in practice:

> Everyone who has been in a tough wage negotiation where the stakes were high knows that the bargain is never struck until one minute before midnight when there is no place else to go, nothing left to do, no possible escape from choosing between a strike and a compromise. In the final analysis collective bargaining works as a method of fixing terms and conditions of employment only because there comes a time when both sides conclude that the risks of losses through a strike are so great that compromise is cheaper than economic battle. And when one side or both miscalculate and conclude that the risks are worth running and a strike occurs, it is settled only when each side is convinced that continuing the struggle will cost more than acceptance of the terms the other offers. (Cox et al. 2011: 438)

In addition, the trade-offs are facilitated by long negotiations which permit the narrowing of issues of disagreement amongst the parties (Cox et al. 2011: 438; Cox 1958: 1409). While these factors apply in Australia as well, reaching agreement is assisted by the existence of stronger legal sanctions for violating good faith obligations and more extensive protections for bargaining representatives than in the United States. Even so, trade-offs and the threat of economic weapons are important catalysts for agreement in each country. In the United States, there are protections for trade union members exercising their bargaining rights. These protections against unfair labour practices are enforced by the National Labour Relations Board (NLRB) in quasi-judicial hearings. However, the sanctions for unfair labour practices are largely regarded as ineffective. Only limited sanctions are available, the most typical being a 'cease and desist' order (Kaufman et al. 2000: 278). As the NLRB is an administrative body, it cannot provide judicial relief such as compensatory or punitive damages (Estlund 2007: 598). Estlund (2007: 599) explains that 'as things stand, employers can treat the small and confined risk of an unfair labor practice charge as a minor cost of doing business'. So while the scope of unfair labour practices protections is broad, their effectiveness is limited.

In Australia too, bargaining representatives are protected in exercising their bargaining rights by the Fair Work Commission (FWC), an administrative tribunal. The FWC has specific powers to resolve disputes by conciliation and arbitration and has a supervisory function to facilitate agreement making. This includes a power to make tailored orders (Creighton and Stewart 2010: 137). For instance, bargaining representatives must meet the good faith bargaining obligations when negotiations for an agreement begin (FWA 228; EM para 950). If those obligations are not met, the FWC can make a 'bargaining order' requiring the representatives to comply with their statutory obligations (FWA ss 229–31; EM paras 954–65). A review of the FWA's use between 2009 and 2011, conducted by the FWA Review Panel in 2012, concluded that the good faith provisions had successfully contributed to extending the coverage of collective agreements to an additional 440,000 employees (FWA Review Panel 2012: 153). Accordingly, protections for bargaining representatives are more extensive and more effective in Australia than in the USA.

EMPLOYEE VOICE REGULATIONS IN CONTEXT

Labour law, as discussed above, plays a significant role in shaping the forms and structures of employee voice through provisions promoting or inhibiting union representation and other forms of collective bargaining, and establishing the terms regulating protected industrial action or employment protection (see also Peetz and Preston 2009). Above we have examined in detail the cross-national diversity between American and Australian labour regulations: the American Wagner Act guarantees union exclusivity in employee representation and collective bargaining, whereas the current Australian *Fair Work Act 2009* (Cth) adopts a pluralistic approach, providing opportunities for employee voice represented in all forms (union, non-union and individuals). In this section we review the IR literature and empirical studies to assess voice regulation in the context of the workplace. Significantly, both countries are experiencing continuous declines in union membership and a 'representation gap' (Taras and Kaufman 2006; Gollan 2007); the USA has applied a Human Resource Management (HRM) approach to involving employees more directly in organizational decision-making, whereas Australia has seen the development of non-union employee representation as well as other direct forms of employee participation (Gollan 2006; Kaufman 2004; Kaufman 2014 forthcoming; Pyman et al. 2010).

It is important to note, however, that labour regulations operate in a complex world where their *de facto* enforcement can be affected by factors of different nature and at various levels (national, sector, industry or workplace) (see for example, Ahlering and Deakin 2007; Kaine 2012; Lund et al. 2008; Perrett 2007). As Ahlering and Deakin (2007: 883) suggested when discussing cross-country comparison of labour regulations, 'the social or economic effect of a given legal rule can only be understood by seeing legal rules as part of a system of interlinked norms, some of which are extra-legal in nature'. This principle also applies to the understanding of employee voice regulations. However the literature is scant in linking the legal provisions to their organizational contexts, demonstrating how legislative conditions interact with other key contextual factors, and the subsequent end results at workplaces (see also Bogg and Novitz 2012). To fill the gap, we draw on extant literature and identify some key contextual factors that coexist and interrelate with regulations of employee voice at a workplace level. Investigations at this level will reveal the ultimate intricacy of labour law exerting its influence on employee participation within an intertwined web of internal and external, direct and indirect, formal and informal regulations, as well as other influential factors, such as social and organizational norms, managerial prerogative and motives, union strength and economic/market conditions (see also Kaine 2012; Perrett 2007; Ramsay 1991; Samuel 2007).

Within organizational contexts, managerial prerogatives and labour management cooperation both affect and are affected by employee voice regulations and are hence related to the forms and structures of employee representation (Atleson 1982; Bogg and Novitz 2012; Dundon et al. 2004; Kaine 2012). Despite the difference between the USA and Australia in labour law philosophy regarding topics such as negotiation and consultation, sharing of power in organizational decision-making has never been an easy goal for the collective efforts of employees. Atleson (1982: 97) noted in the US context that traditionally in the mass production industries all matters, such as wages, hours and everything else, had been areas of exclusive managerial authority. 'Management alone directed the enterprise until restrained by law and collective bargaining agreements. Management, however, still retains all those powers which have not been expressly or implicitly restricted by agreements' (Atleson 1982: 95). Under a different legal framework in Australia, Markey and Reglar (1997) also observed that employee participation or industrial democracy has been generally slow to gain acceptance in workplaces, because Australian managers have traditionally been wary of any whittling away at their managerial prerogative.

More recently, three years after the enactment of the FWA in Australia, the 2012 public submissions to the Fair Work Act Review Panel revealed that the scope of issues permitted for collective bargaining had been one of the central debates between businesses and unions: while unions demanded a wider scope for negotiation, businesses were concerned that employee representatives can now bargain and take industrial action over a much wider set of claims. Business groups thus requested amendments for a broader definition of 'unlawful' terms under the FWA, restricting unions' claims and threats of protected industrial action regarding the use of contractors, outsourcing and business restructuring (ACTU 2012; Ai Group 2012; AMMA 2012). The dispute is essentially a reflection of the fundamental conflicts between labour and capital.

At workplace level, Kaine's (2012: 328) case studies on legal regulation and employee voice in the Australian aged-care industry suggest that exposure to a common shift in labour law does not preclude management agency, which highlights the importance of managerial prerogative in determining the expression of voice. In a similar vein, Bogg and Novitz (2012: 325) find that 'workers' "voice" can be instrumentally called for in order to improve employer profitability through improving manufacturing or service processes or consumer satisfaction'. This is typically reflected in the HRM approach which emerged in the USA in the 1980s and has gained worldwide popularity. Therefore Bogg and Novitz (2012: 325) argue, 'although HRM offers a case for employee voice, which is potentially palatable to employers, it does so only to improve "managerial practice and the functioning of organizations" such that "questions directly and indirectly connected to efficiency and effectiveness" are central'. For the authors, this suggests there is little space for consideration of the social normative purposes of employee voice.

These findings have reinforced Dundon et al.'s (2004: 1149) proposal that the meaning and purpose of employee voice is best understood as a complex and 'uneven set of meanings and purposes with a dialectic shaped by external regulation, on the one hand, and internal management choice, on the other'. Consistently, Dundon et al. (2005: 312) claim that 'on the whole, managers decide whether or not workers have voice in these firms, and it is managers rather than employees who decide what mechanisms to utilise'. Relying on their prerogatives, managers use different response strategies to resist and restrict union recognition and activity, or substitute union representation with other forms of employee participation. Employers typically perceive unions as a source of employee power, which provides a compelling reason for them to establish non-union employee representation or other forms of voice arrangements (Taras and Kaufman 2006). In the USA, with defeat of labour law reform in 1978, management opposition to unions had become more openly expressed. Kochan (2012: 304) thus concludes, 'the increase in management opposition and the ineffectiveness of American labour law in redressing illegal employer behaviour account for a substantial portion of union decline'. By the mid-1980s, union coverage had declined so substantially that 'they could no longer rely on strike threats as a source of bargaining power or use pattern bargaining to spread wage increases beyond their specific bargaining units' (Kochan 2012: 305).

In addition, union representation and non-union employee representation at workplaces is less likely to legally coexist under the restrictive Wagner Act. In the USA, Campolieti et al. (2013) find NER presence (as a large all-encompassing system of the joint-consultative variety) is negatively associated with union demand, suggesting that it works as a substitute for union representation (see also Lipset and Meltz 2000). Whereas in Australia, NER demonstrates a high level of complementarity to union representation: organizations with a union at the workplace were overwhelmingly more likely to report the presence of a consultative committee (Pyman et al. 2006). In fact, Boxall and Haynes's (2005) review of recent findings from a linked series of worker surveys conducted in the USA, the UK, Canada, Australia and New Zealand indicates that outside of the USA non-union representation is increasingly complementary to unions in satisfying employee and employer interests. It is worth noting though that the 'substitute versus complement' debate about NER can oversimplify and/or polarize union avoidance strategies that in practice are quite diverse and complex (Dundon 2002).

Other key contextual factors coexist with regulatory obligations at an organizational level, such as industrial relations climate (Deery and Iverson 2005; Pyman et al. 2010; Snape and Redman, 2012), organizational and employee characteristics (Harley et al. 2010), and employer dominance and union strength (Samuel 2007). Yet, how these factors interact with legal regulation of employee voice and the subsequent influences on employee participation require further research.

In sum, examining legal regulation of employee voice in context reinforces the findings from the comparative analyses conducted above (that is, the exclusivity of the US labour law versus the pluralistic labour law in Australia), whereas additional insights are gained when considering the nuances of enforcing labour regulations at workplaces, as a result of the interrelation and interaction of labour regulation with other organizational factors, such as managerial prerogatives and employer strategies toward unions. In the following section we will discuss related implications and directions for future research.

DISCUSSION AND IMPLICATIONS

Employee voice regulation in each jurisdiction is limited when assessed against its practical operation. The effectiveness of such regulation is limited as a result of the partial coverage of employees by enterprise and collective agreements. In the United States, collective bargains covered only 13 per cent of the workforce in 2009 (Venn 2009: 18). This low level of coverage diminishes the significance of the legal right for exclusive union bargaining. In Australia, coverage was significantly higher, extending to 43.4 per cent of the workforce in 2010 (ABS 2010).[18] This coverage of enterprise agreements is indicative of an extensive legal right to bargain. Since the introduction of enterprise bargaining in the early 1990s, the requirements for plurality of bargaining representatives have resulted in a considerable proportion of non-union agreements.[19] The 2012 FWA Review Panel

(2012: 142–3) found that by September 2011, 67 per cent of agreements were union and 33 per cent were non-union. Nonetheless, the extent of coverage of workplace agreements in Australia indicates a continued influence of trade unions in workplace relations.

As noted above, legislation regulates consultation of representatives about major workplace change in the United States and Australia. In Australia, consultation over major workplace change is mandatory under the FWA. No doubt this will enhance pluralism in discussion of topics and the scope of representation in Australian workplaces. Given the mandatory nature of consultation, it is expected that there will be a correlative increase in numbers of representative consultation arrangements over major workplace change. Although no publicly available data exists on the prevalence of committees in workplaces since 2009, data does exist for earlier periods of regulation. The FWA replaced consultation requirements for enterprise agreements introduced by the Keating Labor government in 1993 and abolished by the Howard conservative government in 1996. The Australian Worker Representation and Participation Survey (AWRPS) (2004) conducted in 2003–04 reported a figure of 38.9 per cent of companies with committees of employees (see Teicher et al. 2007: 137). Even when legislative support for such committees had been removed by the conservative government in 1996, employee consultation committees continued to exist in Australian workplaces.

Similar joint consultation committees exist in the United States. Freeman and Rogers reported in 1999 that over a third of the workplaces they surveyed had an established employee participation committee that discussed problems with management on a regular basis (Freeman and Rogers 1999: 92). They found that a large proportion of non-union committees regularly discussed issues such as wages and benefits – this is an unexpected finding as non-union committees are prohibited from discussing these topics by ss 2(5) and (8)(2)(a) of the NLRA (Taras and Kaufman 2006: 516) and operate illegally (Lobel 2006: 1547). The existence of such employer/employee representation committees undermines the principle of exclusivity of union representation in the United States. Overall, the principle of plurality of representation in Australia is a more pervasive principle than exclusive union representation in the United States.

As demonstrated above, labour regulations do not operate in a vacuum but generally in conjunction with other factors; we have primarily focused on the interaction of legal regulations with managerial prerogatives and employer strategies toward unions. However, there are other key contextual factors which coexist with regulatory conditions at an organizational level, such as industrial relations climate (Deery and Iverson 2005; Pyman et al. 2010; Snape and Redman 2012), organizational and employee characteristics (Harley et al. 2010) and employer dominance and union strength (Samuel 2007). Future research needs to investigate how these other key workplace factors interrelate and interact with legal regulations of employee voice and how these dynamics differ across national legal frameworks. Given the comparatively recent enactment of the FWA in Australia, there is relatively limited empirical evidence available, which also calls for research in the future. Such research will provide evaluative support to policymakers for the improvement of the IR system, and inform employers within different jurisdictions of effective employee voice practices, such as dual or multiple channel arrangements.

Another important benefit of studying legal regulation and its interaction with other factors at workplaces is that it can help us understand the possible ambiguity of labour law, as Perret's (2007) case study indicated, and reduce the indeterminacy of legal provisions as Lee and McCann (2011) have suggested. These are potential fruitful directions for future research. Further, Kaine (2012) suggests taking into account not only formal and direct constraints exerted by labour law and managerial decision-making but also informal and indirect regulators such as the location of a workplace and societal expectations about particular groups of workers.

Our study identifies opportunities for the development of Australian and US labour law in the regulation of employee voice. In the USA, many proposals have been advanced in recent years for introducing different forms of employee voice other than trade union representation, and alternative dispute resolution processes (Kochan 2012). Concerned with the failure of current labour law in supporting diffusions of innovation in relation to alternative voice arrangements and management practices, Kochan (2012: 305) proposes the future reform of US labour law to include provisions concerning direct employee participation, self or co-regulation and enforcement, an American style works council and minority representation (see more discussion in Kochan 2012: 312–14).

In Australia, the duality and complementarity of voice arrangements challenges the dichotomist approach to employee voice, such as human resource management versus industrial relations, and individualism versus collectivism (Benson 2000; Gollan 2007; Pyman et al. 2006). The critical issue involved is a configuration of multiple channels of voice rather than a single channel, and to understand how and why the different voice channels complement each other, under what conditions multiple arrangements flourish and the legal underpinnings of the operation of multiple voice channels (Gollan 2007; Pyman et al. 2006: 555).

In summary, both Australian and US regulation of employee voice provide useful and important examples of the tension and complementarity of the legal frameworks in workplace processes and practices. Consideration of legal provisions, in conjunction with their application in individual workplaces, will greatly enhance our understanding of the resultant variance in voice arrangements and subsequent outcomes in terms of organizational efficiency and employee well-being. Such an analysis across the jurisdictions not only addresses a research gap, but also identifies important opportunities for policymakers to improve the IR system and the making of labour law.

NOTES

*   The authors would like to thank Dr Senia Kalfa for her generous research assistance. Glenn Patmore would like to thank Sarah Shrubb who read and offered comments on his contribution and Jason Goliszek, Candice Parr and Collette Downie, who read material to him and provided legal research assistance.
1. In Australia, they are also implemented through awards.
2. This section relates to collective bargaining in Australia in relation to an existing enterprise. Prior to the enactment of the FWA, there were multiple possible streams of agreement making, which had the capacity to result in disputes over which industrial instrument to use (Explanatory Memorandum to the Fair Work Bill 2008, r 117 (herein EM)). The FWA introduced a single stream of collective enterprise agreements to be made between employers and employees (EM r 141). The FWA also maintains the capacity for employers to make green-fields agreements to establish terms and conditions of employment for a genuine new enterprise, but requires that such agreements must be made with one or more unions that would be eligible to represent the employees who will be employed in the enterprise (EM r 142). The FWA also provides a separate multi-employer bargaining stream for low-paid workers, who had not historically had access to collective bargaining (EM r 179).
3. Under FWA s 236, a bargaining representative of an employee who will be covered by a proposed single-

enterprise agreement may apply to the Fair Work Commission for a determination (a *majority support determination*) that a majority of the employees who will be covered by the agreement want to bargain with the employer, or employers, that will be covered by the agreement

4. The more specific process requirements of the good faith obligation, as determined by the National Labor Relations Board under section 8(d) of the NLRA, are similar to the requirements that have been codified in the Australian legislation (see Creighton and Stewart 2010: 729).

5. See also *NLRB v American National Insurance Co.*, 343 US 395, 404 (1952), Vinson CJ.

6. *NLRB v Insurance Agents' International Union*, 361 US 477, 489 (1960), Brennan J.

7. *NLRB v American National Insurance Co.*, 343 US 395, 402 (1952) Vinson CJ.

8. *NLRB v Insurance Agents' International Union*, 361 US 477, 488 (1960), Brennan J.

9. See also *NLRB v Wooster Division of Borg-Warner Corp.*, 356 US 342 (1958).

10. *First National Maintenance Corp. v NLRB*, 452 US 666 (1981), Blackmun J.

11. An enterprise agreement provides terms and conditions that apply to employees covered by the national system. This chapter focuses on single enterprise agreement making, not other forms of agreements covered by the FWA including multi-enterprise agreements, green-fields agreements and the low-paid stream of multi-enterprise agreements. For a discussion of the rules pertaining to various forms of agreement please see chapters 12 and 21 of Creighton and Stewart (2010).

12. *Re Cram; Ex parte NSW Colliery Proprietors' Association Ltd* (1987) 163 CLR 117, 125 (per Mason C.J., Wilson, Brennan, Deane, Dawson, Toohey and Gaudnon J.J.) (*'Re Cram'*).

13. Unlawful terms are: discriminatory terms; objectionable terms; and terms that would be inconsistent 'in certain ways with the FWA provisions relating to unfair dismissal, industrial action and union right of entry' (Creighton and Stewart 2010: 315–17; see s 194 FWA).

14. These terms include: a nominal expiry date (s 186(5)); a dispute settlement clause (s 186(6)) that 'allows [the] Fair Work [Commission], or another person independent of the parties covered by the agreement, to help resolve disputes about matters arising under the agreement and the National Employment Standards' (s 186(6)); a 'flexibility term' that would permit an employee to request a change in their hours of employment (s 202); and a consultation clause (s 205). It is also noteworthy that the Act requires employers to provide new employees with a Fair Work Information Statement (FWA ss 124, 125) and gives employees a right to vote on an enterprise agreement (FWA ss 180, 181).

15. *Re Cram*; *Amalgamated Metals, Foundry and Shipwrights Union v Broken Hill Pty Co Ltd, Whyalla* (1984) 8 IR 34 (*'Termination, Change and Redundancy Case'*).

16. For example in some areas of the transport industry (see Kaufman 2003 for Delta Air Lines case study for an example of NER).

17. This section draws upon Glenn Patmore's previous work.

18. In addition, awards resulting from arbitrated disputes regarding working conditions covered 15.2 per cent of the Australian workforce in 2010 (ABS 2010).

19. Non-union agreements outnumbered union agreements under the coalition's Work Choices legislation (FWA Review Panel 2012:142–3).

REFERENCES

ABS (Australian Bureau of Statistics) (2010), *Employee Earnings and Hours*, Cat: 6306.0, May.

ACTU (Australian Council of Trade Unions) (2012), 'Submission to the post implementation review of the fair work act 2009', available at: http://www.deewr.gov.au/WorkplaceRelations/Policies/FairWorkActReview/Documents/AustralianCouncilofTradeUnions.pdf (accessed 29 April 2012).

Ahlering, B. and S. Deakin (2007), 'Labor regulation, corporate governance, and legal origin: a case of institutional complementarity?', *Law and Society Review*, **41** (4), 865–908.

Ai Group (Australian Industry Group) (2012), 'Fair work act review: removing the barriers to productivity and flexibility', submission to the department of education, employment and workplace relations of the Australian government, available at: https://submissions.deewr.gov.au/sites/Submissions/FairWorkActReview/Documents/AustralianIndustryGroup.pdf (accessed 3 December 2013).

Amalgamated Metals, Foundry and Shipwrights Union v Broken Hill Pty Co Ltd, Whyalla (Termination, Change and Redundancy Case) (1984) 8 IR 34.

AMMA (Australian Manufacturing and Mining Association) (2012), 'Submission to the Fair Work Act review panel: on the post-implementation review of the Fair Work Act 2009', Department of Education, Employment and Workplace Relations (DEEWR), available at: http://www.deewr.gov.au/WorkplaceRelations/Policies/FairWorkActReview/Submissions/Pages/default.aspx (accessed 30 April 2012).

Atleson, J. (1982), 'Management prerogatives, plant closings, and the NLRA', available at: http://www.law.

nyu.edu/ecm_dlv3/groups/public/@nyu_law_website__journals__review_of_law_and_social_change/docu
ments/documents/ecm_pro_070874.pdf (accessed 20 January 2013).

Bamber, G.J. and P. Sheldon (2007), 'Collective bargaining: an international analysis', in R. Blanpain (ed),
Comparative Labour Law and Industrial Relations in Industrialized Market Economies, Alphen aan den Rijn:
Kluwer Law International.

Benson, J. (2000), 'Employee voice in union and non-union Australian workplaces', *British Journal of
Industrial Relations*, **38** (3), 453–9.

Bogg, A. (2012), 'Investigating voice at work', presented at Voice at Work Australasian Meeting Melbourne,
20–21 July 2012.

Bogg, A. and T. Novitz (2012), 'Investigating "Voice" at work', *Comparative Labor Law and Policy Journal*,
33 (3), 323–54.

Boxall, P. and P. Haynes (2005), *Employee Voice in the Anglo-American World: An Overview of Five National
Surveys*, Proceedings of the 57th Annual Meeting of the Labor and Employment Relations Association,
Chicago: University of Illinois Press.

Buchanan, J. and B. van Wanrooy (2009), 'Employment law reform and social inclusion: if the social inclusion agenda was in the Fair Work Act, where would it be?', paper prepared for the Social Inclusion Forum,
University of Melbourne, 25–26 June.

Campolieti, M., R. Gomez and M. Gunderson (2013), 'Does non-union employee representation act as a complement or substitute to union voice? Evidence from Canada and the United States', *Industrial Relations: A
Journal of Economy and Society*, **52**, 378–96.

Cox, A. (1958), 'The Duty to Bargain in Good Faith', *Harvard Law Review*, **71**, 1401.

Cox, A., D. Box, R. Gorman and M. Finkin (eds) (2011), *Labour Law Cases and Materials*, 15th edn,
Westbury, NY: Foundation Press.

Creighton, B. and A. Stewart (2010), *Labour Law: An Introduction*, 5th edn, Abingdon: Taylor and Francis
(includes reference to chapters by A. Forsyth).

Deery, S.J and R.D. Iverson (2005), 'Labor-management cooperation: antecedents and impact on organizational performance', *Industrial and Labor Relations Review*, **58** (4), 588–609.

Directive 2002/14/EC of the European Parliament and of the Council.

Dundon, T. (2002), 'Employer opposition and union avoidance in the UK', *Industrial Relations Journal*, **33**
(3), 234–45.

Dundon, T., A. Wilkinson, M. Marchington and P. Ackers (2004), 'The meanings and purpose of employee
voice', *International Journal of Human Resource Management*, **15** (6), 1149–70.

Dundon, T., A. Wilkinson, M. Marchington and P. Ackers (2005), 'The management of voice in non-union
organisations: managers' perspectives,' *Employee Relations*, **27** (3), 307–19.

Estlund, C. (2007), 'The ossification of American labor law and the decline of self-governance in the workplace', *Journal of Labor Research*, **28** (4), 591–608.

Explanatory Memorandum to the Fair Work Bill 2008.

Fair Work Act 2009 (Cth).

Fair Work Regulations 2009.

First National Maintenance Corp. v National Labor Relations Board, 452 US 666 (1981).

Forsyth, A. (2012), 'Comparing purposes and concepts in United States and Australian collective bargaining
law', in B. Creighton and A. Forsyth (eds), *Rediscovering Collective Bargaining: Australia's Fair Work Act in
International Perspectives*, New York: Routledge, 203–24.

Freeman, R.B. and J. Rogers (1999), *What Workers Want*, New York: Russell Sage Foundation.

Fudge, J. (2008), 'Working-time regimes, flexibility, and work-life balance: gender equality and families', paper
presented at Melbourne Law School, Melbourne, 18 February.

FWA Review Panel (2012), *Towards more productive and equitable workplaces: An evaluation of the Fair Work
legislation*, November 2012, Australian Government, Canberra.

Gollan, P.J. (2006), 'Editorial: consultation and non-union employee representation', *Industrial Relations
Journal*, **37** (5), 428–37.

Gollan, P.J. (2007), *Employee Representation in Non-Union Firms*, London: Sage Publications.

Gollan P.J. and G. Patmore (2006), 'Transporting the European social partnership to Australia', *Journal of
International Relations*, **48** (2), 217–56.

Harley, B., L. Sargent and B. Allen (2010), 'Employee responses to "high performance work system" practices:
an empirical test of the disciplined worker thesis', *Work, Employment and Society*, **24** (4), 740–60.

Harris, L.A., K.B. Olsen and R.J. Walker (2012), 'Role typology for health and safety representatives',
Employee Relations, **34** (5), 481–500.

Kaine, S. (2012), 'Employee voice and regulation in the residential aged care sector', *Human Resource
Management Journal*, **22** (3), 316–31.

Kaufman, B.E. (2004), *The Global Evolution of Industrial Relations: Events, Ideas, and the IIRA*, Geneva:
International Labour Office.

Kaufman, B.E. (2014), 'The historical development of American HRM broadly viewed, *HRM Review*, forthcoming.

Kaufman, B.E., D. Lewin and J.A. Fossum (2000), 'Nonunion employee involvement and participation programs: the role of employee representation and the impact of the NLRA', in B.E. Kaufman and D.G. Taras (eds), *Nonunion Employee Representation: History, Contemporary Practice, and Policy*, Armonk: M.E. Sharpe, pp. 259–86.

Kochan, T.A. (2012), 'Collective bargaining: crisis and its consequences for American society', *Industrial Relations Journal*, **43** (4), 302–16.

Lee, S. (2004), 'Working-hour gaps: trends and issues', in Jon C. Messenger (ed.), *Working Time and Workers' Preferences in Industrialized Countries: Finding the Balance*, New York: Routledge, pp. 29–59.

Lee, S. and D. McCann (2011), 'New directions in labour regulation research', in S. Lee and D. McCann (eds), *Regulating for Decent Work: New Directions in Labour Market Regulation*, New York : Palgrave Macmillan, pp. 1–17.

Lipset, S.M. and N.M. Meltz (2000), 'Estimates of nonunion employee representation in the United States and Canada: how different are the two countries?', in B.E. Kaufman and D.G. Taras (eds), *Nonunion Employee Representation*, Armonk, NY: M.E. Sharpe, pp. 223–30.

Lobel, O. (2006), 'The four pillars of work law', *Michigan Law Review*, **104** (6), 1539.

Lund, J., N. Declercq and M. Childers (2008), 'Finding their voice', *Labor Studies Journal*, **33** (4), 431–52.

Markey, R. (1987), 'Neo-corporatism and technological change in Australia: international perspective', *New Technology, Work and Employment*, **2** (2), 142.

Markey, R. and G. Patmore (2011), 'Employee participation in health and safety in the Australian steel industry', *British Journal of Industrial Relations*, **29** (1), 8–21.

Markey, R. and R. Reglar (1997), 'Consultative committees in the Australian steel industry', in R. Markey and J. Monat (eds), *Innovation and Employee Participation through Works Councils: International Case Studies*, Aldershot: Avebury, pp. 358–88.

Mundlak, G. (2012), 'Human rights-labor rights: why don't the two tracks meet?', Paper from CELRL Seminar at the Melbourne Law School, 18 April.

National Labor Relations Act 29 USC § 151–69.

National Labor Relations Board v American National Insurance Co., 343 US 395 (1952).

National Labor Relations Board v Insurance Agents' International Union, 361 US 477 (1960).

National Labor Relations Board v Wooster Division of Borg–Warner Corporation, 356 US 342 (1958).

Novitz, T. and A. Bogg (2011), 'Outline of voices at work project', available at http://voicesatwork.org.uk/wp-content/uploads/2011/05/VOICES-AT-WORK-outline-1.pdf (accessed 13 January 2012).

Patmore, G. (2010), 'A legal perspective on employee participation', in A. Wilkinson, P.J. Gollan, M. Marchington and D. Lewin (eds), *The Oxford Handbook of Employee Participation*, Oxford University Press: Oxford, pp. 76–104.

Peetz, D. and A. Preston (2009), 'Individual contracting, collective bargaining and wages in Australia', *Industrial Relations Journal*, **40** (5), 444–61.

Perrett, R. (2007), 'Worker voice in the context of the re-regulation of employment: employer tactics and statutory union recognition in the UK', *Work, Employment and Society*, **21** (4), 617–34.

Pitt, G. (2009), *Employment Law*, 7th edn, London: Sweet and Maxwell.

Pyman, A., B. Cooper, J. Teicher and P. Holland (2006), 'A comparison of the effectiveness of employee voice arrangements in Australia', *Industrial Relations Journal*, **37** (5), 543–59.

Pyman, A., P. Holland, J. Teicher and B.K. Cooper (2010), 'Industrial relations climate, employee voice and managerial attitudes to unions: an Australian study', *British Journal of Industrial Relations*, **48** (2), 460–80.

Ramsay, H. (1991), 'The community, the multinational, its workers and their charter: a modern tale of industrial democracy?', *Work, Employment and Society*, **5** (4), 541–66.

Re Cram; Ex parte NSW Colliery Proprietors' Association Ltd (1987) 163 CLR 117.

Rogers, J. (1995), 'United States: lessons from abroad and home', in J. Rogers and W. Streeck (eds), *Works Councils: Consultation, Representation, and Cooperation in Industrial Relations*, Chicago: University of Chicago Press.

Samuel, P. (2007), 'Partnership consultation and employer domination in two British life and pensions firms', *Work, Employment and Society*, **21** (3), 459–77.

Snape, E.D. and T.O.M. Redman (2012), 'Industrial relations climate and union commitment: an evaluation of workplace-level effects', *Industrial Relations*, **51** (1), 11–28.

Taras, D.G. and B.E. Kaufman (2006), 'Non-union employee representation in North America: diversity, controversy and uncertain future', *Industrial Relations Journal*, **37** (5), 513–42.

Teicher, J., A. Pyman, P. Holland and B. Cooper (2007), 'Employee voice in Australia', in R.B. Freeman, P. Boxall and P. Haynes (eds), *What Workers Say: Employee Voice in the Anglo-American World*, Ithaca NY, ILR Press.

Venn, D. (2009), 'Legislation, collective bargaining and enforcement: updating the OECD employment protection indicators', available at: www.oecd.org/els/workingpapers (accessed 20 November 2013).

Walters, D. and K. Frick (2000), 'Worker participation and the management of occupational health and safety: reinforcing or conflicting strategies?', in K. Frick, P.L. Jensen, M. Quinlan and T. Wilthagen (eds), *Systematic Occupational Health and Safety Management: Perspectives on an International Development*, Oxford: Elsevier, pp. 43–66.

23 Voice across borders: comparing and explaining the dynamics of participation in a context of change
Maria González Menéndez and Miguel Martínez Lucio

INTRODUCTION

Kochan (2007) affirms that governments should care about the declining trend of overall worker voice and trade unions because it diminishes the quality of democracies, diminishes standards of employment, increases social inequality and increases conflict. In Kochan's view, public policy changes to address this trend are more likely in other parliamentary systems than in the USA, and more so in countries affected by the European Union's social disciplining of domestic politics and employer behaviour. While the workers' voice is clearly institutionalized in the EU member states to a higher degree than in the USA or in most other countries, as fragmentation of representation increases, the weaknesses in these voice systems are becoming more visible (see Martínez Lucio and González Menéndez 2013). Bridging the democratic deficit in employment relations is unfortunately not a major current political objective in Europe. However, the concern of this chapter is not to reflect on whether workers' voice is a means to an end or an end in itself (see Frege 2005: 154), or whether it is reaching the point where we are witnessing the end of a moment of collective and coordinated voice: rather, the concern of this chapter is to try to map a route through the way that voice is to be studied across boundaries.

The recent comparative literature on industrial relations has generally identified, first, a common trend of decline in workers' voice, and second – and more relevant to this chapter – a significant degree of continuing cross-national diversity in the configuration of instruments for it. Regarding the second point, the dominant perspective is that 'fundamental institutional differences remain' (Frege and Godard 2010: 529). Considering the predominant method of selection of country cases as paradigmatic contrasts (typically the USA versus Germany), paired with a certain analytical conservatism in the field, obsessed with institutional functionalism, system cohesiveness and stability, this may seem something of a foregone conclusion. Yet a perception of workers' voice as a changing space, political and with many levels of regulation (Martínez Lucio 2010), is not completely absent in some comparative work focusing on participation as an institution, perhaps as an inheritance of the 1970s interest in workers' control. This provides a challenge to the study of voice across borders, as we need to balance an understanding of various determinants of an institutional and economic character with an interest in new forms of change and mutation.

In this chapter we present a review of the comparative literature that has tried to analyse systematically employee voice in different countries to discover how and why there are differences across borders. In analysing this literature we shall look mainly at the explicit and implicit explanatory variables used in a range of theoretical and empirical studies of workers' *workplace* voice, the locus of academic debate in recent decades. The chapter is divided into two parts. The first will look at the specific factors and concepts that have been used to explain difference across borders, with the second devoted to the political science approach. After illustrating the presence of ongoing tension in referencing internal and external environmental factors in explaining the nature of, and changes in, workers' voice, more innovative views on the politics and ideology of workers' voice will be reflected upon.

In general terms the chapter will illustrate the key factors that are debated for explaining variance and similitude: legal regulation, labour power (in unionization, mobilization or institutionalization), labour market factors such as unemployment levels, values/ideologies, industrial relations politics and the role of non-industrial relations institutions (ranging from firm organization to the market orientation of the economy) have all been offered as explanatory variables. The focus of study has also oscillated between interest in levels of *de facto* voice (arguments connected to job control, ranging from industrial democracy to the quality of jobs and autonomy), in its performance-enhancement capabilities (from flexibility and innovation to crisis survival), and in the changing contours of formal workers' voice channels (from works councils to manager-controlled individualized mechanisms). In this literature, focusing on comparing processes is unusual (for some exceptions, see Rigby et al. 2009; and Gold 2011). The field has, instead, an abundance of descriptive reviews of (well-known) regulatory contexts and schemes, alternating with (sometimes very superficially theoretical) survey analyses, which allow for little reflection on rationales and tensions in operation and make workers' voices appear both over-determined and under-theorized. At the same time, a range of approaches introduce a greater focus on the role of the *political* and the *state* which has been followed more recently by a greater need for sensitivity towards questions of *language*, *ideology* and the broad range of *interest groups* that frame the meaning and development of participation in different contexts. This chapter will therefore seek to unveil some of these characteristics and try to locate them within an understanding of the political and ideological context.

EXPLANATORY VARIABLES IN CROSS-COUNTRY COMPARATIVE ANALYSES OF WORKERS' WORKPLACE VOICE

At the heart of the representation of the concept of workers' workplace voice are works councils and similar bodies. For some, these are the quintessential instruments of European bargaining and/or consultation. They are the spaces around which class compromise is institutionalized on a routine and ongoing basis but they are also spaces that can become active agents in their own right, intervening in the array of private and public spheres of the organization. They form one of the major dimensions of Western European industrial relations and have become a focal point for discussion (Rogers and Streeck 1995). Their relations with unions also vary, with some contexts having very close relations between them, while in others they may be more ambivalent, even if works councillors are normally trade union members or even activists themselves

(Müller-Jentsch 1995). There may also be competing trade union structures within works councils – this competition is an important element of any serious study of workers' voice. The control of works councils is an ongoing dilemma, as firm-level interests may be articulated in varying ways, with regard to sector-level collective agreements, for example. A study conducted in the early 1990s of works councils in Canada, France, Germany, Italy, the Netherlands, Poland, Spain, Sweden and the USA (Rogers and Streeck 1995) stressed that, as a rule, works councils were initially opposed by managers, unions or both (for a similar finding for formerly socialist countries, see Vaughan-Whitehead 2003), and that the emergence and stable performance of works councils generally required legal-institutional support, a specific juridical guaranteeing of their powers. The view of Rogers and Streeck here is clearly one of economic rather than political exchange: they refer to 'the productivity of democracy' (1995: 104) to justify works councils as an exchange ensuring workers' cooperation, in the view of managers, and ensuring performance, in the view of workers. In fact, the economic modelling of workers' workplace voice as an informational tool with efficiency-enhancing capabilities (Freeman and Lazear 1995) proved to be a more influential analytical approach than any politics-based approach in the following years.

The organized and modern tradition of industrial relations, for a large part of the later twentieth century, was linked to various regulatory practices in Western Europe. A body of collective legal rights and formalized structures of representation at various levels of both the economy and the firm (with varying points of emphasis) underpinned the role of voice within the industrial relations systems of Europe. Increasingly, liberal-democratic industrial relations emphasized and focused on creating a 'social dialogue' through mechanisms of representation, which had a specific presence at the level of the firm and sometimes even the workplace. Alongside the practice of collective bargaining and macro-level political representation there was a general commitment to ongoing social dialogue within the firm. This varied by country but, overall within Western Europe, workers' voice through representatives was a key feature of an industrial relations system. According to Hyman and Mason (1995), the development of worker representation, and voice more generally, was not solely the outcome of economic development and new forms of state intervention in the mid-twentieth century. Extending the logic of representation within the workplace was also inspired by the democratic context after the war, and by broad social and intellectual concerns about the importance of voice and welfare at work. It was also the outcome of political tension between capital and labour, and the changing balance of forces (Ramsay 1983), as well as the growing importance of legal norms that were structuring management prerogative – showing the manner in which specific views and understandings of participation and representation emerge at particular times and in different country contexts (Knudsen 1995; Marchington and Wilkinson 2000). One of the enduring reasons for the stability of workers' workplace collective representation in many of the more organized and unionized systems of industrial relations in Western Europe since the 1950s is that it brought benefits to the different social partners, albeit not always similar ones. Knudsen (1995) outlines how, for unions, the benefits concern being able to influence the social and economic agendas of firms; for the employer there are perceived benefits in terms of efficiency; and for the state there is the prospect of greater social cohesion and dialogue. Hence, it is not simply a case of there being a strong social-democratic consensus or realization of mutual gains that underpins workers' workplace participation, but of there being a set of interests that can be balanced through structured dialogue within the firm and which become institutionalized over time.

However, in the second half of the 1970s, developments in voice mechanisms in the workplace other than collective bargaining were often presented as a reaction to trade union power and a balance of forces that tended towards labour. First, company-based collective mechanisms were seen as a challenge to the influence of labour. Sorge (1976) saw the establishment of works councils by law in several European countries as a concerted effort by the state and employers to contain radicalizing trade unions. A similar logic prevailed in Ramsay's (1983) cycles of control thesis, which proposed that employers' initiatives with regard to workers' workplace voice in the UK waxed and waned with upsurges and declines in labour power. Contemporary with these approaches, a group of researchers drawn to workers' self-management, the Industrial Democracy in Europe International Research Group (IDE), focused instead on analysing the impact of formal regulation of workplace participation on organizational hierarchies and workers' *de facto* voice in the mid-1970s in Israel, Yugoslavia and ten Western European countries. Their study concluded, more optimistically, that institutional norms had a positive impact on the influence of representative bodies at the plant, as well as on the overall distribution of influence between management and labour in organizations (IDE 1981). Hence these early forays into the crisis and changes in collective representation detected the role of political forces – the balance of forces – as an imperative for change and institutional development. They also pointed to the importance of norms and the framing of workers' voice in terms of social or economic purpose.

From the mid-1980s onwards, however, workers' workplace voice was to be associated increasingly by industrial relations researchers with managerial agency, to the point that it was in fact at the core of an influential development in industrial relations theory: the consideration of strategic choice (Kochan et al. 1984: 18–19). Variability in workers' workplace voice practices across borders was seen as being associated with 'the nature of strategic choices informed by wider cultural and ideological meanings, transmitted through public policies and legislative enactments, distinctive institutional practices and given "constellations" of the distribution of power in the "larger" society and amongst the "actors" themselves . . . requiring sophisticated multi-causal explanations' (Poole 1986a: 172). In this view, approaches linking periods of labour unrest to the institutionalization of some form of worker participation, such as Sorge's and Ramsay's, were to be qualified. Poole (1986b: 37) proposed giving prominence to radical shifts in societal values – for example the development of labour rights – as the key explanatory variable. As a consequence, the emergence of distinctive types of participatory machinery in different national contexts was a result of the diversity in values at each critical conjuncture in each context.

In parallel, the IDE research group repeated in the mid-1980s its mid-1970s study in the same establishments in Denmark, Belgium, Germany, Norway, the UK, the Netherlands, Israel, Yugoslavia and Sweden, which allowed them to carry out a longitudinal analysis. The results of this analysis questioned the achievements of the *de jure* mechanisms for workplace participation established before the 1980s with regard to their impact on *de facto* voice. Changes in the unemployment rate and previous levels of workers' influence at the plant, rather than formal regulation, were the key variables for understanding patterns of distribution of workers' influence in organizations over time (IDE 1993). Change in unemployment rates was found to be a significant negative predictor of change in workers' influence, and particularly in establishments where workers' influence had previously (a decade earlier) been stronger. The nature of managerial strategies towards workers and their representatives were thus conditioned by the pre-existing distribution of influence between management and labour within the enterprise and the current labour market conditions. In 1987, only where labour was not particularly strong in 1977 and where unemployment had not increased very much between 1977 and 1987 had workers' influence not changed much. Other factors – the size of the organization, level of automation, skill requirements, product complexity, perceived market dominance, political instability and, as already mentioned, institutional norms – were of little significance in understanding the dynamics of workers' workplace voice. In other words, *very few contingencies* were found to be truly relevant, and there was no inertia or cumulative voice model in operation: 'During a recession, management would actively seek to reduce the power of the influential groups which could appear to threaten the managerial prerogative, while they would not be concerned to take steps against weaker groups' (IDE 1993: 148). These labour market factors have usually been concealed in mainstream approaches which, for good reasons, wish to be supportive of the institutions, and therefore the role of agency, and the hope that change can be directed.

The expansion of direct participation schemes in workplaces in Europe and the Anglo-American countries in the 1990s was in fact perceived by many industrial relations scholars as part of a managerial offensive to co-opt unions and regain the upper hand in the workplace. Some early comparative case studies in Europe clearly identified the introduction of direct participation schemes as an attack on trade unions (Regini 1993) and IDE's (1993) findings could be seen as further proof of this. Yet, by remarking how *low* both the *de facto* and *de jure* levels of influence-sharing were in the countries analysed, the IDE study questioned that line of debate, and others. They questioned the suspicions of managers and trade unions regarding the potential of workplace workers' voice respectively to usurp the right to manage and to weaken collective bargaining, as well as propositions that workers' voice would produce a measurable improvement in organizational profitability or conflict levels (IDE 1993: 149). Workers' influence was too low to sustain any of these arguments, they argued; employers clearly were not very keen on sharing influence, and the regulation of workplace participation in place was likely to be insufficient to generate what could be described as 'a critical mass' of workers' voices sufficient to make a difference. Since workers' voice in the workplace could be seen to be worthwhile in itself as an extension of political democracy, and workers' influence was independent of most contingencies apart from management's strategic use of labour market conditions, the IDE study concluded that 'a reasonable amount of influence distribution, down to the lowest level of the organization' across Europe (IDE 1993: 151) required stronger formal, non-voluntaristic structural support for participation, that is, more regulation.

Yet another observer was explicitly more cautious as to the potential impact of European legislation on an issue that was deeply political. Knudsen's (1995) study of workplace participation in the UK, Denmark, Germany and Spain highlighted the instability of workers' voice as an institution, and the importance of traditional management and union strategies towards it (see also Regalia 1996): 'it is only through historical struggles, experiments and compromises that viable institutions for participation have emerged' (Knudsen 1995: 21). That is also the reason why countries differ substantially regarding whether workers' voice is primarily a mode of regulation 'in a formal sense or also in a real sense' (1995: 27). For Knudsen, workplace workers' voice could not be understood without also understanding management style and industrial relations traditions at both national and company level. The role of history and institutional 'stickiness' is important in appreciating how voice can vary. Similar approaches to that of Knudsen, most often connected to qualitative research, identified local, regional and national union activity and resources, including framework agreements or knowledge of alternatives and their consequences (Smith 1994), systemic differences in the space for regulation and in the politics for its occupation by competing actors (Blyton and Martínez Lucio 1995), or voice structures at the national level different from collective bargaining (Monat and Beaupin 2003) as relevant variables affecting differential developments in workers' voice across frontiers.

From the mid-1990s the 'technological drive' for participation or, more generally, the 'business case' for participation often attached to human resource management propositions became of interest surrounding the analysis of workers' workplace voice, whether it is direct or representative, particularly in quantitative research. The Employee Direct Participation in Organisational Change (EPOC) group cross-sectional survey carried out in ten European countries in the mid-1990s has been particularly exploited to analyse the relationship between workplace direct and representative voice (see Gill and Krieger 1999; Cabrera et al. 2003; Zoghi and Mohr 2011). In many such studies, recourse to different cross-national cultural values is common, particularly when referring to southern countries, as fostering (or not) workplace collaboration and, as a consequence, voice. This is far removed from the ideological viewpoint of Poole (1986a), and even further removed from the 'balancing of interests' game theory political viewpoint of Knudsen (1995). Recourse to cultural factors as explanatory in fact intensifies as management regulation of workers' voice increases.

Amidst these new developments and expansion in the thinking about voice it is unsurprising that the multiple explanations approach was preferred at the turn of the century. Poole et al. (2001: 520) favoured the diffusion of global management concepts, paired with increases in employers' power, as the main variables affecting workers' participation worldwide but could not formulate an explanation for differences in voice across national frontiers: 'we are far from consistently being able to attach weights to variables'. Similarly, for Edwards et al. (2002: 114) country effects such as 'the nature of trade union organization, the legislative supports for employee voice, the structure of corporate finance and control, labour market conditions and the importance attached to employment security' were important, but also the differences within countries as to 'union strength, unions' ability to develop and articulate an independent view of new forms of work organization, the extent and influence of works councils or similar employee participation bodies, the form of competitive pressures and the nature of the production process or service delivery system'. Yet, the same awareness of the shift in the paradigm of voice (indirect to direct, macro to micro, and collective to individual) that gave impulse to multivariable analyses rendered them rather limited in explaining imperatives for change, processes and outcomes.

In effect, a somewhat volatile contingencies approach was substituted by interlocking institutionalist explanations stemming from the varieties of capitalism approach. A new variable, economic *governance* or *co-ordination* – traits of relations between and within firms – and a renewed emphasis on system analysis reopened the space for institutional approaches to workers' voice (see Almond and González Menéndez 2006; Freeman et al. 2007; Gallie 2007; Frege and Godard 2010; Wailes and Lansbury 2010; Marchington and Kynighou 2012). Freeman et al.'s (2007) study of the liberal market economies of the USA, Canada, the UK, Ireland, Australia and New Zealand is particularly salient in this approach and also in their country case selection method of looking at similar (common historic lineage, high market orientation, similar industrial relations institutions and labour market outcomes) rather than at contrasting economies. It is also the most similar to the IDE (1981) study in looking at both *de facto* and desired workers' voice. The main finding of this study was that no single mode of voice fitted the needs of all workers; while many workers desired more union representation, most endorsed direct participation and showed a preference for more cooperation with management. Subsequently, for Freeman et al. (2007), the best regulation regimes were those protecting varied complementary voice mechanisms.

However, employers' resistance to the broad articulation of the varied mechanisms of workers' collective voice offered in broadly defined coordinated market economies (ranging across workers' assemblies, works councils, industry agreements, private and public sector board-level representation, co-management of training funds, social dialogue at regional and national levels), unless they can control them effectively (Colling et al. 2006), is a re-emerging factor. For some time, political orientations to the economy and to workers' voice in contexts with Roman-Germanic state regulation of workers' collective voice have been significantly affected by neo-liberal messages emanating originally from liberal market economies questioning the 'shared understandings' that support the institutions of the political economy (Almond and González Menéndez 2006). In fact, a failing political exchange can be identified in the prevalence of economic analyses of workers' voice as damaging (or not) to economic performance since the 1990s. Moreover, diminished labour power has been met with employer demands to retain the advantages of previous compromises, such as flexibility and a cooperative workforce, while eroding formal powers of organized labour (Almond and González Menéndez 2006). Some have even proposed that direct voice may behave counter-cyclically (Marchington and Kynighou 2012), although following Gallie (2007) it is labour's political influence that is the key explanatory variable of systemic national work organization and workforce job quality fragmentation practices, including in workers' voices.

Finally, against the consideration of certain recent historical junctures (Poole 1986a, 1968b; Wailes and Lansbury 2010) and political compromises between labour and capital (Knudsen 1995) being critical, some analysts favour taking a very long-term historical view on the formation of governance norms such as the conception of the firm, of the state (Frege 2005) and of the rights of labour (Frege and Godard 2010) to explain differences in workers' workplace voice across national frontiers. In this respect, we have come full circle. Initially, the role of law, the political balance of forces, expedience and a broader social strategy were seen as being central to the development and variability of voice. At a time when the collective crystallization of voice was a given, these features were deemed to be significant, yet the 1980s and 1990s focused the spotlight on the development of individual and direct voice mechanisms in the context of a new set of players, logics and strategies (management, the market and new management strategies). The need to look at the workplace as a more contested terrain, and as a space within which a range of agendas and strategies can be observed, emerged. Cultural and organizational factors became more important in the study of voice during this phase. Yet the past decade has seen a further return to an interest in context and governance within and beyond the firm. The issue of economic coordination emerged as a focus of studies on voice, trying to reconcile the question of regulation with new forms and practices in management approaches to it. However, such an institutionalist relational-based deeply political perspective is still vying with a less context-based universalism.

THE QUESTION OF POLITICAL CONTEXT

One of the main weaknesses of the industrial relations and human resource management (HRM) paradigms is that they have concentrated increasingly on the micro and company-specific or workplace-specific levels of participation. The tendency has been to recount the development of new forms of representation and voice, such as quality circles and team-based systems, or the decline of collective and trade-union oriented participation structures within the firm: much of the literature has therefore engaged with a particular dimension of the realities (Martínez Lucio 2010). To this end, the macro-level – to use that somewhat economics oriented term – has not always been consistently discussed when studying variations and developments in voice beyond broad notions of governance. In one respect this can be explained in ethnic terms. The dominance of the Anglo-Saxon debate within the labour process field and within the study of HRM has meant that many of the characteristics of the systems of employment regulation and management in the UK and the USA, with their weak forms of national labour representation, have framed the discussion on voice – for example, the link between micro-level direct and indirect participation, the emergence of team-working, and the tension between HRM and industrial relations. This means that the role of voice in terms of the level of the state, or national level institutions in relation to employers, rarely enters the discussion in an explicit manner in relation to voice but is placed under the heading of the 'political' or 'balance of forces'. The question of corporatism and tripartism is seen as belonging to the realm of the political, the realm of the 'other': this reflects an ever-increasing focus within industrial relations and HRM on firm-based views and experiences of voice. This is ironic, given the manner with which the debates in this area were once engaged in more political terms. The second half of the chapter will therefore look at the role the political economy – especially the varieties of capitalism – approach in helping understand difference across countries. In addition we revert back to the corporatist debate on the way the dialogue and relations between peak actors such as the state, employers' organizations and trade unions can vary and with what effect. Finally, we will focus on national languages, ideologies and agenda in establishing differences and nuances in terms of national contexts of participation and voice. By looking across these dimensions – political economy, the political, ideologies and practices – we can begin to contextualize the factors raised in the first half of the text and understand variation in the traditions and realities of participation.

The Contribution of the Varieties of Capitalism Debate

There have been a range of attempts to link the regulatory and the political into the discussion of voice in a more systematic and theoretically underpinned approach. As stated earlier, one way of engaging the macro-level dimension has been by discussing questions of corporate governance. In this case, the argument follows that, where corporate governance is more open and linked to the stakeholder as opposed to shareholder influence, the political influence of social and economic organizations such as trade unions will be significant. This corporate governance factor may be a result of legal factors that shape these processes. Gospel and Pendleton (2010) point to four dimensions that shape corporate governance and the extent to which it leans in a social or short-term economic direction: the nature of ownership and shareholder involvement, the manner in which boards are structured, the nature of information disclosure and the role of incentives, such as stock options. The combinations of these factors shape the extent of openness and the extent of worker influence within corporate politics. HRM-related strategies or industrial relations processes are influenced by these high-level corporate-related dimensions, which in turn might mediate the extent of individualization within workplace relations and explain the difference between the way companies in countries with a stronger stakeholder approach, such as Sweden, might develop greater commitment to involvement and quality of working life factors compared to those where shareholder influence is key, such as the United Kingdom.

Budd and Zagelmeyer (2010) provide instead the classic landscaping of the industrial relations system as a basis for explaining how systems of voice may differ: they reference the egoist, unitarist, pluralist and critical approaches as allowing 'for different conceptualisations of state action' (2010: 481). We can spot features of these approaches within a national system and then conceptualize them, though there is a challenge as to how we explain them and their origins. In this respect, Budd and Zagelmeyer argue the need to think in terms of how individual and collective structures of participation within an organization can be the subject of different objectives, such as promoting cooperation or employee rights. In their view, this division is pivotal for beginning to explain how the state, in the form of public policies – at the macro-level – frames and drives different forms of employee participation. They argue that the difference between more social and regulated systems emerges as a result of such policy rationales. They introduce sensitivity to the policy and frameworks of policy but also readily admit that there is no clear causal underpinning here. These approaches attempt to incorporate the firm into the analysis on workers' voice but by also including the *political* remain wedded to questions of relations and coordination.

Hence some have opted for the use of the varieties of capitalism approach (see Wailes and Lansbury 2010): synthesizing different streams of concern in terms of governance, regulation, policy and the nature of the firm. This approach (Hall and Soskice 2001) has become a convenient and perhaps much-needed template to explain differences within systems where some are of a liberal/neo-liberal nature and some tend towards coordination and regulation. This analysis focuses on complementarities within institutions, and how these develop and relate to each other across different spheres. Wailes and Lansbury argue that 'patterns of participation and involvement are likely to vary systematically across varieties of capitalism' (2010: 572). Within coordinated systems, the transformation of participation is likely to evolve through the long-term relationship between capital and labour, given the nature of regulation, the structure of corporate governance, and the pattern of economic activity in areas such as learning and training, whereas in more liberal systems it is likely that innovation in participation may be driven by employers and managers with a view to creating more dualities and fewer approaches leaning towards the collective (Wailes and Lansbury 2010: 573). The importance of this approach is that it locates the discussion on workers' voice within the broader context of economic and political relations. It links levels and provides a vehicle for explaining difference across borders in terms of mutually developing relations that sustain themselves to some extent across time, embedded in institutions.

However, we need to understand the macro-level as an external environmental force: the public policy level is something in itself and not just a conduit for explaining the nature of micro-level representation and coordination. The work outlined on the varieties of capitalism has been important in bringing comparative industrial relations into a more proximate sensitivity to the political. Yet, it has functionalized the political as a series of formal relationships for the purpose of understanding the micro-level. Hence, we need to revisit earlier theories of corporatism which engage more fully with the political and its logics and imperatives: such theories are an almost abandoned arena of study in certain key aspects of industrial relations disciplines. The state must enter the discussion as a complex concept and not just as a passive contextual factor.

The Earlier Corporatist Traditions

Corporatism became a central feature of debates on political economy, political science and industrial relations in the 1970s as the European model of regulation appeared to have been developing national-level relations and dialogue between the state, employers and unions. This co-decision-making process on various macroeconomic issues differed from the state-led model of Fascist corporatism in parts of Europe from the 1920s to the 1940s, which liaised with worker organizations dominated by the state and not independent of it (Schmitter 1974). However, in the post-war period it represented a new voice for the labour movement and even for employer bodies, leading some to suggest that it would lead to a new form of political process and economic management. Boreham and Hall (2005) have linked these discussions to the question of economic democracy. Lehmbruch (1984) argued that such a new model of social dialogue and what was termed liberal or societal corporatism varied greatly across countries, and that caution was required in any discussion of its influence. He argued that such processes are linked to the development of centralized peak organizations, the granting of privileged access to government for such bodies, and the development of a social partnership between them to regulate conflict. Stronger corporatism could be seen in countries such as Austria or Sweden, which had strong social welfare states and commitments to social dialogue, while weaker cases were seen to be the UK and Italy, for example, where dialogue was more piecemeal and uneven. In cases such as the USA, the dominant approach was a pluralist one, with no state concession of a special status to trade unions, whereas cases such as Japan were described as corporatism without labour (Lehmbruch 1984: 66). One could detect that in the stronger cases a series of factors appear to have shaped developments: a highly organized trade union, highly structured employer associations, a strong commitment to social consensus, and specific demographic and closed economic features in terms of the structure of the labour market and capital. In addition, the role of *social learning and diffusion* within specific cultures helps to embed these processes (Lehmbruch 1984: 66); what is more, there was a political exchange calculus that also underpins developments (Lange 1984) and where the costs outweigh the benefits then decline may emerge (Regini 1984). Fulcher (1988), in a prophetic paper comparing the UK and Sweden, argued that we need to understand that in proximate terms the nature of employer organizations and trade union bodies – and the pressures each places on the other in organizing and centralizing – may be interesting, but that there are deeper factors accounting for differences, such as a class-wide organization that existed in Sweden but not in the UK, hence forcing employers to respond through a logic of organization and regulation. He also pointed to the importance of the extent of *synchronicity* between the development of industrialism and ideological developments, such as the link between Sweden's late development and the availability of socialist ideas that emphasized regulation and social consensus: the link between these two allowed voice issues to be embedded in the culture and politics of industry. These factors need to be part of any research agenda discussing voice at the macro-level and the way it configures dialogue in terms of its form and content. Voice is not in effect deliberately made: it is also the outcome of circumstances, historical and political calculations that forge systems of participation and regulation.

What is more, the link between macro- and micro-level systems of voice is complex and can follow strategic paths and not always structural ones. Macro-level voice mechanisms may be driven by specific contingencies. Within the European Union, the 1980s saw the development of a more reactive corporatism dealing with economic crisis as well as growth. The 1990s brought an extension of sector-specific forms of dialogue and national engagement across the key 'partners' on issues such as learning and training, which reflected the shift to a supply-side orientation and approach to economic matters, though once more the extent of their embedded nature varied (Payne and Keep 2005). Much varies, with countries with a stronger commitment to social dialogue creating stable overseeing structures and those with a more strategic and piecemeal process working around looser sets of pacts. The relevance to our discussion is that the different tiers of voice can be coupled together and linked in various ways and around various themes depending on political contingencies. The link to the macro-level of voice can help to offset the unevenness of workplace dialogue between unions and management (Martínez Lucio 1998) and assist local workplace and company-based representatives to develop new roles and influences, as with union administered learning funds in Spain, or Union Learning Representatives in the UK who consult on training in various cases (Rainbird and Stuart 2011). In these cases a partial degree of voice at the macro-level was nevertheless developed in relation to specific themes and work-related questions. Hence this macro-level can be of relevance to micro-level participation and needs to be studied as a series of discrete and sometimes focused strategies and structures that can enhance local participation and change its remit of activity. However, there is the possibility that this higher tier may also constrain the local level and limit action through national agreements, especially with regard to pay negotiations (Panitch 1981), or that it may focus on specific aspects of the employment relation such as learning but not really provide more decision-making power for local union representatives. For this reason, the relationship between these levels is a curious dimension of how voice is constructed and made effective in terms of specific contingent themes.[1] Comparative research therefore needs to engage with the way that these levels link together, how they may actually conflict with each other, and how change in economic and institutional terms creates less coordination.

However, while this area of debate helps to 'complete the picture', one must say that such 'political economy' and 'political science' approaches have their own limitations: primarily a lack of sociological sensibility and of blindness to the questions of working people's lives within workplaces and labour markets (the micro, as we have been saying). There is scant regard for the way that such macro-level frameworks determine or shape the nature of relations within the workplace, or the micro-level relations between management and unions and the workforce. Voice is normally understood within such approaches as being structured in terms of formal, legally derived forums, or as a dialogue between formally designated actors and individuals. The role of the informal and the role of dialogue in a broader sense within the firm is normally a side issue. Yet changes in economic, political and institutional terms are forcing the remit and space of the company and workplace to be the subject of greater scrutiny within such approaches, as evidenced by the debates linked to the varieties of capitalism literature.

THE ROLE OF LANGUAGE AND OF 'OTHER BODIES'

The work of Locke and Thelen (1995) asks us to be alert to the sensitivities that might exist regarding work-related issues in different countries and the emphases that are placed on them. It is normally accepted that, across countries, there will be policy frameworks, institutional structures and sets of practices (both formal and informal) that constitute, and in effect contribute to, the development of voice mechanisms. However, the way that voice is understood within a country, or how it is associated with local customs and traditions, has steadily begun to emerge as a salient feature of industrial relations. Understanding the ways in which the language of voice can contribute to its development is important.

First, the way that voice is commonly understood in terms of its different levels can contribute to its legitimacy and sustainability. For example, the role of national dialogue between unions and employers may be seen as constituting a significant part of the national political process or be viewed as part of an obscure process of undemocratic political influence from organizations such as trade unions. The latter was clearly a focus of the new right's political discourse in the 1970s and 1980s in the UK (Hall 1988) and played a vital part in associating collective forms of industrial relations with distorting individual and transparent dialogue within industry. Across nations there may be sensitivities – positive or negative – in relation to the tripartite or bipartite dialogues discussed earlier, and the form and legitimacy of these processes may actually be contested.

Second, particular forms of voice mechanism may be silenced or removed from the play of politics. For example, the lack of dialogue in relation to developing or deepening industrial democracy – for whatever reason, whether it is the economic context and focus on immediate economic problems or the failure of previous experiences in terms of the subject – may lead to the removal of a vocabulary or a lack of familiarization in popular, and even practitioner, spaces. Thus, radical and institutionalized academic discussions on the question of work and employment have focused less on more systematic forms of worker control in the past two decades (Martínez Lucio 2010). Within the UK, key industrial relations concepts such as industrial democracy may be stigmatized – or perceived as becoming stigmatized – to such an extent that they are terms political leaders may prefer not to use, as is the case within elite social democratic circles and the concept of collective bargaining. In effect, the very terminology of voice and its constituent elements may be mobilized for or against, raised or hidden, and praised or stigmatized. These linguistic issues may also become culturally embedded (and perceived to be culturally embedded) to the extent that they shape policy and action independently.

Third, the relevant agents can also be the subjects of these processes. The legitimacy and perceived national role and significance of trade unions, for example, may facilitate their presence in terms of workplace and company-based forums and systems of representation. At the same time, associations between mechanisms of representation, such as works councils and the organizations that stand for election within them, will be tinged with the latter's perceived political legitimacy. In this respect, we can see that the language of industrial relations is important.

Yet it is also important to widen the remit of analysis of voice by engaging with a broader range of representative actors, partly because of the weakening of traditional industrial relations actors (Heery and Frege 2006), but also as a result of adopting a view of industrial relations as a set of regulatory spaces (see MacKenzie and Martínez Lucio 2005 for an introduction of such political science concepts into the study of industrial relations). These spaces are constituted by particular sites which engage a range of actors that are formal but also informal or network-based: for example, no one can study port transportation and industrial relations in the USA for large parts of the twentieth century without understanding the role of organized crime and a range of social networks in terms of their interface with questions of work and employment (MacKenzie and Martínez Lucio 2005). In terms of voice, we can therefore see that there are various regulatory spaces overlapping and linking, and even containing, one another, from the workplace to formal bargaining and forums of interest representation to the national political realm.

In terms of voice we could argue that there are direct and indirect actors. Direct actors are those charged with representing and engaging on behalf of the represented (unions, management and government, for example); then there are action-based indirect actors who engage in voice-shaping in terms of influencing specific instances of participation and representation (for example, law firms engaged with assisting 'union-busting' or aiding trade unions through the provision of specific advice in relation to bargaining); and policy-facing indirect actors who attempt to frame the debates on questions of voice. Let us examine the first type of indirect actor. These have become an increasing feature of the industrial relations and HRM arenas in the form of law firms that have grown from smaller scale and supportive services to international organizations with large resources working alongside national organizations. In terms of the second type of indirect actor, we see state bodies (forms of conciliation and mediation bodies), professional management bodies (such as the Chartered Institute of Personnel and Development, which frames many debates within management), official and network-based academic bodies (formal such bodies include the British Universities' Industrial Relations Association (BUIRA) or the Labor and Employment Relations Association

(LERA) in the USA), and specialist organizations focused on the subject of participation (such as the Involvement and Participation Association (IPA) or the Pension Investment Resources Centre in the UK) which push for particular types of participation on various matters. We also need to take note of the media and other interests in terms of political and social communication which can shape the nature of debates on participation, such as the union avoidance industry/consultancies (Logan 2006). Internationally, there are also bodies such as the OECD, various EU agencies and others who frame debates and attempt to influence agendas. These bodies form a vital and growing part of the industrial relations landscape, which can frame the nature of voice and trends within it (especially 'fashions') in terms of its level, its focus, the link to educational curricula and the terminology used. In addition, state agencies can form a part of this panorama (Martínez Lucio and Stuart 2011). Marchington et al. (1993) have argued that internal management relations (the links between levels of management) and the reputation of management are central to the waves of interest in certain types of employee involvement. Hence, these relations and waves of interests can be understood in much broader terms by referencing the role of external direct and indirect institutional actors. By drawing on these new debates that have emerged we can enhance our ability to study differences in terms of employee voice across national and regional contexts.

CONCLUSION

When studying voice, we need to be alert to the manner in which the elements that contribute to its development and character have been the subject of discussion and polemic. Many different variables can be seen to emerge from the discussions outlined in the first part of this chapter, and these can be used to explain and study voice between countries: legal regulation, labour power, labour market factors such as unemployment levels, technology, values and ideologies, and industrial relations politics. In addition, non-industrial relations institutions such as markets have been identified in approaches as wide as those dealing with job controls, ranging from industrial democracy to the quality of jobs and autonomy, performance-enhancement capabilities and processes, and the changing contours of formal voice channels.

The first part of this chapter focused on the way in which debates on workers' voice have oscillated between a political and legal view on the one hand and more of a market and management view on the other. The external environment has vied with a growing interest in the internal and corporate environment. Some approaches, such as the varieties of capitalism debate, have tried to balance these, though as with previous approaches normative views of regulation have been an issue. The growth of an HRM approach – loosely speaking – to voice has attempted to push the emphasis toward questions of trends, management relations and internal cultural factors in the face of a broad emphasis on the nature of legal regulation and political tensions. There appears to be a growing synthesis, with the balance of factors being encapsulated in some fields such as industrial relations and critical HRM; however, in mainstream and neo-liberal management circles the internal has predominated.

We have argued that the role of the political remains pivotal and can be reconstituted for the purpose of explaining the real landscape and struggles around and for forms of participation. To do this we need to address the importance of the state and public policy, as suggested by others, beyond the relational approach adopted in the varieties of capitalism debate. We need to look at voice at the macro-level and its influence on the micro as a significant sphere in its own right. To do this, we must be aware of political language and frameworks of meaning. The movement towards a contextualized comparison method is therefore an important building block. With such a move, we can also begin to include the narrative of broadening the map of actors in industrial relations by looking at direct and indirect actors and how they graft national trends and highlight particular themes and preferences. This means that we have to be careful of the move to focus on the firm, which may appear to be important on the one hand because firm-based politics and regulation were almost absent within some sociology of work and industrial relations debates in the past, but which can reduce the political to matters of coordination and intra- and inter-firm politics. Instead, we need to complement this by looking at the reality in broader terms and noting that participation is the subject of much political interest, which can distort, refocus and remake it. In this respect, we need to consider actors and language, as much as internal and external factors, as dimensions of participation.

NOTE

1. Many see the period since the early 1990s as witnessing a general decline in such macro-level forms of voice and a growing tension with micro-level company-based and workplace bargaining and representation, which are more exposed to the pressures of the market and face collective action problems in terms of coordination between units of voice (Hyman 2010). This is why micro-corporatism has been seen as a new development, bringing tension within different types of collective and indirect representation.

REFERENCES

Almond, P. and M. González Menéndez (2006), 'Varieties of capitalism: the importance of political and social choices', *Transfer: European Review of Labour and Research*, **12** (3), 407–25.
Blyton, P. and M. Martínez Lucio (1995), 'Industrial relations and the management of flexibility: factors shaping developments in Spain and the United Kingdom', *International Journal of Human Resource Management*, **6** (2), 271–91.
Boreham, P. and R. Hall (2005), 'Theorising the state and economic democracy', in B. Harley, J. Hyman and P. Thompson (eds), *Participation and Democracy at Work: Essays in Honour of Harvie Ramsay*, Basingstoke: Palgrave, pp. 222–47.
Budd, J.W. and S. Zagelmeyer (2010), 'Public policy and employee participation', in A. Wilkinson, P.J. Gollan, M. Marchington and D. Lewin (eds), *The Oxford Handbook of Participation in Organizations*, Oxford: Oxford University Press, pp. 476–504.
Cabrera, E.F., J. Ortega and J. Cabrera (2003), 'An exploration of the factors that influence employee participation in Europe', *Journal of World Business*, **38**, 43–54.
Colling, T., P. Gunnigle, J. Quintanilla and A. Tempel (2006), 'Collective representation and participation', in P. Almond and A. Ferner (eds), *American Multinationals in Europe: Managing Employment Relations Across National Borders*, Oxford: Oxford University Press, pp. 95–118.
Edwards, P., J. Geary and K. Sisson (2002), 'New forms of work organization in the workplace: transformative, exploitative, or limited and controlled?', in G. Murray, J. Belanger, A. Giles and P.-A. Lapointe (eds), *Work Employment Relations in the High Performance Workplace*, London: Continuum, pp. 72–119.
Freeman, R.B. and E.P. Lazear (1995), 'An economic analysis of works councils', in J. Rogers and W. Streeck (eds), *Works Councils: Consultation, Representation and Cooperation in Industrial Relations*, Chicago, IL: University of Chicago Press, pp. 27–52.

Freeman, R.B., P. Boxall and P. Haynes (2007), 'Conclusion: what workers say in the Anglo-American world', in R.B. Freeman, P. Boxall and P. Haynes (eds), *What Workers Say: Employee Voice in the Anglo-American Workplace*, Ithaca, NY: Cornell University Press, pp. 206–20.

Frege, C. (2005), 'The discourse of industrial democracy: Germany and the US revisited', *Economic and Industrial Democracy*, **26** (1), 151–75.

Frege, C. and J. Godard (2010), 'Cross-national variation in representation rights and governance at work', in A. Wilkinson, P.J. Gollan, M. Marchington and D. Lewin (eds), *The Oxford Handbook of Participation in Organizations*, Oxford: Oxford University Press, pp. 526–51.

Fulcher, J. (1988), 'On the explanation of industrial relations diversity: labour movements, employers and the state in Britain and Sweden', *British Journal of Industrial Relations*, **26** (2), 246–74.

Gallie, D. (2007), 'Production regimes and the quality of employment in Europe', *Annual Review of Sociology*, **33**, 85–104.

Gill, C. and H. Krieger (1999), 'Direct and representative participation in Europe: recent survey evidence', *International Journal of Human Resource Management*, **10** (4), 572–91.

Gold, M. (2011), '"Taken on board": an evaluation of the influence of employee board-level representatives on company decision-making across Europe', *European Journal of Industrial Relations*, **17** (1), 41–56.

Gospel, H. and A. Pendleton (2010), 'Corporate governance and employee participation', in A. Wilkinson, P.J. Gollan, M. Marchington and D. Lewin (eds), *The Oxford Handbook of Participation in Organizations*, Oxford: Oxford University Press, pp. 504–25.

Hall, P.A. and D.W. Soskice (eds) (2001), *Varieties of Capitalism: The Institutional Foundations of Comparative Advantage*, Oxford: Oxford University Press.

Hall, S. (1988), *The Hard Road to Renewal*, London: Verso.

Heery, E. and C. Frege (2006), 'New actors in industrial relations', *British Journal of Industrial Relations*, **44** (4), 601–4.

Hyman, J. and B. Mason (1995), *Managing Employee Involvement and Participation*, London: Sage.

Hyman, R. (2010), 'Social dialogue and industrial relations during the economic crisis'. Working Paper 11, Industrial and Employment Relations Department, International Labour Office, Geneva.

IDE (Industrial Democracy in Europe) (1981), 'Industrial democracy in Europe: differences and similarities across countries and hierarchies', *Organization Studies*, **2** (2), 113–29.

IDE (Industrial Democracy in Europe International Research Group) (1993), *Industrial Democracy in Europe Revisited*, Oxford: Oxford University Press.

Knudsen, H. (1995), *Employee Participation in Europe*, London: Sage.

Kochan, T.A. (2007), 'What should governments do?', in R.B. Freeman, P. Boxall and P. Haynes (eds), *What Workers Say: Employee Voice in the Anglo-American Workplace*, Ithaca, NY: Cornell University Press, pp. 198–205.

Kochan, T.A., R.B. McKersie and P. Cappelli (1984), 'Strategic choice and industrial relations theory', *Industrial Relations: A Journal of Economy and Society*, **23** (1), 16–39.

Lange, P. (1984), 'Unions, workers and wage regulation: the rational basis of consent', in J.H. Goldthorpe (ed.), *Order and Conflict in Contemporary Capitalism*, Oxford: Clarendon Press.

Lehmbruch, G. (1984), 'Corporatism in decline?', in J.H. Goldthorpe (ed.), *Order and Conflict in Contemporary Capitalism*, Oxford: Clarendon Press.

Locke, R.M. and K. Thelen (1995), 'Apples and oranges revisited: contextualised comparisons and the study of labour politics', *Politics and Society*, **23** (3), 337–67.

Logan, J. (2006), 'The union avoidance industry in the United States', *British Journal of Industrial Relations*, **44** (4), 651–75.

MacKenzie, R. and M. Martínez Lucio (2005), 'The realities of regulatory change: beyond the fetish of deregulation', *Sociology*, **39** (3), 499–517.

Marchington, M. and A. Kynighou (2012), 'The dynamics of employee involvement during turbulent times', *International Journal of Human Resource Management*, **23** (16), 3336–54.

Marchington, M. and A. Wilkinson (2000), 'Direct participation', in S. Bach and K. Sisson (eds), *Personnel Management*, 3rd edn, Oxford: Blackwell, pp. 340–64.

Marchington, M., A. Wilkinson, P. Ackers and J. Goodman (1993), 'The influence of managerial relations on waves of employee involvement', *British Journal of Industrial Relations*, **31** (4), 553–76.

Martínez Lucio, M. (1998), 'Spain: regulating employment and social fragmentation', in A. Ferner and R. Hyman (eds), *Changing Contours of Industrial Relations in Europe*, Oxford: Blackwell, pp. 428–58.

Martínez Lucio, M. (2010), 'Labour process and Marxist perspectives', in A. Wilkinson, P.J. Gollan, M. Marchington and D. Lewin (eds), *The Oxford Handbook of Participation in Organizations*, Oxford: Oxford University Press, pp. 105–30.

Martínez Lucio, M. and M. González Menéndez (2013), 'Worker voice under pressure: collective workplace representation and the challenge of multiplying spaces and actors', in J. Arrowsmith and V. Pulignano (eds), *The Transformation of Employment Relations in Europe*, London: Routledge, pp. 33–50.

Martínez Lucio, M. and M. Stuart (2011), 'The state, public policy and the renewal of HRM', *International Journal of Human Resource Management*, **22** (18), 2661–771.

Monat, J. and T. Beaupin (2003), 'The role of economic and social councils in social dialogue', in M. Gold (ed.), *New Frontiers of Democratic Participation at Work*, Farnham: Ashgate, pp. 73–98.

Müller-Jentsch, W. (1995), 'Germany: from collective voice to co-management', in J. Rogers. and W. Streeck (eds), *Works Councils*, Chicago, IL: University of Chicago Press, pp. 53–78.

Panitch, L. (1981), 'Trade unions and the capitalist state', *New Left Review*, **125** (January–February), 21–43.

Payne, J. and E. Keep (2005), 'Promoting workplace development: lessons for UK policy from Nordic approaches to job redesign and the quality of working life', in B. Harley, J. Hyman and P. Thompson (eds), *Participation and Democracy at Work: Essays in Honour of Harvie Ramsay*, Basingstoke: Palgrave, pp. 146–66.

Poole, M. (1986a), 'Industrial democracy', in *Industrial Relations: Origins and Patterns of National Diversity*, London: Routledge, pp. 149–72.

Poole, M. (1986b), *Towards a New Industrial Democracy: Workers' Participation in Industry*, London: Routledge.

Poole, M., R.. Lansbury and N. Wailes (2001), 'A comparative analysis of developments in industrial democracy', *Industrial Relations*, **40**, 490–526.

Ramsay, H. (1983), 'Evolution or cycle? Worker participation in the 1970s and 1980s', in C. Crouch and F. Heller (eds), *International Yearbook of Organizational Democracy: Organizational Democracy and Political Processes*, Chichester: John Wiley & Sons, pp. 203–26.

Regalia, I. (1996), 'How the social partners view direct participation: a comparative study of 15 European countries', *European Journal of Industrial Relations*, **2** (2), 211–34.

Regini, M. (1984), 'The conditions for political exchange: how concertation emerged and collapsed in Italy and Great Britain', in J. Goldthorpe (ed.), *Order and Conflict in Contemporary Capitalism*, Oxford: Clarendon Press.

Regini, M. (1993), 'Human resource management and industrial relations in European companies', *International Journal of Human Resource Management*, **4** (3), 555–68.

Rigby, M., S. Contrepois and F. O'Brien Smith (2009), 'The establishment of enterprise works councils: process and problems', *European Journal of Industrial Relations*, **15** (1), 71–90.

Rogers, J. and W. Streeck (1995), 'Workplace representation overseas: the works councils story', in R.B. Freeman (ed.), *Working Under Different Rules*, New York: Russell Sage Foundation, pp. 97–156.

Schmitter, P.C. (1974), 'Still the century of corporatism?', *Review of Politics*, **36** (1), 85–131.

Smith, A.E. (1994), 'New technology and labour regulation', in J. Bélanger, P.K. Edwards and L. Haiven (eds), *Workplace Industrial Relations and the Global Challenge*, Ithaca, NY: Cornell University Press, pp. 157–89.

Sorge, A. (1976), 'The evolution of industrial democracy in the countries of the European Community', *British Journal of Industrial Relations*, **14** (3), 274–94.

Rainbird, H. and M. Stuart (2011), 'The state and the union learning agenda in Britain', *Work, Employment and Society*, **25** (2), 202–17.

Vaughan-Whitehead, D. (2003), 'Worker participation in Central and Eastern Europe: union strategies', in M. Gold (ed.), *New Frontiers of Democratic Participation at Work*, Farnham: Ashgate, pp. 273–94.

Wailes, N. and R. Lansbury (2010), 'International and comparative perspectives on employee participation', in A. Wilkinson, P.J. Gollan, M. Marchington and D. Lewin (eds), *The Oxford Handbook of Participation in Organizations*, Oxford: Oxford University Press, pp. 570–89.

Zoghi, C. and R.D. Mohr (2011), 'The decentralisation of decision making and employee involvement within the workplace: evidence from four datasets', *British Journal of Industrial Relations*, **49** (4), 688–716.

24 Employee silence
Niall Cullinane and Jimmy Donaghey

INTRODUCTION

The theme of employee voice is central to the study and understanding of work, employment and labour management. A vast body of literature exists on the subject, ranging from studies focused around the efficacy of particular voice mechanisms in delivering on workers' interests, to the more 'managerially' driven concerns as to whether voice impacts on firms' profitability (Johnstone et al., 2010; Kim et al., 2010). Whether these are considered separately or in alliance, some semblance of the two has tended to punctuate the study of voice in literature on work and employment. Furthermore, many of these considerations have been characterized by an underlying assumption that managers and organizations *should* encourage workers to voice their concerns. The human resource management literature has maintained that firms should embrace 'employee voice' because of its positive 'performance' benefits (Cotton et al., 1998; Pohler and Luchak, Chapter 12 above). In the pluralist industrial relations literature, voice is advocated partly because it is seen as an 'organizational good': to paraphrase Flanders's (1970) famous dictum, 'managers can only maintain control by sharing it'. Whilst not seeking to disregard these perspectives, it is reasonable to propose, in opposition, that employers are not necessarily interested in, or inclined to encourage, voice (or at least certain variants of it). Indeed there is a long lineage of research which shows how employers, either by design or default, inhibit workers from articulating their voice (Roy, 1980; Dundon, 2002). One noteworthy re-conceptualization of this tendency is the field of research on the antithesis of employee voice: 'employee silence' (Morrison and Milliken, 2003). The focus of this literature is to examine why workers do not exercise voice. This chapter will review the existing terrain of knowledge on 'employee silence', which has tended to evolve from the organizational behaviour and industrial psychology literatures. After outlining the dominant approach of this field, some problems are identified and, with the desire to further dialogue and research, we offer a perspective on silence rooted in the industrial relations and industrial sociology literature: one which casts silence as part of the 'frontier of control' in the workplace (Goodrich, 1920; Edwards, 1990). Before concluding the chapter, some pertinent elements of our reconceptualization to furthering a research agenda are discussed.

CONCEPTUALIZING EMPLOYEE SILENCE

It is not implausible to suggest that employees are frequently loath to offer up information that could be construed as negative or threatening to those above them in the work hierarchy. The disinclination to speak out, and the silence or 'information withholding' that it gives rise to, has led some scholars to argue that it can undermine 'organizational decision-making' and, over time, erode employee trust and 'morale' (Morrison and Milliken, 2000; Brinsfield, Chapter 8 above). Yet, it is recognized that maintaining silence may make sense for the employee who fears that his or her employer will respond adversely to an upward communication of concerns, thus undermining the employee's position in the organization (Bies, 2009). Salient evidence of this can be seen in the aftermath of the global banking crisis of 2007–08. Evidence suggests that many banking employees, often quite senior, had concerns about their institution's trading activities but were afraid to speak to their bosses about these concerns (Treasury Committee, 2009). This case, alongside numerous others, offers a timely reminder of employee discomfort with speaking up about problems and concerns in the workplace.

It is in within the context of these types of concerns that the academic study of employee silence has been located. Brinsfield et al. (2009) identifies three waves of research into employee silence: the forms of silence, the constructs of silence and the organizational effects of silence. Chiefly, this literature has sought to comprehend the ways in which individuals in organizations make a choice to be silent about issues that matter to them and the types of issues employees are likely to be silent about. Typically silence has been conceptualized as the conscious withholding of information by employees, rather than an unintentional failure to communicate or as reflecting a situation in which employees simply have nothing to say. It is therefore a communicative choice which employees may decide to adopt. Thus in one of the pioneering studies, Pinder and Harlos (2001) defined employee silence as withholding genuine expressions about behavioural, cognitive and/or affective evaluations of organizational circumstances from people who seem capable of changing the situation. These authors differentiated between two basic forms of silence: *acquiescent silence* (passive withholding of relevant ideas, based on submission and resignation) and *quiescent silence* (more active withholding of relevant ideas in order to protect the self, based on a fear of management repercussions). In their research, Pinder and Harlos emphasized 'unjust situations' and focused specifically on factors that would cause employees to break the silence and speak up. In another of the pioneering studies, Morrison and Milliken (2000) defined organizational silence as a collective phenomenon where employees withhold their opinions and concerns about potential workplace problems. They argued that in an organization with a 'systematic culture' of silence, employees do not express their ideas and do not speak the truth out of fear of negative repercussions and/or beliefs that their opinions are not valued (see also Pinder and Harlos, 2001). Indeed fear is seen as the key motivator of organizational silence. Milliken et al. (2003) found that employees were very focused on what they saw as the potential negative outcomes, or risks, of speaking up. Their desire to avoid negative outcomes played an important role in their decisions to remain silent. Furthermore, employee silence may stem from a reluctance to convey negative information because of the discomfort associated with being the conveyer of bad news. The hierarchical relationship between subordinate and supervisor appears to intensify this posture (compare Morrison and Rothman, 2009). There are seen to be powerful norms within the workplace that often prevent employees from speaking out. The most frequently anticipated negative outcome related to damaging one's image or being labelled in a negative manner. Many respondents expressed concerns about damaging relationships or fear of retaliation and punishment, such as losing their jobs or being passed over for promotion (compare Milliken et al., 2003: 1462).

Scholars also note that organizations are often intolerant of criticism and dissent, and that employees may withhold information in order to not 'rock the boat' or create conflict. Edmondson (2003), for example, found that employees' willingness to voice work-related concerns and suggestions to their bosses depended on how approachable and responsive they perceived their supervisors to be. Edmondson also found that organizational 'leaders' are important in creating a voice climate wherein employees feel comfortable about raising problems. Adding to these conceptualizations are Van Dyne et al. (2003). Whereas Pinder and Harlos (2001) and Morrison and Milliken (2003) emphasized the withholding of information due to disengagement or fear, Van Dyne et al. (2003) advance a concept of 'ProSocial Silence' which they take from literature on 'organizational sportsmanship' (Van Dyne et al. 2003: 1368). Rather than being a self-interested silence, it is a silence that is 'other-orientated': not complaining, tolerating inconveniences and impositions of work without grievance. Thus, an employee could show cooperation and other-orientated behaviour by protecting proprietary knowledge for the benefit of the organization or by withholding information because it is confidential and not meant for general discussion.

PROBLEMS WITH THE CONCEPTUALIZATION

Although the present conceptualizations of silence have made inroads into the study of the area, the literature to date has been encumbered with a partiality that narrows the kinds of questions it asks and the explanations it offers. Take, for example, the proposition that employee silence can actually be 'beneficial' as it can help decrease managerial information overload and reduce conflict. Van Dyne et al. (2003) and Tangirala and Ramanujam (2008: 38) argue that silence is only 'negative' where it precludes 'continuous process improvement [that] requires the ongoing identification of operational problems that can illuminate faults in existing work practices'. For Morrison and Milliken (2003) unlimited employee voice is not desirable: 'too much input' is seen to overload managerial decision-making processes and impede timely and effective decision-making. All of this is indicative of a strong managerialist bias in the approach, where the study of silence is subjugated to the interests of those managing work organizations. Indeed, silence tends to be conceptualized in a fashion that stresses the withholding of ideas, information and opinions *with relevance to improvements in work and work organization* (Van Dyne et al., 2003) and where 'new ideas facilitate continuous improvement' (Van Dyne and Lepine, 1998). There is an inherent partiality to these conceptualizations.

Furthermore, the inclination of prevailing conceptualizations is to observe silence through the lens of Mayo's 'human relations' assumptions. Employer–employee relations are reduced to a principally interpersonal matter, laden with psychological and emotive characteristics (Brinsfield et al., 2009; Brinsfield, 2013). For example, Morrison and Milliken (2003: 1564) propose that management do not accept or embrace information from employees on the basis of some innate human tendency. Much of this inclination might well stem from their reliance on communication theory as a source of underlying conceptualizations. Obvious examples in this context are Van Dyne et al. (1995), who declare their focus is on employees' actual communicative choices, rather than perceptions of procedural opportunities. Arguably this privileging is somewhat unhelpful as employees' communicative choices are likely to correlate with the existing procedural opportunities to air them. Yet in spite of respondents in Milliken et al. (2003) citing hierarchical structure and organizational characteristics as the second most important reason for remaining silent, they entirely overlook this explanation in their discussion, opting instead to focus on employees' fears of being viewed 'a tattletale'. There is a risk of treating employer obstruction to voice as the consequence of a personality quirk, when it might be more pertinent to attribute it to material interests aiming for unproblematic capital accumulation. The tendency to reduce the problem of silence to interpersonal issues is probably understandable: it fits with the desire to be prescriptive and offer recommendations for employers. Yet this desire to pinpoint 'managerial implications' leads to rather unhelpful conclusions. For example, Huang et al.'s (2005) study of silence concludes by advising management to make 'an extra effort' and 'pay more attention' to reducing silence. If silence is attributed to more enduring structural factors as we will propose below, such prescriptions become somewhat more problematic.

To take our above argument further, if we conceive of voice as something more than just the articulation of ideas, information and opinions pertinent to *work related improvements*, then the notion that silence is something which should concern management, and which they should seek to rectify, becomes more troublesome. If voice is viewed as a means for employees to express concerns over their independent interests in the wage and effort bargain then it is not unlikely that silence in some areas might be expedient for employers. Indeed Morrison and Milliken (2000) illustrate this (and their managerial bias) when they indicate that silence can be functional for management, advising that unrestricted voice is, in fact, 'dysfunctional'. Equally problematic is the tendency to assume that, were it not for faulty employer practice, employees actively seek to voice ideas to the benefit of the organization. It is true that employees in certain positions on the occupational hierarchy may well be keen to advance ideas for the improvement of their organization. But it is equally plausible that many employees do not wish to contribute ideas that might lead to increased effort expenditure. Many of the occupational types studied in the silence literature are professional workers who might be expected to be more inclined to seek some affective commitment in work, for example, management consultants (Milliken et al., 2003) or nurses (Tangirala and Ramanujam, 2008). An engagement with other occupational groupings, like those found in the wider sociology of work, may demonstrate very different interpretations: for example, classic studies of alienated auto workers (Beynon, 1973; Linhart, 1981). Employee silence, therefore, might not necessarily be a consequence of disenchanted employees whose ambitions to improve productivity are stymied only by an obtuse management, but may stem from a deliberate defensive posture in the wage and effort exchange. Silence in this context can often be seen as a survival strategy, whereby employees with a low attachment to the organization mentally withdraw to cope with work's more unpleasant aspects.

ADVANCING THE CONCEPTUALIZATION OF SILENCE

Our argument to this point has been that the managerialist and unitary bias in existing conceptualizations of silence provides a somewhat incomplete picture of the relevant dynamics. This is not to suggest that the current literature has produced little of value, but that what needs to be done is for current understandings of silence to be extended and pursued under a less restrictive remit. Some work in this direction has already been done. Within the critical management studies literature, there has been an acknowledgement that organizations, through their discursive patterns, intentionally place constraints on the willingness of workers to air their concerns to management (Brown and Coupland, 2005). In contrast to the previous approaches, this tack essentially recognizes that management may actively discourage employee voice and thereby produce silence. This might be achieved through 'normal pressures, ideal-types of worker and accounts of overt attempts to quieten them through notional rules and embarrassment' (Brown and Coupland, 2005: 1062). And, unlike the literature reviewed in the last section, silence is seen as dialectically empowering for workers too: in this case of graduate trainees, silence functioned as a resource whereby organizational cultures – discouraging of new ideas for junior personnel – effectively relieved this group of the responsibility to act. That silence might also be a form of power, rather than powerlessness, is evident in Fletcher and Watson (2007). These authors posit that worker silences can be explained by dimensions of social power in the Gramscian and Lukesian sense, but also insert the concept of relationality: social actors' personal ties for example. The relational concept is further extended to the capitalistic exchange of the wage and effort bargain which is seen to play out in the implicit psychological contract. In their case study of subcontracting builders, silences were evidence of self-interested and altruistic dispositions that sought to continue the comforts and rewards of a particular economic arrangement. Whilst meritorious in providing a richer sociological understanding of silence, some problems with these conceptualizations remain. In Brown and Coupland (2005) for example, the materialist organization of production is left out altogether in favour of the discursive reproduction of organizational life. Whilst concepts like power and control are referenced, there is very little sense of the way in which these are related to wider structural patterns or indeed imperatives of organizational reproduction. A focus on self-referential discourse elides the fact that such discursive patterns are not self-sustaining, but are rather a product of particular material arrangements. Although less evident in Fletcher and Watson's (2007) conceptualization, the keenness to disregard the ontological posture of realism for a 'becoming ontology' neglects the significance of independent, enduring social structures in patterning social behaviour. While not denying the language-based character of social formations, they also have powers that are separate from their constituent subjects: these powers do not need to be recognized in language to be influential (Thompson and Vincent, 2010).

Yet despite the drawbacks of critical management studies, this tradition has been more helpful in conceptualizing silence than has the literature of institutional industrial relations. Here much attention has been focused on mechanisms in organizations that give employees a means of expressing their views. Where silence has entered the frame, it is concluded that where voice structures are not present, silence prevails (Bryson et al., 2007; Charlwood, 2006). Thus, Willman et al. (2006) treat silence as synonymous with 'no voice', stating that 'despite the apparent ubiquity of voice-related benefits, there remain "no voice" firms, defined as those where neither union-initiated nor employer-initiated voice mechanisms exist'. The implication of this might be inferred to suggest that workers are not silent where they have a formal voice mechanism. However, in keeping with the organizational behaviour approach, these authors do affirm the centrality of employer choice in determining whether or not there will be space for employees' voices in organizations. Employers play a key role in choosing whether or not workers will be silent.

This insight formed the basis of one of the more recent efforts in conceptualizing silence by the current authors. Combining insights from industrial relations, political science and industrial sociology, we critiqued the unitarist basis of silence in the dominant organizational behaviour literature. Pointing to the fact that silence may well be of benefit to employers and that they can construct organizations in such a way as to deliberately silence unwanted voice, the approach relied on concepts borrowed from Bachrach and Baratz (1962) regarding the two faces of social power. This proposes that institutional bias can operate in that not only might A exercise power over B in overt decision-making, but A may equally exercise power over B by limiting the scope of social exchange to issues that are relatively innocuous to A. The most obvious instance of this is the process of agenda setting, whereby an issue of importance to B is deliberately left off the agenda by A. Not only is power exercised in the arena of decision-making, but it is also exercised by preventing issues from ever reaching that arena. Thus issues of import to B remain unarticulated. To demonstrate this, we drew on industrial relations research into non-union employee representation as an illustrative case (see also Dobbins and Dundon, Chapter 21 above). The argument was that non-union employee representation may in some cases typify the notion that employers deliberately construct silence in organizations through staving off the encroachment of union voice into substantive areas of the managerial prerogative. There is considerable empirical evidence in support of this argument. Gall (2004) found that anti-union employers in the UK frequently created non-union employee representation schemes to reduce the likelihood of outside involvement by unions in organizational decision-making. Even in more juridified systems of worker voice, similar patterns could prevail. Royle (1998) has demonstrated how McDonald's in Germany was able to manipulate the existing system of co-determination by narrowing the scope of the company works council to issues exclusively of employer concern, such as customer service, quality and new working methods. Such outcomes arise not just because of a managerial hostility to sharing power, but simply because employers' views on voice are often cast in unitary forms. Employers frequently view voice as simply a means of increasing company efficiency and promoting an understanding of company policy rather than as a means for articulating the independent, and often diverging, interests of employees. For example, in Dundon et al.'s (2005) study of employer attitudes to voice, the pervasive tendency amongst the sample of interviewees was to view 'voice' as being about the transmission of information to employees so as to improve organizational performance, rather than conceiving it as dialogue or a two-way exchange. Employees were seen as receptacles of knowledge and voice was about ideas that could help improve organizational effectiveness. Indeed, not one employer respondent interviewed in the study mentioned grievance procedures as a form of voice.

Supporting the critique, silence was also elaborated through a more multi-dimensional canvass of how the dynamic might be produced across the workplace. We now turn to a more detailed elaboration of this framework and identify how it might offer a more productive research agenda for examining organizational silences.

RE-CONCEPTUALIZING EMPLOYEE SILENCE

As in Fletcher and Watson (2007), the core of the framework revolves around notions of silence as a relational dynamic – focusing on the way in which the phenomenon might be derived from either management or worker agency. A useful anchor point for such considerations stems from what other scholars have referred to as 'the central indeterminacy of labour potential' (Smith, 2006; Thompson and Smith, 2009). The social relations between employers and workers arise from the fact that the latter enter into contractual arrangements whereby their capacity to work is utilized to produce value for the former. This relationship gives rise to what Hall (2010) calls a 'conversion problem': how can employers transform the potential labour power purchased in the market into actual labour for profitable production. This conversion problem is problematic because, as Edwards et al. (2006) note, it is punctuated by a structural antagonism between employer and employee: the necessity for employers to transform potential labour power into actual labour and the associated requirement for employers to create structures of control over employees, as well as employers' attempts to maximize their side of the wage-effort exchange by minimizing the flow of rents to labour, in aggregate, tend to create a variety of forms of conflict and resistance.

Yet, conversely, employers must be able to engage and rally employees' cooperation, productive powers and consent, whilst employees too have an interest in the sustainability of the organization that employs them. What both parties bring with them to this relational dynamic then is a set of 'concerns': that is employers and employees define their orientations, in particular contexts, through action and evolution in the employment relationship (Belanger and Edwards, 2007). The subjective assessment (on both sides) of what is an 'advantage', and what is not, is constructed in this context. Whilst their concerns are not wholly fixed over time or determined, there are likely to be identifiable tendencies in these concerns that pattern behaviour. For employers, a relatively unproblematic circuit of profitable capital accumulation and the maintenance of managerial rights over the processes of production vis-à-vis hired labour. For employees, at the minimum, a satisfactory return on labour expenditure as well as a certain level of tolerance for how their labour is deployed in production. Whilst employees might also be inferred to hold some interest in the continued survival of the firm for which they work, this is likely to be a more secondary concern and only of interest insofar as it secures those that are more central. As such, both parties are likely therefore to have some concerns over controlling this relational exchange to ensure neither will be disadvantaged by the behaviour of the other (Wright, 2000).

Theoretically, we can categorize this relational exchange more strictly by the well-known characterizations of 'market' relations and 'managerial' relations (Flanders, 1974). The former covering the price of labour, but also hours of work, holidays and pensions rights; the latter the relationships that define how this process takes place: where market relations determine the price for a set number of hours of work, managerial relations determine how much work is performed in that time, at what specific task or tasks, who has the right to define the tasks and so on. Control concerns for employers and employees are therefore likely to preside over both areas of relations, giving rise to what might be described as a 'frontier of control' (Goodrich, 1920). By this it is meant that at any given point in time, there are understandings by the parties over the rightful degree of regulation they should exert on the various elements of market and managerial relations and the extent to which they are able to impose that regulation. This frontier is not static but is shaped by the interaction between employer and employees in pursuing their respective concerns. In addition, we might propose that these concerns for control over market and managerial relations can operate at different levels: from the basis of control over immediate shop floor or workplace issues to control at more strategic levels of determination. Whilst there is much variation within countries and exchanges happen in some companies and sectors across all levels, traditionally the former (market relations) is best exemplified in the Anglo-American institutional industrial relations literature where the employment bargain is fought out over immediate shop floor issues, whilst the latter (managerial relations) is more typically found in European economies, where employees engage employers at a strategic level in the company or indeed industry (Kjellberg, 1998; Shire, 1994).

Where does silence feature in this model? Rather than privileging any one of the actors in our framework, we opt to refer to 'organizational silence' rather than specifically 'employee silence'. Silence can act to the advantage or disadvantage of either party along the frontier of control. By silence, we accept the long-held notion within the organizational behaviour that it refers to the *withholding* of information, ideas and opinions, but we differ in seeing this withholding as something which advantages one party in the pursuit of their particular concerns. In our framework, then, silence can act either for or against either of the parties' concerns, over market and managerial relations across the spectrum of the shop floor up to the level of strategy. One limitation of this conceptualization is that it is difficult to ascertain the degree of confidence we might have in assuming that, say, employers' attempts to construct silence on market relations issues invariably act against the concerns of employees. It might be the case that the withholding of sensitive information on that front serves to maintain the viability of the business in the future. Therefore what might appear to be an action against employees might be to their benefit in the long run. Yet in defence of our conceptualization, it might be said that it is impossible to determine with any certainty whether such a long-run outcome might be traced back to a decision to withhold information at a previous point in time. There are likely to be a great many variables, such as currency fluctuations or patterns of global trade, which will intrude on the long-term outcomes, in this case, firm survival. Therefore it seems reasonably safe to assume that in the short-run, immediate sense, employers' withholding information of material concern to employees can be conceived as acting to employees' disadvantage at that particular moment in time.

Employers then may opt to close off areas for employee incursion on market relations, withhold information and thereby preserve their capacity for control and ensure minimum disruption to the exercise of their prerogative. In this case, the consequence of such activities is that such silence acts against employee concerns over matters covering the price of labour, hours of work, holidays and pensions rights. In a case study of non-union voice, Cullinane et al. (2012) and Donaghey et al. (2012) illustrated an instance of senior management refusing to disclose to staff the salary range in the company, presenting employees with data on 'job families' without individual employees knowing precisely where they sat on individual bands. Management defended their unwillingness to disclose information on salaries as they did not want it released to the market. Employers can similarly enact silence over aspects of managerial relations which adversely act against employees' concerns. A classic example is the Garrahan and Stewart (1992) study of a management inculcated corporate culture that was designed to remove any opportunities for workplace antagonism at Nissan. Even where this consensual ideology failed to be embraced, employee passivity and, in turn, their silence could be guaranteed by the less sophisticated formula of telling employees to simply 'put up or shut up'. Such actions on the part of management may of course be problematic.

Obstructing employee voice may well encourage employees to pursue other avenues for representing their views. The managerial attempt to silence collective employee voice in Mini Steel for example (Bacon, 1999; Dundon, 2002) resulted in workers resorting to alternative means: notably, voice was articulated through a rogue employee known as the 'Scarlet Pimpernel' who engaged in guerrilla style graffiti. The union also adopted innovative tactics to disseminate their message that Mini Steel was an anti-union employer. The company's personnel director was portrayed on 15-foot posters as Arnold Schwarzenegger in the role in 'The Terminator'. However, it may be that employees are not aware of managerial efforts to silence their concerns over aspects of employment relations: they may acquiesce to such actions depending on the particular aspirations they bring to the employment relationship. This potential acquiescence of course makes it problematic to read the construction of silence by management as acting against employees' concerns unless one is prepared to admit that the latter have an objective interest, whether they realize it or not, in receiving information or articulating voice on certain matters.

Silence too can be used to the benefit of advancing employee concerns. The obvious example of this is found in union–management negotiations. In these cases, as Martin (1992: 97) notes, union negotiators will often attempt to maximize their negotiating objectives 'whilst revealing as little as possible' about their own agenda. Union representatives may invariably bluff their position of strength in order to secure a favourable settlement in bargaining. In the context of a work stoppage for example, if the union can effectively withhold information about the strength of its support and solidarity, it might be able to convince the employer that a bigger concession is needed to end the strike (Batstone et al., 1977). In this regard, silence is acting against employers' immediate interest (a lower level of concession). Undoubtedly, of course, the matter becomes more complicated if we assume that the resulting industrial peace is of more long-term value to the employer.

In other ways too, silence can be used by employees to withhold information from employers so as to exert control over the work relationship and not just, as assumed in the organizational behaviour literature, for fear of managerial reprisal. Given that work organizations are composed of antagonistic relations, workers may choose to be silent in order to advance their concerns vis-à-vis management. It may be that workers in particular circumstances come to recognize the importance of information as a resource and opt to withhold it in what are perceived to be zero-sum situations with management. The classic example of this in the industrial sociology literature are the 'games' around restriction of effort and output as workers manipulate output on piece rates to prevent rate-cutting (Lupton, 1963; Burawoy, 1979). Workers have been found to attempt to outwit time-and-motion studies, so that the latter assessments are based on observations of workers deliberately working slowly and withholding 'true' levels of effort. In circumstances where workers feel they can raise output relatively easy and considerably increase their earnings by producing more than guaranteed by the average minimum, they have been found to withhold their working capacity from their employers so as to maintain a sound balance between output level and wage increases, and avoid reaching the highest limit of income based on maximum productivity. Even when the basic rates were well calculated and workers were induced to do extra work, research has found that they did not necessarily claim credit for the extra production, leaving it aside for a later date. Workers subject to fluctuations in earnings based on piecework often seek to prevent this by equalizing output. Such silence over effort expenditure acts against the concerns of employers in denying employers increased production. Again of course there are complications: there is evidence that employers tolerate such behaviour as constraints that they are forced to accept whilst also taking them for granted as ways of getting the work done. However, such behaviour can only be tolerated by management within the 'limits of minimum wages and acceptable profit margins' (Burawoy, 1979: 89).

Finally, it is not implausible to suggest a causal sequence at play in the relational exchange of silence: for example, workers who are aware that their sphere of influence is being curtailed by a recalcitrant employer may respond in turn through disengagement. Employees, on perceiving that employers seek to limit their capacity to exercise influence over their concerns, respond by withholding affective commitment to the organization. This resonates with Fox's (1974) thesis that a management perceived to treat its workforce in a low-trust fashion subsequently engenders low-trust responses from disapproving employees. Under these conditions, managerial ambitions for worker commitment and application to task languish in the face of an organizational silence predicated on employee cynicism and mistrust. For example, management efforts to affect a voice regime under the strictly business oriented remit of quality circles and/or team meetings may fail to take root in infertile soils where employee morale and low commitment are the norm (Rinehart et al., 1997).

CONCLUSIONS

This chapter has presented and critiqued the dominant approach to employee silence in the literature. A case has been made that present efforts suffer from a number of limitations. Principally these were identified as the narrow assumptions underlying the research and the predominant focus on organizational silences from a managerialist perspective. The argument is not that such approaches are necessarily incorrect, but that they miss out on a wider exchange of organizational silences in the employment relationship. Whilst observing silence might be seen to pose challenges with regard to appropriate research instruments and future empirical work, it need not necessarily be the case. The essence of the framework points to the importance of examining employer and worker motivation and behaviour in advancing, curtailing or suspending voice in organizations. Attitudes, behaviours and their underlying motivations in this context can be readily captured through established research methods and in turn reviewed and explained by recourse to the idea of silence as part of the frontier of control. Ultimately, the intention of our review is to refocus existing debate around silence in the context of continued interest on employee voice.

REFERENCES

Bachrach, P. and M. Baratz (1962), 'Two faces of power', *American Political Science Review*, **56** (4), 947–52.
Bacon, N. (1999), 'Union de-recognition and the new human relations: a steel industry case study', *Work Employment and Society*, **13** (1), 1–17.
Batstone, E., I. Boraston and S. Frenkel (1977), *Shop Stewards in Action: The Organisation of Workplace Conflict and Accommodation*, Oxford: Blackwell.
Belanger, J. and P. Edwards (2007), 'The conditions promoting compromise in the workplace', *British Journal of Industrial Relations*, **45** (4), 713–34.
Beynon, H. (1973), *Working for Ford*, Harmondsworth: Penguin.
Bies, R. (2009), 'Sounds of silence: identifying new motives and behaviors. Voice and silence in organizations', in J. Greenberg and M.S. Edwards (eds), *Employee Voice and Silence in Organizations*, Bingley: Emerald Publishing, pp. 157–71.
Brinsfield, C.T. (2013), 'Employee silence motives: investigation of dimensionality and development of measures', *Journal of Organizational Behavior*, **34** (5), 671–97.
Brinsfield, C.T., M.S. Edwards and J. Greenberg (2009), 'Voice and silence in organizations: Historical review and current conceptualizations', in J. Greenberg and M.S. Edwards (eds), *Voice and Silence in Organizations*, Bingley: Emerald Group Publishing Limited, pp. 3–33.
Brown, A.D. and C. Coupland (2005), 'Sounds of silence: graduate trainees, hegemony and resistance', *Organization Studies*, **26** (7), 1049-69.
Bryson, A., R. Gomez, T. Kretschmer P. Willman, P. (2007), 'The diffusion of workplace voice and high-commitment human resource management practices in Britain, 1984–1998', *Industrial and Corporate Change*, **16** (3), 395–426.
Burawoy, M. (1979), *Manufacturing Consent: Changes in the Labour Process Under Monopoly Capitalism*, Chicago, IL: University of Chicago Press.
Charlwood, A. (2006), 'What determined employer voice choice in Britain in the 20th century? A critique of the "sound of silence" model,' *Socio-Economic Review*, **4** (2), 301–9.
Cotton J.L., D.A. Vollrath, K.L. Froggatt, M.K. Lengnick-Hall and K.R. Jennings (1988), 'Employee participation: diverse forms and different outcomes', *Academy of Management Review*, **13**, 8–22.
Cullinane, N., J. Donaghey, T. Dundon and T. Dobbins (2012), 'Different rooms, different voices: double-breasting, multichannel representation and the managerial agenda', *International Journal of Human Resource Management*, **23** (2), 368–84.
Donaghey, J., N. Cullinane, T. Dundon and A. Dobbins (2012), 'Non-union employee representation, union avoidance and the managerial agenda', *Economic and Industrial Democracy*, **33** (2), 163–83.
Dundon, T. (2002), 'Employer opposition and union avoidance in the UK', *Industrial Relations Journal*, **33** (3), 234–45.
Dundon T., A. Wilkinson, M. Marchington and P. Ackers (2005), 'The meanings and purpose of employee voice', *International Journal of Human Resource Management*, **15** (6), 1149–70.
Edmondson, A.C. (2003), 'Speaking up in the operating room: how team leaders promote learning in interdisciplinary actions teams', *Journal of Management Studies*, **40** (6), 1419–52.
Edwards, P. (1990), 'Understanding conflict in the labour process: the logic and autonomy of struggle', in D. Knights and H. Willmott (eds), *Labour Process Theory*, London: Macmillan.
Edwards, P., J. Belanger and M. Wright (2006), 'The bases of compromise in the workplace: a theoretical framework', *British Journal of Industrial Relations*, **44** (1), 125–46.
Flanders, A. (1970), *Management and Unions: The Theory and Reform of Industrial Relations*, London: Faber.
Flanders, A. (1974), 'The tradition of voluntarism', *British Journal of Industrial Relations*, **12** (3), 352–70.
Fletcher, D. and T. Watson (2007), 'Voice, silence and the business of construction: loud and quiet voices in the construction of personal, organizational and social realities', *Organization*, **14** (2), 155–74.
Fox, A. (1974), *Beyond Contract: Work Power and Trust Relations*, London: Faber.
Gall, G. (2004), 'British employer resistance to trade union recognition', *Human Resource Management Journal*, **14** (2), 36–53.
Garrahan, P. and P. Stewart (1992), *The Nissan Enigma: Flexibility at Work in a Local Economy*, London: Mansell.
Goodrich, C. (1920), *The Frontier of Control*, London: Harcourt, Brace and Company.
Hall, R. (2010), 'Renewing and revising the engagement between labour process theory and technology', in P. Thompson and C. Smith (eds), *Working Life: Renewing Labour Process Analysis*, Basingstoke: Palgrave Macmillan.
Huang, X., E. Van de Vliert and G. Van Der Vegt (2005), 'Breaking the silence culture: stimulation of participation and employee opinion withholding cross-nationally', *Management and Organization Review*, **1** (3), 459–82.

Johnstone, S., P. Ackers and A. Wilkinson (2010), 'Better than nothing? Is non-union partnership a contradiction in terms?', *Journal of Industrial Relations*, **52** (2), 151–68.
Kim, J., J.P. MacDuffie and F.K. Pil (2010), 'Employee voice and organizational performance: team versus representative influence', *Human Relations*, **63** (3), 371–94.
Kjellberg, A. (1998), 'Sweden', in A. Ferner and R. Hyman (eds), *Changing Industrial Relations in Europe*, Oxford: Blackwell, pp. 74–117.
Linhart, R. (1981), *The Assembly Line*, London: John Calder.
Lupton, T. (1963), *On the Shop Floor: Two Studies of Workshop Organisation and Output*, Oxford: Pergamon.
Martin, R. (1992), *Bargaining Power*, Oxford: Clarendon Press.
Milliken F.J., E.W. Morrison and P.F. Hewlin (2003), 'An exploratory study of employee silence: issues that employees don't communicate upward and why', *Journal of Management Studies*, **40** (6), 1453–76.
Morrison E.W. and F.J. Milliken (2000), 'Organizational silence: a barrier to change and development in a pluralistic world', *Academy of Management Review*, **25** (4), 706–25.
Morrison E.W. and F.J. Milliken (2003), 'Speaking up, remaining silent: the dynamics of voice and silence in organizations', *Journal of Management Studies*, **40** (6), 1353–8.
Morrison, E.W. and N.B. Rothman (2009), 'Silence and the dynamics of power: voice and silence in organizations', in J. Greenberg and M.S. Edwards (eds), *Voice and Silence in Organizations*, Bingley: Emerald Publishing, pp. 111–34.
Pinder C.C. and K.P. Harlos (2001), 'Employee silence: quiescence and acquiescence as responses to perceived injustice', *Research in Personnel and Human Resources Management*, **20**, 331–69.
Rinehart, J., C. Huxley and D. Robertson (1997), *Just Another Car Factory? Lean Production and its Discontents*, Ithaca, NY: Cornell University Press.
Roy, D. (1980), 'Fear stuff, sweet stuff and evil stuff: management's defenses against unionization in the south', in T. Nichols (ed.), *Capital and Labour: A Marxist Primer*, Glasgow: Fontana.
Royle, T. (1998), 'Where's the beef? McDonald's and its European works council', *European Journal of Industrial Relations*, **5** (3), 327–47.
Shire, K. (1994), 'Bargaining regimes and the social reorganisation of production', in J. Belanger, P.K. Edwards and L. Haiven (eds), *Workplace Industrial Relations and the Global Challenge*, Ithaca, NY: ILR Press.
Smith, C. (2006), 'The double indeterminacy of labour power: labour effort and labour mobility', *Work, Employment and Society*, **20** (2), 389–402.
Tangirala S. and R. Ramanujam (2008), 'Employee silence on critical work issues: the cross-level effects of procedural justice climate', *Personnel Psychology*, **61** (1), 37–68.
Thompson, P. and C. Smith (2009), 'Labour power and labour process: contesting the marginality of the sociology of work', *Sociology*, **43** (5), 913–30.
Thompson, P. and S. Vincent, (2010), 'Labour process theory and critical realism', in P. Thompson and C. Smith (eds), *Working Life: Renewing Labour Process Analysis*, Basingstoke: Palgrave Macmillan.
Treasury Committee (2009), *Banking Crisis: Regulation and Supervision: Responses from the Government and Financial Services Authority to the Committee's Fourteenth Report of Session 2008–09*, London: The Stationery Office.
Van Dyne, L. and J.A. Lepine (1998), 'Helping and voice-extra role behaviours: evidence of construct and predictive validity', *Academy of Management Journal*, **41** (1), 108–19.
Van Dyne, L., L.L. Cummings and J. McLean-Parks (1995), 'Extra-role behaviours: in pursuit of construct and definitional clarity (a bridge over muddied waters)', in L.L.Cummings and B.M. Staw (eds), *Research in Organizational Behavior*, Vol. 17, Greenwich, CT: JAI Press.
Van Dyne, L., S. Ang and I.C. Botero (2003), 'Conceptualizing employee silence and employee voice as multi-dimensional constructs', *Journal of Management Studies*, **40** (6), 1359–92.
Willman, P., A. Bryson and R. Gomez (2006), 'The sound of silence: which employers choose no employee voice and why?', *Socio-Economic Review*, **4** (2), 283–99.
Wright, E.O. (2000), 'Working class power, capitalist-class interests, and class compromise', *American Journal of Sociology*, **105**, 957–1002.

25 Employee voice in the SME context
Muhammad Sameer and Mustafa F. Özbilgin

INTRODUCTION

In this chapter, we show that employee voice in small and medium-sized enterprises (SMEs) is largely absent in academic studies, representing a missing link in the theorization of employee voice. We present a general overview on important contemporary debates in the employee voice literature and locate it in industrial relations and human resource management literatures. Finally, we explore how employee voice in SMEs can be studied. We offer a number of suggestions for the academic and practitioner use of employee voice in the SME sector.

CONTEMPORARY DEBATES IN EMPLOYEE VOICE LITERATURE

In line with the growing evidence that employee voice is broadly necessary and beneficial for organizational longevity and success, contemporary formulations of employee voice emphasize its utility in organizational settings (Gollan, 2007; Gollan and Wilkinson, 2007; Freeman et al., 2007). This is evident from the glut of literature on employee voice, looking into its relationship with organizational performance, climate and commitment (Richardson et al., 2010; Peccei et al., 2010; Pyman et al., 2010; Dundon et al., 2004), job satisfaction and industrial citizenship (Antcliff and Saundry, 2009; Pyman et al., 2006) and high performance work systems (Bryson et al., 2007; Wood and O'Creevy, 2005).

In the past two decades, it is reported that employers have increasingly been adopting direct forms of voice in order to communicate directly with employees on one to one bases (Wilkinson et al., 2010). However, direct voice has been criticized as a tool of 'managerial prerogative', a means of gathering vital information from employees in order to achieve strategic objectives (Bryson et al., 2007). This criticism raises some important questions about the intent of employers in promoting employee voice. From the above literature, it is clear that economic motives are certainly important drivers for wider adoption of direct employee voice.

The collective notions of voice and participation are fundamental to industrial democracy. However, persistent decline of collective voice and trade unions during the last quarter of the twentieth century led to academic interest in other, non-union forms of voice (Budd et al., 2010) in the English speaking world. Nevertheless, the literature on employee voice at individual and collective levels has its origins in the application of Hirschman's (1970) work on exit, voice and loyalty by Freeman and Medoff (1984), which laid the foundations for the association of employee voice with unions in much of the IR literature.

However, these two forms of employee voice have both witnessed significant changes in advanced economies over the last few decades (Marginson et al., 2010). According to Purcell and Georgiadis (2007), there has been a pervasive decline in union membership and representation among workforces in comparison to an upsurge in employers' use of direct forms of voice. This is evident from the findings of the 2004 UK Workplace Employment Relations Survey (WERS), clearly highlighting the 'growing heterogeneity of representational forms within British workplaces' since the 1998 WERS (Charlwood and Terry, 2007: 335). This change is characterized by an upsurge in collective forms of non-union and hybrid structures (which combine union and non-union arrangements in an organization). The 2004 survey also revealed that workplaces have seen a shift from joint consultative voice channels to more direct forms of employee involvement (Kersley et al., 2006: 125–39).

The above changes raise some critical questions with regard to the role of employer preferences in influencing employee voice arrangements. Bryson et al. (2007) argue that there is little evidence in the voice literature to answer these questions, but that much depends on employers' perceptions of the presence, form and scope of voice regimes in the country of operation. Moreover, it is argued that, from a theoretical point of view, this shift in voice practices is a direct result of the innate characteristics of different forms of voice arrangements influencing employer preferences (Cullinane et al., 2012; Charlwood and Terry, 2007).

According to Freeman and Medoff (1984) employers in unionized environments have to forgo discretionary powers in significant proportion in return for low staff turnover costs and improved quality of decision-making. Therefore, employers tend to perceive non-union collective forms of voice as a better substitute for trade unions. They can enjoy the above-mentioned benefits without having to concede power to an independent party (Purcell and Georgiadis, 2007; cited in Marginson et al., 2010).

Contrary to this, proponents of HRM literature (Storey, 1992) have long suggested that direct voice between employer and employees removes all kinds of barriers posed by the collective arrangements of voice; supposedly fostering effective communication and participation measures, catering to individual needs and resulting in lower employee turnover (Marsden, 2010). However, both non-union employee representation and direct voice mechanisms face strong criticism with regard to their role in shifting power from employees to employers (Pyman et al., 2010).

We note that most of the literature on employee voice in industrial relations and human resource management scholarship focuses on large corporations, which have both formalized direct voice mechanisms and collective representation among workers. Voice in the context of SMEs remains a missing aspect of the voice literature as SMEs have fewer formalized mechanisms and generally have low collective representation among workers. As a consequence, scholarship in the fields of human resource management and industrial relations have paid comparatively little interest to employee voice in SMEs.

DEFINING EMPLOYEE VOICE IN THE SME

Definitions of employee voice are not sensitive to the size and scope of sectors of employment. They are underpinned by the notion that voice would be the same phenomenon irrespective of the size and sector of an organization. In this chapter, we contest this assumption. However, in order to do this, we first explore how voice is defined in the mainstream literature. Voice literature is primarily located within the discipline of employment relations. Budd (2004: 23) suggests that the key objectives of the employment relationship between employer and employee are efficiency, equity and voice. As such, efficiency is considered an employer's concern, dealing with the effective use of limited resources in order to maximize productivity, minimize cost and yield optimum profitability. Equity demands fair and just allocation of economic rewards in relation to good management of employment policies. Lastly, voice is the capability of employees to participate in business decisions, both at collective and individual levels (Budd and Alexander, 2008; Budd, 2004: 23). In this formulation, voice is not differentiated by size of organizations or sector of work.

The term employee voice has been used interchangeably in the employment relations context with concepts such as participation, engagement, involvement and empowerment, overlooking the differences in their meanings and practices (Budd et al., 2010; Wilkinson and Fay, 2011). However, voice is a broad term that encompasses a wide range of meanings and definitions and has been explored in various disciplines ranging from IR, ER and HRM to psychology, law and political science; each discipline trying to extract different aspects of voice, albeit in some cases resulting in similar perspectives (Wilkinson et al., 2010). But one thing that is common to all the definitions of voice is that voice provides an opportunity for employees to have their say (Freeman et al., 2007; Marchington, 2008). However, like other management concepts, the term voice can be subject to different interpretations, in the sense that it reflects both the cooperative and conflict faces of IR (Dundon et al., 2005). Arguably, as opposed to the term 'participation', it fails to signify employee influence and acts as antecedent for the latter rather than as a stepping stone (Strauss, 2006).

Dundon et al. (2004) conclude that voice application in a workplace can broadly cover the following domains: at the individual level, voice is used by employees to express their dissatisfaction over a single issue or problem with the management. Gaining strength voice takes the shape of collective bargaining in the form of independent and/ or company unions – this is based on the exit-voice framework, as defined by Freeman and Medoff (1984). Additionally, some voice mechanisms are used to involve employees in the decision-making process at operational or tactical levels by management with the aim of improving efficiency and effectiveness at organizational levels; this is usually related to notions of high performance and high commitment through employee involvement techniques (Boxall and Macky, 2009). Lastly, voice is articulated through employee–employer partnership at organizational level (union and non-union); a possible win-win situation adopted with the aim of achieving long-term survival and sustainability for both parties in the employment relationship (Budd et al., 2010: 305). Across all definitions and explications of voice, there is a common assumption that what we know as voice, which tends to come from studies in medium-sized and large organizations, can be applied to SMEs. We argue that this tendency is fallacious, as the dynamics, form and substance of employment relationship vary by organization size and sector. As such, voice is practised in different ways in SMEs than is the case in larger organizations. We explain below some attempts at how definitions and explanations that are developed for voice in non-union settings are generalized to SMEs. Although understanding voice in non-union settings may help us understand some aspects of voice in SMEs, voice in SMEs should not be reduced to voice in non-union settings as the two phenomena do not fully converge. We first outline voice in non-union environments. The next section explains how voice in SMEs may be different.

INDIVIDUAL VERSUS COLLECTIVE VOICE IN NON-UNIONIZED ENVIRONMENTS: A CRITICAL REVIEW

Dundon and Gollan (2007) suggest that the adoption of certain non-union voice mechanisms is dependent on the relationship between external and internal factors affecting a particular organization. For instance, intensity of competition in any industry provokes calls for innovation, flexibility and efficiency, thereby requiring close working between management and employees (Bae et al., 2011). Thus, direct voice mechanisms such as team briefings or suggestion schemes are fruitful ways of developing employee participation and satisfaction (Holland et al., 2011). Additionally, direct voice channels are important where employees are in direct contact with customers (Benson and Brown, 2010).

Organizational size and ownership patterns also play an important role in shaping voice arrangements. In particular, the individual styles of owners and managers in SMEs have important implications for the perception of employees about voice and the actual mechanisms that exist in the workplace (Harney and Dundon, 2006; Ryan, 2005). Legal factors or the regulatory environment (Dundon and Gollan, 2007) also limit or enhance particular forms of voice. For example, in North America there is strong regulation in support of collective representation, be it unions (historically) or non-union representation in the form of joint consultation committees (Taras and Kaufman, 2006). Similarly in European Union countries there is an EU directive regarding consultation and information which promotes more direct forms of voice in unionized and non-unionized workplaces (Wilkinson et al., 2007).

Similarly, there are internal pressures that also affect the selection of voice mechanisms in an organization (Dundon and Gollan, 2007). The most important of these are managerial strategies, which tend to be wary of independent unions and collective strength and to focus on non-union channels of voice (Gomez et al., 2010). This is evident from the surge in studies discussing managerial motives for using non-union mechanisms for differing purposes. Lavelle et al. (2010) observe that a majority of home-based and foreign-based multinational companies use indirect channels of voice with the aim of suppressing trade unionism. Furthermore, JCCs are seen to be the most popular form, even in unionized workplaces, which suggests that employees also perceive them as positive and effective expressions of voice (Holland et al., 2009).

Managers sometimes use non-union employee representation (NER) with the motive of discouraging the drive to unionization in workplaces, as is evident from the study conducted in Ireland on a single large organization by Donaghey et al. (2011). This is supported by Butler's (2009) study in the UK which argues that NER systems achieve their aim of union avoidance and legitimate change in voice arrangements; although the NER system in this study falls short in contributing to broad business goals. There is a contrasting view available in literature which states that union and non-unions are not substitutes as they serve different purposes. This is evident in a study by Gomez et al.

(2010) on employees' views of union and non-union voice in terms of perception, attitude and behavioural dimensions. The study concludes that non-union representation is complementary to union representation rather than substituting for it.

Work-related identity and group cohesion are another micro-level factor affecting the choice of non-union mechanism, direct or indirect (Dundon and Gollan, 2007). When the organization recognizes the participation of workers at individual level through formal or informal ways, in values and actions, this will lead to deeper strengthening of individual voice channels for a longer period of time (Richardson et al., 2010). This is evident in Richardson et al.'s (2010) comparative study of the UK and Italy which suggests that in spite of the high incidence of voice practices (partly driven by EU legislation and partly by a significant demand for participation), there is nonetheless a gap between the desire for employee participation and the actuality of it. Furthermore, informal relationships between workers and managers seek to enhance trust, which results in more individualized voice arrangements in organizations. This can lead to increases in productivity and healthy employment relationships in the longer term, especially in SMEs (Dundon and Gollan, 2007). Hence it provides more legitimacy to non-union status in small organizations.

EMPLOYEE VOICE IN SMES

There has been an explosion of studies incorporating SMEs in the business and management literatures. However, very few of them have been devoted to employee voice and representation (Ryan, 2005; Moore and Read, 2006; Wilkinson et al., 2007; Bull et al., 2010). A majority of the voice related studies have been contextualized in large firms with corresponding complexities in structure, processes and control (Barrett and Rainnie, 2002). On the other hand, it is widely established that SMEs comprise more than 90 per cent of all enterprises internationally; moreover, SMEs provide the majority of the employment in many key sectors of an economy. Given their increasing importance it is surprising to see this lacuna in SME research, especially on employee voice, involvement and participation (Baron, 2003; Huselid, 2003; Cardon and Stevens, 2004; Mayson and Barrett, 2006; Bull et al., 2010).

Importantly, despite the dominance of SMEs in a majority of developed economies, SME workers have historically been largely deprived of union representation. According to Dundon and Gollan (2007) this may be a result of displaced or outsourced forms of employment practices. Consequently, SMEs are generally classified as non-union, which makes a strong case for research to be conducted on the voice practices adopted by employers and their impact on individual and organization performance. According to Bacon and Hoque (2005) studying employee voice in the SME context is even more important, given the significant contribution of the sector in terms of job creation, innovation and GDP. Similarly, there are huge differences in the contextual factors of large firms and SMEs; as Bryson (1999: 78) suggests, 'the practices and combinations of voice that are most beneficial in small firms are very different'. Contrary to this, Wilkinson et al. (2007: 1282) recommend that voice practices and schemes that are successful in large firms should also be implemented in SMEs, referring to this as 'mimic opportunism'.

In the UK, for example, WERS 1998 and 2004 (Forth et al., 2006) offered some important insights into the nature of employee voice within SMEs (in the private sector).

The survey results show that small firms are mostly non-unionized in nature, and that only 3 per cent of them have union recognition (Millward et al., 2000; Cully et al., 1999). SMEs are less likely to use JCCs than large firms; the statistics reveal that only 17 per cent of SMEs have some or other form of 'representative voice arrangements' as opposed to 71 per cent in large enterprises (Forth et al., 2006; cited in Bull et al., 2010: 10). Moreover, SMEs tend to favour direct voice channels wherever formal voice practices exist. The survey reveals that 80 per cent of SMEs use a variety of forms of one to one communication with employees, of which workers' meetings and team briefings are the most common. Top-down communication channels also exist in SMEs, as 57 per cent of them have reported the use of notice boards and management chain of command channels to communicate with subordinates (Forth et al., 2006).

Marlow and Gray (2005) argue that although formal voice practices exist in SMEs, it is evident from the extant literature that SMEs mainly incorporate informal employment relationships comprising of more direct and informal voice channels between employer and employees. This is mainly credited to factors such as owners/managers performing specialist HR roles; easy access and closeness between employer and employee; close social relations; level of skills and capabilities of employees; and the need for high flexibility in response to customer preferences (Marsden, 2010; Moore and Read, 2006). On the other hand in large firms there exists a long chain of command in the form of hierarchies which makes it more difficult for direct voice channels to perform effectively (Marginson et al., 2010). The frequency of interactions and feedback usually exists at higher level amongst middle-level managers and professionals as they are closer to the senior management governing the whole organization. Contrary to this, small firms enjoy a smoother flow of communication and information, thus making direct voice more prevalent amongst all types of employees (Dundon and Gollan, 2007).

Furthermore, it is argued that the informal relations in small firms encourage heterogeneity in voice practices, which makes it difficult and complex to understand the degree of relationship between voice and organizational performance (Bull et al., 2010). This is a result of the innumerable internal and external factors which impact on the firm and which result in the heterogeneity and intricacy of voice practices. The external factors include the intensity of competition in the market, the type of industry and ownership, the labour and product market (consumer or industrial) characteristics, and the position of SMEs within the supply chain of product/service. Internal factors include the organizational strategy, managerial styles and strategies, and other social processes (Rainnie, 1989; Goss, 1991; Marchington et al., 1992; Bryson, 1999; Cabrera et al., 2003; Moore and Read, 2006; Wilkinson et al., 2007; Gollan and Wilkinson, 2007).

As major employers in the private sector, SMEs have largely remained non-unionized as a result of the paternalistic nature of their employment relationship (Bae et al., 2011). Bryson et al. (2009), in their analysis of voice practices in British private workplaces from 1980 to 2004, observed an increase from 76 per cent to 82 per cent in organizations having voice practices, although the workplaces with no voice (typical of small firms) remained more or less the same for most of the period at 25 per cent. Specifically, union voice recognition and presence has been in decline in the private sector, reflecting a perceived ineffectiveness of unions in representing their members. Concomitantly, there has been a steady increase in non-union forms of voice, particularly the direct voice types (Bryson et al., 2009: 5). This characteristic is shared by a majority of the advanced countries.

Moreover, in a similar study, Gomez et al. (2010) observed that voice practices in the private sector did not decline in spite of an overall decline in union voice in workplaces. Employers in the UK enjoy the advantage of being free to choose voice mechanisms and practices, and most have initiated non-union forms of voice; many have also successfully implemented 'dual channels' (a combination of union and non-union voice). The obvious benefit of the latter is higher labour and financial productivity as compared to union only voice (Gomez et al., 2010). This continuous adoption of voice mechanisms in the workplace affirms their perceived importance to employers, as opposed to workplaces with no voice. Additionally, one of the key findings is that union voice can be most effective when combined with non-union forms, minimizing the shortcomings of the latter while retaining the benefits of independent unions.

However, very little research has looked at the exit intentions of employees in SMEs. Likewise, employee neglect behaviours such as absence, tardiness and reduced work effort have not been addressed in research on small businesses (Pajo et al., 2010). Apart from voice, Pajo et al. (2010) have also discovered a link between the provision of formal training and reduced negative perceptions for exit or 'neglectful behaviour'.

REFRAMING THE MISSING VOICE IN SMES: THE WAYS FORWARD

The discussion on voice in SMEs warrants a shift away from the traditional debate on union versus non-union voice towards a more relevant terminology that can reflect the dynamics of voice in these small establishments. The fact that SMEs are usually characterized under non-union terrain of voice to some extent provides rationality to the silence in the IR literature on varieties of employee voice in the context of SMEs. There are several reasons for this. For instance, there is very little scope for unions to represent SME workers as union membership would have to operate at very low levels. Moreover, characteristic of small firms is an inherent imbalance of power between the owner/ manager and employees which makes the former dominant in all aspects of business – hence further limiting the possibility for collective voice (Burris, 2012). Lastly, the significant increase in the adoption of HRM practices amongst academia and practitioners around the globe for the past two decades has increased opportunities for more direct channels of voice in all organizations. However, formalized HRM frames also offer a poor prescription for the SME sector, as a result of their reliance on informal mechanisms of managing human resources.

Boxall and Purcell (2008) observe that firms inevitably adapt their HRM to their specific context and that they are wise to do so. Similarly, Ram (1991) has argued that all firms combine aspects of formality and informality, and that the nature and extent of informality in small firms are structured by many contextual factors. Authors such as Ebbinghaus (2002) and Benson and Brown (2010) recommend that future researchers in the field of voice should examine employee perceptions of voice in the private sector where there are typically lower levels of union membership (as is the case in SMEs). Attention to this issue is timely in light of recent suggestions that neglect of formal HR practices might well hinder progress toward sustainable competitive advantage in SMEs (Kotey and Folker, 2007). However, some commentators have argued that a continued or exclusive reliance on informal HR practices in SMEs might be problematic as they do not necessarily provide as much scope as formal practices for the recognition and acknowledgement of the value of employees (Mayson and Barrett 2006).

As a result, the non-union label does not reflect the actual interplay of formal/informal relations between employers and employees, which in turn has some important implications for the way in which voice channels can be administered within SMEs. For instance, owners/managers work in close proximity with their employees and in most cases carry out all the important HR activities, ranging from recruitment and selection to appraisal and compensation. Hence, there is an element of trust and personal communication between them which means that any aspect of grievance or advice on work-related issues (employee consultation and participation) is usually dealt with on an individual level, which is rational and time and cost effective for both parties. This is normally termed in the voice literature as direct voice channels, and has no link with the conventional union or non-union debate in the scholarship (Taras and Kaufman, 2006). Bryson (2004: 225–7) found that employees perceived management to be most responsive when the voice mechanisms were direct and of the non-union variety.

Most importantly, the voice mechanisms in SMEs will be shaped according to the specific trust and personal communication level between owners/managers and employees, which in turn are influenced by a range of factors. For example, family ties tend to enhance the affective commitment of employees, which has been discovered to impact positively on job satisfaction and subsequently reduce employee turnover (exit). Many studies have shown that family relationships are of even greater significance when the size of the firm is small; for instance, employees are considered to play a vital role in the success of many small enterprises (Muse et al., 2005; Cardon and Stevens 2004; Katz et al., 2000). Further, Luchak (2003) found that voice and attachment were not one-dimensional constructs and that employees with an 'affective' or emotional attachment to the organization were more likely to use direct voice, while those with a rational or calculated attachment were more likely to use indirect or representative forms of voice. Similarly, kinship ties play roles in the use of varied voice mechanisms, allowing for some voice mechanisms while limiting others. Depending on the nature of the kinship and the power dynamics that are inherent in the kinship relationship, voice mechanisms may vary. Professional hierarchies nonetheless exist between different forms of skill and education. Status differences in terms of skills and education between employer and employee can shape the nature of the voice mechanisms adopted in the SMEs. There are many other factors, such as salient fault lines and diversity categories such as gender, ethnicity, class, sexual orientation, age, disability and religion which can open up or limit the choice of voice available to workers in the context of the SME sector. Our review of the literature suggests that there is need for exploration of employee voice in the SME sector in light of employee–employer demographics and diversity.

CONCLUSIONS AND RECOMMENDATIONS

In this chapter, we explored the reasons why the micro-dynamics of employee voice is comparatively neglected in the context of SMEs. Providing an overview of employee voice in mainstream literature, we provide a critical assessment of voice literature, identifying its central focus on direct voice mechanisms. We also outlined the studies that explored employee voice in SMEs, and identified the main tendencies of these studies.

We note that employee voice in SMEs relies, in the main, on indirect and informal voice mechanisms as a result of low rates of unionization and a general absence of formal employment mechanisms in the sector. Indirect/informal voice mechanisms are micro-dyadic processes which vary extensively according to the particular dynamics of the personal relationship between the employer and employee. As a result, future studies need to consider exploring the dynamics of the personal/professional relationship between employers and employees in the SME sector. A wide range of demographic and personal factors can shape the nature of the relationship between employers and employees in the SME sector. As demography and personal characteristics are highly embedded in the specific context of the business, place and time, there is a need for studies that allow us to garner a situated and contextual understanding of employee voice in the context of SMEs.

REFERENCES

Antcliff, V. and R. Saundry (2009), 'Accompaniment, workplace representation and disciplinary outcomes in British workplaces – just a formality?', *British Journal of Industrial Relations*, **47** (1), 100–121.

Bae, K.-S., H. Chuma, T. Kato, D.-B. Kim and I. Ohashi (2011), 'High performance work practices and employee voice: a comparison of Japanese and Korean workers', *Industrial Relations: A Journal of Economy and Society*, **50** (1), 1–29.

Bacon, N. and K. Hoque (2005), 'HRM in the SME sector: valuable employees and coercive networks', *International Journal of Human Resource Management*, **16** (11), 1976–99.

Baron, R.A. (2003), 'Human resource management and entrepreneurship: some reciprocal benefits of closer links', *Human Resource Management Review*, **13** (2), 253–6.

Barrett, R. and A. Rainnie (2002), 'What's so special about small firms? Developing an integrated approach to analysing small firm industrial relations', *Work, Employment and Society*, **16** (3), 415–32.

Benson, J. and M. Brown (2010), 'Employee voice: does union membership matter?', *Human Resource Management Journal*, **20** (1), 80–99.

Boxall, P. and K. Macky (2009), 'Research and theory on high-performance work systems: progressing the high involvement stream', *Human Resource Management Journal*, **19** (1), 3–23.

Boxall, P. and J. Purcell (2008), *Strategy and Human Resource Management*, 2nd edn, Basingstoke: Palgrave Macmillan.

Bryson, A. (1999), 'The impact of employee involvement on small firms' financial performance', *National Institute Economic Review*, **169** (1), 78–95.

Bryson, A. (2004), 'Managerial responsiveness to union and non-union voice', *Industrial Relations*, **43** (1), 213–41.

Bryson, A., R. Gomez, T. Kretschmer and P. Willman (2007), 'The diffusion of workplace voice and high-commitment human resource management practices in Britain, 1984–1998', *Industrial and Corporate Change*, **16** (3), 394–426.

Bryson, A., R. Gomez, T. Kretschmer and P. Willman (2009), 'Employee voice and private sector workplace outcomes in Britain, 1980–2004', CEP discussion paper 0924, available at: http://cep.lse.ac.uk/pubs/author2.asp?new_authorid=115 (accessed 4 December 2013).

Budd, J.W. (2004), *Employment With a Human Face: Balancing Efficiency, Equity and Voice*, Ithaca, NY: Cornell University Press.

Budd, J.W. and J.S.C. Alexander (2008), 'Improved metrics for workplace dispute resolution procedures: efficiency, equity, and voice,' *Industrial Relations*, **37** (3), 460–79.

Budd, J., P. Gollan and A. Wilkinson (2010), 'New approaches to employee voice and participation', *Human Relations*, **63** (3), 1–8.

Bull, E., M. Gilman, A. Pyman and S. Raby (2010), 'The contours of employee voice in SMEs: implications for performance and HRM theory', Working Paper No. 199, Kent Business School, available at: http://kar.kent.ac.uk/24464/1/Voice_in_SMEs_Bull_Gilman_Pyman_Raby_April_2009_WEB.pdf Kent Business School. ISSN 1748-7595 (accessed 20 November 2013).

Burris, E.R. (2012), 'The risks and rewards of speaking up: managerial responses to employee voice', *Academy of Management Journal*, **55** (4), 851–75.

Butler, P. (2009), 'Non-union employee representation: exploring the riddle of managerial strategy', *Industrial Relations Journal*, **40** (3), 198–214.

Cabrera, E., J. Ortega and A. Cabrera (2003), 'An exploration of the factors that influence employee participation in Europe', *Journal of World Business*, **38** (1), 43–54.

Cardon, M.S. and C.E. Stevens (2004), 'Managing human resources in small organizations: what do we know?', *Human Resource Management Review*, **14** (3), 295–323.

Charlwood, A. and M. Terry (2007), '21st-century models of employee representation: structures, processes, and outcomes', *Industrial Relations Journal*, **38** (4), 320–37.

Cullinane, N., D. Jimmy, T. Dundon and T. Dobbins (2012), 'Different rooms, different voices: double-breasting, multi-channel representation and the managerial agenda', *International Journal of Human Resource Management*, 23 (1), 368–84.

Cully, M., S. Woodland, A. O'Reilly and G. Dix (eds) (1999), *Britain at Work: As Depicted by 1998 Workplace Employee Relations Survey*, London: Routledge.

Donaghey, J., N. Cullinane, T. Dundon and A. Wilkinson, A. (2011), 'Reconceptualising employee silence: problems and prognosis', *Work Employment and Society*, **25** (1), 51–67.

Dundon T. and P.J. Gollan (2007), 'Re-conceptualizing voice in the non-union workplace', *International Journal of Human Resource Management*, **18** (1), 1182–98.

Dundon, T., A. Wilkinson, M. Marchington and P. Ackers (2004), 'The meaning and purpose of employee voice', *International Journal of Human Resource Management*, **15** (6), 1149–70.

Dundon, T., A. Wilkinson, M. Marchington and P. Ackers (2005), 'The management of voice in non-union organisations: managers' perspectives', *Employee Relations*, **27** (3), 307–19.

Ebbinghaus, B. (2002), 'Trade unions' changing role: membership erosion, organisational reform, and social partnership in Europe'. *Industrial Relations Journal*, **33** (1), 465–83.

Forth, J., H. Hewley and A. Bryson (2006), 'Small and medium-sized enterprises: findings from the 2004 Workplace Employment Relations Survey', UK Department of Trade and Industry Economic and Social Research Council, Advisory Conciliation and Arbitration Service, Policy Studies Institute, Small Business Service.

Freeman, R.B. and J. Medoff (1984), *What Do Unions Do?*, New York, Basic Books.

Freeman, R.B., P. Boxall and P. Haynes (eds) (2007), *What Workers Say: Employee Voice in the Anglo-American Workplace*, Ithaca, NY: Cornell University Press.

Gollan, P.J. (2007), *Employee Representation in Non-Union Firms*, London: Sage.

Gollan, P. and A. Wilkinson (2007), 'Contemporary developments in information and consultation', *International Journal of Human Resource Management*, **18** (7), 1133–45.

Gomez, R., A. Bryson and P. Willman (2010), 'Voice in the wilderness? The shift from union to non-union voice in Britain', in A. Wilkinson, P.J. Gollan, M. Marchington and D. Lewin (eds), *The Oxford Handbook of Participation in Organizations*, Oxford Handbooks in Business and Management, Oxford: Oxford University Press, pp. 383–406.

Harney, B. and T. Dundon (2006), 'Capturing complexity: developing an integrated approach to analysing HRM in SMEs', *Human Resource Management Journal*, **16** (1), 48⁻73.

Hirschman, A.O. (1970), *Exit, Voice, and Loyalty: Responses to Decline in Firms, Organizations and States,* Cambridge, MA: Harvard University Press.

Holland, P., A. Pyman, B.K. Cooper and J. Teicher (2009), 'The development of alternative voice mechanisms in Australia: the case of joint consultation', *Economic and Industrial Democracy*, **30** (1), 67–92.

Holland, P., A. Pyman, B.K. Cooper and J. Teicher (2011), 'Employee voice and job satisfaction in Australia: the centrality of direct voice', *Human Resource Management*, **50** (1), 95–111.

Huselid, M. (2003), 'Editor's note: special issue on small and medium sized enterprises: a call for more research', *Human Resource Management*, **42**, 297.

Katz, J., H. Aldrich, T.M. Welbourne and P.M. Williams (2000), 'Guest editor's comments: special issue on human resource management and the SME: Toward a new synthesis', *Entrepreneurship Theory and Practice*, 7–10.

Kersley, B., C. Alpin, J. Forth, A. Bryson, H. Bewley, G. Dix and S. Oxenbridge (2006), *Inside the Workplace: Findings from the 2004 Workplace Employment Relations Survey*, London: Routledge.

Kotey, B. and C. Folker (2007), 'Employee training in SMEs: effect of size and firm type – family and non-family', *Journal of Small Business Management*, **45** (1), 214–38.

Lavelle J., A. McDonnell and P. Gunnigle (2010), 'Patterning employee voice in multinational companies', *Human Relations*, **63** (3), 395–418.

Luchak, A.A. (2003), 'What kind of voice do loyal employees use?', *British Journal of Industrial Relations*, **41** (1), 115–34.

Marchington, M. (2008), 'Employee voice systems', in P. Boxall, J. Purcell and P. Wright (eds), *The*

Oxford Handbook of Human Resource Management, Oxford: Oxford University Press, pp. 231–50.

Marchington. M., J. Goodman, A. Wilkinson and P. Ackers (1992), *New Developments in Employee Involvement*, Vol. 2, London: Department of Employment.

Marginson, P., P. Edwards, T. Edwards, A. Ferner and O. Tregaskis (2010), 'Employee representation and consultative voice in multinational companies operating in Britain', *British Journal of Industrial Relations*, **48** (1), 151–80.

Marlow, S. and C. Gray (2005), 'Information and consultation in small and medium-sized enterprises', in J. Storey (ed.), *Adding Value through Information and Consultation*, Basingstoke: Palgrave Macmillan.

Marsden, D. (2010), 'Individual voice in employment relationships: a comparison under different collective voice regimes', dp1006, Centre for Economic Performance, LSE.

Mayson, S. and R. Barrett (2006), 'The science and practice of HRM in small firms', *Human Resource Management Review*, **16** (4), 447–55.

McCabe, D. and D. Lewin (1992), 'Employee voice: a human resource management perspective', *California Management Review*, **34** (3), 95–111.

Millward, N., A. Bryson and J.A. Forth (2000), *All Change at Work? British Employment Relations 1980–1998, as Portrayed by the Workplace Industrial Relations Survey Series*, London: Routledge.

Moore, S. and I. Read (2006), 'Collective organisation in small and medium sized enterprises – an application of mobilisation theory', *Human Resource Management Journal*, **16** (4), 357–75.

Muse, L.A., M.W. Rutherford, S.L. Oswald and J.E. Raymond (2005), 'Commitment to employees: does it help or hinder small business performance?', *Small Business Economics*, **24** (2), 97–111.

Pajo, K., A. Coetzer and N. Guenole (2010), 'Formal development opportunities and withdrawal behaviors by employees in small and medium-sized enterprises', *Journal of Small Business Management*, **48** (3), 281–301.

Peccei, R., H. Bewley, H. Gospel and P. Willman (2010), 'Antecedents and outcomes of information disclosure to employees in the UK 1990–2004: the role of employee voice', *Human Relations*, **63** (3), 419–38.

Purcell, J. and K. Georgiadis (2007), 'Why should employers bother with worker voice?', in R.B. Freeman, P. Boxall and P. Haynes (eds), *What Workers Say: Employee Voice in the Anglo-American Workplace*, Ithaca, NY: Cornell University Press, pp. 181–97.

Pyman, A., B. Cooper, J. Teicher and P. Holland (2006), 'A comparison of the effectiveness of employee voice arrangements in Australia', *Industrial Relations Journal*, **37** (5), 543–59.

Pyman, A., P. Holland, J. Teicher and B.K. Cooper (2010), 'Industrial relations climate, employee voice and managerial attitudes to unions: an Australian study', *British Journal of Industrial Relations*, **48** (1), 460–80.

Rainnie, A. (1989), *Small isn't Beautiful*, London: Routledge.

Ram, M. (1991), 'Control and Autonomy in Small Firms', *Work, Employment and Society*, **5** (4), 601–19.

Ramsay, H. (1977), 'Cycles of control: worker participation in sociological and historical perspective', *Sociology*, **11** (3), 481–506.

Richardson, M., S. Tailby, A. Danford, P. Stewart and V. Palignano (2010), 'Employee participation and involvement: experiences of aerospace and automobile workers in the UK and Italy', *European Journal of Industrial Relations*, **16** (1), 21–37.

Ryan, A. (2005), 'Representation, consultation and the smaller firm', in M. Ram, S. Marlow and D. Patton (eds), *Managing Labour in Small Firms*, New York: Routledge, pp. 203–21.

Storey, J. (1992), *Developments in the Management of Human Resources*, Oxford: Blackwell.

Strauss, G. (2006), 'Worker participation: some under-considered issues', *Industrial Relations*, **45** (4), 778–803.

Taras, D.G. and B.E. Kaufman (2006), 'Non-union employee representation in North America: diversity, controversy and uncertain future', *Industrial Relations Journal*, **37** (5), 513–42.

Wilkinson, A. and C. Fay (2011), 'Guest editor's note: new times for employee voice?', *Human Resource Management*, **50** (1), 65–74.

Wilkinson, A., T. Dundon and I. Grugulis (2007), 'Information but not consultation: exploring employee involvement in SMEs', *International Journal of Human Resource Management*, **18** (7), 1279–97.

Wilkinson, A., P. Gollan, M. Marchington and D. Lewin (2010), 'Conceptualising employee participation in organisations', in A Wilkinson, P. Gollan, M. Marchington and D. Lewin (eds), *The Oxford Handbook of Participation in Organizations*, Oxford: Oxford University Press, pp. 1–25.

Wood, S. and M. Fenton-O'Creevy (2005), 'Direct involvement, representation and employee voice in UK multinationals in Europe'. *European Journal of Industrial Relations*, **11** (1), 27–50.

26 Diversity management and missing voices
Jawad Syed

INTRODUCTION

Much of the literature on employee voice assumes that workers are homogeneous, and voice vehicles are designed in a very generic way. However, organizations are dominated by and voice vehicles are generally designed for mainstream employees (for example, white Anglo-Saxon, Protestant, heterosexual persons in the UK, USA and Australia). Workers are diverse, and their opportunity and propensity to voice may vary by gender, race, sexuality and so on. These voices may be missing in the workplace or they may express themselves in different ways. Depending upon the national or organizational context, there may be voices that are not heard or situations in which there is little in the shape of vehicles to enhance such voices. In particular, diverse employees' perspectives and insights may remain ignored, suppressed or missing in decision-making in organizations.

This chapter offers a critical review of the literature covering missing voices in organizations. It identifies diversity management as a missing theoretical paradigm in the literature on employee voice, and illustrates the cases of women, lesbian, gay, bisexual and transgender (LGBT) persons and ethnic minorities in the workplace. The chapter is structured as follows. First it examines the notion of employee voice and also explains various vehicles or mechanisms used to enable employee voice. It then describes the notions of missing voices and diversity and looks at the reasons why diverse employees' voices may be missing, suppressed or ignored in organizations. The chapter then describes the missing voices of three diverse groups, women, ethnic minorities and LGBT persons. Finally, a summary of practitioners' insights is offered followed by practical and theoretical implications.

EMPLOYEE VOICE AND ITS IMPORTANCE

Hirschman (1970: 30) defined voice as 'any attempt at all to change, rather than to escape from, an objectionable state of affairs, whether through individual or collective petition to the management directly in charge, through appeal to a higher authority with the intention of forcing a change in management, or through various types of actions and protests, including those that are meant to mobilize public opinion'. Bell et al. (2011) note that studies of employee voice often treat voice as a universal concept that applies to all workers. As such, the voices of non-mainstream workers, for example, ethnic minorities, women and LGBT employees, have been neglected in much of the theoretical framing and organizational interventions on employee voice.

According to Wilkinson and Fay (2011), the term 'voice' refers to the way in which employees are able to have a say in routine work activities and important decision-making matters at work. The authors note that practitioners and academics also use other terms for employee voice, for example, participation, engagement, involvement, empowerment. Freeman et al. (2007) note that employees want some form of voice at work which will help them deal with problems. In particular, they want more cooperative styles of engagement with management which may help improve their firm performance and their working lives (Purcell and Hall, 2012).

Industrial relations research has traditionally viewed trade unions as the primary mechanism for employee voice. Unions are often seen as employees' collective voice in the determination of the terms and conditions of their employment (Freeman and Medoff, 1984). With the decline in unionism over the past two decades, new non-union voice mechanisms have been encouraged by governments and employers (Benson and Brown, 2010). However, unions have traditionally ignored the voices of non-mainstream employees, and scholars' and practitioners' focus on mechanisms for employee voice does not always take into account the missing voices of diverse employees.

Having a voice, and being listened to, is now acknowledged as an important antecedent of employee engagement (Purcell and Hall, 2012). Recent scholarship on employee participation and engagement has placed emphasis on those aspects of the employment relationship and management that enable employees to become committed to, and engaged with, their work and organization. According to Jones (1997), one way to encourage employees to improve firm performance is through employee voice and participation. Apart from formal unionization, direct participation and consultation mechanisms may provide employees with voice, ownership and a feeling of belonging to the organization and its decision-making processes. Transparent and fair policies may allow redress for grievances where employees feel they have been wronged by management or colleagues (Evans, 2010).

There are several benefits to a firm of enabling employee voice. Strong employee voice mechanisms are an integral part of high performance HRM systems which are 'designed to maximize the quality of human capital in the organization' (Becker et al., 2001). Voice mechanisms may allow employees to provide valuable feedback and thus contribute to business success. They may also help in safeguarding the rights of employees. However, employees may be hesitant to raise their voice for fear of retribution by management (Evans, 2010; Benson and Brown, 2010). While organizations gain from the increased trust that comes from giving employees voice and influence (Pfeffer and Veiga, 1999), at least some managers may be unwilling to share power and control. An open communication does not always translate to genuine employee involvement or influence on actual decision-making processes in the workplace (Gollan, 2010). Hearing employee voice is not the goal per se; due consideration to that voice is what creates an inclusive culture in organizations. Voice without follow up action may offer little value to employees or the firm (Evans, 2010).

In contrast, a legitimate experience of voice and involvement is closely associated with positive employee evaluations of management responsiveness (Bryson et al., 2006). This may, in turn, contribute to increased employee engagement and productivity (Purcell and Hall, 2012).

There are indeed many possible benefits to a firm associated with providing employees with voice. To realize these benefits, organizations must not only provide employees with an adequate outlet to speak, but must also take their voice into account and follow up with visible, meaningful action (Evans, 2010).

Voice Mechanisms and Vehicles

Research suggests that the more extensive the range of voice vehicles or mechanisms used in an organization, the more likely it is that managers will report benefits such as increased performance or decreased absenteeism (Sisson, 2000). Voice mechanisms which combine direct forms of employee–employer interaction with indirect voice (for example, through representative unions or councils) may lead to higher levels of organizational commitment (Purcell and Georgiades, 2007; Purcell and Hall, 2012).

Voice mechanisms in organizations have now expanded beyond formal meetings of trade union representatives with employers. Direct modes of employee–employer communication are more common, and it is likely that the use of social media will further extend the means by which individuals are able to disseminate information and provide feedback. There is an increasing use of consultative committees, in the private sector especially, whether non-union or union or a combination of both, alongside direct methods of employee voice (Purcell and Hall, 2012). In several advanced industrial countries, such as the UK, Norway and Sweden, all employees, including those in non-union firms, have the right to be consulted in specific circumstances, for example in the case of major redundancies and business restructure (Purcell and Hall, 2012). Recent research in Australia by Holland et al. (2011) shows that direct voice is the central voice arrangement underpinning employees' job satisfaction. Bell et al. (2011) suggest that identity-based networks may play a key role in a company's diversity strategy to facilitate voice from minority groups.

The 2004 Workplace Employment Relations Survey study in the UK found that 91 per cent of workplaces with ten or more employees used one or more types of face-to-face communication methods. At least 38 per cent of workplaces held a meeting of all employees addressed by a senior manager 'at least on a monthly basis' with at least some time made available for employee feedback and questions (Kersley et al., 2006; cited in Purcell and Hall, 2012).

Given that formal meetings between unions and employers or consultative committees and employers are less frequent than workforce meetings and briefing sessions (Kersley et al., 2006), employees are more likely to receive timely information direct from their managers than via intermediary channels. However, workforce meetings and briefing sessions are usually designed to disseminate and enforce management agendas and goals, and with only limited and superficial attention to employee feedback and suggestions, there may be little opportunity for meaningful dialogue (Purcell and Hutchinson, 2007; Purcell and Hall, 2012).

Consultation may be seen as a practice (right or expectation) through which employees may be informed of business decisions in advance and have an opportunity to comment prior to their implementation (Budd and Zagelmeyer, 2010). A consultative committee is sometimes established by organizations where representatives of employees, either from trade unions or directly chosen by employees, or both, meet with senior managers to discuss planned business. Trade unions are at times lukewarm towards consultative committees because they may undermine the need or purpose of collective bargaining and are used by at least some employers as substitutes for unions. Employers, for their part, object to legal enforcement of consultative committees, especially where these appear to limit their prerogatives. It is, however, a fact that managers always have the upper hand in consultation since it is they who establish the key parameters of the agenda (Purcell and Hall, 2012).

Regular group and/or one-on-one meetings are another mechanism used by management to hear from employees, for example, to identify what areas are working well and what areas need improvement. When managers meet with employees one-on-one, it may be helpful to make sure the conversation goes both ways. While managers probably have an agenda they want to focus on, employees too may be provided with an opportunity to ask questions and offer comments (Hedayati, 2012).

Other participation systems may be deployed to seek employee input and capitalize on the benefits associated with employee voice and participation. Open-book management may empower employees to review actual organizational situations and provide relevant and helpful input (Case, 1995). Open-door policies are an assurance by the management that employees are welcome to raise issues or provide input at any time. Team mechanisms such as quality circles and total quality management teams enable workers to participate in seeking and implementing better solutions to organizational problems (Evans, 2010).

Increasingly employers use attitude surveys on a regular basis to assess the level of employee engagement and the factors leading to its formation and to identify barriers to it (Purcell and Hall, 2012). Employee surveys can be an economical way to seek input from employees about specific policies or initiatives. However, organizations which survey their workforce without acting on the feedback may negatively affect employee trust and engagement (BlessingWhite, 2011). Anonymity in surveys may encourage employees to offer suggestions without fear of reprisal. Suggestion boxes are equally useful to receive feedback and suggestions from anonymous employees.

The advent of social media may change the way employers communicate with staff and also the way employees express their views to senior management and other colleagues. As Smith and Harwood (2011) recognize, social media has great potential to improve employee voice practices. Its various forms and tools (Facebook, Twitter and the like and their various features) allow rapid sharing of information and views across and outside organizational hierarchies. Two areas likely to be influenced by social media are the potential for managers to share information and consult employees and the potential for employees to gain a stronger collective voice (see Purcell and Hall, 2012). Apparently, not all companies are too sure about the use of social media by their employees. According to news reports, some companies are close to panic when it comes to the use of social media by their managers and employees. Others are actually trying to ban it (Newcombe, 2012a).

DIVERSITY MANAGEMENT AND MISSING VOICES

In today's business environment, a larger presence of women, ethnic minorities, LGBT and other persons in the workplace, an increasing trend towards teamwork, and a greater exposure to international businesses and cultures are constantly challenging employers and employees in all parts of the world. Because of the importance of managing diversity, there is a need to pay attention to the perspectives, insights and concerns of diverse employees in order to ensure their engagement in the workplace and also to maximize organizational performance (Garcia and Martin, 2010).

Members of diverse identity groups bring a variety of perspectives and approaches to the workplace (Thomas and Ely, 1996). Leaders and managers realize that increasing demographic heterogeneity does not in itself enhance organizational performance or effectiveness. Instead, what matters is how a company defines and treats the diversity of its own workforce (Garcia and Martin, 2010).

Hobman et al. (2003) note that diversity may contribute to improved performance when members understand each other and can combine and build on each other's insights and approaches. Interaction processes within a diverse team are crucial to the synergy and integration of diverse voices and opinions. Along these lines, diverse groups may identify the multiple angles of a problem and generate creative solutions. The more openly any problems and issues are recognized and discussed, the better chance there is for diversity to be a factor of organizational success (Garcia and Martin, 2010).

Thomas and Ely (1996) suggest that a more diverse workplace may not only lift employee morale, it may also bring greater access to new segments of the marketplace, and enhance productivity. By leveraging the talent within diverse teams, and approaching diversity as a means to business benefits (for example, efficiency and productivity), organizations may effectively manage diversity to achieve competitive advantage.

Thomas and Ely (1996) offer four paradigms describing management intervention in workforce diversity. (i) Resistance paradigm, in which organizations resist change by maintaining the status quo in the absence of any pressures to increase diversity (Dass and Parker, 1999) and by reproducing inequality (Kirton and Greene, 2005). (ii) Discrimination-and-fairness paradigm, in which organizations focus on equal opportunities and fair treatment through legislative action and by treating everybody the same (Thomas and Ely, 1996). This is demonstrated by concentrating on staff recruitment as a means to address discrimination and employment gaps facing disadvantaged groups (Kandola and Fullerton, 1998). (iii) Access-and-legitimacy paradigm, in which organizations focus on business benefits, maximizing every individual's potential as a source of competitive advantage to the company (Kandola and Fullerton, 1998). This paradigm focuses on matching the demographics of the organization to those of critical consumer or constituent groups. (iv) Learning-and-effectiveness paradigm, in which organizations emphasize the linkages of diversity with work, moving from identity groups towards learning opportunities to gain from diverse forms of knowledge, insights and experiences (Dass and Parker, 1999). In this paradigm, egalitarian organizational culture is seen as a means to higher standards of knowledge and performance in the attainment of which employees are viewed as a valuable resource and strategic asset (Ely and Thomas, 2001). This last paradigm incorporates diverse employee voices and perspectives into the main work of the organization. Organizational learning and growth may be fostered by internalizing different voices and insights offered by diverse employees.

Next, the chapter describes the missing voices of women, LGBT persons and ethnic minorities in the workplace.

Women's Voices

Despite the fact that women today constitute a majority of graduates across many disciplines and constitute approximately one half of all employees in advanced industrial countries, their participation in senior decision-making roles in organizations remains very low. Recent research carried out in the UK (Wearden, 2012) found that only 14.9 per cent of directors at the 100 largest public companies are women. While the percentage is slightly up from 12.5 per cent in 2010, male dominance remains a fact of organizational life. For example, at least ten FTSE 100 companies still operate with men-only boards, mainly mining groups. Other companies continue to lag behind. Just 9.2 per cent of directors on FTSE 250 firms are women, up from 7.8 per cent in 2010 (Wearden, 2012).

Harlos's (2010) empirical study identified gender, work self-esteem and relative power as key determinants of voice in organizations. The study showed that women may be more likely than men to voice to an internal mediator to try to resolve mistreatment. However, women's voice reactions also depend on power relations. The fact that women may be less motivated to voice when the offender is a supervisor instead of co-worker is consistent with gender role norms that point toward differential reactions for men and women.

Recently there has been movement in certain Western countries to increase the number of women in board rooms. Organizations are being encouraged and/or asked to increase the ratio of women in top management. For example in Scandinavian countries, there is currently a legal requirement to raise the number of women in board rooms. A similar legal push, in the shape of positive action, is found in the UK where positive action in favour of women and other protected groups is enshrined in the Equality Act 2010.

Trade unions are an important component in a democratic society, but for decades they have not been able to fully utilize valuable insights and perspectives offered by women that may serve not only women but entire employment sectors (Roberts, 2012). There is also an element of intersectional identity in membership and leadership of trade unions: ethnic minority women, more than white women, remain ignored. The average British trade unionist is a young, degree-educated, white woman working in the professions. At least in some unions, women outnumber men, and women have become vital to the survival of unions. For example, in 2012 Frances O'Grady became the first female general secretary of the Trades Union Congress in 144 years (Roberts, 2012). Increasing women's voices in the decision-making process may not only create a gender-inclusive work environment, it may also help in creating positive business outcomes.

Voluntary networks of working women may be useful not only in safeguarding and promoting women's interests but also in providing useful advice and feedback to employers and businesses. When people are able to talk openly about issues that concern them, to participate in problem-solving and management, and then see how their efforts have a positive impact on their organization, it follows that their job satisfaction increases and their loyalty deepens (Frohlinger, n.d.).

The following is an example of how paying attention to women's voice has its dividends. In order to understand how a women's network may help the bottom line, consider the story of the Women's Initiative (WIN) at Deloitte LLP. Begun in 1992, when the company took on the challenge of identifying the reasons why talented women were leaving the firm, it has not only produced the desired results critical to talent management but led to many other business 'home runs' as well. The WIN (2011) annual report states that in 1993, the firm had fewer than 100 women partners, principals and directors. By 2011, the firm had more than 1000. The firm's gender turnover gap had virtually disappeared. The firm now retains women at the same rate as men, continues to promote women into leadership roles and prepares its partners to sell more effectively to women clients as more women move into decision-making roles (WIN, 2011). Deloitte offers an example of the benefits that may be realized from a women's network that is supported by the top management, given the resources required to succeed and seen as an investment rather than an expense (Frohlinger, n.d.).

LGBT Persons' Voices

Bell et al. (2011) argue that LGBT employees are often silenced by what is perceived as 'normal' in organizations, that is, heterosexist norms and routines. The authors identify some of the adverse outcomes of this silencing and propose ways in which the voices of LGBT employees can be heard. Referring to the 'Don't ask; don't tell' policy of the US military as a lens, Bell et al. (2011) analyse voice, silence and strategies of LGBT employees in organizations. The authors note that heterosexist normativity can foster organizational climates of silence, where the feeling that speaking up is pointless or risky may be common among employees.

Colgan and McKearney's (2012) study shows that LGBT company employee networks provide a mechanism for visibility, community and voice. Such networks are valued by LGBT persons who see them as an important signal for LGBT employees' inclusion in the company and parity of treatment with other equality strands. Colgan and McKearney's study shows that manual, skilled trades and frontline staff are more likely to see the LGBT union group (instead of non-union networks) as their primary means of support. This in part reflects difficulties in attending LGBT network events because of time-off difficulties. Nevertheless, most LGBT employees consider the network provides them with a positive route to visibility and voice. Aside from providing advice on individual issues, such networks are often represented on organization diversity committees (often alongside unions) and are able to feed into discussions on organizational policy and practice (Colgan and McKearney, 2012). Within 'good practice' organizations, managers see the LGBT networks as a valuable platform through which to interact with and seek feedback from LGBT employees. Such networks help in shaping and driving the company's sexual orientation equality agenda (Colgan and McKearney, 2012).

Given the lack of physical markers to differentiate LGBT persons from heterosexuals, the absence of legal protections in many countries or states, the relative lack of union support and negative societal attitudes toward homosexuality may result in more silence for LGBT employees (Bell et al., 2011). Researchers have suggested that defensive silence, the result of fear, or acquiescent silence, the result of giving up hope for change, may result in further disengagement, withdrawal and resignation (Brinsfield et al., 2009; Pinder and Harlos, 2001).

The notion of *quiescent* or *defensive voice*, that is, speaking out to protect oneself from abuse or mistreatment (Ellis and Van Dyne, 2009; Pinder and Harlos, 2001) may be particularly relevant to LGBT employees, as it may occur in environments that are hostile and heterosexist. In contrast, *acquiescent voice* refers to a disengagement, which may manifest as LGBT staff's withdrawing or partial or full resignation from social aspects of work. Van Dyne et al.'s (2003) notion of *pro-social voice* (that is, voice based on cooperative motives that expresses ideas, information and opinions in constructive ways to improve work and organizations) may be seen in conjunction with the notion of

Table 26.1   Implementing voice mechanisms for LGBT employees

Types of voice	Mechanisms of voice at work for LGBT employees (and other invisible minorities)
Articulation of individual dissatisfaction	● Providing anonymous complaint mechanisms ● Allowing feedback free from harassment ● Scrutinizing all policies and practices for sexual orientation bias ● Providing a safe place for LGBT networking (which may sometimes need to be off-site) and allowing staff time for participation
Expression of collective organization	● Creating inclusive diversity councils ● Establishing intra-organizational LGBT networks (virtual or real) ● Union representation that includes LGBT employees
Contribution to management decision-making	● Making an explicit commitment for issues unique to LGBT employees to be considered in decision-making processes ● Allocating adequate staff and financial resources to sexual orientation equality efforts ● Integrating LGBT employees' voice in training and development programs ● Including sexual orientation questions in human resource monitoring systems
Mutuality	● Building representatives of internal and external LGBT networks ● Joining LGBT equality initiatives to bring external scrutiny to the organization ● Identifying and promoting champions of sexual orientation equality

Source: Bell et al. (2011: 140).

LGBT workers as 'tempered radicals' (Meyerson, 2001). That is, LGBT persons may be seen as subscribing to unstated radical plans for positive social change (in wider society and the workplace); however, their radicalism is curbed by organizational (and societal) norms (Bell et al., 2011).

Bell et al. (2011) argue that increasing workforce diversity necessitates new and different voice mechanisms. In their paper, they offer a typology of recognized voice mechanisms, which may be used to give voice to LGBT individuals at work to create a culture of voice and inclusion (see Table 26.1).

While there are anti-discrimination laws to protect LGBT employees from harassment and discrimination in several countries, there are still quite a few countries and areas where the law is either silent on anti-LGBT discrimination or is itself discriminatory against them. Even in those countries where legal protection is available, most organizations limit their action to minimal compliance with legal requirements and do not make an effort to include LGBT employees in designing and implementing organizational policies and strategies. This may lead to stereotyping and discrimination of LGBT employees, which may be caused by a lack of awareness, allowing social distancing within the workplace.

Even though several organizations in the West claim to have policies in place to deal with LGBT employees, LGBT employees remain under-represented in leadership and senior roles. LGBT networks have been instrumental in raising their voices but have not been able to implement strategies that would develop a supportive and inclusive culture.

Some organizations have been successful in providing voice to LGBT staff. They look at managing LGBT employees efficiently as a competitive advantage and as a business case. They encourage LGBT employees to create their own network groups and encourage the hosting of awareness events and forums. Looking at organizational examples, both Accenture and Ernst and Young have been managing LGBT employees very well. The following is a brief overview of the sexual orientation diversity management in each company.

Accenture (2013)

- By creating Global LGBT Network, the company has been able to bring its LGBT community and LGBT Allies together for networking, collaboration and mentoring.
- By creating Local LGBT Network, the company has been able to prevent discrimination and has also raised awareness of sexual orientation or gender identity and expression discrimination within the workplace.
- During 2012, thousands of Accenture employees joined the network as allies, taking equal responsibility for helping make our working environment inclusive of LGBT employees.
- Recruitment procedures of the company reflect an open and proactive acceptance of LGBT applicants.
- The company pays special attention to supporting LGBT careers through adequate training and inclusive climate.
- Corporate Communications are designed to foster a sense of community among members and educate within and beyond the network by building awareness of LGBT issues.

Ernst and Young (2012)

- The company has created the EYGLES network for LGBT employees and their allies. The network was named as one of Stonewall's 'Star Performer Network Groups'.
- The company promotes the concept of inclusive leadership.
- The company sponsors National Student Pride to promote diversity.
- The company regularly engages with clients about sexual orientation as a workplace issue.
- The company has an explicit, strong commitment to diversity and inclusiveness as a business goal and competitive advantage.

Ethnic Minorities' Voices

Race is the 'outward appearance of a person because most people view race as colour and/or outward physical appearance of a person' whereas ethnicity is the 'shared cultures, values, beliefs, foci of control, language and the spirituality of a particular group of individuals' (Balcazar et al., 2010: 82–3). However, racism is considered an umbrella term that covers both race and ethnicity and is defined as 'a belief that some races or ethnic groups are superior to others, used to devise and justify actions that create inequality between racial groups' (Mistry and Latoo, 2009: 20).

In the UK, the Equality Act 2010 provides a legal framework to ensure equal access and employment to all workers regardless of their race, ethnicity and other dimensions of diversity. However, it is an organization's responsibility to adopt and implement a diversity policy that promotes the interests of ethnic minorities in the workplace.

It is a fact that in many organizations, top management teams involved in organizational decision-making do not represent the diversity of wider society and as such ethnic minorities are not given the opportunity to voice their interests in the decision-making process.

Some organizations, such as Goldman Sachs, set up employee networks as a remedy to such issues. The STEP Leadership Development programme at Goldman Sachs supports black African and black Caribbean employees to 'Succeed, Transform, Excel and Perform' in their roles, and aims to develop future black leaders in Europe, the Middle East and Africa (Race for Opportunity, 2012). The formation of LGBT, black, Asian and women's networks is not unusual in such organizations and they are reported as having widespread support. They have multiple strategies that have been constructed to deal with issues of this nature. There are a number of implications. At the group level, initiatives such as employee networks may be supported by the management and encouraged to resolve issues faced by ethnic minorities in the workplace. At the legal level, policies should remain in conformance with legal requirements and duties. At the organizational level, companies may provide adequate structural and cultural support to the creation of ethnic minority networks, and enable regular engagement with ethnic minority employees in order to gain their feedback on organizational policies and strategies.

There is also an issue of intersectionality between age and ethnicity. For example, in Europe, older migrants and ethnic and religious minorities are reported to face specific challenges, for instance, in accessing care, the labour market and so on. Recently, think-tanks and activists have called on the EU to adopt targeted measures and to encourage initiatives in this area (Age, 2012). The EU is home to a significant population of older migrants and ethnic minorities, many of whom are in their fifties or above, having settled in European countries during their early-working or childhood years. However, governments across Europe do not seem to pay much attention to this population group, who face higher risks of discrimination, poverty and health problems. For example, pensioner poverty affects older migrants and ethnic and religious minorities in particular, especially in the current economic crisis, as pensions are being reduced and migrants blamed for economic downturns. In the UK, for example, nearly one in two Bangladeshi and Pakistani pensioners live in poverty, as do one in four older black Caribbean people, compared to one in six white UK pensioners (Age, 2012).

Statistics in the UK have shown that 677,000 people in the UK define themselves as mixed race. In addition, 14.6 per cent of the minority ethnic population are mixed race, a larger group than people of Bangladeshi, African-Caribbean, African or Chinese origin (Bagilhole, 2009: 216). This confirms the fact that organizations need to take into account the diversity within diversity.

Bristol City Council in the UK offers a worthy example of encouraging and making use of ethnic minorities' voice. The council has taken the following action to advance race equality (BCC, 2013). (i) Their BME workforce is currently 9 per cent (738) (for comparison the percentage of the BME population of Bristol is 16 per cent). Positive action is intended to improve the proportionate representation in the workforce. (ii) The council continue to invest in the BME staff network using positive action, having developed a detailed plan to address specific issues affecting BME staff. (iii) Dissemination of training to all senior managers with the council evolved into a three-year training strategy for all staff. (iv) The council work with other public bodies to increase the visibility and influence of BME staff within the public sector. (v) They assist in the promotion of and support to specific community events such as Black History Month. (vi) Finally, continued support is offered to the BME Voice and Influence Steering group as it transitions to form a new agency to take race equality forward for Bristol.

In research into black and minority ethnic (BME) community organizations' views on trade unions, it was reported that 86 per cent of organizations surveyed said that they had never worked with trade unions to promote BME interests and 96 per cent said that unions had never contacted them for advice or consultation (Perrett and Lucio Martinez, 2006). Yet these same community organizations reported that racism, discrimination and marginalization were the greatest difficulties facing BME groups in respect of employment. Further, when asked where they thought BME individuals went for advice on employment related problems only 13 per cent said trade unions, compared to 27 per cent who said that individuals went to Citizens Advice Bureaux. The authors of the research conclude that 'there remains a deficiency in the level of employment support for BME workers' and that the BME voluntary sector represents an access point for trade unions to make contact with BME communities and workers which could be of potential benefit to unions (Perrett and Lucio Martinez, 2006: 21–3; cited in Holgate et al., 2008).

The UK trade union movement's response to the involvement of BME workers within its ranks has not always been positive and, in some cases, despite official policy statements in opposition to discrimination, it has been objectively racist in practice (Phizacklea and Miles, 1987; Radin, 1966). There has, at times, been an unwillingness to acknowledge the racism experienced by BME workers, leading some BME union members to believe that trade unions do not adequately represent their interests (Bradley et al., 2002; GLC, 1984; WEA, 1974, 1980). Only since the late 1970s, as a consequence of challenges from BME activists and anti-racists, have trade unions been forced to re-evaluate their so-called 'colour-blind' stance, whereby they regularly asserted that there was 'no difference' between the experiences of BME and white workers (CIR, 1974; CRE, 1985; Radin, 1966). Ignoring the racialized nature of the labour market and the structural racism within their own organizations, trade unions made little effort during this period to specifically target BME workers for recruitment and organization (Holgate et al., 2008).

During the 1980s, a number of researchers (Lee, 1984; Lee and Loveridge, 1987; Phizacklea and Miles, 1987; WEA, 1980) investigated BME workers' relationship with unions. This body of research reinforced earlier findings, and concluded (Holgate et al., 2008) that black members are denied many of the benefits of their union membership because the movement inhibits full participation; unions fail to take up the grievances of their black members; low levels of participation by black members are due to lack of interest and lack of understanding of trade unionism; there is evidence of direct and passive collusion of shop stewards and officials with employers in discriminatory practices; more often than not 'race' issues do not appear on trade union agendas; unions do not keep records of their ethnic minority membership and are therefore not in a position to respond adequately to black members' needs; and that the prevalent attitude among trade unions is still that of colour blindness.

The 1980s also saw the development of self-organization as a strategy to increase BME involvement in trade unions. The Black Trade Unionist Solidarity Movement (BTUSM), which described itself as a 'pressure group', held its first conference in June 1983, and aimed to bring about a change in the trade union movement and to encourage BME workers to join an appropriate trade union (Holgate et al., 2008).

The UK union movement is known to have few BME union organizers or officials, which, if unions are serious about increasing the organizing of BME workers, could prove a hindrance in future campaigns. The experience from the USA suggests that if union renewal is to be successful the unions must become an integral part of the community and the communities need to become part of the union movement (Sciacchitano, 1998; Holgate et al., 2008).

There have been few union initiatives specifically directed at organizing among the Asian communities of West London (for exceptions see Holgate, 2004), yet there remain a substantial number of trade unionists in the area, and on a number of occasions there have been outbreaks of industrial militancy. The general union, the GMB, has been particularly active within the Asian communities of north-west London, initiating a number of organizing campaigns through the use of community and social networks. By employing Asian union organizers from the locality, the union has been able to build a relationship of trust with many workers who had felt that the unions were not interested in them or the issues they faced at work (Holgate et al., 2008).

In the absence of adequate voice mechanisms, ethnic minority workers may turn to informal intra-work networks, anti-racist organizations, external community-based organizations, faith-based groups and so on as alternative sources of support and guidance (EMRAW, 2013).

Kamenou and Fearfull's (2006) study of ethnic minority women in the UK shows that ethnic minority women are often required to fit into the existing organizational culture as an unstated prerequisite to career development and advancement. Their study suggests that employers must acknowledge and better understand religious and cultural differences instead of requiring their employees to fit into a narrow monoculture.

HRM PRACTITIONERS' PERSPECTIVES

Increasingly, there is a realization that HR needs to play a more proactive role in championing employee voice in the organization. According to Alex Lewis, HR director of BAE systems (a global company engaged in the development and support of defence, security and aerospace systems):

> Voice is important because it is addressing the largest challenge facing HR at the moment, which is retaining and attracting talent. Employees aren't just looking for a job anymore they are looking at a company to have a relationship with, and a relationship isn't a mute thing, a relationship involves having a voice from both parties, that for me is really critical. We now have a generation of people who are looking for a relationship and don't come into a company and look up to senior management and see a hierarchy. This creates conflict because leaders in

organisations tend to be people who work their way up the chain and buy into the concept of hierarchy. So that's why 'voice' can be important as it acts as a counterbalance to both parties. Because like any relationship the way of resolving conflict is by talking. Employee voice is a real business function and it simply drives better business performance.

(Quoted in Newcombe, 2012b)

Similar views were expressed by Nita Clarke, director of the Involvement and Participation Association (IPA):

A lot of the old management paradigms of command and hierarchy are not fit for purpose and the voice is one of the things we need to really think about to change that old paradigm and bring trust back in our organisation. If you have effective employee voice you will know what is going on in your organisation. Silent working is one of the greatest challenges to engagement.

(Newcombe 2012a)

A recent report ('Releasing voice for sustainable business success': IPA, 2012) notes that having a voice is an important matter for employees. However, the report notes that there aren't many companies that have found ways of encouraging and supporting employees to speak up (Newcombe, 2012a). Some of the key findings in the report are as follows: (a) Voice is the foundation of sustainable business success. It increases employee engagement, enables effective decision-making and drives innovation. (b) Voice is about both culture and structures; first you need to get the culture right, then you need to provide the processes and channels through which voice can be expressed. (c) Authenticity and trust are essential. Employees will only speak up when they feel safe and when they know their opinions are both valued and will be acted on. (d) Organizations need to use a variety of channels to access employee voice, and ensure they support both the individual and collective voice of employees. (e) There is some unease about voice and social media; seven in ten organizations either forbid or discourage the use of social media to express opinions about the company (Newcombe, 2012a).

The following is a list of recommendations for HRM practitioners and employers:

- Top management's commitment to diversity management through creating inclusive and meaningful consultation with and enabling the influence of diverse employees in decision-making.
- HRM mechanisms to put equality, diversity and inclusion at the heart of strategic decision-making and service delivery by frequent consultations with employees of diverse backgrounds.
- Establishment of intra-organization diversity networks with a clear schedule of regular meetings and periodical consultation with top management on organizational culture, structure and policies
- Creation of campaigns, bulletins, forums and employee resource groups to enhance diversity awareness and sensitivity in the organization
- Encouraging and enabling of an inclusive culture in the organization. HRM should foster good relations, keeping in view its legal, ethical and organizational responsibilities towards under-represented and historically disadvantaged groups.
- Development and implementation of anti-discrimination and positive action policies.

- Reformation of organizational structure and mandate, making people responsible for diversity management and providing them with adequate resources and authority.
- Provision of project-focused and practical training on diversity management.
- Representation of diverse staff on the executive board to ensure participation in senior-level decision-making.
- Celebration of diversity in the workplace to create general awareness, enhance diverse employees' motivation and inculcate a culture of acceptance and inclusion.
- Positive action to match the organization's demographic composition, across different levels of hierarchy, with that of the local population.

LOCATING DIVERSITY MANAGEMENT IN THEORETICAL PARADIGMS OF EMPLOYEE VOICE

In their recent review of literature on employee voice, Wilkinson and Fay (2011) identify four main strands. The first relates to HRM literature focused on performance. Here the argument is that informing and allowing employees an input into work and business decisions can help create better decisions and more understanding and hence commitment. A second strand of literature from political science sees voice in terms of rights, linking this to notions of industrial citizenship or democratic humanism. A third strand, drawing from the industrial relations literature, sees voice as a representative (and largely union) voice. A fourth strand is rooted in the organizational behaviour literature and relates to task autonomy in the context of work groups acquiring a greater degree of control (see Table 26.2).

The present chapter has highlighted a fifth, relatively ignored strand of literature on employee voice, which is ironically related to missing voices (of diverse employees) in organizations. The fifth strand (added as the last row in Table 26.2) serves as a gist of the current chapter through its summarizing of scheme, focus, vehicle and philosophy of employee voice through the lens of diversity management. Intra-organizational diversity networks, strategic equality-promotion councils and diversity-celebrating activities may be seen as key schemes of diversity management in an organization. The focus of such schemes is not only on anti-discrimination and positive action but also on reaping the benefits of diversity (commonly known as the business case of diversity management). Similarly, the voice vehicles are not only individuals but also collective groups of various dimensions of diversity. Finally the underpinning philosophy of paying attention to the missing voices of diverse employees is the pursuit of social justice as well as efficiency. This author agrees with Wilkinson and Fay's (2011) acknowledgement that the categorization in Table 26.2 may have some overlaps, but it is a useful heuristic device, representing how each of the strands of literature covers the dimensions of voice, the types of schemes typically discussed, the focus and forms of these vehicles, and the underlying philosophy.

A word of caution about the tendency of some organizations and/or managers to resort to tokenism and pseudo-voice. Recent research by de Vries et al. (2012: 29) shows that offering voice opportunity to employees may be counterproductive if employees suspect their organization lacks a genuine interest in considering their voices. This type

Table 26.2   Theoretical paradigms of employee voice

Theoretical strand	Schemes	Focus	Vehicle	Philosophy
HRM	Briefing, open door policy; suggestion schemes	Performance	Individual	Efficiency
Industrial relations	Collective bargaining; works council; social partnership; non-union employee representation	Power	Control; representative	Countervailing power
Industrial democracy	Workers on boards	Decision-making	Representative	Rights
Organizational behaviour	Teams; groups	Job redesign	Individuals and groups	Autonomy and human needs
Diversity management	Intra-organization diversity networks; equality promotion councils; celebrating diversity	Anti-discrimination; positive action; performance	Individuals and groups	Social justice; efficiency

Source: Adapted with some changes from Wilkinson and Fay (2011: 68).

of managerial insincerity in listening to voices with no intention of action is described as pseudo-voice. Perceived pseudo-voice may lead to reduced voice behaviour and increased intragroup conflict.

Burris's (2012) study shows that managers consider employees who engage in more challenging forms of voice as poor performers and that they are less inclined to endorse their ideas than the ideas of those who support management policies and opinions. Employees well recognize the sometimes futile nature of trying to change the status quo (Detert and Trevino, 2010) and the personal risks involved in speaking up (Milliken et al., 2003). Bowen and Blackmon (2003) suggest that an organizational culture that discourages employee voice may more severely affect members of an invisible minority such as LGBT and other diverse employees who may opt to suppress or conceal their identity or voice to escape disadvantage and discrimination at work. This view is supported by Noelle-Neumann's (1991) 'spirals of silence' theory that explains how a person's willingness to express opinion is shaped not just by their own personal opinions but also by the external environment and the perceived 'climate of opinion' (Colgan and McKearney, 2012). The onus clearly is on employers to create a trustworthy and inclusive climate in which diverse employees may freely express their voice and identity without any fear of reprisal or backlash.

REFERENCES

Accenture (2013), 'Accenture Lesbian, Gay, Bisexual and Transgender (LGBT) Network', available at: http://careers.accenture.com/us-en/working/overview/diversity/diverse-workforce/Pages/gay-lesbian-transgender-2010.aspx (accessed 20 February 2013).

Age (2012), 'The voices of older ethnic minorities and migrants are not heard in Europe', Brussels, 12 November, available at: http://www.age-platform.eu/en/age-a-the-media/age-communication-to-the-media-press-releases/1571-the-voices-of-older-ethnic-minorities-and-migrants-are-not-heard-in-europe (accessed 25 November 2013).

Bagilhole, B. (2009), *Understanding Equal Opportunities and Diversity: The Social Differentiations and Intersections of Inequality*, Bristol: The Policy Press.

Balcazar, F., Y. Suarez-Balcazar, C. Keys and T. Taylor-Ritzler (2010), *Race, Culture and Disability: Rehabilitation Science and Practice*, Sudbury, MA: Jones and Bartlett.

BCC (2013), 'Bristol black and minority ethnic voice and influence', Bristol City Council, available at: http://www.bristol.gov.uk/page/community-and-safety/race-and-ethnicity-equality (accessed 25 November 2013).

Becker, B.E., M.A. Huselid and D. Ulrich (2001), 'Making HR a strategic asset', *Financial Times*, November.

Bell, M.P., M.F. Özbilgin, T.A. Beauregard and O. Sürgevil (2011), 'Voice, silence, and diversity in 21st century organizations: strategies for inclusion of gay, lesbian, bisexual, and transgender employees', *Human Resource Management*, **50** (1), 131–46.

Benson, J. and M. Brown (2010), 'Employee voice: does union membership matter?', *Human Resource Management Journal*, **20** (1), 80–99.

BlessingWhite (2011), 'Employee engagement report 2011', available at: http://www.blessingwhite.com/eee_report.asp (accessed 10 December 2013).

Bowen, F. and K. Blackmon (2003), 'Spirals of silence: the dynamic effects of diversity on organisational voice', *Journal of Management Studies*, **40** (6), 1393–417.

Bradley, H., G. Healy and N. Mukerjee (2002), 'Inclusion, exclusion and separate organisation: black women activists in trade unions', Working Paper 25, ESRC.

Brinsfield, C.T., M.S. Edwards and J. Greenberg (2009), 'Voice and silence in organizations: historical review and current conceptualizations', in J. Greenberg and M.S. Edwards (eds), *Voice and Silence in Organizations*, Bingley: Emerald Group, pp. 1–33.

Bryson, A., A. Charlwood and J. Forth (2006), 'Worker voice, managerial response and labour productivity: an empirical investigation', *Industrial Relations Journal*, **37** (5), 438–55.

Budd, J. and S. Zagelmeyer (2010), 'Public policy and employee participation', in A. Wilkinson, P. Golan, M. Marchington and D. Lewin (eds), *The Oxford Handbook of Participation in Organisations*, Oxford: Oxford University Press, pp. 476–503.

Burris, E.R. (2012), 'The risks and rewards of speaking up: managerial responses to employee voice', *Academy of Management Journal*, **55** (4), 851–75.

Case, J. (1995), *Open-Book Management: The Coming Business Revolution*, New York: Harper Business.

CIR (1974), 'Mansfield Hosiery Mills', Commission on Industrial Relations, No. 76.

Colgan, F. and A. McKearney (2012), 'Visibility and voice in organisations: lesbian, gay, bisexual and transgendered employee networks', *Equality, Diversity and Inclusion*, **31** (4), 359–78.

CRE (1985), 'Trade union structures and black workers' participation: a study in central Lancashire', Commission for Racial Equality, London.

Dass, P. and B. Parker (1999), 'Strategies for managing human resource diversity: from resistance to learning', *Academy of Management Executive*, **13** (2), 68–80.

de Vries, G., K.A. Jehn and B.W. Terwel (2012), 'When employees stop talking and start fighting: the detrimental effects of pseudo voice in organizations', *Journal of Business Ethics*, **105**, 221–30.

Detert, J.R. and L.K. Trevino (2010), 'Speaking up to higher-ups: how supervisors and skip-level leaders influence employee voice', *Organization Science*, **21**, 249–70.

Ellis, J.B. and L. Van Dyne (2009), 'Voice and silence and observers' reactions to defensive voice: predictions based on communication competence theory', in J. Greenberg and M.S. Edwards (eds), *Voice and Silence in Organizations*, Bingley: Emerald Group, pp. 37–61.

Ely, R.J. and D.A. Thomas (2001), 'Cultural diversity at work: the effects of diversity perspectives on work group processes and outcomes', *Administrative Science Quarterly*, **46** (2), 229–73.

EMRAW (Ethnic Minority Representation at Work) (2013), 'The influence of identity, "community" and social networks on ethnic minority representation at work', available at: http://www.workinglives.org/research-themes/wlri-project-websites/$-emraw/emraw_home.cfm (accessed 25 November 2013).

Ernst and Young (2012), 'Ernst and Young named top gay-friendly employer in the country', available at: http://www.ey.com/UK/en/Newsroom/News-releases/13-01-17---EY-named-leading-gay-friendly-employer-by-Stonewall (accessed 28 February 2013).

Evans, L. (2010), 'Selecting and managing your team; providing employee voice and influence', *Business Fundamentals*, available at: http://cnx.org/content/m35392/latest/ (accessed 25 November 2013).

Freeman, R.B. and J. Medoff (1984), *What Do Unions Do?*, New York: Basic Books.

Freeman, R.B., P. Boxall and P. Haynes (2007), *What Workers Say: Employee Voice in the Anglo-American Workplace*, Ithaca, NY: Cornell University Press.

Frohlinger, C. (n.d.), 'Why women's networks are good for you', *20–First*, available at: http://www.20-first. com/632-0-the-power-of-womens-networks.html (accessed 25 November 2013).

Garcia, H.N.S and N. Martin (2010), 'Managing differences in organizations', *Business Fundamentals*, available at: http://cnx.org/content/m35392/latest/ (accessed 12 December 2013).

GLC (1984), 'Racism within Trade Unions', Anti-racist Trade Union Working Group, Greater London Council.

Gollan, P. (2010), 'Employer strategies toward non-union collective voice', in A. Wilkinson, P. Golan, M. Marchington and D. Lewin (eds), *The Oxford Handbook of Participation in Organizations*, Oxford: Oxford University Press, pp. 212–36.

Harlos, K. (2010), 'If you build a remedial voice mechanism, will they come? Determinants of voicing interpersonal mistreatment at work', *Human Relations*, **63** (3), 311–29.

Hedayati, S. (2012), 'Amplifying the employee voice', *Women on Business*, 17 March, available at: http://www. womenonbusiness.com/amplify-the-employee-voice (accessed 25 November 2013).

Hirschman, A.O. (1970), *Exit, Voice, and Loyalty: Responses to Decline in Firms, Organizations and States*, Cambridge, MA: Harvard University Press.

Hobman, E.V., P. Bordia and C. Gallois (2003), 'Consequences of feeling dissimilar from others in a work team', *Journal of Business and Psychology*, **17** (3), 301–25.

Holgate, J. (2004), 'Organising black and minority ethnic workers: trade union strategies for recruitment and inclusion', unpublished PhD thesis, University of London.

Holgate, J., A. Pollert, J. Keles and M. Jha (2008), 'Ethnic minority representation at work: an initial review of literature and concepts', Working Lives Research Institute, London Metropolitan University.

Holland, P., A. Pyman, B.K. Cooper and J. Teicher (2011), 'Employee voice and job satisfaction in Australia: the centrality of direct voice', *Human Resource Management*, **50** (1), 95–111.

IPA (2012), 'Releasing voice for sustainable business success', available at: http://www.ipa-involve.com/ resources/publications/releasing-voice-for-sustainable-business-success/ (accessed 10 December 2013).

Jones, D. (1997), 'Employees as stakeholders', *Business Strategy Review*, **8** (2), 21–4.

Kamenou, N. and A. Fearfull (2006), 'Ethnic minority women: a lost voice in HRM', *Human Resource Management Journal*, **6** (2), 154–72.

Kandola, R. and J. Fullerton (1998), *Managing the Mosaic: Diversity in Action*, 2nd edn, London: Institute of Personnel Development.

Kersley, B., A. Carmen, J. Forth, A. Bryson, H. Bewley, G. Dix and S. Oxenbridge (2006), *Inside the Workplace: Findings from the 2004 Workplace Employment Relations Survey*, London: Routledge.

Kirton, G. and A. Greene (2005), *The Dynamics of Managing Diversity. A Critical Approach*, 2nd edn. Oxford: Elsevier Butterworth-Heinemann.

Lee, G. (1984), 'Trade unionism and race', University of Aston Management Centre, Birmingham.

Lee, G. and R. Loveridge (1987), *The Manufacture of Disadvantage*, Milton Keynes: Open University Press.

Meyerson, D.E. (2001), *Tempered Radicals: How People Use Difference to Inspire Change at Work*, Boston, MA: Harvard Business School Press.

Milliken, F.J., E.W. Morrison and P.F. Hewlin (2003), 'An exploratory study of employee silence: issues that employees don't communicate upward and why', *Journal of Management Studies*, **40**, 1453–76.

Mistry, M. and J. Latoo (2009), 'Uncovering the face of racism in the workplace', *British Journal of Medical Practitioners*, **2** (2), 20–24.

Newcombe, T. (2012a), '"Employee voice" is a key to a successful business, says Nita Clarke', *HR Magazine*, 11 December, available at: http://www.hrmagazine.co.uk/hro/news/1075669/-employee-voice-key-successful-business-nita-clarke (accessed 25 November 2013).

Newcombe, T. (2012b), 'HR needs to be the function that "champions employee voice" in the organisation, says BAE Systems HRD', *HR Magazine*, 11 December, available at: http://www.hrmagazine. co.uk/hro/news/1075668/hr-function-champions-employee-voice-organisation-bae-systems-hrd (accessed 25 November 2013).

Noelle-Neumann, E. (1991), 'The theory of public opinion: the concept of the spiral of silence', in J.A. Anderson (ed.), *Communication Yearbook*, Newbury Park, CA: Sage, pp. 256–87.

Perrett, R. and M. Lucio Martinez (2006), 'Trade unions and BME communities in Yorkshire and the Humber: employment representation and community organisation in a context of change', Bradford University School of Management.

Pfeffer, J. and J.F. Veiga (1999), 'Putting people first for organizational success', *Academy of Management Executive Journal*, **13**, 37–48.

Phizacklea, A. and R. Miles (1987), 'The British trade union movement and racism', in G. Lee and R. Loveridge (eds), *The Manufacture of Disadvantage*, Milton Keynes: Open University Press, pp. 21–30.

Pinder, C. and K. Harlos (2001), 'Employee silence: quiescence and acquiescence as responses to perceived injustice', in G. Ferris (ed.), *Research in Personnel and Human Resources Management*, Greenwich, CT: JAI Press, pp. 331–69.

Purcell, J. and K. Georgiadis (2007), 'Why should employers bother with employee voice?', in R.B. Freeman, P. Boxall and P. Haynes (eds), *What Workers Say: Employee Voice in the Anglo-American Workplace*, Ithaca, NY: ILR Press, pp. 181–97.

Purcell, J. and M. Hall (2012), 'Voice and participation in the modern workplace: challenges and prospects', Acas Future of Workplace Relations discussion paper series, available at: http://www.acas.org.uk/media/pdf/g/7/Voice_and_Participation_in_the_Modern_Workplace_challenges_and_prospects.pdf (accessed 25 November 2013).

Purcell, J. and S. Hutchinson (2007), 'Front-line managers as agents in the HRM-performance causal chain: theory, analysis and evident', *Human Resource Management Journal*, 17 (1), 3–20.

Race for Opportunity (2012), 'Awards 2012 Goldman Sachs – Leadership Award', available at: http://race-foropportunity.bitc.org.uk/our-resources/case-studies/rfo-awards-2012-goldman-sachs-leadership-award (accessed 25 November 2013).

Radin, B. (1966), 'Coloured workers and British trade unions', *Race*, VIII (2).

Roberts, Y. (2012), 'The women changing Britain's unions', *Guardian*, 5 August, available at: http://www.guardian.co.uk/politics/2012/aug/05/women-changing-union-movement-tuc (accessed 25 November 2013).

Sciacchitano, K. (1998), 'The union is forever: a comparison of leadership development in SEIU's Dignity Campaign against Beverly Enterprises and SHARE's Campaign at the University of Massachusetts Medical Center', paper presented at the UCLEA/AFL–CIO Annual Conference, San Jose, California, 1 May.

Sisson, K. (2000), 'Direct participation and the modernisation of work organisation', European Foundation for the Improvement of Living and Working Conditions, Dublin.

Thomas, D.A. and R.J. Ely (1996), 'Making differences matter: a new paradigm for managing diversity', *Harvard Business Review*, 74 (5), 79–90.

Van Dyne, L., S. Ang and I.C. Botero (2003), 'Conceptualizing employee silence and employee voice as multi-dimensional constructs', *Journal of Management Studies*, 40 (6), 1359–92.

WEA (1974), *Trade Unions and Immigrant Workers*, London: Workers Educational Association.

WEA (1980), 'A report of a conference held in October 1980: black workers and trade unions', Workers Educational Association, London.

Wearden, G. (2012), 'Record number of women in UK boardrooms', *Guardian*, 10 January, available at: http://www.guardian.co.uk/business/2012/jan/10/record-numbers-of-women-on-uk-boards?newsfeed=true (accessed 25 November 2013).

Wilkinson, A. and C. Fay (2011), 'Guest editors' note: new times for employee voice?', *Human Resource Management*, 50 (1), 65–74.

WIN (2011), 'Deloitte Women Network Annual Report 2011', available at: http://www.deloitte.com/assets/Dcom-UnitedStates/Local%20Assets/Documents/WAR_sm%20FINAL.pdf (accessed 25 November 2013).

27 E-voice: how network and media technologies are shaping employee voice

Nikola Balnave, Alison Barnes, Craig MacMillan and Louise Thornthwaite

INTRODUCTION

Web-based technologies are impacting on the development and expression of individual and collective voice at the workplace. While there is much anecdotal and media coverage concerning the use made of these technologies, the pace of technological development has outstripped academic research on its implications for employee voice. Media coverage often swings between enthusiasm about the capacity of social media to transform contemporary workplaces and concern about privacy and civil liberties raised by examples of the heavy-handed policing of employees' use of social media. Recent media coverage of internet trolls highlights another emerging concern. While still in its infancy, scholarly literature on the implications of internet communication for voice is identifying a range of potentially positive and negative effects. The objective of this chapter is to gather together these preliminary findings and analyses as a basis for considering potential short- and long-term consequences for the expression of voice by both individual employees and unions.

As social media spreads its tentacles through society, employees increasingly use internet forums to express opinions about their working lives. Social media also facilitate a blurring of boundaries between work and non-work life, making it ever more likely that comments made outside work will find their way into the workplace. Individual expressions of voice, both within and outside work, have led to well-publicized instances of employee termination. One of the more notorious examples was the dismissal of Heather Armstrong from a dot.com start-up company in the United States for publishing online satirical pieces about her work. Armstrong subsequently established a website for dismissed and disgruntled employees to vent their dissatisfaction (dooce.com). Armstrong's dismissal, however, was not an isolated example. A recent article in 'The Conversation', a website designed to give academics 'a greater voice in shaping scientific, cultural and intellectual agendas', noted that social media blurs 'boundaries between expressions of academic freedom and obligation to their institutions', and highlighted instances where academics have been disciplined or dismissed for criticizing university management online (Mewburn, 2012). Similarly, a long-term employee of transport company Linfox was dismissed for posting comments about his managers on his 'private' Facebook page. The industrial tribunal at the subsequent unfair dismissal hearing found in his favour, noting that the comments were 'within the employee's right to free speech' but warned that his claims of limited understanding of how Facebook works 'are likely to be viewed less favourably in the future as more and more people join social media websites' (Cullen, 2012).

While at first glance such examples may appear to be unrelated to employee voice, individual expressions of dissatisfaction are one of the prime developments around social media and voice. On the flip-side, government, industry and human resource management advisory bodies point to the ways in which social media can enhance voice. Business Link, a British government online resource for business, suggests that social media provide employees with additional channels such as blogs and network sites that can be used to facilitate voice. The 'tell Colin' programme is cited as an initiative designed to solicit cost-savings suggestions from staff, and 'Magical Thinking' is named as another instance of employees using the intranet to raise suggestions that 'magicians' would then make happen (Business Link, 2011).

Social media allows users to upload video, photo and written text easily and immediately, thus potentially disseminating information and images rapidly to wide audiences. The enhanced capacity to reach geographically disparate communities of users has ramifications for collective as well as individual expressions of voice. During a recent riot at the infamous Foxconn plant in China, authorities 'moved quickly to have photographs and videos of the incident removed from microblogging site Sina Weibo' (Bell, 2012). Presumably this was done in order to quell dissent and/or halt the spread of critical commentary at a national and international level. As *New York Times* reporters noted,

> worker unrest in China has grown more common because workers are more aware of their rights, and yet have few outlets to challenge or negotiate with their employers. When they do, though, the results can be ugly and, because of social media and the Web, almost instantly transmitted to the world in their rawest and most unfiltered form. (Barbosa and Bradsher, 2012)

It is not surprising, therefore, that scholars predict that internet technologies will have a myriad of implications for collective voice by providing effective new channels for union organizing, communication and campaigning, as well as enhancing union democracy (Greer, 2002). The internet also provides the capacity for trade unions to extend campaigns across national borders far more rapidly and easily than in the past. Thus, for instance, following fires in two Pakistani factories in mid-September 2012, the international website LabourStart coordinated a global online campaign with individuals petitioning the Pakistani prime minister in an effort to build pressure for compensation to victims and families, wages for those now without employment, and legal action against the employer and government department officials who had failed to ensure health and safety standards had been met (www.Labourstart.org). This chapter explores these themes through an examination of unions' use of social media and other internet channels to conduct international and local campaigns for labour rights. Individuals also use anonymous blogs to vent frustration and raise awareness of their conditions of work. Campaigns that seek to highlight labour exploitation may damage the reputation of companies, but may also encourage greater corporate social responsibility. Opponents, however, may also exploit social media to discredit such campaigns. Likewise, union members can utilize social media to voice dissent with their union. For example, in February 2013, teachers in Ottawa used Twitter and Facebook to challenge the union leadership's failure to consult with members (Pilieci and Stark, 2013).

Much of the emerging academic work provides salient, if limited, examples of the use of web-based technology for developing employee voice. These examples often point to the benefits of emerging technology for 'e-voice'. A rich body of work critically ana-lysing the use and impact of network and media technologies, however, has yet to be developed. This chapter aims to capture current debates and provide an overview of academic work that is building an understanding of how these technologies facilitate or hinder the expression of voice. We initially look at the relationship between individual voice and new technologies such as intranets, Facebook, Twitter and blogs. These voice mechanisms may be organizationally sanctioned or not. The chapter then explores the literature on web-based technology and collective voice, with a particular emphasis on unions. The ways in which these technologies aid information sharing, campaigning and organizing and internal union democracy are examined. For both individual and collec-tive voice, new technologies present many opportunities but also an array of challenges.

NEW TECHNOLOGY, ORGANIZATIONS AND INDIVIDUAL VOICE

This section examines the impact that new forms of technology have had on the expres-sion of individual employee voice both within the workplace and outside work in employees' personal lives. Miles and Muuka (2011: 92) note that 'at its most basic level employee voice is the expression of opinions and concerns about organisational phenom-ena that may reveal content (agreement, suggestions, argument, support) or discontent (disagreement, contradictory opinions and/or divergent views)'. Thus voice may include individual employee contributions to management decision-making that range from mere participation to the upward expression to managers of 'challenging but construc-tive opinions, concerns or ideas on work-related issues' (Tangirala and Ramanujam, 2012: 251–2). It may also involve the expression of complaints and grievances (Miles and Muuka, 2011: 92; Tangirala and Ramanujam, 2012: 253–4). While individual expres-sions of voice may be 'driven by a sense of personal agency to proactively effect changes to the status quo' (Tangirala and Ramanujam, 2012: 254), equally they may involve spontaneous expressions of opinion or emotion.

Employee voice may be communicated through either organizationally sanctioned or unsanctioned media (Miles and Muuka, 2011: 93). The advent of new technologies has meant that collective voice systems found in unions, and the traditional voice mecha-nisms instituted by organizations, such as consultative committees and grievance proce-dures, are no longer the only options available to employees. With the invention of Web 2.0 interactive platforms, which include features such as online chatting, content crea-tion, tagging and blogging, new opportunities emerged for communication, networking and collaboration. (Mcafee cited in Vuori, 2012: 157). While many organizations have since begun adopting such technologies to facilitate vertical and horizontal communica-tion in the workplace, social media also enables 'interaction between people who create, share, exchange and comment' about work 'in virtual communities and networks' (Toivonen cited in Vuori, 2012: 157). Thus, individual workers now have options for expressing voice through a range of non-sanctioned mechanisms as well as organization-ally sanctioned channels (Miles and Muuka, 2011: 93).

Research on Organizationally Sanctioned Voice Mechanisms Using New Technology

With the proliferation of social media forms and use, a number of scholars have commented on the potential ways in which organizations may use information technologies to provide new organizationally sanctioned forms of communication and employee voice (for example, Vuori, 2012; Arvanitis and Loukis, 2009). For some organizations, adopting social media and other new technologies for such purposes is hindered by such factors as a lack of information-technology capability and support, concerns about legal liability, and lack of CEO and senior management support because of comfort with existing methods (Nancherla, 2010; D'Aprix, 2011: 29). Many organizations, however, have reportedly powered ahead, establishing a range of new technology-based employee involvement mechanisms.

Nonetheless, there has been no systematic scholarly study of the extent, forms and outcomes of such uses of these technologies. Some researchers have considered the implications that new voice mechanisms may have for organizations and individual employees as a result of their impact on changing modes of communication (Vuori, 2012; Arvanitis and Loukis, 2009). Klaas et al. (2012: 337) for instance argue that if social media and other new technologies have made it easier for suggestions and complaints to be registered, particularly where they can be shared anonymously, this may reduce the extent to which raising concerns with multiple levels of managers is seen as provocative or an escalation of conflict. In the process, norms within organizations about the appropriateness of submitting concerns to 'skip-level managers' may also change (Klaas et al., 2012: 337). But given that social media provides an avenue for employees to voice concerns about their employer more broadly within the community and the potential for such communication to go viral, it also provides new opportunities for employees to impose costs on employers through adverse publicity in the pursuit of restorative or retributive justice (Klaas et al., 2012: 337). Moreover, the proliferation of social media channels means that employees' options for voice mechanisms are no longer the preserve of the organization they work for. Miles and Muuka (2011) recommend that managers adopt a strategy for the effective management of employee voice, which should involve the careful choice and orchestration of organizationally sanctioned voice mechanisms to assist in managing the messages conveyed by employees through non-sanctioned mechanisms.

For the most part, however, despite the proliferation of alternative channels for voice, recent studies about internal organizational communication and voice have tended to confine their attention almost exclusively to the formal structures for employee representation and participation, and to employees 'speaking out' to supervisors in face-to-face encounters, to the neglect of voice methods using social media and other new technologies (for example, Pauksztat and Wittek, 2011; Tangirala and Ramanujam, 2012). Thus, for example, Vuori (2012: 160–61) examined the range of internal social media applications established in Nokia, including discussion forums and wikis for sharing expertise and enabling dialogue and interaction between people across departmental and geographic boundaries. According to Vuori, all Nokia employees also had the opportunity to discuss work and ideas in their own blogs, with more than 1400 active blogs at the beginning of 2011. All internal company blogs were collected into a blog platform. While internal wikis were used largely for communicating and informing employees about internal projects, a company social networking service helped employees to meet and engage in discussions online. In addition, an internal 'idea crowd sourcing' service enabled employees to generate, discuss and share new ideas or to suggest changes to practices, services and products. The extent, however, to which these applications provided for active employee voice as opposed simply to communication and project-based collaboration, remains unexplored.

Naslund (2010) discussed the ways in which the multinational electronics retailer Best Buy has used internal social media to open lines of communication through employee social networks and has built wikis to empower employees to contribute ideas to improve company performance. Naslund observed that the internal social networks and communities established through social media have provided broader, more interactive and democratic discussions in the organization. Roush (2005) and Naslund also reported positive outcomes for other companies of internal communication and networking strategies using social media, including Sun Microsystems' employee blog, GE's social network, 'SupportCentral', Nissan's 'N-Square Network', IBM's 'Beehive', and Dell's 'Employee Storm'. The focus of such analyses, however, is almost exclusively on the way social technologies, such as Facebook-like online communities, wikis, idea-sharing tools such as User Voice, blog-based suggestion boxes and message boards, have facilitated employee collaboration, product improvement and customer responsiveness in these companies, rather than on the expression of critical opinion and concerns.

The Case of Blogs and Facebook

Blogs and Facebook have attracted the most attention among scholars examining individual employee use of social media platforms for voice. Research has focused largely on Workblogging and Facebook use outside the workplace, in employees' personal time, and the implications this might have for employing organizations and for employees themselves. To date, much of the discussion about these forums has occurred in scholarly legal journals, with scholars attempting to identify the legal rights and obligations of parties to the employment relationship where social media conduct is an issue in employment law cases.

According to Lee et al. (2006: 318) 'the nature of blogs, characterised as a "breakthrough form of democratic self-expression" (Nardi et al. 2004) has resulted in disputes between employee bloggers and management about what is appropriate blogging content'. This has spilled over into employer attempts to regulate the behaviour of employees on social media sites within the workplace and during their personal time. One of the responses has been for companies to sponsor employee blogging on company-owned domains. Lee et al. (2006) observed that, while employee blogs within organizations can be useful for extending organizational citizenship and tapping into employees' latent potential, an organization's adoption of such blogs raises control issues. Individuals who participate in them must surrender some autonomy. Organizations have tended to adopt one of two blogging strategies: a bottom-up (company-wide) strategy, which explicitly allows any employee to blog inside company-owned domains, and top-down practices, which provide for more limited employee involvement and autonomy. Overall, however, few have supported the higher levels of autonomy associated with bottom-up blogging strategies. The space for employee voice through company blogs has, therefore, mostly remained heavily constrained. Lee et al. (2006: 328) also noted that the objective for many companies which have adopted blogs and encouraged employees to share their thoughts about work was to reduce the incidence of employees venting their feelings in public forums by providing a mechanism that extends some autonomy to employee bloggers. There has, however, been no detailed research on whether blogs have such a substitution effect in practice.

Most employee blogs are hosted independently of company websites. Early research on work blogging suggested it might be a method by which employees could overcome increased isolation in the workplace (Gely and Bierman cited in Richards, 2008: 96). Alternatively, Schoneboom (2007) argued that work blogging is, for some participants, a form of creative written expression. Richards's (2008) detailed ethnographic analysis of work bloggers examined the pursuit of work blogging by employees on a number of levels. Richards argued that while blogging was primarily aimed at communication about work and provided a means for coping with work it might also play an important role as a form of employee resistance to work. He argued that for many employees, blogging is a way to share experiences and ideas about their work, offer realistic views about what their profession involves and interact with their occupational or workforce community. But for many blogging is also a means to vent grievances and frustrations in cyberspace rather than via conventional modes of expression such as grievance procedures and representative bodies. Richards maintained that *venting* may also provide a means for coping with work, with workers reconciling themselves to situations they cannot alter or resolve. In addition, Richards suggested that, as other avenues for resistance disappear, work blogging may provide a fertile ground for trading information about employers, challenging managerial discourse and fomenting broader resistance.

This potential is illustrated by the activities of the Greedy Associates Boards (GA) in the United States. The GA Boards were among the earliest blog sites, then known as internet message boards, on which individual workers exchanged complaints about their jobs, employers, salaries and work environment. Established by young lawyers, GA Boards became a focus for junior lawyers in law firms to complain about salaries (Taras and Gesser, 2003). Young lawyers saw themselves as underpaid compared to peers in comparable sectors such as the finance industry, and the GA Boards evolved into a forum for agitating for a redistribution of income within law firms from partners to associates. The GA Boards established salary benchmarks, made explicit salary demands, reported members' successes in negotiating higher salaries, vilified firms that refused to raise salaries and posted the recruitment pages of those firms that cooperated. For Taras and Gesser (2003: 25), the GA phenomenon represented a distinct form of internet activity. They argued that while participants engaged in information exchange and 'concerted sniping' and the boards lent bargaining power to junior lawyers, there was no collective negotiation and individuals were left to negotiate their own salaries with employers. As well, GAs were unconcerned that working conditions tended to decline as associates' wages grew. Thus, rather than providing the benefits of unionism, the boards essentially empowered individuals who shared 'an extraordinarily strong self-efficacy and a sense of entitlement' to achieve a limited set of financial objectives (Taras and Gesser, 2003: 26).

The dismissal of employees for comments made on Facebook, blogs and other social media forums both during and outside work is a growing phenomenon (Lee et al., 2006; Thornthwaite, 2013). In the United States, such dismissals have attracted their own colloquial term – getting 'dooced' – the word that Heather Armstrong adopted for her blog (dooce.com) after being dismissed for blogging in 2002 (Cote, 2007: 123). While courts are generally reluctant to overturn dismissals where an employee's online conduct has included abusive and insubordinate behaviour, case law is emerging in such countries as the United States and Australia that hostile and unsavoury comments about employers and managers will not necessarily disqualify employees from legal protection. Further, consistent with twentieth-century developments in employment law that limited the extensive regulation of employees' lives outside work that had been associated with traditional master and servant law, the termination of employees for private online conduct will generally be lawful only when a clear connection exists between the conduct and the individual's employment (Thornthwaite, 2013; Gely and Bierman, 2007).

Employer Policy Responses

Increasingly, employers are implementing social media policies in attempts to regulate employee behaviour in social media forums, often trying to extend their control to conduct outside the workplace. This has sparked discussion about the extent to which employers can constrain employees' personal lives. In Australia, the Commonwealth Bank came under employee, union and public criticism in 2010 when it adopted a social media policy whose provisions included a requirement that employees should immediately report any 'inappropriate or disparaging' comments about the company made by friends or other people on any social media network. The bank subsequently negotiated amendments to the most contentious provisions (Rochfort, 2011; Tindal, 2011). In the United States, dismissals of employees for social media conduct and employers' social media policies have attracted widespread scholarly and legal concern because of their potential to violate national industrial law. In a growing number of cases, the National Labor Relations Board has ruled that provisions in the National Labor Relations Act that protect employees from adverse employment actions when engaged in 'concerted activities' for the purposes of 'mutual aid and protection' will apply to social media use and company policies concerning such conduct in certain circumstances (Cote, 2007). Professional magazines have provided recommendations on the desirable content of social media policies, but there has not yet been any substantial scholarly research or critical analysis of such policies and their impact.

Given that social media platforms have emerged only very recently, it is not surprising that discussion of the implications of these new technologies for employee voice has been limited or that much of what has been written on the topic remains at the level of conjecture. What we do know is that employing organizations and employees are together and independently exploring the uses to which these technologies can be put as forums for voicing work-related matters. This is already raising significant legal issues and questions about control and autonomy. Some scholars have also cautioned that while new technologies have opened up new avenues for voice they may also be reducing opportunities for meaningful and effective employee interaction within organizations (Barnes, 2012: 129). As Kupritz and Cowell (2011: 74–5) observed, face-to-face communication remains preferable in certain situations because it best facilitates social presence and media richness. Barnes's (2012: 128) study of the implementation of information and communication technologies in a hi-tech firm also noted that many employees throughout the organization believed that, as communication technology tools had become more embedded, the shift from face-to-face to online interactions had increased their experience of alienation and isolation in the organization.

Whilst IT provides management with a tool to enhance employee voice, this can pose a threat to unionized voice. Communication technology such as intranets provide an avenue for workers to express their concerns directly to management and offer feedback to management proposals, thus potentially leading to 'voice substitution' away from union voice towards direct voice (Chaison, 2002, 2005) and, ultimately, to a reduction in the visibility of the union in the workplace. The following section explores the opportunities and challenges that new technologies present for union voice.

TECHNOLOGY, UNIONS AND COLLECTIVE VOICE

A number of researchers have pointed out that the IT revolution has provided unions with a variety of avenues through which to strengthen union voice (Aalto-Matturi, 2005; Lee, 2000; Lucore, 2002; Shostak, 1999, 2005). Lee (2000: 56, 60) notes that '[n]ew communication technologies create new possibilities for trade unions. In the nineteenth century they made unions possible or at least unions that went beyond a single location', and in this century the internet can play a significant role 'in reviving and strengthening the labour movement'. E-voice has evolved in unions through website chat rooms, discussion forums such as Twitter, Facebook and discussion boards, as well as via website surveys and direct emails between the rank and file and officials (Greer, 2002). Although web-based technology is not seen as the 'magic bullet' (Shostak, 2002: 237) that will miraculously turn around declining union density in those countries experiencing this trend, a survey of the literature suggests that it facilitates information sharing, campaigning and organizing, and enhances internal union democracy. Yet, just as technological developments present many opportunities to enhance voice, they also pose challenges for unions.

Information, Organizing and Campaigning

Access to information is important in facilitating the expression of members' voice within trade unions as, through increasing members' awareness and understanding of issues, it empowers them to engage meaningfully and confidently with officials and other members. Once electronic modes of communication are established, they can be less expensive than traditional forms of print media and allow the union and its activists to communicate developments in real time to the broader membership (Lucore, 2002). A potential drawback is that members may be more likely to ignore an email than they might print media if they receive a high level of email messages.

In terms of union organizing, the internet has enabled unions to establish websites which prospective members can visit in order to gather information on union services and perspectives, have commonly asked questions answered via FAQ pages and download membership forms. As noted above, by enabling non face-to-face interaction, communication technology tools may contribute to reducing employee alienation. This may be particularly useful where employees work remotely, outside the office and from home – a growing labour market phenomenon which has itself been fuelled by developments in internet technologies. As Chaison (2005) reported, by the early 2000s in the United States approximately 19 million people worked from home and relied on the internet to keep them connected with their employer. These workers are sometimes psychologically as well as physically removed from their workplaces. While increasingly enabling paid work to take place remotely, new technologies may also have positive consequences for union organizing because they permit unions and workers to overcome temporal and spatial boundaries. If used effectively, the internet can assist unions to reach and organize such workers, facilitate regular contact between unions and workers and provide avenues for expressing concerns and opportunities to attend virtual meetings, thus giving remote workers a voice while also strengthening unionism. The same applies to labour market groups, such as shift workers, and temporary, casual and agency workers, whom unions have often found difficult to recruit because of their peripheral attachment to the labour market or location in small and dispersed workplaces.

One documented example of such use of the internet at a workplace and industry level to provide voice to precarious and fragmented workers is the Justice for Janitors campaign in the United States which began in 1985. During this campaign, 'electronic bulletin boards' have been used to reach workers who may never have met the people who clean their offices (Newman, 2005). Gely and Bierman (2007) noted that social media forums such as blogs may give employees who belong to historically disadvantaged groups the same ability to communicate as those in positions of authority. Stevens and Greer's (2005) study of web use by American unions also highlighted the potential to open up communication with members from different language groups. A related implication of the reach of these technologies is that web-based communication avenues may facilitate the unionization and subsequent mobilization of workers in industry sectors that are disproportionately characterized by peripheral workforces and, in some cases, are traditionally poorly unionized, such as the hospitality and tourism industries, which are growing rapidly in many Western economies.

Technology may also assist unions in formulating and running campaigns. Greer (2000) and others have commented on the value of online membership surveys for identifying members' opinions on industrial issues. Unions can also use websites to 'rally the troops' and manage members' concerns during industrial action when their commitment to the union can be significantly tested. Forums such as email and Twitter enable unions to take the membership's temperature on key issues during campaigns and to quickly organize meetings and determine member availability to take part in pickets, rallies and other actions. Prior to the arrival of the internet and email this required the deployment of considerable numbers of union officials and delegates.

The literature provides numerous examples of the ways unions use technology for these purposes at local, national and international levels. Internationally, web-based technologies have facilitated alliances between unions and community organizations. Newman (2005: 386) provided examples of alliances around fair trade and trade treaties which emerged in the 1990s. Web-based technologies have also been used to draw international attention to labour abuses by multinational corporations and to campaign against offending organizations through, for example, online petitions and email templates. Nike famously became 'a symbol of sweatshops' in the 1990s. The internet provided coalitions of unions and activists across the globe with opportunities to keep each other up to date with information and share and develop campaigning material and tools such as standardized letters and emails that could be used to place pressure on Nike to change its labour practices (Newman, 2005). As Lee optimistically argues, 'the internet internationalizes unions and is leading to a rebirth of classic trade union internationalism' (Lee, 2000: 60).

A notable example of the internet being used to express international voice is the website LabourStart, a labour news service established in 1998, and run by volunteers, which is published in 27 languages and has more than 100,000 direct subscribers and 500 syndicated unions globally. LabourStart has assisted unions on many campaigns (Gundogan, 2008). These have included a campaign seeking support for striking Suzuki workers in India, which led to the company and union resuming negotiations and ending a lengthy, bitter strike, and an email campaign calling for the release of two jailed Fijian trade unionists. Recently, LabourStart also established a social media platform, Unionbook.org that provides a central hub for dialogue between union members on Twitter, discussion boards and Facebook, as well as a forum for domestic unions to discuss campaigns. The 'Your Rights at Work' campaign in Australia is an example of the use of a 'virtual' campaign to raise awareness of draconian industrial laws and to bring about a change of government. Spearheaded by state and national peak union bodies, the 'virtual' campaign played an important role in strengthening the more traditional aspects of the campaign. Not only did the Australian Council of Trade Unions (ACTU) establish a website, MySpace and Facebook were also used to raise awareness and encourage people 'to share ideas and talk to each other'. As an online campaign officer stated, for the campaign to be successful, workers and concerned citizens 'have to be able to continue to talk to the ACTU, and we'll have to get better at talking back. The union movement traditionally do this well in workplaces and on the ground – doing it online is the next logical step' (Muir, 2008: 80).

While this is a powerful example of how technology can help unions and their members, it also serves to highlight some of the challenges presented by web-based voice. A key emerging challenge includes sabotage by hostile online participants. On occasion conservative 'trolls' tried to flood 'Your Rights at Work' campaign internet sites with provocative messages. Moreover, conservative politicians occasionally turned the words of rank and filers and activists against the campaign. This led to the ACTU introducing a time delay to allow posts to be edited. Although this effectively stopped opponents sabotaging the campaign, it also generated criticism that the union movement was stifling grassroots voice (Muir, 2008).

The potential for online communication as an organizing tool also has significant limitations, particularly given the vast differences in access to the required technologies both within countries and across the globe. Workers in developed countries increasingly have access to information technology, although even here access is not universal. More than 60 per cent of American union members have a computer, and 75 per cent have internet access (Hart, cited in Pinnock, 2005: 458). However, even where workers have access to information technology, it cannot be assumed that they have uniform levels of general literacy let alone the information technology literacy to use it effectively as a voice mechanism (Shostak, 2002). As well, even the most networked, computer-literate union member may suffer from information overload (Aalto-Matturi, 2005). Nevertheless, as the preceding discussion of sweatshop activism demonstrates, the internet may still play a role in improving working conditions globally. The extent to which this becomes a practical reality will depend heavily on the methods that collective organizations develop to surmount these challenges.

While scholars have identified the potential for internet technologies to bring unions and members closer together, some have suggested that use of these communication channels may have a distancing effect. Indeed, there is a risk that unions will simply become virtual customer service centres. Chaison (2005) argued that, as unions become more reliant on the internet for communicating with members, they run the risk of virtual meetings replacing face-to-face organizing.

> Organizing will simply become a matter of developing a website to attract potential members, connecting them with online organizers who can answer their questions, and collecting digital signatures on union authorization cards. As unions distance themselves from their members by relying on the Web, the members will react by evaluating the unions in terms of an exchange relationship . . . This evaluation will not be based on whether the union promotes social welfare or if supporting it is the right thing to do. Rather, unions will have turned themselves into websites, albeit very attractive and sophisticated ones, without realizing it. (Chaison, 2005: 399)

Freeman and Rogers (2002: 17) noted that 'Even cyber-supported members need some hands on attention. Members' loyalty and willingness to act on behalf of others, even more to recruit others, requires human contact and engagement and the shared experience of struggle.' Likewise, Shostak (1999) argued that more traditional forms of one-on-one and face-to-face interaction must, where possible, continue to be unions' primary mode of organizing and lobbying, with web-based communications acting as a support system.

Internal Democracy

A number of writers have suggested that 'e-voice' has the potential to facilitate union democracy (Stevens and Greer, 2005; Diamond and Freeman, 2002; Aalto-Matturi, 2005; Lee, 2000; Lucore, 2002; Newman, 2005). Lee (2000) argues that the internet 'democratizes unions, decentralizes them, makes them more transparent and open, weakens entrenched bureaucracies, and provides new tools for [the] rank-and-file activist'. Perhaps the most comprehensive early research on the subject was Greer's (2002) 'E-voice: How information technology is shaping life within unions', which, in addition to being a detailed source of primary research on early union websites, speculated extensively on the likely future implications of the internet for union democracy. Other scholars have commented on the potential that internet technologies have to empower union members both by facilitating communication between union members and improving communication between rank-and-file union members and senior union officials (Lucore, 2002). Generally this is seen as a positive development that has the capacity to re-energize unions. Scholars have, however, noted that it also has the capacity to undermine union solidarity and member confidence.

It is not the purpose of this chapter to enter into debates on the meaning of union democracy. In examining the implications of new technologies for union democracy we are referring to their impact on aspects of union democracy that may be most affected by information technology. These include members' participation and involvement in decision-making and in the development of policy, organizational priorities and union activities, and in their capacity to influence decisions and actions (Fairbrother, 1986).

Empirical evidence from the United States (Pinnock, 2005) and Finland (Aalto-Matturi, 2005) suggests that unions have been very effective at using the internet and email to improve downward, one-way communication within unions, from officials to their members. There is less evidence, however, of unions fully realizing the potential of the internet for two-way interaction between unions and their members. This point is illustrated by Stevens and Greer (2005) who studied the websites of 63 national unions in the United States, comparing the use made of these websites in 2001 and again in 2004–05. They found evidence of a statistically significant increase over the four years in the proportion of material posted on these sites that was concerned with member issues. Stevens and Greer interpreted this as indicating that unions were becoming more democratic and representative. But they did not find a significant change in the proportion of unions soliciting input from members through their websites on issues to do with employment negotiations, or in the proportion that had chat rooms or discussion board facilities. Indeed, fewer than one in five unions were actively soliciting members' views on negotiation or governance issues through online forums. Given the enormous growth in internet coverage and use since 2005, these patterns may have changed considerably since the research was done. Nonetheless, the study's findings do point to patterns that may be more enduring and warrant further examination, in particular, a disparate use of the web by different unions and a greater emphasis on its use for downward communication of information than for facilitating two-way dialogue.

Developments in information communication, however, do provide opportunities to enhance two-way voice (Aalto-Matturi, 2005; Lucore 2002). Greer (2002: 218) has observed that 'with the Internet there is now potential for the town meeting form of union democracy in cyber space, which Strauss (1991) noted was not feasible in larger unions only a few years ago'. Blogging is one example of how IT developments might facilitate not only information sharing, but also enhanced internal democracy and accountability, in the process providing a virtual meeting place. Pinnock (2005) reported that a number of unions and worker organizations in the United States had started to make use of blogs to widen and deepen communication with members and potential members. Examples include the postal workers (see Postalblog.com), the Teamsters (Teamsternation.blogspot.com), the Service Employees International Union's 'Unite to Win' blog, and the American Federation of Government Employees (AFGE) 'UnionBlog.com'. According to Pinnock (2005: 462), AFGE's UnionBlog 'is meant to be a tool by which workers can use their most authentic voice to share thoughts and views about things the union is involved in or concerned with'. In particular, the AFGE's blog aimed to gain the attention of younger members. Pinnock (2005) conducted interviews with AFGE officials and found considerable support for the effectiveness of UnionBlog. Pinnock quoted a communication specialist at AFGE:

> In my humble opinion, the greatest weakness of the traditional lines of communication . . . is that they are one-way. Information and ideas flow down from the top, but under traditional organizational models they are hindered from flowing upward. The traditional structure of organization . . . creates pressure to stifle ideas coming from below. Without a doubt, open lines of communication could generate a lot of dumb and bad ideas, but those . . . ideas could provide a spark for absolutely brilliant thoughts. Because UnionBlog enables open commu-

nications from the public, readers can learn . . . from so-called real people. (Pinnock, 2005: 462)

Not only do blogs offer unions the opportunity to gather and share information, and thus strengthen voice, they also help unions identify emerging trends and views through the analysis of blog comments. Blogs, however, are not without their drawbacks. Pinnock (2005: 463) pointed out that because blogs are open to commentary from anyone and the censorship of content is typically viewed with 'intense suspicion', unions will 'have to accept the fact that much of the experience will be out of their control'.

Web-based technology may enhance the voice of rank-and-file members, but may have unintended consequences for union leaders. Lucore (2002: 212) argued that unions must now be vigilant 'to answer unsubstantiated rumours and misinformation rapidly' as they are disseminated in cyberspace. A number of examples exist where a small group of union members have been able, through the use of web and email technology, to get rank-and-file members to mobilize against positions advocated by union leaders on particular issues. Both Lee (2000) and Lucore (2002) instanced a late 1990s campaign involving flight attendants at Northwest Airlines. A collective agreement that had been negotiated over a long period of time and recommended to members by union leaders was rejected following an online campaign initiated by a lone flight attendant who directly emailed other union members pointing out the inadequacies of the proposed agreement. Lee (2000) reported that something similar had occurred at American Airlines and in the United Kingdom with the Communication Workers Union.

Web-based technology can be used by individuals to push their own agendas. Greer (2002) observed that e-voice provides union members not only with an opportunity to air dissent at low cost, but also to establish and maintain blocs through factional websites from which they can project dissident views. It may be that the existence of factions is a criterion of union democracy, but, not surprisingly, it may also be a source of concern for union bureaucracies. Newman (2005) and Shostak (2005) have both noted that senior union officials were uneasy about the negative potential of the internet to fragment the 'unity' of union voice on an issue, but this must be set against the possibility that union leaders do not like the challenges to the status quo that the internet clearly facilitates. Future research may shed further light on how the internet might facilitate internal union democracy through enabling rank-and-file challenges to corrupt or inept union hierarchies.

CONCLUSION

The uptake of social media has outstripped analysis of its impact on employee voice. To date, much of the literature is speculative but raises many issues that warrant further investigation. This chapter serves as a starting point for researchers interested in web-based technologies and voice. It demonstrates the many opportunities that new technologies present for employees, managers and unions to enhance existing voice mechanisms. Web-based technologies are, however, a double-edged sword and present an array of challenges for the various actors. Employers and HR managers may introduce a range of new technologies, but if they are not properly resourced or employees are unsure how to access or use them, employee cynicism about the genuineness of management's voice initiatives may result, and, ultimately, voice mechanisms may fail to meet expectations. Web technologies also pose new challenges for management, such as the need for organizations to implement social media policies governing the use of these technologies, in light of the legal ramifications which may flow from social media use.

Internet technology also provides opportunities and challenges for collective voice, the nature and extent of which are still in their infancy. Proliferating social media have the potential to expand the scope, speed and reach of dialogue between unions and their members and to facilitate existing and new forms of industrial action. But the costs of developing online tools and facilities can be considerable and come at a time when union density and hence resources have been severely depleted in many countries.

Employees who express opinions on social media run the risk of damage to their reputation, which may affect their current or future employment opportunities. Social media are tools that are being used by activists and disenfranchised workers to draw attention to exploitative work conditions and thus pose a reputational risk for miscreant organizations. The recent suspension of all advertising from the radio programme of Australian 'shock jock' Allan Jones demonstrates the power of online campaigning. A sustained online campaign that included petitions and Facebook updates urging supporters to email organizations advertising on the programme quickly achieved its aim, but was also plagued by 'trolls'. Web-based technology is not the exclusive preserve of just one viewpoint.

Although this and previously mentioned examples highlight a range of potential consequences for employment relations actors, the existing literature remains too heavily based in speculation and description. Many of the existing studies to date adopt a normative approach, highlighting the potential of network and media technologies to enhance voice. To aid both understanding and practice, we need further in-depth research on how web-based technologies are shaping the development of employee voice, and the challenges, hurdles and solutions that are emerging along the way.

REFERENCES

Aalto-Matturi, S. (2005), 'The internet: the new workers' hall, the internet and new opportunities for the Finnish trade union movement', *Working USA: The Journal of Labor and Society*, **8** (4), 469–81.

Arvanitis, S. and E. Loukis (2009), 'Information and communication technologies, human capital, workplace organization and labour productivity: a comparative study based on firm-level data for Greece and Switzerland', *Information Economics and Policy*, **21** (1), 43–61.

Barbosa, D. and K. Bradsher (2012), 'Riot at Foxconn factory underscores rift in China', *New York Times*, 24 September, available at: http://www.nytimes.com/2012/09/25/business/global/foxconn-riot-underscores-labor-rift-in-china.html (accessed 26 September 2012).

Barnes, S. (2012), 'The differential impact of ICT on employees: narratives from a hi-tech organisation', *New Technology, Work and Employment*, **27** (2), 120–32.

Bell, K. (2012), 'Foxconn riot much worse than first thought: 10 reported dead', available at: http://www.cultofmac.com/192461/foxconn-riot-much-worse-than-first-thought-10-reported-dead/#UicijwxwA10tifGH.99 (accessed1 October 2012).

Business Link (2011), 'Establish employee voice in your business', http://www.businesslink.gov.uk/bdotg/action/layer?topicId=1084699063 (accessed 19 September 2012).

Chaison, G. (2002), 'Information technology: the threat to unions', *Journal of Labor Research*, **23** (2), 249–59.

Chaison, G. (2005), 'The dark side of information technology for unions', *Working USA: The Journal of Labor and Society*, **8** (4), 395–402.

Cote, M. (2007), 'Getting dooced: employee blogs and employer blogging policies under the National Labor Relations Act', *Washington Law Review*, **82** (1), 121–48.

Cullen, S. (2012), 'Linfox loses appeal over Truckie's Facebook comments', ABC News, 3 October, http://www.abc.net.au/news, accessed 3 October 2012.

D'Aprix, R. (2011), 'Cultivating a culture of open communication', *Communication World*, **28** (4), 28–32.

Diamond, W.J. and R.B. Freeman (2002), 'Will unionism prosper in cyberspace? The promise of the internet for employee organization', *British Journal of Industrial Relations*, **40** (3), 569–96.

Fairbrother, P. (1986), 'Union democracy in Australia: accommodation and resistance', *Journal of Industrial Relations*, **28** (2), 171–90.

Freeman, R.B. and J. Rogers (2002), 'Open source unionism: beyond exclusive collective bargaining', *Working USA: The Journal of Labor and Society*, **5** (4), 8–40.

Gely, R. and L. Bierman (2007), 'Social isolation and American workers: employee blogging and legal reform', *Harvard Journal of Law and Technology*, **20**, 287–331.

Greer, C. (2002), 'E-voice: how information technology is shaping life within unions', *Journal of Labor Research*, **23** (2), 215–35.

Gundogan, N. (2008), 'The trade union movement and the internet', unpublished conference paper, Midwest Political Science Association Congress, Chicago, 3–6 April.

Klaas, B., J. Olson-Buchanan and A. Ward (2012), 'The determinants of alternative forms of workplace voice: an integrated perspective', *Journal of Management*, **38** (1), 314–36.

Kupritz, V. and E. Cowell (2011), 'Productive management communication: online and face-to-face', *Journal of Business Communication*, **48** (1), 54–82.

Lee, E. (2000), 'How the internet is changing unions', *Working USA:The Journal of Labor and Society*, **4** (2), 56–72.

Lee, S., T. Hwang and H. Lee (2006), 'Corporate blogging strategies of the Fortune 500 companies', *Management Decision*, **44** (3), 316–34.

Lucore, R.E. (2002), 'Challenges and opportunities: unions confront the new information technologies', *Journal of Labor Research*, **23** (2), 201–14.

Mewburn, I. (2012), 'Academics behaving badly? Universities and online reputations', 'The Conversation', 27 September, available at: http://theconversation.edu.au/academics-behaving-badly-universities-and-online-reputations-9827 (accessed 29 September 2012).

Miles, S. and G. Muuka (2011), 'Employee choice of voice: a new workplace dynamic', *The Journal of Applied Business Research*, **27** (4), 91–103.

Muir, K. (2008), *Worth Fighting For: Inside the Your Rights at Work Campaign*, Sydney: UNSW Press.

Nancherla, A. (2010), 'Don't delete the e-messenger', *T+D*, **64** (2), 26.

Naslund, A. (2010), 'Social media from the inside out', *Communication World*, **27** (5), 36–9.

Newman, N. (2005), 'Is labor missing the internet third wave?', *Working USA: The Journal of Labor and Society*, **8** (4), 383–94.

Pauksztat, B. and R. Wittek (2011), 'Representative voice in different organizational contexts: a study of 40 departments of a Dutch childcare organization', *International Journal of Human Resource Management*, **22** (10), 2222–44.

Pilieci, V. and E. Stark (2013), 'Angry teachers take to social media to blast union over extracurricular activities', available at: http://www2.canada.com/ottawacitizen/news/city/story.html?id=6d5b159f-0d1c-4dd2-a236-e37aa035c3c2 (accessed 9 December 2013).

Pinnock, S.R. (2005), 'Organizing virtual environments: national union deployment of the blog and new cyberstrategies',*Working USA: The Journal of Labor and Society*, **8** (4), 457–68.

Richards, J. (2008), '"Because I need somewhere to vent": the expression of conflict through work blogs', *New Technology, Work and Employment*, **23** (1–2), 95–110.

Rochfort, S. (2011), 'CBA relaxes social media rules', *Sydney Morning Herald*, 24 May, available at: http://www.smh.com.au/business/cba-relaxes-social-media-rules-20110524-1f1kt.html (accessed 9 December 2013).

Roush, W. (2005), 'Sun Microsystems: blog heaven', *Technology Review*, April, 38.

Schoneboom, A. (2007), 'Diary of a working boy: creative resistance among anonymous workbloggers', *Ethnography*, **8** (4), 403–23.

Shostak, A.B. (1999), 'Organized labor's best bet? Cyberunions!', *Working USA: The Journal of Labor and Society*, **3** (4), 120–33.

Shostak, A.B. (2002), 'Today's unions as tomorrow's cyberunions: labor's newest hope', *Journal of Labor Research*, **23** (2), 237–48.

Shostak, A.B. (2005), 'On the state of cyberunionism: an American progress report', *Working USA: The Journal of Labor and Society*, **8** (4), 403–21.

Stevens, C.D. and C.R. Greer (2005), 'E-voice, the internet, and life within unions: riding the learning curve', *Working USA: The Journal of Labor and Society*, **8**, 439–55.

Tangirala, S. and R. Ramanujam (2012), 'Ask and you shall hear (but not always): examining the relationship between manager consultation and employee voice', *Personnel Psychology*, **65** (2), 251–82.

Taras, D. and A. Gesser (2003), 'How new lawyers use e-voice to drive firm compensation: the "Greedy Associates" phenomenon', *Journal of Labor Research*, **24** (1), 9–29.

Thornthwaite, L. (2013), 'Social media, unfair dismissal and the regulation of employees' conduct outside work', *Australian Journal of Labour Law*, October, **26** (2), 164–84.

Tindal, S. (2011), 'CBA gives in to union social media pressure', *ZDNet*, 24 May, available at: http://www.zdnet.com/cba-gives-in-to-union-social-media-pressure-1339315569/ (accessed 9 December 2013).

Vuori, M. (2012), 'Exploring uses of social media in a global corporation', *Journal of Systems and Information Technology*, **14** (2), 155–70.

28 Being psychologically present when speaking up: employee voice engagement
Jamie A. Gruman and Alan M. Saks

INTRODUCTION

Employee voice has important implications in organizations. Many serious organizational calamities, such as the crash of United Airlines flight 173, the Columbia space tragedy, and BP's Deepwater Horizon drilling rig explosion, were caused or intensified by the failure of employees to engage in voice about problems and anomalies (Morrison, 2011). In addition to having consequences for organizations, voice is also associated with individual-level outcomes such as job satisfaction and affective organizational commitment (Thomas et al., 2010).

Employee voice has been the subject of scientific inquiry since Hirschman's (1970) pioneering work on the outcomes associated with customer dissatisfaction (for example, Brinsfield et al., 2009). In this chapter, we extend the literature on employee voice by incorporating ideas from the employee engagement literature and introduce a new construct that we call employee voice engagement. First, we review the research on voice behavior and employee engagement and make note of some similarities between the two areas. Second, we introduce the construct employee voice engagement. We then develop a model of employee voice engagement in which we integrate the literature on employee engagement and employee voice. The chapter concludes with a discussion of the implications of our model for research and practice.

EMPLOYEE VOICE

The literature on employee voice presents no consensus on the definition of the construct. To begin, voice can be understood at two levels of analysis. First, it can represent a structural phenomenon that includes arrangements such as trade unions, collective bargaining, and grievance systems (Dundon et al., 2004). Second, it can represent an individual or group process that involves speaking up in organizations (Morrison, 2011). The present chapter discusses voice from the latter perspective.

LePine and Van Dyne (1998: 853) define voice as 'speaking out and challenging the status quo with the intent of improving the situation.' Similarly, Detert and Burris (2007: 869) suggest that voice involves 'the discretionary provision of information intended to improve organizational functioning to someone inside an organization with the perceived authority to act, even though such information may upset the status quo of the organization and its power holders.' Building on the work of Van Dyne et al. (1995), Liang et al. (2012) distinguish between promotive voice, which involves expressing ideas for improving an organization, and prohibitive voice, which involves speaking up to stop harm from occurring. However, not all definitions of voice involve the same degree of helpfulness. Brinsfield et al. (2009: 4) define voice more simply as 'the expression of ideas, information, opinions or concerns.'

The fact that voice has been defined in so many ways and examined from many different perspectives has led to confusion in the field (Brinsfield et al., 2009). In their review of the literature, Brinsfield et al. (2009) describe 18 different key concepts in the study of voice and silence in organizations, such as whistle-blowing, issue selling, and complaining. To provide focus and clarity, they propose three key features for distinguishing between the different forms of voice and silence: content (what is, or is not, being said?), target (to whom is, or is not, the message being said?), and motive (what is the intent of the behavior?). However, the degree to which such features provide focus and clarity is unclear because they are discrepant from other features recommended in an attempt to accomplish the same end. Specifically, Klass et al. (2012) suggested that the important features of voice are formality (whether or not structured processes or formal mechanisms are used), focus (whether voice is pro-social or justice-oriented), and identifiability (whether the sender of the message is identifiable or anonymous).

Morrison (2011: 375), building on the commonalities among numerous definitions of voice, defines the construct as 'discretionary communication of ideas, suggestions, concerns, or opinions about work-related issues with the intent to improve organizational or unit functioning.' This definition is consistent with the general sense in the literature that voice is a pro-social, voluntary act that has the goal of improving organizational functioning. However, as noted above, not all conceptualizations of voice include all these pro-social elements. In their typology of the different forms of voice and silence, Van Dyne et al. (2003) postulate what they refer to as acquiescent voice, which, motivated by employee resignation, involves the expression of ideas, but with no intention to improve the organization. Morrison (2011) takes issue with Van Dyne et al.'s (2003) notion of acquiescent voice, arguing that because it does not involve conveying suggestions for improvement it falls outside the definition of voice.

We argue, however, that Morrison's (2011) criticism is misguided. It is not only the act of speaking up that matters in organizations, but the *quality* of the ideas and concerns that are spoken. Because acquiescent voice reflects resignation, the quality of the ideas, suggestions, and other information conveyed by employees expressing acquiescent voice is likely to be inferior in quality to those expressing voice that reflects more constructive motives and involvement with work. It is important for organizations to understand the various factors that lead not only to voice, but to committed voice that reflects engagement with work. For example, an employee who has learned from experience that her supervisor is uninterested in hearing anyone else's ideas is likely to acquiesce to the supervisor's suggestions, reluctantly express agreement with his ideas, and only offer new suggestions that are in line with the boss's existing agenda. Thus, the employee may express voice, but not of a quality likely to foster innovation or learning, which is one of the main advantages of the expression of voice (Edmondson, 2003). We agree with Van Dyne et al. (2003) that acquiescent voice is an important topic.

In the present chapter, voice is conceptualized simply as speaking-up behavior (Van Dyne et al., 2003). In the next section, we review the literature on employee engagement in an effort to begin to think about what it means to be engaged in voice and to make a distinction between voice behavior and voice engagement.

EMPLOYEE ENGAGEMENT

In the past decade, there has been a significant increase in research on employee engagement (Albrecht, 2010). It has often been suggested that engagement is the key to an organization's success and competitiveness. Some have even suggested that engagement is 'essential' for contemporary organizations given the many challenges they face (Schaufeli and Salanova, 2007: 156). Engagement has been shown to be a key driver of individual attitudes, behavior, and performance as well as organizational performance, productivity, retention, financial performance, and even shareholder return (Bates, 2004; Baumruk, 2004; Harter et al., 2002; Richman, 2006). Two recent meta-analyses found that engagement is positively related to organizational commitment, task performance, contextual performance and health, and negatively related to turnover intentions (Christian et al., 2011; Halbesleben, 2010).

Although there is no agreement among scholars or practitioners on a specific definition of engagement, there exist both theoretical arguments and empirical evidence that engagement is a distinct psychological construct independent of other constructs such as organizational commitment and job satisfaction (Bakker et al., 2011). With this in mind, perhaps the most common mistake made by both practitioners and academics in conceptualizing and measuring engagement is conflating engagement with other, established constructs.

Both consulting firms and academics routinely incorporate constructs such as affective organizational commitment, proactive behavior, job satisfaction, and extra-role behavior in their definitions of engagement (Leiter and Bakker, 2010; Schaufeli and Bakker, 2010). However, Rich et al. (2010) found a different pattern of relationships between several antecedents and job involvement, job satisfaction, and intrinsic motivation compared to engagement in support of the distinctiveness of the engagement construct. They also found that engagement fully mediated the relationships between antecedents and performance even with the three other constructs included in the model. In line with Leiter and Bakker (2010) and Saks (2008), for conceptual, empirical, and practical reasons, we believe it preferable to regard employee engagement as a specific, well-defined motivational state that may be related to, but is independent of, other established constructs.

Leiter and Maslach (1998) view engagement as the opposite of burnout. They define engagement as 'an energetic experience of involvement with personally fulfilling activities that enhance a staff member's sense of professional efficacy' (Leiter and Maslach, 1998: 351) and consider it to be comprised of energy, involvement, and efficacy (Maslach et al., 2001).

Schaufeli et al. (2002) also view engagement as the conceptual opposite of burnout but view these constructs as independent states with dissimilar structures that must be measured with different instruments. They regard engagement as 'a positive fulfilling, work-related state of mind that is characterized by vigor, dedication, and absorption' (Schaufeli et al., 2002: 74). Rothbard (2001) and Saks (2006) similarly regard absorption as a critical component of engagement (the other component being attention).

Shaufeli and Salanova (2007) suggest that engaged employees are energetically and effectively connected to their work. This can occur through the investment of one's 'self' in work activities. In his study on engagement, Kahn (1990: 694) suggested that engagement involves 'the harnessing of organizational members' selves to their work roles.' By contrast, disengagement involves an extrication of organizational members' selves from their work roles. Kahn (1990: 700) further notes that:

> Personal engagement is the simultaneous employment and expression of a person's 'preferred self' in task behaviors that promote connections to work and to others, personal presence (physical, cognitive, and emotional), and active, full role performances.

Engagement involves high levels of energy and identification with one's work, in contradistinction to burnout which involves low levels of both (Schaufeli and Salanova, 2007). When engaged, people become physically involved in their tasks, cognitively alert, and ardently connected to others in ways that demonstrate their individuality (for example, thoughts, feelings, values, and so on). Enagagement allows people to simultaneously express their preferred selves and completely satify their role requirements (Kahn, 1990).

More generally, engagement means to be psychologically present when occupying and performing an organizational role (Kahn, 1990, 1992). When people are psychologically present they feel attentive, connected, integrated, and focused in their role performances (Kahn, 1992). People vary in the extent to which they draw on themselves in the performance of their roles or what Kahn (1990) refers to as 'self-in-role.' Thus, when people are engaged they keep their selves within the role they are performing. As described in the next section, there are some similarities between employee engagement and voice behavior.

EMPLOYEE VOICE BEHAVIOR AND EMPLOYEE ENGAGEMENT

In many ways, employee voice behavior and engagement are similar. In one of the few studies to link these topics, LePine and Van Dyne (1998) found that when highly satisfied employees worked in favorable group conditions (small or self-managed groups) they displayed more voice than their less satisfied counterparts. LePine and Van Dyne (1998) drew on Kahn's (1990) work on engagement to explain this finding. Specifically, they noted that when employees are engaged they are more mindful and vigilant in their work. They surmised that the satisfied employees in their study may also have been higher in engagement and that this led them to be more attentive and sensitive to information regarding group context, which signaled the appropriateness, desirability, or acceptability of engaging in voice.

As noted earlier, in their typology of the forms of voice and silence, Van Dyne et al. (2003) discuss what they refer to as acquiescent silence and acquiescent voice. Both constructs are related to engagement in that each reflects *dis*engagement as a result of resignation. Acquiescent silence involves intentionally passive, uninvolved behavior, and is reflected in employees' unwillingness to speak up. Van Dyne et al. (2003) explicitly note that this form of silence represents disengagement as per Kahn's (1990) original formulation. Acquiescent voice involves disengaged behavior reflecting the perception of being unable to make a difference and is reflected in employee comments such as 'that's fine with me' or 'whatever you think' (Van Dyne et al., 2003). One implication of Van Dyne et al.'s (2003) typology is that if organizations want to foster meaningful, valuable voice they need to have engaged employees. In short, higher quality voice might be a form of employee engagement.

Burris et al. (2008) hypothesized that employees who were psychologically attached to their organizations would demonstrate higher levels of voice to supervisors, and that conversely, those who were psychologically detached would demonstrate lower levels of voice. They explained that this would occur partly because attachment and detachment should be associated with employee engagement and disengagement respectively. However, Burris et al. (2008) operationalized attachment using a measure of affective organizational commitment, and detachment using a measure of intention to leave. They did not measure engagement directly. Thus, although they provide interesting speculations, their results do not shed light on the empirical relations between engagement and voice, but do suggest an association.

In his conceptual discussion of the conditions that may foster voice, Beugré (2010) suggests that because voice increases perceptions of fairness, employees who are offered the opportunity to express voice are more likely to be engaged. Beugré also suggests that four boundary conditions may influence this association: the value of voice, the degree to which voice is considered by decision-makers, the degree to which voice is expected, and the degree to which voice corresponds to cultural values. Thus, in contrast to the sequence suggested by Van Dyne et al. (2003), the implication in Beugré's work is that voice may lead to engagement.

More recently, Kassing et al. (2012) examined the relationship between engagement and dissent, a form of voice that involves sharing disagreement about workplace practices and polices. Specifically, using a convenience sample of 137 full-time employees, Kassing et al. (2012) explored the associations between engagement, turnover intentions, and three forms of dissent: voice directed towards superiors (upward dissent), voice directed towards co-workers (lateral dissent), and voice directed to people outside of work (displaced dissent). Results revealed that upward dissent was positively associated with engagement. However, lateral dissent was negatively associated with engagement and positively associated with turnover intentions. These results suggest that voice directed upwards in organizations may reflect higher levels of engagement, but voice directed towards co-workers may reflect reduced engagement and general dissatisfaction, and may be an early signal of intentions to leave.

Finally, a recent study by Rees et al. (2013) found that employee perceptions of voice behavior directed at the group were positively related to employee engagement. Furthermore, this relationship was partially mediated by trust in senior management and the employee–line manager relationship. In other words, employees who speak up are more engaged, in part because they trust senior management and have a stronger relationship with line managers.

Thus, although relatively little attention has been given to the relationship between voice and engagement, a few conceptual and empirical works have suggested an association. There are, in fact, a number of reasons to believe that voice and engagement should demonstrate some degree of association. First, both voice and engagement are associated with similar antecedents and consequences. Building on Hirschman's (1970) pioneering work, Farrell (1983) suggested that job dissatisfaction can lead to a number of outcomes including voice or neglect. What Farrell (1983) termed neglect – a passive form of conduct involving 'lax and disregardful behavior . . . temporary abandonment and psychological inattention' (Farrell, 1983: 598) – would today be referred to as disengagement. Considered in a more positive light, job satisfaction has been shown to be associated with both voice (Thomas et al., 2010) and engagement (Saks, 2006; Schaufeli et al., 2008). Thus, voice and engagement share similar if not overlapping nomological networks of antecedents and outcomes.

Second, voice and engagement may be related because they share construct space. For example, both voice and engagement involve expressing the self. As noted earlier, Kahn (1990) described personal engagement as involving the expression of an individual's self in the performance of a role. Similarly, Ashford and Barton (2007) note that voice can take the form of identity-based issue selling in which employees speak up because it is important to their identities. Thus, both engagement and voice can be manifestations of the expression of oneself in one's work role.

A third reason that voice and engagement may be related is because both can be outcomes of favorable social exchanges, and represent forms of repayment for resources an organization provides. Social exchange theory posits that, over time, relationships develop into mutual commitments, based on particular exchange rules, such as reciprocity (Cropanzano and Mitchell, 2005). Saks (2006) argues that when employees receive resources from their employers, one way for them to repay the organization is through engagement. Similarly, employee voice can be considered as a way to repay an organization for providing resources that employees want or that they need in order to do their work (LePine and Van Dyne, 1998; Tucker et al., 2008). In a similar vein, Rees et al. (2013) note that employees build reciprocal relationships with managers and when they are provided with opportunities for voice they respond with heightened engagement. Klaas et al. (2012) suggest that, particularly when employees have positive attitudes towards their supervisors, they may feel obliged to reciprocate in the form of pro-social voice.

In summary, there is both conceptual and empirical evidence to suggest that employee voice and work engagement are related and that they both represent an expression of one's true self in the performance of a role or task. Although some have suggested that employee engagement might be an antecedent of voice behavior (Van Dyne et al., 2003) or that opportunities for voice might be an antecedent of engagement (Beugré, 2010), we argue that one can conceive of voice behavior as a specific form of work engagement. In other words, if employees vary in their engagement when they perform their work roles, they are also very likely to differ in how engaged they are when they speak up. As described in the next section, we refer to this form of employee engagement as employee voice engagement.

EMPLOYEE VOICE ENGAGEMENT

What is the difference between voice behavior and voice engagement? As indicated earlier, voice behavior is simply the act of speaking up. By contrast, voice engagement reflects the degree of absorption, attention, and self-in-role when speaking up, and is similar to employee engagement. Employee engagement has been described as a form of discretionary behavior (Macey and Schneider, 2008) and so has voice behavior. That is, employees make a conscious and deliberate decision regarding whether they will speak up (Morrison, 2011). As described by Morrison (2011: 375), 'voice is defined as discretionary behavior. Individuals choose whether or not to engage in this behavior at any particular moment in time, a choice that is affected by a variety of factors.' Thus, employees choose to engage or not to engage in the performance of a role (Kahn, 1990) and they choose whether or not to speak up or voice about important workplace issues (Morrison, 2011).

As described by Kahn (1990: 694), when engaged, individuals bring themselves fully into a role and they 'employ and express themselves physically, cognitively, and emotionally during role performances.' Furthermore, when individuals are disengaged, they remove their personal selves during their performance. According to Kahn (1990: 694), 'in personal disengagement, people withdraw and defend themselves physically, cognitively, or emotionally during role performances.' The notion of withdrawal is akin to acquiescent silence as described earlier. As described by Morrison (2011: 377), 'An employee displays silence when he or she possesses input that could be valuable to share but does not do so, typically because of fear, concerns about negative repercussions, or feelings of futility.' This is in effect a form of disengagement. Thus, one can think of voice engagement as a continuum from absolute silence (disengagement) to being fully absorbed in the employment and expression of one's true self when speaking up (engagement).

In the context of Kahn's (1990) definition of engagement, voice can be considered a form of self-expression in which individuals vary in terms of the extent to which they are attentive, absorbed, and involved in the act of speaking up. Thus, just as employees can bring varying degrees of themselves to the performance of a work role (Kahn, 1990), they can employ varying degrees of themselves when they speak up. And just as employees can vary in the extent to which they are psychologically present in the performance of a role, they can vary in the extent to which they are psychologically present when they speak up.

Therefore, we argue that voice behavior is the act of speaking up, and some employees speak up more than others. Voice engagement, however, is the depth and degree to which an individual employs and expresses his or her true voice when speaking up. In other words, employees not only differ in terms of whether or not they speak up (that is, voice behavior), but they can also differ in terms of how engaged they are when they do speak up. Thus, employees can vary in the extent to which they express and employ their true and personal selves when they speak up.

How then do we distinguish or differentiate voice behavior from voice engagement? We suggest that voice behavior is just the act of speaking up whereas voice engagement has to do with the extent to which an individual fully employs and expresses his/her true self when speaking up. Thus, voice engagement involves the expression of one's real identity, thoughts, and feelings; when fully engaged in voice, individuals do not shy away from exhibiting what they really think and feel about something. When individuals speak up but are not engaged, they hide their true identity, thoughts, and feelings (Kahn, 1990).

Furthermore, we argue that voice engagement is a function of four dimensions of voice that have been recognized in the voice literature: voice frequency, voice type, voice target, and voice quality. We argue that higher scores on each of these dimensions represent increasing depths or degrees of voice engagement. As described below, voice engagement can be treated as an individual-level as well as an organizational-level construct. In other words, just as individuals can vary in terms of how engaged they are in voice, so can organizations. In the remainder of this section, we describe the four dimensions of voice engagement.

Voice Frequency

The first and most basic dimension of voice engagement is the frequency or the amount of voice behavior exhibited by an individual. As noted by Morrison (2011), much of the research on voice behavior has been concerned with factors that increase or decrease the amount of voice behavior engaged in by employees. Thus, voice engagement is partly a function of the frequency with which an employee speaks up. Employees who speak up more often are exhibiting a higher degree of voice engagement than those who only occasionally or rarely speak up. At the organizational level, voice engagement is greater in organizations where employees as a group frequently speak up.

Voice Type

A second dimension of voice engagement is the content of voice, otherwise referred to as the type of voice. Various types of voice have been identified in the voice literature, such as how to improve an organizational problem, unfairness or misconduct, or any issue of importance (Morrison, 2011). Klass et al. (2012) have noted that research has examined a wide variety of voice types such as pro-social voice, grievance filing, whistle-blowing, informal complaints, and participation in suggestion systems. Morrison (2011) identified three types of voice: suggestion-focused voice, problem-focused voice, and opinion-focused voice. Regardless of the typology employed, the point is that some employees will engage in one or few types of voice while others will engage in many types of voice. Employees who participate in more types of voice are thus exhibiting a higher degree of voice engagement. Organizations in which employees use many types of voice have higher voice engagement.

Voice Target

The third dimension of voice engagement is voice target. Employees can speak up to various targets such as their direct supervisor, co-workers, members of other departments, management, and so on. Some employees choose to limit what they have to say to just one target (for example, supervisor) while others choose to voice their ideas or concerns to several targets (for example, co-workers, other members of the organization, and so on). Therefore, the extent to which an employee is engaged in voice behavior is also a function of the number of targets that they speak up to. An employee who directs his/her voice behavior to many targets is more engaged in voice. When an employee limits his/her voice to only one target s/he is less engaged in voice behavior. Similarly, organizations in which employees speak up to many targets have a higher degree of voice engagement than those where employees limit their voice to one or few targets.

Voice Quality

The fourth dimension of voice engagement is voice quality. As indicated earlier, voice behavior can vary in terms of the quality of the ideas and concerns that are spoken. The quality dimension captures the amount and substance of the contribution made by an employee when s/he engages in voice behavior. For example, two employees might speak up about a matter of importance to the organization but differ in terms of how much information they provide and the substantive nature of what they communicate. The employee who provides more information and information that is more substantive is providing greater voice quality than the employee who says very little or offers very shallow or limited comments. The employee who provides more information and more substantive information is more fully expressing his/her true beliefs and feelings and is therefore more engaged in voice behavior. When employees say very little and what they say is not very deep, they are less engaged in voice behavior. Similarly, organizations in which employees provide more information and more substantive information when they speak up have a higher level of voice engagement.

Summary

In summary, we have argued that voice behavior can vary from individual to individual (and across organizations) in terms of the extent to which an individual fully engages him or herself when exhibiting voice behavior. Individuals who exhibit high levels of voice engagement are frequently involved in voice behavior, exhibit many different types of voice behavior, direct their voice to many targets, and provide quality information when they speak up. This of course begs the question, why are some individuals more engaged in voice than others? In the next section, we try to answer this question and develop a model of employee voice engagement.

A MODEL OF EMPLOYEE VOICE ENGAGEMENT

Research on employee voice has often focused on the determinants of voice behavior (Klaas et al., 2012). As noted by Liang et al. (2012), most models of voice contend that selected psychological variables are causal antecedents of voice, but voice may, in fact, be an outcome, in addition to a precursor of certain psychological variables.

Morrison (2011) suggests that contextual (for example, leadership style) and individual (for example, role definitions) factors lead employees to consider two key issues in deciding whether or not to speak up. The first issue is the perceived costs versus safety of voice, which reflects an employee's judgment of the risks associated with speaking up. The second issue is the perceived efficacy versus futility of voice, which reflects an employee's beliefs about whether speaking up will be effective. In their review of the determinants of alternative forms of voice, Klaas et al. (2012) identified a number of commonalities and differences with respect to different forms of voice. Some of the commonalties of voice include traits, issues of risk and safety of using voice, and the utility of voice.

We suggest that some of the determinants of voice behavior will also be important for voice engagement, as will some of the determinants of employee engagement. Thus, the extent to which employees fully place themselves into the act of speaking up and are psychologically present will also be a function of the factors that are associated with employee engagement. In other words, some determinants of voice engagement will have their basis in the engagement literature to the extent that voice engagement is a specific form of employee engagement.

To understand what factors might determine voice engagement, we refer to Kahn's (1990) ethnographic study of personal engagement. Kahn (1990) suggested that three psychological conditions serve as antecedents of personal engagement: psychological meaningfulness, psychological safety, and psychological availability.

Psychological meaningfulness refers to one's belief regarding how meaningful it is to bring oneself into a role performance. It is associated with incentives to engage and the perception that one is receiving a return on investment of one's 'self-in-role.' Psychological meaningfulness is achieved when people feel worthwhile, valuable, useful, and that they matter and are not taken for granted. Kahn (1990) found that employees' experiences of psychological meaningfulness were associated with higher levels of engagement.

Psychological safety involves the perception of how safe it is to bring oneself into a role peformance without fear of negative consequences to one's self-image, status or career. It is associated with reliable, predictable social environments that have clear boundaries of acceptable conduct in which people feel safe to risk self-expression. Kahn (1990) found that higher levels of psychological safety were associated with engagement.

Psychological availability pertains to one's perception of how available one is to bring oneself into a role. It involves the perception of having the physical, emotional, and psychological resources needed to invest and engage oneself in role performances. It has to do with how ready one is to engage in the performance of a role. Kahn (1990) found that employees were more likely to engage themselves in situations in which they were more psychologically available.

May et al. (2004) operationalized Kahn's (1990) psychological states and developed a scale to assess the expression of self physically, cognitively, and emotionally in a work role. In support of Kahn's (1990) model, they found that meaningfulness, safety, and availability were significantly related to engagement. They also found that job enrichment and role fit were positive predictors of meaningfulness; rewarding co-worker and supportive supervisor relations were positive predictors of safety while adherence to co-worker norms and self-consciousness were negative predictors; and having resources available was a positive predictor of psychological availability while participation in outside activities was a negative predictor.

Research on voice behavior has found that some of Kahn's psychological conditions are important for voice. For example, using a two-wave panel design, Liang et al. (2012) examined three antecedents of promotive and prohibitive voice: psychological safety, felt obligation for constructive change, and organization-based self-esteem. They found that, after controlling for a number of variables, all three antecedents positively predicted changes in both forms of voice six weeks later. Like Morrison's (2011) precursors, the antecedents of voice examined by Liang et al. (2012) map neatly onto the psychological conditions that Kahn (1990) identified as antecedents of engagement.

Specifically, psychological safety is, itself, one of the psychological conditions advanced by Kahn (1990). Felt obligation for constructive change involves the extent to which employees believe that they are required to produce productive changes (Morrison and Phelps, 1999). Such feelings will increase the significance and meaningfulness of the work in which one engages, thus satisfying Kahn's (1990) condition of psychological meaningfulness. Organization-based self-esteem reflects the degree to which employees have a sense of 'personal adequacy' and self-perceptions of being 'effectual and worthwhile' at work (Pierce et al., 1989: 625). Thus, organizational-based self-esteem is a personal resource that satisfies Kahn's (1990) condition of psychological availability.

We suggest that Kahn's (1990) psychological conditions for producing personal engagement may also reflect the conditions necessary for promoting employee voice engagement. Of note is that assessments of the perceived cost versus safety of speaking up are similar to Kahn's (1990) psychological safety condition for producing engagement. Employees' beliefs regarding the value of speaking up are similar to believing that it is meaningful to invest oneself in one's role, which Kahn (1990) also found was a precursor of engagement.

Therefore, to be fully engaged when speaking up in organizations, employees need to feel safe (psychological safety), they need to feel that speaking up will be worthwhile (psychological meaningfulness), and they need to feel that they have the organizational and/or personal resources necessary to speak up (psychological availability). The presence or absence of these conditions will contribute to an organizational climate fostering the expression of employees' selves in their voice, or voice engagement.

Organizational climate pertains to collective perceptions about the policies, practices, and behaviors that are rewarded and encouraged in a particular work environment (Kuenzi and Schminke, 2009). Scholars within both the engagement and voice literatures have suggested that the climate of an organization will influence the relative levels of these phenomena. Bakker et al. (2011) argue that when organizations create a climate in which employees perceive that that their psychological needs are being met, they are more likely to become engaged. Similarly, Morrison (2011) suggests that voice climate is a phenomenon that may influence voice behavior. In an empirical investigation, Morrison et al. (2011) found that group voice climate was a strong predictor of voice behavior, even after controlling for individual attitudes (satisfaction and identification) and individual perceptions of climate. Thus, shared perceptions of voice climate had a significant effect on the display of voice.

However, the question of whether climate should be conceptualized as involving shared perceptions or a shared group of conditions is an unresolved issue in the climate literature (Denison, 1996). Nonetheless, there is evidence that members of work groups develop collective beliefs about the safety and efficacy of voice that impact individual voice behavior (Morrison, 2011). Along these lines, we propose that Kahn's three psychological antecedents of engagement serve as a useful set of conditions that help to create an organizational climate that is favorable to promoting voice engagement.

Furthermore, Kahn (1990) described how employees unconsciously ask themselves three questions in each situation and then decide to engage or disengage depending on the answers. We suggest that in the context of voice engagement, employees ask themselves three similar questions when deciding if they should engage in voice: 1. *How meaningful is it for me to speak up in this situation?* 2. *How safe is it to speak up in this situation?* And 3. *How available am I to speak up in this situation?*

Figure 28.1 depicts a model of employee voice engagement. Below we briefly review

Antecedents of the psychological   Psychological conditions   Voice engagement
conditions for voice climate   (voice climate)

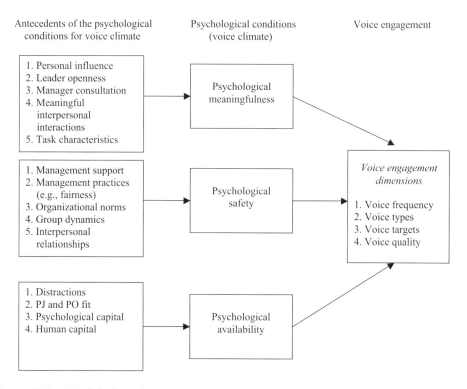

Figure 28.1   Model of employee voice engagement

some of the antecedents that can satisfy Kahn's (1990) three psychological conditions and discuss how each condition may serve as an antecedent of employee voice engagement. Note that in the context of voice behavior, each of the psychological conditions is specific to voice. In other words, we are concerned with the extent to which employees believe that it is meaningful and safe for them to engage in voice and that they have the necessary resources to engage themselves in voice behavior.

Psychological Meaningfulness

Kahn (1990) observed that, among other things, psychological meaningfulness is promoted via role characteristics that allow people to exercise influence. Being influential gives people a sense of being valued. He also observed that meaningful interpersonal work interactions that encourage dignity and a sense of being useful and valued promote meaningfulness.

Psychological meaningfulness may also be a predictor of employee voice engagement. It seems reasonable to expect that employees will be more likely to be engaged when they speak up if they believe that their input is important and valued, and that they can be influential in their team, work unit or organization. Indeed, one of the reasons employees fail to exercise voice in organizations is that they believe it is futile – that speaking up will not make a difference (Milliken et al., 2003). Burris et al. (2008) have shown that employee perceptions of the futility of voice are, in fact, negatively associated with supervisors' ratings of employee voice. Conversely, Venkataramani and Tangirala (2010) demonstrated that employee work-flow centrality increases voice. These authors note that work-flow centrality provides employees with personal influence, which may motivate them to speak up about work-related matters. In fact, Venkataramani and Tangirala (2010) found that personal influence fully mediated the relationship between work-flow centrality and voice.

Leader openness is positively associated with voice. Klass et al. (2012) suggest that leader openness will influence voice not only because of its role in producing psychological safety (discussed below), but also because it signals that the input employees provide will actually be used. They also note that the exercise of voice may be associated with feelings of being a valued and respected member of a group. All of these factors will satisfy the antecedent condition of psychological meaningfulness.

Tangirala and Ramanujam (2012) suggest that managers who consult with employees on work-related matters will engender voice because employees will feel more influential by having a greater impact on outcomes. In a test of their hypothesis, Tangirala and Ramanujam (2012) surveyed nurses about the degree to which their managers consulted with them on work-related issues, and their perceived influence, in addition to other variables. Managers rated the frequency with which nurses engaged in upward voice. Results revealed that, as expected, manager consultation was positively related to employee voice. Further, nurses' perceived influence fully mediated the relationship between manager consultation and employee voice. These results provide strong evidence that psychological meaningfulness may be a significant antecedent of voice engagement.

Kahn (1990) also found that task characteristics influence psychological meaningfulness. Employees were more likely to experience meaningfulness when they were doing work that was challenging and somewhat autonomous. In the employee engagement literature, job characteristics have been found to be a strong predictor of engagement (Christian et al., 2011; Saks, 2006). As indicated earlier, May et al. (2004) found that job enrichment was positively related to meaningfulness. We expect that job characteristics that provide employees with control and autonomy will be especially important for meaningfulness in the context of voice engagement. That is, employees will experience greater meaningfulness when they have control over their work, which will in turn motivate them to fully engage themselves in voice.

Psychological Safety

Voice often involves risk (Morrison, 2011) so employees look for cues in the work environment that suggest whether or not the organizational context is favorable for speaking up (Dutton et al., 2002). Specifically, employees try to ascertain whether or not it is safe for them to express themselves. Liang et al. (2012: 77) suggest that psychological safety represents the 'baseline condition' for voice to occur. However, many of the conditions that encourage employee perceptions of safety remain unknown (Klaas et al., 2012). Insight into the conditions that foster perceptions of safety may be gleaned from Kahn's (1990) study of the precursors of engagement. Recall that like voice, engagement also involves a consideration of the potential negative consequences to one's self-image, status or career.

Among the factors that Kahn (1990) found influenced perceptions of psychological safety were management practices, interpersonal relationships, organizational norms, and group dynamics. Kahn (1990) found that management practices that fostered psychological safety were supportive, open, clear, consistent, and predictable. Supportive managerial environments allowed employees to experiment without fear of the consequences. A recent meta-analysis found that social support as well as transformational leadership and leader–member exchange were positively related to work engagement (Christian et al., 2011). The same conditions and leadership style appear necessary to promote workplace voice. Employees need to feel as though their managers are supportive and open to hearing comments and suggestions, that management will be consistent in entertaining and encouraging divergent opinions, and will not retaliate if their own positions are threatened.

There is a fair amount of research demonstrating the importance of supportive management practices in fostering voice, and a general consensus that such practices are necessary for voice to occur (Detert and Burris, 2007; Edmondson, 2003; Walumbwa and Schaubroeck, 2009). According to Morrison (2011), one of the most important cues about whether it is safe to voice is the behavior of the immediate supervisor. Further, perceptions of one's supervisor affect the frequency of voice behavior. Consistent with the practices identified by Kahn (1990), Saunders et al. (1992) argued that voice to supervisors is more likely to occur when employees perceive that their supervisors are consistent and fair in decision-making, easy to approach, and will not seek retribution when employees speak up. In support of their hypothesis, Saunders et al. (1992) found that employees who perceived their managers in this favorable way were indeed more likely to engage in voice.

Other research has specifically examined the relationships between management practices, psychological safety, and voice. For example, Detert and Burris (2007) found that manager openness and transformational leadership were positively related to subordinates' levels of voice, and that these relationships were partially mediated by psychological safety. In a second study, Detert and Burris (2007) found that psychological safety fully mediated the relationship between manager openness and voice. Similarly, Walumbwa and Schaubroeck (2009) found that psychological safety partially mediated the relationship between ethical leadership and employee voice.

Specific management practices that help to foster psychological safety include downplaying status differences and displaying humility (Edmondson, 2003), being fair and just in decision-making (Hsiung, 2012), providing individualized consideration and other components of transformational leadership (Liu et al., 2010), and being open to input (Detert and Burris, 2007).

Kahn (1990) observed that psychological safety was also associated with behavior that conformed to organizational norms. Organizational norms involve rules of conduct concerning appropriate and inappropriate behavior (Cialdini et al., 1990). Organizational climates that are favorable to producing voice engagement will likely be characterized by organizational norms that make speaking up a safe and acceptable form of behavior. In environments in which organizational norms favor speaking up, those who demonstrate voice are perceived as having more pro-social motives and as more likable (Whiting et al., 2012). As noted by Korte (2009), one of the primary sources of learning about norms for appropriate behavior is an employee's supervisor. Supervisors who create an environment in which employees feel free to express themselves are likely to foster norms that favor voice.

Kahn's (1990) research also uncovered the fact that group dynamics played a part in producing psychological safety. He observed that the members of groups manifest unconscious roles that define their status and this status makes it more or less safe to engage oneself. These roles were part of larger 'plays' that connected members through unconscious coalitions (Kahn, 1990: 709). Once occupying a particular role, employees had varying amounts of latitude to safely express themselves in their role. For example, Kahn (1990) found that organizational tenure influenced the unconscious role occupied by members and that old and new members felt safer interacting in situations involving members of their own cohort. The various levels of psychological safety fostered by group dynamics may similarly influence employee voice engagement. For example, Tangirala and Ramanujam (2012) found that employees with longer tenure in their organizations tended to display more upward voice. Longer serving members may unconsciously perceive themselves as occupying a more privileged, higher status position in the organizational 'family' and thus have more latitude with respect to their ability to safely express themselves. This may also explain why the relationship between the opportunity to express oneself and intent to remain is lower for employees with longer tenure (Avery et al., 2011). Longer tenured employees, who already have higher privilege and status, may be relatively indifferent to privilege afforded by being given the opportunity to speak up.

Taken together, the preceding discussion suggests that psychological safety will be more common in organizational climates that feature managers who are open to voice and implement practices that make this clear to employees, strive to develop workgroup norms that encourage voice, develop trusting and supportive relationships, and are sensitive to the roles played by various group members, some of whom may be reluctant to speak up.

Psychological Availability

The third antecedent of engagement that Kahn (1990) identified was psychological availability, which reflects the extent to which employees are able to engage themselves at work as a result of the level of various resources they have available to them. He suggested that four distractions compromised psychological availability: depletion of physical energy, depletion of emotional energy, outside lives, and insecurity. These distractions interfere with people's ability to cope successfully, which is what psychological availability supports.

These same distractions may affect employee voice engagement. Being physically fatigued may reduce employees' ability or motivation to speak up. Depletion of emotional energy from, for example, handling customer complaints may leave employees emotionally exhausted and interfere with the expression of voice. Distractions at home that produce work–family conflict may hinder employees' ability or willingness to consider workplace improvements and engage in voice.

The one distraction that has received some attention in the voice literature is insecurity. As described by Kahn (1990), insecurity which interferes with engagement can occur because employees are self-conscious, ambivalent about their fit with the organization, or lack self-confidence. Self-consciousness interferes with engagement because it leads people to be preoccupied with the judgments of other people, and to be focused on managing impressions instead of freely engaging in their role. The voice literature has considered the political aspects of speaking up (for example, Milliken et al., 2003; Morrison and Rothman, 2009), thus addressing aspects of self-consciousness. However, there is a dearth of work in the voice literature pertaining to employees' perceived fit with their organizations.

Person–job (PJ) fit and person–organization (PO) fit are associated with numerous organizational outcomes including job satisfaction, commitment, and intent to quit (Kristof-Brown et al., 2005). When employees feel that there is some degree of congruence between themselves and their jobs and/or organizations they may be less distracted and more motivated and able to consider ideas and offer suggestions.

Another aspect of distraction that has received some attention in the voice literature relates to the personal resource of self-confidence. It is possible that employees who lack the perceived skill or confidence in their work-related knowledge may resist speaking up in the workplace (Tangirala and Ramanujam, 2012). The self-confidence-related construct that has received the most attention in the voice literature is self-esteem (LePine and Van Dyne, 1998; Liang et al., 2012; Premeaux and Bedeian, 2003). LePine and Van Dyne (1998) found that, after partialling out a number of control variables, global self-esteem was a marginally significant predictor of voice six months later. They also found that global self-esteem interacted with group size and management style in predicting voice behavior, such that employees with low self-esteem displayed less voice when working in a large group or under a traditional management style. Similarly, as noted earlier, Liang et al. (2012) found that organization-based self-esteem was a predictor of voice measured six weeks later.

A more direct measure of confidence is self-efficacy, which refers to 'an individual's conviction or confidence about his or her abilities to mobilize the motivation, cognitive resources, and courses of action needed to successfully execute a specific task within a given context' (Stajkovic and Luthans, 1998: 66). Saks and Gruman (2011) found that self-efficacy was positively related to the engagement of organizational newcomers. It would appear that self-efficacy may be an important personal resource that helps employees to be psychologically available to engage in voice.

Self-efficacy has recently been included as part of a higher-order construct known as psychological capital, or PsyCap, which is also comprised of hope, optimism, and resiliency (Luthans and Youssef, 2004). Recent research has demonstrated that the variables that comprise PsyCap are positively associated with engagement (Avey et al., 2008; Bakker and Demerouti, 2008; Xanthopoulou et al., 2007).

PsyCap, and the variables that comprise it, may also influence employees' psychological availability and have an effect on voice engagement. For example, optimists tend to take credit for successes (Sweetman and Luthans, 2010). Employees who are optimistic may be more likely to believe that their input will lead to a successful outcome and may be more likely to fully engage themselves when they speak up. Hope involves a belief that one can think of pathways to achieve goals and develop the motivation to pursue them (Sweetman and Luthans, 2010). Employees who are hopeful may be more creative in thinking of ways to benefit the organization and methods to implement improvements, and thus be more likely to engage themselves in voice. Resiliency involves the ability to recover from adversity and successfully address difficulties (Sweetman and Luthans, 2010). Employees who have higher resiliency may be better able to handle challenges to their ideas and be more likely to persist in offering thoughts and suggestions at work. Thus, psychological capital may represent an important personal resource for employees that helps to satisfy Kahn's (1990) condition of psychological availability which we expect will be associated with higher levels of employee voice engagement.

Finally, we also expect that human capital will be an important factor leading to psychological availability. Human capital refers to individuals' knowledge, skills, and abilities. Education, experience, and training are important for the development of human capital which plays an important role in performance (Crook et al., 2011). In the context of voice engagement, human capital is an important resource as one's ability to provide meaningful voice will be influenced by one's human capital. In other words, employees with greater human capital will be more psychologically available to fully engage themselves in voice.

Summary

In summary, we have proposed that Kahn's (1990) three psychological conditions for personal engagement can also be considered important conditions of voice engagement and in combination represent a climate for voice. Further, as shown in Figure 28.1, we have identified a host of factors that are likely to facilitate each of the psychological conditions and promote a positive voice climate.

IMPLICATIONS FOR RESEARCH AND PRACTICE

In this chapter, we have attempted to extend the domain of voice behavior by introducing the construct of employee voice engagement. Based on Kahn's (1990) work on personal engagement, we defined employee voice engagement as the extent to which employees fully employ and express their true selves when they engage in voice behavior. Further, we suggest that employee voice engagement is a function of the frequency, types, targets, and quality of voice behavior. Specifically, employees who are fully engaged in voice behavior speak up more frequently, use numerous types of voice, direct their voice to many targets, and the information they convey when they speak up is of high quality.

In addition to expanding the domain of employee voice, the voice engagement construct also extends the literature on employee engagement. Most of the research on employee engagement has treated engagement as a general and broad construct even though engagement can vary as a function of a specific task or role (Saks, 2008). For example, a professor might be highly engaged when s/he works on research but much less engaged when teaching. In this chapter, we have suggested a more precise and specific form of engagement in the workplace, which is associated with voice behavior. This represents an extension of the engagement construct beyond the more broad and general form of work engagement that has been the focus of engagement research.

Research on employee voice has focused on whether or not employees speak up rather than the degree or extent to which they do so. The voice engagement construct offers a number of new directions for future research on employee voice. For starters, there is a need to develop a measure of voice engagement. This should follow from the four dimensions of voice engagement described in this chapter. Thus, separate scales need to be developed to measure the frequency of voice behavior (for example: How often do you express your ideas about organizational problems?); the type of voice behavior (for example: To what extent have you expressed your feelings or beliefs through each of the following methods – suggestion system, informal complaints, grievance, and so on); the target of voice (for example: To what extent have you expressed your feelings and beliefs to each of the following persons – fellow co-workers, direct supervisor, upper management, and so on); and the quality of voice (for example: When you speak up at work, to what extent do you provide a lot of detail and information?).

Future research on employee voice might benefit from the inclusion of voice engagement. This will help to establish the validity of these two related but distinct constructs and aid in understanding how they differ with respect to determinants and outcomes. Perhaps most importantly, future research is needed to test the propositions suggested by our model of voice engagement. Along these lines, future research could test the extent to which each of Kahn's (1990) psychological conditions predict voice engagement as well as the extent to which the antecedents of the model predict the psychological conditions.

Although we did not discuss outcomes of voice engagement, we would expect that many of the outcomes of voice behavior and employee engagement will also be outcomes of voice engagement. Therefore, future research might investigate the extent to which voice engagement predicts employee attitudes (for example, job satisfaction), intentions (for example, intention to quit), and behaviors (for example, organizational citizenship behaviors). Future research might also consider the relationship between voice engagement and work engagement. Given that a number of voice-related variables such as participation in decision-making, decision latitude, job control, and autonomy are associated with work engagement (Bakker and Demerouti, 2008; Demerouti et al., 2001), we would expect voice engagement to be positively related to work engagement. In other words, as employees become more engaged in voice they will in turn become more engaged in their work. This might then lead to more voice engagement resulting in a reciprocal relationship between voice engagement and work engagement that begins with voice engagement.

In terms of practice, our model provides organizations and managers with guidelines for increasing employee voice engagement. Accordingly, managers should create a climate in which employees feel safe, find meaning in their work and membership in the organization, and have the resources they need to engage in voice behavior. The model also provides some suggestions for how organizations can enhance the experience of the psychological conditions. For example, supportive and caring supervisors help to ensure psychological safety; work that provides employees with control and autonomy helps to create meaningfulness; and providing employees with training that strengthens their human and psychological capital will provide them with a sense of psychological availability required to engage in voice. To the extent that employees experience these psychological conditions, they will become more engaged in voice behavior and organizations will have a higher level of voice engagement. Furthermore, as we indicated above, as voice engagement increases so should work engagement. Thus, by increasing voice engagement organizations can potentially also increase work engagement.

CONCLUSION

Although research on voice behavior has a long history and much has been learned about the determinants of employee voice, much less is known about how employees differ in the extent to which they are fully engaged when they speak up. In this chapter, we have attempted to extend the literature on employee voice by introducing a new construct that we refer to as employee voice engagement. By integrating Kahn's (1990) research on personal engagement with the literature on voice behavior, we have developed a model to explain the conditions required for employees to fully engage themselves in voice behavior. Our main contention is that when employees speak up, what matters most is not that they choose to voice, but rather, how engaged they are when they do speak up.

In conclusion, employee voice engagement and the accompanying model presented in this chapter extend both the voice and engagement literatures and offer new directions for research and practice on employee voice and employee engagement. We believe that promoting and facilitating high levels of employee voice engagement is likely to have substantial benefits for employees, work groups, and organizations.

REFERENCES

Albrecht, S.L. (2010), 'Employee engagement: 10 key questions for research and practice', in S. L. Albrecht (ed.), *Handbook of Employee Engagement: Perspectives, Issues, Research and Practice*, Cheltenham, UK and Northampton, MA, USA: Edward Elgar, pp. 3–19.

Ashford, S.J. and M.A. Barton (2007), 'Identity-based issue selling', in C.A. Bartel. S. Blader, and A. Wrzesniewski (eds), *Identity and the Modern Organization*, Mahwah, NJ: Lawrence Erlbaum Associates, pp. 223–44.

Avery, D.R., P. McKay, D.C. Wilson, S.D. Volpone and E.A. Killham (2011), 'Does voice go flat? How tenure diminishes the impact of voice', *Human Resource Management*, **50**, 147–58.

Avey, J.B., T.S. Wernsing and F. Luthans (2008), 'Can positive employees help positive organizational change? Impact of psychological capital and emotions on relevant attitudes and behavior', *Journal of Applied Behavioral Science*, **44**, 48–70.

Bakker, A.B. and E. Demerouti (2008), 'Towards a model of work engagement', *Career Development International*, **13**, 209–23.

Bakker, A.B., S.L. Albrecht and M.P. Leiter (2011), 'Key questions regarding work engagement', *European Journal of Work and Organizational Psychology*, **20**, 4–28.

Bates, S. (2004), 'Getting engaged', *HR Magazine*, **49** (2), 44–51.

Baumruk, R. (2004), 'The missing link: the role of employee engagement in business success', *Workspan*, **47**, 48–52.

Beugré, C.D. (2010), 'Organizational conditions fostering employee engagement: the role of "voice"', in S.L. Albrecht (ed.), *Handbook of Employee Engagement: Perspectives, Issues, Research and Practice*, Cheltenham, UK and Northampton, MA, USA: Edward Elgar, pp. 174–81.

Brinsfield, C.T., M.S. Edwards and J. Greenberg (2009), 'Voice and silence in organizations: historical review and current conceptualizations', in J. Greenberg and M.S. Edwards (eds), *Voice and Silence in Organizations*, Bingley: Emerald Publishing, pp. 3–33.

Burris, E.R., J.R. Detert and D.S. Chiaburu (2008), 'Quitting before leaving: the mediating effects of psychological attachment and detachment on voice', *Journal of Applied Psychology*, **93**, 912–22.

Christian, M.S., A.S. Garza and J.E. Slaughter (2011), 'Work engagement: a quantitative review and test of its relations with task and contextual performance', *Personnel Psychology*, **64**, 89–136.

Cialdini, R.B., R.R. Reno and C.A. Kallgren (1990), 'A focus theory of normative conduct: recycling the concept of norms to reduce littering in public places', *Journal of Personality and Social Psychology*, **58**, 1015–26.

Crook, T.R., S.Y. Todd, J.G. Combs, D.J. Woehr and D.J. Ketchen Jr (2011), 'Does human capital matter? A meta-analysis of the relationship between human capital and firm performance', *Journal of Applied Psychology*, **96**, 443–56.

Cropanzano, R. and M.S. Mitchell (2005), 'Social exchange theory: an interdisciplinary review', *Journal of Management*, **31**, 874–900.

Demerouti, E., A.B. Bakker, F. Nachreiner and W.B. Schaufeli (2001), 'The job demands–resources model of burnout', *Journal of Applied Psychology*, **86**, 499–512.

Denison, D.R. (1996), 'What is the difference between organizational culture and organizational climate? A native's point of view on a decade of paradigm wars', *Academy of Management Review*, **21**, 619–54.

Detert, J.R. and E.R. Burris (2007), 'Leadership behavior and employee voice: is the door really open?', *Academy of Management Journal*, **50**, 869–84.

Dundon, T., A. Wilkinson, M. Marchington and P. Ackers (2004), 'The meanings and purpose of employee voice', *International Journal of Human Resource Management*, **15**, 1149–70.

Dutton, J.E., S.J. Ashford, K.A. Lawrence and K. Miner-Rubino (2002), 'Red light, green light: making sense of the organizational context for issue selling.', *Organization Science*, **13**, 355–69.

Edmondson, A.C. (2003), 'Speaking up in the operating room: how team leaders promote learning in interdisciplinary action teams', *Journal of Management Studies*, **40**, 1419–52.

Farrell, D. (1983), 'Exit, voice, loyalty and neglect as responses to job dissatisfaction: a multidimensional scaling study', *Academy of Management Journal*, **26**, 596–607.

Halbesleben, J.R.B. (2010), 'A meta-analysis of work engagement: relationships with burnout, demands, resources, and consequences, in A.B. Bakker and M.P. Leiter (eds), *Work Engagement: A Handbook of Essential Theory and Research*, New York: Psychology Press, pp. 102–17.

Harter, J.K., F.L. Schmidt and T.L. Hayes (2002), 'Business-unit level relationship between employee satisfaction, employee engagement, and business outcomes: a meta-analysis', *Journal of Applied Psychology*, **87**, 268–79.

Hirschman, A.O. (1970), *Exit, Voice, and Loyalty: Responses to Declines in Firms, Organization and States*, Cambridge, MA: Harvard University Press.

Hsiung, H.-H. (2012), 'Authentic leadership and employee voice behavior: a multi-level psychological process', *Journal of Business Ethics*, **107**, 349–61.

Kahn, W.A. (1990), 'Psychological conditions of personal engagement and disengagement at work', *Academy of Management Journal*, **33**, 692–724.

Kahn, W.A. (1992), 'To be fully there: psychological presence at work', *Human Relations*, **45**, 321–49.

Kassing, J.W., N.M. Piemonte, C.C. Goman and C.A. Mitchell (2012), 'Dissent expression as an indicator of work engagement and intention to leave', *Journal of Business Communication*, **49**, 237–53.

Klaas, B.S., J.B. Olson–Buchanan and A.-K. Ward (2012), 'The determinants of alternative forms of workplace voice: an integrative perspective', *Journal of Management*, **38**, 314–45.

Korte, R.F. (2009), 'How newcomers learn the social norms of an organization: a case study of the socialization of newly hired engineers', *Human Resource Development Quarterly*, **20**, 285–306.

Kristof-Brown, A.L., R.D. Zimmerman and E.C. Johnson (2005), 'Consequences of individuals' fit at work: A meta-analysis of person–job, person–organization, person–group, and person–supervisor fit', *Personnel Psychology*, **58**, 281–342.

Kuenzi, M. and M. Schminke (2009), 'Assembling fragments into a lens: a review, critique and proposed research agenda for the organizational work climate literature', *Journal of Management*, **35**, 634–717.

Leiter, M.P. and A.B. Bakker (2010), 'Work engagement: introduction', in A.B. Bakker and M.P. Leiter (eds), *Work Engagement: A Handbook of Essential Theory and Research*, New York: Psychology Press, pp. 1–9.

Leiter, M.P. and C. Maslach (1998), 'Burnout', in H.S. Friedman (ed.), *Encyclopedia of Mental Health*, Vol. 1, New York: Academic Press, pp. 347–57.

LePine, J.A. and L. Van Dyne (1998), 'Predicting voice behavior in work groups', *Journal of Applied Psychology*, **83**, 853–68.

Liang, J., C.I.C. Farh and J.-L. Farh (2012), 'Psychological antecedents of promotive and prohibitive voice: a two-wave examination', *Academy of Management Journal*, **55**, 71–92.

Liu, W., R. Zhu and Y. Yang (2010), 'I warn you because I like you: voice behavior, employee identifications, and transformational leadership', *Leadership Quarterly*, **21**, 189–202.

Luthans, F. and C.M. Youssef (2004), 'Human, social and now positive psychological capital management: investing in people for competitive advantage', *Organizational Dynamics*, **33**, 143–60.

Macey, W.H. and B. Schneider (2008), 'The meaning of employee engagement', *Industrial and Organizational Psychology*, **1**, 3–30.

Maslach, C., W.B. Schaufeli and M.P. Leiter (2001), 'Job burnout', *Annual Review of Psychology*, **52**, 397–422.

May, D. ., R.L. Gilson and L.M. Harter (2004), 'The psychological conditions of meaningfulness, safety and availability and the engagement of the human spirit at work', *Journal of Occupational and Organizational Psychology*, **77**, 11–37.

Milliken, F.J., E.W. Morrison and P.F. Hewlin (2003), 'An exploratory study of employee silence: issues that employees do not communicate upward and why', *Journal of Management Studies*, **40**, 1453–76.

Morrison, E.W. (2011), 'Employee voice behavior: integration and directions for future research', *Academy of Management Annals*, **5**, 373–412.

Morrison, E.W. and C.C. Phelps (1999), 'Taking charge at work: extra-role efforts to initiate workplace changes', *Academy of Management Journal*, **42**, 403–19.

Morrison, E.W. and N.B. Rothman (2009), 'Silence and the dynamics of power', in J. Greenberg, and M.S. Edwards (eds), *Voice and Silence in Organizations*, Bingley: Emerald Publishing, pp. 111–33.

Morrison, E.W., S.L. Wheeler-Smith and D. Kamdar (2011), 'Speaking up in groups: a cross-level study of group voice climate and voice', *Journal of Applied Psychology*, **96**, 183–91.

Pierce, J.L., D.G. Gardner, L.L. Cummings and R.B. Dunham (1989), 'Organization-based self-esteem: construct definition, measurement and validation', *Academy of Management Journal*, **32**, 622–48.

Premeaux, S.F. and A.G. Bedeian (2003), 'Breaking the silence: the moderating effects of self-monitoring in predicting speaking up in the workplace', *Journal of Management Studies*, **40**, 1537–62.

Rees, C., K. Alfes and M. Gatenby (2013), 'Employee voice and engagement: connections and consequences', *The International Journal of Human Resource Management*, **24**, 2780–98.

Rich, B.L., J.A. LePine and E.R. Crawford (2010), 'Job engagement: antecedents and effects on job performance', *Academy of Management Journal*, **53**, 617–35.

Richman, A. (2006), 'Everyone wants an engaged workforce how can you create it?', *Workspan*, **49**, 36–9.

Rothbard, N.P. (2001), 'Enriching or depleting? The dynamics of engagement in work and family roles', *Administrative Science Quarterly*, **46**, 655–84.

Saks, A.M. (2006), 'Antecedents and consequences of employee engagement', *Journal of Managerial Psychology*, **21**, 600–619.

Saks, A.M. (2008), 'The meaning and bleeding of employee engagement: how muddy is the water?', *Industrial and Organizational Psychology*, **1**, 40–43.

Saks, A.M. and J.A. Gruman (2010), 'Getting newcomers engaged: the role of socialization tactics', *Journal of Managerial Psychology*, **26**, 383–402.

Saunders, D.M., B.H. Sheppard, V. Knight and J. Roth (1992), 'Employee voice to supervisors', *Employee Responsibilities and Rights Journal*, **5**, 241–59.

Schaufeli, W.B. and A.B. Bakker (2010), 'Defining and measuring work engagement: bringing clarity to the concept', in A.B. Bakker and M.P. Leiter (eds), *Work Engagement: A Handbook of Essential Theory and Research*, New York: Psychology Press, pp. 10–24.

Schaufeli, W. and M. Salanova (2007), 'Work engagement: an emerging psychological concept and its implications for organizations', in S.W. Gilliland, D.D. Steiner and D.P. Skarlicki (eds), *Managing Social and Ethical Issues in Organizations*, Greenwich, CT: Information Age Publishing, pp. 135–77.

Schaufeli, W.B., M. Salanova, V. Gonzalez-Roma and A.B. Bakker (2002), 'The measurement of engagement and burnout: a two sample confirmatory factor analytic approach', *Journal of Happiness Studies*, **3**, 71–92.

Schaufeli, W.B., T.W. Taris and W. van Rhenen (2008), 'Workaholism, burnout, and work engagement: three of a kind or three different kinds of employee well-being?', *Applied Psychology: An International Review*, **57**, 173–203.

Stajkovic, A.D. and F. Luthans (1998), 'Social cognitive theory and self-efficacy: going beyond traditional motivational and behavioral approaches', *Organizational Dynamics*, **26**, 62–74.

Sweetman, D. and F. Luthans (2010), 'The power of positive psychology: psychological capital and work engagement', in A.B. Bakker and M.P. Leiter (eds), *Work Engagement: A Handbook of Essential Theory and Research*, New York: Psychology Press, pp. 54–68.

Tangirala, S. and R. Ramanujam (2012), 'Ask and you shall hear (but not always): examining the relationship between manager consultation and employee voice', *Personnel Psychology*, **65**, 251–82.

Thomas, J.P., D.S. Whitman and C. Viswesvaran (2010), 'Employee proactivity in organizations: A comparative meta-analysis of emergent proactive constructs', *Journal of Occupational and Organizational Psychology*, **83**, 275–300.

Tucker, S., N. Chmiel, N. Turner, M.S. Hershcovis and C.B. Stride (2008), 'Perceived organizational support or safety and employee safety voice: the mediating role of coworker support for safety', *Journal of Occupational Health Psychology*, **13**, 319–30.

Van Dyne, L., L.L. Cummings and J. McLean Parks (1995), 'Extra-role behaviours: in pursuit of construct and definitional clarity (a bridge over muddled waters)', in L.L. Cummings and B.M. Staw (eds), *Research in Organizational Behavior*, Vol. 17, Greenwich, CT: JAI Press, pp. 215–85.

Van Dyne, L., S. Ang and I.C. Botero (2003), 'Conceptualizing employee silence and employee voice as multidimensional constructs', *Journal of Management Studies*, **40**, 1359–92.

Venkataramani, V. and S. Tangirala (2010), 'When and why do central employees speak up? An examination of mediating and moderating variables', *Journal of Applied Psychology*, **95**, 582–91.

Walumbwa, F.O. and J. Schaubroeck (2009), 'Leader personality traits and employee voice behavior: mediating roles of ethical leadership and work group psychological safety', *Journal of Applied Psychology*, **94**, 1275–86.

Whiting, S.W., T.D. Maynes, N.P. Podsakoff and P.M. Podsakoff (2012), 'Effects of message, source, and content on evaluations of employee voice behavior', *Journal of Applied Psychology*, **97**, 159–82.

Xanthopoulou, D., A.B. Bakker, E. Demerouti and W.B. Schaufeli (2007), 'The role of personal resources in the job demands–resources model', *International Journal of Stress Management*, **14**, 121–41.

29 The future of employee voice
John W. Budd

As recently as perhaps 25 years ago, employee voice was narrowly conceived. In the research literature, employee voice was largely seen as an extension of Hirschman's (1970: 30) conception of voice as a means to 'change, rather than escape from [that is, exit], an objectionable state of affairs.' In industrial relations, this was most influentially articulated through Freeman and Medoff's (1984) collective voice face of labor unions. Consistent with this, employee voice in practice was largely seen as something best delivered through labor unions. In retrospect, it is easy to see what should have been articulated 25 years ago as a future course for employee voice. Specifically, one should have called for broader definitions of employee voice, more diverse disciplinary perspectives on broader aspects of voice, and greater recognition of individual and non-union forms of voice in practice.

Thankfully, that is where we are today, as witnessed by the breadth and depth of the chapters in this handbook and other recent collections of employee voice research (for example, Budd et al. 2010). So while the future of narrowly conceived voice and the closely associated institution of labor unionism are perhaps questionable at best, there is a strong future for richer and broader conceptualizations and forms of employee voice. Ironically, this new breadth and depth of contemporary research on employee voice makes it more challenging to lay out its future, and it is impractical as well as redundant to cover all of the future directions raised by the chapters in this handbook. I will instead propose some areas where I think particular attention is warranted, but the reader is again encouraged to read the others chapters in the handbook with an eye toward thinking critically about future directions for employee voice in both research and practice.

PUSHING THE CONCEPTUAL BOUNDARIES OF VOICE

Academics and practitioners have many different conceptualizations of employee voice. As noted above, Hirschman (1970) defined voice as a complaint mechanism. In this way, some employers see suggestion boxes as a voice mechanism. Advocates of high performance human resource practices embrace an employee involvement perspective in which voice can improve organizational performance through problem-solving teams and other methods. A neoliberal, free market perspective sees voice as exercised by one's feet in the form of quitting. To labor advocates, collective bargaining and other activities pursued by labor unions are viewed as the only legitimate forms of employee voice.

In my work, I have advocated for an inclusive definition that sees employee voice as expressing opinions and having meaningful input into work-related decision-making (Budd 2004; Befort and Budd 2009). This broad conceptualization of voice should include individual and collective voice, union and non-union voice, and voice mechanisms that cover not only employment terms, but also work autonomy and business issues (see also Budd et al. 2010; Dundon et al. 2004). To be blunt, the traditional indus-trial relations emphasis on collective voice through collective bargaining is excessively narrow. Richer understandings have and continue to come from including non-union collective voice as well as various dimensions of individual voice within our conceptual-ization of employee voice. Similarly, the frequent approach of starting with Hirschman's (1970) definition of voice is excessively narrow because employee voice is then linked so strongly with complaining rather than broader conceptualizations of input, expression, autonomy, and self-determination.

Consequently, future work on voice should continue to push the conceptual bounda-ries of employee voice in order to further broaden and deepen the theorizing on and understanding of employee voice. For example, one organizational development profes-sional claims that 'voice is only active if we have a culture where people feel they can communicate in an open and honest way, upwards, downwards, and sideways' (quoted in Clarke and Manwaring 2011: 11). The idea that voice can potentially be expressed upwards, downwards, and sideways offers a useful way to think about pushing the conceptual boundaries of employee voice. In particular, I believe that sideways or peer-to-peer voice has been overlooked (more on this later). At the same time, we need to be vigilant to avoid letting the definition of voice become so broad that it risks losing meaning. For example, downward communication from organizational leaders without opportunities for employees to respond might better be seen as communication rather than voice. Admittedly, the boundaries of employee voice might be porous and blurred, but researchers could continue to push and identify these boundaries.

Future work on voice should also address the extent to which voice is conceptual-ized as an intrinsic or as an instrumental activity. In other words, there is an unresolved tension over the extent to which voice needs to be effective in changing something in order to be considered voice. I have argued for an intrinsic definition to voice based on innate human needs for self-determination (Budd 2004) whereas, for example, Hyman (2005: 127) has countered that 'voice is an effective means to achieve one's aims, or it is a charade.' Admittedly, if voice never achieves an instrumental end nor leads to something of substance (including something as simple as a deeper understanding), it is reasonable to hypothesize that individuals will not desire or exercise voice, and it is appropriate to question whether voice is meaningful. But this does not mean that voice must be concep-tualized solely in instrumental terms. In other words, I assert that it is a mistake only to consider something as voice when it is instrumentally effective. Voice does not need to be effective 100 percent of the time; some of the time it can solely have intrinsic worth. But if voice never achieves instrumental ends, one can seriously question whether it is true voice. So where is the dividing line? This is another nebulous conceptual boundary that future work on voice needs to wrestle with.

EXIT-VOICE REDUX

While I have criticized the literature's over-reliance on Hirschman's (1970) approach to voice, it nevertheless remains true that, in the words of Meardi (2012: 186), 'to understand "voice" we need to understand "exit".' In the traditional literature on employee voice, exit is seen narrowly as quitting one's job. Meardi (2012), however, has significantly expanded exit to be three-dimensional. The first dimension is exit from effectively contributing to one's organization. This includes not only the traditional focus on quitting, but also what Meardi (2012) terms 'internal exit' and what some organizational behavior scholars have labeled 'neglect' (Farrell 1983; Mellahi et al. 2010) – organizational misbehavior, informal resistance, and low levels of commitment, loyalty, and engagement. The second dimension of an expanded perspective on exit is exit from one's local geographical area. In the context of work, this type of exit occurs through worker migration to areas with better work opportunities and conditions. For some, this might include seeking more desirable workplace voice mechanisms. Meardi's (2012) third dimension of exit is exit from the political arena such as through voter apathy and low levels of voter turnout. This can be related to the work context because political exit might be caused by political parties' lack of responsiveness to workers' concerns.

This broadened approach to exit can provide a useful framework for future work on voice. For starters, future research should consider how different forms of voice can serve as a counterweight to these dimensions of exit. Specifically, are there different voice mechanisms that alleviate the need for organizational exit, geographical exit, and political exit? Moreover, we can question whether the repression of certain forms of voice leads to different forms of exit, and ask what types of demands for voice arise from limitations on various forms of exit. Are these behaviors driven by workers, managers, the state, or others? Also, there is recognition that labor union voice in the workplace can contribute to political participation (Budd forthcoming), but less is known about how other forms of employee voice might make such contributions. Deeper answers to these and related questions can contribute to our understanding of voice while also helping societies design more robust institutions of voice.

Similarly, while exit is one practical alternative to voice, and therefore one conceptual foil for voice, silence is another. That is, just as workers can choose exit or voice, they can also choose silence or voice. The research literature on silence, however, tends to be distinct from the research literature on voice, with the former largely the domain of organizational behavior scholars and the latter the domain of employment relations scholars and sociologists. In this way, the literature on silence tends to implicitly employ a unitarist frame of reference, while the literature on voice is rooted in pluralist or critical thought (Donaghey et al. 2011; for a description of the unitarist, pluralist, and critical approaches to employment relations scholarship, see Budd and Bhave 2008, 2010). As such, there appear to be ripe areas for integrating these perspectives which could enhance our understanding of both voice and silence. For example, the literature on silence has used communicative theory (for example, Van Dyne et al. 2003) which has not yet been systematically integrated into the traditional literature on employee voice.

The literature on silence has also devised a more fine-grained differentiation of types of motivation for silence than is common in the voice literature (for example, Van Dyne et al. 2003; Detert and Edmondson 2011). This depth could be profitably applied to the voice literature, not only to better understand types of voice, but also their potentially different implications. For example, Burris (2012) finds that managers respond differently to employees who are perceived to be using voice in a way that supports the organization's policies and practices than they do to employees who are perceived to be using voice in a way that challenges the organization's status quo.

The issue of silence also begs questions about whether workers want opportunities for voice and what influences their participation. As noted by Markey et al. (2012), the extent to which employees perceive that they have influence and the extent to which they desire influence in the workplace are important issues that have not received a lot of research attention. These authors therefore survey workers about their perceived and desired influence, and find that organizational characteristics are more important than personal characteristics. Their results also uncover an interesting relationship between learning new things and wanting more influence. Cregan and Brown (2010) also find an interesting pattern of results in which willingness to participate in a voice mechanism depends on the types of issues valued by workers. Future work on voice should continue this line of research, investigating what determines the extent to which employees desire more voice and more influence, and what determines a willingness to exercise voice in the workplace. Indeed, returning to Meardi's (2012) expansion of exit, voice research should expand these inquiries beyond the workplace as well.

ROOTING VOICE IN THE NATURE OF WORK

Much research on work-related issues has lost its connections with what work actually is. Moreover, academic research as well as human resources policies tend to homogenize work to the extent that both theory and practice are implicitly rooted in particular, albeit unstated, conceptualizations of what work is and why workers work. These limitations are present in the literature on employee voice, such as when one research stream focuses exclusively on voice as a form of industrial democracy while another stream focuses solely on voice as a way to enhance organizational performance. Future work on voice within both academic and practitioner circles needs to be more careful to connect voice to concepts of work. And being more explicit in these connections would, in turn, improve cross-disciplinary conversations about work and facilitate deeper, multidisciplinary understandings.

As a broad foundation for this needed effort, Table 29.1 summarizes ten conceptualizations of work that are found in the literature on work across the humanities and the social and behavioral sciences: work as a curse, disutility, a commodity, freedom, personal fulfillment, occupational citizenship, identity, a social relation, caring for others, and service (Budd 2011). As further shown in Table 29.1, these conceptualizations yield diverse implications for thinking about employee voice.

If work is seen as a curse, then work as a lousy state of affairs is a pre-ordained fait accompli. From this perspective, there is little that can be done to change or improve work, so employee voice is not important. Workers should instead seek fulfillment or other rewards outside of work so perhaps non-work voice is important, but not employee voice. In a similar, albeit perhaps more modern, vein, conceptualizing work as disutility, such that work is simply tolerated to earn income, also implies that employee voice is not an important construct because the focal point is money or other extrinsic rewards, not participation and self-determination. This is reinforced by the fact that modeling work as disutility in economic scholarship is typically accompanied by a complementary conceptualization of work as a commodity exchanged in competitive labor markets. Exit, not voice, is prioritized in market-mediated transactions so voice is embraced only to the extent that it can be seen as the freedom to quit and thus facilitate efficient market

Table 29.1   Relating voice to conceptualizations of work

Work as . . .	Definition	Implications for voice
1. A curse	An unquestioned burden necessary for human survival or maintenance of the social order.	No voice warranted. Accept work as lousy.
2. Disutility	A lousy activity tolerated to obtain goods and services that provide pleasure.	No voice warranted. Accept work as solely a source of income.
3. A commodity	An abstract quantity of productive effort that has tradable economic value.	Voice as freedom to quit.
4. Freedom	A way to achieve independence from other humans, or from nature by expressing human creativity.	Voice as freedom to quit and freedom of speech. Also, creativity-enhancing voice.
5. Personal fulfillment	Physical and psychological functioning that (ideally) satisfies individual needs.	Satisfaction-enhancing voice (where desired) and productivity-enhancing voice (where effective).
6. Occupational citizenship	An activity pursued by human members of a community entitled to certain rights.	Voice as industrial democracy and self-determination over employment conditions.
7. Identity	A method for understanding who you are and where you stand in the social structure.	Voice for self-determination as part of healthy human identity.
8. A social relation	Human interaction embedded in social norms, institutions, and power structures.	Peer-to-peer voice. Militant voice for resistance. Radical voice for systemic change.
9. Caring for others	The physical, cognitive, and emotional effort required to attend to and maintain others.	Need for 'meta-voice' about what work means, and therefore desired forms of work.
10. Service	The devotion of effort to others, such as God, household, community, or country.	See caring.

exchanges. In other words, voice is weakly seen as something exercised by one's feet, not through deeper expressive actions.

Work can also be conceptualized as a source of freedom. This conceptualization has different strands. First, work can be a source of economic freedom. This yields a perspective on employee voice that is similar to the one derived from seeing work as a commodity – specifically, voice is the freedom to quit. Second, work can be a source of political independence from others. In this way, employee voice includes not only the freedom to quit, but also the freedom of speech within the workplace. Unfortunately, free speech rights for workers are often overlooked in discussions of employee voice (Befort and Budd 2009). Third, work can also be a source of freedom from the dictates of nature. From this perspective, employee voice should serve human creativity, such as through individual autonomy and the peer-to-peer exchanges of ideas.

Work can also be conceptualized as a source of personal fulfillment through achievement, mastery, self-esteem, and self-worth, though this also goes hand-in-hand with the possibility that work with mindless repetition, abusive co-workers or bosses, excessive physical or mental demands, or other factors that comprise lousy work can have negative psychological consequences. Human resource management scholarship builds on this conceptualization of work as personal fulfillment by assuming that to be effective, human resource management practices must satisfy workers' psychological needs by managing their cognitive and affective functioning. Voice, then, is typically seen as something that can enhance job satisfaction and employee engagement which simultaneously enhances individual productivity and organizational performance.

Industrial relations theorizing goes further by seeing work as an activity undertaken by human beings who are entitled to certain rights. This occupational citizenship conceptualization of work then goes beyond the satisfaction and efficiency aspects of voice to also value human needs, even when employee voice does not improve productivity. When paired with a belief that imperfect labor markets render individual employee–employer relations unequal, industrial relations scholarship traditionally prioritizes collective voice as providing self-determination and industrial democracy, especially through independent labor unions and collective bargaining. Labor unions are also privileged in industrial relations because their bargaining power is seen as providing necessary economic protection for workers who are individually disadvantaged in their dealings with their employers.

Work can also be a source of identity which helps individuals understand who they are and where they fit into the broader world. To the extent that individual self-determination is seen as an innate human need, the identity conceptualization of work indicates that employee voice should provide autonomy and self-determination in support of the construction of healthy, positive identities. This suggests that a lack of or repression of employee voice which stifles self-determination can prevent the development of positive identity. This conceptualization of work, therefore, should prompt analyses of the deep importance of voice, especially when contrasted with views that see work as a curse, disutility, or commodity.

Another conceptualization of work is as a social relation in which work consists of human interactions that are experienced in and shaped by social networks, social norms and institutions, and socially-constructed power relations. At a micro-level, this emphasis on human interactions suggests that employee voice should include peer-to-peer interactions. At a macro-level, the social relations theorizing on work is often accompanied by a belief that the employment relationship is characterized by deeply-conflicting, antagonistic employee–employer interests. In other words, work is viewed as contested terrain in which employers and employees continuously seek control and make accommodations. Employee voice, then, is seen as an institution that should provide capacity for resisting and re-shaping managerial control strategies. Moreover, in selected radical traditions employee voice in the form of militant trade unions and other worker organizations is seen as radical, syndicalist voice that can help replace capitalism with an alternative socio-economic system.

Lastly, work can be seen as a way to care for and serve others. Workers in caring and serving occupations might value some or all of the preceding forms of voice illuminated by the other conceptualizations of work. But by themselves, these ways of thinking about work, which are typically outside the mainstream in Western scholarship on work, suggest the need for a new, higher-level form of voice in which workers can influence what work means to them. I propose to call this 'meta-voice.' Meta-voice can be exercised, for example, when workers choose to see work as a way to care for or serve others rather than seeing work in more typical Western ways. Another form of meta-voice is employees expressing a desire to their employers to have more time and support for volunteering.

As summarized in Table 29.1, if we consider a broad pattern of ways to model work, and in turn explicitly root our thinking about employee voice in a broad framework, then we can advance the literature on employee voice in two ways. First, the theoretical foundations of employee voice can be strengthened by a more careful linkage to the nature of work, and second, forms of voice that are commonly overlooked, such as employee free speech, peer-to-peer voice, and a newly-proposed meta-voice, are revealed as worthy of additional research. With that said, note carefully that the entries in Table 29.1 are intended to be read as complements, not substitutes. We should seek to further integrate the forms of voice that emerge from Table 29.1 rather than treating them in isolation. In this way, an explicit rooting of voice in theories of work can help stimulate more interdisciplinary research on voice.

EMERGING INSTITUTIONS AND FUTURE RESEARCH

In addition to the new conceptual directions I have proposed, voice research should continue to confront and analyze issues that result from changing and emerging institutions of voice. The decline of a key institution of employee voice, labor unions, has been well documented for a variety of countries (Addison et al. 2011; Charlwood and Haynes 2008; Godard 2009; Pinto and Beckfield 2011). This has given rise to interesting studies on unmet demand for union voice (Pyman et al. 2009), employers' roles in determining voice regimes (Gollan 2010; Willman et al. 2006), the development of alternative voice mechanisms (Holland et al. 2009), and numerous other issues related to employee voice.

Yet there is more to be done. The importance of corporate governance structures and financial markets in shaping employee voice are worthy of additional attention. In a trend that has been labeled 'financialization,' corporations are increasingly focused on financial concerns such as boosting stock prices to satisfy Wall Street expectations and to increase the value of executive stock options. Financialization also includes an increased pursuit of profits through financial transactions rather than through the delivery of valuable goods and services (Dore 2008). Financialization can affect voice by shaping corporate goals which in turn shape strategies toward employee issues generally, and labor unions specifically, including decisions on how corporations allocate resources; for example, by using corporate cash reserves to repurchase stock rather than investing in new equipment (Lazonick 2009). More generally, the voice literature would benefit from a deeper understanding of the relationship between models of corporate governance and ownership, corporate decision-making, and employee voice structures.

The decline of labor unions also raises important questions about the ability of employee voice to provide checks and balances to shareholders and managers in corporate governance. Among shareholders, managers, and employees, three patterns of conflict might occur: (1) class conflict in which shareholders and managers align against employees over compensation and other terms and conditions of employment; (2) accountability conflict in which shareholders and employees align against low-performing managers; and (3) insider-outsider conflict in which managers and employees align against shareholders over takeovers or other restructuring issues (Jackson et al. 2005). Strong forms of employee voice, especially via collective bargaining, have traditionally been advocated as a way to bring a balance to the class conflict dimension, but a labor union or some other form of institutionalized power can also enhance social welfare by making employees an effective actor in balancing these other conflicts (Dau-Schmidt 2011). The decline in labor unions begs the question of whether other forms of employee voice can effectively play these roles in corporate governance.

In the public policy arena, the decline of unionized voice has been accompanied by an increased emphasis on soft law in the European Union (Peters 2011) and corporate self-regulation in the United Sates (Estlund 2010). In the context of the US workplace, Estlund (2010) advocates for the need for 'regulated self-regulation' or 'co-regulation' rather than unadulterated corporate self-regulation. In this way, the weakening of the hard law of the state can potentially be offset by bolstering the regulatory role of non-governmental actors, including, for employment issues, workers themselves. A popular example in many countries is a health and safety committee. Notably for this chapter, the questions that surround the participation of employees in the regulatory process are essentially questions of voice. For example, to ask what types of employee participation are necessary to ensure that corporate compliance is more than cosmetic is to ask what forms of voice would be effective. There is scope for much research on the types of support that are needed to make these arrangements meaningful, such as protections against reprisals and the assistance of outside monitoring agents, or whether this is a hollow exercise because of corporate power (Secunda 2010).

Related issues arise in the context of soft law approaches that provide weaker obligations for organizations than under hard law. For example, Britain, Australia, New Zealand, and various European countries have implemented laws granting employees the right to request a flexible or altered work schedule. This can be seen as a form of soft law because employers' only obligations are to consider these requests. Within this type of framework in which workers are given more choice, 'it is crucial to understand the conditions under which that choice is made and how choice is exercised and managed' – in other words, we need to understand employee voice in the presence of certain parameters around employee choice (Donnelly et al. 2012: 188).

There are many other areas where it is important for future research on voice to intersect with evolving practices and institutions. On a workplace level, for example, the increased diversity in voice mechanisms gives rise to a greater diversity of types of roles beyond traditional shop stewards and other union positions. Identifying the challenges of these positions and the skills required to be successful are important issues for future research. In representative systems, for example, how do representatives find a balance between being a delegate who simply voices workers' views and being a representative who takes a confident, leadership role in shaping as well as reflecting views? Related to this, what types of training do both worker representatives and managers need in order to make consultation and other voice arrangements effective (Hall and Purcell 2012)?

On more of a macro-level, voice research should continue to follow developments in multi-level voice and governance mechanisms and their intersections with public policy and multinational corporations (Marginson and Sisson 2004; Marginson et al.

2010). Voice research should also continue to follow developments in employee voice in developing countries in Asia, Africa, and elsewhere. Will these countries follow Western models or some other path, and what determines what type of path is followed? What are the implications for workers, their communities, their organizations, and their political systems?

Lastly, the implications for voice of changing technologies is an important issue for future research. For starters, the tremendous use of social networking technologies by so many individuals seemingly supports the contention of voice researchers that it is human nature to want to engage in voice. Through blogs, tweets, online comments, and other tools, so many want to be heard. Through Facebook, LinkedIn, and other sites, so many want to connect with others. Our research on voice practices needs to keep pace with these developments. Are they complements or substitutes to more traditional voice mechanisms? Are they particularly useful for certain types of employees or issues? Why are companies so concerned with these voice behaviors, and what are the ramifications of different organizational responses?

Changes in employee voice brought on by new information technologies should also prompt a re-evaluation of our conceptual approaches to employee voice. We could start with the fact that our traditional categories of employee voice seemingly overlook a major category of social media: employee-to-employee interactions such as voicing concerns with each other, sharing common experiences, griping, supporting each other, and sharing tips and techniques. Indeed, while overlooked in research, this form of voice has likely been occurring for centuries in guildhalls, union halls, pubs, bowling alleys, company cafeterias, and other venues where workers gather to socialize and talk shop. It seems that our conceptual as well as empirical research on voice should pay more attention to various forms of peer-to-peer or sideways voice.

CONCLUSION

Employee voice is not a new issue. Two thousand years ago, at least one Roman farmer consulted with his slaves about changes in their work because 'they are more willing to set about a piece of work on which they think that their opinions have been asked and their advice followed' (Columella 1941: 93). In the late nineteenth century, a banner for the Newcastle, England, blacksmith's union proclaimed that the union was 'a voice from the forge.' But academic interest in employee voice has perhaps never been higher than it is today. This is visibly demonstrated by the breadth of the chapters in this handbook. These chapters draw from diverse intellectual traditions and theoretical perspectives, analyze numerous voice processes, and identify a broad range of intersections and implications.

At the same time, traditional, collective-oriented forms of employee voice in practice are either stagnant or declining in many parts of the world while individual and/or technology-based forms of voice are seemingly on the rise. So the future of employee voice is mixed. The challenge for researchers and practitioners is to continue to deepen our scholarship and broaden our practices so that employee voice remains a vibrant area of research and practice that engages with cutting-edge theory as well as with workers and their organizations in their everyday lives.

REFERENCES

Addison, John T., Alex Bryson, Paulino Teixeira and André Pahnke (2011), 'Slip sliding away: further union decline in Germany and Britain', *Scottish Journal of Political Economy*, **58** (4), 490–518.
Befort, Stephen F. and John W. Budd (2009), *Invisible Hands, Invisible Objectives: Bringing Workplace Law and Public Policy into Focus*, Stanford, CA: Stanford University Press.
Budd, John W. (2004), *Employment with a Human Face: Balancing Efficiency, Equity, and Voice*, Ithaca, NY: Cornell University Press.
Budd, John W. (2011), *The Thought of Work*, Ithaca, NY: Cornell University Press.
Budd, John W. (forthcoming), 'Implicit public values and the creation of publicly valuable outcomes: the importance of work and the contested role of labor unions', *Public Administration Review*.
Budd, John W. and Devasheesh Bhave (2008), 'Values, ideologies, and frames of reference in industrial relations', in Paul Blyton, Nicolas Bacon, Jack Fiorito and Edmund Heery (eds), *Sage Handbook of Industrial Relations*, London: Sage, pp. 92–112.
Budd, John W. and Devasheesh Bhave (2010), 'The employment relationship', in Adrian Wilkinson, Tom Redman, Scott Snell and Nicolas Bacon (eds), *Sage Handbook of Human Resource Management*, London: Sage, pp. 51–70.
Budd, John W., Paul J. Gollan and Adrian Wilkinson (2010), 'New approaches to employee voice and participation in organisations', *Human Relations*, **63** (3), 303–10.
Burris, Ethan R. (2012), 'The risks and rewards of speaking up: managerial responses to employee voice', *Academy of Management Journal*, **55** (4), 851–75.
Charlwood, Andy and Peter Haynes (2008), 'Union membership decline in New Zealand, 1990–2002', *Journal of Industrial Relations*, **50** (1), 87–110.
Clarke, Nita and Tony Manwaring (2011), 'Rethinking voice for sustainable business success', report published by the Centre for Tomorrow's Company and IPA.
Columella, Lucius Junius Moderatus (1941), *De Re Rustica*, trans. Harrison Boyd Ash, London: William Heinemann.
Cregan, Christina and Michelle Brown (2010), 'The influence of union membership status on workers' willingness to participate in joint consultation', *Human Relations*, **63** (3), 331–48.
Dau-Schmidt, Kenneth G. (2011), 'Promoting employee voice in the American Economy: a call for comprehensive reform', *Marquette Law Review*, **94** (3), 765–836.
Detert, James R. and Amy C. Edmondson (2011), 'Implicit voice theories: taken-for-granted rules of self-censorship at work', *Academy of Management Journal*, **54** (3), 461–88.
Donaghey, Jimmy, Niall Cullinane, Tony Dundon and Adrian Wilkinson (2011), 'Reconceptualising employee silence: problems and prognosis', *Work, Employment and Society*, **25** (1), 51–67.
Donnelly, Noelle, Sarah B. Proctor-Thomson and Geoff Plimmer (2012), 'The role of "voice" in matters of "choice": flexible work outcomes for women in the New Zealand public services', *Journal of Industrial Relations*, **54** (2), 182–203.
Dore, Ronald (2008), 'Financialization of the global economy', *Industrial and Corporate Change*, **17** (6), 1097–112.
Dundon, Tony, Adrian Wilkinson, Mick Marchington and Peter Ackers (2004), 'The meanings and purpose of employee voice', *International Journal of Human Resource Management*, **15** (6), 1149–70.
Estlund, Cynthia (2010), *Regoverning the Workplace: From Self-Regulation to Co-Regulation*, New Haven, CT: Yale University Press.
Farrell, Dan (1983), 'Exit, voice, loyalty, and neglect as responses to job dissatisfaction: a multidimensional scaling study', *Academy of Management Journal*, **26** (4), 596–607.
Freeman, Richard B. and James L. Medoff (1984), *What Do Unions Do?*, New York: Basic Books.
Godard, John (2009), 'The exceptional decline of the American labor movement', *Industrial and Labor Relations Review*, **63** (1), 82–108.
Gollan, Paul J. (2010), 'Employer strategies towards non-union collective voice', in Adrian Wilkinson, Paul Gollan, Mick Marchington and David Lewin (eds), *The Oxford Handbook of Participation in Organizations*, Oxford: Oxford University Press, pp. 212–36.
Hall, Mark and John Purcell (2012), *Consultation at Work: Regulation and Practice*, Oxford: Oxford University Press.
Hirschman, Albert O. (1970), *Exit, Voice, and Loyalty: Responses to Declines in Firms, Organizations, and States*, Cambridge, MA: Harvard University Press.
Holland, Peter, Amanda Pyman, Brian K. Cooper and Julian Teicher (2009), 'The development of alternative voice mechanisms in Australia: the case of joint consultation', *Economic and Industrial Democracy*, **30** (1), 67–92.

Hyman, Richard (2005), 'Striking a balance? Means, ends and ambiguities', *Employee Responsibilities and Rights Journal*, **17** (2), 127–30.

Jackson, Gregory, Martin Höpner and Antje Kurdelbusch (2005), 'Corporate governance and employees in Germany: changing linkages, complementarities, and tensions', in Howard F. Gospel and Andrew Pendleton (eds), *Corporate Governance and Labour Management: An International Comparison*, Oxford: Oxford University Press, pp. 84–121.

Lazonick, William (2009), *Sustainable Prosperity in the New Economy? Business Organization and High-Tech Employment in the United States*, Kalamazoo, MI: Upjohn Institute.

Marginson, Paul and Keith Sisson (2004), *European Integration and Industrial Relations: Multi-Level Governance in the Making*, Basingstoke: Palgrave Macmillan.

Marginson, Paul, Paul Edwards, Tony Edwards, Anthony Ferner and Olga Tregaskis (2010), 'Employee representation and consultative voice in multinational companies operating in Britain', *British Journal of Industrial Relations*, **48** (1), 151–80.

Markey, Raymond, Katherine Ravenswood, Don J. Webber and Herman Knudsen (2012), 'Influence at work and the desire for more influence', unpublished paper, Macquarie University.

Meardi, Guglielmo (2012), *Social Failures of EU Enlargement: A Case of Workers Voting with their Feet*, New York: Routledge.

Mellahi, Kamel, Pawan S. Budhwar and Baibing Li (2010), 'A study of the relationship between exit, voice, loyalty and neglect and commitment in India', *Human Relations*, **63** (3), 349–69.

Peters, Anne (2011), 'Soft law as a new mode of governance', in Udo Diedrichs and Wolfgang Wessels (eds), *The Dynamics of Change in EU Governance*, Cheltenham, UK and Northampton, MA, USA: Edward Elgar, pp. 21–51.

Pinto, Sanjay and Jason Beckfield (2011), 'Organized labor in European countries, 1960–2006: persistent diversity and shared decline', in David Brady (ed.), *Research in the Sociology of Work*, Vol. 22, Bingley: Emerald Group Publishing, pp. 153–79.

Pyman, Amanda, Julian Teicher, Brian Cooper and Peter Holland (2009), 'Unmet demand for union membership in Australia', *Journal of Industrial Relations*, **51** (1), 5–24.

Secunda, Paul M. (2010), 'Book review of *Regoverning the Workplace: From Self-Regulation to Co-Regulation*', *Industrial and Labor Relations Review*, **64** (1), 203–5.

Van Dyne, Linn Soon Ang and Isabel C. Botero (2003), 'Conceptualizing employee silence and employee voice as multidimensional constructs', *Journal of Management Studies*, **40** (6), 1359–92.

Willman, Paul, Alex Bryson and Rafael Gomez (2006), 'The sound of silence: which employers choose no employee voice and why?', *Socio-Economic Review*, **4** (2), 283–99.

Index